The Ties That Bind:
Bruce Springsteen
A *to* E *to* Z

The Ties That Bind:

BRUCE SPRINGSTEEN

A *to* 🔲 *to* Z

Edited by Gary Graff

Forewords by Damon Gough (aka Badly Drawn Boy)
and Mike Mills (of R.E.M.)

VISIBLE
INK
PRESS

Detroit

The Ties That Bind: Bruce Springsteen A to E to Z

Copyright 2005 by Visible Ink Press®

This publication is a creative work fully protected by all applicable copyright laws, as well as by misappropriation, trade secret, unfair competition, and other applicable laws.

Visible Ink Press®
43311 Joy Rd. #414
Canton, MI 48187-2075

Visible Ink Press is a registered trademark of Visible Ink Press LLC.

Most Visible Ink Press books are available at special quantity discounts when purchased in bulk by corporations, organizations, or groups. Customized printings, special imprints, messages, and excerpts can be produced to meet your needs. For more information, contact Special Markets Director, Visible Ink Press, at www.visibleink.com or (734) 667-3211.

Art Director: Mary Claire Krzewinski
Typesetting: The Graphix Group
ISBN 1-57859-157-0

Printed in the United States of America

10 9 8 7 6 5 4 3 2

CIP on file with the Library of Congress

PHOTO CREDITS
Robert Alford: Cover, back cover, xiv, xv, xviii, xix, xx, xxi, xxiii, xxiv, xxv, xxvi, xxviii, xxix, xxxiii, xxiv, xxxv, xxxvi, 1, 23, 25, 36, 65, 85, 86, 103, 106, 121, 147, 148, 159, 179, 192, 202, 205, 225, 226, 237, 253, 266, 269, 273, 295, 315, 317, 371, 384, 389, 393, 397, 409, 423
AP/Wide World Photos: 2, 9, 16 ,19, 33, 55, 59, 75, 81, 94, 130, 135, 137, 144, 166, 177, 183, 186, 199, 206, 207, 228, 242, 268, 285, 291, 293, 308, 310, 324, 333, 338, 342, 354, 355, 362, 364, 366, 372, 386, 399, 411, 421
David Belisle: xvii
Bill Green: xv
Paul Natkin: 44, 84, 97, 110, 118, 190
Ken Settle: xvii, xxvii, 40, 66, 71, 151, 160, 234, 262, 263, 279, 290, 296, 319, 340, 359, 400, 426
Jim Shive: 13, 51, 128, 129, 215, 245, 303, 375, 419
Tom Weschler: 335

782.42166
T

For Harry, whose wheels became wings far too early.

Contents

Foreword by Damon Gough *xiii*   Foreword by Mike Mills *xvii*
Introduction *xix*   Acknowledgments *xxiii*
Contributors *xxv*   Glory Days: A Timeline *xxxi*

Contents

Contents

T

U

V

W

YZ

PHOTOS

Contents

PHOTOS

ENCORES

The day I discovered Bruce Springsteen, my life changed. I felt different, I felt excited. Bruce had a profound impact on me, but it was also very subtle, if that's possible. I felt inspired but I didn't immediately grab the broomstick and strike poses in the mirror as though with a guitar, as I think Bruce may have done when he discovered Elvis.

I was fourteen and music was generally an important part in my life. At that point the Smiths were the band I followed most closely; before that it was the Police, the Specials, the Jam, and any other decent music that came across the airwaves on British radio. I loved all kinds of music and enjoyed it as an important factor in my life. Why was it, though, that Springsteen's music came along and totally eclipsed everything I had heard before? I wasn't looking for anything. I wasn't unhappy. We were never rich, and certainly never poor. I had two parents who were and are the best in the business, a brother and two sisters who loved me. I didn't need anything. I didn't need saving. But when I heard "Thunder Road" for the first time, I felt saved from something. I also didn't know at this point that music would become my life. I didn't start playing guitar until I was nineteen.

The point of my discovery of Bruce happened quite randomly and kind of by accident (I think this may have been important in fueling my fascination, maybe not). It was Christmastime in 1984. I was flicking channels for something to watch on TV. I'd never really heard of Bruce Springsteen, but the success of *Born in the U.S.A.* had spawned a documentary that was showing on BBC2, a program called "The Old Grey Whistle Test." David Hepworth was interviewing Bruce backstage after a gig in Philadelphia, I think. This was interspersed with video clips and songs, old and new.

I flicked past this show several times before I finally stopped on it. I instinctively grabbed a blank videotape (we'd just acquired our first VCR) and forced it into the player. It was footage from *No Nukes* in 1979, and the harmonica/piano intro of "Thunder Road" is what caused this reaction. I taped the remainder of the documentary and then rewound the tape to watch this particular song again. I still have that tape; the footage is wobbly at the start and takes a few seconds to even out, missing the first few bars. I watched that version of "Thunder Road" maybe 100 times over the next few days, and became totally fascinated with the song itself and separately fascinated with the performance, which I think is incredible.

Springsteen himself comes over as an unpretentious, uncalculated natural performer, exuding enthusiasm, excitement, and real emotion, and looking like he really gives a shit. Springsteen's disregard for rock posturing, together with his sense of irony and brilliant humour, resulted in Bruce probably being the coolest guy on the planet at that point in history.

I feel lucky now that this was my introduction to Bruce Springsteen. Otherwise, is it possible I could have written him off as a flag-waving, muscle bound, gravel-voiced guy shouting "Born in the U.S.A."— which many people did at the time? I'd like to think I would have discovered Bruce's music at some point or another, but you never know. Twenty years on and I still feel that moment was supposed to happen; it was a point of fate in my life.

Over a period of months I went out and bought all the albums in more or less chronological order, each time discovering gems I'd never known before. Imagine hearing "Incident on 57th Street" for the first time, the breakdown in the middle with the narrative, then the beautiful piano outro, then "Rosalita" kicking in. Then songs like "Lost in the Flood," "The Angel," "Meeting Across the River," and countless others. I had a lot of discovering to do. At times I felt cheated that I hadn't got to this stuff earlier, but I was always excited to hear what Bruce did next.

Once I'd absorbed all the official releases, I embarked on the world of bootlegs. In those days you could only get these from record fairs that traveled around the country. I'd spend most of my spare cash on as many tapes as I could get my hands on. Around that period I also read the biography *Born to Run* by Dave Marsh, which was something of a bible to me at the time. That, coupled with the bootlegs, kept me constantly fascinated, and I didn't really listen to much other music for a good few years.

I became particularly obsessed with finding versions of "Thunder Road." I'd always skip straight to "Thunder Road" on every bootleg, just to hear what the version was like, how the phrasing altered or the mood differed. Sometimes there were radically different arrangements, like the early one from the Main Point in Philadelphia, when the song was titled, "Wings for Wheels."

I've seen Bruce Springsteen play live around twenty times now, and I can't wait for the next. Around five years ago my girlfriend Clare and I met Bruce for the first time after a show in Manchester. We decided to stay in a hotel in town and make a night of it. I'd half thought Bruce would stay there himself. I didn't think for a minute that it would work out, and I feel guilty that it did. Bruce came over to us in the lobby bar and we spoke for about twenty minutes. He was as gracious and charismatic as you'd hope him to be. I offered him a signed copy of my fourth EP, *It Came from the Ground,* by way of thanks.

In 2003 Bruce played again at the Manchester Cricket Ground, about a mile away from my house. This time, amazingly, his promoter, Harvey Goldsmith, invited us to say hello before the show. Between the two meetings, Clare and I had two children. We asked Bruce how his kids were and we told him about ours, Edith and Oscar Bruce, before he took the stage. Midway through the show he said, "This one goes out special to Oscar Bruce," and then played "Thunder Road." Imagine that. I was totally overwhelmed, to the point where, after the show, I'd thought I'd imagined it.

Tom Sheehan, a photographer friend, managed to find me a bootleg copy of the show. Just like when I was fourteen, I skipped straight to "Thunder Road," and there was the dedication as clear as a bell. I have to admit I cried; it encapsulated the emotion of twenty years of being a Springsteen fan.

Once again Bruce was responsible for one of THE moments of my life. I wrote the song "Life Turned Upside Down" in tribute to that moment. Bruce Springsteen single-handedly gave me the courage and inspiration to start a journey and work hard for something I could be proud of. If my chosen career had been flower arranging, it would have been the same inspiration that would've made me strive to be good at that. It just so happens that my chosen career turned out to be music, so the connection to Bruce is an easier one to make.

Few people have the power, conviction, and passion to inspire the way Springsteen still does. Thanks once again, Bruce, for showing me the way.

Always your fan,
Damon Gough
aka Badly Drawn Boy

Badly Drawn Boy's debut album, Hour of the Bewilderbeast, *won Great Britain's prestigious Mercury Music Prize for the year's best album in 2000. His subsequent releases include the score for the film adaptation of Nick Hornby's* About a Boy *(2002),* Have You Fed the Fish? *(2002), and* One Plus One Is One *(2004). The latter contains the song "Life Turned Upside Down." Gough resides in Manchester, England, with his girlfriend and two young children.*

Foreword by
Mike Mills of R.E.M.

I knew, after the first hour, that the voice wasn't going to last. I was even more certain after the second hour that it was going to collapse like a dynamited building, but by the time the third hour rolled around I was beginning to have serious doubts about my assessment. Then, as the fourth hour approached, I realized that the voice wasn't going anywhere; indeed, it was as strong as it had been all night. I also knew that I would never think of rock 'n' roll in the same way again.

Seeing Bruce Springsteen and the E Street Band at the Fox Theater in Atlanta in 1978 was a watershed experience for me. I watched someone rock as hard for four hours as I'd ever seen anyone rock at all. The passion, the commitment, all the things I've associated with Bruce over the years were there, and in very large doses. In following Bruce over the years, I've realized that he understands rock 'n' roll as well as anyone ever has—the beauty and power that it has, and the energy and commitment it takes to both corral and unleash that power. And all this from one of the kindest, most thoughtful people I've met in all my years in music.

Bruce's decision to involve himself in the Vote for Change tour was no shock, but it was a surprise given his previous disinclination to endorse a particular political candidate or position. The degree to which he involved himself, however, was no surprise at all. He went in giving 100 percent commitment to the cause, just as he gives in everything he agrees to do. I was and am proud to have been a part of the Vote for Change tour with Bruce, and humbled (and way psyched) to have shared the stage with him and the fabulous E Street Band. A master songwriter, kick-ass musician, and kind and genuine person all rolled into one rock 'n' roll icon—that's Bruce Springsteen to me.

Mike Mills

Mike Mills cofounded R.E.M. in 1980 in Athens, Georgia, playing bass, keyboards, and guitar and singing on the group's seventeen albums. Mills has also appeared on albums by the Indigo Girls, Warren Zevon, the Troggs, Smashing Pumpkins, Liz Phair, Kevin Kinney, Robbie Robertson, Christy McWilson, and Victoria Williams, and he participated in the 2003 Tell Us the Truth tour.

Introduction

Three decades after *Born to Run* and thirty-three years since *Greetings from Asbury Park, N.J.*, there are certain things we know about Bruce Springsteen. He is one of the most important and accomplished singers and songwriters in rock 'n' roll history (not to mention a pretty fair guitar player, too). He is a versatile and adventurous craftsman who has struggled to avoid being trapped or pigeonholed by any one creative direction he has pursued. He hates being called The Boss, and he is a valid pick for the most dynamic live performer on the planet. All told, he is simply one of the greats, an artist who has transcended hype and fashion and has attained—whether he wanted it or not—the iconic status of those he may have revered himself.

How did he get there? Honesty. Because, after all the analysis and assessments and accolades, Springsteen *means* it, and always has. He writes, plays, and performs with the sincerity and the passion of a '69 Chevy with a 396, barreling down Highway 1, 9, 29, or 31. But we're not talking about the bottled or manufactured kind of emotions that some—okay, many—rock acts have been able to trade on as genuine passion; rather, Springsteen testifies to a redeeming and life-saving quality in the music, creating a sonic landscape in which ideals and experiences collide and there's a potential, and a *need*, to find light even in the darkest of places.

In the spring of 2001, in the afterglow of his reunion tour with the E Street Band, Springsteen talked to me about "that job we do" and the overwhelming sense of purpose behind it. "I guess you'd say we've devised a language by which we assist ourselves and our audience in making sense of the world and their lives, and in finding both our and their place in the world," he explained. "It's a passing of energy and of thought. I think the basic idea is to enhance understanding or to just pull you out to say, 'Hey, you're not alone, I'm not alone' ... And I think that's what people come for; they want to be lifted up and grounded at the same time. The band is idealistic, and yet it deals regularly with the world as it stands, and in the end, hopefully, we open up possibilities and the idea of possible worlds."

Springsteen has indeed taken us, and himself, on a trip for the better part of four decades, speaking first through the characters that populated his early work and then, starting with *Darkness on the Edge of Town*, narrating through first-person experiences. He has given us the realm of human emotion with a poet's grace and a garage rocker's exuberance, from teen angst to adult anxiety and all aspects of life—cars, crime, courtship, marriage, parenthood, and politics included—without ever losing sight of "The Promised Land" that he sang about in 1978. Across fifteen albums he has fashioned a kind of social history, not of the world but about one person's place in it. In doing so, he reflects some vestige of all our experiences, whether we've tracked alongside him on our own ride into adulthood or are still teenagers (or younger) yearning to roll down the window and let the wind blow back our hair.

And then there's the live show, the truest portal to Springsteen of any. It's a roller coaster that climbs and plunges and soars and only very rarely coasts to allow us—and the band—to catch our breath. Even his solo acoustic shows of 1995–97 had the intensity of something being played out in front of us, a theme we could certainly feel if not necessarily verbalize while we were dancing in the dark. And, oh yeah, the big, electric shows are also a hell of a lot of fun, with a greater sense of humor than is often demonstrated on record, one of the reasons you find so many folks willing to hit the highway and travel to more than just the one that plays in their hometown.

Through this work, this "job" that he does, Springsteen has created a sprawling, complex life story. Though the parts of that story are as intriguing as the whole, in the myriad writing that's been done about Springsteen they've never really been broken down and examined in their own right. And a good part of the fun with Springsteen has been that shared history through the years as his audience has grown up with him.

So welcome to *The Ties That Bind: Bruce Springsteen A to E to Z*. Beneath this dirty hood is an examination of all things relevant to Mr. Springsteen, the E Street Band, and the ghosts of Asbury Park. With nearly 300 entries, we've sifted out the many individual fragments of Springsteen's life and career—the characters (real and created), the albums, the singles, the band members, the family members, and all the adjunct personalities, places, events, and even myths that are often referred to in the context of Springsteen lore. This is a book for those who may want to know more about

Mike Appel or the Palace, Asbury Park or the Hollywood Hills, the Firecracker Show or the Bomb Scare Show.

It is our hope that *The Ties That Bind* will enhance and enrich the connection any fan, longtimer or novice, has with Springsteen and his music. This book contains a wealth of information that should leave you with a better sense of someone who set out to do more than just record songs and play shows—someone who has, in fact, been able to shake the world a little bit.

So sit tight and take hold. We're pulling out of here to win....

Gary Graff
garygraff@visibleink.com

Acknowledgments

The roots for *The Ties That Bind: Bruce Springsteen A to E to Z* were planted in January 1996, when I first met Visible Ink Press publisher Marty Connors at—where else?—a Springsteen show at the Fox Theatre in Detroit, Michigan. Marty is one of *those* Springsteen fans, a Brucehead who figures that when Springsteen's on tour, his place is on the road as well. A subsequent lunch led to the *MusicHound Essential Album Guide* series, but there was even at that time an expressed interest in doing some kind of Springsteen book. Nine years and eleven *MusicHounds* later, this bus is finally stopping on 82nd St., and Mr. Connors is, I hope, doing a joyful E Street Shuffle. I hoist a Guinness in his direction.

The full-time and adjunct staff at Visible Ink Press was, as always, a pleasure to work with on this project—professional, creative, and contagiously enthusiastic. Terri Schell kept us "honest" as only the strongest of project managers and Springsteen fanatics could and made sure we never got waist-deep in "The Big Muddy." My friend Dean Dauphinais's keen eye and resourcefulness helped to make sure the photo end of this book rocked. Christa Gainor, Brad Morgan, Larry Baker, and Jim Craddock provided a range of top-notch editorial support, while Mary Claire Krzewinski, Bob Huffman, and Jake Di Vita handled all matters relating to design, art, and composition. Roger Jänecke and Mary Beth Perrot patiently and skillfully harnessed the energy of all the Bruce geeks involved with the book to make sure there was really a "Reason to Believe." And a special thanks to Jeff Becker and Jill Connors, whose uninhibited curiosity and embrace of all things Bruce helped inspire this project.

Another benefit of a project like this is the opportunity to work with writers who are both peers and friends and willing to take a "Leap of Faith" to be part of it. Dan Durchholz, my brother from another mother, Erik Flanni-gan, and Chris *"Backstreets"* Phillips served as valuable go-to guys who gave *The Ties That Bind* priority within their busy lives. Lynne Margolis stepped up like a journalistic pack mule every time she got the call. And my deep grati-tude goes to everyone else who contributed great work—Robert Bader, Steve Knopper, Matt Lee, Michael Norman, Jonathan Pont, Robert Santelli, Jeff Zaslow, Ben Rocher, Shari Deeken: Your best was *always* good enough. Pho-tographers Robert Alford, Paul Natkin, Jim Shive, Ken Settle, and Tom Weschler combed their archives to provide the project with their outstanding work, and Marcia Schiff at AP/Wide World Photos led her organization's cooperation with the book.

Many thanks to Badly Drawn Boy (Damon Gough) and R.E.M.'s Mike Mills for sharing the kind of warm and insightful feelings about Bruce Spring-steen that could only come from fans who are also fellow recording and tour-ing musicians. Both of their forewords, and the discussions we had while they were writing them, deepened my own appreciation for Springsteen.

Thanks also go out to other colleagues and supervisors (the guys *I* call The Boss) whom I work with on a day-to-day basis and who both knowing-ly and unwittingly indulged me the time and space I needed to complete the book: Robert Musial at the *Oakland Press*; Laura Demarco at the *Cleveland Plain Dealer*; Dia Stein, Dave Ankers, Bruce Simon, and the rest of the Launch Radio Networks crew; Ken Calvert and Bill Stedman at WCSX Detroit; Sean Elliott, Bob Madden, Brian Nelson, and Eric Jensen at WLZR Milwau-kee; Gayden Wren at the *New York Times'* Starbeat syndicate; and everyone at *Revolver*, *Guitar World*, and Red Flag Media.

My father, Milton Graff, was still alive when we started this book in the fall of 2003, and his encouragement and pride sustained me even after he passed away. My in-laws Miriam and Henry Brysk never failed to inquire about the progress of the book and provided an inspiring rooting section. And all my love goes to my true beautiful rewards—my wife Judy, daughter Hannah, and stepsons Ben and Josh for their support and for putting up with the time demands, the endless flow of Springsteen music, and the profound-ly chaotic state my office reached over the course of this project.

Gary Graff

Contributors

Editor

Gary Graff turned his attention to journalism after an unsatisfying encounter with ninth-grade biology convinced him that it might be wise to steer a career path away from medicine. Over the years, Graff has written award-winning music articles and criticism for the *New York Times* Features Syndicate, *Guitar World*, *Revolver*, *Rolling Stone*, *People*, Reuters, UPI, *Replay*, *Request*, *Launch*, *Hit Parader*, *Hits*, *Billboard*, *Backstreets*, *Beatlefan*, *Country Song Roundup*, *ICE*, *BMI Music World*, Mr. Showbiz, Compuserve WOW!, the Microsoft Network, Red Flag Media, and for myriad newspapers, including the *Cleveland Plain Dealer*, *San Francisco Chronicle*, *Dallas Morning News*, *Boston Globe*, *Detroit Free Press*, *Pittsburgh Post-Gazette*, *Atlanta Journal-Constitution*, *San Diego Union Tribune*, *Oakland Press* (Mich.), and the *Detroit Journal* and *Sunday Journal*. Graff is the founding editor of the award-winning *MusicHound Essential Album Guide* series and was also the editor of Thomson Gale's *Popular Music* annual. Graff is also cofounder and board member of the Motor City Music Awards Foundation, and he reports on rock news for the New York–based Launch Radio Networks, Detroit's WCSX-FM, and Milwaukee's WLZR-FM. A graduate of the University of Missouri–Columbia, Graff lives with his wife, daughter, and twin stepsons in suburban Detroit, where he can sometimes be found flailing at racquetballs, golf balls, softballs, floor hockey pucks, and bass guitars. **Favorite Springsteen Song**: "The Promised Land." **Favorite Springsteen Album**: *Born to Run*. **Favorite Springsteen Show**: September 22, 1984, Civic Arena, Pittsburgh, PA.

Contributors

Robert Bader is the editor of *Groucho Marx and Other Short Stories and Tall Tales*, an anthology of the comedian's lost writings. He is also a television producer and a regular contributor to *Backstreets*. He lives in New York City. **Favorite Springsteen Song:** "Kitty's Back." **Favorite Springsteen Album:** *The Wild, the Innocent & the E Street Shuffle.* **Favorite Springsteen Show:** June 3, 1978, Nassau Coliseum, Long Island, NY.

Marty Connors saw his first Bruce Springsteen show at Detroit's Michigan Palace in 1975. After that, he was never the same. Most people think that this new state of not being the same was an improvement. Regardless and ever since, he's been attending Springsteen shows with religious dedication, and has often connected to the big song in the sky during "She's the One." When his daughter, Jane, was eight, she attended her first show during the Tunnel of Love Express tour; this helped put an end to her obsession with Olivia Newton-John. Because of Springsteen, Connors has seen places he never would have seen, like Cincinnati and East Rutherford, New Jersey. As the publisher of Visible Ink Press, he's been hoping for this book to see the light of day for quite some time. **Favorite Springsteen Songs:** "She's the One" and "Something in the Night." **Favorite Springsteen Album:** *Darkness on the Edge of Town.* **Favorite Springsteen Show:** November 17, 1978, Michigan State University, East Lansing, MI.

Daniel Durchholz spends his time hiding on the backstreets of Wildwood, Missouri, where he lives with his wife, Mary, and four children. He is co-editor (with Gary Graff) of *MusicHound Rock: The Essential Album Guide.* He is a frequent contributor to *Stereophile* magazine, the *St. Louis Post-Dispatch*, *Chicago Tribune*, and radio station KMOX. **Favorite Springsteen Song:** "Thunder Road." **Favorite Springsteen Album:** *Born to Run.* **Favorite Springsteen Show:** February 28, 1977, Fox Theatre, St. Louis, MO.

Erik Flannigan first wrote about Bruce Springsteen for *Backstreets* in 1986 (he remains a senior editor to the magazine) and later served as contributing editor to *Backstreets: Springsteen: The Man and His Music* (Harmony). He's also co-author (with Charles R. Cross) of *Led Zeppelin: Heaven and Hell* (Harmony) and a frequent contributor to *No Depression*. Some say he bears a passing resemblance to Lynn Elder. **Favorite Springsteen Song:** "Stolen Car." **Favorite Springsteen Albums:** *Darkness on the Edge of Town* and *Tunnel of Love.* **Favorite Springsteen Show:** Christic Institute Benefit Concert, November 16, 1990, Los Angeles, CA.

Steve Knopper, who enjoyed his first kiss at a Springsteen show on a frigid Denver night in 1985, covers the music industry for *Rolling Stone* magazine. He has also written for *Spin, Esquire, Entertainment Weekly*, the *Chicago Tribune, Newsday*, and many others. He is the editor of *MusicHound*

Swing!: The Essential Album Guide (Visible Ink Press) and *MusicHound Lounge: The Essential Album Guide* (Visible Ink Press), and co-author of *The Complete Idiot's Guide to Starting a Band* (Alpha). **Favorite Springsteen Song:** "Roulette." **Favorite Springsteen Album:** *Nebraska.* **Favorite Springsteen Show:** September 1985, Mile High Stadium, Denver, CO.

Matt Lee is a recovering musician now engaged in public relations in Detroit with an emphasis on media placement. **Favorite Springsteen Song:** "Zero & Blind Terry." **Favorite Springsteen Album:** *Born to Run.* **Favorite Springsteen Show:** December 30, 1978, Cobo Arena, Detroit, MI.

Lynne Margolis left her native Pittsburgh (home of Joe Grushecky) for Austin, Texas, in late 2003. The freelance music journalist does, however, bemoan missing a pair of 1975 Springsteen concerts in the Steel City and then having to stand on a chair to get out of the way of 5,500 stampeding students entering an April 13, 1976, Springsteen show at Penn State University—her first-ever rock concert. It would not be the last time she stood on a chair at a Springsteen concert. **Favorite Springsteen Song:** "Sad Eyes." **Favorite Springsteen Albums:** *Greetings from Asbury Park, N.J.* and *The Wild, the Innocent & the E Street Shuffle.* **Favorite Springsteen Shows:** Three performances with Joe Grushecky & the Houserockers at Nick's Fat City in Pittsburgh, PA.

Michael Norman has been the arts and entertainment editor of the *Cleveland Plain Dealer* since 1999. He covered pop music for the newspaper from 1992–99. A graduate of Ohio State University, he resides in Medina, Ohio, with his wife, Ann, and two daughters, Katie and Madeline. **Favorite Springsteen Song:** "Badlands." **Favorite Springsteen Album:** *Darkness on the Edge of Town.* **Favorite Springsteen Show:** November 14, 1999, Gund Arena, Cleveland, OH.

Christopher Phillips is the editor of *Backstreets: The Boss Magazine* (celebrating its twenty-fifth year of publishing in 2005) and webmaster of Backstreets.com. The son of a Jersey Girl, he lives with his wife, Laura, in Chapel Hill, NC. **Favorite Springsteen Song:** "Tunnel of Love." **Favorite Springsteen Album:** *Nebraska.* **Favorite Springsteen Show:** December 7, 1984, Tallahassee, FL.

Jonathan Pont is a New York–based journalist who has written about music for *Backstreets*, the *Los Angeles Times*, and *No Depression*. **Favorite Springsteen Song:** Has not yet been written. **Favorite Springsteen Album:** *Nebraska.* **Favorite Springsteen Shows:** The two Christic Institute benefit concerts, November 1990, Los Angeles, CA; June 12, 2000, Madison Square Garden, New York, NY; and September 6–7, 2003, Fenway Park, Boston, MA.

Robert Santelli, a New Jersey native, has been writing about Springsteen and the Asbury Park music scene since 1973, when he became the rock critic for the *Asbury Park Press* and began freelancing for *New Jersey Monthly*, *Rolling Stone*, *Musician*, *Modern Drummer*, *Billboard*, and many other publications. He taught popular music history and American studies at Monmouth and Rutgers universities in New Jersey before moving to Cleveland in 1995 to become vice president of education and public programs at the Rock and Roll Hall of Fame and Museum. Santelli became the director of the Experience Music Project in Seattle in 2000. He is also the author and editor of numerous books on American music and travel, including *The Big Book of Blues* (Penguin), *Hard Travelin': The Life and Legacy of Woody Guthrie* (Wesleyan University Press), *American Roots Music* (Harry Abrams), and *The Jersey Shore: A Travel Guide* (Globe Pequot Press). Santelli also co-authored *The Big Beat: Conversations with Rock's Great Drummers* (Contemporary) with E Street Band drummer Max Weinberg and worked with Bruce Springsteen on his book *Songs* (Avon). Currently Santelli is completing a book on the history of the Asbury Park music scene. He lives on Bainbridge Island, Washington, with his wife and three children. **Favorite Springsteen Song:** "Tunnel of Love." **Favorite Springsteen Album:** *Born to Run.* **Favorite Springsteen Show:** December 11, 1975, Seton Hall University, West Orange, NJ.

Jeffrey Zaslow is a columnist for the *Wall Street Journal*. Previously, as advice columnist at the *Chicago Sun-Times*, he often advised readers by quoting a Springsteen lyric. Zaslow lives in suburban Detroit with his darling wife, Sherry, whose wedding ring is inscribed, "I'd drive all night." They have three daughters, all of whom have seen Springsteen from the pit. **Favorite Springsteen Song:** "Thunder Road." **Favorite Springsteen Album:** *The River.* **Favorite Springsteen Show:** August 9, 1985, Soldier Field, Chicago, IL.

Photographers

Robert Alford's career as an entertainment photographer spans thirty-five years. His work has taken him on world tours with dozens of bands. Some of his shots of over 500 different artists and groups have become album covers and posters, and his work has been featured in hundreds of publications the world over. He resides in Canton, Michigan.

Paul Natkin is a rock 'n' roll photographer who has been photographing musicians for twenty-eight years. His work has been published in many magazines and newspapers, including *Newsweek*, *People*, *Rolling Stone*, and *Creem*. His photo of Springsteen graced the cover of *Newsweek* in August 1985. He lives in Chicago, Illinois.

Ken Settle is a Detroit-area photographer who has specialized in music photography for three decades. His photos have been published worldwide in magazines such as *Guitar Player, Rolling Stone,* the original *Creem* magazine, *People,* and *Playboy.* Numerous album, book, television, and video projects have featured his work, including Grand Funk's live album *Bosnia,* Tom Wheeler's *The Stratocaster Chronicles,* and VH1's "Behind the Music" and "Driven" series.

Jim Shive has been a photographer for over twenty-five years with his rock 'n' roll archives housing some of the most exclusive images from the 1970s and 1980s. His work has appeared on television and in magazines, books, and newspapers. Check out more images, including limited edition prints, at www.SpringsteenGallery.com.

Thomas Weschler started his career shooting photos of the Beatles from his TV screen on February 9, 1964; he developed them himself and the next morning took them to school where many, many girls wanted them. At age fifteen his life's work began with a simple thought: "Photography, music, girls, why not?" He is still working as a photographer in the Detroit area shooting music-related projects.

Glory Days:
A Timeline

1949

September 23: Bruce Frederick Springsteen is born at Monmouth Memorial Hospital in Long Branch, NJ. Tipping the scales at nearly six and one-half pounds, he is the first child of Douglas and Adele Springsteen. The family resides in Freehold, NJ.

1950

December 8: Springsteen's sister Virginia is born.

1955

September: Springsteen begins the first of an eight-year sentence at St. Rose of Lima parochial school in Freehold, acquiring an abundance of Catholic imagery that proves useful later.

1956

September 9: A seed is planted as Springsteen watches Elvis Presley shake, rattle, and roll for the first time on the Ed Sullivan Show. The show is viewed by a record 60 million people or more than 80 percent of the television audience.

1958

Adele Springsteen rents her son a guitar, with the provision that he take lessons.

1959

Guitar lessons don't agree with Springsteen, who quits and begins pursuing a more random form of musical apprenticeship.

1962

September 7: Sister Pamela is born in Freehold.

1963

Springsteen becomes the proud owner of a guitar he purchases for $18 at the Western Auto Store in Freehold.

1964

Freshman Springsteen attends Freehold Regional High School and joins his first band, the Rogues. The band has a few local gigs, mostly at teen dances.

1965

The down payment on the future of rock 'n' roll is made when Adele Springsteen takes out a $60 loan to buy her son a six-string guitar and a small amplifier for Christmas.

When the lead singer of the Castiles, George Theiss, falls for Springsteen's sister Ginny, Springsteen earns an audition with the band, which is managed by Tex and Marion Vinyard. Bidding adieu to the Rogues, Springsteen joins the Castiles, eventually becoming lead guitarist. The group's first paying job at a local swim club earns them $35.

1966

May: The Castiles record a single, "Baby I" b/w "That's What You Get," co-written by Springsteen and Theiss. The single is never released.

1967

The Castiles perform at Greenwich Village's Cafe Wha and a variety of other gigs, including the opening of a supermarket.

June: Springsteen graduates from Freehold High School. He does not attend his graduation.

August: The Castiles play their final show in Red Bank, NJ.

September: An aspiring poet, Springsteen briefly attends Ocean County Community College in Toms River, NJ.

November: Springsteen meets fellow long-hair and Jersey Shore musician Steve Van Zandt.

1968

The Castiles break up. Springsteen forms Earth, a power trio featuring Springsteen on lead vocal and guitar covering songs by Cream, the Doors, Jimi Hendrix, and other popular groups.

1969

Springsteen's family moves to San Mateo, CA, but he and sister Ginny remain in New Jersey. Later in the year, Springsteen moves to Asbury Park.

Springsteen fails his U.S. Army physical exam with a 4-F status, partly due to injuries sustained in a timely 1967 motorcycle accident.

Earth lasts only a few months. Springsteen joins Child, an Asbury Park blues-rock band whose members include Vini Lopez and Danny Federici. Based at the Upstage in Asbury Park, Child morphs into Steel Mill after Springsteen and Lopez discover another local band known as Child.

1970

Steve Van Zandt joins Springsteen and Steel Mill. The band is managed by Carl "Tinker" West, a local surfboard manufacturer. Steel Mill broadens Springsteen's reach both artistically and geographically, as he writes almost all the songs and the band gains popularity outside its Jersey Shore stomping grounds, including regular stops in Richmond, VA.

January 13: Steel Mill heads west to perform at the Matrix in Berkeley, CA.

February 22: Springsteen and Steel Mill record three demos for concert promoter and manager Bill Graham at Fillmore Recording Studios in San Francisco, CA, but they turn down Graham's offer for a recording contract, deciding the $1,000 advance is insufficient.

1971

February: Steel Mill breaks up as Springsteen tires of their blues-rock sound in favor of a new musical direction. He forms the short-lived big band Dr. Zoom and the Sonic Boom with Asbury Park regulars, including Steve Van Zandt, Danny Federici, David Sancious, Vini Lopez, Garry Tallent, and Johnny Lyon. Later that year, he assembles the Bruce Springsteen Band, an eleven-piece multi-racial rock and soul outfit, which also includes Federici, Van Zandt, Tallent, and Sancious.

November: At a meeting arranged by Carl West, Springsteen plays two songs for Mike Appel and Jim Cretecos, Tin Pan Alley songwriters who aspire to be talent managers and producers. The response is cool.

1972

February: Now a solo act, Springsteen returns from a visit to his family in California and auditions once more for Appel and Cretecos, who are much more taken with his abilities.

March: Appel and Cretecos form Laurel Canyon Ltd., a production and management company. Springsteen signs on as the only client.

May 2: Springsteen auditions for Columbia Records executive John Hammond at his office in New York City.

May 3: Hammond takes Springsteen into the studio to record a dozen demos, including "It's Hard to Be a Saint in the City," "Mary Queen of Arkansas," "Growin' Up," "Does This Bus Stop at 82nd Street?," "The Angel," "If I Was the Priest," "Cowboys of the Sea," and "Arabian Nights."

June 9: Springsteen signs with Columbia and receives a $25,000 advance. Several days later, Mike Appel takes Springsteen to see Elvis Presley at Madison Square Garden.

Springsteen begins recording his debut at tiny 914 Sound Studios in Blauvelt, NY, during the summer, supported by a posse of familiar Asbury Park musicians.

October 28: First show billed to Bruce Springsteen and the E Street Band is held in West Chester, PA. Members include Garry Tallent, Clarence Clemons, Danny Federici, and Vini Lopez. The band takes its name from the Belmar, NJ, address of David Sancious's mother, where it had rehearsed for the album. Sancious, though a player on the album, does not begin touring with the group until mid-1973.

1973

January 5: Springsteen releases his debut album, *Greetings from Asbury Park, N.J.*

May 30: Springsteen begins a twelve-date tour of arenas opening for Chicago. During the summer, work begins on the second album with the core group of Tallent, Clemons, Federici, Lopez, and Sancious at 914 Sound Studios.

November 5: Springsteen releases his second album, *The Wild, the Innocent & the E Street Shuffle.*

1974

Early in the year, Jim Cretecos leaves Laurel Canyon.

February 14: Springsteen fires E Street Band drummer Vini Lopez.

February 23: New E Street Band drummer Ernest "Boom" Carter debuts. During his brief tenure he's involved in studio work for the next album.

May 9: Springsteen's opening show for Bonnie Raitt at the Harvard Square Theater in Cambridge, MA, is reviewed by music critic Jon Landau, who proclaims in the May 22 edition of the *Real Paper*, "I saw rock 'n' roll future and its name is Bruce Springsteen." The band performs a new song, "Born to Run."

August: "Born to Run" is recorded at 914 Sound Studios with Ernest "Boom" Carter on drums. Carter and David Sancious leave the E Street Band to form a new group, Tone.

September: Responding to an ad in the *Village Voice*, pianist Roy Bittan and drummer Max Weinberg join the E Street Band.

Hoping to generate buzz, manager Mike Appel leaks copies of the single, "Born to Run," to supportive radio DJs in New York, Philadelphia, and Boston. Sales of the first two albums have been disappointing at approximately 90,000 units total.

September 18-19: The first shows with Bittan and Weinberg in the band take place at the Main Point, Bryn Mawr, PA. Sharing their debut is Suki Lahav, the band's first female member, on violin.

1975

March 9: Lahav has last show with the band before moving to Israel with her husband.

May: Guitarist Steve Van Zandt joins the E Street Band.

July 20: *Born to Run* tour starts in Providence, RI.

July 25: The single "Born to Run" is released.

August 13: Springsteen and the E Street Band begin a revelatory ten-set, five-night stand at the Bottom Line in New York City.

September 1: Springsteen releases his third album, *Born to Run*

October 27: *Time* and *Newsweek* magazines both feature Springsteen on their covers.

November 18: Springsteen plays his first show abroad at the Hammersmith Odeon in London, England.

December 12: Live version of "Santa Claus Is Coming to Town" is recorded at C.W. Post College in Brookville, NY, as part of a proposed live album that never surfaces. "Tenth Avenue Freeze-Out" is released as a single.

1976

March: Springsteen begins a year of regular touring with a show at the Beacon Theatre in New York.

April 29: Springsteen scales the fence at Elvis Presley's Graceland estate in Memphis, TN, and is escorted off the premises by guards.

July 27: Springsteen files suit against Mike Appel and Laurel Canyon in federal court in Manhattan for fraud, breach of trust, and undue influence.

July 29: Appel countersues Springsteen and wins a preliminary injunction barring Springsteen from recording.

November 26: Springsteen closes the year by joining Patti Smith for two shows at the Bottom Line in New York City.

1977

February 7: Chicken Scratch tour begins in Albany, NY.

Winter: *Thunder Road*, the first Springsteen fanzine, is founded by Ken Viola and Lou Cohan.

February 19: Springsteen's "Blinded by the Light" is a No. 1 hit for Manfred Mann's Earth Band.

March 22–25: Chicken Scratch tour concludes with shows at Music Hall, Boston, MA.

May 28: Springsteen and Appel settle their lawsuits. Springsteen immediately enters the studio with new co-producer/manager Jon Landau to start recording his fourth album.

1978

May 19: *Darkness on the Edge of Town* tour kicks off at the Paramount Theatre in Asbury Park.

June 6: Springsteen releases his fourth album, *Darkness on the Edge of Town.*

June 9: "Prove It All Night" is the first single released from the new album.

August 14: "Badlands" is the second single released.

1979

January 1: *Darkness* tour concludes in Cleveland, OH.

April: Recording begins on a fifth album at New York's Power Station.

September 22–23: Springsteen performs at the Musicians United for Safe Energy (MUSE) No Nukes benefit concerts at Madison Square Garden in New York City.

1980

April: The General Assembly of New Jersey debates the title of New Jersey Pop Music Ambassador to America for Springsteen and the adoption of "Born to Run" as "the unofficial rock theme of our State's youth." The measures fail.

October 3: *The River* tour opens in Ann Arbor, MI, with Bob Seger joining Springsteen for an encore version of "Thunder Road."

October 17: Springsteen releases *The River*, his fifth album. Shortly thereafter, the first single, "Hungry Heart," is released, and becomes Springsteen's first Top 5 single.

October 24: The first edition of *Backstreets* newsletter is handed out for free at Springsteen show in Seattle, WA.

1981

February 3: "Fade Away" is the second single from *The River.*

April 7: Springsteen and the E Street Band begin their second tour of Europe in Hamburg, West Germany.

August 20: Springsteen leads the Night for the Vietnam Veteran benefit concert for the Vietnam Veterans of America at the Los Angeles Sports Arena in California.

1982

January 3: Springsteen begins recording what will become the *Nebraska* album on a Teac Tascam Series 144 four-track cassette recorder in his rented home in Colts Neck, NJ. The cassette spends a considerable amount of time in Springsteen's jeans pocket before it is engineered for release.

September 20: Springsteen releases his sixth album, *Nebraska*.

1984

May: Steve Van Zandt formally departs the E Street Band.

May 9: "Dancing in the Dark" single is released, peaking at No. 2 on charts.

June: Nils Lofgren and Patti Scialfa join the E Street Band.

June 4: Springsteen releases *Born in the U.S.A.*

June 29: *Born in the U.S.A.* tour begins in St. Paul, MN.

August 5: Springsteen begins ten shows at Brendan Byrne Arena, East Rutherford, NJ.

August 18: "Cover Me" is released as second single.

October: Booking agent Barry Bell introduces Springsteen to model/actress Julianne Phillips. "Born in the U.S.A." is released as single.

1985

January 28: Springsteen takes part in the recording of the all-star famine relief single "We Are the World" at A&M Studios in Hollywood, CA.

February 4: "I'm on Fire" is released as a single and charts in the Top 10.

March 21: *Born in the U.S.A.* tour moves to Australia.

April 10–22: Springsteen plays series of dates in Japan.

May: Another Top 5 hit, "Glory Days" is released as the fifth single from *Born in the U.S.A.*

May 13: Springsteen marries Julianne Phillips in a late-night ceremony in Lake Oswego, OR.

June 1: European leg of *Born in the U.S.A.* tour opens in Dublin, Ireland.

August: Springsteen begins a stadium tour of U.S. in Washington, DC. "I'm Goin' Down" is released as a single and charts in Top 10.

October: *Born in the U.S.A.* tour ends in Los Angeles, CA. Springsteen joins Artists United Against Apartheid for the single "Sun City."

November 21: "My Hometown" is released as a single and breaks the Top 10.

1986

October 13: Springsteen joins Neil Young at Bridge School Benefit concert.

November 10: Springsteen releases five-LP, three-CD box set *Live/1975–85*.

1987

January 21: Springsteen inducts Roy Orbison into the Rock and Roll Hall of Fame at the Waldorf-Astoria Hotel in New York City.

September: "Brilliant Disguise" is released as a single, cracking the Top 5.

September 30: Springsteen joins Orbison and an all-star band for filming of *A Black & White Night* at the Coconut Grove in Los Angeles, CA.

October 6: Springsteen releases *Tunnel of Love*, his eighth album. Title track is released as a single that month, reaching the Top 10.

October 22: Springsteen performs "Forever Young" at a memorial service for John Hammond in New York City.

December 7: Springsteen participates in a tribute to Harry Chapin at Carnegie Hall in New York City.

1988

January 20: Springsteen inducts Bob Dylan into the Rock and Roll Hall of Fame at the Waldorf-Astoria Hotel in New York City.

February: "One Step Up" is released as a single, peaking at No. 13 on charts.

February 25: Tunnel of Love Express Tour begins in Worcester, MA.

June: Paparazzi catch Springsteen and E Street Band singer Patti Scialfa canoodling on a hotel balcony during the Roman stop of the European leg of the Tunnel of Love Express Tour.

August: Springsteen releases *Chimes of Freedom* EP to promote upcoming Human Rights Now! tour for Amnesty International.

August 30: Phillips files for divorce from Springsteen, citing irreconcilable differences.

September 2–October 15: Springsteen and the E Street Band headline the six-week Amnesty International Human Rights Now! tour with Sting, Peter Gabriel, Tracy Chapman, and Youssou N'Dour.

1989

February: Springsteen releases *Video Anthology 1978–88.*

March 1: Phillips divorce is finalized.

October 18: Springsteen disbands the E Street Band with a phone call to each member.

1990

April: Springsteen buys a $14 million estate in Beverly Hills, CA.

July 25: Evan James Springsteen is born to Springsteen and Patti Scialfa.

October 29: Springsteen joins the jamming at fortieth birthday party for Tom Petty.

November 16–17: Springsteen joins Bonnie Raitt and Jackson Browne at Christic Institute benefit in Los Angeles, CA.

1991

June 8: Springsteen marries Patti Scialfa.

December 30: Jessica Rae Springsteen is born.

1992

March 4: The single "Human Touch" is released.

March 31: Springsteen simultaneously releases two albums, *Human Touch* and *Lucky Town.*

May 9: Springsteen make first live television performance on "Saturday Night Live."

June 5: Springsteen performs nationally broadcast radio concert with his new band.

June 15: Springsteen begins world tour in Stockholm, Sweden.

July 23–August 10: American leg of tour begins with eleven shows at Brendan Byrne Arena, East Rutherford, NJ.

September 22: Springsteen tapes MTV "Plugged" episode in Los Angeles, CA.

November 11: MTV airs Springsteen's "Plugged" performance.

1993

January 12: Springsteen inducts Creedence Clearwater Revival into the Rock and Roll Hall of Fame at the Century Plaza Hotel in Los Angeles, CA.

March 31: Springsteen begins another tour in Europe in Glasgow, Scotland.

April 12: Springsteen releases *In Concert MTV Plugged* album and home video.

June 24: Springsteen headlines A Concert to Fight Hunger benefit in East Rutherford, NJ.

June 25: Springsteen appears for the first time on *Late Night with David Letterman,* the final show of that program.

June 26: Springsteen holds the Kristen Ann Carr Fund benefit in New York City.

1994

January 5: Sam Ryan Springsteen is born.

Spring: "Streets of Philadelphia," written for the film *Philadelphia*, is Springsteen's first Top 10 single since "Tunnel of Love" in 1987.

March 21: Springsteen wins an Academy Award for Best Song for "Streets of Philadelphia."

1995

January: Springsteen and the E Street Band reunite in the studio and cut three new songs for Springsteen's *Greatest Hits* album: "Secret Garden," "Blood Brothers," and "This Hard Land."

February 28: Springsteen releases *Greatest Hits.*

Spring: "Secret Garden" is released as a single, eventually reaching the Top 20.

March: *Blood Brothers*, a documentary by Ernie Fritz chronicling the recording of new tracks by Springsteen and the E Street Band for the *Greatest Hits* collection, airs on the Disney Channel.

April 5: Springsteen appears on *The Late Show with David Letterman.*

September 2: Springsteen and the E Street Band perform at the Concert for the Rock and Roll Hall of Fame in Cleveland, OH.

October 17: Springsteen kicks off a six-show run as a member of Joe Grushecky & the House-rockers in Asbury Park, NJ.

November 19: Springsteen performs at eightieth birthday party for Frank Sinatra in Los Angeles, CA.

November 21: Springsteen releases *The Ghost of Tom Joad.*

November 26: Springsteen begins solo acoustic tour in Los Angeles, CA.

1996

March 25: Springsteen sings "Dead Man Walking" from the film of the same name at the 68th Annual Academy Awards. It fails to win the Best Song category, however.

October 26: Springsteen receives the John Steinbeck Award at San Jose State University in San Jose, CA.

November 1: Springsteen performs a benefit concert at St. Rose of Lima in Freehold, NJ.

November 19: Springsteen releases *Blood Brothers* home video.

1997

May 5: Springsteen receives the prestigious Polar Music Prize from the Royal Swedish Academy of Music.

1998

April 26: Douglas Springsteen dies at age seventy-three.

November 10: Springsteen releases *Tracks* box set.

December 10: Springsteen plays at a show marking the fiftieth anniversary of Amnesty International's Declaration of Human Rights in Bercy, France.

1999

March 15: Springsteen is inducted into the Rock and Roll Hall of Fame by U2 frontman Bono.

April 9: Springsteen and the E Street Band begin their reunion tour in Barcelona, Spain.

April 13: Springsteen releases *18 Tracks*.

2000

June: After Springsteen performs "American Skin (41 Shots)," a song that references the fatal shooting of an unarmed African immigrant by New York police officers, at earlier shows, the Patrolmen's Benevolent Association of New York City calls for a boycott of Springsteen's concerts at Madison Square Garden.

2001

January 16: Springsteen releases *The Complete Video Anthology/1978–2000*.

April 3: Springsteen releases *Live in New York City*.

April 7: "Bruce Springsteen & the E Street Band Live in New York City" debuts on HBO.

September 21: Springsteen performs "My City of Ruins" for the "America: A Tribute to Heroes" telethon to benefit the victims of the September 11 terrorist attacks.

November 6: Springsteen releases *Live in New York City* home video and DVD.

2002

May: Independence for New Jersey launches a drive to place Springsteen's name on the general election ballot as a possible candidate for the U.S. Senate. Springsteen declines.

May 18: Springsteen speaks at the dedication of Vinyard Park in Freehold, NJ, named for Castiles manager Tex Vinyard and his wife, Marion.

July 16: "The Rising," the first single from the forthcoming album, is released.

July 30: Springsteen releases *The Rising*, marking his first release of entirely new studio material recorded with the E Street Band since 1984.

August 5: *The Rising* tour begins in East Rutherford, NJ.

September 22: *Springsteen: Troubadour of the Highway* photo exhibit opens at the Frederick R. Weisman Art Museum in Minneapolis, MN.

2003

July 15–27: Stadium leg of *The Rising* tour begins with seven shows at Giants Stadium in East Rutherford, NJ.

September: Zagat's first music guide ranks *Born to Run* as the No. 1 most popular album. *Darkness on the Edge of Town* also makes the Top 10.

September 6–7: Springsteen and the E Street Band play the first concert in thirty years at venerable Fenway Park in Boston, MA.

October 4: Bob Dylan joins Springsteen for the final show of *The Rising* tour at Shea Stadium in Flushing, NY.

November 11: Springsteen releases three-CD retrospective *The Essential Bruce Springsteen*.

November 18: Springsteen releases *Live in Barcelona* DVD.

2004

March 15: Springsteen inducts Jackson Browne into the Rock and Roll Hall of Fame at the Waldorf-Astoria Hotel in New York City.

October 1: Springsteen is one of the headliners on the Vote for Change tour, beginning in Philadelphia, PA.

October/November: Springsteen plays at a series of rallies for Democratic presidential candidate John Kerry in Wisconsin and Ohio.

November 9: Springsteen releases *In Concert MTV Plugged* on DVD.

2005

February 13: Springsteen wins Grammy for Solo Rock Vocal Performance for "Code of Silence."

March 14: Springsteen inducts U2 into the Rock and Roll Hall of Fame at the Waldorf-Astoria in New York City.

April 4: Springsteen tapes an acoustic performance for broadcast on VH1 "Storytellers" later in the month.

April 5: "Devils & Dust" single is released.

April 25: In Detroit, Springsteen launches a thirty-three-date international solo acoustic tour to support *Devils & Dust*.

April 26: *Devils & Dust*, Springsteen's nineteenth album, is released.

Academy Awards

Film industry honors

he Academy Awards have been presented annually by the Academy of Motion Picture Arts and Sciences since 1929. They honor achievements in film and film-related activities, including music. Bruce Springsteen entered the Oscar realm with songs for two socially conscious films. He won the Academy Award for Best Original Song in 1994 for "Streets of Philadelphia."

The song was written for Jonathan Demme's 1993 film *Philadelphia,* about a lawyer (played by Tom Hanks, who won an Oscar for his performance) fired by his law firm when it is revealed he is dying of AIDS. Springsteen's song mentions AIDS only obliquely, but it is ultimately a much-needed plea for understanding of the disease and those who suffer from it. The song was a Top 10 hit and also won four Grammy Awards.

Springsteen was again nominated in the Best Song category for the title track to Tim Robbins's 1995 capital punishment film *Dead Man Walking.* It lost to "Colors of the Wind," a song from Disney's animated blockbuster *Pocahontas.* —DD

Alabama 3. See A3.
Zachary Alford. See 1992–93 Bruce Springsteen Touring Band.

Springsteen celebrates his Oscar win for Best Original Song for "Streets of Philadelphia" backstage at the 66th Academy Awards on March 21, 1994, with presenter (and fellow Jersey native) Whitney Houston.

Alliance of Neighbors Concerts

Fundraising concerts for Monmouth County, New Jersey, victims of September 11 terrorist attacks, October 18 and 19, 2001

ruce Springsteen opted not to perform at two major concerts held the third weekend of October 2001 related to the September 11 terrorist attacks—the Paul McCartney–organized Concert for New York City at Madison Square Garden and What More Can I Give? in Washington, D.C. Instead he stayed home and played three benefit shows for the Alliance of Neighbors, a charity founded to assist the families of September 11 victims from Monmouth County, New Jersey. Springsteen was joined by fellow Monmouth County resident Jon Bon Jovi along with Joan Jett, the Rascals' Felix Cavaliere, former members of Elvis Presley's band, Phoebe Snow,

John Eddie, Joe Ely, the Smithereens, and others. E Street Band bassist Garry Tallent was the music director for the shows. Two shows, with tickets priced from $50 to $500, were originally scheduled; one was slated for October 20, the same night as the Concert for New York City, and was moved to not conflict with that event and its live VH1 broadcast. An open rehearsal was subsequently added for the afternoon of October 18 in order to allow younger children from the victims' families to see the performers, and the front section of seats was held especially for them.

On each of the two nights, Springsteen sang "Tiger Rose" with the Elvis crew—Sonny Burgess, Jerry Scheff, D.J. Fontana, and Kevin Kennedy— "All Just to Get to You" with Ely, and "Light of Day" with Jett. For his own short set, Springsteen was backed by E Streeters Tallent, drummer Max Weinberg, and wife Patti Scialfa on "Bobby Jean," "Land of Hope and Dreams," and "Thunder Road," while the Pilgrim Baptist Church Celestial Choir joined for "My City of Ruins." Springsteen also led the full-company ensemble version of Ben E. King's "Stand by Me" that closed the shows.

An estimated $700,000-plus was raised by the shows, which was broadcast to cable subscribers in the Northeast. —*GG*

Eric Alterman

College professor, author, political and media columnist

A plethora of Bruce Springsteen biographies were already on the market when Eric Alterman published *It Ain't No Sin to Be Glad You're Alive: The Promise of Bruce Springsteen* in 1999. But Alterman's entry—which won the 1999 Stephen Crane Literary Award—earned special praise from reviewers and peers for going beyond the traditional format and placing Springsteen and his music in a greater level of cultural context, making it the most widely praised Springsteen tome next to Dave Marsh's biographies and, of course, Springsteen's own *Songs*.

As the media critic of *The Nation*, Queens, New York, native Alterman has written frequently about Springsteen, including one essay entitled "Boss of My Hometown." He's also written several other books about the media and politics, including the award-winning *Sound & Fury: The Making of the Punditocracy* in 1992, *Who Speaks for America? Why Democracy Matters in Foreign Policy* in 1998, *What Liberal Media? The Truth about Bias and the News* in 2003, *The Book on Bush: How George W. (Mis)leads America* (with Mark Green) in 2004, and also in 2004, *When Presidents Lie: A History of Deception and Its Consequences*. He's written columns for *Rolling Stone, Mother Jones,* and other periodicals, and he publishes a regular blog, "Altercation," for MSNBC's website.

Alterman's day job is in academia, however. With a Ph.D. in U.S. history from Stanford University, he's an English professor at Brooklyn College of the City University of New York and a senior fellow at both the Center for American Progress, a nonpartisan research institute "dedicated to promoting a strong, just and free America," and at the World Policy Institute at New School University in Manhattan. —GG

"America: A Tribute to Heroes"

September 11 benefit telethon broadcast September 21, 2001

Ten days after the September 11, 2001, terrorist attacks on New York City and Washington, D.C., the entertainment industry mobilized for an unprecedented cooperative effort—"America: A Tribute to Heroes," which was carried on all three major networks and any other broadcast outlet that wished to participate. The telethon was viewed by nearly sixty million people and raised an estimated $150 million for the September 11th Telethon Fund, which distributed money to related charities. Bruce Springsteen opened the two-hour program with "My City of Ruins," a song he had originally written about the decline of Asbury Park, New Jersey; he recorded it with the E Street Band during sessions in the fall of 2000 and debuted it on December 17, 2000, at one of the Asbury Park holiday shows. Springsteen intended to perform a new song, "Into the Fire," on the show, but he felt it wasn't complete enough to perform (he finished it in time to include on 2002's *The Rising*). Altering the lyrics slightly, he performed "My City of Ruins" surrounded by candles at Sony International Recording studio in Manhattan, accompanied by his wife, Patti Scialfa, E Street Band members Steve Van Zandt and Clarence Clemons, Scialfa's former Trickster bandmates Soozie Tyrell (who would later join the E Street Band on *The Rising* tour) and Lisa Lowell, and Dee and Layonne Holmes from Holiday Express, a charity based in Monmouth County, New Jersey. Also taking part in "America: A Tribute to Heroes" were Neil Young (on his own and with Pearl Jam's Eddie Vedder), Billy Joel, U2 (with Nelly Furtado and Eurythmics' Dave Stewart), Willie Nelson, Paul Simon, Alicia Keys, Dave Matthews, members of Limp Bizkit and the Goo Goo Dolls, Stevie Wonder, Tom Petty & the Heartbreakers, the Dixie Chicks, Faith Hill, Sheryl Crow, Enrique Iglesias, and Bon Jovi, along with actors such as Tom Hanks, Julia Roberts, Tom Cruise, Al Pacino, Chris Rock, Jimmy Smits, Kelsey Grammer, Jim Carrey, Will Smith, Clint Eastwood, Robert De Niro, and Robin Williams. The event was preserved on an album and DVD, with proceeds from sales also going to the charitable fund. —GG

American Music Masters

Educational series at Rock and Roll Hall of Fame and Museum, Cleveland, Ohio

The Rock and Roll Hall of Fame and Museum in Cleveland kicked off its annual American Music Masters series in September 1996 with a ten-day celebration of the life and music of folk legend Woody Guthrie. Bruce Springsteen, then on his solo acoustic tour to promote *The Ghost of Tom Joad*, headlined the celebration's grand finale, an all-star tribute concert on September 29 at Cleveland's Severance Hall. The event was hosted by actor Tim Robbins and also featured Pete Seeger, Arlo Guthrie, the Indigo Girls, Billy Bragg, Ramblin' Jack Elliott, Ani DiFranco, Joe Ely, Soul Asylum's Dave Pirner, and others. Springsteen opened his set with Guthrie's "Tom Joad," then teamed with Texas singer-songwriter Ely on a rollicking version of "Going Down the Road (I Ain't Going to Be Treated This Way)." The pair was later joined by Arlo Guthrie for a romp around "Oklahoma Hills." Springsteen, whose forty-minute set was the longest of the evening, lightened the mood with a funny take on Guthrie's children's song, "Riding in My Car (Car Song)," sang a powerful rendition of "Plane Wreck at Los Gatos (Deportee)," and capped his set with one of his own songs, "Across the Border." Springsteen came back for the show's encore, an all-star jam that featured sing-along renditions of Guthrie's "Hard Travelin'," "I Got to Know," "Hobo's Lullabye," and, of course, "This Land Is Your Land."

The E Street Band's rhythm section, drummer Max Weinberg and Garry Tallent, were part of the following year's American Music Masters tribute to Jimmie Rodgers, performing at separate shows that also included Guy Clark, Steve Earle, Ricky Skaggs, Iris Dement, John Prine, Jimmie Dale Gilmore, Levon Helm, Junior Brown, and Lynyrd Skynyrd. —*MN*

"American Skin (41 Shots)"

Controversial song inspired by 1999 Amadou Diallo shooting in New York City

With the title track of 1984's *Born in the U.S.A.*, Bruce Springsteen experienced the radical misinterpretation of one of his songs. But it was not accompanied with the kind of vitriol that greeted "American Skin (41 Shots)," which he premiered on June 4, 2000, at Philips Arena in Atlanta. The song was inspired by an incident on February 4, 1999, in New York's Bronx borough, when four police officers fired forty-one shots at unarmed African immigrant Amadou Diallo, who didn't understand the officers' instructions; speculation is that he thought they were asking for ID and was reaching for his wallet, but they thought he was going for a weapon. Nineteen of the bullets hit him, killing Diallo and sparking allegations of excessive force and racial profiling. In February 2000, the officers were cleared of any wrongdoing, resulting in even more public debate.

Springsteen wrote "American Skin" about more than just the Diallo shooting, though the song makes several direct references to it. But it made a broader thematic statement about decision and consequences; the *New York Times* described it as "a resonant elegy and a reflection on how fear can become deadly." "Because a lot had been written about the case in magazines and newspapers," Springsteen explained later, "I was just setting out to basically continue writing about things that I'd written about for a long period of time, which is, Who are we? What's it mean to be an American? What's going on in this country we live in? It was asking some questions that were hanging very heavy in the air … And it was extension of just a lot of my other work." He added, however, "I think it dealt very directly with race, and that's a subject that pushes a lot of buttons in America." That it did—especially in the New York police community.

After sound-checking the song several times, Springsteen and the E Street Band rolled it out at the June 4 Atlanta show and it was promptly posted on file-sharing Internet sites, with the media picking up on it as well. The first police reaction came from Patrick Lynch, president of the 27,000-member Patrolmen's Benevolent Association; though he hadn't heard the song, Lynch posted a letter on the organization's website on June 8 accusing Springsteen of "trying to fatten his wallet by reopening the wounds of this tragic case" and urging New York officers to neither attend nor work as moonlighting security guards at Springsteen's upcoming ten-show stand at Madison Square Garden. New York City Police Commissioner Howard Safir told the *New York Daily News*, "I personally don't care for Bruce Springsteen's music or his song," while Bob Lucente, president of the New York State Fraternal Order of Police, called Springsteen a "fucking dirtbag" and declared, "He goes on the boycott list."

Other police factions came to Springsteen's defense. A group called 100 Blacks in Law Enforcement spoke out in support of him, with spokesman Lt. Eric Adams telling the Associated Press, "We commend Bruce Springsteen, and we believe that he is courageous in the position that he is taking." Another police lieutenant, Michael J. Gorman, wrote a letter to the *New York Times* noting, "[T]rying to muzzle those who refer to this tragedy is wrong. Mr. Springsteen has generally been a supporter of police officers, giving generously to police charities. Attacks on him are not only unfair but also counterproductive." A New York patrolman, meanwhile, brought a sign to one of the Garden shows that declared, "Here sits a NYC policeman who still loves Bruce!!" (Springsteen spotted him and said from the stage "Now there's a sign I like!")

For his part, Springsteen said he was "surprised ... there were so many people willing to comment so quickly about something they've never heard. That was just somewhat puzzling to me, because we'd only played the song once, in Atlanta, and there was no recorded version of it ... There was a lot of misrepresentation and comment about something that I don't think a lot of people had heard, and the song wound up being misrepresented by quite a few people." Springsteen played the song, without comment, at each of the ten Madison Square Garden shows, and he included it on his *Live in New York City* album and DVD in 2001. After the first night's show, on June 12, he met with Diallo's parents, who expressed their appreciation for the song. —*GG*

Amnesty International Human Rights Now! Tour

Fall 1988

Following its successful (but short) Conspiracy of Hope tour in 1986 featuring U2 and the Police, Amnesty International had loftier goals to celebrate the fortieth anniversary of the Declaration of Human Rights document. A longer tour was in order, one that criss-crossed the globe rather than just playing in North America. Bruce Springsteen agreed to headline the jaunt, which ran from September 2 in London, England, to October 15 in Buenos Aires, Argentina. Springsteen announced his involvement in the Human Rights Now! tour during his internationally broadcast Tunnel of Love Express concert in Stockholm, Sweden. Springsteen told the crowd he'd be joining Sting, Peter Gabriel, Tracy Chapman, and Youssou N'Dour, then played a rendition of Bob Dylan's "Chimes of Freedom" that was subsequently released on an EP, the proceeds of which went to Amnesty International. (Other tracks on the EP included live version of "Tougher Than the Rest," "Be True," and the acoustic "Born to Run.")

The nineteen shows on the tour marked Springsteen and the E Street Band's first-ever performances in Africa, India, and South America. Each concert began with the tour participants singing Bob Marley's "Get Up, Stand Up." Springsteen's set was much shorter than usual, ranging from seventy to eighty minutes, which fans were ambivalent about; it wasn't nearly long enough for the Bruceheads, of course, but they were undeniably intense and passionate, given to occasional surprises such as Woody Guthrie's "I Ain't Got No Home." The full cast trooped on stage again at the end of Springsteen's sets for "Chimes of Freedom."

Springsteen and Sting, who had taken part in the Conspiracy of Hope tour, became fast friends during Human Rights Now! Early in the tour Sting began joining Springsteen each night to sing on "The River." Within two weeks Springsteen was also part of Sting's set, joining for the Police hit "Every Breath You Take." "I think there were friendships forged on that tour that have lasted to the present day," Sting recalls. "For the first time in any of our careers, we were kind of forced to share the bubble—sharing hotels, sharing the plane, sharing dressing rooms, sharing the stage. It made us feel much less isolated than you normally feel as a sort of rock icon. We'll all say it was our favorite tour ever; it was just so much fun to play with your peers."

There were musical highlights beyond the Sting duets. The Tunnel of Love Express horn section rejoined the E Streeters for the September 19 stop in Philadelphia. U2's Bono, sporting a cowboy hat, was a guest for "Chimes of Freedom" on September 21 in Los Angeles. Gabriel led the crowd in singing "Happy Birthday" to Springsteen at the September 23 show in Oakland, California; at the same show Springsteen joined Joan Baez for Dylan's "Blowin' in the Wind." Other musicians—including original E Street Band keyboardist David Sancious (then in Gabriel's band), as well as violinist Shankar and percussionist Mino Cinelu from Sting's band became adjunct E Street Band members most nights. And at the final show in Buenos Aires— which was aired live on radio and filmed for an HBO special—Gabriel and Sting dressed up as Springsteen in black vests, jeans, and boots for a joyous "Twist and Shout" finale.

At press conferences along the tour route, Springsteen made some of his most forthright political comments to date. Even though he said at one gathering, "My job on the Amnesty tour was to come out at the end of the night and rock the house," he noted by the end that Human Rights Now! "was about trying to assert myself as a world citizen ... This tour marks my graduation of sorts. And I hope that I will be able to go back home and, in my music, write about a different sensibility that I felt on this tour."

Springsteen beat the Amnesty International drum again on December 10, 1998, at the Paris Concert for Amnesty International, a concert celebrating the fiftieth anniversary of the Declaration of Human Rights. He joined Human Rights Now! tour mates Gabriel, Chapman, and N'Dour in reprising "Get Up, Stand Up," then played his own four-song acoustic set that included "The Ghost of Tom Joad," "Born in the U.S.A." (which he had to stop and start again due to sound problems), "Working on the Highway," and "No Surrender." The concert was broadcast in the U.S. via pay per view on April 3, 1999, and was then sold on DVD. —*GG*

Ten years after he and the E Street Band toured the world as part of the Human Rights
Now! effort, Springsteen again asserted his support for Amnesty International with a solo
acoustic performance in Paris on December 10, 1998, at a concert marking the fiftieth
anniversary of the Declaration of Human Rights.

Michael Antrim

New Jersey youth, art contest winner

I n December 2002, Michael Antrim, a seventeen-year-old high school student from Red Bank, New Jersey, won a Best in Show award at the annual Freehold Public Library art contest—with a portrait of Bruce Springsteen entitled, "Hometown Hero." Following the win, Elaine Smith, a Freehold artist who organizes the contest, wrote a letter to Springsteen about Antrim, a National Honor Society student who also suffered from a serious form of Crohn's disease and was a participant in Make-A-Wish Foundation activities. Springsteen wrote back quickly, sending a congratulatory note to the youth, apologizing for not being able to make it to the art show. He said he would love to see the prize-winning portrait some other time.

That time came on June 29, 2004, when Springsteen paid a visit to Antrim's home. During the course of the ninety-minute visit, Springsteen chatted with the boy and his mother, Kathleen Antrim, played guitar with the youth—including "The Promised Land," his mom's favorite—and complimented the "Hometown Hero" portrait. Springsteen signed the original copy to Michael, inscribing it, "Keep the Faith," and also autographed a print for teacher Smith, "To Elaine. We did it!" He departed with a handshake and hug for the young artist and a kiss on the cheek for mom. —*GG*

Mike Appel

Springsteen manager and coproducer

I t's easy to portray Mike Appel as the ogre in the Bruce Springsteen story. He signed the fledgling rock hero to a prototypically exploitive management and production contract. And when he began losing his grip on his artist, Appel threw up barriers that held Springsteen in limbo at one of the most crucial times of his career. Yet it was Appel's faith and tireless energy that got Springsteen in the door with John Hammond and Columbia Records, that snuck out early copies of "Born to Run" to build hype for a third album no one was sure the label wanted, and that engineered—for better and for worse—the simultaneous *Time* and *Newsweek* covers that vaulted Springsteen into the pop culture consciousness. As Springsteen noted at his 1999 induction into the Rock and Roll Hall of Fame, "Mike kicked the doors down when they needed kicking."

It's impossible, and probably wrong, to say that without Appel there would be no Springsteen, but he was unquestionably a vital element of the success story. Born October 27, 1942, in the Flushing section of Queens, New York, Appel started playing guitar when he was fourteen and formed his first band, the Humbugs, when he was sixteen. He went to St. John's University and received a bachelor's degree in business arts in 1965; after graduation he joined the marine reserves, working six months as a platoon secretary before going to weekends only. Appel was then signed as a producer, songwriter, and artist with H&L music, where he wrote "Soul Searchin'" for Bobby Lewis. Appel befriended Jim Cretecos, a veteran of the Broadway *Hair* cast, and the two struck a partnership, moving to the Wes Farrell Organization and writing the Partridge Family hit "Doesn't Somebody Want to Be Wanted," as well as songs for the Partridges' David Cassidy, "Chain Reaction" for Aretha Franklin's sister Carolyn, and some commercials. But Appel and Cretecos craved more legitimacy in the rock world, so they started working with a hard-rock band named Sir Lord Baltimore, then with a vocal harmony group called Montana Flintlock. The latter introduced them to Carl "Tinker" West, who knew the partners wanted to work with a singer-songwriter. He pointed them to Springsteen, who had been in bands West managed. Springsteen played two songs for them in November 1971 in their New York offices; Appel was not impressed with the material—"They were the worst two songs I ever heard in my life," he told *Backstreets*—but Springsteen's performance of them resonated. "Even though the songs were as dull as hell, I heard a voice in my head that said, 'This kid's a superstar,'" he recalled. His advice to Springsteen was to a) write more songs and b) write more commercial songs.

Four months later Springsteen returned from visiting his family in California with those songs. Appel didn't remember him at first, but he soon set up another audition, and songs such as "It's Hard to Be a Saint in the City," particularly the lyrics, won him over. Appel and Cretecos made plans to quit the song factory and form a new production company, Laurel Canyon, to handle Springsteen; they invited fellow employee Bob Spitz to come with them and handle the song-publishing end. They started shopping Springsteen around to record companies, getting rejected by Elektra and A&M but scoring an audition with Hammond at Columbia; this impressed Springsteen, who had just read Anthony Scaduto's biography of Bob Dylan and knew that Hammond had signed Dylan to the label. When they walked into Hammond's office, the brash Appel threw down a gauntlet: "You're the guy who discovered Bob Dylan, huh? Well, we want to find out if that was just luck or if you really have ears." Springsteen was mortified, but his songs wowed Hammond and led to a deal. And Hammond respected Appel's passion for his client: "Appel is as offensive as any man I've ever met," he told *Time* magazine, "but he's utterly selfless in his devotion to Bruce."

The contracts Springsteen signed with Appel, meanwhile, included management, album production, and song publishing rights. Naive and unconcerned at this point with business matters, Springsteen waived a great deal of control, a move he would come to regret in just a few years. Springsteen signed a one-year deal with four one-year options for Laurel Canyon, during which time he was required to make five albums for the company; interestingly, Laurel Canyon had contracted with Columbia for ten albums. Laurel Canyon's remuneration was three times what Springsteen would get. Appel also cut costs on the recording of *Greetings from Asbury Park, N.J.* by doing it at the cut-rate 914 Sound Studios in Blauvelt, New York—where *The Wild, the Innocent & the E Street Shuffle* and the song "Born to Run" were also recorded. But, Appel has pointed out, he paid Springsteen a regular salary—$350 a week—and handled all front costs of touring even when no money was coming in from record sales. Before *Greetings* was out, Appel hyped the National Football League (unsuccessfully) to let Springsteen perform an anti-war song, "Balboa vs. the Earth Slayer," before the Super Bowl. When radio stations weren't playing Springsteen's single, he sent out a Christmas card featuring a photo of Springsteen sitting on Santa Claus's lap with a note warning that anyone who didn't play the record would get coal for Christmas—and made good on the threat by sending out charcoal briquettes with "coal" painted on the sides. Appel also took Springsteen to see Elvis Presley perform at Madison Square Garden in 1972. And he gave him the leather jacket off his back for the *Born to Run* album cover shoot.

The Appel-Springsteen relationship began to unravel in April 1974. Springsteen met music critic Jon Landau outside of Charley's in Cambridge, Massachusetts—ironically while he was reading a copy of Landau's review of *The Wild, the Innocent & the E Street Shuffle* in Boston's *Real Paper*. He brought Landau inside to meet Appel, who immediately harangued the writer about his criticisms of the album's production. After Landau wrote his essay proclaiming, "I saw rock and roll future and its name is Bruce Springsteen," he and Springsteen struck a friendship, and Landau soon became a trusted confidant. Ultimately, Springsteen asked Landau to coproduce the *Born to Run* album, which did not sit well with Appel. "Landau had it in his mind all along, once he saw Springsteen and declared him rock and roll's future, to produce Bruce and eventually take over his management," Appel told Marc Eliot, author of the book *Down Thunder Road: The Making of Bruce Springsteen.* "The best I can say about Landau as producer, prior to working with Bruce, was he was a heck of a critic."

Appel may have bristled over what was going on in Springsteen's creative world, but he continued to hustle to promote his career. With Columbia indifferent to Springsteen after poor sales of the first two albums, Appel decided to release early tapes of a new song, "Born to Run," to friendly radio stations in order to generate some buzz for a third album. It worked. So did his ploy to get Springsteen on the cover of both *Time* and *Newsweek* in October 1975; "I conned the goofball editors into that and backed them into a

While his court battle with former manager Mike Appel prevented him from recording, Springsteen maintained his rigorous touring schedule in support of *Born to Run* while performing new unreleased material such as "Something in the Night" (which would later appear on *Darkness on the Edge of Town*) at shows including a six-night run at the Palladium in New York City in November 1976.

corner until they had no way out," Appel recalled to *Backstreets*. He also claimed to have negotiated an opportunity for Springsteen to earn $1.5 million to fill in on an NBC TV special that was supposed to have starred Bob Dylan—which Springsteen turned down, as well as a lucrative July 4 headlining show at Giants Stadium in East Rutherford, New Jersey. Appel was hatching an idea for an inventive, circus-style tent tour when the relationship severed in early 1976.

As *Born to Run* took off, however, Springsteen began asking questions about money and other business matters and demanded accountings from Laurel Canyon. Then he told Appel he wanted Landau to produce the next album. Appel balked, based on the exclusive contract Springsteen had signed with him, and thus began one of the most bitter legal battles in rock 'n' roll history. Springsteen filed suit against Appel and Laurel Canyon on July 27, 1976 in federal court in Manhattan, claiming fraud, breach of trust, and undue influence. Appel countersued on July 29 in New York State Supreme Court, asking the court to prohibit Springsteen and Landau from working together in the studio. His contractual right to choose Springsteen's album producers was upheld; he defeated two subsequent appeals by Springsteen, effectively keeping his client from recording his next album unless it was done under Appel's supervision. The case raged for nine months, finally settling out of court on May 28, 1977. Appel received a reported $800,000 to relinquish management and production rights; he agreed to reduce his per-album percentage to two percent, and kept fifty percent of the publishing rights to Springsteen's already-released songs. He sold that stake back to Springsteen six years later for a reported $425,000. Eliot's *Down Thunder Road* was published in 1992, "with the participation of Mike Appel." Afterwards, Springsteen told *Rolling Stone* magazine that he disagreed with Appel's contention that Landau stole Springsteen from him: "What happened was Mike and I had kind of reached a place where our relationship had kind of bumped up against its limitations. We were a dead-end street. And Jon came in, and he had a pretty sophisticated point of view, and he had an idea how to solve some very fundamental problems, like how to record and where to record. But Mike turned Jon into his monster, maybe as a way of not turning me into one."

Eliot's book reveals that Appel—who went on to work with other artists—patched things up with Springsteen in 1986 after contacting Landau to request a meeting. The two men had lunch together on November 20 in Los Angeles, according to Appel, and have stayed in touch ever since. Returning the favor of the *Born to Run* leather jacket, Springsteen gave Appel a similar garment as a present to Appel's son, who Appel promised would one day pass it on to Springsteen's son Evan. And when Appel stopped backstage in New York during the *Tunnel of Love* tour, Springsteen reportedly loaned him $175,000. The reconciliation was cemented at the Hall of Fame induction. "I consider him my friend," Springsteen said during his acceptance speech. "I want to say Mike, thanks for everything—mostly everything—and thanks for being my guest here tonight. I'm glad you're here with me." —GG/LM

Asbury Park Convention Hall

Landmark Jersey Shore concert venue

T hough many rock legends—including the Rolling Stones, the Who, Janis Joplin, and the Doors—had graced the Asbury Park Convention Hall stage, Bruce Springsteen didn't play there till 1999, when he and the E Street Band used it for rehearsals before embarking on their 1999–2000 reunion tour. Springsteen began his tradition of doing charity shows there when he and the band performed three dress rehearsal/tour preview shows on March 11, 18, and 19, 1999. (On March 15, he stopped by the Waldorf-Astoria Hotel in New York to get inducted into the Rock and Roll Hall of Fame.) He had used the adjoining, more intimate Paramount Theater for three shows on his *Ghost of Tom Joad* solo tour in November 1996, but at 3,600 seats, the convention hall holds more than double the capacity of the Paramount. The 1999 shows were announced just a couple of days in advance and all tickets were priced at $20.

Springsteen also held charity shows on a cobill with the Max Weinberg 7 & Friends on December 3, 4, 6, 7, and 8, 2001; July 25, 26, and 30 and August 2 and 5, 2002 (July 30 also included a live "Today" broadcast to celebrate the release of *The Rising*); and December 5, 7, and 8, 2003. (A planned December 6 show was canceled because of a blizzard.) They were all announced just days ahead of time; by 2001, tickets had risen to $50 and $100. But since they began doing the shows, Springsteen and company have raised hundreds of thousands of dollars for local charities and community projects. The *Asbury Park Press* reported the 2003 concerts alone raised more than $200,000 for a new Asbury Park community center, as well as $18–$20,000 for twelve other nonprofit groups, including homeless and women's shelters, substance abuse centers, food banks, health clinics, and recreational and educational organizations. The Boys and Girls Clubs of Monmouth County, the Save Tillie Foundation, the Asbury Park Chamber of Commerce, a local high school band, and a Pee-Wee football team on which the Springsteen boys played have all received cash from the concerts.

The convention hall complex itself is an area landmark. The building, erected in the 1920s and opened July 11, 1930, with performances by the Marx Brothers and Ginger Rogers, is a mix of late nineteenth- and twentieth-

Springsteen and members of the E Street Band greet their fans gathered on the beach out-side Convention Hall in Asbury Park, New Jersey, where the band had performed live on the "Today" show to celebrate the release of *The Rising*. Appearing at the July 30, 2002, show were (from left) band members Roy Bittan, Clarence Clemons, Springsteen, Patti Scialfa, Steve Van Zandt, Garry Tallent, and Danny Federici.

century revival and renaissance styles. Designed by architects Warren and Wetmore, the same pair who designed New York's Grand Central Station, the hall is on the National Register of Historic Places. A large boardwalk arcade runs between the hall and theater. The complex is owned by the City of Asbury Park but is leased to and operated by Asbury Partners LLC, the company that is redeveloping the city's shoreline properties. —*LM*

Asbury Park, New Jersey
Jersey Shore resort town, est. 1871

Asbury Park, the faded resort city on the New Jersey Shore, is deeply rooted in the rock 'n' roll legacy of Bruce Springsteen. Even before he named his 1973 debut album *Greetings from Asbury Park, N.J.*—spurning the advice of publicists and executives from Columbia Records to reject his Jersey roots and instead make himself identifiable with New York—Asbury Park played an important role in Springsteen's career. Not only did the city supply him with a rich landscape of characters, stories, locales, and subcultures for his songs, but Asbury Park's raw, blue-collar image, its racial tensions and economic problems, and its broken dreams did much to put Springsteen, as an artist, in touch with the underbelly of America. In contemporary pop culture, in fact, Asbury Park and Bruce Springsteen are practically synonymous.

The roots of Asbury Park's music tradition extend back to the 1920s, long before Springsteen's arrival in the city. From the Jazz Age on, Asbury Park has had a strong link to American popular music, though the city's music scene grew especially hot when Springsteen began writing and performing there in the late '60s. Although a far cry creatively from the '70s heyday when Springsteen, Southside Johnny Lyon, Steve Van Zandt, and Jon Bon Jovi were first drawing international attention to it, Asbury Park retains its rock 'n' roll allure.

The origins of Asbury Park, however, hardly indicate a rich musical heritage would be in the making. The city was founded in 1871 by James A. Bradley, a New York brush manufacturer. Bradley named his 500-acre settlement Asbury Park in honor of the first Methodist bishop in America, Francis Asbury. Bradley envisioned a city by the sea free of gambling and liquor— the vices, he believed, that had corrupted two of New Jersey's other resort towns, Long Branch and Atlantic City. Bradley believed Asbury Park should be more in line with its neighbor, Ocean Grove, where religion, morals, patriotism, and family life were celebrated. Bradley spent the remainder of his life realizing his dream. By the time of his death in 1921, Asbury Park had become a pleasant middle-class resort with beautiful homes, gardens, a thriving business area, and a bustling boardwalk. Concerts by brass bands and orchestras provided cultural nourishment during Bradley's years. But in the 1920s, as the transformation of American popular music enabled jazz to take hold practically everywhere, Asbury Park broadened its musical reach. William "Count" Basie, the pianist born in nearby Red Bank, cut his musical teeth in Asbury Park clubs, as did Long Branch drummer Sonny Greer, who would keep the beat for Duke Ellington for many years. In the '30s and '40s, swing bands and pop singers—including Benny Goodman, Glenn Miller, and Frank Sinatra—performed in Asbury Park, making the city a stop-off for touring acts coming out of New York and on their way to Atlantic City and Philadelphia.

The opening of the Garden State Parkway in 1957 made it easier for Asbury Park to attract daily vacationers from northern New Jersey. With a boardwalk that had matured into a major tourist attraction rivaled only by the Atlantic City boardwalk farther south, Asbury Park enjoyed prosperity as a major seaside resort. In the '60s, Asbury Park's Convention Hall began presenting rock concerts, and by the end of the decade such artists as the Beach Boys, the Four Seasons, Bob Dylan, the Rolling Stones, the Dave Clark Five, the Doors, Jefferson Airplane, Janis Joplin, and the Who had all performed there, enabling both vacationers and local teens the chance to see in-person rock's biggest stars without having to travel to New York or Philadelphia. In 1968 the first Asbury Park rock club, the Upstage, opened its doors above a shoe store on Cookman Avenue. An after-hours musicians' club that featured late-night jams, the Upstage attracted the best of the area's rock musicians. Springsteen, Lyon, Billy Chinnock, and future E Street Band members such as Van Zandt, David Sancious, Garry Tallent, Danny Federici, Vini "Mad Dog" Lopez, and Ernest "Boom" Carter were Upstage regulars. As one Upstage musician put it, "This was the place to be heard, to be seen, and to make your mark. More bands formed out of the Upstage than any club around. It was absolutely the most important place in the development of the Asbury Park music scene, the one everyone came to know in the '70s."

The popularity of the Upstage, like Asbury Park itself, came to a halt in 1970 when the city was racked by race riots that all but destroyed the downtown area and permanently tarnished its reputation as a first-class resort. Almost overnight, vacationers who had been coming to Asbury Park for years chose other Jersey Shore towns such as Pt. Pleasant Beach and Seaside Heights from which to enjoy the region's sun, sand, and surf. Like other clubs and businesses, the Upstage could not weather the impact of Asbury Park's racial violence and closed in 1971, leaving the city's vibrant rock scene without a flagship club. Many musicians moved out of Asbury Park: Southside Johnny, Sancious, Carter, and Tallent headed to Richmond,

In the early 1900s, Asbury Park, New Jersey, boasted a thriving beachfront, which was the centerpiece of the picturesque resort town that later became the birthplace of Springsteen's musical career.

Virginia; Van Zandt went on tour with a Philadelphia doo-wop group, the Dovells; Chinnock moved to Maine; and Springsteen began making nightly jaunts to New York City, performing in clubs as a solo artist. Things changed dramatically when Springsteen was offered a recording contract by Columbia Records in 1972 and began preparations to record his debut album. Still living in Asbury Park, Springsteen called many of his musician friends back to the city to help him make the album. One good thing, at least from a musician's point of view, resulted from the 1970 race riot: apartment rents grew cheap, enabling struggling musicians to relocate there from other parts of the Shore.

Although *Greetings from Asbury Park, N.J.* was not a commercial success, it did garner critical praise, and it drew curious attention to the city and its recovering music scene. *Greetings* and Springsteen's follow-up album, *The Wild, the Innocent & the E Street Shuffle*, were rich with references to Asbury

Park's people and places while the sound conveyed the R&B–influenced, urban-inspired flavor of the Jersey Shore's unique beach and boardwalk culture. In the course of one very creative year, 1973, Springsteen had released two albums that defined the Asbury Park music scene.

In 1974, a new club called the Stone Pony opened on Ocean Avenue in Asbury Park. Its owners, Butch Peilka and Jack Roig, hired Southside Johnny and his new group, the Asbury Jukes, to be the house band. Led by Steve Van Zandt, who had returned to the Jersey Shore after his road stint with the Dovells, and Lyon, whose blues and R&B knowledge went unchallenged in Jersey Shore music circles, the Asbury Jukes' sound was an infectious mix of rock, soul, blues, R&B, and reggae, driven by a blaring horn section that kept the Pony dance floor crowded until closing, three nights a week. When Springsteen and his E Street Band came off the road, the musicians found comfort hanging out at the Stone Pony, listening to their friends perform.

A year after the Stone Pony opened, Asbury Park went from a locally hip rock 'n' roll town to an international music destination. In late 1975, *Time* and *Newsweek* published simultaneous cover stories on Springsteen, luring many rock fans, writers, and record company executives to Asbury Park to see for themselves if this Jersey Shore town, home to rock's next "messiah," as *Newsweek* put it, was the next Liverpool. Overnight, the Stone Pony became one of the best-known rock clubs in America, while the city became the keeper of the future of rock 'n' roll. Like no other time since the early '60s, when Beatlemania and the British Invasion launched what seemed like a hundred new bands on the Jersey Shore, Asbury Park and other Shore communities were awash with R&B and soul-inflected rock bands inspired by Springsteen and the E Street Band and Southside and his Jukes. In May 1976 the Jukes kicked off the release of their debut album *I Don't Want to Go Home* with a live broadcast party/concert at the Stone Pony. Musically, things got even hotter at the Shore.

With Asbury Park's music scene nationally known by the end of the 1970s, media attention naturally included the sorry condition of the city. Though the race riots that ruined Asbury Park's economy had occurred several years earlier, the city had made little progress toward rejuvenating itself. But Asbury Park was not without visionaries who believed their projects would get the city back on track. In the 1980s there was a flurry of rebirth activity in Asbury Park, despite the continued loss of major businesses— including the *Asbury Park Press* newspaper, which in 1985 relocated to nearby Neptune Township. Local builder Henry Vaccaro and Connecticut developer Joseph Carabetta were two of the first to sink money into what they hoped would be Asbury's renaissance. Country singer Johnny Cash and pop superstar Michael Jackson also had their own plans for the city: Cash saw beautiful condos on the Asbury Park oceanfront; Jackson hoped to build a state-of-the-art recording studio and entertainment center there. Neither project panned out. On the rock 'n' roll front, however, a number of new clubs opened; the Fast Lane in particular quickly rivaled the Stone Pony for supremacy. In 1986 two Springsteen fans and collectors, Billy Smith and Steve Bumball, opened up the Asbury Park Rock & Roll Museum nearly a decade before Cleveland premiered the Rock and Roll Hall of Fame and Museum. Yet by the end of the decade, Asbury Park still resembled a poster city for the dangers posed by urban blight and economic decay.

Asbury Park fared no better in the 1990s. More development plans passed through city council chambers, but none of them got off the ground. First-time visitors to Asbury Park, lured there by the city's connection to Springsteen, were shocked to see the shambles it was in. The Stone Pony, one of the few meaningful businesses in the city, went bankrupt, only to open, close, and open again—but it was never able to recapture the excitement that regularly flowed off its stage. Convention Hall once again hosted rock concerts, but the venue was in such need of a facelift and acoustic improvements that it never established itself as anything more than a one-off special event venue. Even Springsteen's use of the venue for rehearsals and occasional concerts couldn't jumpstart Convention Hall into a full-time concert facility.

Today, Asbury Park continues to suffer. Still other developers have presented plans to city leaders; the most optimistic of them—including a coalition of builders and preservationists called Asbury Partners—believe a change of fortune for the city is imminent. But even Asbury Park's most popular advocate has his limits. When developers adopted The Rising as the name of a condominium complex in 2004, Springsteen responded with a letter in Asbury Park's *triCityNews*, appealing to planners and city leaders to respect the song title's connection to the events of September 11 and "to place both my and my song's names out of the running for any new buildings, streets, hot dog stands (well, maybe hot dog stands) as the city moves toward its exciting future." The developers immediately obliged.

Musically, the Asbury Park music scene rests on past laurels; although the Stone Pony remains open, it has lost much of its original character. Few young bands carry on the city's long-standing love affair with R&B-drenched rock. Instead, the scene relies on veteran outfits, manned by musicians who recall the glory days of the '70s, to keep the flame burning. Perhaps Springsteen, the city's favorite son and its most important advocate, described the city best when he wrote in his song, "My City of Ruins": "Young men on the corner/Like scattered leaves/The boarded up windows/The empty streets." But also in the song, Springsteen described the city's undying faith when he repeatedly exhorts, like an impassioned preacher: "Come on, rise up!"—exactly what Asbury Park's residents and the state's rock fans have been hoping for more than three decades now. —*RS*

A3

Genre-blending British band, aka Alabama 3

The politically focused British electronic rock band A3 (aka Alabama 3) got the attention of Bruce Springsteen fans in 1999, when the makers of the HBO mob series "The Sopranos"—which features E Street Band guitarist Steve Van Zandt as hitman Silvio Dante—adopted the group's "Woke Up This Morning" as its theme song. But the group really raised eyebrows when the track listing for its 2002 release *Power in the Blood* showed a forty-seven–second snippet of Springsteen's "Badlands." As it turns out, however, that wasn't the song. "We got the bloody title wrong—it's 'Nebraska,'" noted A3's Rob Spragg (aka Larry Love). "It was a copy fuckup."

The album also included an original song called "Woody Guthrie," and Spragg said he felt the strong connection between the two artists. "Whatever my opinions on American imperialism were," he explained, "I think people like Springsteen and Woody Guthrie always have something to say. It's important to remind the world, or our small audience in that world, that America does have cultural commentators who have something valid to say. It's not all Sylvester Stallone. I do like Springsteen; I think he's a major writer."

Formed in the mid-'90s after its three main members met in rehab, A3 won critical acclaim for its blend of electronic, country, gospel, and blues, which played as well in dance clubs as it did to serious listeners—though the American country group Alabama sued the collective over its name, after which Spragg and company adopted the A3 moniker in the U.S. "Woke Up This Morning" appeared on the group's debut album, 1997's *Exile on Coldharbour*. —*GG*

Backstreets Magazine

Springsteen fan magazine

Long before any music lover with time and a web server could be the president of an international fan club, Charles R. Cross of Seattle created a fanzine devoted to Bruce Springsteen. His first edition of *Backstreets* was a four-page newsletter, which he handed out for free at Springsteen's Seattle Coliseum show on October 24, 1980. He parlayed that initial effort into a full-fledged (though officially unsanctioned) Springsteen magazine.

Backstreets grew into a quarterly publication of journalism strictly for the Springsteen fan, expanding its staff and subscriber base in the early '80s and upgrading from newspaper to magazine format with its tenth issue. Also known as *The Boss Magazine*, *Backstreets* has scored exclusive interviews with members of the E Street Band and Springsteen's crew, kept an eye on the Jersey Shore music scene and related artists, and consistently offered in-depth analysis of Springsteen's work. In 1989, the editors published a *Backstreets* book, *Springsteen: The Man and His Music*, which was updated in 1992. Still publishing quarterly, *Backstreets* magazine has continued to grow, adding glossy pages and full color, with an international circulation of 15,000 and rising. While numerous other Boss fanzines have been published around the world (many of which have been gathered in the Asbury Park Library, part of a Springsteen Special Collection organized and donated by *Backstreets* in 2001), *Backstreets* magazine is by far the longest running.

Cross, meanwhile, became a prominent music writer. In 1986, he became the editor of Seattle's entertainment paper, the *Rocket*, where he stayed for fourteen years. He has also published articles in *Rolling Stone*, *Esquire*, *Playboy*, *Spin*, and *Tracks*, and has written three other books, notably 2001's *Heavier Than Heaven: The Biography of Kurt Cobain*.

Current publisher and editor Christopher Phillips was hired as *Backstreets'* managing editor in 1993, after being an avid reader for many years. Phillips worked with Cross for the next five years, starting the magazine's website and soon becoming editor. In 1998, Cross completely passed the reins to Phillips, who eventually relocated *Backstreets* to the East Coast, most recently to North Carolina. In addition to now serving as publisher, Phillips continues to write for, edit, and design each issue of the magazine.

Phillips also maintains the magazine's website, Backstreets.com, launched in 1995. While it remains an independent fan effort, it tends to get the biggest exclusives. When the Vote for Change tour was announced in August 2004, Phillips was one of the first reporters to talk to Springsteen—his first interview specifically for *Backstreets*. It's certainly the most reliable site for Springsteen news: After any given Springsteen concert, the setlist link is filled with commentary from fans. The site also sells official Springsteen merchandise (vinyl, CDs, T-shirts, books, and posters) and hosts online message boards, including BTX: The Backstreets Ticket Exchange. Originally developed by Phillips as a scalping-free ticket trading post, BTX evolved into an online chat forum that connects the *Backstreets* community of fans.

At eighty issues and counting, *Backstreets* remains largely subscriber supported (averaging sixty pages per issue, with very little advertising), with color photography from professionals and fans alike. What began as one man's appreciation for an inspirational artist has grown into a place where thousands participate in an ongoing discussion of all things Springsteen. —*SK/CP*

"Badlands"

Single release: August 14, 1978
Album: *Darkness on the Edge of Town* (Columbia, 1978)
Also on: *Live/1975–85* (Columbia, 1986), *Greatest Hits* (Columbia, 1995), *Live in New York City* (Columbia, 2001), *The Essential Bruce Springsteen* (Columbia, 2003)
Chart peak: No. 42

The second single from the *Darkness on the Edge of Town* album did not crack the *Billboard* Top 40 but became a fast favorite of Bruce Springsteen's audiences, a fist-waving anthem that opened many a show on the *Darkness* tour. Named after director Terrence Malick's 1973 film that starred Martin Sheen as a killer running from the law, "Badlands" is

Springsteen performs at the Masonic Temple in Detroit, Michigan, on September 1, 1978, on the *Darkness* tour, for which an anthemic version of "Badlands" was a frequent show opener.

infused with political and social consciousness voiced in lines such as, "Poor man wanna be rich/Rich man wanna be king/And a king ain't satisfied/Till he rules everything." At the same time, it's an optimistic song in which Springsteen declares, "I believe in the love that you gave me/I believe in the faith that can save me" and "It ain't no sin to be glad you're alive."

One particularly memorable performance of "Badlands" had definite political implications, however. It came on the night after Ronald Reagan was elected president in November 1980; introducing the song, Springsteen told the audience, "I don't know what you guys think about what happened last night, but I think it's pretty frightening. You guys are young. There's gonna be a lot of people depending on you coming up, so this is for you," then launched into the song, the recording of which was used on *Live/75–85*. Like many of the songs on *Darkness*, "Badlands" took a great deal of time to write and record; the version that appears on the album is generally considered to be Take 23. In the U.S. the single was backed by "Streets of Fire," while another *Darkness* track, "Something in the Night," was the U.K. B-side. —*GG*

Arthur Baker

Dance music producer and remixer

A pioneer in dance and hip-hop production, Arthur Baker was named Producer of the Year by *Rolling Stone* magazine and received the Trendsetter Award from *Billboard*. Thanks to his extended dance remixes of *Born in the U.S.A.* material, however, Baker's role in Springsteen history is a contentious one. After DJ-ing in his hometown of Boston, Baker joined the staff of Tommy Boy Records in the early 1980s. He was, with Afrika Bambaataa, the mastermind behind the Soul Sonic Force's "Planet Rock" in 1981—the first twelve-inch single to go platinum, the beginning of electro-funk, and one of the enduring landmark recordings of the hip-hop genre. Baker also discovered, signed, and produced New Edition. As the 1980s progressed, with club music and twelve-inch dance mixes entering the mainstream, Baker was on the forefront as one of the decade's most prominent remixers, producing for New Order and soon remixing tracks for mainstream pop and rock artists such as Cyndi Lauper, Fleetwood Mac, the Cars, and the Rolling Stones.

According to Chuck Plotkin, it was Springsteen's label that "had this idea [for a remix] and were intent on giving it a shot." After CBS presented work from several prominent remixers, Springsteen chose Baker, liking what he had done with Lauper's "Girls Just Want to Have Fun." As Plotkin told *Billboard*, "It was adventuresome enough to constitute something new, but also kept in mind the meaning of the original." And so Baker was hired to bring Bruce to the dance floor.

"Dancing in the Dark," as it appears on *Born in the U.S.A.*, was originally conceived as a single—even, as Jon Landau reportedly whispered in Max Weinberg's ear before recording the album track, a "dance record." Baker's mix took that whispered suggestion to (and possibly past) its logical conclusion. Baker told the *Los Angeles Times*, "When I first heard 'Dancing' I thought it was a great song, but I thought there was something missing in the record. I thought it was real one-dimensional—very straight, especially the bass line. I tried to give the record more dimension. I wanted to make it more like Bruce's old stuff—I remember what 'Born to Run' was like—with the fuller sound and the bells." Baker deconstructed the Springsteen song, replacing the rhythm tracks with synthesized drums and new bass lines, adding female backing vocals, chimes, and reverb in his remixes for "Dancing in the Dark (Blaster Mix)," "Cover Me (Undercover Mix)," and "Born in the U.S.A (Freedom Mix)." There were also dub and radio versions of each, along with two dub mixes for "Cover Me."

The "Dancing in the Dark" remix twelve-inch was released on June 29, 1984, the same day the *Born in the U.S.A.* tour began; the other two followed later that year. Love 'em or hate 'em, they remain the most anomalous recordings in Springsteen's canon; the official release of the semi-Sousafied "Born in the U.S.A. (Freedom Mix)" provides perhaps the best argument that Springsteen wasn't blameless when it came to that song's widespread misinterpretation.

In 1985, Baker collaborated with Little Steven on the anti-apartheid "Sun City" record; Baker donated studio time and his mixing prowess, and the two coproduced the protest song. "Steve played me his original demo, and I liked it," Baker recalled. "A few days later, we went right in, cut the track, added a few things." Springsteen was recruited for the political project (along with an array of rock, hip-hop, jazz, and reggae artists), which benefited the Africa Fund.

In 1987, Baker utilized tape edits in "Put the Needle to the Record," helping pioneer (along with Double Dee & Steinski) the sampling genre of "cut and paste." That influence was strongly felt in Little Steven's 1992 remixes of Springsteen's "57 Channels (and Nothin' On)," which featured sound bites from the L.A. riots.

The *Born in the U.S.A.* remixes have never been officially issued on compact disc, though a pirate release titled *The Remix Album* compiles all ten Baker creations (along with Little Steven's three reworkings of "57 Channels" and the hip-hop influenced "Streets of Philadelphia"). Baker has released solo albums of his own and continues to DJ and produce; the latest in a string of his own labels (Streetwise, Criminal, Minimal) is Whacked. —*CP*

Bobby Bandiera

New Jersey guitarist and songwriter; member of Southside Johnny & the Asbury Jukes

Since the early '80s, when he was a member of the Stone Pony house band Cats on a Smooth Surface, Bobby Bandiera has been one of Bruce Springsteen's most frequent non–E Street Band musical mates. With Cats he backed Springsteen on drop-in appearances in the '80s, mostly at the Stone Pony but also at other clubs around the Jersey Shore. And since he left to join Southside Johnny & the Asbury Jukes in the late '80s, Bandiera has continued to be beckoned by Springsteen for periodic shows, including his birthday parties and his now-annual benefit concerts for the Rumson Country Day School. Springsteen, meanwhile, joined Jon Bon Jovi, Gary U.S. Bonds, Southside Johnny, and others at the Hope Concert on April 29, 2003, at the Count Basie Theater in Red Bank, New Jersey, to raise money for Robert Bandiera, Jr., who suffers from a rare neurological disorder.

Like many of his New Jersey musical colleagues, Bandiera Sr. grew up on a diet of classic rock and R&B. He rushed home from his Catholic school's Sunday evening services to see the Beatles perform on *The Ed Sullivan Show* and filled his collection with albums by the Jimi Hendrix Experience, Cream, the Yardbirds, and the Young Rascals. He learned to play guitar to those records and began playing in bands, including Holme, before Cats on a Smooth Surface. Besides his role as an Asbury Juke, he's recorded with Jon Bon Jovi, Cyndi Lauper, and Springsteen's wife, Patti Scialfa, and he did one tour with Bon Jovi. Bandiera has also appeared on stage with B.B. King, Stevie Wonder, Eric Clapton, and the Rolling Stones' Keith Richards. He leads his own Bob Bandiera Band and has recorded three solo albums, the most recent of which is 2004's *Is My Father There?*, featuring guest appearances by several of the Jukes.

Cats on a Smooth Surface is still together and working, and it's still known mostly for Springsteen's numerous guest appearances at Jersey Shore clubs. Vinnie Danielle now leads the band after the departure of Bandiera and its other high-profile alumnus, onetime Styx member Glenn Burtnick. Cats continues to play club shows as well as private parties and corporate gigs. *—GG*

Mike Batlan and Doug Sutphin

Former Springsteen crew members, plaintiffs in 1987 lawsuit

Mike Batlan and Doug Sutphin were veteran members of the E Street Band road crew—serving thirteen and ten years respectively—when they quit "in disgust" in October 1985 following the end of the *Born in the U.S.A.* world tour. Batlan also had the distinction of being the man who "recorded" the *Nebraska* album, the spare January 1982 demo tape that wound up becoming Springsteen's sixth album and first solo effort. The parting was clearly not amicable, and two years later the pair sued Springsteen for back wages they claimed he owed them, as well as $6 million in punitive damages. "We are suing him for massive violations of this country's labor laws, which resulted in our being cheated out of hundreds of thousands of dollars in wages," Batlan explained in a letter to *Q* magazine. "I alone am suing him for abrogating contractual promises he made to me in the earliest years of his career, regarding how I would be paid."

Those alleged "violations" included unpaid overtime and what the roadies claimed were "illegal" fines—for testing Nils Lofgren's guitar without authorization, missing an air-conditioning cue during a concert at Pittsburgh's Three Rivers Stadium, and "somehow being responsible for a hurricane-force storm that washed away [Springsteen's] canoe," resulting in a $311.11 penalty. Batlan claimed that he and other Springsteen employees were forced to sign an "unconscionable" Waiver of Rights clause in their contracts that he said absolves Springsteen of "any and all ... monies, debts, damages, obligations ... any and all oral promises" he may have made to them. Batlan also expressed anger that Springsteen spent a reported $2 million in legal fees to fight their suit. "Can a man be a hero to the working class while simultaneously spending millions of dollars in a legal battle to keep the workers of his own industry exempt from the protections of labor law?" he fumed in the *Q* letter. "Is a man compassionate and understanding of a working person's plight in this world when he snatches [a]... weekly paycheck from his own employees' wallets? Is a man truly philanthropic if the money he donates to charity (with maximum publicity) is in reality merely the wages he illegally failed to pay his own employees?"

The case dragged on for nearly four years. Batlan and Sutphin acknowledged that Springsteen paid them $250,000 in severance in 1985 (even though they quit), and Batlan admitted taking tapes of unreleased Springsteen recordings and four notebooks containing some unreleased song lyrics, selling the latter for $28,000. In April 1989 a judge threw out the punitive damages claim but left the overtime issue intact. In September 1991 Springsteen settled out of court with the roadies for $200,000, just six days before the case was to go to trial, according to Marc Eliot's *Down Thunder Road: The Making of Bruce Springsteen*. At the time, a statement by the Parcher and Hayes law firm, which represented Springsteen, termed the settlement "a matter of principle." It also meant Springsteen would not be compelled by the court to reveal the inner-workings of his operations.

In a *Rolling Stone* magazine interview eleven months later, Springsteen called the lawsuit "disappointing. I worked with these two people for a long time, and I thought I'd really done the right thing. And when they left, it was handshakes and hugs all around, you know. And then about a year later, *bang!* I think that if you asked the majority of people who had worked with me how they felt about the experience, they'd say they'd been treated really well. But it only takes one disgruntled or unhappy person, and that's what everyone wants to hear ... If you spend a long time with someone and there's a very fundamental misunderstanding, well, you feel bad about it." —*GG*

"Because the Night." See Patti Smith.

Barry Bell

Springsteen booking agent, 1973–present

In 1973, when Bruce Springsteen signed with the William Morris Agency to handle his concert bookings, Barry Bell was working as an assistant to Sam McKeith, the agent in charge of Springsteen's affairs. In 1976 Bell and Springsteen's manager, Mike Appel, discussed forming their own agency, though the conversation ceased after Springsteen and Appel counter-sued each other that year. Strapped for cash, Springsteen asked William Morris for a loan, which the company refused; Frank Barsalona's Premier Talent, however, offered a $100,000 advance, wooing away Springsteen—and, subsequently, Bell—in early 1977. Bell's efforts in booking tour dates helped keep Springsteen financially afloat while the lawsuit raged, and he's also credited as a vital ingredient in Springsteen's career ascent through his shrewd and aggressive strategies. Bell credited Springsteen's success as a live act to the fact that he changed the shows nightly, telling biographer Dave Marsh, "I would go there and I would be surprised every night. With somebody else, after seeing the act two nights in a row, you'd say, 'Okay, let's go home.' But here, you know, I wanted to be there the next night, to see what the new surprise was gonna be, what the new innovation was gonna be, what the new material was gonna be, where he would jump this time, what would he do crazy next time."

In his Rock and Roll Hall of Fame induction speech in 1999, Springsteen thanked both Bell and Barsalona for "a great job." Bell also has the distinction of introducing Springsteen to his first wife, actress-model Julianne Phillips, in the fall of 1984. He knew Phillips through friends at the Elite Modeling Agency, where she was a client. They also frequented the same Manhattan restaurant, Cafe Central. Bell arranged for a dinner date after one of Springsteen's shows at the Los Angeles Sports Arena; as they dated, became engaged, and married in May 1985, Bell called it "a good booking"—although the couple divorced in 1989. —*GG*

Before the Fame. See Prodigal Son.

Bob Benjamin

Artist manager, activist

ob Benjamin is known among Bruce Springsteen fans as the man who created the now-annual Light of Day benefits for the Parkinson's Disease Foundation. A Parkinson's sufferer himself, Benjamin also manages Joe Grushecky & the Houserockers, a Pittsburgh, Pennsylvania–based band. Grushecky and Springsteen occasionally write and perform together, and Springsteen produced one of Grushecky's albums, *American Babylon*, in 1995. A former *Billboard* magazine researcher, Benjamin created Marketing Dept., an agency that does retail marketing for record labels, in 1991 and has worked extensively with New York–based Razor & Tie Records. He met Grushecky in 1992, during Grushecky's first stint as a Razor & Tie artist, and they joined forces while Grushecky was working on his *American Babylon* album. (Grushecky's original deal with the label had ended by then, but they partnered again for that release.)

Benjamin first met Springsteen in 1977, when he asked Springsteen for an autograph outside of a Toronto show. In 1978 Benjamin managed to work his way up to Springsteen's hotel room before a Buffalo show by telling a bellhop he was working on a story for *Thunder Road*, the first Springsteen fanzine. He was invited in, and Springsteen, who was just starting to get involved in merchandising, quizzed Benjamin about what might appeal to young fans. Benjamin went to lunch with Springsteen and E Street Band members Garry Tallent and Roy Bittan; he walked them over to the theater for sound check, and wound up with a front-row seat for the show. That night, he also met Jon Landau.

When Benjamin organized the first official Light of Day benefit in 2000, Springsteen showed up to support his friend's cause. He subsequently coordinated *Light of Day: A Tribute to Bruce Springsteen*, which was released in 2003 on Benjamin's Schoolhouse Records label; proceeds from the album are split between the Parkinson's foundation and the Kristen Ann Carr Fund, dedicated to the late daughter of Springsteen's co-manager, Barbara Carr. As for his *Thunder Road* story, it never ran—which could be because Benjamin is not sure it even got written. —*LM*

Chuck Berry

Singer, guitarist, songwriter, icon

ne of the fathers of rock 'n' roll, Chuck Berry has occasionally descended to merely being its deadbeat dad. The songs he recorded from the mid-to-late '50s through the early '60s, including "Maybellene," "Roll Over Beethoven," "School Days," "Rock & Roll Music," "Sweet

Little Sixteen," and "Johnny B. Goode," form the genre's very foundation. The familiar guitar licks that open many of his songs are a clarion call to rock, while his carefully crafted lyrics transcend the commonness of the topics he often wrote about: girls, cars, and playin' guitar like ringin' a bell.

But Berry's personal demons—including a preternaturally nasty disposition (he's alienated nearly everyone around him and even punched out his greatest fan and acolyte, Keith Richards of the Rolling Stones), mercenary touring habits (he often travels alone, playing with unrehearsed pickup bands, and insists on being paid in cash, in advance), a taste for young women (one of his several trips to prison was for transporting a minor over state lines), and sexual deviance (he was sued by female employees of a restaurant he owned for hiding video cameras in the women's restroom)—have denied him much of the love and respect owed to one whose contributions to music have been so great. Bruce Springsteen was a fan and grew up on Berry's music just as he had the music of Elvis Presley, the Beatles, and the Rolling Stones. As he became an artist in his own right, Springsteen wrote songs that drew certain parallels to Berry's: they were concerned with the open road and the possibilities of what lay ahead; they were populated with colorfully named, unforgettable characters (Berry's included Johnny B. Goode and the "Brown Eyed Handsome Man," Springsteen's featured the denizens of Greasy Lake, Jack the Rabbit, and Weak-Kneed Willie, among many others); and both had more than a passing interest in cars. Berry once specified a "coffee-colored Cadillac," while Springsteen rhapsodized about a "'69 Chevy with a 396, Feulie heads and a Hurst on the floor." Springsteen even appropriated a couple of song titles from Berry, "Promised Land" and "Downbound Train." In fact, Berry has a cowriting credit on "Johnny Bye Bye," which shares lyrics with Berry's "Bye Bye Johnny."

Springsteen and Berry met on stage in the early '70s. Chances are that Berry doesn't remember it, but the story is so indelibly etched in Springsteen's memory that he recounted it in the 1987 Berry documentary *Hail! Hail! Rock and Roll!* Springsteen and his band were hired to open a show for Berry and Jerry Lee Lewis at the University of Maryland Field House in College Park on April 28, 1973. They volunteered to back him up as well, thrilled to be playing with their idol—even for free. Berry blew in the stage door five minutes before the performance, collected his money, and plugged in. Springsteen asked him what songs they were going to do, and Berry answered, "We're going to do some Chuck Berry songs." He started playing and let the chips fall where they may; at one point, Springsteen recounted, Berry turned to the band and said, "Play for that money, boys"—though the group wasn't getting an additional fee for playing with Berry. When Berry was finished, he left immediately. It's not a particularly flattering story, yet for some reason Berry transcribed it and used it for the introduction to his autobiography, going so far as to preface Springsteen's remarks with, "Now here

Springsteen and Chuck Berry perform Berry's song "Johnny B. Goode" to open the Concert for the Rock and Roll Hall of Fame and Museum in Cleveland, Ohio, on Saturday, September 2, 1995. More than forty different acts played during the concert, which was held at Cleveland Municipal Stadium in honor of the long-awaited opening of the Rock Hall.

is a guy who speaks what God loves, which is the truth." Springsteen and the E Street Band later backed Berry for his appearance at the Rock and Roll Hall of Fame gala opening concert in 1995. —*DD*

"Better Days"

Single release: March 4, 1992
Album: *Lucky Town* (Columbia, 1992)
Also on: *MTV Plugged* (Columbia, 1993/1997), *Greatest Hits* (Columbia, 1995)
Chart peak: No. 16

 f this comes off as one of the most optimistic songs in Bruce Springsteen's cannon ... well, it is. "With a young son and about to get married (for the last time), I was feelin' like a happy guy who has his rough days rather than vice versa," he writes in the liner notes to *Greatest Hits*. He could also have added that he was about to become a father again, with daughter Jessica Rae's arrival just a couple of months after he recorded the song. No wonder that in the lyrics he even presents himself as a "fool" who's "halfway to heaven and just a mile out of hell." The song certainly reflects the overwhelmingly bright tone of the *Lucky Town* album, a set that was written and recorded in a lightning two-month blast in the fall of 1991, following the arduous creation of its companion piece *Human Touch*.

Technically, the title track from *Human Touch* was the A-side of the single, but Columbia promoted both tracks to radio in order to hype both of the simultaneously released albums. That said, "Better Days" was considered Springsteen's first album track B-side since 1978, when he began backing his singles with unreleased material. —*GG*

The Big Beat

1984 book by E Street Band drummer Max Weinberg

hile "down time" was hard to come by in the first decade of the E Street Band's existence, drummer Max Weinberg took advantage of his to research and write (with author and music historian Robert Santelli) *The Big Beat*, the subtitle of which—*Conversations with Rock's Greatest Drummers*—pretty much sums up its contents.

Weinberg focused on fourteen fellow skin-pounders in the book, including Elvis Presley veterans D.J. Fontana and Hal Blaine, the Beatles' Ringo Starr, the Rolling Stones' Charlie Watts, the Rascals' Dino Danelli, the Band's Levon Helm, Johnny "Bee" Badanjek from Mitch Ryder's Detroit Wheels, Dave Clark, the Faces' Kenney Jones, and studio legends such as Earl Palmer, Bernard Purdie, Russ Kunkel, and Jim Keltner.

"It's a book of conversations with drummers who represent, to me, that original spirit of rock 'n' roll," Weinberg explained. "Drummers are generally in the back and never have the opportunity to tell their story. We got almost a history of where rock drumming has come from."

The Big Beat was first published in 1984, in time for the *Born in the U.S.A.* tour. It's gone in and out of print over the years; a 1991 edition featured a new foreword by Springsteen, and the most recent reissue was in May 2004. —*GG*

Roy Bittan

Keyboardist, E Street Band member 1974–present

esponding to a *Village Voice* ad Bruce Springsteen placed for a pianist, "The Professor" joined the E Street Band in late 1974, in the middle of the laborious *Born to Run* sessions, and immediately stamped his character onto the classic record. Without Bittan's extended, classically styled piano introductions for "Thunder Road" and "Jungleland," the album would lack crucial playfulness and drama. Bittan—a Rockaway Beach, New York, kid who originally studied to be a doctor—has filled that role ever since for Bruce Springsteen, both within and outside of the E Street Band.

"I think what happened there was when I joined the band, Bruce's material brought out something in me ... I hit Bruce at the time when I was able to be very creative within his framework and he was looking for that kind of input," Bittan said in 1993's out-of-print *Local Hero: Bruce, In the Words of His Band*. "I felt very strongly about what he was writing about. I didn't come from the Jersey Shore, but I came from the New York shore, and when he talked about the boardwalk in Asbury Park, New Jersey, I had the boardwalk in Playland, in Rockaway Beach, and it was very similar. I was relating very strongly to the things that he talked about ... He was writing about themes that touched me deeply." Since *Born to Run*, Bittan is the only E Streeter to have performed on every Springsteen album. His "Born in the U.S.A." synthesizer line is perhaps the most distinctive in rock 'n' roll, and he provided important texture on songs such as "Tunnel of Love" and the Oscar-winning "Streets of Philadelphia." After The Boss dismissed the E Street Band in 1989 and subsequently fell into a "creative funk," it was Bittan he recruited to come to his home studio and help him shake his malaise. (They came up with "Roll of the Dice" and "Real World," which became the heart of the *Human Touch* album and for which Bittan shares a cowriting credit.)

Born in 1949, Bittan took accordion and piano lessons as a child. He attended pre-med classes at Brooklyn College, but for extra cash, he played in bands a few nights a week. His reputation as a session pianist grew quickly, however, and he switched his major to music education, then abandoned both medicine and teaching for rock 'n' roll. After David Sancious left the E Street Band for a solo career, Bittan answered Springsteen's Village Voice ad seeking someone who could play "classical to Jerry Lee Lewis."

Along with Max Weinberg, who answered the same ad and replaced drummer Ernest "Boom" Carter around the same time, Bittan quickly ingratiated himself with the band. In the studio, he was the perfect combination of classical virtuosity and epic rock grandeur; on stage, his receded hairline, studious glasses, and stoic manner won him the nickname "The Professor." "Roy's playing formed the signature sound of some of my greatest records," Springsteen explained as he was inducted into the Rock and Roll Hall of Fame in 1999. "He can play anything. He's always there for me. His emotional generosity and his deep personal support mean a great, great deal to me."

Roy Bittan (right, at piano) and Springsteen on stage in Detroit in August 1981. Bittan provided what Springsteen has called "the signature sound of some of my greatest records."

After *Born to Run*, session offers piled up for Bittan; although he receives very little fanfare for it, he performed on '70s landmarks such as Jackson Browne's *The Pretender*, Meat Loaf's *Bat Out of Hell*, David Bowie's *Station to Station*, and Peter Gabriel's first self-titled album. He has continued to supplement his E Street work with other projects over the years, appearing on albums by Stevie Nicks, Donna Summer, Dire Straits, Bob Seger, and Bon Jovi. He also coproduced Lucinda Williams's 1998 country-rock masterpiece *Car Wheels on a Gravel Road.*

Tellingly, aside from Springsteen's wife and backup singer Patti Scialfa, Bittan was the only E Streeter to perform on The Boss's early-'90s albums *Human Touch* and *Lucky Town* and the subsequent tour to support them. When the E Street Band reunited for 1995 sessions and a 1999 tour, of course, Bittan maintained his spot on the piano bench.

So what's the secret to longevity in Springsteen's band? Being ready, according to Bittan. "Bruce has always been the consummate master of putting together a set. There's so much to draw from in terms of the catalog," he told the *Rocky Mountain News* in a rare interview in 2003. "Sometimes he just calls one, and in the ROM of our minds, we're able to pull it out. Other times we try to make our way through it at sound check and then we have to refer back to the record after sound check. Then we do it, you know?" —*SK*

A Black & White Night. See Roy Orbison.

Blood Brothers

Documentary and home video, released 1996

In 1995, Bruce Springsteen and the E Street Band reunited in the studio for the first time in eleven years. The occasion was the recording of new songs to be included on Springsteen's *Greatest Hits* album, which ultimately included four of the numbers—"Secret Garden," "Murder Incorporated," "Blood Brothers," and "This Hard Land." Producer/director/photographer Ernie Fritz was given complete access to the sessions, and *Blood Brothers* is his documentary of the event. Much of the film shows the minutia that must be dealt with when releasing an album—photo shoots, picking the album cover, tweaking the press release, etc. Springsteen can also be seen trying to work his career in around the demands of his personal life; at one point he directs manager and coproducer Jon Landau to schedule a session for later in the day because he has to take his kids to see the Broadway production of *Beauty and the Beast* in the afternoon.

Of more immediate interest to fans is seeing how hard Springsteen works on every aspect of his music, from the extra time he puts into writing lyrics to the attention he pays to achieving the perfect musical accompaniment and getting the right mix. The film includes interviews with E Street Band members and footage of the video shoot for "Murder Incorporated," which was done live at Tramps in New York City. That completed video, as well as the clip for "Secret Garden" (which features actors), are included on the DVD. Early in the film, record producer Chuck Plotkin frets, "This could be amazing or this could be a catastrophe." He needn't have worried; the *Greatest Hits* CD, which debuted at No. 1 on the *Billboard* charts, and the documentary both turned out to be the former.

Blood Brothers was broadcast on the Disney Channel in March 1996 and released on video disc and VHS that fall, accompanied by a five-song EP. The DVD arrived in October 2003. *—DD*

Off of E Street ... Roy Bittan

Bon Jovi, *Bon Jovi* (1984)
Gary U.S. Bonds, *Dedication* (1981), *On the Line* (1982)
David Bowie, *Station to Station* (1986), *Scary Monsters* (1980)
Jackson Browne, *The Pretender* (1976)
Tracy Chapman, *Matters of the Heart* (1992)
Chicago, *Chicago 25: The Christmas Album* (1998), *Christmas: What's It Gonna Be* (2003)
Rick Derringer, *Good Dirty Fun* (1983)
Celine Dion, *Falling into You* (1996)
Dire Straits, *Making Movies* (1980)
Bob Dylan, *Bootleg Series, Vols. 1–3: Rare and Unreleased 1961–1991* (1991)
Peter Gabriel, *Peter Gabriel* (1977), *Peter Gabriel* (1978)
Ian Hunter, *You're Never Alone with a Schizophrenic* (1979)
Andrew Lloyd Webber, *Now and Forever: The Andrew Lloyd Webber Box Set* (2001)
Meat Loaf, *Bat Out of Hell* (1977), *Dead Ringer* (1981), *Bat Out of Hell II: Back into Hell* (1983)
Stevie Nicks, *Bella Donna* (1981), *Wild Heart* (1983), *Street Angel* (1994)
Lou Reed, *Set the Twilight Reeling* (1996)
Patti Scialfa, *Rumble Doll* (1983)
Bob Seger & the Silver Bullet Band, *The Distance* (1982), *The Fire Inside* (1991), *It's a Mystery* (1995)
Patty Smyth, *Patty Smyth* (1992)
Jim Steinman, *Bad for Good* (1981)
Barbra Streisand, *Emotion* (1984)
Donna Summer, *Donna Summer* (1982)
The Thorns, *The Thorns* (2003)
Bonnie Tyler, *Faster than the Speed of Night* (1983), *Secret Dreams & Forbidden Fire* (1986), *Bitterblue* (1991)
Lucinda Williams, *Car Wheels on a Gravel Road* (1998)

The Bomb Scare Show

October 2, 1975, in Milwaukee, Wisconsin

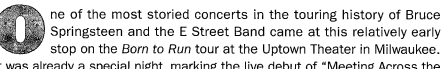

ne of the most storied concerts in the touring history of Bruce Springsteen and the E Street Band came at this relatively early stop on the *Born to Run* tour at the Uptown Theater in Milwaukee. It was already a special night, marking the live debut of "Meeting Across the River"—which, interestingly, was the opening song. But seven songs into the show, the theater management and local police stopped the concert because of a bomb threat, evacuating the venue with the promise that fans would be readmitted after the premises were inspected. Springsteen and company waited the delay out in a nearby bar and returned to the stage notably, and noticeably, loose, restarting the show with Chuck Berry's "Little Queenie" and winding up with Gary "U.S." Bonds's "Quarter to Three." —*GG*

Jon Bon Jovi

New Jersey rock star

fter Bruce Springsteen, Jon Bon Jovi is the most successful and most well-known rock artist to rise out of the Asbury Park music scene. During the course of his two-decade-plus recording career, his self-named band has sold 100 million albums, completed numerous U.S. and world tours, sold out Giants Stadium at the Meadowlands complex in New Jersey many times, and performed at Super Bowl XXXVII in San Diego in 2003. Almost singlehandedly, Bon Jovi—the band—has kept alive '80s-style pop-metal in the twenty-first century, finding a way to make the mostly teen-driven themes of the genre relevant, beyond just nostalgia, to fans now in their forties. Individually, Jon Bon Jovi has gone from a pretty, pop-metal poster boy to a superstar artist whose talent for writing hit songs, leading an incredibly successful band, and routinely delivering potent, high energy rock shows now goes unquestioned and is even celebrated. Bon Jovi has also launched a film career, including well-received roles in *U-571, Moonlight and Valentino, The Leading Man*, and TV's "Ally McBeal." He purchased an Arena Football League franchise for Philadelphia in 2003 and, like Springsteen, has become a New Jersey rock 'n' roll icon, a faithful advocate for his home state who lives less than twenty-five miles from where he grew up (and not far from Springsteen in Rumson, New Jersey).

Born John Bongiovi in Sayreville, New Jersey, in 1962, Bon Jovi missed out on the earliest days of Asbury Park's emerging rock music scene. He was a boy when the area's first important club, the Upstage, opened in 1968. He was still underage when another Asbury Park club, the Stone Pony, began attracting national attention, thanks to the dramatic rise of Springsteen in

1975. However, that didn't stop him from lying about his age so that his band, the Atlantic City Expressway, could occasionally play the Pony. From the start, Bon Jovi took as his mentors Asbury Park's three most influential artists—Springsteen, Steve Van Zandt, and Southside Johnny Lyon. Although the music for which Bon Jovi would eventually become famous bears little resemblance to the R&B–heavy, soul-inspired rock those musicians played, Bon Jovi learned much from his forebears about performing, creating an image, developing a fan base, and keeping close to one's roots. He's acknowledged that Springsteen casts something of "a shadow" over his standing in the rock pantheon, but he never hesitates to identify himself as an avid fan and Springsteen as "someone who I've watched closely and learned a lot from over the years. And I enjoy the hell out of his stuff."

Early, post–Atlantic City Expressway bands such as the Rest and John Bongiovi & the Wild Ones eventually led to Bon Jovi signing his own deal in 1983—after sweeping up his cousin Tony Bongiovi's Power Station recording studio in New York City—and the release of the group's self-titled debut album a year later. In 1986, the multiplatinum *Slippery When Wet* and a handful of hit singles like "You Give Love a Bad Name" and "Livin' on a Prayer" vaulted Bon Jovi to superstar status, and his band was considered to be the hottest of the early MTV age. Two years later Bon Jovi released what would become the album most closely connected to his Jersey Shore roots and publicly put him in closer allegiance to Springsteen, Van Zandt, and Southside Johnny. Although it was thick with pop and hard-rock songs, *New Jersey* celebrated Bon Jovi's home state in emphatic fashion at a time when Springsteen's link to the state was unrivaled. In a 1990 interview, Bon Jovi said, "I didn't call the album *New Jersey* just because I was born and raised there and still live there. The thing is, people who live in New Jersey have a certain attitude; there's something about people who've been the butt of jokes about their state for a long time and still keep their pride. A lot of people who've lived in Jersey all their lives tend to put loyalty pretty high on their list of priorities. I like that. I always have. And I like to have my songs and the way I live my life reflect that."

Bon Jovi and guitarist Richie Sambora were credited with helping to inspire MTV's popular "Unplugged" series with their acoustic performance at the 1989 MTV Video Music Awards in Los Angeles. Bon Jovi continued to release albums throughout the '90s, including the solo outing *Blaze of Glory* (the soundtrack to the film *Young Guns II*), *Keep the Faith*, and *These Days*. While the group suffered a slight drop in fan interest in the alt-rock '90s, 2000's *Crush* was a double-platinum triumph, while 2002's *Bounce*, not unlike Springsteen's *The Rising*, drew inspiration from the human impact of the September 11 terrorist attacks.

Over the years, Bon Jovi has performed numerous times with Spring-steen and Southside Johnny, particularly on Jersey stages. In 1991, after

Although a Jersey Shore icon of a different era, Jon Bon Jovi draws strongly on his Springsteen influence in his stage performance and songwriting.

touring with the band, he was part of Southside Johnny & the Asbury Jukes' comeback album, *Better Days*, singing on it and appearing in the video shot at the Stone Pony. On a semi-regular basis, he has presented Christmas con-

certs at the Jersey Shore, raising many thousands of dollars for local charities; on January 31, 1998, Springsteen, most of the E Street Band, and
Southside Johnny joined Bon Jovi for Come Together: Jon Bon Jovi & Friends,
a benefit for a slain New Jersey police officer. More recently, Bon Jovi has
been a guest performer at Springsteen's holiday shows. —RS/GG

Gary U.S. Bonds

Singer, songwriter

 orn Gary Anderson in Jacksonville, Florida, early '60s rock 'n' roll
shouter Gary U.S. Bonds got his moniker from Norfolk,
Virginia–based producer/label owner Frank Guida, who thought it
might get his artist's records a few more spins if DJs mistook them for public
service announcements. As it turned out, Bonds's fervent performances were
all that was necessary to turn "New Orleans," "Quarter to Three," and "School
Is Out" into Top 10 hits in 1961. Success was fleeting, though, and Bonds was
eventually relegated to playing the oldies circuit. One young artist who was
inspired by the manic energy and multi-tracked vocals of Bonds's early hits was
Bruce Springsteen. For years, he and the E Street Band played "Quarter to
Three" as an encore number. E Streeter Steve Van Zandt had also met Bonds
years earlier, when Van Zandt was playing guitar with the Dovells. Springsteen
and Van Zandt got a chance to honor their influence by coproducing Bonds's
comeback album *Dedication* in 1981. Springsteen contributed three songs,
"Your Love," the title track, and "This Little Girl Is Mine," which charted at No.
11 (marking the longest time spent between Top 20 hits by any artist). Bonds
and Springsteen also dueted on the Moon Mulligan song "Jole Blon."

Bonds says the success of the *Dedication* project, which came out in
the wake of Springsteen's *The River*, gave him a sense of what lay ahead for
his young friend. "I knew he was gonna be big," Bonds says. "I knew that
was gonna happen. Once I heard 'This Little Girl,' I knew he was headed for
something even bigger than what he'd already done."

A year later, Springsteen and Van Zandt coproduced Bonds's follow-up
On the Line, which featured seven Springsteen songs: "Hold On (To What You
Got)," "Out of Work," "Club Soul City," "Love's on the Line," "Rendezvous,"
and "Angelyne." "Out of Work" charted, nearly reaching the Top 20, but the
album flopped and Bonds was dropped by his label.

Another twenty years passed before Bonds resurfaced. In 2004, he
released *Back in 20*, featuring Springsteen and Southside Johnny Lyon helping out on the Bonds-penned "Can't Teach an Old Dog New Tricks." Bonds
notes that Springsteen is "such a good friend, such a kind man, that he said
yes without even a hesitation. He didn't want to produce it or anything; he

was on tour at the time. I said, 'Don't worry, I'll write it. I'll produce it. I just need you to sing and play.' He said, 'Fine, I'll go with that.'" —*DD/GG*

Bono. *See* **U2.**

Bootleg Police
Lynn Elder, Rich Breton, Jan Rodenrijs, Fred Mills

This foursome, and many others who shall remain nameless, provide consumer protection to the underground as the Bruce Springsteen bootleg reviewers of record. No one is quite sure if Lynn Elder is a he or a she, but regardless, Elder helped establish the protocol for reviewing Springsteen boots with the three-book series *You Better Not Touch* (subtitled *The Honest and Accurate Guide to Bruce Springsteen on Bootleg Compact Disc*), published by *Backstreets* magazine. Opinionated and some might even say downright cranky, Elder's conservative ratings helped set a standard of criticism for others to follow. Elder's last volume, published in 1997, covers recordings through *The Ghost of Tom Joad* acoustic tour.

Rich Breton took bootleg reviewing to the web in a big way with his massive archive Brucelegs, which now resides at Brucelegs.com. It remains the most exhaustive database for Springsteen bootleg information; unfortunately, Breton has elected not to update his site further (brucebase.com is trying to pick up where Breton left off). Rodenrijs is the publisher of *Wanted* magazine out of Holland and the author of a magazine and book series reviewing Springsteen bootlegs with a seasoned and savvy collector's eye. The most recent issue of *Wanted,* published in late 2003, covers most of the dates on *The Rising* tour. Finally, Fred Mills has taken up residency as *Backstreets'* main man on the bootleg beat. When he's not writing about Brucelegs, you can find his work about other artists in the pages of *Magnet, ICE*, and other publications. —*EF*

Born in the U.S.A.

Released: June 4, 1984
Producers: Bruce Springsteen, Jon Landau, Chuck Plotkin, Steve Van Zandt
Tracks: "Born in the U.S.A.," "Cover Me," "Darlington County," "Working on the Highway," "Downbound Train," "I'm on Fire," "No Surrender," "Bobby Jean," "I'm Goin' Down," "Glory Days," "Dancing in the Dark," "My Hometown"
Chart peak: No. 1 (seven weeks)

Springsteen calls *Born in the U.S.A.* "one of my purest pop records," and he's not kidding. Released in the late spring of 1984, with the first single, "Dancing in the Dark," cruising up the charts, Springsteen's seventh album was an iconic pop smash, launching seven Top 10 singles and selling more than twenty million copies. It also vaulted Springsteen from American rock 'n' roll icon to worldwide sensation, playing to stadiums packed with many fans who had perhaps heard *of* him but had not heard him in the past.

It was an experience Springsteen viewed with great ambivalence. He was not necessarily keen on the ephemeral and superficial nature of pop stardom; as much attention was paid to his physique—which had been bulked up at the gym—as to his songs. Nor did he like seeing himself or his music co-opted for commerce and political gain, particularly when President Ronald Reagan tried to alter Springsteen's message and then attach himself to it during his reelection campaign of 1984. *"Born in the U.S.A.* changed my life and gave me my largest audience," Springsteen wrote in *Songs.* "It forced me to question the way I presented my music and made me think harder about what I was doing."

Springsteen actually thought pretty hard about what he wanted to do with *Born in the U.S.A.* in the first place, resulting in one of the most difficult albums he's ever made. Material wasn't a problem; finding the *right* material was. Following the success of *The River* and "Hungry Heart," Springsteen was uncertain about where he wanted to take his music—and whether he wanted to proceed down the pop hit path that he'd tripped upon in 1980–81. The one-man *Nebraska* project ultimately became a vehicle to temporarily back away from that, as well as a kind of model for *Born in the U.S.A.* "I wanted to take that record and electrify it," Springsteen wrote. He actually convened the E Street Band in May 1982 for sessions that yielded a band version of *Born in the U.S.A.*'s title song along with tracks such as "Cover Me," "I'm on Fire," "I'm Goin' Down," "Darlington County," "Downbound Train," and "Glory Days." *Nebraska* idled things until May 1983, when the group got together again for sessions that were prolific but less satisfying; future B-sides and fan favorites like "Pink Cadillac," "Stand on It," "Janey Don't You Lose Heart," "Murder Incorporated," "This Hard Land," "Shut Out the Light," Springsteen's take on Elvis Presley's "Follow That Dream," and "Protection," which he had written for Donna Summer, were committed to tape, but Springsteen was having trouble finding a cohesive album amidst the material.

There were many discussions with manager Jon Landau and producer Chuck Plotkin, and much hand-wringing over the situation. Gradually, however, the decision to make a "rock 'n' roll album" came into focus and additional songs—"No Surrender," "Bobby Jean," "My Hometown"—brought a greater sense of direction. Springsteen also took the unusual move of polling band and crew members and friends about which of the seventy songs under consideration should make the album—and even asking them to suggest sequences. "No Surrender" and "Dancing in the Dark"—the lat-

Springsteen's "working man" look for the *Born in the U.S.A.* tour became his trademark image in the mid-1980s. That album's seven Top 10 singles brought Springsteen his largest concert crowds ever.

The Ties That Bind

ter a testy answer to Landau's call for something with hit potential—were late additions.

In its final released form, *Born in the U.S.A.* is both poppy and profound, its abundant hooks delivered with the most urgent, in-your-face production Springsteen had achieved on an album up to that point. Like "Born in the U.S.A.," whose true meaning was perhaps obscured by the song's pounding, power rock fervor, the darker messages of other songs were also mitigated by smooth synthesizer riffs ("Dancing in the Dark") or buoyant guitar grind ("I'm Goin' Down"). "No Surrender" and "Bobby Jean" are anthems to faith, devotion, and friendship, while the good-humored "Glory Days" and the mournful "My Hometown" offer different nostalgic turns. And while his storytelling knack is in fine form on tracks like "Darlington County" and "Working on the Highway," Springsteen delves ever deeper into inner emotions, from the smoldering sexual desire of "I'm on Fire" to the pleading despair of "Cover Me" and creative angst of "Dancing in the Dark."

Springsteen's hindsight perspective on *Born in the U.S.A.* remains ambivalent. He considers it a "grab-bag" kind of album that doesn't have the thematic unity of some of his earlier releases. "I put a lot of pressure on myself over a long period of time to reproduce the intensity of *Nebraska* on *Born in the U.S.A.*," he wrote. "I never got it ... The framework of that idea can be found ... with the title song and 'My Hometown.' But it really didn't flesh out like I had hoped it would."

For twenty million–plus buyers, however, it fleshed out just fine. —*GG*

"Born in the U.S.A."

Released: October 1984
Album: *Born in the U.S.A.*(Columbia, 1984)
Also on: *Live/1975–85* (Columbia, 1986); *Greatest Hits* (Columbia, 1995); *Tracks* (Columbia, 1998); *18 Tracks* (Columbia, 1999); *Live in New York City* (Columbia, 2001)
Chart peak: No. 9

The anthemic third single from the *Born in the U.S.A.* album—which Bruce Springsteen considers "one of my five or six best songs"— began life in 1981 when filmmaker Paul Schrader sent Springsteen a script entitled *Born in the U.S.A.* for what later became the movie *Light of Day*, starring Joan Jett and Michael J. Fox. Springsteen had recently read Vietnam veteran Ron Kovic's memoir *Born on the 4th of July* and had also played a benefit for the Vietnam Veterans of America in Los Angeles on August 20, 1981, a show considered by fans to be one of best he has ever played. Both of these experiences inspired the content of the song, which was originally called "Vietnam." Springsteen noted that "the sound of 'Born in the U.S.A.' was martial, modal, and straight ahead. The lyrics dealt with the problems Vietnam vets faced when they came back home after fighting in 'the only war that America had ever lost.' In order to understand the song's intent, you needed to invest a certain amount of time and effort to absorb both the music and the words."

Springsteen recorded his first version of "Born in the U.S.A." in January 1982 for his solo effort *Nebraska* but was not happy with it. He brought it out for the first full-band sessions for the *Born in the U.S.A.* album in May 1982 and wound up using the third take, recorded live in the studio. Drummer Max Weinberg said cutting the song was "the greatest single experience I've ever had recording."

"Born in the U.S.A." became one of Springsteen's most misunderstood songs, with many listeners—along with politicians, including President Ronald Reagan—embracing it as patriotic anthem. He also had to fend off numerous offers from companies wanting to use the song as an ad slogan. "Born in the U.S.A.'"'s dark theme was more readily evident on his earlier recordings of it (one of which surfaced on the *Tracks* collection), but Springsteen felt that the *Born in the U.S.A.* version put the song "in its most powerful presentation. If I tried to undercut or change the music, I believe I would have had a record that might have been more easily understood, but not as good." John Sayles directed the song's video, including out-of-sync concert footage from a ten-night stand at the Los Angeles Sports Arena in the summer of 1984. Springsteen returned the favor for "Born in the U.S.A.'"'s inspiration to filmmaker Schrader by writing the title song for *Light of Day*. Springsteen allowed the controversial rap group 2 Live Crew to sample "Born in the U.S.A." for its song "Banned in the U.S.A.," while the song was also licensed for the closing credits in the 1987 documentary *Dear America: Letters Home from Vietnam*. And its B-side, "Shut out the Light," is appropriately enough another song about a Vietnam veteran struggling to adjust to post-war life. At the 2000 Summer Olympic Games in Sydney, Australia, the U.S. team used the song for its theme as it marched in for the Opening Ceremonies.   —*GG*

Born on the Fourth of July

Book by Vietnam veteran Ron Kovic; made into 1989 film by Oliver Stone.

During one of his cross-country road trips in the late '70s, Bruce Springsteen stopped at a drugstore near Phoenix and picked up a copy of a book titled *Born on the Fourth of July*. Ron Kovic wrote the book after a tour of duty in Vietnam left him wheelchair-bound and disillusioned. He went from being a gung-ho marine sergeant to a hardcore anti-war activist; the chronicle of his experiences and conversion was released on July 4, 1976, the bicentennial celebration of America's independence— which also marked another of his birthdays.

Ironically, shortly after he bought the book, Springsteen was lounging by a pool at the same Los Angeles hotel where Kovic was saying. Kovic introduced himself; Springsteen initially thought he was a fan making conversation until he referenced *Born on the Fourth of July.* Springsteen told Kovic he had just finished the book, and the two spoke at length. Through Kovic, Springsteen met other Vietnam veterans, including Vietnam Veterans of America founder Bobby Muller. Springsteen also referenced the book in concert while introducing songs, including "Darkness on the Edge of Town."

Kovic's book and their subsequent interactions motivated Springsteen to assist disenfranchised veterans, which in turn led to his 1984 song "Born in the U.S.A." These actions thrust him to a new level of fame and into a political spotlight he had previously avoided. Kovic subsequently cowrote a film script based on his story with director Oliver Stone; the *Born on the Fourth of July* film was released in 1989 and won Golden Globe awards for Best Film, Best Actor (Tom Cruise), Best Screenplay, and Best Director. It was also nominated for several Oscars. There were, however, no Springsteen songs on the film soundtrack, which was comprised of era-specific songs by Bob Dylan, Van Morrison, the Shirelles, and others. —*LM*

Born to Run

Released: September 1, 1975
Producers: Bruce Springsteen, Jon Landau, Mike Appel
Tracks: "Thunder Road," "Tenth Avenue Freeze-Out," "Night," "Backstreets," "Born to Run," "She's the One," "Meeting Across the River," "Jungleland"
Key outtakes: "A Love So Fine," "Linda Let Me Be the One," "Lonely in the Park," "Walking in the Street"
Chart peak: No. 3

B*orn to Run* is the album that put Bruce Springsteen on the map— on the pop charts, on the cover (simultaneously) of *Time* and *Newsweek*, and, most importantly, in the ears of fans located far beyond his faithful enclaves of New Jersey and eastern Pennsylvania. But it was also a protracted, pressured, and arduous project that left Springsteen in tears some nights, frustrated at the difficulties he was having in realizing on tape what he heard in his head. And as it took his career to a higher level, it also signaled a changing of the guard in his camp, from original manager and coproducer Mike Appel to former music critic Jon Landau. "The tension making that record I could never describe," Springsteen told a Dutch interviewer in 1975. "It was killing, almost; it was inhuman. I hated it. I couldn't stand it. It was the worst, hardest, lousiest thing I ever had to do." Harsh words for what many consider to be one of the best rock 'n' roll albums of all time.

There was no small degree of pressure on the album, of course. After sales of less than 90,000 copies of his first two albums, Columbia Records was no longer enamored with the highly touted Springsteen. *Born to Run* seemed a make-it-or-break-it proposition, a sentiment echoed in "Thunder Road"'s declaration, "We got one last chance to make it real/To trade in these wings on some wheels."

It did have a promising start, however. The title track, which Springsteen road-tested with the E Street Band in 1974 and recorded in August of that year—with Ernest "Boom" Carter on drums—was leaked to a few sympathetic radio stations and became an underground hit, stoking expectations for the third Springsteen album. That, however, became something of an albatross as Springsteen changed the band lineup—bringing in new keyboardist Roy Bittan and drummer Max Weinberg—and weathered the departure of Jim Cretecos, who coproduced his first two albums. His new creative partner would be Landau, a supportive journalist who gave Columbia a heaven-sent promotional hook when he famously declared in a May 1974 concert review, "I saw rock and roll future and its name is Bruce Springsteen." Though Springsteen himself loathed the hype campaign that employed the line, he and Landau struck up a friendship that helped to broaden Springsteen's worldview and perspectives on popular culture.

The new association rankled Appel, who surmised, "Landau had it in his mind all along, once he saw Springsteen and declared him rock and roll's future, to produce Bruce and eventually take over his management." Appel also told Springsteen biographer Marc Eliot (*Down Thunder Road*) that he felt like a scapegoat for his client's creative problems: "Bruce had lost his direction, his energy and to some extent his confidence ... It was easy to start shifting the blame as to why things weren't happening." However, Springsteen contended that Landau nevertheless brought focus and enthusiasm back to the project, encouraging him to change studios—from 914 Sound Studios in Blauvelt, New York, to the more state-of-the-art Record Plant in New York City—and bringing in Jimmy Iovine as the album's engineer. "(Landau) helped me step in and get the job done," Springsteen wrote in *Songs*. "We stripped down the songs and streamlined the arrangements. We developed a more direct sound with cleaner lines."

Though Springsteen had already recorded "Born to Run" and an eventual outtake, "A Love So Fine," in 1974, the bulk of the *Born to Run* sessions took place between March and July 1975—when the band stayed off the road for its longest stretch to that point. *Born to Run*—whose alternate titles included *The Legend of Zero & Blind Terry, From the Churches to the Jails, The*

Hungry and the Hunted, and *War & Roses*—also began as a concept album, a kind of day-in-the-life song cycle that would start with an alarm clock going off and a spare, acoustic version of "Thunder Road" and finish with a full-band take on the same song. That idea was scrapped, but Springsteen's ambitions remained high: "The characters … are less local than on *Greetings* and *The Wild, the Innocent*," he explained in *Songs.* "They could have been anybody and everybody. When the screen door slams on 'Thunder Road,' you're not necessarily on the Jersey Shore anymore. You could be anywhere in America. These were the beginnings of the characters whose lives I would trace in my work for the next two decades … It was the album where I left behind my adolescent definitions of love and freedom."

Born to Run is, in fact, rich with themes of escape, from the frequent car imagery to the after-work catharsis of "Night" and the willingness to do anything to achieve freedom—even criminal acts—voiced in the hushed, cinematic "Meeting Across the River." The epic grandeur of some of the tracks—including "Thunder Road," "Backstreets," "Born to Run," and "Jungleland"—also pay tribute to influences such as Roy Orbison and "wall of sound" producer Phil Spector. Some of the songs besides the title track had also been road-tested by Springsteen and the band, including "She's the One," "Jungleland," and "Thunder Road," which early on was titled "Wings for Wheels."

The latter brought another new collaborator into the Springsteen camp—guitarist Miami Steve Van Zandt, who had played with Bruce in earlier Jersey bands such as Steel Mill, Dr. Zoom and the Sonic Boom, and the Bruce Springsteen Band. When Springsteen decided to use a full horn section for "Tenth Avenue Freeze-Out," he called in Van Zandt, who was managing, producing, and playing in the brass-heavy Southside Johnny & the Asbury Jukes. Van Zandt told the horn players—including the seasoned brothers Michael and Randy Brecker—to put away their written charts and proceeded to sing each player the parts he wanted them to play. After that display, according to biographer Dave Marsh, Springsteen told Appel, "Okay, it's time to put the boy on the payroll. I've been meaning to tell you—he's the new guitar player."

The *Born to Run* sessions came to a crashing end. Springsteen—who was pacifying disgruntled girlfriend Karen Darvin, holed up in a Holiday Inn near the studio—has acknowledged tossing one proposed mix of the album out a window and at one point thought about scrapping what had been recorded and just taping the songs in concert. It wasn't until Landau put his foot down and told him, among other things, "You are not supposed to like it. Do you think Chuck Berry sits around listening to 'Maybelline'?" that Springsteen was persuaded to let go of the work. Even then, the final few days were spent 24-7 in the studio; on the final morning, July 20, Springsteen was recording

"It is a magnificent album that pays off in every bet ever placed on him—a '57 Chevy running on melted down Crystals records that shuts down every claim that has been made. And it should crack his future wide open."
                    —*Rolling Stone*

"Street-punk image and all, Bruce Springsteen is an American archetype, and *Born to Run* will probably be the finest record released this year ... If I seem to OD on superlatives, it's only because *Born to Run* demands them."
                    —*Creem*

"Born to Run gets us closer still to what Bruce Springsteen is all about. The range is as wide as either of the earlier albums, from poignancy to street-strutting cockiness to punk poetry to quasi-Broadway to surging rock anthems ... All this observer can say is that on repeated hearings ... *Born to Run* seems one of the great records of recent years."
                    —*New York Times*

"He is the purest glimpse of the passion and power of rock 'n' roll in nearly a decade. His *Born to Run* album comes to grips with the emotional essence of rock 'n' roll so well that I think it could give even Elvis chills."
                    —*Los Angeles Times*

the lead vocal for "She's the One" in one studio, mixing "Jungleland" in another, and rehearsing with the band for a concert that night in Providence, Rhode Island—Van Zandt's first with the E Street Band.

Born to Run was largely greeted as an instant classic, an irony since, as Springsteen told the Dutch reporter, "I hated it for the few first few times I heard it ... People legitimately liked the record, which I couldn't fathom at the time because I hated it so much." —*GG*

"Born to Run"

Released: July 1975
Album: *Born to Run* (Columbia, 1975)
Also on: *Live/1975–85* (Columbia, 1986); *Chimes of Freedom* EP (Columbia, 1988); *Greatest Hits* (Columbia, 1995); *Live in New York City* (Columbia, 2001); *The Essential Bruce Springsteen* (Columbia, 2003)
Chart peak: No. 9

 orn to Run" is arguably the most famous and important song in Bruce Springsteen's career. Without question, it's the song that put him on the mainstream rock 'n' roll map—his first bona fide hit single, after all—and set up the breakthrough he would experience with the subsequent *Born to Run* album. The making and marketing of the song are also legends in themselves.

Having been tested on the road, it was the first song recorded for the *Born to Run* album, done in August 1974 at 914 Sound Studios in Blauvelt, New York, with an E Street Band that still included David Sancious on piano and Ernest "Boom" Carter on drums. There was a certain amount of urgency and duress, since Springsteen's first two albums had sold a combined 90,000 copies at that point and Columbia Records was losing interest in his career. In the liner notes to his *Greatest Hits* album, Springsteen even notes that "Born to Run" was "my shot at the title—a twenty-four-year-old kid aiming at 'the greatest rock 'n' roll record ever.'"

Springsteen performs at the Palladium in New York City in November 1976, on the second
leg of the *Born to Run* tour.

In his *Songs* book, Springsteen, who spent six months working on the song, writes that "Born to Run" "was the first piece of music I wrote and conceived as a studio production. It was connected to the long, live pieces I'd written previously by the twists and turns of the arrangement. But 'Born to Run' was more condensed; it maintained the excitement of 'Rosalita' while delivering its message in less time and with shorter bursts of energy. This was a turning point, and it allowed me to open my music up to a far larger audience."

He can thank then-manager and producer Mike Appel for that. Shortly after "Born to Run" was recorded, Appel leaked copies of "Born to Run" to supportive radio DJs in New York, Philadelphia, and Boston; they began playing it and generated a buzz that made Columbia take notice. The label eventually ponied up an estimated $250,000 in advertising and promotion support for the album, a huge sum for an unknown and relatively unsuccessful artist. Interestingly, former Hollies singer Allan Clarke was impressed enough by the song to record a cover version and release it as a single in Europe in the fall of 1974—months before Springsteen's own version came out. (In 1975 the Hollies would also cover Springsteen's "4th of July, Asbury Park [Sandy]," which hit No. 85 on the *Billboard* Hot 100—better than any Springsteen single had done to that point, too.)

In March 1980, fans launched a petition drive to make "Born to Run" the official state song of New Jersey. Springsteen, according to disc jockey Carol Miller—one of the leaders of the drive—"laughed, but he seemed very pleased about it." On June 12, the state legislature acknowledged the public sentiment and named "Born to Run" the state's "Unofficial Youth Rock Anthem."

"Born to Run"—which was named the No. 1 Springsteen song of all time in a 2003 poll by Britain's *Uncut* magazine—has remained a staple of Springsteen's live performances, usually as an encore, although he chose it as a show-opener for the December 9, 1980, show he and the E Street Band played the night after John Lennon was assassinated. He delivered it in a spartan acoustic arrangement for the 1988 Tunnel of Love Express Tour. The song has also been covered by Melissa Etheridge, Cowboy Mouth, Frankie Goes to Hollywood, and Suzi Quatro. —*GG*

The Boss

Springsteen nickname

By most recollections, Bruce Springsteen came to be known as The Boss in the early '70s, when he took control of the payroll for bands such as Steel Mill, Dr. Zoom and the Sonic Boom, and his own Bruce Springsteen Band. In 1999 he told Britain's *Mojo* magazine that back then, "Everybody had to have a nickname, there was no one in Asbury Park that did not have a nickname." In the Sonic Boom days, Springsteen was also known as The Doctor, joining a cast of colorful monikers that included Southside for Johnny Lyon's love of Chicago blues and Miami, which was bestowed upon Steve Van Zandt when he returned from a trip to Miami with a Hawaiian-style shirt. Springsteen said he became The Boss as "a result of paying them at the end of the week."

A different viewpoint came from Van Zandt in the 1975 *Time* magazine cover story. The guitarist said that Springsteen's prolific writing and natural leadership tendencies earned him the nickname as much as his role as paymaster: "Bruce was writing five or ten songs a week. He would say 'I'm gonna go home tonight and write a great song,' and he did. He was The Boss then, and he's The Boss now."

Springsteen also told *Mojo* that The Boss nickname "was never meant for public dissemination. I personally would have preferred that it had remained private." However, Northeast area concert promoter John Scher, who promoted many Springsteen shows since the days of Steel Mill and became a friendly associate, told *Backstreets* magazine that as they shared a hot dog at Mrs. Jay's in Asbury Park in the mid-'70s, Springsteen seemed comfortable with the label. "I said ... 'Do you know that people have called you (The Boss) for a long time behind your back?'" Scher related. "He said 'Yeah, I know.' 'Did it bother you?' He said, 'No. When I was growing up, somebody else always was the boss. My dad had a boss. The boss had control of people's lives.' Then he gave me a big smile and said, 'Now I'm The Boss.'" However, Springsteen also told *Creem* magazine, "I hate bosses. I hate being called The Boss ... I always hated being called 'boss.'"

In a 1978 *Rolling Stone* interview, however, Springsteen acknowledged that he left no question about who's in charge. "Anybody who works for me, the first thing you better know is I'm gonna drive you crazy," he said. "Because I don't compromise in certain areas. So if you're gonna be in, you better be ready for that." —*GG*

The Boss Club

Ad hoc Los Angeles club night dedicated to Springsteen

n 1984 Seth Marsh was a frustrated club DJ playing the latest dance hits by Michael Jackson, Madonna, and Prince; in his heart, Marsh was a rocker who would occasionally slip some different songs, particularly those by Bruce Springsteen, into his set. The favorable response from some of his regular patrons gave him an idea—a once-a-week club night dedicated to Springsteen music. "I figured there would be a few people who would get a kick out of it," said Marsh, who's attended more than 300 Springsteen shows in twenty-five cities over the years.

That would prove to be an understatement. Marsh and his business partner, Dave Krask, launched the Boss Club on Tuesday nights at Imperial Gardens, a Japanese restaurant on Hollywood's Sunset Strip, in the fall of 1984—just as Brucemania was taking hold thanks to the *Born in the U.S.A.* album. Playing officially released and bootleg material from his vast personal collection, Marsh established the Boss Club with a crowd of about fifty regulars. But when the *Los Angeles Times* mentioned the weekly gathering, the crowd swelled to 200–300, including celebrity Springsteen fans such as Sean Penn, Rob Lowe, Prince, and Rick James. Springsteen's mother and younger sister Pamela even came in one night, "dancing to every song," according to Marsh. After the release of the all-star "We Are the World" famine relief single, in the spring of 1985, the Boss Club held a benefit night for USA for Africa.

Columbia Records supplied the Boss Club with CDs, posters, and other giveaway prizes. The Springsteen camp, meanwhile, showed its appreciation by inviting Marsh and Krask to one of the summer 1985 shows at Giants Stadium in East Rutherford, New Jersey, putting them up at the E Street Band's hotel and giving them prime seats with the group members' families. And after Krask committed suicide in 1988, Springsteen—alerted to the news by a letter from a Boss Club regular—called Marsh and spent ninety minutes on the phone commiserating.

The Boss Club stayed open as a weekly concern until 1992, when the Imperial Gardens was sold and became the famed Roxbury dance club. After that Marsh switched gears, hosting several special Boss Club gatherings each year and bringing in live acts including E Street Band guitarist Nils Lofgren and saxophonist Clarence Clemons, as well as Jersey Shore fixtures such as John Eddie, longtime Springsteen cohort Joe Grushecky, and an assortment of Springsteen tribute bands. Marsh, who now runs a private auction company, maintains a mailing list of about 3,000 people, and he still hosts original patrons who bought lifetime VIP passes he sold to them to raise money in 1984. —*GG*

The Bottom Line

Famed New York City nightclub, 1974–2004

here is perhaps no series of concert dates more important in Bruce Springsteen's history than his ten-set, five-night stand August 13–17, 1975, at the Bottom Line in New York's Greenwich Village that launched the *Born to Run* album. These performances were so frenzied and revelatory that *Rolling Stone* magazine titled its review "A Rock Star Is Born," while

The Bottom Line in New York's Greenwich Village was the site of a five-night stand by Springsteen and the E Street Band in 1975 to support the release of *Born to Run* that the *New York Times* ranked "among the great rock experiences." The club, shown here in 2003, was closed for financial reasons on January 22, 2004, by then-owner New York University.

the *New York Times* declared that the shows "will rank among the great rock experiences of those lucky enough to get in." Bottom Line co-owner Allan Pepper told *Tracks* magazine, "Bruce set the bar for how good you could be. Nobody ever reached what he did." Springsteen himself later told *Rolling Stone*, "The band cruised through them shows like the finest machine there was. There's nothin'—nothin'—in the world to get you playing better than a gig like that. The band walked out of the Bottom Line twice as good as when they walked in."

And Springsteen did walk out of those shows a star, thanks to the hype generated by writer, *Born to Run* coproducer, and future manager Jon Landau's "I have seen rock and roll future" proclamation in Boston's *Real Paper* in 1974 and the temerity of Columbia Records to buy a quarter of the 500 tickets available to each show to expose Springsteen to company employees, journalists, and radio folks. The first set on August 15 was aired live on New York's WNEW-FM to further spread the word. Previewing *Born to Run* with selections such as the title track, "She's the One," "Night," "Tenth Avenue Freeze-Out" and "Thunder Road" and dishing out covers like "Quarter to Three," "When You Walk in the Room," and "Then She Kissed Me," Springsteen succeeded in generating an enormous buzz that set *Born to Run* off on a sprint.

The 1975 shows weren't Springsteen's only notable visits to the Bottom Line, however. Though Max's Kansas City was his club of choice, Springsteen played his first Bottom Line dates July 12–14, 1974—after turning down opportunities to open for ZZ Top and Chuck Berry and canceling a booking at the Ozark Music Festival in Missouri to play the shows. He debuted "Jungleland" during the stand as well. After the '75 stand, he returned on November 26, 1976, to play guitar and piano during Patti Smith's two shows. When he attended a show at the Bottom Line by singer Rachel Sweet, so many people wanted to buy Springsteen a drink that his table was jammed with full Heineken bottles by the time he left.

Pepper and partner Stanley Snadowsky opened the Bottom Line in 1974 after booking acts into other clubs around Greenwich Village. The two envisioned a stylistically open room and achieved it with a gamut of artists that included Bob Dylan, Bill Monroe, Little Richard, the New York Dolls, the Talking Heads, Tom Petty & the Heartbreakers, Dolly Parton, Tammy Wynette, the Police, Buddy Guy, and Ringo Starr—as well as famous cameos by Neil Young, Eric Clapton (with Carl Perkins), the Rolling Stones' Keith Richards (briefly, with Rockpile), and Bonnie Raitt and Linda Ronstadt (with George Jones). Johnny Cash made a rare late-career appearance there with June Carter Cash in July 1999. The Bottom Line shut down on January 22, 2004, after its lease expired with New York University, which owned the building at West 4th and Mercer streets. —*GG*

Bridge School Benefit Concerts

Fund-raising shows for San Francisco Bay–area school for impaired children

Widely considered one of the coolest annual concert events in the country, the Bridge School benefits have over the years attracted A-list artists performing acoustically and sometimes in rare combinations. Some surprise reunions have also taken place at the shows, which are hosted by Neil Young.

The San Francisco Bay–area school was created in 1986 to help speech- and physically impaired children find alternative ways to communicate. The school was founded by Pegi Young, wife of Neil and mother of his second cerebral palsied child, Ben (the first, Zeke, was with ex-wife Carrie Snodgrass); James Forderer, also the parent of a handicapped child; and speech-language pathologist Dr. Marilyn Buzolich. Buzolich specializes in augmentive and alternative communication (AAC), which helps children convey their thoughts via nonverbal means. Almost every one of the concerts, started in 1986 and held every year since 1988, has occurred at the Shoreline Amphitheater in Mountain View, California, south of San Francisco. Bruce Springsteen has played at two of them: the inaugural concert, which also featured Nils Lofgren, Don Henley, Tom Petty, Robin Williams, and a surprise Crosby, Stills, Nash & Young reunion; and the ninth edition in 1995. In 1986, he performed "Helpless" with Neil Young, then performed his own set, which began with an a capella "You Can Look (But You Better Not Touch)" and a solo "Born in the U.S.A." Lofgren and fellow E Street Band member Danny Federici joined him on several songs in the set, which concluded with a rendition of "Hungry Heart" that featured harmonies by CSNY. Springsteen joined the other performers at the end of the night to sing CSNY's "Teach Your Children."

The 1995 Bridge School benefit bill, in addition to Springsteen and Young, included Beck, Emmylou Harris with Daniel Lanois, the Pretenders, Blind Melon, and Hootie & the Blowfish. Anticipating his forthcoming *The Ghost of Tom Joad* album and the solo tour to support it, Springsteen's set previewed "The Ghost of Tom Joad" and "Sinaloa Cowboys," along with "Seeds," "Adam Raised a Cain," "Point Blank," and "This Hard Land." He joined Young for a duet on "Down by the River" and joined the entire company for an evening-ending "Rockin' in the Free World." *—LM/GG*

"Brilliant Disguise"

Released: September 1987
Album: *Tunnel of Love* (Columbia, 1987)
Also on: *Greatest Hits* (Columbia, 1995); *The Essential Bruce Springsteen* (Columbia, 2003)
Chart peak: No. 5

The first single from *Tunnel of Love*, "Brilliant Disguise" went to No. 5 on the *Billboard* Hot 100 chart and offered a strong indication of the stark, brooding tone that dominated the album. Springsteen considered "Brilliant Disguise" the album's "center," and explained in *Songs*, "Trust is a fragile thing; it requires allowing others to see as much of ourselves as we have the courage to reveal. But you drop one mask and find another behind it, until you begin to doubt your own feelings about who you are. It's the twin issues of love and identity that form the core of *Tunnel of Love*."

But while many listeners assumed that "Brilliant Disguise"—with its references to a marriage—was about Springsteen and his then-newlywed wife, actress-model Julianne Phillips, he denied it, claiming that the song, like most of *Tunnel of Love*, was "not literally autobiographical."

Though *Tunnel of Love* was billed as a Springsteen solo album, he did employ members of the E Street Band in different configurations. While he played guitar, bass, and keyboards on "Brilliant Disguise," Springsteen also brought in Roy Bittan on piano, Danny Federici on organ, and Max Weinberg on drums. But the video, directed by Meiert Avis, features Springsteen alone, singing "Brilliant Disguise" live as the camera gradually pans in for an extreme close-up of his face. —*GG*

Jackson Browne

Singer-songwriter, Rock and Roll Hall of Fame member

When Bruce Springsteen inducted Jackson Browne into the Rock and Roll Hall of Fame in 2004, he recounted meeting the singer and getting up on stage with him at Max's Kansas City in the early 1970s. He watched and listened carefully, and in the end came up with two conclusions: "My first thought was, 'Damn, he's good,'" Springsteen said. "My second thought was, 'I need less words.'" In fact, many words have flowed from Browne's pen over the years, but what has carried his songs the most were the emotions expressed—of lost love, shattered idealism, and political outrage on the one hand and steely resolve on the other. Browne songs are about weathering life's vagaries and carrying on in spite of the pain and the seemingly insurmountable odds—not unlike Springsteen's own work.

Browne grew up in southern California. As a teenager, he joined an early version of the Nitty Gritty Dirt Band. In 1967–68 he lived in New York, where he backed Tom Rush and Velvet Underground chanteuse Nico in Greenwich Village clubs. Nico recorded his song "These Days," and soon other artists—including Linda Ronstadt, the Byrds, and Bonnie Raitt—covered his work. He signed with David Geffen's fledgling Asylum Records and recorded his eponymous debut album, which produced a Top 10 hit in "Doctor My Eyes" and also contained a version of the Eagles' hit "Take It Easy," which was cowritten by Browne.

Subsequent albums *For Everyman, Late for the Sky,* and *The Pretender* (produced by Springsteen's manager, Jon Landau) explored personal relationships and broad social themes. His 1977 album *Running on Empty* was a concept album about life on the road and was recorded in hotel rooms, on the tour bus, and in concert.

Browne and his music became more politicized in the late '70s—and he in turn helped to bring Springsteen out of his political shell, playing a key role in convincing his New Jersey friend to join him at the 1979 No Nukes

Springsteen introduces singer-songwriter Jackson Browne at Browne's induction into the Rock and Roll Hall of Fame in New York City on March 15, 2004.

concerts in New York City organized by Musicians United for Safe Energy (MUSE). Browne sang "Stay" with Springsteen and the E Street Band on the nights they played. Springsteen and Browne also collaborated at the Rally for

Nuclear Disarmament on June 12, 1982, before a crowd of more than 500,000 at New York City's Central Park.

Browne's '80s albums, *Lawyers in Love, Lives in the Balance,* and *World in Motion,* focused on U.S. military involvement in Central America and issues of poverty and homelessness. Browne joined Springsteen and Bonnie Raitt in a pair of November 1990 benefit concerts for the Christic Institute, a California organization that focuses on public interest issues in the U.S. and Central America, including litigation and legislation. At each of the shows the performers played solo acoustic sets and collaborated at the end of the night. Browne—who also produced early releases by Warren Zevon—has endured occasional bouts of negative publicity, too, brought on when his first wife committed suicide in 1976, and during his all-too-public breakup with actress Daryl Hannah in 1992, during which she accused him of assaulting her. In Springsteen's speech inducting Browne into the Rock and Roll Hall of Fame, he mused, "The Beach Boys and Brian Wilson, they gave us California as paradise and Jackson Browne gave us *Paradise Lost.* Now I always imagine, what if Brian Wilson, long after he'd taken a bite of that orange the serpent offered to him, what if he married that nice girl in 'Caroline No?' I always figured that she was pregnant anyway, and what if he moved into the valley and had two sons? One of them would have looked and sounded just like Jackson Browne. Cain, of course, would have been Jackson's brother in arms, Warren Zevon. But, Jackson to me, Jackson was always the tempered voice of Abel; toiling in the vineyards, here to bear the earthly burdens, confronting the impossibility of love, here to do his father's work." —*DD/GG*

Bruce Springsteen & the E Street Band Live in New York City
HBO program and home video release

Air date: April 7, 2001
Release date: November 6, 2001
Tracks: HBO/Disc 1—"My Love Will Not Let You Down," "Prove It All Night," "Two Hearts" (incl. "It Takes Two"), "Atlantic City," "Mansion on the Hill," "The River," "Youngstown," "Murder Incorporated," "Badlands," "Out in the Street," "Tenth Avenue Freeze-Out," "Born to Run," "Land of Hope and Dreams," "American Skin (41 Shots)." Disc 2—"Backstreets," "Don't Look Back," "Darkness on the Edge of Town," "Lost in the Flood," "Born in the U.S.A.," "Jungleland," "Light of Day," "The Promise," "Thunder Road," "Ramrod," "If I Should Fall Behind"
Extras: "New York City Serenade" tour documentary, photo gallery

oward the end of Bruce Springsteen's 1999–2000 reunion tour with the E Street Band, he and manager Jon Landau realized they hadn't documented much of the outing on film. Landau suggested that could be easily remedied; Springsteen told VH1 that Landau "said 'Look, Sony will give us these cameras and the last couple of nights we can film the thing. If you like it, great, if not, okay.' ... I had a few suggestions about the lighting and this, that, and the other thing. I didn't think about it after that, because it wasn't super-expensive. If it didn't come out good, it didn't come out good."

The final two shows of the tour, June 29 and July 1 at New York City's Madison Square Garden, were filmed. And fortunately Springsteen was satisfied with the results, which yielded a two-hour concert special on HBO titled *Bruce Springsteen & the E Street Band*, and a home video seven months later that appended *Live in New York City* to the title.

Springsteen told VH1 that his main caveat for approving the filming was that "it doesn't get in the way of doing the last shows" at the Garden. He rejected standard tools such as cranes and camera tracks; this presented a challenge to director Chris Hilson, who had previously directed concert films for the British pop groups Boyzone and Wet Wet Wet. "We had no choice but to stay focused on the performance—which is the beauty of this project," Hilson told *Sound & Vision* magazine. "We had a handheld camera on stage and two steady-cams near the stage, but that was as fancy as it got." As HBO executive Nancy Geller told *Rolling Stone*, "It's shot the way Bruce performs, which is just in your face."

There were initial expectations that the home video, and companion live album, would be ready for release in time for the holiday season of 2000. But the HBO deal pushed the project into 2001 and also brought about some changes—most notably Springsteen's decision to add "Born to Run" to both the broadcast and the live album. HBO's exclusive period to show the footage also gave Springsteen and his team time to create a more thorough home-video package, adding eleven songs—including the six "bonus" tracks that were on the live album—and a tour documentary. Some retailers were provided with a special CD, featuring exclusive live versions of "My Hometown" and "This Hard Land," to use as a sales promotion.

Bruce Springsteen & the E Street Band was nominated for six Emmy Awards, including Outstanding Variety, Music or Comedy Special for producers Springsteen, Landau, and George Travis. It took home two trophies, for Outstanding Lighting Direction and Outstanding Multi-Camera Picture Editing for a Miniseries, Movie or Special. —*GG*

Bruce Springsteen Special Collection

Materials housed at the Asbury Park Public Library

t's impossible to calculate how many trees have died to fill fans' insatiable need for information about Bruce Springsteen and the E Street Band. But one can get a small sense of the enormity of print material produced at the Asbury Park Public Library's Bruce Springsteen Special Collection. Even Springsteen could probably learn a thing or two about himself by combing through the collection, which contains more than 2,000 books and periodicals dedicated to his life and music.

The collection started with about 1,000 items donated by fans from around the world at the request of *Backstreets* magazine, the most prominent of dozens of Springsteen fanzines. When *Backstreets* editor Christopher Phillips turned the collection over to the library on December 8, 2001, he said the goal was to bring together and make available "the truly essential works by biographers, critics, scholars, journalists, and fans. To music fans around the world, Asbury Park is a special place, for its influence on Springsteen personally and artistically, and for the way he incorporates those influences into his music. This donation reflects our deep ties to Asbury Park, and our belief that music heritage can be a strong force in the community's future."

During a concert that night at the Asbury Park Convention Hall, Springsteen said, "I want to thank all you folks who showed up at the library today for our little section there ... The collection has ... more stuff than every place except my mother's basement!"

Through the efforts of *Backstreets*, the Save Tillie preservation group, and individual fans, the archive has since more than doubled in size. It contains printed matter from thirty countries, including books, magazines, tour programs, songbooks, and even comic books, along with collections of rare fanzines prized for their exhaustive coverage. The library's website contains a complete list of current holdings and "wanted" items, as well as usage instructions and restrictions. The collection is accessible by appointment only. Copies of material are available via interlibrary loan and a library-linked worldwide electronic document transfer network. For more information, call (732) 774-4221 or visit www.asburypark.lib.nj.us/bruce.htm. —*LM*

Bruce Springsteen's America: The People Listening, A Poet Singing. See **Robert Coles.**

Bruce Springstone and the Bedrock Band

1982 Springsteen parody

ruce Springstone and the Bedrock Band are a case study in the Springsteen musical adage, "From small things big things one day come." The project, an off-the-cuff parody hatched by some staffers at Johns Hopkins University in Baltimore and their friends, featured Springsteen-styled parodies of two popular songs—the theme from "The Flintstones" cartoon and "Take Me Out to the Ballgame." Thanks to Springsteen's growing commercial stature in the wake of *The River*, the songs captured people's imagination and wound up receiving major media attention, right around the same time Springsteen released the *Nebraska* album. Marshall Crenshaw asked the ad hoc group to open his show in the spring of 1983 at Hopkins, and Dr. Demento even featured "Bedrock Rap/Meet the Flintstones" on his syndicated Sunday night radio program and included it as part of his *Greatest Novelty Hits of All Time* compilation box set.

Bruce Springstone was Tom Chalkley, who provided the vocals on the two songs. Chalkley was in a Baltimore band called the Reason with Hopkins instructor and music critic Craig Hankin; along with another friend, Jimmy Owen, they cooked up the Springsteen-style "Flintstones" theme for a St. Patrick's Day 1982 comedy show on the university campus and played it again when opening for comedian Robert Klein at the school's annual spring fair. Two DJs at the latter gig—including Howard Stern, who was then working in Washington, D.C.—said they'd play the parody on the air if the trio recorded it. They recorded a demo with Suzy Shaw, who worked in the Hopkins library, on keyboards, and the local Clean Cuts label offered them a deal to put it out.

The Bedrock Band expanded for the actual recording, adding bassist Gabor Lutor from the Reason and drummer John Ebersberger, who also drew the cover image—a knock-off of the *Born to Run* cover with Dino as Clarence Clemons. The group also brought in a couple of ringers—saxophonist Ron Holloway from Gil Scott-Heron's band and a fledgling rocker named Tommy Keene, who had just signed his first recording contract, on lead guitar. The two songs were recorded on a four-track machine at the low-fi Hit & Run studio in rural Maryland.

Hanna-Barbera gave the troupe permission to use the "Flintstones" images, and no opposition came from the Springsteen camp, either. Hanna-Barbera reversed its position as the disc became more popular, however, and refused to let the Bedrock Band release a video it had filmed or distribute any merchandise related to the song. Clean Cuts, meanwhile, sued Major League Baseball for unauthorized use of its version of "Take Me Out to the Ballgame" and won an out-of-court settlement that included a lifetime private box for Baltimore Orioles games. Springsteen's reaction? After hearing numerous reports that he loved the parody, Hankin sent him a letter asking how he felt about it. It took some time, but he eventually received a postcard on which Springsteen wrote, "The record is great! I love it! Keep rockin!" *—GG*

Kevin Buell

Springsteen guitar technician, 1987–present

evin Buell replaced Mike Batlan as Bruce Springsteen's guitar technician and aide de camp following Batlan's acrimonious departure after the *Born in the U.S.A.* tour. Buell first went on the road with Springsteen and the E Street Band on 1988's Tunnel of Love Express Tour and has been a fixture ever since. For the 1995–96 solo tour he played subtle keyboard parts offstage on certain songs, and he was credited as a "project coordinator" for 2002's *The Rising* album. —*GG*

Brendan Byrne Arena. *See* **Continental Airlines Arena.**

John Cafferty and the Beaver Brown Band

Jersey Shore group bearing a striking stylistic similarity to Springsteen and the E Street Band

ohn Cafferty and the Beaver Brown Band formed in Narragansett, Rhode Island, in 1972. A fixture on the Boston club circuit for many years, the group began as a cover band and was originally known as Beaver Brown—after the paint color in its first rehearsal studio. The original members—John Cafferty (vocals, guitar), Gary "Guitar" Gramolini (guitar), Robert Cotoia (keyboards), Pat Lupo (bass), and Kenny Jo Silva (drums)—were joined in 1977 by saxophone player Michael "Tunes" Antunes. Constant touring around New England and eventual visits to the Jersey Shore area built a loyal following, and the sextet began to incorporate Cafferty's original songs into its set.

Bruce Springsteen took notice of the band and, along with Clarence Clemons, made a surprise guest appearance with the group at Toad's Place on August 25, 1978, in New Haven, Connecticut, following his own show that night at the New Haven Coliseum. Beaver Brown's debut single was released in 1980 on the independent Coastline label, and its show at New York's Bottom Line was broadcast over WNEW-FM, the same station that broadcast Springsteen's landmark show there five years earlier. By this time Beaver Brown was getting a lot of attention; unfortunately much of it was because the group was perceived as an E Street Band knockoff. The WNEW broadcast was hyped with a "decide-for-yourself" promotion. "I never took that in any other way than positive," Cafferty said of the Springsteen comparisons. "I was lucky enough to meet Bruce,

John Cafferty was a Jersey Shore staple as part of the band Beaver Brown when he and the group achieved national attention with their music on the soundtrack of the 1983 movie *Eddie and the Cruisers.*

around 1973. The guys in my band became friends with the guys in his. When we'd play at the Jersey Shore, they would always come down and get onstage with us ... Over the years, Bruce has given us a lot of advice and encouragement. He helped me become better at what I do."

In July 1981 Clarence Clemons opened a club in Red Bank, New Jersey, and Big Man's West became a regular stop for Beaver Brown. Springsteen sat in with the group there seven times in 1982 and also guested at the Fast Lane in Asbury Park. Despite the attention, Beaver Brown simply could not land a record deal until producer Kenny Vance (formerly a member of Jay and the Americans) hooked the group up with film director Martin Davidson. Cafferty wrote the songs for the fictional band in the 1983 film *Eddie and the Cruisers* and Beaver Brown recorded the soundtrack, which became its first album—though Antunes was the only band member to appear in the film, and actor Michael Pare, as Eddie Wilson, lip-synced Cafferty's vocals. The film didn't do especially well and was forgotten until it became a hit on cable television network HBO in the summer of 1984. In an unusual bit of chart history, the single "On the Dark Side," which had peaked at No. 64 on the *Billboard* Hot 100 in October 1983, reached the Top 10 in September 1984.

With its name officially changed to John Cafferty and the Beaver Brown Band, the group released *Tough All Over* (1985) and *Roadhouse* (1988) on the Scotti Brothers label and toured extensively, sometimes opening for major acts such as the Beach Boys. A few other singles charted ("C-I-T-Y" in the Top 20 in 1985) and the group appeared frequently on television, but the success was short-lived. In 1989 Cafferty and company again provided the songs and sounds for the fictional movie band in the ill-conceived sequel *Eddie and the Cruisers II: Eddie Lives.* The second soundtrack album was followed by two more albums under the Eddie and the Cruisers moniker, with photos of the actors from the movies on the covers.

The years that followed saw personnel changes and occasional touring. Cafferty, Gramolini, and Antunes continue to form the core of the band.

In 2003 they contributed a recording of "The E Street Shuffle" to *Light of Day: A Tribute to Bruce Springsteen*, a charity album to benefit the Parkinson's Disease Foundation and the Kristen Ann Carr Fund. Gramolini's brother Joel was a member of Southside Johnny & the Asbury Jukes from 1978–81. Cafferty's cousin is Steve Smith of Steve Smith and the Nakeds, another Rhode Island band that has worked with Clarence Clemons on occasion. —*RB*

Barbara Carr

Springsteen co-manager

arbara Carr has co-managed Bruce Springsteen since 1980 as a partner in Jon Landau Management. She also is married to journalist and author Dave Marsh, who serves as Springsteen's most familiar biographer.

Born in 1946 in Trenton, New Jersey, Carr grew up in Texas and Oklahoma, and attended Marymount College and the London School of Economics. She met Marsh and Landau, still a practicing journalist at the time, while she was working as head of publicity at Atlantic Records, where she went to work after returning from London with her then-husband, journalist Patrick Carr (the couple had two children, Kristen and Sasha).

Carr eventually went to work at Champion Entertainment, a management company. She left there to manage singer/songwriter Ellen Shipley. Landau offered her some working space at his New York office and eventually invited her to work in tandem with him. Carr and Landau share management of Springsteen's career, but they each have individual roles as well; she oversees Springsteen's song publishing and his charitable work, among other details. The company also manages the band Train and at one time represented country star Shania Twain.

In 1993, Carr's oldest daughter, Kristen, died at age twenty-one from a rare form of cancer called liposarcoma. Her family established the Kristen Ann Carr Fund in her honor; Springsteen continually helps to raise funds for the charity.

The family resides in Connecticut and New York City. —*LM*

Kristen Ann Carr Fund/Musicians on Call

Organization benefiting sarcoma research and support

risten Ann Carr was the daughter of Barbara Carr, Bruce Springsteen's co-manager, and the stepdaughter of Dave Marsh, Carr's husband since Kristen was three years old and Springsteen's biographer. With her parents, sister Sasha, and fiancé Michael Solomon by her side, Kristen died on January 6, 1993, at the age of twenty-one, a victim of a rare form of connective-tissue cancer called liposarcoma. At her request, the foursome created the Kristen Ann Carr Fund, a nonprofit organization that sponsors sarcoma research and support programs for teens and young adults with cancer. The summer before her death, Kristen and Solomon worked on the European leg of Springsteen's world tour, organizing bar trips and sightseeing expeditions for his new band. The couple had planned to use Springsteen's "If I Should Fall Behind" as their wedding song, but Springsteen and his wife, Patti Scialfa, wound up singing it at her funeral. Springsteen also decided that the last concert of his tour would be a benefit to help endow the fund. Held June 26, 1993, at Madison Square Garden in New York City, the Concert for the Kristen Ann Carr Fund featured one of Kristen's favorite artists, Terence Trent D'Arby (who wasn't well-received), along with Joe Ely and future E Street Band adjunct Soozie Tyrell. The show opened with the traditional "That Lonesome Valley," and memorial bouquet of white roses sat on the stage for the entire shows. Ticket sales and donations raised $1.5 million, more than enough to finance a research fellowship and patient support groups.

The fund has been sustained via concert ticket auctions and events such as annual winter semi-formals; the Springsteens were among sponsors for the ten semi-formals, and Bruce has donated signed guitars, tour jackets, and other memorabilia for its silent auctions. And anyone who wanted to spring for a $100 ticket got the chance to hobnob with the Springsteens, E Streeters, Sting, and other celebrities. A 2003 double-CD compilation called *Light of Day: A Tribute to Bruce Springsteen*, split its proceeds between the Carr fund and another charity Bruce supports, the Parkinson's Disease Foundation. When Bruce accepted his Grammy Award for Song of the Year for "Streets of Philadelphia" in 1995, he thanked Kristen and said, "(her) spirit is in this song."

Solomon and his friend Vivek Tiwary subsequently started Musicians on Call, an outgrowth of the Carr fund, after Tiwary lost both parents and an aunt within five years. The organization's mission is to help seriously ill patients heal or manage their pain via music. It was established after Solomon and Tiwary had arranged for musicians to perform at Memorial Sloan-Kettering Cancer Center in New York; a nurse explained that some patients were too sick to come to the lounge and listen and asked if the musicians could stop in their rooms to play. The experience was so powerful for all involved that Tiwary and Solomon decided to make it happen on a regular basis.

To raise start-up funds for the new organization, Springsteen donated several pairs of front-row seats and backstage passes for shows on his E

Street Band reunion tour in 1999–2000, and they were sold in VH1's first online auction. A pair of tickets to the tour finale show at Madison Square Garden, face value $135, went for $26,330. (The figure earned a listing in *Business Week*.) Musicians on Call has since auctioned dozens of tickets and passes donated by artists including Sting, John Mellencamp, John Mayer, Norah Jones, Billy Joel, James Taylor, the Who, Britney Spears, and the E Street Band. Jones and Nils Lofgren are among several high-profile artists who have also performed for patients.

More information on both charities is available at www.sarcoma.com and www.musiciansoncall.com. —*LM*

Ernest "Boom" Carter

E Street Band drummer, 1974

 rnest "Boom" Carter is best known as the E Street Band drummer who played the famous roll that begins Bruce Springsteen's 1975 signature song, "Born to Run." Carter was born and raised in Asbury Park, New Jersey, where he was formally trained in music, ultimately settling on drums and percussion as his principal instruments. Carter's best friend growing up on the Jersey Shore in the late '60s was original E Street Band pianist David Sancious—who, like Carter, also played guitar. Their instrumental versatility meant Carter and Sancious were frequent members of the jam scene at the Asbury Park after-hours musicians' club the Upstage, where the foundation of so many of the city's rock groups—including the E Street Band—was formed.

After race riots tore through Asbury Park in 1970, the city's vibrant music scene temporarily fragmented. Carter and Sancious, along with future E Street Band bassist Garry Tallent and harmonica player Southside Johnny Lyon, left New Jersey for Richmond, Virginia, where they worked as session players in a local recording studio. During their time in Virginia, Carter and Sancious also formed a duo called Cinnamon and played small Richmond clubs. Then, in mid-1972, Springsteen called Sancious and invited him to play keyboards on his debut album, *Greetings from Asbury Park, N.J.* With Sancious heading back to the Jersey Shore, Carter moved to Atlanta and accepted a job playing drums in a group called Little Royal and the Swing Masters, a James Brown–influenced soul revue that toured the South. In February 1974, Sancious contacted Carter and inquired if he'd be interested in joining Springsteen's E Street Band; original drummer Vini "Mad Dog" Lopez had just left the group, and Springsteen, touring to support his second album *The Wild, the Innocent & the E Street Shuffle*, needed a quick and capable replacement. Carter met Sancious and Springsteen when the E Street Band played Atlanta shortly thereafter and agreed to become its new drummer. Already familiar with Springsteen and all of the members of the E Street Band from his Asbury Park days, Carter easily settled in behind the drums, giving the band a more jazz- and soul-influenced drum sound than Lopez, a hard-rock hitter, had contributed to the group.

Despite Springsteen's satisfaction with his playing, Carter remained with the E Street Band for only about ten months. For most of that time he was on the road, touring with the group during the critical period when Springsteen was experimenting onstage with the songs that would ultimately comprise the *Born to Run* album. Carter recorded just one song with Springsteen and the E Street Band, *Born to Run*'s title track, in sessions held from August to October 1974. He recalled that the drum roll beginning "was Bruce's idea. He told me what he wanted, and I played it." When Sancious secured a recording contract of his own and left the E Street Band to form the jazz-rock fusion group Tone, Carter went with him. Carter, who was replaced in the E Street Band by North Jersey drummer Max Weinberg, continued to perform and record with Tone until the band's breakup in the early '80s. After Tone, Carter logged time with bluesman Paul Butterfield, Southside Johnny & the Asbury Jukes, and finally the Fairlanes, a popular Asbury Park blues-rock band led by guitarist Billy Hector. In the late '80s, Carter left New Jersey and moved to San Francisco. —*RS*

Johnny Cash

Singer, songwriter, pop culture icon

Few figures cast as long a shadow over popular music—indeed, over popular culture—as Johnny Cash. A member of both the Country Music Hall of Fame and the Rock and Roll Hall of Fame, Cash was a rockabilly hellion, a country "outlaw" (long before such a term existed), a singer of gospel songs and folk music, and a writer of hundreds of original songs (he is a member of the Songwriters Hall of Fame as well). Cash was an author, an actor and, for a couple of years, the host of the most popular television show in America. There really was no one else like him.

He was an influence on countless artists, Bruce Springsteen among them. You can't necessarily hear it on Springsteen's early albums, but by *Nebraska*, with its stark, resolute songs about good and evil, and the rockabilly fervor that powers some of the music that followed (not to mention Springsteen's penchant for black clothes), you could tell that Cash made a heavy impact on The Boss.

Respect between the two artists was mutual. Cash admired Springsteen's songwriting and made his song "Johnny 99" the title track of a 1983

Johnny Cash professed his admiration for Springsteen's songwriting, recording "Johnny 99," "I'm on Fire," and "Highway Patrolman" in the later years of his legendary career.

album. Springsteen's "Highway Patrolman" appeared on the same disc. Cash later recorded "I'm on Fire," which appeared on the tribute album *Badlands: A Tribute to Bruce Springsteen's Nebraska.*

Springsteen joined other performers to fete Cash in 1999 on "An All Star Tribute to Johnny Cash," which aired on cable channel TNT in 2000. In it, he praised Cash for "taking the social consciousness from folk, the sense of humor from country, and the sense of rebellion from rock and roll." Springsteen also contributed a version of "Give My Love to Rose" to the 2002 album *Kindred Spirits: A Tribute to the Songs of Johnny Cash.*

Cash was born to sharecroppers in Kingsland, Arkansas, on February 26, 1932. He sang in church and learned to play the guitar, and appeared on the local radio station as a teenager. After trying factory work in Detroit, he joined the air force and served in Germany. Afterwards, he married, moved to Memphis, and worked as an appliance salesman. Persistence won him a recording contract with Sun Records owner Sam Phillips, and Cash recorded the hits "Cry, Cry, Cry," "Folsom Prison Blues," and "I Walk the Line." He signed with Columbia and moved his family to the West Coast in 1958; the hits kept coming, including "Ring of Fire," which was cowritten by his future wife, June Carter.

The pressures of ceaseless touring led to Cash's trouble with alcohol and amphetamines, and he was arrested trying to smuggle pills over the Mexican border in 1965. Further misadventures led to the disintegration of his marriage. He relocated to Nashville and moved in with fellow country singer (and substance abuser) Waylon Jennings. After bottoming out, Cash got sober with help from June Carter, a frequent duet and touring partner. They married in 1968. Cash's live album *At Folsom Prison* went platinum, and he began hosting his own TV program, *The Johnny Cash Show*, on ABC, using it to champion young artists such as Bob Dylan, Joni Mitchell, Neil Young, Linda Ronstadt, and Stevie Wonder.

Cash held strong Christian beliefs and did not shy away from controversial causes. He opposed the war in Vietnam, yet traveled there to entertain the troops. He also spoke up for Native American rights and appeared at evangelist Billy Graham's "crusades." In the late '70s and early '80s, Cash's hits were few and far between, yet he continued to be a popular touring act. Columbia Records dropped him, ending a twenty-five-year relationship. He moved to Mercury with mixed results and justifiably felt betrayed by an industry his work had helped create and bolster for so many years.

It was the rock 'n' roll crowd that put him back on top. In 1993, U2 invited Cash to sing on "The Wanderer," a track from their album *Zooropa*. A year later, producer Rick Rubin signed him to his American Recordings label and produced his album, also titled *American Recordings*. With Cash singing songs by Tom Waits, Nick Lowe, Glenn Danzig, and others, he was embraced by a new generation. Three more volumes followed in the *American Record-*

ings series; the definitive collection of that creative collaboration is captured in the five-disc box set *Cash Unearthed*, released in 2003.

Cash died on September 12, 2003. Springsteen paid tribute by opening his concerts the next two nights with "I Walk the Line." —*DD*

The Castiles

Springsteen's first "professional" band, 1965–68

Bruce Springsteen was a member of the teen rock group, the Castiles from 1965–1968. A fourteen-year-old Freehold (New Jersey) High School sophomore and aspiring singer/guitarist, Springsteen joined the Castiles after the breakup of the very first band he played in, the Rogues. The Castiles' lead singer and rhythm guitarist, George Theiss, was romantically interested in Springsteen's sister, Ginny; Theiss asked Springsteen to audition for a spot in the Castiles as a way to get to know her.

The Castiles had been together, albeit loosely, for a few months prior to Springsteen's arrival. The band formed largely at the urging of Tex and Marion Vinyard, a Freehold couple who loved music and kids. The Castiles practiced in the Vinyards' living room, with Tex and Marion becoming practically surrogate parents to the members of the Castiles, especially Springsteen. Originally the Castiles grew out of another Freehold band, the Sierras, and consisted of Theiss, bass player Paul Popkin, and drummer Bart Haynes—all local high school kids—as well as lead guitarist Frank Marziotti, a local musician in his mid-20s who was looking for a gig and content to play with musicians much younger than he was. After Springsteen joined the Castiles—who took their name from a popular brand of shampoo—Marziotti found himself in the role of mentor, giving guitar tips to the young upstart. Marziotti eventually relinquished his place as the Castiles' lead guitarist to Springsteen and left the band.

The Castiles' first public performance was at Freehold's West Haven Swim Club in 1965. Playing a broad selection of mostly British Invasion rock, the Castiles set list was sprinkled with songs by the Animals, the Dave Clark Five, Them, the Who, the Yardbirds, and the Rolling Stones. As the band's popularity increased, it played high school and CYO (Catholic Youth Organization) dances, battles of the bands, parties, and a new mid-'60s creation, teen clubs. Eventually, the Castiles broadened their reach and performed in neighboring towns along the Jersey Shore, including Middletown and Keyport.

"We went out and played with confidence," Theiss told *Backstreets* magazine. "We played without being afraid of blowing it. It was the feeling of thinking we were good which was the thing that made us good. We certainly weren't the best musicians around, but often we sounded like we were—

because of our confidence." In the spring of 1966 the Castiles cut a self-produced single in nearby Brick Township. The two songs the band recorded— "That's What You Get" and "Baby I"—were written by Theiss and Springsteen. The single was never released. During this time the band added organ player Bob Alfano to broaden its sound. Other changes occurred as well: Curt Fluhr replaced Popkin on the bass, though Popkin remained in the band playing some guitar, tambourine, and singing backup. Original drummer Haynes left the band and joined the army (he was killed in combat in Vietnam); he was replaced by Vinny Manniello. Theiss and Springsteen remained the front figures, with Springsteen playing a larger role as a singer and assuming all the lead guitar chores.

In 1967 the Castiles performed at the Cafe Wha?, one of the hippest clubs in New York City's Greenwich Village. Despite its increasing success, the band struggled to stay together after Springsteen, Theiss, and other members of the Castiles had graduated from high school. By early 1968, the Castiles had broken up. With his parents moving to California, Springsteen left Freehold for Asbury Park and short-lived residencies in other Jersey Shore towns. Future post-Castiles bands for Springsteen included Earth, Child, Steel Mill, Dr. Zoom and the Sonic Boom, and the Bruce Springsteen Band before he finally signed his deal with Columbia Records and formed the E Street Band.

The Castiles finally found themselves on the radio nearly forty years after they broke up. In 2004 Episcopal priest Fred Coleman discovered reel-to-reel tapes from two shows he hired the band to play at the Left Foot, a Freehold teen center; portions aired on National Public Radio's *All Things Considered* on September 16, the thirty-seventh anniversary of the first performance. The NPR broadcast included new interviews with Theiss and Alfano; the network's website featured longer samples of the Springsteen-Alfano original "Mr. Jones" and covers of Donovan's "Catch the Wind" and Leonard Cohen's "Suzanne"—all of which featured lead vocals by Springsteen. —*RS/GG*

Harry Chapin

Singer, songwriter, humanitarian

Before Band Aid and Live Aid and USA for Africa and the other assorted mid-'80s famine relief benefits, there was Harry Chapin and World Hunger Year (WHY). Singer-songwriter Chapin founded the charity in 1975 with talk show host and former priest Bill Ayres, and Chapin spent much of his time promoting and raising money for WHY—and lobbying on hunger issues in Washington, D.C.—until he suffered a fatal heart attack while driving to a performance in July 1981. His manager, Ken Kragen, helped organize the USA for Africa "We Are the World" recording project in Chapin's honor, and Chapin's widow, Sandy, who continues WHY, accepted a Congressional Medal of Honor for his efforts posthumously in 1987.

Bruce Springsteen was a supporter of WHY and a fan of Chapin's. He took part in a concert on December 7, 1987—what would have been Chapin's forty-fifth birthday—at New York's Carnegie Hall, playing an acoustic version of Chapin's "Remember When the Music" and incorporating a few comments encouraging the audience to continue supporting WHY. The concert—which also featured performances by Pete Seeger, Richie Havens, Judy Collins, and Peter, Paul & Mary, as well as other artists—was released on an album called *Tribute* in 1990, with a PBS special airing in 1991. In addition to Springsteen, WHY's website (www.worldhungeryear.org) lists E Street Band members Max Weinberg, Clarence Clemons, and Steven Van Zandt individually as active supporters, along with *Backstreets* magazine and other New Jersey musicians, including Southside Johnny & the Asbury Jukes.

Harry Chapin (1942–1981) performs at Avery Fischer Hall in New York City in 1976. Springsteen was among the performers who honored Chapin, who founded the World Hunger Year (WHY) charity, at a 1987 concert in the singer's honor.

A New York City native and son of a jazz drummer, Chapin sang in the Brooklyn Boys Choir and logged time at the Air Force Academy and Cornell University. In the mid-'60s, however, he started performing in Greenwich Village clubs while also making documentary films; one, *Legendary Champions*, was nominated for an Academy Award. Chapin began recording in 1972, winning a devoted fan base for narrative songs such as "Taxi" and his chart-topping "Cats in the Cradle." Chapin also wrote a Tony-nominated musical, "The Night that Made America Famous," served as a delegate to the 1976 Democratic National Convention, and was designated as one of the 10 Most Outstanding Young Men in America by the Jaycees. —*LM/GG*

Chicago

Brass-fortified rock band, hitmakers

You can count on one hand the number of other artists and groups Bruce Springsteen opened for after he began recording for Columbia Records in 1973. And he only *toured* as the opener for one—popular, brass-toting labelmates Chicago, for whom Springsteen warmed up ten shows in the spring of 1973, supporting his debut album *Greetings from Asbury Park, N.J.* He hated the experience—though it didn't have anything to do with Chicago itself. "The guys in Chicago were great," he told Philadelphia DJ Ed Sciaky in 1978. "They were some of the nicest people I ever met." But Springsteen felt that constraints of being an opening act—a half-hour set, which allowed for six or seven songs to be played each night—and the sheer size of the arenas where Chicago was headlining were not adequate conditions for his music or his band.

"I went crazy. I went insane during that tour," he told *Crawdaddy* magazine founder Paul Williams. "It was the worst state of mind I've ever been in, I think, and just because of the playing conditions for our band ... I couldn't play those big places. It had nothing to do with anything, but I couldn't do it. It had nothing to do with anything that had anything to do with me, those big arenas." Springsteen went on to promise, "I won't go to those places again," and to say, "We don't want to get bigger" than 3,000-seat venues—comments he had to backpedal on when he had to start playing regularly in arenas during the early 1980s.

Chicago, of course, was unfazed by its brief experience with Springsteen. The group continued to rack up hits throughout the 1970s and 1980s and has weathered personnel changes, including the loss of key members and lead singers such as guitarist Terry Kath, who accidentally shot himself in 1978, and bassist Peter Cetera, who left in 1984. The group remains active and in 2004 staged a successful joint headlining tour with Earth, Wind & Fire. —*GG*

"Chicken Lips and Lizard Hips"

Songwriters: Nancy and John Cassidy
Album: *For Our Children* (Disney, 1991)
Also on: *For Our Children 10th Anniversary* (Disney, 1999)
Chart peak: No. 31 (album)

In the spring of 1991, Bruce Springsteen agreed to contribute a song to *For Our Children,* a benefit album for pediatric AIDS prevention that Disney was putting together. He came up with an original called "Pony Boy," which he wrote as a lullaby for his newborn son, Evan. But at the last minute Springsteen decided to keep that song and instead recorded a cover of "Chicken Lips and Lizard Hips" by Nancy and John Cassidy, which he found on a copy of Nancy Cassidy's *KidsSongs* that was in Evan's nursery.

The Palo Alto, California–based Cassidy released "Chicken Lips" on *KidsSongs,* her first album, in 1986; John Cassidy said that it was intended as an homage to the popular children's song "Great Green Gobs." Nancy Cassidy has subsequently recorded four other children's albums as well as two collections of her original folk music. John Cassidy, meanwhile, "retired" from songwriting after his one and only credit. "To have Bruce record it, I just can't imagine how to top that, so I'm out," he said. He does, however, continue to publish children's and family books through his publishing company, Klutz.

For Our Children also included contributions from Bob Dylan, Paul McCartney, Elton John, Barbra Streisand, Little Richard, and Sting, among others. A tenth anniversary edition of the album came out just eight years later in October 1999. *—GG*

Chicken Scratch Tour

Early 1977 concert tour

nable to record—at least on his own terms—due to his lawsuits with manager Mike Appel, Bruce Springsteen hit the road in early 1977 on what was dubbed the Chicken Scratch Tour in order to make some money and keep the E Street Band together and working. It was a memorable thirty-three-date excursion, featuring the five-piece Miami Horns section that had played some latter dates on the 1976 *Born to Run* tour as well as the premiere of much of the new material Springsteen was working on at the time.

The tour kicked off February 7, 1977, at the Palace Theater in Albany, New York, and hopped around the East Coast and Midwest before finishing on March 25 in Boston with a show *Backstreets* magazine founder Charles Cross called "another candidate for greatest show ever." Playing between thirteen and twenty songs each night, Springsteen gave the audiences a taste of fresh numbers such as "Action in the Streets," "Don't Look Back," and "Something in the Night." Ronnie Spector and Flo and Eddie were guests at the February 17 show in the Cleveland suburb of Richfield, Ohio, on "Baby I Love You," "Walking in the Rain," "Say Goodbye to Hollywood," and "Be My Baby."

Springsteen was still in legal limbo after the Chicken Scratch Tour wrapped up. He was finally able to get back in the studio, with new producer (and future manager) Jon Landau, on June 1, four days after reaching an out of court settlement with Appel. *—GG*

Child

Late '60s hard rock band with Danny Federici and Vini Lopez

he late 1960s was an active period for Bruce Springsteen. In early 1968 his Jersey Shore high school teen rock band, the Castiles, broke up. In its wake Springsteen formed a hard-rock trio, Earth, which featured Springsteen in both lead guitar and lead singer roles. Earth lasted only a few months before Springsteen ended it to join Child, a band not unlike Earth in its penchant to play heavy blues-rock. However, the group featured all new musicians, included a keyboard player, and was based not in Freehold, Springsteen's hometown, but in his newly adopted residence of Asbury Park.

Child was conceived in 1968 at the Upstage, the Asbury Park after-hours musicians' club where Springsteen and the rest of the Jersey Shore's top rock players jammed on weekends. The band consisted of Springsteen on lead vocals and guitar, bass player Vini Roslyn—formerly of one of the Jersey Shore's most popular mid-'60s bands, the Motifs—drummer Vini Lopez, and organ player Danny Federici, late of another Shore band, the Moment of Truth. Lopez and Federici would go on to become original members of Springsteen's E Street Band.

Playing with Lopez, whose style had direct links to Cream's Ginger Baker and the Who's Keith Moon, and with Federici, who learned at once how to give guitarist Springsteen both space and support, made Springsteen a more complete musician. It was in Child that Springsteen's reputation as an adept guitar player became more established; by the time Child had run its course, Springsteen was the most revered guitar player on the Jersey Shore, and the Upstage musician most in-demand for late-night jams.

When Springsteen and Lopez heard that another area band was also going by the name Child, they decided to change their name. Chuck Dillion, a mutual friend from the Jersey Shore town of Bay Head, suggested the name Steel Mill. Thus was born what many longtime Springsteen fans believe to be the best of his pre–E Street bands. —RS

Chimes of Freedom EP

Released: August 1988
Producers: Bruce Springsteen, Jon Landau, Chuck Plotkin
Tracks: "Tougher Than the Rest," "Be True," "Chimes of Freedom," "Born to Run"

n July 3, 1988, performing an internationally broadcast Tunnel of Love Express Tour stop in Stockholm, Sweden, Bruce Springsteen told the crowd that he would participate in Amnesty International's

Human Rights Now! tour that fall. He followed the announcement with a performance of Bob Dylan's "Chimes of Freedom." The song became the title track for a four-song EP Springsteen released to promote the tour and raise money for Amnesty International. Besides "Chimes of Freedom," the EP includes live recordings of "Be True" from the March 28, 1988, show at Detroit's Joe Louis Arena, and two songs from an April 27, 1988, concert at the Los Angeles Sports Arena: "Tougher Than the Rest" and the acoustic "Born to Run" that Springsteen was performing on the tour.

Though not promoted in the same manner as a standard album release, "Chimes of Freedom" did manage to make it to No. 16 on *Billboard*'s Mainstream Rock Tracks chart. The first American CD pressing was as a three-inch disc that featured an edited version of "Tougher Than the Rest"; Canada got the full-length "Tougher" on a proper five-inch disc. Current pressings correct the original problem. —*GG*

Christic Institute Benefit Concerts

1990 fundraising shows

On November 16–17, 1990, Bruce Springsteen joined Bonnie Raitt and Jackson Browne at the Shrine Auditorium in Los Angeles to perform a benefit for the Christic Institute, an interfaith public interest law and political action group that tried to expose the CIA's involvement in Iran/Contra drug smuggling activities. The institute filed a $24 million federal lawsuit using the Racketeer and Corrupt Influence Organizations (RICO) Act. But the charges were thrown out of court and the institute was hit with large fines, eventually causing its demise.

Backstreets magazine founder Charles Cross dubbed Springsteen's Christic shows "two of the most important and dramatic concerts of his career." They were, first of all, solo acoustic dates—two of the few he'd done up to that time. They also marked his first announced performances since he dismissed the E Street Band nearly a year before. And because he had not released an album in three years, fans were hot for new material—which they got, as Springsteen debuted six new songs during the two-night stand, including "Red Headed Woman," "When the Lights Go Out," "57 Channels," "Real World," "The Wish," and "Soul Driver."

Other gems from the Christic shows: Springsteen's first-ever acoustic rendering of "Darkness on the Edge of Town"; his first solo treatment since 1975 of "Tenth Avenue Freeze-Out"; the first performances since 1985 of "Reason to Believe," "My Father's House," "Atlantic City," and "Nebraska"; and "Wild Billy's Circus Story," which had been on the bench since 1974. He also flubbed the words to "Thunder Road" at the November 16 show.

Browne and Raitt closed the show with Springsteen each night with "Highway 61" and "Across the Borderline." A number of bootlegs came out of the shows; the *Boston Globe* later reported that some were so good that Springsteen and manager Jon Landau considered making an album from them. —*LM/GG*

Chrysler Corporation

Automotive manufacturer

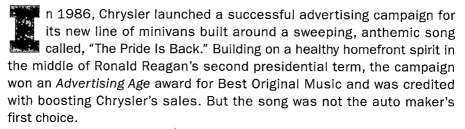 n 1986, Chrysler launched a successful advertising campaign for its new line of minivans built around a sweeping, anthemic song called, "The Pride Is Back." Building on a healthy homefront spirit in the middle of Ronald Reagan's second presidential term, the campaign won an *Advertising Age* award for Best Original Music and was credited with boosting Chrysler's sales. But the song was not the auto maker's first choice.

If "The Pride Is Back" seemed like a knock-off of Bruce Springsteen's "Born in the U.S.A.," that's because it was. Chrysler had actually drawn up a campaign using Springsteen singing "Born in the U.S.A." in TV and radio ads and reportedly offered him $12 million. Company executives hoped that Springsteen would be willing to endorse Chrysler Chairman Lee Iacocca, who *Rolling Stone* magazine had called "the Bruce Springsteen of business," in his efforts to lead the company out of financial ruin—with the help of government loans and union concessions. Springsteen, of course, has never endorsed a product and certainly wasn't about to at that time, especially when the memory of both 1984 presidential candidates trying to glom on to his *Born in the U.S.A.* fame was still fresh.

So instead Chrysler decided to co-opt the Springsteen attitude with "The Pride Is Back." Joan Neary, who cowrote the song with Marc Blatte, admitted to the *Phoenix New Times* that "The Pride Is Back," with its chorus of "The pride is back, born in America," was intended to ape "Born in the U.S.A." "We knew from the start that Chrysler really wanted 'Born in the U.S.A.' So obviously we didn't want to go way in the opposite direction … But the commercial didn't really copy his song. It's just got the *spirit* of his music."

"The Pride Is Back" was sung by Kenny Rogers (who, like Springsteen, was part of the "We Are the World" benefit single in 1985) and Sandy Farina. Rogers also recorded a version of the song as a single, without much success. —*GG*

Gia Ciambotti. *See* 1992–93 Bruce Springsteen Touring Band.

The Chrysler Corporation's plan to spur automobile sales by leveraging Springsteen's image as an American icon fell flat when he rejected the car company's request to use "Born in the U.S.A." in radio and TV ads. The company settled for Kenny Rogers and an award-winning campaign with the theme "The Pride Is Back."

Bob Clearmountain

Springsteen mixing engineer

Prior to hooking up with Bruce Springsteen for *Born In the U.S.A.*, mixing engineer Bob Clearmountain already had impeccable hit-making credibility—in the '70s, he cofounded New York City's Power Station studio, which gave the world Chic's "Good Times," Sister Sledge's "We Are Family," Roxy Music's *Avalon*, and the Rolling Stones' *Tattoo You*, among many others. In his Rock and Roll Hall of Fame acceptance speech, Springsteen praised Clearmountain as a "great mixer who helped me bring my music to a wider audience."

Clearmountain grew up in Connecticut, playing bass in high school bands. A fellow musician introduced him to an engineer at New York's Mediasound. Clearmountain, who had always been the guy in the band who recorded the shows, fell in love with the knobs and dials and spent so much time at Mediasound that the studio hired him as an "assistant's assistant." Working on jingles by day and R&B by night, he soaked up the atmosphere and helped make hits such as Kool & the Gang's "Funky Stuff."

In 1977, shortly after a group of prominent engineers formed the Power Station in New York, Clearmountain became its chief recording engineer. He had a reputation for speed, impressing artists such as Chic's Nile Rodgers, and built enough of a reputation and a resume of hits to go independent in the early '80s. By 1983, after his sparsely produced *The River* (recorded at the Power Station) and *Nebraska* albums, Springsteen came calling. "He has a very clear vision of getting his point across, and he taught me that the song and its central character are always the most important," Clearmountain, who has also mixed *Live/ 1975–85, Tunnel of Love, Tracks,* and the Oscar-winning "Streets of Philadelphia" track, told *Mix* magazine in March 2004. "Everything in the mix needs to complement that. Most of Bruce's songs are about someone's tribulations or joys of life. The connection between the character as portrayed by the singer and the listener can never be broken. Everything needs to add to the connection and not take away from it. From a mixing standpoint, that means you have to connect with the song first before you even start."

After building his Mix This! home studio in California in the mid-1990s and moving into it full-time, Clearmountain continues to work with Springsteen and the E Street Band. Over the years, he has continued to mix and produce high-profile projects for artists big and small, including pop hitmakers such as Bryan Adams, Counting Crows, and the Pretenders, singer Shelby Lynne, and "American Idol" star Clay Aiken. —*SK*

Clearwater Festival

Annual environmental fundraising festival in Asbury Park, New Jersey

ruce Springsteen has quietly been a member of Clearwater, a New Jersey environmental protection organization, for years. But when the group decided to move its annual fundraising festival to Asbury Park after twenty-five years in nearby Sandy Hook on April 18, 2001, Springsteen showed his approval by turning up to play a thirty-minute acoustic set that included the (at the time) unreleased "My City of Ruins" (which he introduced as "a prayer for my city"), "Bobby Jean," "This Hard Land," "Does This Bus Stop at 82nd Street?," and "Blinded by the Light." He brought several fans on stage to help him sing the latter. Springsteen praised Asbury Park's newly elected city council from the stage and told the *Asbury Park Press*, "It's great (Clearwater) brought the festival here. It's part of the city's revitalization." —*GG*

Clarence Clemons

King of the world, master of the universe, E Street Band saxophonist since 1971

he E Street Band's super-sized sax man and, for years, Bruce Springsteen's primary onstage foil, Clarence Clemons's signing on with the E Street Band has become the stuff of legend. Much of that legend was propagated by Springsteen himself with a story he often told in concert to preface "The E Street Shuffle." In it, Springsteen and Little Steven Van Zandt are down on their luck, walking home on the boardwalk from a poor-paying gig. It's raining and the wind is whipping, and through the mist comes a stranger—a huge man all dressed in white and carrying a saxophone. They think he means to rob them and they cower in a doorway, throwing down their money and even Springsteen's tennis shoes. But all the Big Man wants to do is shake his hand.

In reality, what happened was that Clemons went to see Springsteen perform in Asbury Park; he had been told about Springsteen by Karen Cassady, the singer in Norman Seldin & the Joyful Noise, the band Clemons was playing in at the time. The Bruce Springsteen Band was playing at the Student Prince nearby. It was indeed a rainy and windy night, and when Clemons opened the door to the club, a gust of wind blew it right off the hinges. Clemons told Springsteen he wanted to join the band and Springsteen, somewhat intimidated, agreed. Clemons got onstage with them and "the magic began," as he tells *Backstreets* magazine—with an early version of

Clarence Clemons (left) is a commanding presence as Springsteen's on-stage foil, and his soulful saxophone solos are a critical element of the E Street Band's signature sound.

"Spirit in the Night." Springsteen recalled the event at his Rock and Roll Hall of Fame induction, noting, "a sound came out of his horn that seemed to rattle the glasses behind the bar and threatened to blow out the back wall ... I knew I'd found my sax player."

Born January 11, 1942, in Norfolk, Virginia, Clemons is the son of a Baptist minister and a family that thought rock 'n' roll was "the devil's music," even though one Christmas they gave him a saxophone rather than the train he'd requested. At home he was influenced by gospel music and some R&B, including the Coasters, Otis Redding, and especially saxophonists King Curtis, Junior Walker, and Boots Randolph. At University of Maryland Eastern Shore he "majored in football, but I always had my sax in my car, looking for what I really wanted to do. I wanted to play music."

A few years older than the other E Streeters, Clemons's saxophone brought a funky, King Curtis–style flavor to the band. Onstage, Springsteen and Clemons were polar opposites: Springsteen, small of stature, and the

Clarence Clemons wails his trademark saxophone sound at the March 1988 Tunnel of Love Express Tour stop in Detroit, Michigan.

The on-stage schtick between The Big Man and The Boss is a highlight of E Street Band performances.

Big Man, well, big. Springsteen wore jeans, T-shirts, and leather jackets; Clemons wore white three-piece suits. Springsteen was the gregarious life of the party, Clemons the strong, silent type. Guitar/sax, black/white, and so on. Yet they worked for a common purpose, and when they came together, whether onstage or in the recording studio, Springsteen's lyric came true—sparks flew on E Street. "Something happened when we stood side by side," Springsteen noted in 1999. Some of Clemons's saxophone solos are as highly regarded and well-known by Springsteen fans as the songs they adorn—"Rosalita," "Spirit in the Night," "Born to Run," "Jungleland," "The Promised Land," and many others. Original Springsteen manager and coproducer Mike Appel told *Backstreets* that Clemons "was a great 'feel' guy" but said that Springsteen was actually responsible for many of those solo spots, such as the one on "Jungleland," singing them to Clemons note by note.

Clemons remained with Springsteen throughout the E Street Band's original run and joined in whenever they've reunited. "Whatever he needs, I try to provide," Clemons—whose dressing room on tour is known as the Temple of Soul—told *Backstreets*. When the E Streeters are on downtime, Clemons maintains a solo career, starting in 1983 with *Rescue*, which is credited to Clarence Clemons and the Red Bank Rockers—a group that ended in 1984, when drummer Wells Kelly died. (Springsteen sat in on guitar for the track "Savin' Up," which he also wrote.) *The Chief* was released in 1984 and *Hero* in 1985, the latter album yielding a hit single in "You're a Friend of Mine," a duet with Jackson Browne that was about and originally intended for Springsteen. Clemons's other albums include *A Night with Mr. C* (1989), *Peacemaker* (1995), and two *Live from Asbury Park* CDs released in 2002 and 2004, featuring his Temple of Soul band and with Springsteen jamming on Eddie Floyd's "Raise Your Hand" on the second volume. During the early '80s Clemons also operated a club called Big Man's West in Red Bank, New Jersey, which hosted many Springsteen guest appearances.

As an actor, Clemons has had roles in film and on TV. His credits include Martin Scorsese's *New York, New York*, *Bill & Ted's Excellent Adventure*, *Blues Brothers 2000*, and TV's "Nash Bridges" and "The Wire." And he's enjoyed a prodigious career as a guest musician, lending a hand to Steve Van Zandt and Nils Lofgren, appearing on albums by rock legends such as Carl Perkins and Roy Orbison, playing the solo on Aretha Franklin's hit "Freeway of Love," and serving in Ringo Starr's inaugural All-Starr Band in 1989. Clemons also considers himself a spiritual "seeker" who has studied various religions. A guru (Sri Chinmoy) gave Clemons his spiritual name Mokshagun. His domestic life has not been quite as smooth as some of his solos, however. Twice married—the second taking place in May 2004 to Dr. Meg Yanhong in her hometown of Fushon City, China—Clemons found himself in legal trouble in December 1996 when then-girlfriend Sharlene Smalley accused him of domestic battery. Clemons settled the matter before it went to trial, agreeing to counseling, making a $1,000 donation to charity, and writing a letter of apology to Smalley. —*DD/GG*

Off of E Street ... Clarence Clemons

Joan Armatrading, *Me Myself I* (1980)
Gary U.S. Bonds, *Dedication* (1981), *On the Line* (1982)
Jim Carroll, *World Without Gravity* (1994)
Carlene Carter, *Two Sides to Every Woman* (1979)
Joe Cocker, *Unchain My Heart* (1987)
Aretha Franklin, *Who's Zoomin' Who* (1985)
Great White, *Sail Away* (1994)
Dan Hartman, *Images* (1976)
Ian Hunter, *All of the Good Ones Are Taken* (1983)
Janis Ian, *Night Rains* (1979)
Dave Koz, *Lucky Man* (1993)
Greg Lake, *Greg Lake* (1981)
Alvin Lee & Ten Years After, *Pure Blues* (1995)
Little Steven & the Disciples of Soul, *Men Without Women* (1982)
Nils Lofgren, *Silver Lining* (1991)
Roy Orbison, *King of Hearts* (1992)
Carl Perkins, *Go Cat Go* (1996)
Todd Rundgren, *Nearly Human* (1989)
Ringo Starr, *All-Starr Band* (1990)
Zucchero, *Zucchero* (1986), *Diamante* (1995)

The Cleveland Boys

Fanatical quartet from the banks of Lake Erie

Bruce Springsteen has inspired plenty of big fans over the course of his career. But it's doubtful many are as fanatic as the Cleveland Boys, four men from Cleveland who began a unique relationship with Springsteen in 1976, bonding through music—and softball. Legend has it that Jim Kluter was introduced to Springsteen's second album *The Wild, the Innocent & the E Street Shuffle* by a friend, and immediately got hooked. After *Born to Run*, he became obsessed and convinced pals Joe Juhasz and Bill Spratt to journey to Asbury Park over the July 4, 1976, weekend to see if they could track Springsteen down. The truck drivers from Ohio hopped a plane and headed for the Stone Pony. Their quest was rewarded on the second night, when Springsteen showed up to jam with Southside Johnny & the Asbury Jukes. They found out he and the band would be playing softball the next day at a high school field against a team from *Crawdaddy* magazine. Spotting Springsteen playing catch, Kluter approached him and said, "Hey, Bruce! I love you!" and hugged him. Springsteen laughed. As the game began, Springsteen's team, the E Street Kings, was short a few players. "Bruce points up to us and says, 'How 'bout those Cleveland boys?'" Kluter recalled. They played—and won a double-header. Springsteen asked them to return the next weekend for another game; this time, John Kusznier took Spratt's place. When Springsteen asked them where they were staying, they said they didn't know, so he asked them if they wanted to bunk at his place. Kluter said Springsteen was renting a large house, but it was completely unfurnished; the only room with carpeting was the music room, where they slept next to guitars and pages of half-written songs.

The quartet soon became renowned for their dedication. When Springsteen and the E Street Band performed in 1977 at the suburban Richfield Coliseum, a poster advertising the shows read: "WMMS 101 FM proudly presents the rock and roll event of the year—The Cleveland Boys with special guest Bruce Springsteen." It featured a photo of Springsteen surrounded by the four men wearing "The Cleveland Boys" T-shirts. At one time they had Springsteen's home phone number, and he periodically showed up at their parties, with the E Street Band and tour bus in tow in one case. Some of the guys spent a month touring with Springsteen in the late '70s, riding the band bus on a West Coast swing from San Francisco to Los Angeles. At some of his Cleveland performances, Springsteen would head into the crowd on one of the Boys' shoulders. After an August 1978 show at the Richfield Coliseum, the Cleveland Boys invited Springsteen to go out drinking; instead of getting on the bus Springsteen hopped into Kluter's Chevy Malibu for the trip to the Royal Knight, a now-closed shot-and-a-beer hangout in Parma, Ohio. Kluter told one reporter that Springsteen started drinking Pabst Blue Ribbon and peppermint Schnapps as word of mouth spread and the bar slowly filled with other fans. On the way back to the Cleveland hotel where Springsteen was staying, Kluter played a bootleg tape from one of his shows, and soon they were all singing along to "Spirit in the Night." E Street Band drummer Max Weinberg gave the Boys a shout-out during the grand opening Concert for the Rock and Roll Hall of Fame on September 2, 1995.

During the 1999–2000 E Street Band reunion tour, Springsteen was still dedicating songs to them in performances, and when they could get through increasing layers of bureaucracy, they still scored backstage passes and prime tickets. In the book *Rock 'n' Roll and the Cleveland Connection*, Kluter marveled, "He doesn't have to give us the time of day. But that's the kind of guy he is. When you talk to him, even after all this time as a rock star, he's a just regular guy. He still has that knack for making you feel like you're one of his best friends. But it's funny to look back and think, 'Wow, we really kinda grew up with him. How'd we do that?'" *—LM*

Jimmy Cliff. *See* "Trapped."

Natalie Cole

R&B and pop singer with legendary genes

he daughter of incomparable jazz and pop legend Nat "King" Cole, Natalie Cole followed in her father's footsteps, but not before pursuing a career in R&B and contemporary pop. She had a string of No. 1 R&B hits, including "This Will Be," "Inseparable," "Sophisticated Lady," "I've Got Love on My Mind," and "Our Love," all of which were Top 40 pop hits as well. She won the Best New Artist Grammy in 1976. But by the turn of the decade, the hits stopped coming.

Cole reemerged in 1987 with the album *Everlasting*, which yielded hits in "Jump Start," "I Live For Your Love," and Bruce Springsteen's "Pink Cadillac," the popular *Born in the U.S.A.* outtake that wound up as the B-side of "Dancing in the Dark" and subsequently appeared on 1998's *Tracks* box set. Though Cole's version of the song glosses over its central metaphor—did she actually think he was writing about a *car?*—her single reached to No. 5 on the *Billboard* Hot 100 and to No. 9 on the R&B chart.

In recent years, Cole has taken on the role of chanteuse, singing pop standards such as her father's "Unforgettable," which produced a No. 14 pop hit and a popular video that featured Cole "duetting" with her late father. The multi-platinum 1991 album *Unforgettable with Love* won six Grammys, including Record, Album, and Song of the Year. —*DD*

Robert Coles

Psychiatrist, professor, author

obert Coles is a child psychiatrist, Harvard professor of social ethics, a Presidential Medal of Freedom honoree, and publisher of a Boston-based documentary magazine called *DoubleTake*. Coles is also a Pulitzer Prize–winning author of more than sixty books, including the 2003 release, *Bruce Springsteen's America: The People Listening, A Poet Singing*.

Bruce Springsteen and Coles met each other through Will Percy, the nephew of author Walker Percy—a fan who had written a letter to Springsteen before dying of cancer in 1989. Eight years later, Springsteen read Walker Percy's *The Moviegoer* and met Will Percy backstage at a concert. Springsteen then responded to Walker Percy's note by writing one to his widow. Later that year, Will Percy wrote a piece about Springsteen for *DoubleTake,* then introduced him to Coles, who had once written about Walker for the *New Yorker* magazine. Springsteen and Coles became friends, sharing a belief that stories about ordinary people can, in Springsteen's words, "establish a commonality by revealing our inner common humanity." Meanwhile, the magazine, which started in 1995, was going broke. In an attempt to stem the cash crisis, Springsteen performed two fundraising concerts on February 19–20, 2003, at the Somerville Theater outside Boston; they raised nearly $1 million, but despite the publicity and influx of cash, *DoubleTake* went on hiatus that year.

The downtime apparently gave Coles a chance to compile the book, which consists of ten fans' personal—and apparently unedited—accounts of how Springsteen's music affects them, each introduced by Coles's own comments and recollections. The almost uniformly panned book also aroused suspicion in some quarters that quotes were doctored or fabricated. When music journalist David Hajdu pursued his hunch that Coles may have embellished the content of his conversations with Walker Percy, he talked to Will Percy, who said his uncle would never have spoken in the manner described by Coles. —*LM*

Come Together: Jon Bon Jovi & Friends

1998 all-star benefit concert for family of slain New Jersey police officer

Bruce Springsteen and Jon Bon Jovi were the faces of New Jersey rock throughout the '80s and into the '90s. So it was only fitting that when Bon Jovi organized the Come Together benefit for the family of a slain New Jersey police officer, he invited Springsteen and much of the then-disbanded E Street Band crew to participate.

Held January 31, 1998, at the Count Basie Theatre in Red Bank, New Jersey, Come Together: Jon Bon Jovi & Friends was a benefit for the family of Sgt. Patrick King, the most decorated officer in the history of Long Branch, New Jersey; on November 20 of the previous year King was fatally shot by a fugitive who had vowed to kill himself and a police officer rather than be captured and returned to jail. Bon Jovi organized the show in short order and raised more than $112,000 for King's widow and their two sons.

Joining the bill with Springsteen were his wife, Patti Scialfa, former E Street Band guitarist Steve Van Zandt, saxophonist Clarence Clemons, keyboardist Danny Federici, and drummer Max Weinberg. Other notables included Southside Johnny Lyon and the other members of Bon Jovi. Actor Danny DeVito was the emcee.

The entire company—which had rehearsed for two nights prior—kicked things off with Southside's "This Time It's for Real" and finished the evening with John Fogerty's "Rockin' All Over the World," Roy Head's "Treat Her Right," and Springsteen's "Thunder Road." Springsteen, meanwhile, spent much of the night onstage; he sang "Badlands" on his own before hooking up with Bon Jovi on "Tenth Avenue Freeze-Out," "You Give Love a Bad Name," "Wanted Dead or Alive," and "Forever." Springsteen and Van Zandt partnered on "Two Hearts," "Until the Good Is Gone," "The Promised Land," "Bobby Jean," and "Backstreets." Southside Johnny sang "The Fever" with Springsteen, who wrote the song; Van Zandt then joined them for "It's Been a Long Time," and Bon Jovi made the trio a quartet on "Born to Run." Springsteen also backed Scialfa on her own "Love's Glory." —GG

The Complete Video Anthology 1978–2000

Released: January 16, 2001
Tracks: Disc 1—"Rosalita (Come Out Tonight)," "The River," "Thunder Road," "Atlantic City," "Dancing in the Dark," "Born in the U.S.A.," "I'm on Fire," "Glory Days," "My Hometown," "War," "Fire," "Born to Run," "Brilliant Disguise," "Tunnel of Love," "One Step Up," "Tougher Than the Rest," "Spare Parts," "Born to Run" (acoustic); Disc 2—"Human Touch," "Better Days," "57 Channels (And Nothin' On)," "Leap of Faith," "Streets of Philadelphia," "Murder Incorporated," "Secret Garden," "Hungry Heart," "Dead Man Walking," "The Ghost of Tom Joad," "The Ghost of Tom Joad" (from *The Tonight Show with Jay Leno*), "Highway Patrolman," "If I Should Fall Behind," "Born in the U.S.A." (from *Charlie Rose*)

*T*he Complete Video Anthology expanded the out-of-print 1989 home video release *The Video Anthology*, adding an additional fifteen pieces to bring the collection up to date. It kicks off with the rowdy 1978 performance video of "Rosalita (Come Out Tonight)" and goes through all of Bruce Springsteen's promotional videos to that point. It also includes some rare gems, including Springsteen's performance of "Hungry Heart" with Germany's Wolfgang Niedecken and members of his Leopardefellband (Leopard Skin Band), an acoustic rendition of "Born in the U.S.A." from his 1998 appearance on PBS's *Charlie Rose,* and a couple of collaborations with some of Springsteen's film buddies—Sean Penn, who directed "Highway Patrolman" for his film *Indian Runner*, and Tim Robbins, who directed "Dead Man Walking" for his *Dead Man Walking*. —GG

The Concert for the Kristen Ann Carr Fund. *See* **Kristen Ann Carr Fund.**

The Concert for the Rock and Roll Hall of Fame

September 2, 1995, Cleveland, Ohio

*T*he Rock and Roll Hall of Fame and Museum in Cleveland celebrated its long-awaited grand opening on September 2, 1995, with a star-studded concert at Cleveland Municipal Stadium on the shores of Lake Erie. By the time the final note sounded at 2:10 a.m. on September

3, forty-one different combinations of artists had taken the stage, playing sixty-eight songs over the course of six hours and forty minutes. The bill included Bruce Springsteen and the E Street Band, Bob Dylan, Chuck Berry, Jerry Lee Lewis, Johnny Cash, Aretha Franklin, John Mellencamp, Bon Jovi, Eric Burdon, Melissa Etheridge, Dr. John, Al Green, the Pretenders, Jackson Browne, John Fogerty, Lou Reed, Sheryl Crow, George Clinton & the P-Funk All-Stars, the Kinks, Heart, Natalie Merchant, Robbie Robertson, Bruce Hornsby, Booker T. & the MGs, Sam Moore, the Allman Brothers Band, Slash, Boz Scaggs, James Brown, Martha & the Vandellas, Little Richard, and others.

Springsteen and the E Street Band were at the center of the action much of the evening. They opened the concert in proper style, teaming up with Chuck Berry on "Johnny B. Goode." They also backed Jerry Lee Lewis on "Great Balls of Fire" and "Whole Lotta Shakin' Goin' On." In their own set, they paid tribute to Hall of Fame inductee Big Joe Turner and Bill Haley with "Shake, Rattle and Roll" and gave props to inductee Bo Diddley by preceding "She's the One" with a snippet of "Bo Diddley." The group also performed "Darkness on the Edge of Town," after which an overzealous young fan jumped onstage at the end of the song, grabbing Springsteen around the neck and giving him a kiss. As security guards rushed to the rescue, Springsteen tried to call them off; "Hey, that's rock 'n' roll," he said to the crowd. Bob Dylan showed up around midnight as a surprise guest, and Springsteen joined him on a rendition of "Forever Young."

The Boss also played a bit part in the show's botched encore; the plan was to have Chuck Berry fire up the crowd for the show's big finale by playing "Rock and Roll Music" with Springsteen, Melissa Etheridge, and Booker T. & the MGs. But Berry botched the lyrics and didn't play the song in the same key as his supporting players. The show ended with a planned all-star jam on the Beatles' "Come Together" and Dylan's "Like a Rolling Stone." —*MN*

Continental Airlines Arena

Sports and entertainment complex in East Rutherford, New Jersey

hen it first opened its doors on July 2, 1981, the Continental Airlines Arena in East Rutherford, New Jersey, was formally known as the Brendan Byrne Arena; informally, it was called the House that Bruce Built. It has been the site of more Bruce Springsteen concerts than any other venue—including six shows that served as the arena's grand opening in 1981. He went on to play ten nights there in 1984, eleven in 1992, a benefit show to fight hunger in 1993, fifteen in 1999 (launching the North American portion of the E Street Band "rededication" tour), the opening show of *The Rising* tour in 2002, and the last show of the Vote for Change tour in October 2004. There was also a rehearsal show in 2002, and Springsteen appeared as a surprise guest at the Holiday Express Christmas concert there in 2001. It has become common practice for fans from all over the world to make the pilgrimage to the Meadowlands to see Springsteen at his home arena, with the flags of many nations flying in the parking lots during ritual pre-show tailgate parties.

The multiple-night engagements at the arena usually result in Springsteen making a special effort to vary the set lists. Numerous rarities and one-off performances have been highlights of shows at the arena over the years. Special guests inevitably hop on stage, too, including Gary U.S. Bonds, Steve Van Zandt and Clarence Clemons (when they were not members of Springsteen's band), J.T. Bowen of Clemons's Red Bank Rockers, the late Who bassist John Entwistle, Southside Johnny, and Joe Ely. Springsteen's personal haberdasher played bongos on "Spirit in the Night" at a 1999 show, with Springsteen telling the crowd, "I owe him some money on the suits, so he's gonna play here tonight."

Named originally for New Jersey Governor Brendan Byrne, the arena became commonly know as the Meadowlands Arena even though the name was not officially changed until Continental Airlines purchased the rights in January 1996. Tickets for the 1981 Springsteen shows listed the venue as the Byrne Meadowlands Arena; by the time he returned in 1984 the tickets simply read Meadowlands Arena. The facility was built primarily for the New Jersey Nets of the National Basketball Association, but it became the home to the National Hockey League's New Jersey Devils in 1982 when that franchise moved from Colorado.

In addition to the Meadowlands arena shows, Springsteen has performed sixteen times at the larger Giants Stadium just across the road. —*RB*

Elvis Costello

Multi-faceted British singer, musician, songwriter, composer, and performer

 lvis Costello tended to be lumped in with the punk rock/New Wave explosion taking place in Great Britain when he emerged in 1977 with *My Aim Is True*. But that's only one part of an extremely diverse career. The truth is that Costello (real name Declan McManus) has long been a music fan with broad tastes—including an early fondness for Bruce Springsteen, who Costello acknowledged "we were copying" when he was in the mid-'70s band Flip City. "When Bruce came to London ... in 1975, we were like, 'Who are these johnny-come-latelies?'" Costello told *Rolling Stone* magazine. "We'd been digging him for years. I loved *The Wild, the Innocent & the E*

English singer Elvis Costello (right) has been a longtime fan of Springsteen and the E Street Band. The two have played together many times, including here at the 2003 Grammy Awards, where they joined Dave Grohl and Steve Van Zandt in a roaring version of the Clash's "London Calling" to honor that band's recently deceased guitarist Joe Strummer.

Street Shuffle. The songs are so operatic. Then he narrowed it down. I learned something from that. When he wanted to get over, he wrote 'Born to Run.'" When *Vanity Fair* asked Costello to name 500 essential albums in 2000, he put four Springsteen titles on the list—*The Wild, the Innocent & the E Street Shuffle*, *The River*, *Tunnel of Love*, and *The Ghost of Tom Joad*.

Costello and Springsteen have shared the stage on several occasions. They both took part in Roy Orbison's *A Black & White Night* concert in 1987, and Springsteen invited Costello to be part of his 2001 holiday shows; Costello played on December 8, with Springsteen joining him for a medley of Costello's "Alison" and Smokey Robinson & the Miracles' "Tracks of My Tears" and "Tears of a Clown," while Costello backed Springsteen on "Christmas (Baby, Please Come Home)" and "Santa Claus Is Comin' to Town." Costello and Springsteen played the Clash's "London Calling" together at the 2003 Grammy Awards, and Costello also contributed his cover of Springsteen's "Brilliant Disguise"—originally released as a B-side in the U.K.—to the 2003 *Light of Day* tribute album.

Born in London in 1954, Costello, the son of a big band leader, built on his initial blast of brash, acerbic albums with forays into country and classical (chamber and symphonic), touches of jazz and blues, and lush pop with fellow composer Burt Bacharach. His production credits include ska-rockers the Specials, Celtic rockers the Pogues, and Swedish mezzo-soprano Anne Sofie Von Otter. Costello and his band the Attractions were inducted into the Rock and Roll Hall of Fame in 2003. —*GG*

"Cover Me"

Single released: August 18, 1984
Album: *Born in the U.S.A.* (Columbia, 1984)
Also on: *Live/1975–85* (Columbia, 1986)
Chart peak: No. 7

The second single from the *Born in the U.S.A.* album came dangerously close to being the Bruce Springsteen song that was given to Donna Summer for her self-titled 1982 album, rather than "Protection." Springsteen wrote "Cover Me" in Los Angeles in the spring of 1982 after music mogul David Geffen suggested he write something for Summer, who was then on Geffen Records; in *Songs*, Springsteen wrote, "She could really sing and I disliked the veiled racism of the anti-disco movement," hence his willingness to come up with something for the disco diva.

When Springsteen coproducer and manager Jon Landau heard "Cover Me," however, he intervened and suggested that Springsteen keep it for himself. Springsteen and the E Street Band recorded it in May or June 1982 at the Power Station in New York City. Like its predecessor, "Dancing in the Dark,"

"Cover Me" hit the *Billboard* Top 10, while remixer Arthur Baker gave the song a major sonic overhaul for the dance clubs. An alternate studio take of the track has circulated among collectors featuring a radically different arrangement and lyrical variations, dubbed "(Drop on Down and) Cover Me." —*GG*

Cowboy Junkies
Canadian rock group

anada's Cowboy Junkies have quietly become one of the most prolific younger bands that demonstrate an appreciation for Bruce Springsteen's music. As singer Margo Timmins noted, "We're all huge Springsteen fans." The group has covered Springsteen three times on its albums: a version of "State Trooper" appears on their 1986 debut *Whites Off Earth Now!*; a rendition of "My Father's House" was included as a hidden track on the 1999 compilation *Rarities, B-Sides and Slow Sad Waltzes*; and "Thunder Road" is part of a bonus disc of covers that accompanied the 2004 studio set *One Soul Now*.

Timmins said that she was especially anxious to get a version of "Thunder Road" onto tape: "I've always loved that song; it's one of the most beautiful songs ever written. To me, 'Thunder Road' is a real woman's song. It speaks of aging and losing certain dreams that you might have as a young woman that I don't think young men have. It's just a song I've always wanted to sing from my perspective, a woman's perspective." Timmins said the group actually tried to record it several years ago but wasn't satisfied with the results. "I don't think I had the skill to do what I wanted to do with it," she says. "I knew how I wanted to do it but just didn't have the talent yet. So we waited and brought it back. I'm very happy with this take on it; it has a nice balance between the sadness and the beauty I think is part of that song."

Timmins and her brothers Michael and Peter formed Cowboy Junkies in 1985 in Toronto with friend Alan Anton. The group released *Whites Off Earth Now!* independently but signed with RCA in 1987. They broke through the following year with *The Trinity Sessions*, a critically acclaimed set recorded in a single fourteen-hour session at an old church. The group has continued to tour and record, leaving the major label world in 2000 to sign with the smaller Zoe/Rounder. The Springsteen songs they've recorded frequently pop up in their live shows. —*GG*

Courteney Cox-Arquette
Actress, video star

n 1984, director Brian De Palma chose Courteney Cox from among 300 women as the stunned fan Springsteen would lure on stage to dance with him in the video for "Dancing in the Dark." She reportedly was paid

In 1984, before she became one of America's "Friends," Courteney Cox-Arquette (then just plain Courteney Cox) became famous as the wide-eyed fan that Springsteen calls up on stage to be his dance partner in the "Dancing in the Dark" video.

$350 for the clip, which was filmed in St. Paul at the start of the *Born in the U.S.A.* tour. "It was scary," Cox-Arquette told NBC's "Dateline" in May 2004. "I just imitated what (Springsteen) did. Whatever he did, I followed."

The appearance helped jump-start her career, which included playing Michael J. Fox's girlfriend on the "Family Ties" TV series. In 1994, she won the role of Monica Geller on "Friends," which made her a rich star and a beloved Thursday-night TV fixture for ten years. She also starred in the popular *Scream* series of horror spoof movies.

Before she married fellow actor David Arquette, Cox dated Adam Duritz of the band Counting Crows, who put her in her second music video, for the band's "Long December." Cox-Arquette has also had relationships with actor Michael Keaton and Ian Copeland, brother of former Police drummer Stewart and manager Miles. The Copelands' uncle, Hunter Stewart, is Cox-Arquette's stepfather. —*LM*

Creedence Clearwater Revival

Iconic '60s and early '70s rock band, Rock and Roll Hall of Fame member

Creedence Clearwater Revival is one of Bruce Springsteen's prime American rock touchstones. Though CCR was at the opposite end of the rock 'n' roll spectrum from the singer-songwriters, most notably Bob Dylan—of whom Springsteen was initially seen as a stylistic descendant—its spare, economical style, performing fervor, and occasional political subtext are elements Springsteen gleaned from the group. CCR's "Who'll Stop the Rain," which became an anthem of sorts for Vietnam veterans, is one of Springsteen's favorite in-concert covers, and he's also performed group leader John Fogerty's "Rockin' All Over the World."

However, Springsteen became unwittingly embroiled in some of CCR's inner turmoil at the 1993 Rock and Roll Hall of Fame induction ceremony in Los Angeles. He inducted the group into the Hall, then played three songs with an ad hoc band put together by Fogerty—who harbors such great animosity towards his former bandmates that he's refused to play with them since 1971. Not surprisingly, this greatly offended bassist Stu Cook, drummer Doug Clifford, and the family of the late guitarist Tom Fogerty; Cook said that Springsteen subsequently apologized for the slight.

Springsteen and Fogerty continued their friendship, however. In October 2004, Fogerty joined Springsteen and the E Street Band as their special guest on the politically themed Vote for Change tour; playing with the E Street crew, Fogerty performed some of his solo and CCR songs and dueted with Springsteen each night on "The Promised Land."

CCR came into existence in 1967, though the band actually formed in 1959 as the Blue Velvets. It signed with Fantasy Records in 1964 and became the Golliwogs before adopting the CCR moniker in 1967, after John Fogerty and Clifford returned after being drafted into military service. In its heyday, CCR was one of rock's quintessential singles bands, churning out songs that sounded great blasting out of an AM transistor radio and ruling the charts for much of 1969 and 1970. With heavy guitar riffs, rhythms that approximated supercharged rockabilly, and John Fogerty's impassioned vocals, CCR took songs like Dale Hawkins's "Suzie Q" and its own "Proud Mary," among many others, to the upper reaches of the pop charts. But CCR was also able to work the political unrest and societal upheaval of the late '60s and early '70s into equally radio-ready anthems such as "Fortunate Son," "Bad Moon Rising," "Run Through the Jungle," and "Who'll Stop the Rain."

Resentful of his brother's dominant role in the band, Tom Fogerty left in 1971. The rest of the group splintered the following year. Tom

Springsteen and fellow roots rocker John Fogerty, who was the lead singer for Creedence Clearwater Revival before launching his solo career, perform during the Vote for Change tour in October 2004.

recorded several albums with his band Ruby before dying of AIDS-related respiratory failure in 1990. Cook and Clifford worked with Doug Sahm and the country band Southern Pacific, and since the mid-'90s, have toured as Creedence Clearwater Revisited, much to John Fogerty's displeasure.

As for the erstwhile Creedence frontman, he's recorded sporadically over the years, often hampered in his efforts by legal hassles with Fantasy. His solo albums include *Centerfield* (1985), *Blue Moon Swamp* (1997), and *Déjà Vu All Over Again* (2004). In the fall of 2004, Fogerty appeared as part of the Vote for Change tour, performing with Springsteen in the midst of his set. Besides duetting with Springsteen on "The Promised Land," Fogerty performed "Fortunate Son," "Déjà Vu," "Proud Mary," "Bad Moon Rising," and "Travelin' Band" with the E Street Band throughout the tour. —*DD*

Jim Cretecos

Springsteen coproducer, 1973-74

Despite playing a significant role at the beginning of Bruce Springsteen's recording career, Jim Cretecos has become something of a footnote in the story; he helped build the foundation but wasn't around for the housewarming party. He was, however, the coproducer of record on Springsteen's first two albums, *Greetings from Asbury Park, N.J.* and *The Wild, the Innocent & the E Street Shuffle*, and someone who helped Springsteen, as a fledgling recording artist, learn the ropes in the studio.

Cretecos was a Tin Pan Alley songwriter; he partnered with Jeff Barry on "Lay a Little Lovin'," a Top 10 hit for *Hair* star Robert McNamara. In 1967 McNamara introduced Cretecos to Mike Appel, another songwriter; the two hit it off and began working together. "I liked Jimmy," Appel told *Down Thunder Road* author Marc Eliot. "He was very quick-witted, funny, and a very talented guy, a tech-head who loved to work the console knobs." When Appel signed on with the Wes Farrell Organization, he brought Cretecos in as his songwriting partner, though Cretecos never signed a contract with the organization. The duo were considered the "house hippies," more interested in hard and experimental rock than pop songs and commercial jingles; they began working with the groups Sir Lord Baltimore and Tumbleweed, but both became disappointing business situations. When early Springsteen manager Carl "Tinker" West sent his client to meet Appel and Cretecos in 1971, the two were initially cool to him. But when Springsteen returned in February 1972, they found him to be greatly matured as a songwriter and decided to make him their sole full-time concern, forming Laurel Canyon Ltd. as a management, production, and publishing company.

Appel handled the "daytime operations" while Cretecos—who was present at Springsteen's audition for CBS Records' John Hammond—focused on the studio, and he went on the road with Springsteen and his band as well. But early in 1974, Cretecos left Laurel Canyon. According to Appel, Cretecos was frustrated with the company's beleaguered finances and advocated a return to writing and producing other artists in addition to Springsteen. Cretecos had also recently married and, Appel said, his wife did not like him going out on the road or keeping late hours at the studio. "Jimmy kind of gave up," Appel said. The parting was amicable—initially; Appel paid Cretecos $1,500 for his share of Springsteen's publishing and the two agreed to work together on future projects. Later, however, Appel said the two men "had a falling out over the agreement. I had to settle with him again years later," although he did not specify the terms of that settlement.

Cretecos effectively disappeared from Springsteen's world after leaving Laurel Canyon; Springsteen did not acknowledge him in any way in his

Rock and Roll Hall of Fame induction speech in 1999. Cretecos surfaced in 1998, however, when some labels who were trying to distribute a collection of early Springsteen recordings—*Prodigal Son* and other collections—cited him as the source of the material. Cretecos denied having sold the tapes to anybody. —*GG*

"Dancing in the Dark"

Single release: May 9, 1984
Album: *Born in the U.S.A.* (Columbia, 1984)
Also on: *Greatest Hits* (Columbia, 1995), *The Essential Bruce Springsteen* (Columbia, 2003)
Chart peak: No. 2

The first single from *Born in the U.S.A.* was also the final song written and recorded for the album. After protracted recording sessions that dated back to May 1982, Bruce Springsteen felt he finally had the record together in March 1984. But coproducer and manager Jon Landau didn't; he told Springsteen that he felt they lacked a sure-fire hit single. An angry, exasperated Springsteen has acknowledged snapping at Landau, "I've written seventy songs. You want another one, *you* write it." The argument proved to be just the spark Springsteen needed to light his creative fire, however. He went back to his hotel in Los Angeles (where Bob Clearmountain was mixing tracks for the album) and poured out "Dancing in the Dark," a song that took stock of the isolation he felt after *The River*'s success and the frustrations he encountered in trying to come up with an album that satisfied him. While it was embraced as a feel-good pop anthem—"It went as far in the direction of pop music as I wanted to go—and probably a little farther," Springsteen noted in *Songs*—it was a dark and angry lament in which he declares, "I ain't nothing but tired/Man I'm just tired and bored with myself."

Springsteen and the E Street Band approached the song a couple of different ways, fiddling with the instrumental attack before coming up with the synthesizer-led arrangement that made the album, with Clarence

Clemons's saxophone taking the song into the fade. But Steve Van Zandt, who had left the E Street Band by this point but was still a close friend and confidant, did not hear its hit potential, telling Springsteen biographer Dave Marsh, "I said, 'This is a big mistake … If you're gonna throw something out, throw out ["Dancing in the Dark"] and "No Surrender" should be the first single.' That's how much I know."

"Dancing in the Dark" wound up being Springsteen's biggest hit to date, reaching No. 2 on the *Billboard* Top 100 (kept out initially by Duran Duran's "The Reflex" and then for many weeks by Prince's "When Doves Cry") and No. 4 in the U.K. It also snared Springsteen his first Grammy Award, for Best Rock Vocal Performance, Male, and was handed off to Arthur Baker for Springsteen's first-ever dance remix. The song's video, meanwhile, was directed by Brian De Palma and filmed at the opening date of the *Born in the U.S.A.* tour, on June 29, 1984, in St. Paul, Minnesota. A pre-"Friends" Courteney Cox appears as the fan who Springsteen yanks out of the front row to dance with him at the end of the song, a ritual he'd continue throughout the tour.

In the liner notes for *Greatest Hits*, Springsteen refers to it as "My big smash!" and recalls, "A bunch of autograph seeking Catholic schoolgirls came rushing up to me in the streets of N.Y.C., screaming they'd seen the video. Teen idol status at thirty-five! I enjoyed it." *—GG*

Darkness on the Edge of Town

Released: June 6, 1978
Producers: Jon Landau, Bruce Springsteen
Tracks: "Badlands," "Adam Raised a Cain," "Something in the Night," "Candy's Room," "Racing in the Street," "The Promised Land," "Factory," "Streets of Fire," "Prove It All Night," "Darkness on the Edge of Town"
Key outtakes: "Because the Night," "Don't Look Back," "Fire," "Frankie," "Hearts of Stone," "I Wanna Be With You," "Preacher's Daughter," "The Promise," "Rendezvous," "The Way"
Chart peak: No. 5

Shortly before Bruce Springsteen's fourth album, *Darkness on the Edge of Town*, was released, he told the *New York Times*, "I didn't want to do another album right away. If you start worrying about putting out a follow-up album, you get caught up in the machine of the industry." Maybe so, but it's fair to say that he didn't anticipate that *Darkness* would follow 1975's *Born to Run* by more than two-and-a-half years, mostly due to a bitter lawsuit with former manager Mike Appel that kept Springsteen out of the studio for a year.

Recording for *Darkness* formally began on June 1, 1977, four days after the lawsuit with Appel was settled, at Atlantic Studios in New York City.

But Springsteen and producer Jon Landau hardly started from a blank slate; though depression and frustration over the delay caused by the lawsuit affected his songwriting, Springsteen still came in with a healthy rash of first-rate tunes, including "The Promise," "Something in the Night," "Frankie," "Rendezvous," "Don't Look Back," and the album's eventual title track—some of which had already been road-tested by the perpetually touring band. The pent-up creative juices flowed quickly in the early days of recording, yielding songs such as "Fire," "Because the Night," "Drive All Night," an early version of "Sherry Darling" (later to surface on *The River*), and two numbers ("Candy's Boy" and "The Fast Song") that would morph into "Candy's Room."

Nevertheless, Springsteen notes in *Songs*, "The songs were difficult to write ... The songs came together slowly, line by line, piece by piece ... After *Born to Run*, I wanted to ensure that my music continued to have value and a sense of place ... I was searching for a tone somewhere between *Born to Run*'s spiritual hopefulness and '70s cynicism." Other influences on his writing as well this time, he explained, came from the "early pop class consciousness" of the Animals' "It's My Life" and "We Gotta Get Out of This Place," from a newfound interest in country music and Hank Williams, and from films such as John Ford's adaptation of *The Grapes of Wrath* and Jacques Tourneur's *Out of the Past.*

Writing mostly at a farm he was living on in Holmdel, New Jersey, Springsteen also tapped into childhood memories of watching his parents struggle to make ends meet. Combining all of this, he wrote about characters who "feel weathered, older, but not beaten. The sense of daily struggle in each song greatly increased. The possibility of transcendence or any sort of personal redemption felt a lot harder to come by." But he did not feel that the album was a downer, either. "I put on the first few seconds of "Badlands," the first song of the album," he told *Rolling Stone*, "those lines about 'I believe in the love and the hope and the faith.' It's there on all four corners of the album." But, he acknowledged, the album *was* intended to be "relentless." "On *Born to Run* there was the hope of a free ride. On *Darkness*, there ain't no free ride," he told *Crawdaddy*. "You wanna ride, you gotta pay. And maybe you'll make it through, but you ain't gonna make it through 'til you been beat, you been hurt, until you been messed up. There's hope, but it's just the hope of, like, survival."

Springsteen was also looking for an album that would "sound leaner and less grand than *Born to Run*," which was achieved by Chuck Plotkin and Jimmy Iovine, who mixed the album. Not everyone was impressed, however; E Street Band guitarist Steve Van Zandt, who was credited with "production assistance," is one who felt that *Darkness* was disappointing: "That record really is a shame; it didn't sound very good. It has some of his best and most important songs, some of his best guitar playing, and a terrible produc-

Springsteen and Steve Van Zandt perform in Detroit on the *Darkness* tour in on September 1, 1978. Although credited with "production assistance" on *Darkness*, Van Zandt has expressed his disappointment with that album's sound.

tion. The first thing I said to him when he told me about the *Greatest Hits* record was, 'Please let me go in and remix the *Darkness* songs.' He said, 'If we start that, man, this thing will come out in 2010.'"

Darkness, which switched from Atlantic Studios to New York's Record Plant, could actually have been a very different type of album as well. By most estimates Springsteen, Landau, and the E Street Band worked on some three dozen songs, including what Springsteen told *Rolling Stone* was "an album's worth of pop songs" such as "Rendezvous," "Fire," "I Wanna Be with You," and "Don't Look Back" (which was reportedly on the album until the last minute, when it was switched for "Darkness on the Edge of Town"). "There was a lot of variation in the material we recorded," he confirmed in *Songs*, "but I edited out anything I thought broke the album's tension." He told *Rolling Stone* that the ten tracks that made the final cut "were the most important for me to get out. I wanted to put out stuff that I felt had the most substance and yet was still an album." He did, however, hold back "The Promise" because he feared it would be misinterpreted as being about the lawsuit with Appel.

The album almost came out in the fall of 1977, titled *Badlands*; cover art was actually prepared, but Springsteen wasn't yet satisfied. Meanwhile, there was a swirl of outside activity involving Springsteen music: Southside Johnny & the Asbury Jukes were recording some of his songs for their *Hearts of Stone* album, which Van Zandt was producing; Robert Gordon took "Fire"; and Iovine, who was producing Patti Smith's *Easter*, snared "Because the Night," which became her biggest hit. Smith, meanwhile, introduced Springsteen to photographer Frank Stefanko, a meat-market worker by day who took the eventual cover shot for *Darkness* in his bedroom. Knowing that the long gap since *Born to Run* would result in plenty of scrutiny, Springsteen was overseeing every aspect of the album, including graphics; a month before its release he ordered a remix of "The Promised Land" with a new solo by Van Zandt, which meant remastering an entire side of the album.

Several titles were also considered for the album; besides *Badlands*, Springsteen also considered *Racing in the Streets*. Two more possibilities, *American Madness* and *History Is Made at Night*, came from good-naturedly flipping through the Andrew Sarris film textbook *The American Cinema: Directors and Directions 1929–1968*.

The excitement awaiting *Darkness* manifested itself in radio stations jumping the gun as soon as they got their copies. The Century Broadcasting Group, with outlets in Los Angeles, San Francisco, St. Louis, and Detroit, aired it first, on May 18, and CBS sent cease-and-desist telegrams the next morning. Other stations in

"**D**arkness passes the romantic delirium of *Born to Run*, cuts deeper, lingers longer."
—*Time*

"**I**f these songs are about experienced adulthood, they sacrifice none of rock 'n' roll's adolescent innocence ... It poses once more the question that rock 'n' roll's epiphanic moments always raise: Do you believe in magic? And once again, the answer is yes. Absolutely."
—*Rolling Stone*

"... an artful, passionate, rigorous record that walks a fine line between defeat and defiance, and if it had considerably more of the go-for-broke recklessness that it celebrates, it might have also been a great record."
—*Creem*

"**I**f it breaks the spell of high expectations imprisoning him, this debacle may yet enable Springsteen to give himself more of the psychological space he obviously needs to create music that sounds genuinely felt rather than hopefully contrived."
—*New Times*

"**P**ain never used to show on him ... But now he is owning up to it, doing for desperation what he did for release. The effect is unsettling, then staggering ...."
—*Crawdaddy*

"**A**n important minor artist or a rather flawed and inconsistent major one."
—*Village Voice*

New York and Cleveland and on Long Island also slipped the album on the air early.

And Springsteen, who started the *Darkness* tour two weeks before the album's release, told *Rolling Stone* that he was comforted in Philadelphia when "some kids ran backstage and said, 'Hey, that one was good, it was worth the wait.'" —*GG*

Clive Davis

CBS Records president 1967–73

Clive Davis was already a major player in the music industry when Bruce Springsteen auditioned for John Hammond in May 1972. At the head of the label since 1967 after coming up through its legal department, Davis had helped transition CBS Records into the rock era—doubling its sales in the process—by giving priority to existing artists such as Bob Dylan and also by signing Big Brother & the Holding Company (with Janis Joplin), the Electric Flag, Laura Nyro, the Chambers Brothers, Sly & the Family Stone, Chicago, and Blood, Sweat & Tears. His major rock signings also included Pink Floyd and Billy Joel. His oft-spoken motto was, "Creativity is king. Content is king." Davis concurred with Hammond's high opinion of Springsteen but admitted to *Backstreets*, "I never really knew the totality of what the artist could grow into. I knew about his writing skills, his poetry and lyrics, but I did not know this solitary figure would grow into the incredible live performer he would become. You sign people you feel are unique and have vision … but you don't know everything they will become as they evolve." Davis was highly impressed with Springsteen's steadfast devotion to his artistry but knew he wasn't dealing with a sucker, either; when he heard the first tapes for *Greetings from Asbury Park, N.J.*, Davis told Springsteen it lacked a "breakthrough radio cut." "Most artists, if you discuss that, they get very defensive," Davis noted, "but he said, 'You know, you're right. Let me spend some time with this.'" Springsteen then turned in "Blinded by the Light" and "Spirit in the Night." Davis, meanwhile, did his part in trying to break Springsteen, getting him an opening spot with Chicago (which proved to be a mistake) and also booking him on an attention-getting 1973 show in Los Angeles with Miles Davis and the Mahavishnu Orchestra.

When Davis was fired in May 1973, Springsteen lost a valuable supporter. Davis's chilly relationship with CBS Inc. president Arthur Taylor led to his dismissal from the label; the company sued him for expense account violations and intimated that Davis's business practices had resulted in governmental investigations into the record division. Davis has long denied the allegations. It didn't take him long to get back on his feet, however; he founded

Arista Records in 1974, building a strong lineup that over the years included Patti Smith, the Kinks, Barry Manilow, Whitney Houston, the Grateful Dead, Aretha Franklin, Sean "Puffy" Combs, Toni Braxton, Sarah McLachlan, Annie Lennox, Alicia Keys, and—for the multi-platinum, Grammy-gobbling *Supernatural* album—Santana, his onetime Columbia signing.

Davis was run out of Arista in 2000 after it was purchased by the German-owned Bertelsmann Group (BMG); as part of his severance agreement he set up J Records within the BMG fold and, after enjoying great success there, was made the head of RCA Records (which owned BMG) in 2003 and became a guiding force in all BMG operations—which in 2004 included a distribution merger with Sony Music, which had purchased CBS Records years before.

On January 28, 1997, Davis received a star on the Hollywood Walk of Fame. On March 6, 2000, he was inducted—by Patti Smith—into the Rock and Roll Hall of Fame as a nonperformer. —*GG*

Brian De Palma

Film and video director

It's hard to think of a less likely director for Bruce Springsteen's first conventional music video than Brian De Palma. Known mostly for his work in the suspense and horror genres, De Palma was nonetheless tapped to direct the clip for Springsteen's 1984 blockbuster "Dancing in the Dark." A devotee of Alfred Hitchcock, De Palma often emulated techniques made famous by his hero and even went so far as to hire Hitchcock's music director, Bernard Hermann, to score his 1973 film *Sisters*. De Palma's breakthrough was the 1976 adaptation of the Stephen King novel *Carrie*. He also directed *Blow Out*, *Body Double*, the gory cult classic *Scarface*, *The Untouchables*, and the disastrous *Bonfire of the Vanities*. He staged a commercial comeback, though, with the first *Mission: Impossible* film in 1996.

With the single already in heavy rotation on radio, the "Dancing in the Dark" video was filmed in St. Paul, Minnesota, during the first show of Springsteen's *Born in the U.S.A.* tour. Springsteen performed the song twice to accommodate filming, the only known time he's repeated a song in succession in a single concert. Some Springsteen fans were taken aback by the finished product, in part because it was the first time Springsteen made any concessions to the medium of music videos—such as lip-syncing. They also found it to be a bit too clean-cut and polished, from Springsteen's incessant grin to his ungainly jig to his plucking of a clean-scrubbed Courteney Cox (pre-"Friends" and pre-Arquette) from the front row for an onstage dance that became a ritual during the tour.

Noted film director Brian De Palma (left) oversees filming of the "Dancing in the Dark" video, shot live during a concert in St. Paul, Minnesota. Springsteen had to perform the song twice to accommodate filming—the only time he's ever played the same song two times in a row in the same concert.

Those concerns aside, the clip proved popular on MTV (which, after all, was the whole idea) and helped drive "Dancing in the Dark" to No. 2 on the *Billboard* Hot 100. —*DD*

"Dead Man Walking"

Song from 1995 movie of the same name

ruce Springsteen received his second Academy Award nomination for writing "Dead Man Walking," the desolate ballad that opens the soundtrack to his friend Tim Robbins's 1995 death-row movie of the same name. But, as he predicted, he didn't win a follow-up Academy Award to 1994's "Streets of Philadelphia." "Oh, I don't know; when those Disney pictures are out there (*Pocahontas*, the eventual winner), you don't stand a chance," he said, laughing, in a preceremony 1996 interview with *The Advocate*. "'Dead Man Walking' is another song that's pretty offbeat, so I am not really expecting one."

Springsteen performed the piece after the politically outspoken writer-pro-ducer-director Robbins and actress Susan Sarandon sent a letter to musicians they admired asking for contributions to the project. After viewing a screening in New York, Springsteen agreed, as did Steve Earle, Lyle Lovett, Eddie Vedder of Pearl Jam, Suzanne Vega, Tom Waits, Patti Smith, and Johnny Cash. "All these people have in some way inspired me to write, to make up stories," Robbins, the son of folk singer Gil Robbins, told the *Los Angeles Times*. "Bruce Springsteen's *Nebraska* is a big inspiration. Eddie's music has a real importance to it. So all these people writing for this film, it's like completing a circle."

Acclaimed as a multifaceted actor as well as a writer and director, Robbins's career started on TV (including bit parts in "Hill Street Blues" and "St. Elsewhere"), then turned to film in the mid-'80s, eventually leading to star turns in *Bull Durham*, *The Player*, *The Shawshank Redemption*, and *Short Cuts*. He was nominated for an Academy Award for Best Director for *Dead Man Walking*; Penn was nominated for Best Actor and Sarandon took home the trophy for Best Actress. Robbins later won the Oscar for Best Supporting Actor for 2003's *Mystic River*. He and his band Gob Roberts appeared on a bill including Pearl Jam as part of the Vote for Change tour in October 2004.

With its swirling background keyboards, provided by then-on-hiatus E Street Band organist Danny Federici, "Dead Man Walking" recalled the feel of "Streets of Philadelphia." Springsteen's acoustic guitar was much more prominent, however, and the lyrics are in narrative style, not dreamy first person. With a lyric that also appears in "Downbound Train," Springsteen sings, "I had a job, I had a girl," in the voice of a death-row inmate similar to Sean Penn's film character. "But between our dreams and actions lie this world." During *The Ghost of Tom Joad* tour, Springsteen frequently performed "Dead Man Walking" along with the new dark-and-sparse folk songs he had been doing solo on acoustic guitar. A few years later, he took a break from all that solemnity. The *New Musical Express* suggested he resembled Penn's charac-ter, and he responded: "I do? I didn't realize that. Help! I'm going home ... I don't have as much hair as he does, for a start." *—SK/GG*

Jonathan Demme

Film and video director

 n Academy Award–winning director (for the 1991 thriller *The Silence of the Lambs*), Jonathan Demme has done his share for capturing the excitement of rock 'n' roll on film as well. He directed the Talking Heads' groundbreaking concert movie *Stop Making Sense* as well as Neil Young's *The Complex Sessions* and Robyn Hitchcock's *Storefront Hitchcock.* Demme started out writing and directing low-budget movies for famed B-movie auteur Roger Corman (including the immortal women-in-prison flick *Caged Heat*). Eventually, he was trusted with weightier material, including quirky efforts such as *Melvin and Howard* and *Swimming to Cambodia*, the latter being a filmed version of Spaulding Gray's one-man show. *Something Wild* and *Married to the Mob* were offbeat, yet did respectable box office business. Demme's true critical and commercial breakthrough, though, was with *Silence*, which was a blockbuster hit and earned him an Oscar for Best Director.

In 1993, Demme asked Bruce Springsteen to write a song for *Philadelphia*, the story of a lawyer who is fired by the homophobic partners of his law firm when it is discovered he has AIDS. Springsteen won an Academy Award for his song "Streets of Philadelphia," which plays over the film's opening credits. Demme also directed the video for the song, which includes clips from the movie and a most unusual live vocal from Springsteen recorded as he walked the streets of the city. He would work with Springsteen again, directing the video for "Murder Incorporated," shot live in the New York City nightspot Tramps. He also got behind the cameras in 2000 to film a concert performance of Springsteen and the E Street Band's new arrangement of "If I Should Fall Behind." Demme has also directed videos for New Order and Fine Young Cannibals and produced such films as *Adaptation, That Thing You Do!* (a music-oriented flick starring Springsteen pal Tom Hanks), and *Mandela.* —*DD*

Carolyn Dennis. *See* **1992–93 Bruce Springsteen Touring Band.**
"Detroit Medley." *See* **Mitch Ryder.**
Amadou Diallo. *See* **"American Skin (41 Shots)."**

The Dixie Chicks

Country trio, political activists

 atalie Maines, the lead singer of the Texas country trio the Dixie Chicks, knew she'd probably ruffle a few feathers on March 10, 2003, when she told an audience in London, England—in the midst of the U.S. military buildup in the Persian Gulf—"Just so you know, we're ashamed the president of the United States is from Texas." The crowd in Britain, where the pending invasion of Iraq was vociferously opposed, appreciated Maines's remark. But back home the firestorm started almost before the Chicks (which also includes Emily Robison and Martie Maguire) reached their encore.

Radio stations removed the Chicks' music from their playlists and sponsored anti-Chicks demonstrations. Sales of their then-current album, *Home*, fell significantly. Fellow artists such as Lyle Lovett, Charlie Daniels, and Toby Keith criticized Maines. The South Carolina House of Representatives passed a motion calling on the group to perform for troops based in their state as a gesture of apology. The group was booed at the 2003 Academy of Country Music Awards ceremony.

Bruce Springsteen, however, was one of the few voices—along with Sheryl Crow, Vince Gill, and Faith Hill—that came to the Chicks' defense. While he didn't take a position on what Maines said (though he made his own stance against the war clear), he defended her right to say it in a posting on his brucespringsteen.net website: "The Dixie Chicks have taken a big hit lately for exercising their basic right to express themselves. To me, they're terrific American artists expressing American values by using their American right to free speech. For them to be banished wholesale from radio stations, and even entire radio networks, for speaking out is un-American. The pressure coming from the government and big business to enforce conformity of thought concerning the war and politics goes against everything that this country is about—namely freedom. Right now, we are supposedly fighting to create free speech in Iraq, at the same time that some are trying to intimidate and punish people for using that same freedom here at home. I don't know what happens next, but I do want to add my voice to those who think that the Dixie Chicks are getting a raw deal, and an un-American one to boot. I send them my support."

Maines ultimately issued an apology of sorts, saying that "it was the wrong wording" and noting that "whoever holds that office should be treated with the utmost respect." She did not, however, apologize for opposing the war. Bush, meanwhile, told NBC that the group was "free to speak their mind."

In October 2004, the Chicks joined Springsteen, Pearl Jam, R.E.M., John Mellencamp, Jackson Browne, and other artists on the Vote for Change tour, sharing a bill with James Taylor. "We must put an end to Mad Cowboy Disease," said Maines at the grand finale show in Washington, D.C., before the group's performance of "Truth No. 2." —*GG*

Dr. Zoom and the Sonic Boom

Short-lived early '70s band with horns, baton twirlers, and Monopoly players

 he brainchild of Bruce Springsteen, Dr. Zoom and the Sonic Boom was a short-lived hodgepodge of Asbury Park–area musicians and characters Springsteen knew from the boardwalk and local rock clubs.

Springsteen blended music with onstage histrionics that created a circuslike atmosphere whenever Dr. Zoom and the Sonic Boom performed—which wasn't often. The band, if it could be called that, had no set number of musicians; rather, Dr. Zoom and the Sonic Boom was loosely organized under the assumption that the crazy onstage antics and wall of sound the band produced would somehow be entertaining. "We had everybody I knew that could play an instrument ... and some that couldn't!" Springsteen told *Crawdaddy* magazine in 1973.

Springsteen formed the Sonic Boom in 1971, after the breakup of Steel Mill, his popular hard rock outfit that evolved from jams at the Asbury Park after-hours musicians' club, the Upstage. Not certain what to do next musically, Springsteen created a musical menagerie of rock, blues, and soul, not unlike that of Joe Cocker's then-popular Mad Dogs and Englishmen. Springsteen made the Sonic Boom unique by having musicians share the stage with baton twirlers, an emcee, and a table full of Monopoly players— the latter of which was a popular offstage activity for Jersey Shore musicians, with Springsteen known as a particularly cutthroat Monopolyist. Springsteen and some of the other members of the band even asked a local mechanic to work on a car engine onstage while they performed, but in the end it proved too much trouble and the idea was scratched.

The Sonic Boom played only a handful of dates before disbanding a few months after its inception. One of the band's performances occurred at the Asbury Park club the Sunshine Inn, where it opened for the Allman Brothers Band. In addition to Springsteen, other members of Dr. Zoom and the Sonic Boom were future E Street Band members Danny Federici and David Sancious (keyboards), Vini Lopez (drums), Garry Tallent (bass), and Steve Van Zandt (guitar), along with Southside Johnny Lyon (harmonica), Big Bobby Williams (drums), Kevin Connair (emcee), Big Danny Gallagher (Monopoly player), backup singers known as the Zoomettes, assorted local horn players, and whoever else was around to challenge Big Danny in the Atlantic City–themed board game.

Never meant to be anything musically meaningful or permanent, Dr. Zoom and the Sonic Boom did convince Springsteen that his next musical endeavor ought to include horns and backup singers. As the Sonic Boom faded, a new outfit, the Bruce Springsteen Band, took its place. —*RS*

DoubleTake **Benefit Concerts**

Music and conversation, February 2003

 oubleTake magazine first came to many Bruce Springsteen fans' attention with its twelfth quarterly publication. In that Spring 1998 issue, Springsteen was interviewed by Will Percy (nephew of the late Walker Percy, a writer Springsteen admires) in a wide-ranging discussion that's probably the most philosophical of his career. Percy and Springsteen discussed literature (the elder Percy's and more), pop culture, the role of writing and art in society, and the cult of celebrity. That issue's editorial also included something of a mission statement, illustrating why Springsteen would be drawn to the magazine (particularly at the tail end of *The Ghost of Tom Joad* era) and vice versa: "[W]e drew our founding inspiration from the collaborative Depression-era work of James Agee and Walker Evans, of Dorothea Lange and Paul Taylor, of photographers and writers who together explored aspects of a troubled nation's social reality, and then, in their different, yet complementary ways did compelling justice to what they had heard and witnessed."

Springsteen soon became friendly with *DoubleTake* founding editor Dr. Robert Coles, later praising Coles's book *A Secular Mind* and sitting in on one of his classes at Harvard. When *DoubleTake* began to flounder in 2003—the magazine was forced to take a "publishing break" following its Spring 2003 edition—Springsteen pitched in with a pair of benefit concerts for the magazine. On February 19 and 20, 2003, he played the tiny (900 capacity) Somerville Theatre in the magazine's hometown of Somerville, Massachusetts. Billed as "an intimate evening of music and conversation with Bruce Springsteen," each of the two nights found Springsteen playing solo, on brief hiatus from his tour supporting *The Rising* with the E Street Band. Introduced by Coles, Springsteen proceeded to strip down an even mix of songs from his entire catalog, on both acoustic guitar and piano—more akin to the legendary 1990 Christic Institute benefits than the more recent solo acoustic tour for *The Ghost of Tom Joad*.

What made the *DoubleTake* benefits truly unique was the unprecedented "conversation" element of the shows. Springsteen made a point of talking explicitly about his craft, touching on the creative process and genesis of songs as he went. After a lengthy absence, Springsteen the storyteller was back (he had remained relatively mum onstage for the recent E Street Band tours), and he clearly put a great deal of thought into these "master class"–style performances. As if line-by-line explications of "Growin' Up," "Blinded by the Light," and "Does This Bus Stop at 82nd Street?" weren't enough, Springsteen upped the ante by holding Q&A sessions from the stage after each performance. Unfortunately, the unmoderated questions devolved by the second night, to the point where Springsteen had to throw up his hands. Still, he more than held up his end of the "conversation" in Somerville, and many fans can only hope he'll try it again.

After the Somerville shows, in October 2003, Coles published *Bruce Springsteen's America: The People Listening, A Poet Singing* (Random House).

The benefit concerts didn't enable the magazine to resume publishing right away, however. After soliciting additional financial donations from supporters, the magazine officially ceased publishing by the fall of 2004. —*CP*

Drive All Night
Musical based on Springsteen songs

rive All Night, a musical based on Bruce Springsteen's songs, was the brainchild of actor-director Darrell Larson (he played the lead in the film *Mike's Murder*) and his collaborator, Stephanie Kerley Schwartz. They sculpted their plot from nearly three dozen tunes, raging from favorites such as "Hungry Heart," "Thunder Road," and "Brilliant Disguise" to rarities like "If I Was the Priest," "Protection," and "The Honeymooners." Even the then-fresh "Land of Hope and Dreams" was included as the closing number. The story traced the relationship of Eddie and Mary through their courtship and the rigors of married life.

Developed under the auspices of the Culture Project in New York City, a "reading" of the musical was held on March 12, 2002, in the Theater at St. Clement's. Springsteen, however, did not authorize *Drive All Night* to proceed further into full production, bringing the project to a quick end. —*GG*

Bob Dylan
Revered rock and folk troubadour

ruce Springsteen wasn't the first artist to be hailed as the "new Dylan," and he probably won't be the last. But he might be the only one of the "new Dylans" to create a body of work that could allow him to be considered worthy of the comparison. From the moment he signed with Columbia Records, Springsteen was likened to Bob Dylan and anointed his heir apparent. There were parallels to base that upon: like Dylan a decade before, Springsteen had also been signed to Columbia by John Hammond; and at the time of his meeting with Hammond, Springsteen had just read Anthony Scaduto's biography of Dylan. He told *Rolling Stone* magazine, "It was amazing to me, reading that book and then I find myself sitting there in that office."

The comparisons to Dylan could not have been surprising to Springsteen. The record company waged a full-scale promotional campaign based on the "new Dylan" hype. A 1973 *Rolling Stone* article said, "Much about Springsteen reminds people of Dylan—the slept-in appearance, the foggy manner, the twang, the lyrics, and the phrasing of his songs. It seems only natural that Hammond would have signed him." In the same article Hammond said of Springsteen, "He's much further along, much more developed than Bobby was when he came to me." A *Rolling Stone* review of Spring-steen's second album stated that his "debut album sounded like 'Subter-ranean Homesick Blues' played at 78, a typical five-minute track bursting with more words than this review." Eventually other "new Dylans" came along and the press allowed Springsteen his own identity.

Born Robert Allen Zimmerman in Duluth, Minnesota, Dylan emerged from New York's Greenwich Village folk scene to become not-so-arguably the most impactful singer-songwriter in contemporary music. He merged rock 'n' roll and folk sensibilities, creating an electric kind of social consciousness that gave his messages great relevance to the '60s counterculture—and beyond. His body of work spans more than four decades, has gone through periodic stylistic swings and movements (even embracing Christianity at one point in the late '70s), but has managed to endure and remain vital. As recently as 1998 he won a Grammy Award for Album of the Year for *Time Out of Mind.*

Springsteen never hid his admiration for Dylan, though some of his initial comments—like those in a 1974 interview with *Crawdaddy* founder Paul Williams—were somewhat dismissive; Springsteen said that he was mostly influenced by *Bringing It All Back Home, Highway 61, Blonde on Blonde,* and *John Wesley Harding,* but, at that point, had stopped listening to Dylan albums. But while inducting Dylan into the Rock and Roll Hall of Fame on January 20, 1988, Springsteen explained, "When I was a kid, Bob's voice somehow thrilled me and scared me, it made me feel kind of irresponsibly innocent—it still does—when it reached down and touched what little worldliness a fifteen-year-old high school kid in New Jersey had in him at the time. Dylan was a revolutionary. Bob freed the mind the way Elvis freed the body. He showed us that just because the music was innately physical did not mean that it was anti-intellectual. He had the vision and the talent to make a pop song that contained the whole world. He invented a new way a pop singer could sound, broke through the limita-tions of what a recording artist could achieve, and changed the face of rock 'n' roll forever."

Although they met on several occasions, Springsteen and Dylan appeared together publicly for the first time at the all-star recording of "We Are The World" on January 28, 1985, which was captured in a television doc-umentary and a music video. They were also on Little Steven's 1985 anti-apartheid record "Sun City," but their parts were recorded at separate ses-sions. They were both part of a star-packed jam session at the 1988 Rock and Roll Hall of Fame induction, but their first real performance together occurred on October 20, 1994, at Dylan's concert at New York's Roseland Ballroom; Dylan brought Neil Young and Springsteen on stage to play guitar

Springsteen is one of many musicians to be called "the new Dylan," but he's also one of the few to possibly live up to the billing. Here the two rock icons jam together at the Concert for the Rock and Roll Hall of Fame in Cleveland, Ohio, in September 1995.

at the end of the show. Nearly a year later, on September 2, 1995, Dylan and Springsteen shared the stage again in Cleveland, Ohio, at the Concert for the Rock and Roll Hall of Fame; during his set Dylan playfully introduced Springsteen, saying, "Now a buddy of mine is gonna come up and play one of my old songs—Mr. Bruce Springsteen. Let me hear you say 'Bruuuuce.'" The event was broadcast live over the cable network HBO, but their duet on "Forever Young" was inexplicably omitted from the CD release of the concert. (Springsteen had previously performed the song at a memorial service for John Hammond.) Two months later they both appeared at Frank Sinatra's eightieth birthday celebration at the Shrine Auditorium in Los Angeles, California, but performed separately.

Springsteen again honored Dylan on December 7, 1997, at the Kennedy Center Honors in Washington, D.C. He performed Dylan's "The Times They Are A-Changin'" at the televised event, introducing the song as a "beautiful call to arms in the struggle for social justice." Over the years Springsteen has performed several Dylan compositions, with "Chimes of Freedom" being the only one to see official release. "Highway 61 Revisited" was the song they performed together when Dylan was Springsteen's guest at the final show of *The Rising* tour on October 4, 2003, at New York's Shea Stadium.

For his part, Dylan thus far has performed only one Bruce Springsteen composition; a one-time 1990 concert version of "Dancing in the Dark." But "Tweeter and the Monkey Man," one of Dylan's contributions to the Traveling Wilbury's first album, is a song filled with Springsteen imagery and direct lyrical references.

In the Rock and Roll Hall of Fame induction speech, Springsteen assessed Dylan's tremendous influence while effectively making the case they there's never been a need for any "new Dylans." To this day, whenever great rock music is being made, there is the shadow of Bob Dylan. Bob's own modern work has gone unjustly underappreciated because it's had to stand in that shadow. —*RB*

The E Street Band

"The heart-stoppin', earth shakin', earth-quakin', heart-breakin', air-conditioner-shakin', history-makin', legendary" touring and recording band

ruce Springsteen's "longtime compadres and collaborators and great friends," as he described its members in 2002, the E Street Band is easily one of rock 'n' roll's longest running, most esteemed group of musicians. The band backed Springsteen at every step from 1972 through 1988, becoming so seemingly inseparable from his music that the majority of fans—as well as band members—were bewildered when he chose to work with other musicians in 1989. Though Springsteen distanced himself from the band in the late '80s and for much of the '90s, and he was inducted into the Rock and Roll Hall of Fame without them, his legacy will always be entwined with these "blood brothers." As the E Street Band's 1999 "rededication" suggests, Springsteen wouldn't have it any other way.

Post-punk detractors have derided the E Street Band as too baroque, with its signature saxophone and twin keyboards (and, upon occasion, accordion, glockenspiel, and even tuba). But the experience, versatility, and adaptability of these crack musicians have increasingly made any notion of an "E Street sound" an elusive one. Over the years they have been able to conjure up nearly any music Springsteen had in his head—from the carnival jangle of the Asbury Park boardwalk to the wall of sound of Phil Spector, from jazz-inflected R&B to lean rockabilly, from plaintive country ballads to driving rock 'n' roll. In every case, their power, precision, and professionalism have been a hallmark of Springsteen's recordings and performances. Beyond their musicianship, the E Street Band came to embody much of what was in the music, as Springsteen recently observed: "They were symbols of a lot of what I wrote about: trust, loyalty, friendship. In some ways they were the physical realization of the community I imagined and sang about in the songs."

Though it's hard to imagine his career without the E Street Band, Springsteen was signed to Columbia Records as a solo artist. He had fronted an evolving series of bands in the late '60s and early '70s—Child became Steel Mill, then Dr. Zoom and the Sonic Boom, then the Bruce Springsteen Band—but by the spring of 1972 Springsteen was going it alone. That's how manager Mike Appel envisioned his music, and that's how John Hammond signed him to the label. Recording for his debut that summer, however, Springsteen insisted on bringing some of his Asbury Park compatriots into the studio. While the resulting *Greetings from Asbury Park, N.J.* was a midpoint between a solo and a band effort, the E Street Band soon became as integral to Springsteen's recordings as to his live shows.

Originally the core of the Bruce Springsteen Band, the 1972 E Street Band included Garry W. Tallent (bass), Clarence Clemons (saxophone), Danny Federici (organ), and Vini "Mad Dog" Lopez (drums). Prior to recording with Springsteen, Clemons played in Norman Seldin's band, Joyful Noyze. The others had been with Springsteen longer—Lopez and Federici since Child in 1969, Tallent since Dr. Zoom in 1971. Following the *Greetings* sessions, they played their first show billed as the E Street Band on October 28, 1972, in West Chester, Pennsylvania. The group had rehearsed for the *Greetings* album at the Belmar home of piano player David Sancious's mother, and they took their name from that address: 1105 E Street. Sancious himself, previously part of the Bruce Springsteen Band and a player on *Greetings*, didn't become a touring E Street Band member until mid-1973. With his official addition on June 22, joining the band for a stand at Fat City in Seaside Heights, New Jersey, the E Street foundation was complete. The band immediately began work on a second album.

The lineup of Tallent, Clemons, Lopez, Federici, and Sancious only survived for one Springsteen record, and appropriately his jazziest—*The Wild, the Innocent & the E Street Shuffle*. Just a few months after the album's November 1973 release, the departure of Lopez in early 1974 was the first of several major changes to the group that year. Though his loose drumming style might have been a poor fit with Springsteen's next direction, it was Lopez's "Mad Dog" behavior that ultimately got him fired after a fight with Mike Appel's brother. "(We) had a few words," Lopez later told *Backstreets* magazine. "I pushed him and he went down. After that, I was told I was to leave the band." Lopez has since been an occasional guest drummer at

Springsteen's New Jersey shows. He formed Steel Mill Retro in 2003 to revisit pre–E Street tunes (with Springsteen's blessing).

Lopez's last show was February 12, 1974. Although the drummerless E Street Band had to cancel a couple of dates, it returned to the stage a mere eleven days later with new drummer Ernest "Boom" Carter, a friend of Sancious who played his first gig with the E Street Band on February 23 after two days of rehearsal. His stint with the band would be brief but busy, between nonstop gigging and studio work for Springsteen's next record. Only one song with Carter would end up on the third album, but it would be a classic: the title track to *Born to Run*. Two months in the making, "Born to Run" was finally finished in August. Sancious then left to pursue a solo career, and he took his drummer pal with him. Sancious and Carter played their last show with the E Street Band on August 14; they formed Tone, a jazz fusion band that also featured future E Streeter Patti Scialfa on vocals. Sancious would record with Springsteen again in the early '90s, playing keyboards on a couple of songs from the *Human Touch* sessions.

Heading into the fall of 1974, and with a third album far from finished, only three members of the E Street Band remained. To fill out the roster, Springsteen placed a classified in the *Village Voice*. The ad called not only for a drummer ("no jr. Ginger Bakers, must encompass R&B and jazz") and pianist ("classical to Jerry Lee Lewis"), but also trumpet and violin players. To replace Carter and Sancious, Springsteen auditioned thirty drummers and thirty piano players at Studio Instrument Rentals in New York. He found Roy Bittan, a technically advanced pianist soon dubbed "The Professor," and "Mighty" Max Weinberg, a powerful drummer who shared the band's Jersey roots. Pointing to the importance of the stage show, both Bittan and Weinberg had experience on Broadway (Weinberg was fresh from the pit of *Godspell*; Bittan had toured with *Jesus Christ Superstar*). The pair would join Federici, Tallent, and Clemons as permanent fixtures of the E Street Band to the present day. Weinberg recalled the invitation from Springsteen: "If you want the job you can have it. It pays seventy-five dollars a week." Weinberg: "I'll take it."

After canceling a few gigs to rehearse in early September, the E Street Band's first shows with Bittan and Weinberg were on September 18–19, 1974, at the Main Point in Bryn Mawr, Pennsylvania. Also making her E Street debut on those nights was the band's first female member, Suki Lahav on violin. Not part of the *Village Voice* auditions, she was the wife of engineer Louis Lahav, who worked on Springsteen's first two albums. Her run with the band lasted only as long as Carter's (her last show was March 9, 1975) before she moved to Israel with her husband. During that period, Lahav also took part in the *Born to Run* sessions, making her mark on "Jungleland." More than twenty-five years would pass before another violinist would be among the E Street ranks.

The final piece of the E Street puzzle came during the grueling *Born to Run* recording sessions in late spring of 1975. "Miami" Steve Van Zandt— one of Springsteen's oldest friends and a musical cohort who had played in Steel Mill and Dr. Zoom and the Sonic Boom—had a knack for arrangements, and he came to the studio to help out with horns as the band struggled with "Tenth Avenue Freeze-Out." Before long, Van Zandt would officially join the band on guitar and vocals, supplementing Springsteen in style on both counts and joining Clemons, "The Big Man," as a second onstage foil when the *Born to Run* tour began on July 20, 1975.

The addition of Van Zandt solidified a lineup that would last into the next decade. This is the E Street Band that would go with Springsteen from small clubs to arenas to international stardom. While that was a gradual process, the "hype" started fast and furious soon after Van Zandt's arrival, and it wouldn't be just for Springsteen. After now-legendary shows that August at the Bottom Line in New York City, *Rolling Stone* magazine declared, "This group may very well be the great American rock & roll band," while the *New York Times* called it "one of the best rock bands anybody has ever heard."

Just when the hype might have gotten to be too much, a contractual dispute between Springsteen and Appel following the *Born to Run* tour put the brakes on. Since the lawsuit kept them out of the studio, delaying a fourth album, the band gigged constantly in 1976–77, both to make a living and to stave off boredom. The Chicken Scratch Tour, named for its haphazard itinerary, began on March 25, 1976—with occasional stops in the studio, not for Springsteen but for Van Zandt's continuing production of the Asbury Jukes and for a version of Billy Joel's "Say Goodbye to Hollywood" with Ronnie Spector. On the road at that time the E Steeters were supplemented by two versions of the Miami Horns, so named because they were directed by Van Zandt.

The resolution of the lawsuit in mid-1977 ushered in a golden era for the E Street Band. After finally recording a fourth album, they embarked on the *Darkness on the Edge of Town* tour in 1978, playing theaters and arenas around the U.S.—a seven-month trek that many considered the apex of Springsteen's performing career (even if, on tours that followed, he has seemed to provide nightly evidence to the contrary). Within four months of the *Darkness* tour's end, the band was back in the studio for *The River*, with Van Zandt joining Springsteen and Jon Landau as coproducer. Partly due to the guitarist's influence, sessions focused on capturing the band's live sound, often with the group recording together in one room. For both *Darkness* and *The River* (1980), Springsteen's legendary songwriting prolificacy was at its height, and the band recorded copious amounts of material. *The River* swelled to a double album, with numerous E Street recordings left over and unreleased (and later forming arguably the strongest portion of the 1998 outtakes collection, *Tracks*).

The tour that followed, beginning October 3, 1980, was the largest yet in scope. While the *Darkness* tour mixed theaters with a few larger venues, the tour for *The River* moved into sports arenas and coliseums around the U.S. Lasting nearly a year (in the middle of which they were picked by *Rolling Stone* readers as Band of the Year), it also took the E Street Band on a full-scale European tour for the first time. The group had played a handful of dates in Europe in 1975 to mixed reviews and didn't leave North America for another five-and-a-half years; when it crossed the Atlantic again in 1981, it was for a triumphant thirty-four-show run in twelve countries that cemented Springsteen's status as an international rock star.

Ironically, the unequivocal triumph of the 1980–81 tour presented a new and difficult challenge to Springsteen and the band—how to move forward once a dream becomes reality. Springsteen would later describe that post-tour period as a time "when I had to put my old dreams down, because I had grown beyond them." As, presumably, had Van Zandt, who accepted an offer from EMI-America to record a solo album, a decision that would lead to him leaving the group—though not until 1984, making it the E Street Band's first personnel change in nearly nine years. But Van Zandt was still on board for studio sessions in the early '80s. Following *The River*, the E Street Band recorded two albums with Gary U.S. Bonds—his comeback *Dedication* in 1981 (recorded between legs of *The River* tour), and *On the Line* in 1982. Van Zandt coproduced both records along with Springsteen; meanwhile, though still an E Street Band member, he worked on his first solo album, *Men Without Women*.

In April 1982, following the *On the Line* sessions, Springsteen and the E Street Band began work on their follow-up to *The River*. More than half of the songs that would eventually be on *Born in the U.S.A.* were recorded by the band that May, but that full-band album would still be two years in the making. It was delayed by an unanticipated solo album that was a vast departure for Springsteen—*Nebraska*, a collection of stark solo performances that Springsteen recorded as demos at home on a four-track recorder. Springsteen tried the *Nebraska* material with the band but was unable to capture the spirit of those home recordings. He decided to put the demos out as is, and *Nebraska* became Springsteen's first detour off E Street.

Eschewing any kind of tour for *Nebraska*, Springsteen resumed the full-band sessions for a rock record that would be far different in tone. Van Zandt was again on board as coproducer, taking the live-in-the-studio aesthetic from *The River* to its ultimate conclusion. In the spring of 1984, just months before the release of *Born in the U.S.A.*, Van Zandt—who had ditched the Miami moniker and was now known as Little Steven—left the E Street Band. He announced his departure in April, and a May 29 press release made it official. "The split was amicable," read the EMI release, "and Van

Zandt and Springsteen remain the best of friends." With a summer tour around the corner, the empty slot was quickly filled by guitarist extraordinaire Nils Lofgren, well known for his previous work with Neil Young and as an artist in his own right (both solo and with his band Grin). Lofgren joined the E Street Band on May 15, playing his first show on June 8 at the Stone Pony in Asbury Park, New Jersey, after a few weeks of rehearsal; this warm-up show was the E Street Band's first gig in thirty-three months.

Also joining the E Street Band for the *Born in the U.S.A.* tour was Patti Scialfa on backing vocals. A graduate of Asbury Park High School, Scialfa went on to study music in Miami and New York, and had previously auditioned for Springsteen when he was considering taking backup singers on the road in the '70s. Making a go of it as a singer/songwriter in the late '70s and early '80s, she gradually reconnected with Asbury musicians, sang with Southside Johnny & the Asbury Jukes, and performed at the Stone Pony. On June 25, 1984, a mere four days before the tour opener in St. Paul, she became the band's first female member since Suki Lahav.

The *Born in the U.S.A.* tour made Springsteen and the E Street Band a truly global concern. On a tour lasting more than sixteen months, the band played its first shows in Japan and Australia, eventually graduating to stadiums. Longtime fans embraced Lofgren and Scialfa, and the E Street Band was again named Band of the Year in the *Rolling Stone* Music Awards, this time by both readers and critics. Even in the thick of his solo career, Van Zandt couldn't resist making occasional guest appearances: his presence in the "Glory Days" video, for one, made it seem like he'd never left the band; and the August 20, 1984, show at Brendan Byrne Arena in East Rutherford, New Jersey, featured the return of both Van Zandt and yet another version of the Miami Horns. Van Zandt also guested at a Giants Stadium show a year later, as well as in Memphis, Atlanta, and London. For these brief moments, what would become the quintessential modern-day E Street Band was onstage—Federici, Tallent, Clemons, Weinberg, Bittan, Lofgren, Scialfa, and Van Zandt. Capping the *Born in the U.S.A.* extravaganza was Springsteen's first live release, 1986's *Live/1975–85.* Comprised of five LPs, the box set was heavily edited and occasionally disjointed, but it finally captured the band live, collecting a decade's worth of its finer performances. Appropriately, and finally, it was the first album to officially bill the E Street Band.

The 1987 release of *Tunnel of Love* marked a significant change in Springsteen's recording style and showed perhaps the first sign that he was moving away from his longtime collaborators. While the solo nature of *Nebraska* had been happenstance, for the *Tunnel* album Springsteen "wanted to get back to the intimacy of home recording." While each E Street Band member appeared on the album (most notably Weinberg, who overdubbed percussion on eight of the twelve tracks), it was largely recorded by Springsteen himself in his home studio. The album was released on October 6, 1987, and within a few weeks the E Street Band, less familiar with the new material than usual, began rehearsals for a tour that wouldn't start for another four months. When the Tunnel of Love Express Tour began on February 25, 1988, the band's line-up was unchanged from the *Born in the U.S.A.* tour. But there was one addition: the Horns of Love, the first horn section on a Springsteen tour since 1977. Springsteen also changed the E Street Band musicians' positions on stage for the tour—most notably bringing Scialfa down front, where she played a much more intrinsic role in the performances. The Express Tour, having once again moved to stadiums by its end, wrapped up on August 3 in Barcelona, Spain. A month later, the E Street Band went back out with Springsteen for Amnesty International's Human Rights Now! tour (sans horns, except for a show in Philadelphia). Coincidentally, the Amnesty tour reunited them with Sancious, by then a member of Peter Gabriel's band. For a month and a half, the E Streeters toured the world, playing countries (even continents) they never had before, including Costa Rica, India, Greece, Zimbabwe, Brazil, and Argentina. Not bad for a swan song. The October 15, 1988, tour closer in Buenos Aries would be their last show together as a full band before the greatest paradigm shift of their careers. For the next year, Springsteen and the band were on unofficial hiatus, with some members occasionally playing together, but largely doing their own thing while waiting for the next E Street Band project. Springsteen recorded "Viva Las Vegas" for an Elvis Presley tribute album with other musicians in September 1989, but the phone call each E Streeter received the next month still came as a shock.

On October 18, 1989, Springsteen telephoned each E Street Band member to tell them that they should "feel free to accept other offers." To some degree, this was merely stating the obvious; Springsteen had been moving in this direction for some time, with *Born in the U.S.A.* the only full-band studio recording since 1980, and band members had consistently recorded with other artists during lulls in E Street activity. Their history together, as well as Springsteen's choice of words, suggested that this wasn't a permanent rift; as Weinberg told the *Asbury Park Press*: "The concept of being fired doesn't even apply after almost two decades of working with Bruce." But "Bruce Fires E Street Band" was how the story became told, and for all intents and purposes, Springsteen broke up the band with that phone call. Looking back on it in 2002, Federici told NBC's "Today," "It was a shock. I didn't expect it. It was a surprise." Weinberg called it "earth-shattering." Clemons said, "It broke my heart." In 2001, however, Springsteen said he didn't think his decision led to any kind of long-term grudge: "I'm sure they didn't like it, but there wasn't really that kind of (angry) feeling ... I think we've had such a long history; I think that over a long period of time, the

The E Street Band, including (from left) Clarence Clemons, Max Weinberg, Springsteen, and Garry Tallent, headlined a free outdoor show at Kean College in Union Township, New Jersey, on September 22, 1974.

totality of our relationships have been so positive. We've done so much for each other in so many different ways that it was just part of the whole thing."

As if to immediately say "no hard feelings," Springsteen joined Clemons and his solo band on stage for a few songs before the end of 1989. But over the next five-plus years, only Roy Bittan would work with Springsteen on any kind of consistent basis (besides Scialfa, of course, who married Springsteen in 1991). Bittan and Springsteen cowrote two songs for 1992's *Human Touch*, and Bittan was the sole E Street carryover to Springsteen's 1992–93 touring band. Springsteen didn't address the split publicly until 1992, when he told *Rolling Stone*, "I played with the E Street Band— some of the guys—since we were eighteen. I felt like I'd gone a long time really playing with the same people, and I hadn't had a chance to go out and see what other people are going to bring to what I'm doing. And I think there's some responsibility to try and step out a little bit."

There's never a shortage of silly showmanship at an E Street Band performance. From left, Clarence Clemons, Springsteen, Garry Tallent, and Steve Van Zandt ham it up at a December 31, 1980, show at Nassau Coliseum in Uniondale, New York.

On the other hand, he added, "When you've spent that kind of time with people, it's like an imprint on your soul, that never goes away." Illustrating that fact, members of the E Street Band made guest appearances throughout the 1992–93 tour. But it wasn't until early 1995, after Springsteen's Academy Award–winning solo success with "Streets of Philadelphia," that another phone call finally brought the band back together. The occasion was Springsteen's *Greatest Hits*, the first such collection of his career, and he wanted to reunite the band to add new studio tracks to the collection. The calls came on January 5; four days later, the entire band, now including both Van Zandt and Lofgren on guitar, was recording at the Hit Factory in New York City. Springsteen soon told VH1, "I think everybody plays together better now than we did when we stopped. People had gotten better at their instruments and better as an ensemble." As Lofgren put it, "We clicked right off the bat." This first reunion was documented by filmmaker Ernie Fritz in the feature-length *Blood Brothers*, its title taken from a

Springsteen and the band closed out the successful 2002–2003 tour in support of *The Rising* with a series of concerts at Shea Stadium in New York City, including this show on October 1. With Springsteen front and center on guitar, the rest of that iteration of the band included Max Weinberg (rear, on drums) and (left to right) Nils Lofgren, Clarence Clemons, Steve Van Zandt, Patti Scialfa, and Garry Tallent.

new song from these sessions that was inspired by Springsteen's relationship with the band.

In conjunction with *Greatest Hits*, Springsteen took the E Street Band back to the concert stage as well, performing several New York shows together in early 1995—February 21 at Tramps, April 5 on "The Late Show with David Letterman," and later that same night at Sony Studios. But a tour was not in the cards, and Springsteen made it clear that his solo itch wasn't behind him. He told the *New York Times*: "I simply want to do both things, like what Neil Young does with Crazy Horse. He'll go and do a project with different musicians, and then he'll come back and play with Crazy Horse when he has something that feels right for them." As if to demonstrate, Bruce played one more show with the E Street Band that year, inaugurating the Rock and Roll Hall of Fame and Museum on September 2 in Cleveland—before

The E Street Band opens a ten-show stand at Giants Stadium on July 15, 2003. From left: Nils Lofgren, Clarence Clemons, Springsteen, Max Weinberg (on drums), Steve Van Zandt, Patti Scialfa, and Garry Tallent.

embarking on his first solo acoustic tour to support *The Ghost of Tom Joad*, which continued well into 1997.

The E Street Band's next performance together would be another Rock Hall event, three-and-a-half years later: Springsteen's own induction as a performer on March 15, 1999. A more permanent reunion was just around the corner; within days, Springsteen and the E Street Band would be hitting the road together, their first tour in more than a decade. But there was a touch of controversy regarding the Hall of Fame induction. Springsteen was nominated as a solo artist, for his entire body of work since 1973. The lack of a similar honor for the E Street Band became the subject of much debate among many in the rock world—critics, fans, and industry-types alike. Technically, Hall of Fame rules dictate that artists "become eligible for induction twenty-five years after the release of their first record." Since the E Street Band wasn't officially listed as the artist on a Springsteen release until the *Live/1975–85* box in 1986, Hall of Fame Foundation officials argued that it still had another thirteen years to wait (though it might be argued that the 1977 single with Ronnie Spector would meet the criteria). The Hall's Side Men category was introduced the following year, to accommodate similarly overlooked players.

While the E Street Band members have yet to be inducted, either as Performers or Side Men, their contributions didn't go unnoticed on the night of Springsteen's honor. In his induction speech, U2's Bono made sure to note that Springsteen "surrounded himself with fellow believers. The E Street Band wasn't just a great rock group, or a street gang. It was a brotherhood." Springsteen himself thanked each member by name, from Lopez on up, and even acknowledged the controversy: "Everybody wants to know how I feel about the band. Hell, I married one of 'em!" He went on to conclude: "My wife, my great friends, my great collaborators, my great band. Your presence tonight honors me, and I wouldn't be standing up here tonight without you, and I can't stand up here now without you. Please join me."

After performing three songs with Springsteen that night, the main event started a few days later as they embarked on a full-scale U.S./European tour. The reunion tour would last through July 2000. Opening with a warm-up show before an Asbury Park crowd on March 18, Springsteen made his intent clear: "This is kind of a special night for us, because its a rededication of our band, and the job that we do, and our commitment to serve. So it's a big, big night." Over the course of the tour, the E Street Band debuted several new songs, including "Land of Hope and Dreams," "Further On (Up the Road)," "American Skin (41 Shots)," "Code of Silence," and "Another Thin Line." The group revisited Springsteen's vast back catalog, giving the first live airing of long-lost E Street outtakes from the newly released *Tracks* box set. The musicians also put their stamp on Springsteen's off–E Street material, such as "Youngstown," "Human Touch," and "If I Should Fall Behind." At the tour's final show (July 1, 2000, at Madison Square Garden), an emotional "Blood Brothers" led to an impromptu chant from the audience that seemed to surprise and touch everyone on stage: "E Street Band! E Street Band!" The 1999–2000 tour was documented on the *Live in New York City* album and DVD, both of which, like *Live/1975–85*, were credited to Bruce Springsteen and the E Street Band.

Of the reunion tour, Springsteen said, "I felt it was the best E Street Band that I ever stood on stage with. To be able to do that, to grapple with the subjects we grappled with for our whole career, to stand there with your great friends and to take those ideas forward, and to give people some new experience and hopefully new inspiration, that's what we're always trying for. It doesn't get any better."

Seen as a "going concern" by both Springsteen and the band members, the group entered the studio together following the tour. *The Rising*, released in 2002, marked the first studio album fully recorded with the E Street Band since 1984's *Born in the U.S.A.* The resulting 2002–03 tour brought one more addition to the roster: Scialfa's old friend Soozie Tyrell on violin and vocals. Featured prominently on *The Rising*, Tyrell had been a contributor to Springsteen recordings for some time—from "Shut Out the Light" in the early '80s to *Lucky Town* (1992) and *The Ghost of Tom Joad* (1995); she'd also performed live with Springsteen on the *Tom Joad* acoustic tour and at his Asbury Park holiday shows. Whether or not *The Rising* tour made her a full-fledged E Street Band member remains a question—even to Tyrell herself. She told *Backstreets* mid-tour, "I don't think that officially I am, but when I'm up there playing with them I feel a part of the band. Probably by the second or third tour, if I'm ever asked again, I may be." In any case, Tyrell's violin added a dimension to the band's sound that had been largely missing since 1975. In addition to Europe and North America, *The Rising* tour took the E Street Band to Australia (for the first time since 1985) and New Zealand. Once again, they filled massive stadiums, nearly two decades after the height of the *Born in the U.S.A.* craze.

With two lengthy international tours in four years, Springsteen made it clear that the "rededication" of the E Street Band was not to be taken lightly. Ever since those 1989 phone calls, it's been on the table that Springsteen will keep his options open but that the E Street Band will likely remain a going concern for the rest of his career. "I don't think I'd want to have to choose between the band and the solo stuff," he wrote in *Songs*. "I'd like to have both. One of the things I realized when I saw the guys [in 1995] was that we're like each other's arms and legs." However the E Street Band factors into Springsteen's plans, Van Zandt promised in early 2004, "We will make another record, and we will be back for sure." In October 2004, the band headlined seven shows as part of the Vote for Change tour.

Particularly in the world of rock 'n' roll, the band's longevity is remarkable; prior to *The Rising* tour, Springsteen remarked, "One of the things I'm proudest about in my life right now is that everybody survived, is alive and healthy. It's a business where that's rare." Yet, as opposed to many wizened rock acts, survival is only a starting point when it comes to their performances. Springsteen described the E Street Band's post-rededication goal: "We're gonna go out, and we're gonna be better than we ever were. We're not gonna be just as good, we're gonna fight to be better than we ever were." That philosophy, instilled by Springsteen from the early days, is what makes the E Street Band great. "We're very aware of going onstage and playing each show as if it's our last show," Weinberg said in 2002. "With that kind of energy, that kind of inspiration that you pull out from your gut, I think that's the core of the E Street Band experience. And Bruce taught us all that in the beginning. I remember him saying very early on, 'It's one night for us, but the person out there, they might have been waiting a month to see the show.' We owed it to ourselves and to them to put on our best show, and play it as if it's our last." —*CP*

Steve Earle

Singer, songwriter, performer, playwright

J ust as Bruce Springsteen got tired of the "new Dylan" comparisons, Steve Earle was anxious to peel off "the hillbilly Bruce Springsteen" sticker that critics slapped on him when he released his first album, *Guitar Town*, in 1986. But Earle, whose early work made him something of a country insurgent, has freely admitted the magnitude of Springsteen's influence on that album, particularly via *Born in the U.S.A.*

Virginia native Earle caught a Springsteen show on the 1985 tour promoting that album two weeks before he started writing songs for his disc. "It's one of the best shows I've ever seen to this day and it influenced me as a performer for the rest of my career," he told the *Chicago Tribune*. Earle said Springsteen's work gave him the revelation that he could make a thematically unified album, something that was meant to be heard in its entirety. And he could do it regardless of what the Nashville establishment thought. Ever since then, Earle—who bridged the rock-country divide after doing a stint in jail for drug possession in 1994—has been committed to doing it his way, both musically and politically. He's an outspoken advocate of banning the death penalty and land mines, and a tenacious fighter for welfare rights. He's had more freedom to do that since forming his own E-Squared record label and hooking up with Artemis Records, run by fellow human rights advocate and major-label refugee Danny Goldberg.

Earle credits Springsteen not only with inspiring his work but with elevating his profile dramatically just by buying that first album. E Street Band bassist Garry Tallent, a Nashville resident, knew some of Earle's band members and obtained the record. He tipped Springsteen off about it, and Springsteen—at the height of his fame—went to a record store and picked it up. Someone saw him, and word of his purchase ended up in *Billboard* magazine. It was a quiet but effective endorsement. Earle, meanwhile, has paid tribute to Springsteen on record. His 2002 reissue of *Guitar Town* added his live cover of Springsteen's "State Trooper," which had previously been part of a twelve-inch single from the original album. Earle has also covered "Nebraska" and performed "Racing in the Street" live with its author. Springsteen showed up as a surprise encore guest during Earle's February 6, 1998, show at the former Tradewinds club in Sea Bright, New Jersey; they did Carl Perkins's "Everybody's Trying to Be My Baby," the Rolling Stones' "Sweet Virginia" and "Dead Flowers," and Earle's own "Guitar Town," "I Ain't Ever Satisfied," and "Johnny Come Lately."

When he taught a class at Chicago's Old Town School of Folk Music in 2000, Earle discussed how some of today's best songwriters share a lineage tracing directly back to traditional folk. A class participant reported that Earle devoted an entire session to *Nebraska* and called "State Trooper" "the scariest fucking song I've ever heard." He also played the album's title tune for the class, saying, "and this is the second scariest song." One of the more intriguing aspects of their relationship has nothing to do with their own interactions, but the dichotomy between Springsteen's elevation to the pedestal of post–September 11 musical hero and the media-fueled demonization of Earle as his evil opposite. Springsteen was able to question American and worldwide reactions to September 11 on his 2002 album *The Rising*, which was seen as an unflinching but not antagonistic examination of events—and more importantly, a catharsis for a wounded nation. Earle almost simultaneously released *Jerusalem*, an album that also contained songs expressing his take on the September 11 tragedy and was occasionally reviewed in tandem with *The Rising*. Significantly, the song "Jerusalem" conveys Earle's wish for peace. But in "John Walker's Blues," which gained notoriety even before the album came out, he peers into the heart of John Walker Lindh, a young American who became a Taliban soldier captured during the subsequent military invasion of Afghanistan. Earle neither supported nor condemned Lindh's actions; he simply tried to examine the mindset of a boy who could turn on his own country.

Singer-songwriter Steve Earle, shown here in New York City in 2000 before the release of his album *Transcendental Blues*. Earle admits that his early records were influenced by Springsteen's work, especially the album *Born in the U.S.A.*

But the song was seen as sympathetic to Lindh and gave conservative commentators a goldmine of fodder with which to attack Earle. In his liner notes to the album, Earle makes the frequently overlooked point that those who dare to question their government's actions are its true patriots. Woody Guthrie, an influence on both Earle and Springsteen, would have approved. Springsteen took a similar tack on "Paradise," a song from *The Rising*, in which he takes on the persona of a suicide bomber, but with none of the backlash Earle experienced. —*LM*

The Early Years. See Prodigal Son.

Earth

Late '60s power trio led by Springsteen on vocals and guitar

Bruce Springsteen formed the group Earth in early 1968 following the demise of the Castiles, the group he had played in for most of his high school years. Springsteen graduated from Freehold (New Jersey) High School in 1967; a few months later, the Castiles, one of Freehold's most popular teen rock bands, broke up. The Castiles' sound, deeply influenced by groups from the first British Invasion (the Rolling Stones, the Animals, the Kinks, etc.), had grown stale. With the rising popularity in America of the British psychedelic supergroup Cream, a trio that featured the guitar muscle of Eric Clapton backed by bass player Jack Bruce and drummer Ginger Baker, Springsteen was eager to lead his own power trio. In Earth, Springsteen assumed all guitar and vocal chores, backed by two other young Jersey Shore musicians, bassist John Graham and drummer Michael Burke.

Earth performed in local high schools and teen clubs and at parties, and the trio ventured to New York City to play on at least one occasion. The group's repertoire featured songs from Cream, the Doors, Jimi Hendrix, and other blues-based groups popular in 1967–68, as well as more than one song from the psychedelic folk singer Tim Buckley. With Earth, Springsteen developed as a lead guitarist and singer, having to rely on no one but himself for both duties.

Earth barely lasted a year before Springsteen ended it to join a new band, Child, which included two future E Street Band members—keyboardist Danny Federici and drummer Vini Lopez. By this time, too, Springsteen had left his hometown of Freehold for good and moved to Asbury Park, where the music scene was heating up thanks to a popular after-hours musicians' club called the Upstage. —*RS*

John Eddie

Singer, songwriter, Jersey rocker

Just as Bruce Springsteen had to endure the "new Dylan" label, John Eddie (born John Edward Cummings) became one of the legions of New Jersey rockers caught in the catch-22 of "next Springsteen" comparisons. Eddie's family moved from Virginia to Cherry Hill, New Jersey, when he was a preteen. He wound up quitting school, joining the navy, then forming a band called the Front Street Runners, which quickly became a regular at the Stone Pony in Asbury Park. They were frequently joined onstage by Springsteen, one of their loyal fans.

Eddie admits to being inspired by seeing Springsteen play a 1974 community college gig (he told a *Philadelphia Inquirer* writer that he had been a huge David Bowie fan, but seeing Springsteen made him realize that one could be theatrical and rock out "without having to wear women's clothing"). But he was far from a copycat act; when he began recording in the mid-'80s, he admitted in the *Inquirer*, "I used to say that I wanted to be the E Street Wham!"

A New York showcase that exhibited Eddie's songwriting strength and enormous stage presence caused a bidding war that landed him at Springsteen's label, Columbia, in 1986. His self-titled debut yielded the modest hit "Jungle Boy," but the subsequent *The Hard Cold Truth* scored no hits. Then-manager Tommy Mottola got him out of his Columbia contract, and Elektra Records stepped in. But Elektra never released the albums he recorded there, including one he did with legendary Neil Young producer David Briggs. (The label did place his cover of the Cure's "Inbetween Days" on its 1990 anniversary collection.)

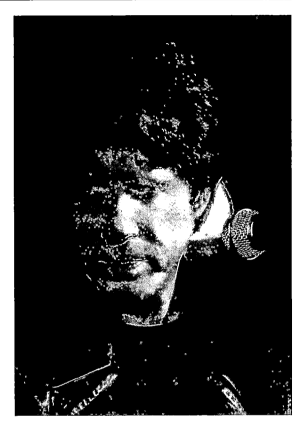

John Eddie has had to endure the pressure of being "the next Springsteen" since emerging from the Jersey music scene in the mid-1980s. Here he prepares for a sound check at the East Village's Mercury Lounge on May 16, 2003, when he was touring to support his first album in fourteen years, *Who the Hell Is John Eddie?*

Eddie wound up back on the regional circuit, releasing his own albums, *Seven Songs Since My Last Confession, Happily Never After*, and *Guy Walks into a Bar*, a live disc that provided a sense of his outsized performing capability. Then he hooked up with Luke Lewis, who was forming Lost Highway Records. In 2003, Lost Highway released *Who the Hell Is John Eddie?* As the title indicates, it's filled with self-deprecating humor and fall-down-funny sarcasm, alternated with songs of Nashville-worthy heartbreak, played out on a foundation of Memphis soul, Jersey R&B swagger, a little folk, and rockabilly. One critic called the breakup tune "Let Me Down Hard" "one of the best songs that Springsteen never wrote"; and in one of his more hilarious tunes, the aging lament "Forty," Eddie teased, "I guess I'm fucking forty/That's what my mamma said/But Bruce Springsteen's fucking 53/And the Stones are almost dead." —*LM*

Dave Edmunds

British singer, guitarist, songwriter, producer

When British rock veteran Dave Edmunds went to see Bruce Springsteen play in the spring of 1981 at Wembley Arena, he expected a good show but not necessarily a new song to record. "I was backstage in the hospitality area after the gig," Edmunds remembered, "and one of his crew or road managers tapped me on the shoulder and said, 'Bruce wants to meet you.' I went back and had this great talk with him, and he played me this song and said, 'I'd like you to do this, if you like it.' He said he'd send me the tape, which he did." The song was "From Small Things (Big Things One Day Come)," an energetic rocker that Edmunds recorded and used as the opening track of his 1982 album *DE7*, augmenting the arrangement with two horn players. It was released as a single and didn't chart, but the presence of a previously unrecorded Springsteen song in the wake of *The River*'s success was enough to give Edmunds the highest-charting album of his career (No. 56 on the *Billboard* Top 200). Springsteen finally released his own version of the song, as originally recorded for *The River*, on 2003's *Essential* collection.

A native of Wales, Edmunds launched his solo career after his band, Love Sculpture, broke up in 1969. He scored an early hit with 1970's chart-topping "I Hear You Knocking" and quickly faded into relative obscurity, though he enjoyed strong critical support. He formed another group, Rockpile, with Nick Lowe in 1976, which basically supported the two men on their own albums and recorded just one under the group moniker. Edmunds also produced albums for the Stray Cats and Shakin' Stevens, and he scored a Top 40 hit in 1983 with the Jeff Lynne–produced "Slippin' Away." —*GG*

18 Tracks

Released: April 13, 1999
Producers: Bruce Springsteen, Chuck Plotkin
Tracks: "Growin' Up," "Seaside Bar Song," "Rendezvous," "Hearts of Stone," "Where the Bands Are," "Loose Ends," "I Wanna Be With You," "Born in the U.S.A.," "My Love Will Not Let You Down," "Lion's Den," "Pink Cadillac," "Janey Don't You Lose Heart," "Sad Eyes," "Part Man, Part Monkey," "Trouble River," "Brothers Under the Bridge," "The Fever," "The Promise"
Chart peak: No. 64

When Bruce Springsteen's *Tracks* box set came out in the fall of 1998, fans celebrated but quickly—and not surprisingly—began grousing about what *wasn't* among the selection of rare and unreleased material. One song was almost unanimously singled out—

"The Promise," a song he wrote after *Born to Run* and played at shows in 1976–77. It was one of the first songs recorded for *Darkness on the Edge of Town*, but Springsteen decided not to put it on the album for fear it would be interpreted as being about the lawsuit with former manager Mike Appel that kept him out of the studio for a year. And when it came time to assemble *Tracks*, Springsteen said he didn't have a version of "The Promise" that he liked enough to release. But bowing to the furor, he cut a new version of the song—a solo rendition accompanying himself on piano—at his Thrill Hill Recording studio in New Jersey for inclusion on *18 Tracks*, a single-disc distillation of the bigger box set. The presence of "The Promise," of course, gave those who had purchased *Tracks* motivation to buy *18 Tracks* as well. So did a pair of other non-*Tracks* tracks: a May 1973 version of "The Fever," which Springsteen subsequently gave to Southside Johnny & the Asbury Jukes; and "Trouble River," recorded in 1990 during sessions for the *Human Touch* album. The remaining fifteen songs were all included on the *Tracks* box. —*GG*

Electric Nebraska

E Street Band versions of eventual *Nebraska* songs

I n early 1982, nearly six months removed from the end of the long tour supporting *The River*, Bruce Springsteen was writing songs at a record clip—a collection of bleak, desolate tunes that reflected the darkness of the times (post-Vietnam, the start of the Reagan administration) and the man (now thirty-two, unmarried, and arguably at a crossroads with impending superstardom).

Using a four-track recorder, Springsteen cut home demos to cassette, the very master tape that would later become the source for *Nebraska*. But before the decision was made to release the material as a solo album,

"('The Promise' and 'The Fever') are worth the price of admission alone, though *18 Tracks* also collects several of the box set's highlights ... Of course, it'd kill sales of the box set to include all the best stuff here, perhaps explaining why a frat-house rocker like "Where the Bands Are" is included at the expense of more powerful and personal numbers such as "The Wish" and "The Honeymooners."
—*Calgary Sun*

"*18 Tracks* is a condensed version of the enormous *Tracks* boxed set, so people can save money by not buying either ... Which is a shame because, in amongst the studio flotsam and live jetsam, there are wonderful moments ..."
—*Q*

"(A) single-disc distillation of the box set that's satisfying for casual fans not willing to shell out for the whole thing but essential for hardcore Springsteen followers needing ('The Promise' and 'The Fever') to complete their collection."
—*Amazon.com*

"... *18 Tracks* is ultimately most essential for those hardcore fans who already shelled out for most of the material in question anyway; and though it's appalling to force the devoted to buy a full-length album for just three new songs, at least each is excellent ...."
—*All Music Guide*

Springsteen and the E Street Band recorded several of the songs we know from *Nebraska* in electric arrangements. One song written with the rest of *Nebraska* that was ultimately judged even more powerful in its electric arrangement was "Born in the U.S.A.," but several other songs were also cut with the E Streeters—"Johnny 99," "Atlantic City," "Open All Night"—and it is this collection of unreleased, full-band arrangements that collectors refer to as *Electric Nebraska.*

Did *Electric Nebraska* come close to release? It appears not too close, though certainly the idea that these songs would form the basis of Springsteen's next album was there, even as the decision eventually came down to release the solo *Nebraska* and keep working on the next full-band album. A year later, in fact, it appeared they had that record primed for release (see the entry for *Murder Incorporated*), only to pull back once again, and wait still another year to cull together band recordings from 1982, 1983, and 1984 to form *Born in the U.S.A.*

Electric Nebraska is unbootlegged and remains the ultimate holy grail to Springsteen collectors. Some speculate that the full-band live arrangements of "Atlantic City" and the 2003 tour version of "Johnny 99" closely resemble the *Electric Nebraska* versions. —*EF*

Joe Ely

Texas singer, songwriter, musician

he term Americana not only defines Joe Ely's music, it evokes the sorts of experiences the Amarillo, Texas, native writes and sings about in albums with titles such as *Honky Tonk Masquerade*, *Lord of the Highway*, and *Letters to Laredo*, in projects with his alt-country "supergroup" the Flatlanders (with Jimmie Dale Gilmore and Butch Hancock), or in projects like a twelve-CD set of spoken word pieces based on his road diaries. Nurtured in the musical incubator of Lubbock, Ely's colorful life has included friendships with Stevie Ray Vaughan and the Clash, a stint tending animals with the Ringling Bros. and Barnum & Bailey Circus, months spent performing as a musician member of the original *Stomp* cast, tours with the Kinks and the Rolling Stones, a spot on the Buddy Holly Walk of Fame, a performance of Holly songs with Paul McCartney, and cowriting thirteen new national anthem candidates and performing them at the Smithsonian Institute in Washington, D.C. He's also a visual artist and novelist and is part of the all-star musical collective Los Super Seven.

And he has a good friend and trusted colleague in Bruce Springsteen, who's gone out of his way to be one of Ely's most enthusiastic patrons in the mainstream rock world. Springsteen contributed to Ely's revered 1995 album, *Letter to Laredo*, providing harmonies on the songs "All Just to Get to You" and "I'm a Thousand Miles from Home." They've shared stages frequently as well: at a pair of benefits Springsteen staged in 1993—the Concert to Fight Hunger on June 24 at the Meadowlands and the Concert for the Kristen Ann Carr Fund on June 26 at Madison Square Garden; at the 1996 Rock and Roll Hall of Fame and Museum conference *Hard Travelin': The Life and Legacy of Woody Guthrie*; and almost always when Springsteen performs in Austin, where Ely now resides.

Springsteen was also a guest in a twenty-minute documentary about an Amtrak train trip Ely took up the West Coast from San Diego to Seattle, and the shows he performed along the way. The piece, which aired in 1997 on VH1 in Europe, included a performance by Ely and Springsteen at Johnny Depp's Viper Room in Hollywood. The film won a European VH1 Award, but Springsteen's management requested that it not be shown in the states. There were no hard feelings, however. Ely and Springsteen again shared a stage on October 19, 2001, during a benefit concert for the Alliance of Neighbors, a group organized to help families of 160 Monmouth County residents lost in the September 11 terrorist attacks that was organized by E Street Band bassist Garry Tallent. Ely and Springsteen dueted on "All Just to Get to You"; the show, which was held at the Count Basie Theater in Red Bank, New Jersey, and carried to cable subscribers in the Northeast, raised more than $700,000.

When the *Light of Day* Springsteen tribute album was compiled in 2003, Ely chose to record a version of "Working on the Highway" from the *Born in the U.S.A.* album because he and Bruce had done it earlier that year at a Springsteen show in Austin; just as it closed that concert, it also closes the double disc. —*LM*

Maria Espinosa

First kiss

 hen Bruce Springsteen called out, "Maria Espinosa, baby, where are you tonight?" while performing in 1996 at his old elementary school in Freehold, New Jersey, she was not in attendance. But afterwards she told the *Asbury Park Press*, "I can't believe he remembers my name. I was flattered when I found out." Then again, who *doesn't* remember a first kiss? Springsteen and Espinosa locked lips during a dance at the local YMCA canteen in downtown Freehold. She pegged their ages at fifteen; Springsteen recalled it as thirteen in a verse remembering the smooch in the song "In Freehold." "It must have lasted about a minute," she said. "It was good. I dreamed about it afterward." It was apparently good for Springsteen, too, who sang, "I walked home with a limp but I felt just fine, that night in Freehold." Espinosa kept the kiss secret until Springsteen's November 8, 1996, performance at St. Rose of Lima in Freehold: first it was because her parents didn't allow her to have a boyfriend, so she'd be in trouble; then, after Springsteen became famous, she didn't think anyone would believe her. Still, she always had a fondness for the "hippie" and "loner" who was "the only guy with a leather jacket and long hair back then, but he was kind of nice, and I thought he was cute. And he was not prejudiced." The Espinosas were the second Puerto Rican family to settle in Freehold, moving there in 1958. Espinosa went on to marry (becoming Maria Espinosa Ayala) and have four children; she also has several grandchildren. —*GG*

The Essential Bruce Springsteen

Released: November 11, 2003
Producers: Bruce Springsteen, Jon Landau, Mike Appel, Roy Bittan, Jimmy Cretecos, Brendan O'Brien, Chuck Plotkin, Steve Van Zandt
Tracks: Disc 1—"Blinded by the Light," "For You," "Spirit in the Night," "4th of July, Asbury Park (Sandy)," "Rosalita (Come Out Tonight)," "Thunder Road," "Born to Run," "Jungleland," "Badlands," "Darkness on the Edge of Town," "The Promised Land," "The River," "Hungry Heart," "Nebraska," "Atlantic City"; Disc 2—"Born in the U.S.A.," "Glory Days," "Dancing in the Dark," "Tunnel of Love," "Brilliant Disguise," "Human Touch," "Living Proof," "Lucky Town," "Streets of Philadelphia," "The Ghost of Tom Joad," "The Rising," "Mary's Place," "Lonesome Day," "American Skin (41 Shots)" (live), "Land of Hope and Dreams" (live); Bonus Disc—"From Small Things (Big Things One Day Come)," "The Big Payback," "Held Up Without a Gun," "Trapped," "None but the Brave," "Missing," "Lift Me Up," "Viva Las Vegas," "County Fair," "Code of Silence," "Dead Man Walking," "Countin' on a Miracle" (acoustic)
Chart peak: No. 14

ruce Springsteen's *Greatest Hits* set in 1995 was pretty much what the title indicated, a singles-oriented collection that didn't run too deep—though it did have four new tracks to lure in the faithful. *The Essential Bruce Springsteen*, on the other hand, offers a more comprehensive overview, drawing from all of Springsteen's studio albums plus *Live in New York City*, and even picks up his Oscar-winning "Streets of Philadelphia." Even better, it contains a bonus disc of rarities that brought much celebrating from the faithful.

In his liner notes for *Essential*, Springsteen wrote that the project was inspired by the "new faces" he and the E Street Band saw in the audiences for their 2002–2003 world tour. And while he noted that "one man's coffee is another man's tea" in terms of song selection, Springsteen explained that "the idea was to present a little bit of what each album has to offer." Those offerings were also enhanced by Bob Ludwig, who remastered the material and greatly improved some songs for which audio quality had been lacking on previous CDs. The bonus disc was the greatest enhancement, of course—a dozen tracks for which Springsteen also provided some background detail in the liner notes. The songs include the movie soundtrack songs "Missing" (from *The Crossing Guard*), "Dead Man Walking" (*Dead Man Walking*), and "Lift Me Up" (*Limbo*); "From Small Things (Big Things One Day Come)," which was written and recorded in 1979 and subsequently given to Dave Edmunds; rare recordings "County Fair" and "The Big Payback"; live recordings of "Held Up Without a Gun," "Trapped," and "Code of Silence" (the latter cowritten with Joe Grushecky and recipient of a Solo Rock Vocal Performance Grammy in 2004); the *Born in the U.S.A.* outtake "None but the Brave"; a rendition of "Viva Las Vegas" from the 1990 *New Musical Express* benefit album *The Last Temptation of Elvis*; and the acoustic version of "Countin' on a Miracle" that was played at the end of many shows on the 2002–2003 *The Rising* tour.

Initial pressings of the collection were flawed, however, by some liner note mistakes that misidentified the recording dates of a couple of live songs, gave credit to engineer Ludwig for playing bass on "Viva Las Vegas" (it was really Bob Glaub), and misidentified E Street Band members Garry Tallent and Danny Federici in one photo. The errors were corrected in subsequent editions. —*GG*

Melissa Etheridge

Singer-songwriter, gay rights activist

 hen New York radio personality Scott Shannon dubbed Melissa Etheridge "the Bruce Springsteen of women rockers," he might not have known how great a

"*T***he Essential Bruce Springsteen is less bloated and more rewarding than the '98 outtakes box, *Tracks*. The frenetic 'Held Up Without a Gun,' the troubled 'Missing,' the wistful 'County Fair' and the Asbury Park reminiscence 'None but the Brave' deserved rescue from the vaults. Except for a few duds (the field-holler version of 'Countin' on a Miracle'), Disc 3 is as engaging a ride as any through Springsteen's '80s peaks, '90s valleys and current rebirth."**

—*Entertainment Weekly*

"... in trying to be all things to all people Springsteen has missed a chance to make this compilation truly outstanding ... (I)t always frustrates when an artist of Springsteen's magnitude tries to accommodate 'new fans' at the expense of those of us who have been around long enough to tell his best work from a simple album-to-album anthology ... If they just wanted to produce a sampling from all his albums, which they have done here, they shouldn't have called it *The Essential Bruce Springsteen*.

—*Jam! Showbiz*

"Springsteen is neither glamorous nor mysterious, but as this three-disc compilation demonstrates, he is an extremely talented and important artist ... *The Essential Bruce Springsteen* is a fine introduction to his work and it atones for the shoddy 1995 compilation *Greatest Hits* ... The meat of this collection is enough to chew on for a lifetime. The two discs get the Springsteen story as right as is possible in 150 minutes, and if they don't work, then Springsteen is definitely not for you."**

—*Pitchfork Media*

Once dubbed "the Bruce Springsteen of women rockers," Melissa Etheridge became friends with Springsteen after the release of her second album *Brave and Crazy* and has since performed with him several times. Here she performs his classic "Born to Run" at the Concert for New York at Madison Square Garden on October 20, 2001.

compliment he was actually giving her. Springsteen became Etheridge's favorite musician while she was growing up in Leavenworth, Kansas, where her creative leanings and her (then hidden) sexual orientation isolated her from other youths. Listening to Springsteen's music, she said, "took me some place else, made me feel like I wasn't alone and allowed me to dream of getting somewhere beyond where I was." Meeting, befriending, and even performing with Springsteen was not among those dreams—but they all happened over the course of her career.

Etheridge, who had been writing songs since the age of eight, blew out of Kansas after high school to study at Berklee College of Music in Boston. In 1982, on her twenty-first birthday, she headed to Los Angeles to pursue a recording contract, courting label interest with her club gigs and showcases around town and eventually signing with Chris Blackwell's Island Records, which released Etheridge's self-titled first album in 1988. Her second album,

1989's *Brave and Crazy*, hadn't been out long when she first met Springsteen in a Los Angeles restaurant; Etheridge was sitting at the bar and Springsteen was picking up a take-out order and, she recalled "he *waved* at me. I didn't think anyone knew who I was at the time, so to have him wave at me and then wave me over so we could talk just blew my mind." They became friendly and Springsteen was among Etheridge's supporters when she came out publicly as a lesbian at the January 1993 Triangle Ball that was part of President Bill Clinton's inauguration celebration.

When Etheridge was tapped to perform on an episode of MTV's "Unplugged" series in 1995, the network asked her for some potential duet partners. She requested Springsteen but assumed he wouldn't do it. He did. They taped the show on February 15 at the Brooklyn Academy of Music, performing "Thunder Road" together. Etheridge was so excited about performing with Springsteen that she forgot the lyrics on the first take and almost botched them again on the second; Springsteen actually backed away from the mic when the troublesome line—"So Mary climb in ..."—came around to let Etheridge sing it herself. "It was like, 'OK, let's see if you remember it this time,'" Etheridge remembered. "There's, like, a beat and then I step up and sing it, and Bruce is standing there laughing." Etheridge subsequently joined Springsteen and the E Street Band—along with Jon Bon Jovi and Richie Sambora—on August 12, 1999, at the Continental Airlines Arena in East Rutherford, New Jersey, for a rendition of "Hungry Heart." They were both nominated in the Best Rock Song category at the 2000 Grammy Awards, Etheridge for "Angels Would Fall" and Springsteen for "The Promise" (the Red Hot Chili Peppers won for "Scar Tissue").

Etheridge and her former partner, Julie Cypher, have two children—Bailey (1997) and Beckett (1999)—who were fathered with sperm donated by fellow singer-songwriter David Crosby. The couple split up in 2001 and Etheridge later hooked up with actress Tammy Lynn Michaels. A tour to support Etheridge's 2004 release *Lucky* was postponed as she sought treatment for breast cancer. But Etheridge, still bald from the effects of chemotherapy, was the highlight of the 2005 Grammy Awards when she partnered with Joss Stone in a powerful performance of Janis Joplin's "Piece of My Heart." —*GG*

"Fade Away"

Single release: February 3, 1981
Album: *The River* (Columbia, 1980)
Chart peak: No. 20

 oth at the time and in retrospect, "Fade Away" seemed an odd choice for a second single from *The River.* With the tour in support of the album in full gear, any number of other tracks from the album were generating more familiarity and fan support; Springsteen didn't even perform "Fade Away" live until December 1, 1980—nearly two months into the tour. And it's never been included on any of the subsequent compilations or live albums. That said, "Fade Away"—which by all accounts was recorded in 1980, after Springsteen had abandoned the proposed *The Ties That Bind* single-disc set—reached the Top 20, albeit barely. It may have been a bit of a letdown after "Hungry Heart"'s No. 5 showing, but it was still Springsteen's second highest-charting single to that point. The B-side was "Be True," an outtake from *The River* sessions, which would eventually form the back end of a one-two punch with "Tunnel of Love" as the opening salvo of 1988's Tunnel of Love Express Tour shows. —*GG*

Danny Federici

aka "Phantom," E Street Band keyboardist 1972–present

hough Steve Van Zandt may be Bruce Springsteen's oldest friend in the E Street Band, keyboardist Danny Federici enjoys the distinction of the longest tenure playing with Springsteen.

Springsteen performs at Detroit's Cobo Arena in October 1978.

The two met in 1968, introduced by drummer Vini "Mad Dog" Lopez during an after-hours jam at the Upstage in Asbury Park. Federici was so impressed that he cast his lot with Springsteen almost immediately, playing with him in Child, Steel Mill, Dr. Zoom and the Sonic Boom, and the Bruce Springsteen Band before the E Street Band was dubbed in 1972, following the release of Springsteen's first album, *Greetings from Asbury Park, N.J.* "I just always felt there was something truly special about Bruce," Federici told *Backstreets* in 1990. "He had a drive and a determination that was so strong that I believed in what he believed in ... I didn't care if I made any money."

Born January 23, 1950, in Flemington, New Jersey, Federici was the adopted only child of a New York City doorman and a "stage mom." Federici began playing piano at an early age and spent fifteen years studying accordion. "My mother was Polish and my father was Italian, so there was a big emphasis on the accordion," Federici told *Backstreets*. That said, his father never quite saw the wisdom of pursuing a career in music until he attended a Springsteen show in the '70s at the Philadelphia Spectrum. "I was duded up in a suit with some fancy shoes, and we were in the dressing room, and my father was walking around bragging about me," Federici recalled in 1997. "So I looked at him and said 'So—doing pretty good, huh? The bum; he's never gonna go anywhere, huh?' And there was this big smile on his face, right under that big Italian nose. I'll remember that always."

With his mom "pulling me by my ear to play here and play there," Federici was a seasoned performer by the time he as an adolescent, playing polkas, Italian folks songs, and, with his own bands, rock 'n' roll at Elks lodges, Moose halls, political rallies, and even on WABC-AM in Manhattan. Of course, he also discovered there was a difference between being the guitar player and the guy with an accordion strapped around his shoulders. "The girls were not going for the squeeze box," Federici said. "I remember I had an accordion that was like an accordiovox; Gary Lewis & the Playboys used to play one of these things. You didn't have to squeeze it; I could lay it down on my amplifier and play it like it was a little organ. As soon as I could do that, I did, 'cause squeezing this thing was not hip at all—especially not if you wanted to be a rock 'n' roller."

Nicknamed Phantom for his low-key, retiring personality, he indeed became a rock 'n' roller with Springsteen; during his Rock and Roll Hall of Fame induction speech, Springsteen called Federici "the most instinctive and natural musician I've ever met," whose playing "brought the boardwalks of Central and South Jersey alive in my music." Former Springsteen manager and producer Mike Appel seconded that, calling Federici "a flawless performer. He never dropped a note as far as I can remember." Appel told *Backstreets* that Federici apparently knew how to dress the rock 'n' roll part, too; he recalled a college gig at which Federici showed up in a baseball uniform and David Bowie–style makeup. Springsteen ordered him to ditch the makeup, according to Appel. Springsteen also did quite a bit of directing in terms of the keyboard parts Federici and Roy Bittan played; "He heard little riffs in his head," Federici told *Backstreets*. "If anything, we'd probably play too busy, and then Bruce would say, 'No, no, no. Simplify it.' Bruce got more defined as to what he wanted as the years went on."

There was a dark side to Federici's rock 'n' roll life, however. He developed a drinking problem—"I was born Irish, which helped," he cracked—that led to two stints in rehab before he became sober in 1983. During some of his binges he even quit the band several times over what he described as "petty" matters. It was so bad that on one visit to Los Angeles to see Springsteen he never made it out of the hotel bar. Nevertheless, he told *Backstreets* that Springsteen "stuck by me through thick and thin. He never said a word to anyone about my problems ... Bruce was there for laughing and crying."

Given their long association, it's stands to reason that Federici was one of the most shocked members of the E Street Band when Springsteen called in 1989 to say he was going to work with other people. But Federici said that after battling his drinking as well as a bad marriage, and with a new marriage in place at the time of the call, he was in a better place to deal with it. He even voiced some ambivalence about Springsteen's success to *Backstreets*: "We started out as a band which turned into a super, giant corporate money-making machine. That was an amazing thing for me to go through as a musician."

Federici didn't waste much time getting into other musical situations, however. He and drummer Max Weinberg toured in Dave Edmunds's band in 1990. He also formed some bands with fellow Jersey musicians, including Stone Hill (which included Bon Jovi drummer Tico Torres) and World Without

Off of E Street ...
Danny Federici

Joan Armatrading, *Me Myself I* (1980)

Gary U.S. Bonds, *Dedication* (1981), *On the Line* (1982)

Garland Jeffreys, *Escape Artists* (1981)

Evan Johns & His H-Bombs, *Evan Johns & the H-Bombs* (1986), *Bombs Away* (1989), *Love Is Murder* (1997)

Little Steven & the Disciples of Soul, *Men Without Women* (1982)

Graham Parker, *The Up Escalator* (1980), *No Holding Back* (1996)

Walls, and was part of the House of Blues house band. Still, he noted, "I had no idea what I wanted to do. I didn't want it to be, 'Oh, look, there's another of those E Street guys doing something.' It really took me many, many years to pull my head out of the sand and say, 'Who am I, and what's going on here?' I had forgotten who I was as a musician. You forget when you're making a lot of dough, and you've got all the perks and private jets and all this stuff; it's like, 'Wait a minute! Now I've got to get to work.'" Federici found his voice with his first solo album, a set of jazz-influenced instrumentals titled *Flemington*, after his central Jersey hometown, which was released in 1997 on Federici's own Deadeye Records label. It was rereleased by Hip-O Records in 2001 as *Danny Federici*, remastered and adding one song, "Erica," written for his wife. —*GG*

Fender Esquire

Springsteen's primary electric guitar

ruce Springsteen's main guitar is a Fender Esquire—a single-pickup version of the popular Telecaster model that was one of the first electric guitars designed by Leo Fender and his partner, George Fullerton (it first went on sale in 1950). What isn't as clear is the actual vintage of the well-worn instrument, which Springsteen purchased in 1969. Printed reports said it's a 1952, 1953, or 1954 model; Fender contends it's a 1952. Complicating matters is the fact that the Fender decal was incorrectly placed on the guitar's headstock; it thus was considered a "second" and its serial number was rubbed out, although former guitar tech Mike Batlan told *Musician* magazine that there was a serial number with an asterisk next to it, indicating it was indeed a flawed guitar.

Springsteen did modify the Esquire, changing the standard Fender input and adding a humbucking input in its neck. Before he went wireless Springsteen also installed a battery-operated impedance transformer to accommodate the long cable lengths that allowed him more freedom of movement on stage.

According to Fender, Springsteen also applies household sealants over the cavities of all his guitars—including the Esquire. This dates back to

Springsteen wields his trademark Fender Esquire at an August 1992 show in Auburn Hills, Michigan.

his '80s in-concert habit of keeping a full water bucket on stage into which he'd dip his head to cool off—drenching the guitar in the process. The sealant protected the pickups and wiring from water damage. According to the manufacturer, Springsteen tests his sealing jobs by pouring a two-liter bottle of Evian over the guitars and then plugging them in. —*GG*

"57 Channels (And Nothin' On)"

Single released: June 1992
Album: *Human Touch* (Columbia, 1992)
Chart peak: 68

The version of "57 Channels (And Nothin' On)" that Bruce Springsteen debuted at the November 1990 Christic Institute Benefits didn't quite prepare listeners for the eventual recorded version of the song that surfaced a year and a half later. At the Christic shows Springsteen played it with a spirited rockabilly abandon that hammed up the song's humorous rumination on the explosion of communication and home entertainment. On the *Human Touch* album, however, it takes on a more sinister and foreboding tone, with Springsteen accompanying himself on bass and plenty of reverberation to make his howls and yips sound like some sort of pained, spectral creature in the mix.

Already topical, the song took on additional weight with a pair of Little Steven remixes by former E Street Band member Steve Van Zandt. Between the album's release and that of "57 Channels" as a single, the city of Los Angeles—where Springsteen was living as well as rehearsing with his band—erupted in violence after four police officers were found not guilty in the beating of black motorist Rodney King. Van Zandt incorporated the "no justice, no peace" that was chanted by rioters and demonstrators into the song to give it an even sharper political edge.

It was hoped that "57 Channels" would help restore some commercial luster to *Human Touch* and its simultaneously released companion album, *Lucky Town*, as they slid down the charts in the summer of '92. Unfortunately it didn't work, as the song only reached No. 68 on the *Billboard* Hot 100 chart. —*GG*

"Fire"

Single released: February 1986
Album: *Live/1975–85* (Columbia, 1986)
Chart peak: No. 46

By the time Bruce Springsteen finally released his own recorded version of "Fire"— from a December 16, 1978, San Francisco performance for the *Live/1975–85* box set—he was practically doing a cover version. The song was a No. 2 hit for the Pointer Sisters in 1979, while rockabilly singer Robert Gordon had some success with it the previous year (Springsteen played piano on Gordon's recording of the song). Legend has it that Springsteen even sent a demo of the song to Elvis Presley, shortly before The King's death in August 1977, but there's no hard evidence to support that claim.

"Fire" was considered for inclusion on *Darkness on the Edge of Town,* and E Street Band keyboardist Roy Bittan once observed, "Everybody agreed 'Fire' was one of the best songs he wrote for that album. But he would not put it on because it's not what he wanted to say on *Darkness.*" Springsteen did perform the song live, however, and some have noted that he was a bit ambivalent at the Pointers' success with the song—happy for the success as a songwriter but resentful that, pre–*The River,* he wasn't scoring Top 10 hits as an artist. He didn't have much success with his version of "Fire," either; it was Springsteen's first single since "Badlands" in 1978 to miss the Top 40.

"Fire" has also been covered by Babyface and Des'ree, while comedian/actor Robin Williams did a parody in his act of the song as sung by Elmer Fudd, which he performed at the October 13, 1986, Bridge School Benefit concert near San Francisco at which Springsteen also appeared. The promotional video for "Fire" was shot at that show, capturing Springsteen's spare arrangement of the song with E Street band members Nils Lofgren on guitar and Danny Federici on accordion. —*GG*

The Firecracker Show

December 31, 1978, in Richfield, Ohio

ruce Springsteen and the E Street Band rang out 1978 with a bang—literally. Performing at Richfield Coliseum outside Cleveland, before an exuberant New Year's Eve crowd, Springsteen asked from the stage, "(If) you guys brought any firecrackers and stuff, I'd appreciate it if you didn't set 'em off, 'cause I don't want people getting hurt ... So if you just keep 'em in your pocket or something, I'd really appreciate it."

The crowd mostly complied until just after Springsteen counted into the New Year, when someone in the upper deck threw a firecracker towards the stage, and it detonated near Springsteen's head. Furious, Springsteen snapped, "Well, I almost lost my eye thanks to some asshole ... But that ain't gonna ruin my New Year, and I hope it don't ruin yours." After playing the next song, "Good Rockin' Tonight," he left the stage without a word, put on a clean shirt and then returned to rock. By all accounts, the incident inspired Springsteen and the band to turn things up another notch, bringing the show to a furious conclusion in the wee hours of 1979.

The next night, January 1, Springsteen closed the *Darkness on the Edge of Town* tour with a thirty-one-song, three-and-a-half-hour marathon—at the time, his longest performance ever. —*GG*

John Fogerty. *See* **Creedence Clearwater Revival.**
Shane Fontayne. *See* **1992–93 Bruce Springsteen Touring Band.**
John Ford. *See The Grapes of Wrath.*

Richard Ford

Prize-winning novelist and sports writer

When sports writer and novelist (and Bruce Springsteen fan) Richard Ford was looking for a title for the sequel to his 1986 book *The Sportswriter*, he settled on *Independence Day*, borrowed from Springsteen's 1980 album *The River*. "To most Americans, I think, to be independent means to have no ties, to be separate, isolated," Ford explained to the *Providence Journal*. "And as a novelist, what I wanted to do was to recalibrate the word, to see if it was possible to give it an affirming quality. Independence can mean freedom from mistakes, regrets, freedom to go forward together with others."

The book, which was published in 1995, was the first book ever to win both the Pulitzer Prize and PEN/Faulkner award for fiction. It picks up the story of *The Sportswriter's* protagonist Frank Bascombe, who's dealing with divorce, single parenting, and a career change to real-estate home sales. At "a curving point" of his life, Bascombe takes a redemptive, soul-searching trip to several sports halls of fame with his teenage son.

Ford, a Jackson, Mississippi, native who was raised in Arkansas, published two novels before joining the staff of *Inside Sports* magazine. He wrote *The Sportswriter* after that publication was sold and wrote a collection of short stories and another novel between that and *Independence Day*. Based in New Orleans, he continues to write and has also taught classes at Princeton University, the University of Michigan, and Williams College. —*GG*

Al Franken

Writer, comedian, actor, commentator

Al Franken had received plenty of critical praise for his book *Lies and the Lying Liars That Tell Them: A Fair and Balanced Look at the Right*—along with slams from the political right wing—when it was published in 2003. Bruce Springsteen was among those who gave it an exuberant thumbs-up, recommending it to audiences at several shows on the stadium leg of *The Rising* tour. The ultimate plug: Springsteen brought Franken on stage for a brief cameo during "Mary's Place" at the October 3 concert at Shea Stadium in Franken's native New York.

That was a mark of how far Franken has come since his days as a writer and extra for NBC's "Saturday Night Live," where he ultimately graduated into a full-fledged Not Ready for Prime Time Player best known for his new age-y character Stuart Smalley. But the Harvard-educated Franken's greatest fame came from his sharp, satiric political commentary, starting in 1988 when CNN hired him to help cover the Democratic National Convention. He also wrote for Comedy Central's *Politically Incorrect*, launched an NBC series called "Lateline" about a TV news program, and, with 1996's *Rush Limbaugh Is a Big Fat Idiot*, began writing a series of humorous but hard-line political tomes that included *Why Not Me? The Making and Unmaking of the Al Franken Presidency* (1999) and, of course, *Lies and the Lying Liars*, which spent seven weeks at No. 1 on the *New York Times* best-sellers list.

In 2004 Franken took his spiel to the liberal talk network Air America Radio, co-hosting "The O'Franken Factor" with Katherine Lampher. Franken also turned bits from the show into an album released that September—but which didn't nearly sell as well as, say, a Springsteen record. —*GG*

Freehold, New Jersey

Springsteen's hometown

reehold, New Jersey, the hometown of Bruce Springsteen, is located in western Monmouth County, some fifteen miles from Asbury Park and other beach communities on the Jersey Shore. Settled before the Revolutionary War, Freehold is steeped in colonial history. In 1778, the Battle of Monmouth, a turning point in America's war for independence, was fought not far from the village center. During the battle, American forces under General George Washington fought British troops led by General Henry Clinton to a draw, forcing the redcoats to flee across New Jersey to the safety of New York City. Prior to the early summer battle, Washington's troops had spent a miserable, demoralizing winter at Valley Forge in Pennsylvania; the victory at Monmouth gave the Americans a renewed sense of purpose and proved they could hold their own against the better trained and better equipped British regulars.

In the late nineteenth century Freehold became an important commerce center in central New Jersey. Farms thrived outside of town, producing a wide array of crops, while inside Freehold, factories and mills provided jobs for newly arrived immigrants and other blue-collar workers. Freehold continued to grow into the mid-twentieth century, but with the 1961 closing of the

Karagheusian Rug Mill, the town's biggest employer, Freehold began a period of gradual economic decline that is, in part, still felt today.

Although actually born at a hospital in nearby Long Branch, Springsteen spent his formative years in Freehold, living in a lower-middle-class section of town called Texas, which was settled by Appalachian refugees and white ethnics. The 1939 *WPA Guide to New Jersey* observes of the town, "[I]n an unobtrusive way it seems to embody America's growth from farm to factory." Yet Freehold was largely bypassed by the prosperity enjoyed by much of white America in the 1950s and 1960s. Most of the available work came from the local 3M factory, a rug mill, a Nescafe factory, and a number of much smaller manufacturers. Deeply segregated, Freehold's whites and blacks lived, respectively, on the "right" and "wrong" side of an actual railroad track. To Springsteen, his hometown was "a small, narrow-minded town … very conservative … stagnating … There really wasn't much." The Springsteens' first Freehold residence was at 87 Randolph Street, which is where the future rocker watched in awe in 1956 as Elvis Presley performed for the first time on *The Ed Sullivan Show*. Shortly thereafter he would ask his parents for a guitar and begin his life-long love of rock 'n' roll. The Springsteen family also lived for a while at 39 Institute Street before moving to a nondescript two story house at 68 South Street, next to a gas station.

Springsteen attended St. Rose of Lima grammar school in Freehold (where he performed a special show in 1996) and had learned to play guitar well enough to join his first band, the Rogues, when he was thirteen years old. The group played some school dances and community socials in and around Freehold. In 1964 Springsteen entered Freehold Regional High School. After the breakup of the Rogues, Springsteen joined the Castiles during his sophomore year. Given the Rogues' amateurish standing, the Castiles is often credited as Springsteen's first true rock 'n' roll band. Springsteen's first performance with the Castiles occurred in 1965 at the now defunct Woodhaven Swim Club on East Freehold Road in neighboring Freehold Township. (Freehold is officially Freehold Borough, thus separating it from Freehold Township.) The Castiles was one of Freehold's most popular teen rock groups; being a member gave Springsteen valuable experience as a performer (he sang and played guitar), since the band performed regularly, not just in Freehold, but also at teen clubs, battles of the bands, and school dances in other Jersey Shore towns. During his time with the Castiles Springsteen also began to dabble in songwriting.

Springsteen left Freehold for good in 1968, going on to live in a number of other Jersey Shore communities before finally settling in upscale Rumson. One of Springsteen's hits, "My Hometown" from the *Born in the U.S.A.* album, recalls life in Freehold in the early and mid-'60s. "'My Hometown' was based on childhood memories of driving down Main Street on my dad's lap, the closing of a local mill and a racial incident that occurred near my house during my adolescence," Springsteen related in *Songs.*

Over the years Springsteen has quietly supported a number of Freehold charities, including the purchase of a fire truck for the city, and has kept a mostly low profile connection to his hometown. He resisted a mid-'90s effort to erect a statue of him in the city, and after the city council rejected the idea on the basis of cost, Springsteen included a verse in his good-humored song "In Freehold" (as yet unreleased but performed in concert a handful of times), thanking the council "for saving me from humiliation by demonstrating the good hard common sense that we learned in Freehold." —*RS*

Freehold Regional High School

Springsteen's alma mater; graduated June 1967

fter an oppressive eight years in parochial school at St. Rose of Lima, Bruce Springsteen found comparative freedom at the public Freehold Regional High School. But his time there was fairly undistinguished: one classmate noted that he was "a real quiet boy, not someone who made a big impression on you." Maria Espinosa Ayala, who gave Springsteen his first kiss, recalled him as "the only guy with a leather jacket and longer hair back then, but he was nice, and I thought he was cute." Springsteen told the *Los Angeles Times,* "I didn't even make it to class clown. I had nowhere near that amount of notoriety. I didn't have … the flair to be the complete jerk. It was like I didn't exist. It was the wall, then me. But I was working on the inside all the time. A lot of rock 'n' roll people went through this solitary existence."

Springsteen didn't even feel enough of an attachment to attend his graduation in June 1967. Then again, he might not have been welcome; prior to the ceremony, a teacher, balking at his long hair, told his classmates that if he was allowed to accept his diploma looking like that, it would be disrespectful. No one spoke up in Springsteen's support. He did, however, have warm feelings for at least one instructor, English teacher Robert Hussey: In 1999 the *New York Daily News* reported on a yearbook that was being sold for $10,000 with Springsteen's inscription to Hussey, which read: "This page is too small for me to write a fraction of the complimentary things I would like to say to you. You have taught me things I could not get from any book. You have helped me understand people so much more than I had previously. You have gained my utmost respect and appreciation. For all this I can say but a mere thank you. But it is a thank you that is felt deep within my heart."

Occasional Springsteen sightings at Freehold High football games were reported after his graduation—even as late as 1984, after *Born in the*

U.S.A.'s release. Since moving back to New Jersey in the '90s he has also attended some of his class reunions. And in hometown ode "In Freehold," he mused, "Well the girls at Freehold Regional yeah, they all looked pretty fine/Had my heart broke at least a half a dozen times/I wonder if they miss me, do they still get the itch...." —*GG*

Doug Friedline

Professional political campaign aide who spearheaded "Springsteen for Senate" drive in 2002

ost people in New Jersey would elect Bruce Springsteen God if they could. But Doug Friedline was happy to settle for U.S. Senator in 2002. Friedline, a campaign aide to former-pro-wrestler-turned-Minnesota-governor Jesse Ventura, formed the political group Independence for New Jersey, and launched a drive to "draft" Springsteen to run for a New Jersey senate seat. He circulated to get the 800 signatures needed to put Springsteen on the ballot for the 2002 general election. Springsteen, however, brought a quick end to the campaign; reaching back to a history lesson from his school days and, with his tongue planted firmly in his cheek, he announced, "If nominated, I will not run. If elected, I will not serve." —*GG*

"From Small Things (Big Things One Day Come)." *See* Dave Edmunds.

The Ghost of Tom Joad

Released: November 21, 1995
Producers: Bruce Springsteen, Chuck Plotkin
Tracks: "The Ghost of Tom Joad," "Straight Time," "Highway 29," "Youngstown," "Sinola Cowboys," "The Line," "Balboa Park," "Dry Lightning," "The New Timer," "Across the Border," "Galveston Bay," "My Best Was Never Good Enough"
Key outtakes: "Brothers Under the Bridge," "Back in Your Arms"
Chart peak: No. 11

n 1995, Bruce Springsteen fans were hopeful that his triumphant *Greatest Hits* reunion with the E Street Band signaled a full-scale resumption of the group enterprise. They almost got it; Springsteen acknowledged that he did more recording with the E Streeters, including a rocking, full-band arrangement of "The Ghost of Tom Joad." But, he said at the time, "I just wasn't sure of my rock voice. I wasn't sure of what it sounded like or what it was going to be doing or what its purpose was at that moment. The band wasn't functioning at the time, so I kind of went to where I thought I could be most useful." That was back home to Los Angeles, where he began working alone with an acoustic guitar. "I had 'Straight Time,' 'Highway 29.' I began to get into that groove, kind of film noir. So I started to write, and I said, 'That's the kind of record I think I want to make. I want to make a record where I don't have to play by the rules, I don't have any singles or none of that kind of stuff. I can make whatever kind of music I want to make.' I hadn't done that in a real long time. I guess I wanted to see if I could do it again."

Springsteen hit the road with only his guitar and harmonica to support the release of *The Ghost of Tom Joad*, playing small theaters and adopting a more somber stage presence.

Springsteen wound up writing a batch of spare, folk-like narratives drawn from a variety of sources—and, in many ways, grounded in the themes of all his work up to that point, particularly that which was influenced by the

The Ties That Bind

book and subsequent movie adaptation of *The Grapes of Wrath* (which, of course, inspired the title track). There were other sources at work as well: "Youngstown," a parable about the decay of industrialized America, was inspired by *Journey to Nowhere: The Saga of the New Underclass*, an American travelogue by writer Dale Maharidge and photographer Michael Williamson; parts of "Sinaloa Cowboys" came from a man Springsteen met in the Arizona desert during a motorcycle trip who told him about the death of his brother; other portions of "Sinaloa Cowboys" and "Balboa Park" were rooted in *Los Angeles Times* articles about illegal aliens and the drug trade. Elements of *The Grapes of Wrath* author John Steinbeck's *Of Mice and Men* could be found in "The New Timer," while "Galveston Bay" delved into the lingering personal and cultural politics of the Vietnam war. The Southwest and particularly California provided settings for these songs, and in *Songs* Springsteen acknowledged doing "a good amount of research to get the details of the region correct."

"The stories in *The Ghost of Tom Joad*," he told *DoubleTake* magazine, "were ... stories about brothers, lovers, movement, exclusion—political exclusion, social exclusion—and also the responsibility of these individuals—making bad choices, or choices they've been backed up against the wall to make. The way all those things intersect is what interests me." And despite the dark terrain, Springsteen contended that there was plenty of hope in these songs: "There's something being revealed—about (the characters), about you. That's always exciting. Even if the stuff is dark, even if there's tragedy involved, it's still exciting. The truth is always hopeful, it's always inspiring, no matter what it is."

Once he had the songs together, Springsteen began recording them with a small group of musicians—including his wife, Patti Scialfa, E Street

"**B**y climbing into their hearts and minds, Springsteen has given voice to people who rarely have one in this culture. And giving voice to people who are typically denied expression in our other arts and media has always been one of rock 'n' roll's most important virtues. As we move into the rough times and badlands that lie ahead, such acts will count for more than ever before."

—*Rolling Stone*

"**O**n the surface, Springsteen's story-song approach is a smart, thoughtful move ... But for all its nobility, *The Ghost of Tom Joad* still feels like a disappointing step back ... Springsteen took a similar lo-fi approach on his 1982 album *Nebraska*, but at least that album had the sheer force of 'Atlantic City' and a few stray rockabilly licks and whoops to vary its morose pace. In comparison, *The Ghost of Tom Joad* sounds downright depressed."

—*Entertainment Weekly*

"**T**his is campfire music ... Tom Joad's ghost shares sonic space with the spirit of Woody Guthrie—and the continuing influence of Bob Dylan. *Tom Joad* actually sounds better over headphones, not for sound quality but because its intimacy requires the listener to get as close as possible rather than pumping it over the big speakers."

—*Detroit Sunday Journal*

Band members Danny Federici and Garry Tallent, future E Streeter Soozie Tyrell, and drummer Gary Mallaber. Even coproducer Chuck Plotkin played some keyboards for the project. Comparisons to the musical approach of the even more spare *Nebraska* were apt; as Springsteen wrote in *Songs*, "The music was minimal; the melodies were uncomplicated, yet played an important role in the storytelling process. The simplicity and plainness, the austere rhythms defined who these characters were and how they expressed themselves." It was not a commercial sound, and Springsteen wrote in *Songs*, "I knew that (it) wouldn't attract my largest audience. But I was sure the songs on it added up to a reaffirmation of the best of what I do."

That it did. *The Ghost of Tom Joad* received a Grammy Award for Best Contemporary Folk Album (he played the title song at the awards ceremony). On the heels of the project he also received the esteemed Polar Music Prize in Sweden for "an outstanding career as a singer and stage performer." Springsteen supported *Tom Joad* with one of the most daring tours of his career, a solo acoustic presentation that found him reinventing some of his previous songs as well as trying out new material—including the mass media commentary "Sell It and They Will Come," the slyly ribald "Temple of Love," and the irreverent hometown salute "In Freehold." The tour led him to special performances as well, including benefits for the John Steinbeck Research Center in San Jose, California, and for the new Hispanic Community Center at his childhood parish, St. Rose of Lima, in Freehold. —*GG*

"Glory Days"

Single released: May 1985
Album: *Born in the U.S.A.* (Columbia, 1984)
Also on: *Greatest Hits* (Columbia, 1995); *The Essential Bruce Springsteen* (Columbia, 2003)
Chart peak: No. 5

he fifth single from *Born in the U.S.A.* , "Glory Days" hit No. 5 on the *Billboard* Hot 100. It was also one of the first songs Bruce Springsteen conceived for the album, recording it in May 1982 and considering it one of the project's cornerstone songs. In the song, Springsteen pokes fun at nostalgia, with two vignettes. In the liner notes to *Greatest Hits*, he writes, "The 1st verse (about meeting a high school baseball player) actually happened, the 2nd verse (about a high school classmate and single mother) mostly happened, the 3rd verse, of course, is happening now." The video for the song, a performance clip set in a pool hall, was filmed at various sites in New Jersey and directed by filmmaker John Sayles. Steve Van Zandt, who left the E Street Band after the recording of *Born in the U.S.A.*, made a cameo appearance in the video, as did Springsteen's then-newlywed bride Julianne Phillips and The Boss's biographer Dave Marsh. —*GG*

Lynn Goldsmith

Photographer, former girlfriend

ynn Goldsmith, a world-renowned rock photographer who started her career at *Rolling Stone* magazine, first captured images of Springsteen in 1972 when he was an unknown but buzzed-about artist and she was still in the early stages of her career. After that she had many more opportunities to photograph him—enough to publish two books, 1984's *Springsteen* and 2000's *Springsteen: Access All Areas*, the latter a chronicle of his 1978 *Darkness on the Edge of Town* tour. At the time the photos were taken, Goldsmith was also Springsteen's girlfriend, balancing sometimes competing professional ambitions and personal desires.

"You don't have to live with Bruce Springsteen, specifically, to learn the lesson of being with a person and not really hearing their needs because you're wrapped up in yourself," Goldsmith told *Backstreets* magazine. She also acknowledged that she struggled with being known as Springsteen's girlfriend more than for her own work. "I was always hiding it. My identity as a photographer was more important to me than being with the person I care about."

Goldsmith was already well established in music industry circles when Patti Smith set her up with Springsteen in 1977. A Detroit native and graduate of the University of Michigan, she worked for Joshua Television and, in 1972, was a director for ABC's "In Concert." The following year she directed a short documentary, *We're an American Band*, which was shown in theaters. In her 1995 book *Photodiary* she revealed details about her relationship with Springsteen, describing how calculated his look was, how the two of them scrutinized photos of Bob Dylan to study what he did, and how Springsteen would buy vintage clothes and distress them further by driving over them. She wrote that he didn't want her to sell photos in which he was smiling, and that he was upset that the Pointer Sisters had a hit with "Fire," because they were more successful with his music than he was. She's also spoken about him as "incredibly possessive," trying to limit her fraternization with E Street Band members and even governing how she dressed when she was with him.

Goldsmith also wrote about how much she loved Springsteen and how she thought they were meant to be together—but that her steadfast independent streak proved to be their undoing. When he asked her to accompany him on a press trip to promote the just-released *Darkness*, she refused because she had assignments and berated him for thinking her career was less important than his. This, she wrote, left the door open for another woman to walk in, although Goldsmith takes responsibility for breaking things up. "*I* didn't want to be in that relationship," she told *Back-*

streets. "It's not that it didn't work out; I think it worked out the way it was supposed to … The only thing I regret is not being there for someone who really cared about me. I don't regret losing the relationship. I just regret those moments that someone said they needed me and I wasn't there for really dumb reasons."

Springsteen's resentment led to a particularly dramatic scene at the second of his performances at the Musicians United for Safe Energy (MUSE) No Nukes concerts on September 23, 1979, at Madison Square Garden in New York, which has gone down in Springsteen history as perhaps the worst of his few incidents of bad concert behavior. Goldsmith volunteered her services to MUSE before Springsteen signed on to the shows. According to her account in *Photodiary*, they met and decided he would not show up at the venue until 10 p.m. She promised not to go backstage. (Other accounts mention that she also promised not to shoot from the photo pit in front of the stage, though she only alludes to that in her retelling.) At the second show, which took place on his thirtieth birthday, Springsteen was not in a good mood; he even threw a fan-proffered birthday cake back into the audience, hitting someone in the face, then flung his harmonica into the crowd. He later started pointing at Goldsmith and sent security guards to remove her; when they didn't, he motioned for her to come to the stage, but she didn't want to abandon her shooting position. Springsteen jumped offstage, grabbed her, pushed her onstage to the microphone and announced, "This is my ex-girlfriend!"—the one thing that would upset her most, she wrote. Springsteen then shoved her into the wings. Though humiliated, she did not sue him for $3 million as one newspaper reported the next day.

In a subsequent *Rolling Stone* Random Note item about his uncharacteristic display, Springsteen said: "It was just between her and me, boyfriend and girlfriend. She was doin' something she said she wouldn't do. I tried to handle it in other ways, but she avoided them. So I had to do it myself."

Over the years Goldsmith has voiced support for Springsteen, and particularly for his music and performances—though she's noted that she didn't own his albums even when they were dating. The No Nukes incident had no lasting damage, either; she went on to found the LGI Photo Agency, which represented hundreds of photographers around the world until she sold it in 1997. Goldsmith is the youngest member ever to be inducted into the Director's Guild of America, and her work has appeared in the popular *A Day in the Life of …* series. In 1983, under the name Will Powers, she released an album, *Dancing for Mental Health*—featuring songs cowritten with Sting, Steve Winwood, Nile Rogers, and Todd Rundgren—and had a minor hit with the single "Kissing to Be Clever." She's also published books about pop groups the Police and New Kids on the Block. —*GG/LM*

Robert Gordon

Rockabilly singer and performer

ockabilly singer Robert Gordon is another product of the underrated Washington, D.C., music scene that's produced a number of notable guitarists—Danny Gatton, Roy Buchanan, Link Wray, and E Street Band member Nils Lofgren—as well as Emmylou Harris and Mary Chapin Carpenter.

After an aborted early '70s stint in the punk band Tuff Darts (he left before they recorded anything), Gordon met record producer Richard Gottehrer ("My Boyfriend's Back," "Hang on Sloopy," "I Want Candy"). Gottehrer teamed Gordon with kindred spirit Wray (creator of the 1958 hit "Rumble"); they worked together on 1977's *Robert Gordon with Link Wray* and on 1978's *Fresh Fish Special*.

The latter contained "Fire," a tune written and handed off by rockabilly fan Bruce Springsteen—who was in a nonrecording purgatory due to legal circumstances and intended to give the song to Elvis Presley. Springsteen also stopped in the studio to play piano on Gordon's recording. The song never caught fire in the marketplace, however—at least not in Gordon's hands; the Pointer Sisters' 1979 version reached No. 2 on the charts.

Gordon's partnership with Wray ended after *Fresh Fish Special*; he subsequently worked with British guitarist Chris Spedding. Gordon still records and performs intermittently. *—LM*

Graceland. See Elvis Presley.

Grammy Awards

Recording industry honors

ruce Springsteen's first appearance at a Grammy Awards ceremony was a memorable one; cameras caught him on February 15, 1985, sitting in the front row with his then-girlfriend (and future wife), actress-model Julianne Phillips. It was the couple's first major public outing and created a "Who's that girl?" furor that nearly eclipsed the fact that Springsteen won his first Grammy, Best Male Rock Vocal Performance for "Dancing in the Dark."

Springsteen was on the road with the just-started Tunnel of Love Express Tour on March 2, 1988, when the *Tunnel of Love* album won the Best Rock Vocal Performance trophy. Six years later, on March 1, 1994, he was part of a tribute to Curtis Mayfield, performing a medley with an all-star group that included Bonnie Raitt, Steve Winwood, B.B. King, Steve Cropper, and Don Was.

Springsteen performs "The Ghost of Tom Joad" during the 39th Annual Grammy Awards in New York City on February 26, 1997. Springsteen won the Best Contemporary Folk Album Award for the song; as of 2004, he had won eleven Grammy Awards in categories ranging from folk to rock.

The following year, on March 1, 1995, Springsteen opened the Grammy ceremony with "Streets of Philadelphia," his Academy Award– and Golden Globe–winning contribution to the film *Philadelphia*. Springsteen walked away with four Grammys that night thanks to the song, including Song of the Year, Best Male Rock Vocal Performance, Best Rock Song, and Best Song Written Specifically for a Motion Picture or Television. He was back for the 1997 ceremony, playing "The Ghost of Tom Joad" at New York's Madison Square Garden and accepting a trophy for Best Contemporary Folk Album.

Many expected another major Springsteen sweep at the 2003 Grammy show, again at Madison Square Garden, as *The Rising* had brought him five nominations. He wound up with a not-too-shabby three—Best Rock Album and, for the title track, Best Rock Song and Best Male Rock performance, all off-camera—but his defeats by Norah Jones in the prestigious Album of the Year and Song of the Year categories were considered major upsets. Springsteen's mother, Adele, and his wife, Patti Scialfa, expressed their disappointment to Fox News from Sony's after-show party, and when *Entertainment Weekly* magazine asked Steve Van Zandt if he felt Springsteen was robbed, the E Street Band guitarist replied, "In a word, yeah. But it's all good. It's one of those things where they were all good records, you know?" Springsteen still made his mark on the show, playing "The Rising" with the E Street Band and joining a "London Calling" tribute to the Clash and its recently deceased frontman Joe Strummer with Van Zandt, Elvis Costello, Foo Fighters' Dave Grohl, and Rage Against the Machine/Audioslave's Tom Morello. Springsteen also shared a Grammy at the 2003 ceremony with the late Warren Zevon; "Disorder in the House," their duet on Zevon's posthumous album *The Wind*, received the trophy for Best Rock Performance By a Duo or Group With Vocal. —*GG*

The Grapes of Wrath

Acclaimed novel, film

J ohn Steinbeck's 1939 novel *The Grapes of Wrath* is one of the great achievements of American literature. A year later, it was turned into a classic film by director John Ford that made a tremendous impact on Bruce Springsteen—an influence that showed up in the title track and the overall tone of his 1995 album, *The Ghost of Tom Joad*.

The story follows the Joad family, Oklahoma tenant farmers forced off their land during the Great Depression. They make for California in search of a better life but find conditions quite the opposite of the paradise they'd dreamed of. Along the road and in the labor camps, they encounter acts of courage, kindness, corruption, and cruelty and suffer all manner of hardship and loss. The family stays together for as long as it can thanks in part to the strength of its men, though mostly it is the steadfastness of its women that sees it through. Tom Joad is a prison parolee who makes the journey to California but along the way becomes increasingly embittered about the treatment of his fellow migrants. He gets in a fight with and kills an anti-union vigilante and has to run away. In a memorable scene—reprised, in part, in "The Ghost of Tom Joad"—he says goodbye to his mother, speculating that his story is part of a much larger struggle. He tells her, "Maybe it's like Casey says. A fellow ain't got a soul of his own, just a little piece of a big soul, the one big soul that belongs to everybody, then. Then it don't matter. I'll be all around in the dark. I'll be everywhere, wherever you can look. Wherever there's a fight so hungry people can eat, I'll be there. Wherever there's a cop beatin' up a guy, I'll be there. I'll be in the way guys yell when they're mad. I'll be in the way kids laugh when they're hungry and they know supper's ready and where people are eatin' the stuff they raise and livin' in the houses they build. I'll be there, too."

In 1995, Springsteen told interviewer Bob Costas that it was the film more so than the book that made an impact on him. "Yeah, that picture I guess I saw in the late '70s and it had a really deep effect on me," says Springsteen, who's used the film adaptation of Steinbeck's *East of Eden* as source material for earlier songs such as "Adam Raised a Cain" and "Darkness on the Edge of Town." "I think I'd read some John Steinbeck, probably earlier than that, in high school, and there was something about the [*Grapes of Wrath*] film that sort of crystallized the story for me. And it always stayed with me after that, for some reason there was something in that picture that always resonated throughout almost all of my other work. It was just an image that popped out as I was sitting around on the couch messing around with the guitar." Springsteen added that Joad's speech, delivered by Henry Fonda in the film, made him cry.

In some of the 1996 shows on his acoustic solo tour, Springsteen played "Tom Joad," the Woody Guthrie song inspired by Steinbeck's character, as a prelude to "The Ghost of Tom Joad." He also played a show on October 26, 1996, to benefit San Jose State University's Center for Steinbeck Studies, at which he was also honored with the inaugural Steinbeck Award, presented annually to artists whose work addresses issues of social justice. In addition to performing, Springsteen read from *The Grapes of Wrath.* After the concert, Steinbeck's widow, Elaine, presented Springsteen with a signed, first-edition copy of the book.

Steinbeck was born in Salinas, California, in 1908. His work often dealt with social issues and the economic plight of rural laborers. In addition to *The Grapes of Wrath*, which won the Pulitzer Prize for literature, his most notable works are *Tortilla Flat* (1935), *Of Mice and Men* (1937), *East of Eden*

(1952), and *Travels with Charley* (1962). He was awarded the Nobel Prize for literature in 1962 and died in 1968.

Ford was born Sean Aloysius O'Feeney (possibly O'Fearna) in Cape Elizabeth, Maine, in 1895. Over the course of a long career, he made all kinds of films but was most famous for his westerns, including *Stagecoach* (1939), *My Darling Clementine* (1946), and *The Man Who Shot Liberty Valance* (1962). Ford won six Academy Awards, including one for *The Grapes of Wrath.* He died in 1973. *—DD/GG*

Greasylake.org

Fan website

 amed after the mythical body of water where Crazy Janey and Killer Joe did their thing in Bruce Springsteen's "Spirit in the Night," Greasylake.org is a tribute page run by Danish librarian Karsten Stanley Anderson. (His email address is cosmic_kid@greasylake.org, if you're tallying *Greetings from Asbury Park, N.J.* references.) It's perhaps the most thorough, up-to-date Springsteen fan page on the web, and its riches include a magazine library dating to Jon Landau's famous "Growing Young with Rock 'n' Roll" article from the *Real Paper* in 1974. Also valuable is the catalog of Springsteen's albums, including complete lyrics and trivia nuggets about each song, plus a show-by-show concert history and Springsteen biographical time-line. *—SK*

Greatest Hits

Released: February 28, 1995
Producers: Bruce Springsteen, Jon Landau, Chuck Plotkin, Steve Van Zandt, Mike Appel, Roy Bittan
Tracks: "Born to Run," "Thunder Road," "Badlands," "The River," "Hungry Heart," "Atlantic City," "Dancing in the Dark," "Born in the U.S.A.," "My Hometown," "Glory Days," "Brilliant Disguise," "Human Touch," "Better Days," "Streets of Philadelphia," "Secret Garden," "Murder Incorporated," "Blood Brothers," "This Hard Land"
Chart peak: No. 1

 iven his leaning toward the highly conceptual as a recording artist, a *Greatest Hits* album was not necessarily the kind of venture that came to Bruce Springsteen naturally. But in late 1994, as he strug-gled with a new studio album that wasn't quite coming into "focus," he was open to manager Jon Landau's suggestion of a career overview. "Jon called me one night," Springsteen told VH1, "and he read off a sequence, the sequence that's on (*Greatest Hits*) and it just seemed like a good idea." He also told *Guitar World* that he was not opposed to a hits collection: "I like the

"With the mighty exception of *Born in the U.S.A.* ... Springsteen's standing as a singles artist has seemed an incidental byproduct of his main focus: arraying his songs in theme-driven album-length statements. For this reason, *Greatest Hits* comes across as a collection of familiar songs, each stellar in its own right, that somehow adds up to something less than the sum of its parts."

—*Rolling Stone*

"It's one thing for the media to gauge an artist by his or her commercial success, but for Springsteen to do it is disorienting, if not depressing. The passion and conviction ingrained in his music never needed to be redeemed by sales statistics. Was Springsteen so flummoxed by the public indifference that greeted *Lucky Town* and *Human Touch* that he looks to chart positions for support? ... *Greatest Hits* leaves you wondering whether one of the most exuberant and thoughtful of American rockers believes in his own dreams anymore. It's the music equivalent of yet another factory shutting down."

—*Entertainment Weekly*

" ... we get a very uneven impression of The Boss's career. The earliest albums are ignored; *Born in the U.S.A.*'s songs are over-emphasized; the recent *Lucky Town* should have sent a better delegate than "Better Days." But otherwise one cannot complain. From "Born to Run" to "The River" to "Streets of Philadelphia," this music has heart and it gives heart. Is he, as he once so boastfully proclaimed, 'a cool rocking daddy in the U.S.A.?' Indeed he is all that, and more and deeper things besides."

—*Q*

Continued on next page...

classic idea of hits—it was sort of like *50,000,000 Elvis Fans Can't Be Wrong* ... I wanted to introduce my music to younger fans, who for twelve bucks could get a pretty good overview of what I've done over the years. And for my older fans, I wanted to say, 'This still means something to me now, you still mean something to me now.' It was just kind of a way of reaffirming the relationship that I've built up with my audience over the past twenty-five years."

Timing was on Springsteen's side for such an endeavor as well. He was still riding high on the Oscar-winning triumph of "Streets of Philadelphia," which had also landed a rash of Grammy Award nominations. In fact, *Greatest Hits* would come out the day before Springsteen performed on the 1995 Grammy Awards—and walked away with four trophies, including Song of the Year, Best Rock Song, Best Male Rock Vocal Performance, and Best Song Written for a Motion Picture or Television.

Greatest Hits was more than what its title said, however. In early January 1995 Springsteen decided to call the E Street Band, dismissed in 1989, back into the studio for the first time since the final sessions for *Born in the U.S.A.* to record some new songs for the album. The group—including both guitarists Steve Van Zandt and Nils Lofgren—assembled January 9 at the Hit Factory in New York City, and in *Songs* Springsteen writes, "We ... got behind our instruments and had a great time." The party included an in-studio birthday cake on January 11 for Clarence Clemons, who had canceled his own birthday party—with no complaints.

For the sessions, Springsteen and company rekindled a couple of older selections, the politically charged "Murder Incorporated" from the early '80s and the *Born in the U.S.A.* outtake "This Hard Land." "Secret Garden"—which would later become a hit via the film *Jerry Maguire*, came from the studio album Springsteen was working on at the time, and "Blood Brothers," inspired by the reunion, was written the night before the sessions. Springsteen and the E Streeters worked on some other tracks, including "Back in Your Arms," that didn't make the final cut (although a recording of "Back in Your Arms" from these sessions was subsequently released on *Tracks* in 1998). Interestingly, neither did a number of other bona fide hit singles, including Top 10 entries such as "Cover Me," "I'm On Fire," "War," and "Tunnel of Love."

...Continued

"**I**t is a testament to the continuing depth of Springsteen's writing that none of the new songs sounds at all out of place here. 'Blood Brothers,' especially, comes off as a touching farewell to the very friends he's gathered around him. Lines such as 'We got our own roads to ride' and 'Always movin' ahead and never lookin' back' might not look like much on the printed page but, delivered with a sort of bemused weariness, they ring unerringly true."

—*Toronto Sun*

The *Greatest Hits* project marked a short burst of activity for the E Street Band. Besides the sessions, the group played a February 21 show at Tramps in New York City so Jonathan Demme could film a video for "Murder Incorporated." The group played twice in New York on April 5, on "The Late Show with David Letterman" and then at Sony Studios. The group subsequently disbanded again, however, as Springsteen went back to work on what became *The Ghost of Tom Joad.*

Greatest Hits was Springsteen's second album to debut at No. 1 on the *Billboard* Top 200; the first was *Live/1975–85* in 1986. The CD booklet features his handwritten notes about the songs, as well as full lyrics and performance and production credits. A special promotional edition of *Greatest Hits* was released in a larger packaging format, with a fold-out centerspread displaying the original singles jackets. —*GG*

Greetings from Asbury Park, N.J.

Released: January 5, 1973
Producers: Mike Appel, Jim Cretecos
Tracks: "Blinded by the Light," "Growin' Up," "Mary Queen of Arkansas," "Does This Bus Stop at 82nd Street?," "Lost in the Flood," "The Angel," "For You," "Spirit in the Night," "It's Hard to Be a Saint in the City"
Chart peak: No. 60

ard as it is to relate to more than thirty years later, Bruce Springsteen was once an unknown quantity. A rock 'n' roll newcomer with at best a regional reputation, he was part of a legion of "new Dylans" that were foisted on music fans in the early '70s due to a combination of Bob Dylan's continued absence from the scene and the subsequent explosion of new troubadours such as Neil Young, James Taylor, Van Morrison, and Joni Mitchell. And despite the attention *Greetings from Asbury Park, N.J.* received thanks to an aggressive campaign by Columbia Records, it was a commercially and sonically inauspicious debut that only hinted at the virtues that would become obvious on subsequent releases. It's important to remember that *Greetings* was Springsteen's first step as solo artist. Until 1971 he had been mostly a band leader or member. But feeling that he had taken that avenue as far as he could, Springsteen committed himself to performing under his own name and decided to "write some music to survive on with just myself and the guitar," as he explains in *Songs.* With encouragement from future song publisher and future manager Mike Appel and his partner, Jim Cretecos, Springsteen wrote in the back room of a shuttered beauty parlor on the ground floor of his apartment building in Asbury Park. "They were written in half-hour, fifteen-minute blasts," Springsteen told the *Los Angeles Times.* "A few of them I worked on for a week or so, but most of them were just jets, a real energy situation."

In *Songs,* he mused, "The lyrics and spirit of *Greetings* came from a very unselfconscious place. Your early songs come out of a moment when you're writing with no sure prospect of ever being heard. Up until then, it's just you and your music. That only happens once." *Greetings* was the only time he wrote his lyrics first, Springsteen reveals in *Songs:* "I'd write the verses, then pick up the guitar or sit at the piano and follow the inner rhythm of the words." He came up with a series of "twisted autobiographies ... people, places, hang-outs, and incidents I'd seen and things I'd lived. I wrote impressionistically and changed names to protect the guilty." All the while he kept going to record company auditions in New York City, eventually signing to Columbia Records after a successful audience with John Hammond, the legendary talent scout whose signings included Bob Dylan, Aretha Franklin, and Billie Holiday.

With Appel and Cretecos producing, Springsteen started recording *Greetings* in three weeks in the summer of 1972 at 914 Sound Studios in Blauvelt, New York, with early E Street Band members Garry Tallent on bass, David Sancious on keyboards, and Vini Lopez (billed as Loper but also known as Mad Dog) on drums. Columbia president Clive Davis wasn't initially pleased with the results, however. "I listened for a breakthrough radio cut and didn't hear one," Davis recalled to *Backstreets,* "so I called (Springsteen) ... Most artists, if you discuss that, get very defensive, but he said, 'You know, you're right. Let me spend some time with this.'" Bringing saxophonist Clarence Clemons into the fold, Springsteen added "Blinded by the Light" (at one point titled "Madman's Bummers") and "Spirit in the Night," which became the album's two (unsuccessful) singles.

There were, however, continuing disagreements between Springsteen and the label over his approach on the album. Columbia, which had signed him based on a solo acoustic audition for Hammond, envisioned their artist in that vein, while Springsteen wanted to pursue a louder, rock-band approach more like his previous Jersey incarnations. "The label wanted a folk album," Springsteen told *Guitar World*, "because I was really signed as a folk artist by John Hammond, who didn't know that I ever had a band." One of those bandmates, guitarist Steve Van Zandt, said Springsteen's Jersey posse was disarmed at the direction *Greetings* took: "Everyone was basically going 'What the fuck is *this*?' His first record was a lot softer, a lot lighter, than anything he'd ever done."

Greetings received mixed but mostly positive reviews. Some critics found the album under-produced, as Appel and Cretecos endeavored to hang on to as much of Columbia's $65,000 advance and recording budget as they could. Springsteen's live performances, particularly of "Spirit in the Night" and "Growin' Up," made their recorded counterparts sound like mere sketches. Amidst frequent comparisons to Dylan and Morrison, some also felt Springsteen's lyrics were a bit too wordy and busy, perhaps the result of writing them before the music; Columbia tried to parlay that into an advantage, boasting in one ad, "This man puts more thoughts, more ideas and images into one song than most people put into an album." In a 1973 interview with the *Los Angeles Times*, Springsteen confessed, "I got a lot of things out on that first album. I let out an incredible amount at once— a million things in each song." The album was hardly a commercial behemoth, however, selling just 25,000 copies in its first twelve months of release and not even charting until the summer of 1975, when Columbia revved up the hype machine with the "Born to Run" single, attracting buyers to Springsteen's initial effort. —*GG*

"**D**espite the kiss-of-death 'new Dylan' hype that Columbia has given him, and despite the fact that most of the current crop of singer/songwriters give me a swift pain, I have no doubt that this kid's really got it ... His music is an absolutely haunting kind of mutated sleazy R&B, and his band is fantastic. It reminds me of what Van Morrison might be doing if he ever stopped whining."
—*Stereo Review*

"**T**he jokey lingo and absurdist energy ... are exactly the excesses that made Dylan a genius instead of a talent ... Even urban-mythos rambles like 'Lost in the Flood' are not without charm. And in songs like 'Growin' Up' and 'Blinded by the Light,' there's an unguarded teen-underclass poetry that has Springsteen's name on it."
—*Village Voice*

"**H**e's been influenced a lot by The Band, his arrangements tend to take on a Van Morrison tinge every now and then, and he sort of catarrh-mumbles his ditties in a disgruntled mushmouth sorta like Robbie Robertson on Quaaludes with Dylan barfing down the back of his neck. It's a tuff combination, but it's only the beginning."
—*Rolling Stone*

Patty Griffin

Singer-songwriter

ritically acclaimed singer-songwriter Patty Griffin tends to be covered more than cover. So when she included Bruce Springsteen's "Stolen Car" on her 2002 album *1000 Kisses*, it made news with both her fans and his. "I've been singing that song live in my solo shows for years," Griffin explained at the time. "It's, like, an astonishing song to me. I was told by a few people I should put that one out, so I finally did." Her version of the song was also included on the 2003 benefit album *Light of Day: A Tribute to Bruce Springsteen*.

Springsteen songs were a regular part of Griffin's repertoire when she began performing in Boston-area folk clubs in the early '90s, following a divorce. Her debut, 1996's *Living with Ghosts*, was actually a demo she had been shopping around to labels. After two releases with A&M she signed with Dave Matthews's ATO label. In addition to her own recordings, Griffin has appeared on albums by Emmylou Harris, Bruce Cockburn, the Chieftains, Julie Miller, Jules Shear, Marc Cohn, and others. Griffin's songs have been recorded by many artists, including Harris, the Dixie Chicks, Lucinda Williams, Reba McEntire, and Martina McBride. —*GG*

Joe Grushecky

Singer, songwriter, bandleader

ittsburgh rocker Joe Grushecky has been writing steel-toughened songs about working-class heroes and unshakeable dreams just about as long as Bruce Springsteen has, and his brand of muscular, R&B–laden rock has often been compared to that of Springsteen and fellow Jersey rocker Southside Johnny. Grushecky and his Iron City Houserockers got what appeared to be their big break when they signed with MCA in the late '70s and were teamed with renowned producers such as Steve Cropper, Ian Hunter, Mick Ronson, and E Streeter Steve Van Zandt. But Grushecky, a special education teacher by day, has never been able to step completely out of Pittsburgh and into national prominence, even though he's had help from The Boss himself.

Every time Grushecky releases a new album, Springsteen fans from around the world travel to Pittsburgh for the release party—just in case. Springsteen has shown up—three times, in fact; in each instance, the goal was to help his pal grab some extra publicity, but he also seems to relish the opportunities to revisit his own bar-band roots.

Springsteen and Grushecky first met when Van Zandt produced 1980's *Have a Good Time*, which spurred *Rolling Stone* magazine to hail the

Houserockers as "the best bar band in the land." The Grushecky-Springsteen alliance made perfect sense because their music bears such strong similarities. Grushecky's is filled with imagery scraped from western Pennsylvania's coal mines and forged with memories of disappearing steel mills and jobless underdogs, delivered as touching ballads or blast-it-loud rock 'n' roll. Southside Johnny also shares that musical style, but neither he nor Grushecky could be accused of copying—they merely developed at the same time, from the same sensibilities and experiences.

After his music career slowed in the '80s, Grushecky decided to take one last stab at the big time with 1995's *American Babylon*. His wife suggested calling Springsteen—who had invited Grushecky on stage during some of his Pittsburgh shows—for a little musical support and coattail excitement. Originally, Springsteen was going to help out with one song, then things snowballed; he became the album's producer, cowriting two and performing on eight of the album's twelve songs. Springsteen also became a Houserocker for a brief five-city, six-show tour to launch the album in Pittsburgh, New York, Philadelphia, Chicago, and Asbury Park. Springsteen also cowrote four songs on Grushecky's follow-up, 1998's *Coming Home*, and made an expected "surprise" appearance at the Pittsburgh release party. Grushecky's 1999 concert album *Down the Road Apiece Live* features Springsteen guesting on three tracks—"Talking to the King," "Pumping Iron," and the title track.

Springsteen and the Houserockers have shared other stages, including three Light of Day fundraisers for Parkinson's Disease research produced by Grushecky manager and Springsteen friend Bob Benjamin. They've also continued writing together; during Springsteen's 1999–2000 reunion tour with the E Street Band, he introduced a collaboration with Grushecky called "Code of Silence" and included a live version of it, recorded at New York's Madison Square Garden and later awarded a Grammy for Solo Rock Vocal Performance, on *The Essential Bruce Springsteen* in 2003. Springsteen and Grushecky paired up on Grushecky's home turf on December 2, 2004, at a benefit concert for victims of flooding in the Pittsburgh area from September of that year, at an even aptly titled Flood Aid '04. —*LM*

Woody Guthrie

Singer, songwriter, performer, American folk icon

t a 1996 tribute to Woody Guthrie sponsored by Cleveland's Rock and Roll Hall of Fame and Museum, Bruce Springsteen performed two Guthrie songs, "Plane Wreck at Los Gatos (Deportee)" and "Riding in My Car (Car Song)." Before the latter, Springsteen explained how he chose that children's song: "I'm going through this Guthrie songbook, and I was kind of excited. I said, 'Hmmm, automobiles, that's *my* business, Mr. Guthrie. No disrespect, but that's *my* business." Then he launched into the good-natured tune, cracking at the end, "Shit, why didn't *I* think of that?"

The comment, heard on *'Til We Outnumber 'Em: Woody Guthrie*, the album of the tribute, is indicative of Springsteen's appreciation for Guthrie as a forebearer who knew how to say all the right things in the right ways. Though Springsteen is considered an aesthetic descendant of the folk hero, he's acknowledged that he really didn't begin to investigate Guthrie's work until November 5, 1980, when he was given a copy of Joe Klein's biography, *Woody Guthrie: A Life,* after a concert at Arizona State University. The new appreciation made an immediate impact on Springsteen's 1982 album *Nebraska* and became one of the threads in the fabric of his repertoire, with a more pronounced influence on 1995's *The Ghost of Tom Joad.*

A native of Okemah, Oklahoma, Woodrow Wilson Guthrie learned to play guitar, harmonica, fiddle, and mandolin as an adolescent and spent much of the Great Depression riding the rails, living among migrants of the Dust Bowl and gleaning material that would inform his songs—particularly populist anthems such as "Dust Bowl Refugees," "Grand Coulee Dam," "So Long, It's Been Good to Know You," and the enduring (and misinterpreted) "This Land Is Your Land." Guthrie actually considered himself to be communist, writing a column for the *Communist Daily Worker*, but the party refused his membership because he wouldn't renounce religion.

Guthrie's star rose when he arrived in New York City in 1940 and became a darling of leftist factions. In addition to making music, he continued his studies in politics, economics, and other subjects and was a regular performer at strikes and protest rallies. He was an acknowledged cornerstone for the folk movement that sprung up in Greenwich Village in the '40s and '50s, and he mentored younger talents such as Bob Dylan and Joan Baez. Huntington's disease, a genetic nerve disorder that killed his mother, also claimed Guthrie on October 3, 1967. In addition to his body of work, he also left behind hundreds of unfinished songs, many of which have been completed and recorded by artists such as Wilco, Billy Bragg, and Janis Ian.

Author and historian Robert Santelli, who produced the Rock and Roll Hall of Fame's Guthrie tribute, notes in the book *Hard Travelin': The Life and Legacy of Woody Guthrie*, "[D]espite his late introduction to Guthrie, it is Springsteen who most authentically has carried out the Guthrie influence in modern rock and roll. He has acted as the musical conduit for those younger songwriters seeking a Guthrie-esque style in which music becomes a potent sociopolitical force."

An undated photograph of folk music legend Woody Guthrie. After reading a biography of Guthrie in 1980, Springsteen explored the singer's musical influences, leading him to write and record the stark and haunting acoustic album *Nebraska* **(1982) and later** *The Ghost of Tom Joad* **(1995).**

That embrace of such commentary also indoctrinated Springsteen into Guthrie's experience as a singing spokesman for various causes. Like Guthrie's most famous song, "This Land Is Your Land"—written as a populist response to Irving Berlin's "God Bless America"—Springsteen's "Born in the U.S.A." was misconstrued as a patriotic anthem rather than a protest song. Springsteen, who has performed "This Land Is Your Land" at his concerts, had to turn the pounding anthem into a Guthrie-like folk tune before people started to understand its message, sometimes making the comparison between the two songs himself before he performed it. But it was the police backlash from "American Skin (41 Shots)" that gave Springsteen an even firmer link to Guthrie, Dylan, and other folk singers who earned public wrath for nobly criticizing the establishment or taking on sensitive issues.

Springsteen, who serves on the advisory board of the Woody Guthrie Foundation, has performed several Guthrie songs, including "Tom Joad,"

"Going Down the Road," and, on the 1988 release *Folkways: A Vision Shared—A Tribute to Woody Guthrie and Leadbelly,* "I Ain't Got No Home" and "Vigilante Man," as well as a group-sung rendition of "This Land Is Your Land." Like Guthrie, Springsteen has been the subject of biographies by Dave Marsh, husband of Springsteen co-manager Barbara Carr.

Springsteen has also performed with Guthrie's son Arlo. At the Rock and Roll Hall of Fame tribute, both men joined in on group sings of "Hard Travelin' Hootenanny" and "'Til We Outnumber 'Em (This Land Is Your Land)," and Arlo is also part of the group that sings "This Land Is Your Land" on the *Folkways* album. —*LM/GG*

Hammersmith Odeon

**Site of Springsteen's first European show,
November 18, 1975**

The Bruce Springsteen mania surrounding 1975's *Born to Run* album was not limited to the United States. Over in Europe they were hearing about "rock and roll future" and were ready to see it in the flesh when Springsteen and the E Street Band crossed the Atlantic for the first time ever in November 1975. Unfortunately, the "future" got off to an inauspicious start on those shores.

Springsteen and company arrived in England in mid-November to find the hype in overdrive. Posters plastered around the city proclaimed, "Finally. The World Is Ready for Bruce Springsteen." He tore many of these down himself. He was also upset with buttons that read, "I have seen the future of rock 'n' roll at the Hammersmith Odeon," which were to be distributed at the November 18 show; Springsteen nixed them, and plain *Born to Run* buttons sporting a pair of sneakers were handed out instead. It all had an effect on his debut British performance; even guitarist Steve Van Zandt remarked to *Rolling Stone* magazine, "I've never seen him so subdued," and despite the first performance of "Lost in the Flood" in thirteen months, it was not a show that validated Jon Landau's famous proclamation. Some in the British press were uncharacteristically charitable, however; *Melody Maker* noted that Springsteen "was cast down by a response that was less magnanimous than he usually receives" from the show-me audience, while Robin Denselow wrote in the *Guardian*, "I think he might really be the genius his publicists and managers claim, but they've made it hard to show it. We certainly didn't quite see it last night."

The English got a better look at it when Springsteen returned to the Hammersmith Odeon on November 24, after shows in Sweden and the Netherlands. He pulled out his longest show to date, a three-hour set featuring twenty-one songs and nine encores, some of which was filmed and broadcast on the BBC's "Glory Days" special in 1987. Peter Gabriel has called it the second greatest concert he ever attended, bested only by Otis Redding. *Melody Maker* confirmed, "[I]t was a night on which one's emotions were completely exhausted." —*GG*

John Hammond

Producer and record company talent scout

During his fifty-year career in the music business, John Hammond was credited with discovering a diverse array of artists, including Billie Holiday, Count Basie, Lionel Hampton, Charlie Christian, Aretha Franklin, George Benson, Bob Dylan, Stevie Ray Vaughan, and Bruce Springsteen. In fact, it was Hammond's track record that Springsteen's then-manager Mike Appel used to challenge the venerable record executive at the fledgling artist's May 2, 1972, audition in Hammond's office at Columbia's "Black Rock" headquarters in New York City. As Hammond recalled in *Crawdaddy* magazine, "Mike started yakking. He said, 'I want you to know that we're just, you know, being nice to you because you're the guy who discovered Dylan and we just wanted to find out if that was luck or whether you really have ears.' So I said, 'Stop, you're making me hate you!'" Fortunately, Springsteen's performance, which began with "It's Hard to Be a Saint in the City," won Hammond over. "The kid absolutely knocked me out," Hammond told *Newsweek* in 1975. "I only hear somebody really good once every ten years, and not only was Bruce the best, he was a lot better than Dylan when I first heard him."

One can only imagine how Springsteen felt about the entire Hammond episode; he had just finished reading Anthony Scaduto's Dylan biography and was well aware of Hammond's iconic status. He was appalled at Appel's demeanor—"Before I ever played a note the hype began," he told *Newsweek*—and intimidated by the notion of playing his "beat-up guitar" with no case in front of a bona fide legend. "I went into a state of shock as soon as I walked in," said Springsteen, who used tapes from the audition to begin the 1998 *Tracks* box set. He didn't have much time to recover, either; Hammond rushed him to the Gaslight in Greenwich Village to hear him play live, then championed him to Columbia president Clive Davis.

Born into a prominent and wealthy family on December 15, 1910, Hammond studied piano and violin as a child and continued his musical studies at Yale University. He made frequent trips to New York City, immersing himself in Harlem's rich musical scene and the bohemian lifestyle of Greenwich Village. In 1927 Hammond saw Bessie Smith perform at the Alhambra Theatre, and the performance remained an influence on him throughout the rest of his life. He wrote for various music magazines and, after dropping out of school, became the American correspondent for the English music paper, *Melody Maker*. Hammond recognized the injustice of racism being experienced by the black artists he loved and championed civil rights from the earliest days of his career. He covered the infamous Scottsboro Boys trial for the *New Republic* in 1932 and served on the board of the National Association for the Advancement of Colored People (NAACP) for many years.

At age twenty Hammond produced his first record. He personally funded the recording of pianist Garland Wilson, which sold thousands of copies and brought him his first success. At the height of the Great Depression, Hammond was hired by Columbia Records in England to produce American jazz recordings for the European market. In 1933 Hammond found eighteen-year-old Billie Holiday singing in a Harlem nightclub and arranged for her to record one song with his friend Benny Goodman. (Goodman would later marry Hammond's sister, Alice.) A week after producing Holiday's first recording session, Hammond would produce Bessie Smith's last. He continued to produce jazz sessions with the likes of Fletcher Henderson, Coleman Hawkins, and Benny Carter, and he encouraged Goodman to form his first big band. With Hammond's help the Goodman orchestra became the first racially integrated band, incorporating black musicians such as Teddy Wilson, Charlie Christian, and Lionel Hampton. Hammond discovered Count Basie while randomly turning a radio dial in Kansas City in 1936 and convinced Basie to come to New York.

Hammond produced numerous sessions for Columbia and other labels from 1937–43 before serving in World War II. After the war he continued working as a producer for Vanguard, Keynote, Majestic, and Mercury. In 1954 Hammond became one of the founders of the Newport Jazz Festival and served on its board until 1970. He rejoined Columbia in 1959, discovering another eighteen-year-old singer with a powerful gospel voice, Aretha Franklin, as well as Bob Dylan a couple of years later.

By the time of Springsteen's commercial breakthrough with 1975's *Born to Run*, Hammond was preparing to retire. He continued to do some A&R work for Columbia, and in 1982—at the age of seventy-two—was responsible for signing Stevie Ray Vaughan to Columbia's sister label, Epic.

A Columbia Records in-house tribute video produced in Hammond's honor in 1976 includes the earliest known on-camera interview with Springsteen. And in 1984 Springsteen participated in a documentary project in which he was videotaped in conversation with Hammond. Some of this 1984 footage would appear in the documentary *John Hammond: From Bessie Smith to Bruce Springsteen*, which was completed in 1990, three years after Hammond's death on July 10, 1987. The film also includes some brief footage of Springsteen's August 1972 appearance at Max's Kansas City in New York, opening for Dave Van Ronk. Another Springsteen performance—at a memorial service for Hammond at St. Peter's Church in New York on October 22, 1987—plays over the documentary's closing credits. That day, Springsteen introduced his performance of Bob Dylan's "Forever Young" by saying, "This is a song by another young fellow that John gave a break to." —*RB/GG*

John Wesley Harding

Singer, songwriter

Although British folk singer John Wesley Harding took his name from a Bob Dylan album and his voice recalls the young Elvis Costello, he has a closer relationship with Bruce Springsteen than with either of them. The Harding-Springsteen connection came about after Springsteen heard Harding's fourth album, 1993's *Why We Fight*, and surprised "Wes" a year later by jumping on stage with him at McCabe's in Santa Monica, California. "It's a very nice story—just that he likes my music," Harding said in 2002. "I got to meet him by coincidence, but he knew who I was."

Springsteen, himself in a folk-troubadour phase at the time, invited the San Francisco–based Harding to open two California dates on *The Ghost of Tom Joad* tour—the first time The Boss used an opening act since the 1970s. Later, their duet on Springsteen's "Wreck on the Highway" from the McCabe's show wound up on a reissue of Harding's 1998 CD *Awake*. Harding also covers Springsteen's "Jackson Cage" as a bonus track on the same reissue.

In addition to being a friend, Harding has also become an occasional songwriting confidant for Springsteen. "The thing about Springsteen's songs is, in a sense, they're quite easy to play because the chords are quite easy," he said. "You can work 'em out as a kid, you don't even need a chord book. But they're difficult to do well. To me, growing up as teenager in England, ''69 Chevy with a 396,' he might as well be talking Japanese."

Harding also told the *San Francisco Chronicle* in 1999, "(Springsteen's) music has a totally redemptive belief in rock 'n' roll. The songs are so heavy and overwrought and meaningful. They're like operas, those songs. It's drama that you totally believe. It's triumphant. It's all about rock music, growing up, what goes on between men and women." —*SK*

Emmylou Harris

Singer, songwriter, neo-traditionalist country and roots artist.

A neo-traditionalist country singer and songwriter possessed of a cracked, crystalline soprano voice, Emmylou Harris is an artist whose work has consistently challenged country music's hidebound ways. She is regarded as a godmother of the so-called "alternative country" genre, and her work is readily accepted by rock 'n' roll fans as well. Harris has written a number of songs over the years, but she's especially adept at covering the work of others, including Chuck Berry, Rodney Crowell, Delbert McClinton, Dolly Parton, Daniel Lanois, Neil Young, Townes Van Zandt, Doc Pomus, and Bruce Springsteen. Harris has recorded a number of Springsteen songs over the years. Her version of "The Price You Pay" appeared on her 1981 album *Cimarron*, and "Racing in the Streets" graced 1982's live *Last Date*. She sang "My Father's House" on *Thirteen* in 1986 and "Tougher Than the Rest" on 1990's *Brand New Dance*. "Mansion on the Hill" appeared on another live album, 1992's

Emmylou Harris performs during the Farm Aid 2003 concert at Germain Amphitheater in Columbus, Ohio, on September 7, 2003. A longtime fan of Springsteen's work, Harris has covered his songs numerous times, and on her 2000 album *Red Dirt Girl*, she had Springsteen and Patti Scialfa sing backup on her version of the song "Tragedy."

At the Ryman. For *Western Wall: The Tucson Sessions*, Harris's 1999 collaboration with Linda Ronstadt, the duo covered Springsteen's "Across the Border" as well as Patti Scialfa's "Valerie." Harris enlisted Springsteen and Scialfa, both confirmed fans, to sing backup on "Tragedy," a cut from 2000's Grammy-winning *Red Dirt Girl.*

Born in Birmingham, Alabama, and raised in the Virginia suburbs of Washington, D.C., Harris was discovered by Flying Burrito Brothers' Chris Hillman and mentored by Gram Parsons, who featured Harris prominently on his *GP* and *Grievous Angel* albums. She pursued a solo career in earnest after Parsons's death in 1973, topping the country charts with "If I Could Only Win Your Love," "Together Again," "Sweet Dreams," and "Two More Bottles of Wine." She appeared in The Band's farewell documentary *The Last Waltz* in 1976 and won a Grammy for Best Female Vocal Performance in 1977. *Trio,* her first collaboration with Ronstadt and Dolly Parton, came out in 1987, while *Trio II* came out twelve years later and won a Grammy for Best Country Collaboration with Vocals.

Harris's music changed radically in 1995 with *Wrecking Ball*, which was produced by Daniel Lanois, who had worked with U2, Bob Dylan, and the Neville Brothers. Harris's angelic voice proved a terrific fit for Lanois's moody soundscapes, and the album won a Grammy for Best Contemporary Folk Album. Subsequent albums found Harris continuing in the same sonic vein, but writing more of the material and collaborating frequently with Buddy Miller. —*DD*

High Fidelity

2000 film directed by Stephen Frears

In the middle of *High Fidelity*, John Cusack's character Rob Gordon—a hipster Chicago record-store owner who is existentially confused about women—decides to reconnect with his Top 5 ex-girlfriends. "Just see 'em and talk to 'em," he tells himself. "You know, like a Bruce Springsteen song." And suddenly, in a room with an electric guitar, Springsteen himself shows up to indulge Rob's fantasy. "That's what you're looking for, you know, get ready to start again," Springsteen says, deadpan, in his first-ever dramatic movie appearance. "It'd be good for you." After a conversation, Rob says, "Thanks, Boss."

It's a hilarious dream sequence, especially if you don't know it's coming (which, of course, Springsteen fans did after months of media hints). As it turned out, snagging Springsteen was easier than Cusack expected for the 2000 adaptation of Nick Hornby's British novel. "I knew him. I was friends with him," the actor, who cowrote the screenplay, told the *Buffalo News*. "So I called him and asked him, and he said yes.

"It was kind of a strange Hail Mary. You're asking Bruce to play himself in a way he'd never done in a movie before. It was a funny idea. It might not be funny to Bruce. I had no idea whether he'd want to do it. In fact, I sort of assumed he wouldn't. But I had to ask. I sort of apologized ... I'd go to his concerts forever. He invited me to his birthday party one year. I stayed in contact. I stayed friendly." Springsteen's sequence was nominated for Best Cameo in a Movie at the 2001 MTV Movie Awards but lost out to James Van Der Beek's guest turn in *Scary Movie*.

Although The Boss's film career seems to have ended with *High Fidelity*, a 2002 *Chicago Sun-Times* rumor had Springsteen portraying a local radio DJ who helps suicidal Julia Stiles "straighten out her life." The film, directed by Tom Sierchio (1984's *Delivery Boys*), has yet to make it to the screen. —*SK*

Robert Hilburn

Los Angeles Times **pop music editor and critic,**
1970–present

hough Dave Marsh is the print journalist most closely associated with Bruce Springsteen, Los Angeles–based Robert Hilburn has been a constant correspondent throughout his career and has interviewed Springsteen more times than any of his peers. The first, in fact, was the result of some strong-arming tactics; after an interview request was surprisingly turned down in the summer of 1974, Hilburn was asked by Columbia Records to hold a profile of its recently fired chief, Clive Davis, which was due to run during Columbia's national convention in Los Angeles. Hilburn agreed—if he could get Springsteen. The deal was made, and the interview took place after Springsteen opened for Dr. John on July 25 at the Santa Monica Civic Auditorium—during which, Hilburn recalled, Springsteen spent much of the time wondering if he should do interviews at all and how much he should say about the meanings of his songs. By his own estimate Hilburn has interviewed Springsteen a dozen or so times, and he was tapped by Rolling Stone Press to write the 1985 book *Springsteen*. Hilburn has been at the *Times* since 1970 as chief pop music critic and pop music editor and is widely regarded as the dean of the music journalism world. —*GG/LM*

Holiday Shows

Springsteen tradition circa 1997

ince his residential return to New Jersey from Los Angeles, Bruce Springsteen has regularly held musical holiday gatherings—a tradition that has grown from low-key jam sessions into full-blown almost annual benefit extravaganzas that are as much fixtures on his fans' calendars as the December holidays themselves. It indeed started small, with annual Christmas parties—starting in 1997—at Rumrunners in Sea Bright, New Jersey, at which Springsteen usually hired Asbury Jukes guitarist Bobby Bandiera and his band to play and then wound up joining them onstage for a significant chunk of the evening.

The Holiday Show became a more formal endeavor in 2000, when Springsteen, the Max Weinberg 7, "and Friends" set up shop on December 17 and 18 at the Asbury Park Convention Hall, with proceeds from tickets and merchandise going to a variety of New Jersey area food banks, health-care facilities, civic organizations and charities. Among the "Friends" at these shows were Springsteen's wife, Patti Scialfa; E Streeters Steve Van Zandt, Nils Lofgren, and Garry Tallent; Southside Johnny Lyon; and even Springsteen's manager, Jon Landau. A pattern was established, too, for

In 1997 Springsteen began hosting holiday gatherings in New Jersey for friends and family. By the year 2000, the originally low-key get-togethers had turned into a large-scale series of benefit concerts designed to raise money for Springsteen's favorite charities. Here, he sings with members of the Max Weinberg 7 on December 3, 2001, during the first of five shows held at Convention Hall in Asbury Park.

unique collaborations and rarely played material, both covers and Spring-steen originals—and, of course, "Santa Claus Is Comin' to Town."

In the wake of the September 11 tragedies, the 2001 Holiday Show series got bigger and better—and even more meaningful—with a five-show stand December 3, 4, 6, 7, and 8 at the Convention Hall. The city of Asbury Park, with a new mayoral administration in place, was added to the list of beneficiaries, and the guest list swelled; in addition to Scialfa, Lofgren, and Lyon, Springsteen and company were joined by Elvis Costello on the 8th, Bruce Hornsby—and his accordion-led version of Hot Chocolate's "You Sexy Thing"—on the 7th and 8th, and Garland Jeffreys on the 3rd, 4th, and 6th.

With *The Rising* tour in motion, Springsteen took 2002 off for a real Christmas break but brought the Holiday Show series back in 2003 with three Convention Hall shows on December 5, 7, and 8—the latter a makeup date for December 6, which was canceled due to bad weather. Jeffreys returned, and some new "Friends"—Jon Bon Jovi, Sam Moore, and Jesse Malin—joined the fray. The shows also included a sobering but spirited nod to the U.S. military actions in Iraq, with Nick Lowe's "(What's So Funny 'Bout) Peace, Love and Understanding." The 2004 holiday shows included back-to-back performances on December 19 at Harry's Roadhouse in Asbury Park, benefiting area merchants and charities —*GG*

The Hollies

British rock band

T his British band's 1975 rendition of "4th of July, Asbury Park (Sandy)" was one of the first covers of a Springsteen song ever done—though Hollies singer Allan Clarke actually issued a 1974 solo recording of "If I Were a Priest," a frequently bootlegged track from Springsteen's 1972 Columbia Records demo tape (known then as "If I Was a Priest") for John Hammond. A rendition of "Born to Run," released as a Clarke solo single in France several months before Springsteen's version of the song came out, wound up on reissues of the Hollies' 1976 album *Write On.* Clarke also recorded "Blinded by the Light" for his 1976 solo album *I've Got Time.*

One of the most successful of the mid-'60s British Invasion bands, the Hollies were among many influenced by Buddy Holly—even naming themselves after him when it formed in 1962. The group's most famous member is undoubtedly cofounder Graham Nash, who gained greater fame after leaving the group and subsequently joining Crosby, Stills & Nash (& Young). The Hollies had several hits, notable for their pop vitality and wonderfully tight harmonies. Nash, Clarke, and guitarist Tony Hicks handled songwriting, though they earned early popularity with a chain of mostly well-chosen covers such as Doris Troy's "Just One Look." At their mid-'60s peak, the Hollies produced a string of charming tunes that became hits on both sides of the pond, including "Look Through Any Window," "Bus Stop," and "Carrie Ann."

There were hits after Nash's 1968 departure, including "He Ain't Heavy, He's My Brother," "Long Cool Woman (In a Black Dress)," and "The Air That I Breathe." It was Nash's replacement, Terry Sylvester, who claims credit for bringing Springsteen to the Hollies. The former Swingin' Blue Jeans member signed a publishing deal with Warner/Chappell Music, the same publishing company that handled Springsteen's songs; it was through Sylvester that the Hollies sat down with Warner/Chappell's Adrian Rudge, who played the group a couple of songs by a then-unknown Springsteen, leading to the "4th of July" cover. —*LM*

The Horns of Love

Horn section for the 1988 Tunnel of Love Express Tour

The Tunnel of Love Express Tour in 1988 marked the second time Bruce Springsteen and the E Street Band went on the road with a full horn section; the first was with the Miami Horns for the 1977 Chicken Scratch Tour. One member of the Horns of Love, saxophonist Ed Manion, was part of the original Miami Horns, while two others, trombonist Richie "La Bamba" Rosenberg and trumpeter Mark Pender, were in a one-off Miami Horns section that played "Tenth Avenue Freeze-Out" at Springsteen's August 20, 1984, concert at Brendan Byrne Arena in East Rutherford, New Jersey (it's featured on the *Live/1975–85* album). The Horns of Love were filled out by trumpeter Mike Spengler and saxophonist Mario Cruz. Rosenberg and Pender are now part of the Max Weinberg 7, the house band for NBC's "Late Night with Conan O'Brien." —*GG*

Human Touch

Released: March 31, 1992
Producers: Bruce Springsteen, Jon Landau, Chuck Plotkin, Roy Bittan
Tracks: "Human Touch," "Soul Driver," "57 Channels (And Nothin' On)," "Cross My Heart," "Gloria's Eyes," "With Every Wish," "Roll of the Dice," "Real World," "All or Nothin' at All," "Man's Job," "I Wish I Were Blind," "The Long Goodbye," "Real Man," "Pony Boy"
Chart peak: No. 2

After the Amnesty International Human Rights Now! tour ended in October 1988, Bruce Springsteen came off the road and began making major changes in his life. He finalized his divorce with Julianne Phillips, had his first son (Evan), moved to California, married Patti Scialfa, and gave the E Street Band members their walking papers. What he didn't do much of was music, choosing instead to take some time off to focus on these life changes.

His first post–E Street album began taking shape in January 1990 with "Part Man, Part Monkey" (which had been performed with the E Street Band on 1988's Tunnel of Love Express Tour) and a rendition of "Viva Las Vegas" for the British benefit album *The Last Temptation of Elvis*. But, as Springsteen noted in *Songs*, *Human Touch* was another record that evolved slowly, and it would take him the better part of a year and a half to accumulate and record the material—carefully constructing songs with Roy Bittan, the sole survivor of the E Street purge. In fact, Bittan received cowriting credit on two tracks, "Roll of the Dice" and "Real World," Springsteen's first songwriting collaborations for one of his own albums.

"The record took shape when Roy and I would play together in my garage apartment and make tapes of song and arrangement ideas I came up with," Springsteen explained in *Songs*. "Then we'd go into the studio and set up what essentially was a two-man band ... The two of us could create an entire band sound live in the studio."

To flesh out their basic tracks, Springsteen brought in a rhythm section of one-time Journey bassist (and future "American Idol" judge) Randy Jackson and Toto drummer Jeff Porcaro, who replaced the drum machine patterns Springsteen and Bittan had worked with. An array of well-credentialed guests were deployed as well, including soul singers Sam Moore and Bobby King, Bobby Hatfield of the Righteous Brothers, former E Street Band keyboardist David Sancious, ex-Faces keyboardist Ian McLagan, trumpeter Mark Isham, and Scialfa. The songs on *Human Touch* paralleled Springsteen's life events, chronicling hardships and romantic breakups as well as joyous new directions. "To receive what love delivers," he explained, the song's characters "have to surrender themselves to each other and accept fate. This tension is at the heart of *Human Touch*."

The tension wasn't entirely resolved, however. Springsteen told the *Los Angeles Times* that when he finished in mid-1991, he didn't feel *Human Touch* reflected "someone who felt as thankful and blessed as I did." So he wrote one more song, "Living Proof," that inspired a second, quicker batch of songs that became *Lucky Town*, an album that was released simultaneously with *Human Touch*—a move that surprised both his fans and the music industry, though Springsteen contended that the two groups of songs shared a thematic continuum that made them work as companion pieces. "It just wasn't a double album to us," manager and coproducer Jon Landau told British journalist Patrick Humphries in 1992. "To us they are very distinct—there's no song you could take from *Human Touch* and put it on *Lucky Town* and vice versa, which would flow and feel coherent in that context."

Springsteen announced that the two albums were coming on January 23, 1992, shooting a video for *Human Touch*'s first single, the title track, in

> " ... while breaking no new musical ground on these companion pieces, he has created his most mature and subtle work to date."
> —*San Francisco Chronicle*

> "His most confused records since his debut. It's as though his ability to craft a good record has gone the way of his working-class image."
> —*Entertainment Weekly*

> "For years, expressions of happiness were considered dangerous for rock's great artists because it might bring complacency. But you don't have to sacrifice your artistic instincts when acknowledging moments of comfort and tenderness. In these two albums, Springsteen offers living proof."
> —*Los Angeles Times*

> "The aesthetic and thematic aims of *Human Touch* and *Lucky Town* would have been better realized by a single, more carefully shaped collection that eliminated their half dozen or so least essential songs."
> —*Rolling Stone*

> "The mere presence of these records is uplifting. He's given us a lot of good music at a time when we can use it."
> —*New York Daily News*

Springsteen's tour to support the release of the *Human Touch* and *Lucky Town* albums in 1992 and 1993 marked the first time in nearly two decades he had hit the road without the E Street Band.

New Orleans at the end of the month—at which point he and Landau played the music for Sony executives who were gathered there for a conference. The single, which featured "Better Days" from *Lucky Town* as a B-side, preceded the albums by nearly four weeks. —*GG*

"Human Touch"

Released: March 4, 1992
Album: *Human Touch* (Columbia, 1992)
Also on: *Greatest Hits* (Columbia, 1995), *The Essential Bruce Springsteen* (Columbia, 2003)
Chart peak: No. 16

he first single from the *Human Touch/Lucky Town* joint release boasts a moody, keyboard-based arrangement that sounds like a natural progression from Bruce Springsteen's previous album, *Tun-*

nel of Love. The song winds through an ebb-and-flow arrangement that includes a languid, almost offhanded-sounding guitar solo and emotive wordless vocals by Springsteen and his wife, Patti Scialfa. It's a song about longing that accepts past failings ("So you been broken and you been hurt/Show me somebody who ain't") with a grim determination to move towards something better. As Springsteen wrote in *Songs*, it's about the "search to find some emotional contact, some modest communion, some physical and sexual connection."

"Human Touch" was recorded by the album's core group—Springsteen and E Street Band keyboardist Roy Bittan, with Toto drummer Jeff Porcaro and onetime Journey bassist (and future "American Idol" judge) Randy Jackson. Scialfa is the song's only guest.

"Human Touch" was backed by "Better Days," a track from the companion *Lucky Town* album—the first time since 1978 that Springsteen didn't use a previously unreleased song for a B-side. The "Human Touch" video, directed by Meiert Avis, was filmed in late January 1992 in New Orleans. —*GG*

"Hungry Heart"

Released: October 18, 1980
Album: *The River* (1980)
Also on: *Live/1975–85* (1986), *Greatest Hits* (1995), *The Essential Bruce Springsteen* (2003)
Chart peak: No. 5

ruce Springsteen's first Top 10 single—of his own, at least—was recorded in the spring of 1979, before he and the E Street Band played the No Nukes concerts, at the Power Station in New York City. It almost went the way of "Because the Night" and "Fire," however; in the liner notes of his *Greatest Hits* album, Springsteen explains, "I met the Ramones in Asbury Park and Joey asked me to write a song for 'em. I went home and that night I wrote this. I played it for Jon Landau and, earning his money, he advised me to keep it."

Pay the man double, then. "Hungry Heart"—on which the E Street Band was abetted by lush backing vocals from Flo (Mark Volman) and Eddie (Howard Kaylan) from the Turtles—shot to No. 5 and became a quick concert favorite on which the crowd would sing the first verse while Springsteen "conducted" from the stage. In *Songs*, Springsteen describes it as one of the songs he wrote "to provide fuel for our live show and to create a counterbalance to the ballads that began showing up more and more in my work." It worked; beginning on November 20, 1980, in Chicago, the audience began singing "Hungry Heart" while the E Street Band played and Springsteen laid back, listening to them. It became a ritual that still occurs every time the song is played. The B-side of "Hungry Heart" was a short rocker called "Held

Springsteen plays Detroit's Cobo Arena on October 9, 1980, the fifth stop on the tour for *The River*. **As the tour progressed, the live version of "Hungry Heart" became a fan sing-along favorite.**

Up Without a Gun," which didn't make it onto *The River* and began a tradition of Springsteen using non-LP tracks for his B-sides.

"Hungry Heart" was the first Springsteen song to be used for a movie soundtrack—*Risky Business*, which was Tom Cruise's breakthrough film in 1983. It's been covered by the Beach Boys' Mike Love and Jesse Malin. —*GG*

"I'm Goin' Down"

Single release: August 1985
Album: *Born in the U.S.A.* (Columbia, 1984)
Chart peak: No. 9

he rockabilly-flavored "I'm Goin' Down" was the sixth single to be pulled from *Born in the U.S.A.* and, like its predecessors, made its way into the *Billboard* Top 10. Another dark lyric (about sexual frustration) set to an uptempo instrumental track, it was released to coincide with Bruce Springsteen's stadium dates in the late summer and fall of 1985, which brought the eighteen-month tour supporting the album to a close.

"I'm Goin' Down" was among the tracks recorded in May 1982 at the Power Station in New York City, during the first E Street Band sessions for *Born in the U.S.A.* It was at one point slated to come off the album in favor of "Pink Cadillac," the eventual B-side of "Dancing in the Dark," but while it eventually wound up on the A list it hasn't been included on any subsequent live albums or compilations. But it does turn up in concert on occasion. Another session outtake, "Janey Don't You Lose Heart," was used as the B-side; this marked the first released performance by then-new E Streeter Nils Lofgren, whose backing vocals were recorded and mixed in to replace the originals by Steve Van Zandt.   —*GG*

"I'm on Fire"

Single release: February 4, 1985
Album: *Born in the U.S.A.* (Columbia, 1984)
Also on: *Live/1975–85* (Columbia, 1986)
Chart peak: No. 6

The fourth—and fourth consecutive Top 10—single from *Born in the U.S.A.* was among the songs recorded in the first E Street Band sessions for the album, in May and June 1982 at the Power Station in New York City. In *Songs*, Bruce Springsteen wrote that it was one of the songs he "wrote trying to finish the album." This one, he noted, "came to me one night in the studio when I was just goofing around with a Johnny Cash and the Tennessee Three rhythm." The rollicking "Stand on It," another *Born in the U.S.A.* sessions refugee, appears on the B-side.

The song's video, directed by John Sayles, was initially going to be taken from live footage shot at concerts at the Carrier Dome in Syracuse, New York, Springsteen's first stadium shows. But Sayles and Springsteen went with a concept piece instead—effectively Springsteen's first "acting" role. In it he plays a garage mechanic who's subtly propositioned by a leggy (that's most of what we see of her) customer who asks him to bring the car back to her place—and lets him know her husband won't be home. Springsteen does as he's asked but passes on the sexual advance, instead dropping the car off and walking home as the video fades to black.

Sayles donated his $10,000 directing fee to aid organizations for Sandanistas in Nicaragua. —*GG*

In Concert MTV Plugged

Released: April 12, 1993 (Europe); August 26, 1997 (U.S.)
Producers: Bruce Springsteen, Jon Landau
Tracks: "Red Headed Woman," "Better Days," "Atlantic City," "Darkness on the Edge of Town," "Man's Job," "Human Touch," "Lucky Town," "I Wish I Were Blind," "Thunder Road," "Light of Day," "If I Should Fall Behind," "Living Proof," "My Beautiful Reward"
Chart peak: No. 189
Home video/DVD: "Red Headed Woman," "Better Days," "Local Hero," "Atlantic City," "Darkness on the Edge of Town," "Man's Job," "Growin' Up," "Human Touch," "Lucky Town," "I Wish I Were Blind," "Thunder Road," "Light of Day," "The Big Muddy," "57 Channels (And Nothin' On)," "My Beautiful Reward," "Glory Days," "Living Proof," "If I Should Fall Behind," "Roll of the Dice"

On September 22, 1992, Bruce Springsteen was booked to tape an episode of MTV's popular "Unplugged" series. It was at that point his second-ever "live" TV appearance, and fans were stoked in anticipation for a rare acoustic performance. But Springsteen had other plans. After a solo rendition of the unreleased "Red Headed Woman," Springsteen brought his 1992–93 touring band on stage and put the plug back in to play what was essentially a truncated, ninety-minute edition of the regular stage show, though there were also stripped-down renditions of "Thunder Road" and "Growin' Up."

MTV executives were relatively sanguine about this turn of events, making the best of the situation by crossing the *Un* out on that particular episode's title. "Unplugged" producer Alex Coletti told Britain's *Q* magazine, "When you have the chance to work with Bruce Springsteen, he can do what he wants. It was a fantastic show, and it still had a lot of "Unplugged"'s feel. It was very small, very intimate, very loose—and that's all part of what makes "Unplugged" special. But it was very loud."

The "plugged" session was subsequently turned into a thirteen-track CD— containing the previously unreleased "Red Headed Woman" and "Light of Day"—and a full-length home video release. The CD first came out in April 1993, in Europe only for a limited ninety-day release to promote Springsteen's European dates that year. Nearly four-and-a-half years later—ironically, after his solo acoustic *The Ghost of Tom Joad* tour—it was given a full worldwide release. A home video of the performance, adding three songs not broadcast ("Roll of the Dice," "Living Proof." and "If I Should Fall Behind") was also released and came out on DVD in November 2004. —*GG*

"**E**ric Clapton does *Unplugged* (completely acoustic, famous songs rejigged), issues CD (somewhat reluctantly): result—universal acclaim, mega sales and Grammies by the armful. Bruce Springsteen does *Unplugged* (in a convention-busting Plugged kinda way), issues CD (strictly limited edition, European release only): result—a pretty good Springsteen live album ... With considerable power and occasionally glorious moments, it serves to remind that despite recent reservations (both his and ours) about his ability or his willingness to stay awake at the wheel, there's enough under The Boss's travel-battered bonnet to take him a good few miles further yet down rock 'n' roll highway."
—*Q*

"... an excellent sampling of the 1992 Bruce. His storytelling between songs— especially when he describes writing 'Local Hero' after seeing his image in black velvet at a discount store—is priceless. But his best moments are when he's alone with his guitar or backed by Roy Bittan's piano, doing 'Red Headed Woman,' 'Growin' Up' and 'Thunder Road.' If only there had been more truly unplugged moments like these during the show."
—*Entertainment Weekly*

"**T**he large, post E-Street band is solid but predictable, though all this set does is remind listeners of the big mystery: Why doesn't Springsteen follow the lead of his brilliant *Tunnel of Love* album and find an interesting middle ground between his stadium heritage and today's dry Woody Guthrie routine?"
—*Amazon.com*

Michael Jackson

Pop superstar, personality icon

Three musicians ruled the pop music world in the summer of 1984—Bruce Springsteen, Michael Jackson, and Prince. They shared time at the top of the charts, sold records at multi-platinum levels, and, because each granted few or no interviews, were the subjects of curiosity as intense as their most fervent fans' devotion. The Springsteen-Jackson link was even more pronounced, because both recorded for Sony Music (Springsteen for the Columbia label, Jackson for Epic) and both were criss-crossing North America on separate tours that summer. They connected at the beginning of September 1984. Springsteen was on a short break from his *Born in the U.S.A.* tour and at home in New Jersey when Jackson and his brothers, on their *Victory* tour, swung through Philadelphia. A "Summit Meeting," as *People* magazine headlined it, was set up at Jackson's hotel for a brief and awkward meeting between the two musical superpowers.

Springsteen sported a short-sleeved shirt, jeans, and a red neckerchief and sucked on an ice cube. Jackson wore a pink button-down shirt over a white T-shirt, rose-colored pants that were too long for him, and monogrammed blue slippers. They talked a bit of shop, Springsteen asking about the high number of cues in the *Victory* production, Jackson expressing wonder at the length of Springsteen's shows and at his rapport with the audience. "I tell stories," Springsteen told Jackson, "People like that, I've learned. They like to hear your voice do something besides singing. They go wild when you just ... talk."

Jackson replied, "Oh, I could never do that. It feels like people are learning something about you they shouldn't know."

The meeting's most humorous moment came when Jackson grabbed his secretary, Shari, for a photo with Springsteen. "Shari wants you for Christmas," Jackson said, to which Springsteen cracked, "What's wrong with Thanksgiving?" Jackson took his leave after about fifteen minutes, and Springsteen concluded, "He's just a real nice guy."

The two would meet again nearly five months later at the recording of USA for Africa's "We Are the World" in Los Angeles. Jackson cowrote the song, and both he and Springsteen were featured soloists.

Jackson's life and career have gone through many twists since the orchestrated 1984 encounter with Springsteen. The onetime Motown child prodigy never equalled the commercial zenith he hit with 1982's *Thriller* but still produced a series of blockbusters, including *Bad* and *Dangerous*. But in the mid-'90s his artistic virtues were subdued by controversies, including a brief marriage to Elvis Presley's daughter Lisa Marie and a 1993 child molestation accusation that was settled out of court. Another molestation accusation surfaced in 2003. —*GG*

Randy Jackson

Musician, producer, "American Idol" judge

efore he began his tenure as the *dawg!*matic member of "American Idol"'s; trio of judges in 2003, Randy Jackson was an active musician and label executive. That included eight years as a senior vice-president of A&R with Columbia Records, during which time he played bass on Bruce Springsteen's *Human Touch* and *Lucky Town* albums, which were recorded in the latter part of 1991 at Springsteen's home studio in Los Angeles. Springsteen was another credit on Jackson's already brimming resume, which includes recording and touring with Elton John, Bob Dylan, Mariah Carey, *NSYNC, Celine Dion, Whitney Houston, Madonna and Destiny's Child. He was Journey's bassist in 1986–87 and a senior vice-president of A&R at MCA Records for four years after his Columbia stint. In addition to working "Idol," Jackson manages young singers Nikka Costa and Van Hunt, and in 2004 he published a book, *What's Up, Dawg? How to Become a Superstar in the Music Business.* —*GG*

Garland Jeffreys

Singer, songwriter, performer since mid-'60s

 ans of Bruce Springsteen know Garland Jeffreys for his appearances at the holiday shows in Asbury Park (in 2001 and 2003), as well as two guest spots during *The Rising* tour (July 18, 2003, at Giants Stadium in East Rutherford, New Jersey, and on October 4, 2003, at Shea Stadium in New York). The relationship between the two musicians actually dates back to 1973, when the Brooklyn-born Jeffreys—who had just released his first solo album for Atlantic Records—met Springsteen at Max's Kansas City in New York when Springsteen was sharing the bill with Bob Marley & the Wailers. The two ran into each other at the Record Plant recording studio in the mid-'70s, and Springsteen dedicated a song to Jeffreys at a 1980 Madison Square Garden show that Jeffreys attended. They recon- nected in 2001, prior to the September 11 terrorist attacks, and again afterwards, "comparing notes and feelings," Jeffreys told *Backstreets*. He invited Springsteen to an upcoming appearance in New York; Springsteen, in turn, asked him to partici- pate in the Asbury Park holiday show to play some songs from Jeffreys's 1991 album *(Don't Call Me) Buckwheat*. For *The Rising* shows Jeffreys performed such crowd- pleasers as his remake of ? and the Myste- rians' "96 Tears," Gary U.S. Bonds's "Quar- ter to Three," and the staple "Twist and Shout." Jeffreys also recorded a version of Springsteen's "Streets of Philadelphia" that he sold independently at his concerts.

Singer-songwriter Garland Jeffreys, shown here in 2003, befriended Springsteen in 1973. He has performed at Springsteen's annual holiday concerts and as a special guest during encores of E Street Band shows. He also recorded a popular remake of "Streets of Philadelphia."

Jeffreys started writing and performing in the mid-'60s, after a brief tenure at the Institute of Fine Arts in New York. He performed solo before joining the band Grinder's Switch for one album in 1969, then went out on his own again, signing with Atlantic and enjoying critical praise, though little commercial suc- cess, until "96 Tears" made a splash in 1981. His career since has been marked by long gaps between recordings, though he continues to perform. —*GG*

Jersey Artists for Mankind (J.A.M.)

Mid-'80s charity organization

n 1985, inspired by the benefit fever of Band Aid, USA for Africa, and the Live Aid and Farm Aid concerts, a group of New Jersey musicians, along with longtime Stone Pony disc jockey Lee Mrowicki, formed Jersey Artists for Mankind (J.A.M.). The organization's goal was to record its own single—"We've Got Love"—to benefit local charities, particularly food banks. Bruce Springsteen and E Street Band members Max Weinberg, Nils Lofgren, and Clarence Clemons were among the 450 musicians who participated in the recording of the song—which was produced by E Street Band bassist Garry Tallent—in January 1986 at the Stone Pony. The song was written by Asbury Jukes guitarist Bobby Bandiera, and other participants included Southside Johnny Lyon, John Eddie, and Glenn Burtnick.

Five different mixes of "We've Got Love" were released on Arista Records, and proceeds from the recording as well as J.A.M. T-shirts were directed to the designated charities. J.A.M. also put on the January 19 benefit at the Stone Pony for workers laid off from the 3M plant in Freehold, at which Springsteen and most of the E Street Band performed. —GG

"Jersey Girl." *See* **Tom Waits.**

The Jersey Shore

East Coast vacation destination

The Jersey Shore is the colloquial term for the coastal area of New Jersey, a 127-mile stretch of beach and boardwalk that extends from Sandy Hook, part of the Gateway National Recreation Area, to Cape May, the southernmost Shore town with one of the largest concentrations of Victorian homes in America. In between Sandy Hook and Cape May are nearly fifty resort communities, including Asbury Park and Atlantic City, which collectively contain a culture that is more affected by the dominating presence of the Atlantic Ocean than anything else. Many of Springsteen's song narratives have Jersey Shore settings, and characters that appear in his songs, especially those found on his early albums such as *Greetings from Asbury Park, N.J., The Wild, the Innocent, & the E Street Shuffle*, and *Born to Run,* are based, either directly or indirectly, on Jersey Shore friends and associates. No region of New Jersey or America, for that matter, has impacted Springsteen's songwriting more profoundly and has been reflected more often than the Jersey Shore.

To go "down the Shore" is one of the most common destinations in New Jersey. It is the state's summer playground, a place that sits in stark contrast to the heavily industrialized, more densely populated areas of northern New Jersey where a good portion of the state's nine million residents live. Jersey Shore beaches are some of the most beautiful on the eastern seaboard, with their swerving sand dunes and rolling breakers. Most of the Shore towns have boardwalks, and many of them contain amusement areas, games of chance, arcades, food stands, bars, and carnival-like oddities, all of which make for a striking, blue-collar subculture that isn't found anywhere else in Amerca.

The Jersey Shore is loosely divided into six regions: the North Jersey Shore, which is where many north Jerseyans and New Yorkers vacation during the summer months; the Inland Shore, which includes those communities without direct access to the beach such as Freehold, Bruce Springsteen's hometown; the Bay region, which consists of those communities on or near Barnegat Bay and its estuaries; Long Beach Island, an eighteen-mile barrier island that is some four miles off the mainland; Atlantic City, New Jersey's version of Las Vegas; and the Southern Shore, which is where vacationers from Philadelphia and eastern Pennsylvania spend summers and includes such big resort areas as Ocean City and Wildwood, as well as Cape May.

The Jersey Shore's original inhabitants were the Leni Lenape Indians. In the mid-seventeenth century, Dutch and English farmers and whalers began settling the area. Over time, the New Jersey coast became known for its attractive climate—ocean breezes kept the area cool in the summer, and in the winter somewhat warmer temperatures meant less snowfall. In the 1800s, visitors from New York and Philadelphia frequented summer resort communities such as Long Branch and Cape May, and later Atlantic City, making the Jersey Shore one of America's first vacation regions.

Until the early years after World War II, the Jersey Shore remained primarily a string of resort towns bustling in the summer and practically deserted from Labor Day until Memorial Day. But with the opening in 1957 of the Garden State Parkway, which runs the length of the Shore, the region began a period of unprecedented growth. The Parkway made all Shore towns easily accessible, prompting a major increase in Jersey Shore tourism in the late '50s and '60s. The Parkway also caused the eventual transformation of some beach towns into bedroom communities of New York and Philadelphia.

Today, the Jersey Shore is the foundation of New Jersey's vast tourism industry. While Atlantic City is unquestionably its main attraction, other towns and cities such as Wildwood, Seaside Heights, Cape May, Belmar, Pt. Pleasant Beach, and Ocean City attract hundreds of thousands of vacationers each summer. Other communities not located exactly on the beach have became attractive year-round communities, including Toms River, Lakewood, Brick Township, Red Bank, Rumson, Spring Lake, Sea Girt, and most of the communities located next to or near Atlantic City.

Springsteen was born in Long Branch, a Jersey Shore town a few miles north of Asbury Park, and lived most of his early years in Freehold, a Revolutionary War town near where the important Battle of Monmouth was fought in 1778. Springsteen attended Freehold Regional High School, spent a brief

Hard rocker Joan Jett earned a Top 40 hit with her recording of Springsteen's "Just Around the Corner to the Light of Day" from the film *Light of Day*, in which she starred in 1987.

time at Ocean County College in Toms River, and played teen clubs and bars on the north Jersey Shore. He also lived in Long Branch, Asbury Park, Holmdel, and other Shore towns before settling in Rumson, the most exclusive community on the north Jersey Shore. —*RS*

Joan Jett

Singer, songwriter, musician

Singer/guitarist Joan Jett was a member of the teenage rock 'n' roll girl group the Runaways but rose to even greater fame as a solo artist. Despite difficulty getting a record deal on her own (Jett and her manager Kenny Laguna eventually released her debut album themselves), she broke through with the 1982 single, "I Love Rock and Roll."

Jett's music is heavily influenced by the British glam acts of the early '70s such as T. Rex, Slade, and Suzi Quatro (one of the few female hard rockers that preceded Jett). The extent to which Jett is a genuine fan of the music comes across in her full-throttle live performances and the fact that she is not shy in putting her own stamp on material made famous by others. Her hits include covers of Tommy James and the Shondells' "Crimson and Clover," Sly & the Family Stone's "Everyday People," and Gary Glitter's "Do You Wanna Touch Me (Oh Yeah)." Jett's career intersected with Bruce Springsteen in 1987, when she starred with Michael J. Fox in the Paul Schrader film *Light of Day*. Several years earlier, Schrader had shared an unproduced film script titled *Born in the U.S.A.* with Springsteen, who borrowed the title for one of his biggest hit songs. To repay the debt, Springsteen offered Schrader another song, "Just Around the Corner to the Light of Day," to use in his movie; once the title was truncated, Jett sang the song in the film and it became a Top 40 hit for her that year. Springsteen added the song to his concert repertoire, and it appeared on 1992's *In Concert MTV Plugged*.

Jett remains an active artist today, and has also served as an inspiration to younger acts, particularly "riot grrrl" bands like Bikini Kill and Sleater-Kinney. —*DD*

Journey to Nowhere: The Saga of the New Underclass

1985 book by Dale Maharidge and Michael Williamson

 ruce Springsteen bought a copy of *Journey to Nowhere: The Saga of the New Underclass* in 1985, when it was first published. He put it aside, unread, only to pull it off the shelf one sleepness night in the mid-'90s. He read it cover to cover, and it wound up directly influencing "Youngstown" and "The New Timer," two of the songs that appeared on 1996's *The Ghost of Tom Joad* album. "It's a very powerful book," Springsteen told the *Washington Post*. "It should be out there. It should be read."

Sacramento Bee staffers Dale Maharidge, a writer, and Michael Williamson, a photographer, put together *Journey to Nowhere* to chronicle the new class of unemployed and dispossessed workers that had arisen in the early '80s in the U.S. They spent three years living and traveling with those people in twenty-seven states, riding the rails with modern-day hobos and hearing stories that hearkened back to the 1930s era of the Great Depression, the Dust Bowl, and *The Grapes of Wrath*, a book and film that also exerted great influence on *The Ghost of Tom Joad*. "Youngstown" was drawn directly from the story of laid off Youngstown steelworkers Joe Marshall and his namesake son, who Maharidge and Williamson interviewed and photographed amidst the imploded ruins of the town's Campbell Works; Springsteen included Marshall Sr.'s observation, "What Hitler couldn't do, they (the company) did for him," in the song's lyric. "The New Timer," meanwhile, was inspired by *Journey to Nowhere*'s numerous freight train travelers.

"(The book) puts faces and real-life circumstances on all the statistics that you read about but that remain abstract to a lot of people," Springsteen explained. "It doesn't really tell you what to think, it just shows you things: This is what we found, this is what is out there. And that's kind of what I've tried to do with my record. I don't think you can tell people anything, but you can show 'em something."

Journey to Nowhere had gone out of print by the time Springsteen recorded *The Ghost of Tom Joad*. In an effort "to replay something that meant something to me," he talked about the book at his *Tom Joad* concerts, and when Hyperion decided to reprint it in 1996, Springsteen wrote a new introduction. —*GG*

Cleopatra Kennedy. *See 1992–93 Bruce Springsteen Touring Band.*

John Kerry

Massachusetts senator, 2004 Democratic presidential candidate

Bruce Springsteen had lent his support to political causes prior to the 2004 U.S. presidential election, but he had never before endorsed a major political candidate. That changed when he threw his weight—and active participation—behind Massachusetts Senator John Kerry, the Democratic Party's nominee to challenge incumbent President George W. Bush. He told *Backstreets* magazine, "I like John Kerry a lot. I don't think he has all the answers, or that (running mate) John Edwards has all the answers, but I think they have the experience, the life experience, and I think they have the sincerity to ask the hard questions about America and to try to search for honest solutions. I believe they're going to do that."

Kerry made his fondness for Springsteen's music and message known early in the presidential campaign. He identified "No Surrender," from 1984's *Born in the U.S.A.*, as his favorite song at a September 2003 debate, during which one of his primary election opponents, Congressman Richard Gephardt, announced that *his* favorite song was "Born in the U.S.A." Shortly after that, Kerry, a guitarist, played Springsteen's "Tenth Avenue Freeze-Out" while backed by Moby at a September 2003 fundraiser dubbed John Kerry Unplugged. He subsequently adopted "No Surrender" as his campaign theme; it was played on July 28, 2004, as he arrived by water taxi in Boston

Springsteen took his support of 2004 presidential candidate John Kerry to the stage at the Washington, D.C., Vote for Change concert on October 11, 2004.

for the Democratic Party's national convention and was piped over the speakers the following night as he strode to the podium at the Fleet Center to accept the party's nomination. "Bruce Springsteen had it right: 'No retreat,

Springsteen shakes hands with presidential candidate John Kerry in Madison, Wisconsin, on October 28, 2004, just days before the national election. He appeared with Kerry at several stops during the last days of the campaign, performing a couple of acoustic numbers and voicing his support for the candidate to rally attendees.

no surrender,'" Kerry told reporters. "We are taking this fight to the country, and we're going to win back our democracy and our future." Three months later, at an Election Day eve rally in Cleveland, Kerry praised Springsteen as "a great poet. He sings from his heart, he writes from his heart, and he writes about real people and the struggles of life itself ... I've been a fan of his for a long time, and I'll tell you what, I may be running for president of the United States, but we all know who The Boss really is."

Springsteen stumped for Kerry almost as hard as he campaigns for one of his album releases. He took part in the anti-Bush Vote for Change tour, headlining seven shows in swing states, including a late addition at Continental Airlines Arena in East Rutherford, New Jersey, when Kerry's position seemed to be slipping in Springsteen's home state. Springsteen also wrote an op-ed piece for the *New York Times* about the tour that explained his support for Kerry, and he joined the candidate on the road during the final few days of the campaign, playing at rallies in Madison, Wisconsin (for an estimated 80,000 people), and Columbus, Ohio, as well as Miami and Cleveland. Springsteen played short solo acoustic sets at the gatherings—"The Promised Land" and "No Surrender," with "Thunder Road" added in Cleveland—and introduced Kerry with both humor ("We've had a sax player, I think it's time for a guitar player in the White House!") and passion: "Senator Kerry, since he was a young man, has shown us by having the courage to face America's hard truths, both the good and the bad, that that's where we find a deeper patriotism, we find a more complete view of who we are, we find a more authentic experience as citizens, and that's where we find the power that is embedded only in truth to make our world a better and safer place for our kids to grow up in."

At the Cleveland rally, Kerry exulted that Springsteen gave him one of his guitar picks, telling him to "take it to the White House, this is gonna bring you good luck!" Kerry promised that "this pick is going to play in the White House," but for now it will only be on a visit; he was defeated by Bush in both the Electoral College and popular votes. —*GG*

Kid Leo

Legendary Cleveland radio disc jockey

leveland rocked long before it became home to the Rock and Roll Hall of Fame and Museum (where Bruce Springsteen's is among the inductees' names etched in glass), and much of the beat was provided by WMMS-FM. One of the first FM stations that grew to powerhouse status in the early-'70s free-form rock era, WMMS boasted some nationally renowned disc jockeys and heavily influenced other rock stations. In particular, Kid Leo (Lawrence James Travagliante) is credited with breaking Springsteen and Southside Johnny & the Asbury Jukes on the "North Coast" banks of Lake Erie; because Leo and WMMS wielded so much muscle, other stations followed suit when he began championing the New Jersey musicians.

But Leo didn't work alone. According to *Rock 'n' Roll and the Cleveland Connection*, fellow WMMS DJ David Spero and local rocker Michael Stanley, who led the Michael Stanley Band, also deserve recognition for exposing Springsteen's music to the Midwest masses. Spero said, "Kid Leo and I were always getting into musical battles. He was into glam rock … and I was strictly a rock 'n' roller. So when (*The Wild, the Innocent & the E Street Shuffle*) came out, Michael Stanley called me and said, 'Have you heard this guy, Bruce Springsteen?' Now, I'd seen him as a folkie down at Ohio University (in Athens, Ohio) … That was '74, when he'd just come out with his *Greetings from Asbury Park*. Then once I heard the *E Street* album, I loved it and started playing it on the air. And I'd tell Leo, 'You gotta play this guy.' And he'd say,

'Yeah, when you start playing Roxy Music.' Finally I played a Roxy Music tune I thought was pretty cool, so then he had to play Springsteen. Well, shortly after that I left (the station), and eight months later, *Born to Run* came out, and Leo is credited for breaking Bruce Springsteen." Kid Leo (he adopted "Kid" from popular boxing monikers) was at WMMS from 1973–1988, much of that time as the station's music director. A frequent concert emcee, he introduced Springsteen and the E Street Band at the station's tenth-anniversary concert on August 9, 1978, at the Agora Ballroom as if he were announcing a boxing match: "Round for round, pound for pound, there ain't no finer band around ... Bruce Springsteen and the E Street Band!"

When Kid Leo left WMMS to take a job as vice president of album promotion at Columbia Records (Springsteen's label), Springsteen was one of many celebs who called to wish him luck. Leo ended that shift as he did every Friday afternoon, by playing his happy-hour lead-in, "Born to Run." Leo went on to serve as the label's head of special projects and hosted the national radio broadcast from the July 3, 1988, Tunnel of Love Express Tour stop in Stockholm, Sweden. He left Columbia in 2002. In September 2004, Kid Leo signed on to Steve Van Zandt's Underground Garage channel offered by Sirius satellite radio as a weekend DJ. —*LM*

Greg Kihn

Berkeley-based singer, songwriter, bandleader

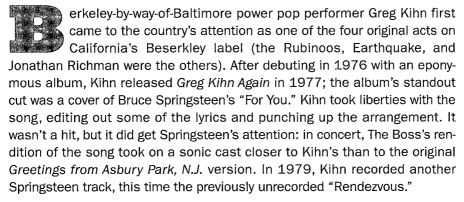erkeley-by-way-of-Baltimore power pop performer Greg Kihn first came to the country's attention as one of the four original acts on California's Beserkley label (the Rubinoos, Earthquake, and Jonathan Richman were the others). After debuting in 1976 with an eponymous album, Kihn released *Greg Kihn Again* in 1977; the album's standout cut was a cover of Bruce Springsteen's "For You." Kihn took liberties with the song, editing out some of the lyrics and punching up the arrangement. It wasn't a hit, but it did get Springsteen's attention: in concert, The Boss's rendition of the song took on a sonic cast closer to Kihn's than to the original *Greetings from Asbury Park, N.J.* version. In 1979, Kihn recorded another Springsteen track, this time the previously unrecorded "Rendezvous."

Kihn's biggest hits have come with songs that he cowrote. In 1981, "The Breakup Song (They Don't Write 'em)" made it to No. 15. Two years later, "Jeopardy," which was bolstered by a humorous video, charted at No. 2. Kihn's popularity waned after the mid-'80s; in recent years he's continued to sing, but his primary creative outlet is writing screenplays, novels, and short fiction. —*DD*

Bobby King. *See* 1992–93 Bruce Springsteen Touring Band.

Suki Lahav

E Street Band violinist, 1974–75

Before Patti Scialfa, there was another first lady of the E Street Band—Suki Lahav, an Israeli-born singer and violinist who was first a studio hand on *The Wild, the Innocent & the E Street Shuffle* and toured with the group from September 1974 through March 1975.

After Lahav and her husband, Louis, arrived in the U.S. in 1971, Louis worked as an engineer at 914 Sound Studios in Blauvelt, New York, where Springsteen recorded his first two albums. Springsteen had an idea to incorporate violin into his music but did not grab his engineer's wife straightaway; rather, he auditioned several players, and only after a children's choir failed to turn up to sing on "4th of July, Asbury Park (Sandy)" did Springsteen give Lahav her shot—as a singer, having her track multiple parts to achieve the choir effect he wanted. Lahav also contributed backing vocals to "Incident on 57th Street." On the road, Lahav's violin became a contrast point to the raucous rock attack that dominated Springsteen's live repertoire. "Bruce used the violin only for the romantic side of him," Lahav recalled to *Backstreets* in 1985. "I played only on the slow songs." She was, however, around long enough to provide the violin introduction to "Jungleland" for 1975's *Born to Run*, while her live contributions were captured on a widely bootlegged February 5, 1975, concert broadcast from the Main Point in Bryn Mawr, Pennsylvania.

Lahav and her husband decided to return to Israel in the spring of 1975, and they later split up. She did not keep in touch with Springsteen, but in the late '80s she called him on behalf of a friend and film producer who wanted to use three Springsteen songs—"Jungleland," "Point Blank," and "Hungry Heart"—in one of his movies. After a friendly chat, Springsteen granted permission for the songs to be used. —*GG*

Jon Landau

Manager, producer

t's true that journalists write the first draft of history, but rarely do they know it at the time. Jon Landau somehow knew, though he certainly had no idea that a single sentence would become one of the most quoted in rock history and would change the course of his life. To say it altered Bruce Springsteen's life as well is an understatement; had it not been for Landau's guidance—as a producer, manager, and friend—Springsteen might not have been a Rock and Roll Hall of Famer (class of 1999), sold millions of records and concert tickets, or become the respected philanthropist and humanitarian he is.

Springsteen first blipped onto Landau's radar in 1973, while Landau was the editor of *Rolling Stone* magazine's album review section. He listened to *Greetings from Asbury Park, N.J.* at the behest of CBS Records chief Clive Davis, liking it enough to assign a review to Lester Bangs. Landau also asked another writer, Stu Werbin, to check out Springsteen's sparsely attended gig at Max's Kansas City in New York. Werbin liked Springsteen so much that he made Landau accompany him the following night.

As Springsteen's buzz grew in the Boston area, native son Landau heard *Greetings*'s followup, *The Wild, the Innocent & the E Street Shuffle*, and liked it, too. The band was slated to appear in Beantown for a series of shows at Charley's. By then, Landau was ready to weigh in with his own opinion. Landau's recollection is quoted in Fred Goodman's book *The Mansion on the Hill*: "I reviewed the album and timed it to appear in the *Real Paper* [a Boston alternative weekly] before the gig because it was a favorable review and I had been told that in Cambridge, I had some marquee value." In the review, Landau called Springsteen "the most impressive new singer-songwriter since James Taylor" and the record "the most under-rated album so far this year, an impassioned and inspired street fantasy that's as much fun as it is deep." But he voiced his criticisms, too: "Next time around, he ought to work a little harder on matching the production to the material, round out a few rough edges, and then just throw down some more hot ones on the vinyl."

Landau and fellow critic Dave Marsh got to the show to find Landau's enlarged review pasted outside the club—and noticed Springsteen reading it. Landau stood next to him, asked him what he thought, and when Bruce admitted the reviewer had accurately noted the album's strengths and deficiencies, Landau introduced himself. Inside the club, Springsteen introduced Landau to his then-manager Mike Appel, who took issue with Landau's printed criticisms. It was shortly afterward, on May 9, 1974, that Landau saw the show that would inspire his famous "rock and roll future" proclamation. Catching Springsteen opening for Bonnie Raitt at the Harvard Square Theater on the night before his twenty-seventh birthday, Landau wrote an essay in which he said that Springsteen's performance rekindled the long-dampened spark of excitement that had ignited his passion for music in the first place: "Tonight, there is someone I can write of the way I used to write, without reservation of any kind. Last Thursday, at the Harvard Square Theater, I saw my rock and roll past flash before my eyes. And I saw something else: I saw rock and roll future and its name is Bruce Springsteen. And on a night when I needed to feel young; he made me feel like I was hearing music for the very first time."

In the wake of the rave—which Columbia Records quickly turned into an advertising campaign—Springsteen contacted Landau and the two spoke for hours. Springsteen asked him what a producer's job really was, and Landau, who had tried his hand at it, gave his explanation. "I thought, 'This is an interesting guy and I don't know any guys like this,'" Springsteen told *Entertainment Weekly* in 2003. "That was my take on him: 'I don't know any guys like this.'"

Springsteen subsequently invited Landau into the studio, where he was working on his third album, *Born to Run*. "So he came in, he had ideas about how the band should be arranged. We listened to records together and we said we like this drum sound, that guitar sound. And it became clear to me that what he was doing was assisting me in doing what I wanted to do. So the security for a young guy like me was suddenly there. I was like, 'Hey, I'm steering the boat, I got some help here.' And I felt comfortable."

Landau quit his *Rolling Stone* job to coproduce *Born to Run*, and has never looked back. But the Lexington, Massachusetts, native's rise to his post as Springsteen's right-hand man wasn't completely smooth. His journalistic story starts with some early bylines in *Crawdaddy* magazine, where his work caught the eye of Jann Wenner, the young San Franciscan who was about to launch a new music periodical, *Rolling Stone*. Landau's pan of the Jimi Hendrix Experience's *Are You Experienced?* appeared in the first issue. But Landau was interested in the other side of music—making it, in his case as a producer. He got to know some key players, including a few major-label honchos; Elektra's Jac Holzman and publicist Danny Fields introduced him to Detroit's anarchy-spouting MC5, and when the band's politics cost them their Elektra deal, they asked Landau to find them a new home. He did, with

Atlantic Records, where Jerry Wexler said he'd sign them if Landau produced the album. Landau lived with the band in Ann Arbor, Michigan, for four months while they recorded the 1970 release *Back in the USA.*

Landau went on to introduce Atlantic to the J. Geils Band and also produced two albums for James Taylor's brother Livingston—*Livingston Taylor* (1970) and *Liv* (1971). Though Landau's efforts weren't hits, he had the ability to speak in a language Springsteen needed to hear. When the recording of *Born to Run* stumbled after the title song was cut, Springsteen sought Landau's advice. Landau told him to record at a better studio than the cut-rate one Appel had steered him to, suggesting the Record Plant in New York City. Springsteen continued to use Landau as part of his brain trust in the studio, and according to his own account in the *Encyclopedia of Record Producers*, Landau "kind of volunteered" to become the album's coproducer, and Springsteen "kind of asked."

Appel wasn't pleased, but together the trio created a masterpiece that's often ranked near the top of any all-time greatest albums list. It not only turned Springsteen into a bona fide star but also cemented Landau's status as a credible producer. Jackson Browne subsequently sought him out to produce *The Pretender*, which became Browne's first million-seller and, many feel, his best work. But when Springsteen told Appel he wanted Landau to produce the next album, Appel brought up the matter of his contractual right to choose the album producers, setting off a lengthy legal battle.

By the time a settlement was reached in 1977, Appel was out and Landau was in—for good. He also became Springsteen's manager and created Jon Landau Management with partner Barbara Carr (Dave Marsh's wife). In 1998, the company took on Shania Twain, helping to turn her third album, *Come on Over*, into the best-selling album ever released by a female solo artist. But just before the 2002 release of *Up!* she sought new management, not wanting to be a second priority to anybody—even Springsteen. Landau Management also has steered the careers of Natalie Merchant, Patti Scialfa, and Train.

Springsteen expressed his appreciation for Landau's efforts during his Rock and Roll Hall of Fame induction acceptance speech in 1999: "I've seen the future of rock 'n' roll management, and its name is Jon Landau ... But Jon's given me something beyond friendship and beyond guidance: his intelligence, his sense of the truth, his recognition of my intelligence. His creative ability as a producer and editor, his ability to see through to the heart of matters, both professional and personal, and the love that he's given me has altered my life forever. What I hope to give to my fans with my music—a greater sense of themselves and greater freedom—he with his talents and his abilities has done that for me. There's no thank you tonight that's gonna do the job, and it's a debt that I can't repay—and one I treasure always. Thank you, Jon. I love you." —*LM*

The Last Temptation of Elvis. See Elvis Presley.
"Late Night with Conan O'Brien." *See* **Conan O'Brien.**
"Late Night with David Letterman." *See* **David Letterman.**
"The Late Show with David Letterman." *See* **David Letterman.**

Laurel Canyon Ltd.

Production, management, and publishing company for Springsteen, 1972–76

Clarence Clemons and Springsteen perform at a free outdoor concert at Kean College in Union Township, New Jersey, on September 22, 1974, while under the management of Laurel Canyon.

Laurel Canyon Ltd. was the company established by Mike Appel and Jim Cretecos in the spring of 1972 to handle production, management, and publishing concerns for their new client, Bruce Springsteen. The company included three separate but intrinsically interwoven divisions; the publishing wing was initially called Sioux City Ltd. but was subsequently changed to Laurel Canyon Music, Ltd. Springsteen signed deals with all three divisions, and it was Laurel Canyon that actually signed the recording contract with Columbia Records in 1972. It was also Laurel Canyon that Springsteen sued—and was sued by—in the famous 1976 court case in which he negotiated his independence.

According to Appel, the Laurel Canyon name came from two sources. One was Joni Mitchell's *Ladies of the Canyon* album, which he happened to see in the window of a Manhattan record store on the same day that Cretecos called him from Newton, Massachusetts, telling Appel how beautiful the laurel was in that area. "The world laurel stuck in my head, along with canyon," Appel told author Marc Eliot. The fledgling company had a name. Laurel Canyon set up offices at 75 E. 55th Street in Manhattan, upstairs from Bob Dylan's manager, Albert Grossman. Appel joked that the building had "the only toilet bowl shared by Dylan and Springsteen."

Cretecos resigned from Laurel Canyon in early 1974. Laurel Canyon Music, Ltd. held interest in Springsteen into 1983, when the artist bought out the remaining share of his song publishing for a reported $425,000. —*GG*

Annie Leibovitz

Photographer

Since she started freelancing for *Rolling Stone* magazine in 1970 at age twenty, photographer Annie Leibovitz has shot hundreds, if not thousands, of portraits for publications all over the world. The *Rolling Stone* cover of John Lennon naked and curled around Yoko Ono—the last photograph taken before he was killed just hours later—is hers. But it's her *Born in the U.S.A.* album cover shot that makes her loom large in the annals of Springsteen history. And it would never have become one of the most renowned images in rock 'n' roll or pop culture iconography if Leibovitz had her way.

Leibovitz, photo stylist Andrea Klein, and Bruce Springsteen had brainstormed mightily, but could not come up with an idea for the album cover. According to biographer Dave Marsh, Springsteen had somehow acquired a huge American flag, and they decided it seemed fitting to build a photograph around an image addressed in the album's songs. Many shots were taken of a blue-jeaned Springsteen in front of that simple flag backdrop. But it was the one Leibovitz snapped as just a "grab shot"—an off-the-cuff, quickie candid—that he and Klein chose. Leibovitz complained that it was out of focus, but Springsteen liked the shot, in which the flag's stripes were echoed in his white T-shirt and the red ball cap stuck in the right pocket of his Levi's. One could tell even from behind that this person had a confident sense of what he was about. And there was no mistaking that it was Springsteen. Dispelling rumors that he was allegedly urinating on the flag, he told *Rolling Stone* that year that "we took a lot of different types of pictures, and in the end the picture of my *ass* looked better than the picture of my *face*, so that's what went on the cover." Marsh wrote that Springsteen was also trying to convey a "loving but critical" message about America's zeitgeist in the mid-1980s Reagan era, though at the time Springsteen said, "I didn't have any secret message."

While the *Born in the U.S.A.* cover is Leibovitz's most famous photograph of Springsteen, she's shot him frequently over the years. She was also responsible for the *Tunnel of Love* album cover in 1987 and the sleeve photos on Springsteen's *Songs* book. She photographed Springsteen at Cadillac Ranch in 1979 in Amarillo, Texas, and has had her work appear on some of his singles.

When Leibovitz became the second staff photographer *Rolling Stone* ever hired, she was still a student at the San Francisco Art Institute. She got her degree in 1971, became the magazine's chief photographer in 1973, and in 1975 was hired by the Rolling Stones to document their world tour. Eventually, she began shooting for several other magazines, including *Time, Newsweek, Vogue, Esquire,* and most recently, *Vanity Fair.* She became that magazine's first contributing photographer in 1983, the same year her first book, *Annie Leibovitz: Photographs*, was published. Leibovitz is widely regarded as one of the top portrait photographers in the world. In 1990, she opened the Annie Leibovitz Studio in New York, and in 1991, the Westport, Connecticut, native became the first woman—and only the second living photographer—to be honored with an exhibit at the Smithsonian Institute's National Portrait Gallery. She has published several books, including: *Olympic Portraits*, a two-year chronicle of athletes in training; *Dancers; Women; Photographs—Annie Leibovitz 1970–1990*; and, in 2003, *American Music*, for which she spent four years traveling across the country shooting artists as legendary as Springsteen and as under-recognized as R.L. Burnside. The book was released in conjunction with an exhibit created by the Experience Music Project in Seattle. It later traveled to the Rock and Roll Hall of Fame and Museum in Cleveland, which is also the home of several pieces of Springsteen memorabilia. —*LM*

Al Leiter

Major league baseball pitcher

 ew Jersey native Alois (Al) Leiter has pitched in Major League Baseball's All-Star Game twice and in seven World Series games. But Leiter says he was far more freaked out to sing "Rosalita" with Bruce Springsteen and the E Street Band at the October 3, 2003, concert in New York's Shea Stadium. "When I pitch, I'm nervous before the game, but once I'm out there I just pitch," Leiter, a New York Mets pitcher at the time, told the *White Plains (N.Y.) Journal News.* "I was way more nervous with Bruce, because I was totally out of my element ... The whole day of the concert I was under some delusional thought he was going to turn to me and say 'Take it away, Al!' and I would freeze up ... I was worried the music was going to stop or something." As it turned out, Leiter did fine, banging on a tambourine and, at Springsteen's direction, hanging close to Patti Scialfa—although Leiter said Steve Van Zandt tried to help him with his tambourine technique.

Leiter, who grew up in Toms River, New Jersey, met Springsteen during the Tunnel of Love Express Tour in 1988; they bonded backstage by talking about their high schools, which were rivals. They stayed in touch, though Leiter noted that he hasn't been able to attend many Springsteen shows over the years because the New York and New Jersey concerts often coincided with the baseball season. Leiter did, however, attend the final show of the E Street Band reunion tour on July 1, 2000, at Madison Square Garden in New York City—after winning the 100th game of his career that afternoon at Shea Stadium. Aware of the pitcher's fondness for Springsteen, the stadium DJ played "Tenth Avenue Freeze-Out" when Leiter came to the mound in the first inning and "Born to Run" each time he batted.

Leiter has been pitching in the major leagues since 1987, when he was a member of the New York Yankees. He went to Toronto in 1989 and Florida in 1996 before joining the Mets in 1998. In addition to his baseball career, he and his wife, Lori, run a charity called Leiter's Landing to provide assistance for needy children. —*GG*

David Letterman

Veteran late-night TV host

When Bruce Springsteen broke his long-held abstinence from live TV performances, it was good news for late-night host David Letterman, a major fan. Letterman snagged his first Springsteen appearance on June 25, 1993, for the farewell episode of "Late Night with David Letterman" on NBC before he moved to CBS; Springsteen played, appropriately, "Glory Days."

Springsteen made his first appearance on "The Late Show with David Letterman"—housed at the Ed Sullivan Theater in New York's Times Square—on April 5, 1995, promoting his *Greatest Hits* album with performances of "Murder Incorporated" and "Secret Garden," and an off-camera rendition of "Tenth Avenue Freeze-Out." Springsteen has made three other stops at "The Late Show": December 14, 1995, to promote *The Ghost of Tom Joad* with a performance of "Youngstown"; and August 1, 2002, to play "The Rising" and "Lonesome Day," the latter of which was taped and broadcast the following night. Springsteen later told *Entertainment Weekly*, "Letterman threw me a little. They said, 'Ya wanna come over and sit on the couch?' I said, 'Ahh, ya sit on the couch ya gotta be funny. That's too much pressure.' But he's funny, so you don't have to be too funny yourself." The five guest spots for Letterman are the most Springsteen has done for any one host. —*GG*

Jerry Lee Lewis

Rock 'n' roll pioneer

They both tried unsuccessfully, on separate occasions, to barge into Graceland and visit Elvis Presley. But other than that, rock 'n' roll pioneer Jerry Lee Lewis and Bruce Springsteen have had very few encounters in common. Springsteen and the E Street Band were the third act on an April 28, 1973, bill with Chuck Berry and The Killer—who, of course, is famous for "Great Balls of Fire," "Whole Lot of Shakin' Goin' On," and other '50s classics. The group then backed Lewis during the 1995 Concert for the Rock and Roll Hall of Fame.

But other than that, and a certain give-everything enthusiasm for rock 'n' roll, Springsteen and Lewis belong to different times and eras. Lewis's direct influence on Springsteen is detectable in a handful of piano-based boogie songs, such as "Ramrod" and "She's the One." In concert, Springsteen covered Lewis's classics "High School Confidential," "Great Balls of Fire," and "Whole Lot of Shakin' Going On."

The Ferriday, Louisiana–born Lewis emerged in Memphis at the same time as Elvis Presley and Carl Perkins, making hits for Sam Phillips's Sun Studio and infamously railing about rock as the devil's music (he was kicked out of a fundamentalist Bible school, and evangelist Jimmy Swaggart is his cousin). After growing up on country music, Lewis learned black gospel and R&B at clubs and churches and developed a flamboyant, over-the-top style of boogie-woogie piano. (He sometimes played with his feet, often while standing up.) His only Top 10 hits were "Great Balls of Fire," "Whole Lotta Shakin' Goin' On," and "Breathless," but Lewis was poised to perhaps succeed Presley as The King when his life took a turn for the melodramatic. He fell in love with his thirteen-year-old third cousin, Myra Gale Brown, and married her in 1957—creating a public-relations debacle that reverberates to this day. Although Lewis soldiered on, making rock, country, blues, and rockabilly records according to his whims, he never approached the same level of stardom.

One of the original Rock and Roll Hall of Fame inductees in 1986, Lewis is the subject of a biographical movie, 1989's *Great Balls of Fire*, starring Dennis Quaid as The Killer and featuring Winona Ryder and X's John Doe. Despite a series of controversies, including the mysterious deaths of two of his wives, tax problems, and substance abuse, Lewis continues to perform and release albums. —*SK*

Light of Day Benefit Concerts

Fundraising events for Parkinson's Disease

ruce Springsteen often shows up to accompany friends at bar gigs, but in early November he makes a point of appearing at a particular event: the annual Light of Day benefit show for the Parkinson's Disease Foundation, organized by his friend Bob Benjamin.

Benjamin, aka New Jersey Bob, was diagnosed with the disease in 1996. In 1998, he turned his November 3 birthday party into a fundraiser for the foundation. The first show was held at the Downtown Cafe in Red Bank, New Jersey; Bobby Bandiera of Southside Johnny & the Asbury Jukes performed, and about $2,000 was raised. After skipping a year, Benjamin gave the event an official name in 2000 and corralled several bands to play. He chose the title of Springsteen's song from the *Light of Day* film soundtrack because the lyric "just around the corner 'til the light of day" embodies the hope that a cure for Parkinson's will be found in the not-too-distant future.

The Light of Day benefits have visited the Stone Pony in Asbury Park, New Jersey, and at the Tradewinds in Sea Bright, New Jersey. The 2003 bash was spread over two nights, and the 2004 event grew to three nights. Springsteen has made it to each one since 2000, often to play with Joe Grushecky & the Houserockers, who Benjamin manages. However, Benjamin points out that The Boss has never been formally scheduled to play at any of the shows. Springsteen didn't make it to the second night of 2003 but had an extra-special surprise for the first night, bringing actor and Parkinson's sufferer Michael J. Fox—who costarred in *Light of Day*—on stage. Fox played guitar on "Light of Day" and "Twist and Shout"—and, according to Benjamin, played very well. In 2004 Springsteen joined the Houserockers' set to play a mix of his own tunes, Grushecky collaborations, and party-band covers.

Since 1998, Benjamin's parties have raised nearly $200,000 for research efforts. While the bills are packed with talent for each one, their popularity is obviously increased by the fact that fans expect Springsteen to attend. In September 2003, Benjamin put together a double album, *Light of Day: A Tribute to Bruce Springsteen*, on his Schoolhouse Records label; the project raised money for the Parkinson's Foundation and the Kristen Ann Carr Fund, dedicated to the late daughter of Springsteen's co-manager, Barbara Carr. —*LM*

Little Steven & the Disciples of Soul. See Steve Van Zandt.

Live in Barcelona

Released: November 18, 2003
Tracks: Disc One—"The Rising," "Lonesome Day," "Prove It All Night," "Darkness on the Edge of Town," "Empty Sky," "You're Missing," "Waitin' on a Sunny Day," "The Promised Land," "Worlds Apart," "Badlands," "She's the One," "Mary's Place," "Dancing in the Dark," "Countin' on a Miracle," "Spirit in the Night," "Incident on 57th Street," "Into the Fire"; Disc Two—"Night," "Ramrod," "Born to Run," "My City of Ruins," "Born in the U.S.A.," "Land of Hope and Dreams," "Thunder Road"
Extras: "Drop the Needle and Pray: *The Rising* On Tour" documentary

 ruce Springsteen's second full-length concert DVD with the E Street Band came from the second show of the European leg of *The Rising* world tour, on October 16, 2003, at the Palau Sant Jordi in

Barcelona, Spain. The first thirteen songs were broadcast live by MTV Networks Europe, and some of that was subsequently aired by CBS in the U.S. The European broadcast was preceded by a one-hour "Countdown to ..." special.

It was a typically spirited E Street Band outing, which guitarist Steve Van Zandt dubbed "rather incredible ... It was one of the most extraordinary audiences in the world, just one of those freaky things where you do a great show the same night you're doing a live broadcast, usually that doesn't happen. They're usually good, but very rarely are they great, for some reason. (Barcelona) was an exception to the rule. Everything just came together. It was amazing." "Mary's Place" from *The Rising* was moved up in the set in order to accommodate the TV broadcast, but the live audience got a few treats that weren't seen until the release of the DVD—including the tour debut of "Spirit in the Night" in a solo piano rendition and an audible for "Thunder Road" as the last song of the night. The DVD also came with a documentary, "Drop the Needle and Pray: *The Rising* on Tour," that included live footage from Boston's Fenway Park and Giants Stadium in East Rutherford, New Jersey, as well as interviews with Springsteen and members of the E Street Band and unpublished photos from *The Rising* tour.

A production snafu on initial pressings of the DVD (catalog number 56390) resulted in a defective second disc, which Sony replaced upon request. —*GG*

Live in New York City

Released: April 3, 2001
Producers: Bruce Springsteen, Chuck Plotkin
Tracks: Disc 1—"My Love Will Not Let You Down," "Prove It All Night," "Two Hearts," "Atlantic City," "Mansion on the Hill," "The River," "Youngstown," "Murder Incorporated," "Badlands," "Out in the Street," "Born to Run"; Disc 2—"Tenth Avenue Freeze-Out," "Land of Hope and Dreams," "American Skin (41 Shots)," "Lost in the Flood," "Born in the U.S.A.," "Don't Look Back," "Jungleland," "Ramrod," "If I Should Fall Behind"
Chart peak: No. 5

Bruce Springsteen's third live album, and second with the E Street Band, came from the final two concerts on the 1999–2000 reunion tour—June 29 and July 1 at Madison Square Garden in New York City. *Live in New York City* was originally intended to be a companion piece for the HBO concert special *Bruce Springsteen & the E Street Band*, the reason why in terms of length it only represents about half of the usual concerts they performed on the tour. Ultimately Springsteen and company decided to fortify the CD with the final six tracks that close out the second disc, including the rare "Lost in the Flood," the hushed, group-sung arrangement of "If I Should

"**T**he reunion tour with the E Street Band was not just a simple celebration of glory days, a nostalgic tribute to past triumphs. It was a contemplation on old friends and the ties that bind. The vitality and joy that these nine musicians share is a palpable part of the production."
—*San Francisco Chronicle*

" ... instead of just cranking out one succinct hit after another, (Springsteen) reinvents songs and lets them unfold for as long as they stay interesting—which makes *Live in New York City* the rare concert album that actually merits a second listen."
—*Dallas Morning News*

" ... a predictably magnificent concert recording. This two-CD set, taped last summer, reminds us that Springsteen is the most heroic composer in modern pop music and demonstrates that the E Street Band can still galvanize his songs into rock-and-roll epiphanies."
—*Washington Post*

Fall Behind," and the rootsy, acoustic-styled version of "Born in the U.S.A."

Springsteen also made the call to add "Born to Run" to both projects—late enough that the song wasn't on advance review copies and isn't listed on the first pressings of the CD. Though it was played during the encores, "Born to Run" appears out of sequence at the end of the first disc of the CD, following "Out in the Street"; in the HBO special and subsequent home video release, it's in a more familiar position, between "Tenth Avenue Freeze-Out" and "Land of Hope and Dreams."

Working with coproducer Chuck Plotkin, Springsteen mastered the package on February 6–7, 2001, at Bob Ludwig's Gateway Mastering Studio in Portland, Maine. Ludwig told *Sound & Vision* magazine that Springsteen was involved hands-on in the lengthy sessions: "He spent a lot of time working in a separate editing room. He would go in there and listen to one of his raps, for instance, and decided to take out a phrase or put something back in. He would just keep going back and forth like that. He cares a great deal about having everything be exactly as he wants it to be."

Part of the mission of the live projects, Springsteen said at the time the CD was released, was to hammer home the idea of the tour as a "rededication" of the E Street Band: "I guess the nicest thing about it was we were able to reconstitute the band as an ongoing sort of creative unit ... I felt the band was more powerful than ever, and to have sort of refound the band in the present and saying, 'Oh yeah, this is a job we have to continue to do. There's a job to be done.'"

Springsteen also gave credit to his cohorts for the new material he came up with before and during the tour, including "American Skin (41 Shots)" and "Land of Hope and Dreams," which were featured on the CD. "The two songs that are on the record are two songs I would not have written if I had not been playing with the band and dealing with those ideas and those issues and going from town to town and trying to continue to define what our band was about and meant to be about," he explained. "It was a big experience, just very satisfying."

When *Live in New York City* was released, Springsteen surprised fans at Jack's Music Shoppe in Red Bank, New Jersey, which stayed open past midnight for those who wanted to buy the album at the first possible minute. "We'd been in California for a week, so I was on California time," Springsteen said. "So I went down and signed some records and talked to some of the fans and things. It was fun. It's just, you know, it's just saying 'hi.'" —*GG*

Live/1975-85

Released: November 10, 1986
Producers: Bruce Springsteen, Jon Landau, Chuck Plotkin
Tracks: Disc 1—"Thunder Road," "Adam Raised a Cain," "Spirit in the Night," "4th of July, Asbury Park (Sandy)," "Fire," "Growin' Up," "It's Hard to Be a Saint in the City," "Backstreets," "Rosalita (Come Out Tonight)," "Raise Your Hand," "Hungry Heart," "Two Hearts"; Disc 2—"Cadillac Ranch," "You Can Look (But You Better Not Touch)," "Independence Day," "Badlands," "Because the Night," "Candy's Room," "Darkness on the Edge of Town," "Racing in the Street," "This Land Is Your Land," "Nebraska," "Johnny 99," "Reason to Believe," "Born in the U.S.A.," "Seeds"; Disc 3—"The River," "War," "Darlington County," "Working on the Highway," "The Promised Land," "Cover Me," "I'm on Fire," "Bobby Jean," "My Hometown," "Born to Run," "No Surrender," "Tenth Avenue Freeze-Out," "Jersey Girl"
Chart peak: No. 1

ntil 1985, Bruce Springsteen held steadfast reasons for not wanting to put out a live album. He told the BBC's "Old Grey Whistle Test" in 1984, "A lot of what we do at this point is about *being there* ... I think it's important that people come out, they come down, they go someplace where there's a bunch of other people. And then ... a live record, a lot of times you're doing things that you've done already. I think it'd probably be a little boring to work on, maybe." He reiterated the latter point to the *Los Angeles Times*, noting that the idea of a live album "wasn't ever interesting enough for me ... I get interested in what I can do next; I get curious and anxious about writing more songs." Of course, the fact Springsteen happened to be not only one of rock's most exciting live performers but also one of its most unpredictable, with set lists that changed nightly, meant that fans wanting souvenirs had to get them from the unreliable and expensive bootleg market—though that underground community had yielded its own share of legendary recordings over the years.

But Springsteen warmed to the live album idea in November 1985, shortly after the mammoth *Born in the U.S.A.* tour closed. His manager and coproducer, Jon Landau, sent him a tape containing four live songs—a cover of

> " ... an unprecedented event in popular recording ... the pop-record equivalent of an epic American novel, its story told in the ungrammatical, rough-hewn vocabulary of rock."
>
> —*New York Times*

> "It's not enough. By anyone else's standards, of course, *Bruce Springsteen & the E Street Band Live/1975–85* is an embarrassment of riches ... Still, Springsteen could have filled a five-record set with what's missing from this one."
>
> —*Rolling Stone*

> "This album is about continuity and honest reassurance, a job very well done. Although it takes some smart chances (e.g., 'War'), it wasn't meant to shock or enlighten or redefine—it was meant to sum up, and it does."
>
> —*Village Voice*

Edwin Starr's "War" that was being considered as a B-side for the forthcoming "My Hometown" single, renditions of "Born in the U.S.A.," a new song called "Seeds," and "The River." Landau included a note suggesting a live album, and when the two began combing through concert tapes and came upon a stark voice-and-piano version of "Thunder Road" from 1975 at the Roxy in Los Angeles, they felt that they could make what biographer Dave Marsh described as something that "wouldn't be a live album or a greatest hits album so much as the next *Bruce Springsteen* album."

Springsteen told Marsh that he was particularly interested in letting people hear how well the E Street Band played in concert. "I was never completely satisfied with any of the recorded versions of things we did—certainly not before *The River*," Springsteen confessed. "On 'Badlands' or 'Darkness,' the live versions are the way that stuff was supposed to sound. And we couldn't have ever got that in the studio, even if we had been playing well—because the audience allows you to attack something with a lot more intensity." Springsteen, Landau, and Chuck Plotkin hit the vaults and started poring through an estimated thirty recorded shows, culling tracks from sixteen of them—including chunks from July 7, 1978, at the Roxy, from three 1981 shows at the Meadowlands Arena, from two 1985 shows at Giants Stadium in East Rutherford, New Jersey, and from September 29, 1985, at the Los Angeles Coliseum. April and May were spent at studios in Los Angeles and New York reviewing masters and overdubbing; mixing with Bob Clearmountain stretched from June to October. Springsteen and company decided on forty songs to be spread over five LPs, three cassettes, and three compact discs. Record advance orders were placed for 1.5 million copies, making it the best-selling box set in history. One mark of the excitement; a truck carrying an estimated 10–15,000 copies of the live set was hijacked in Italy.

While fans and reviewers would have their quibbles with *Live/ 1975–85*, all were thrilled with the inclusion of certain tracks: E Street Band versions of "Fire" and "Because the Night," hits he gave away to the Pointer Sisters and Patti Smith, respectively; full-band versions of some *Nebraska* tracks; unre-

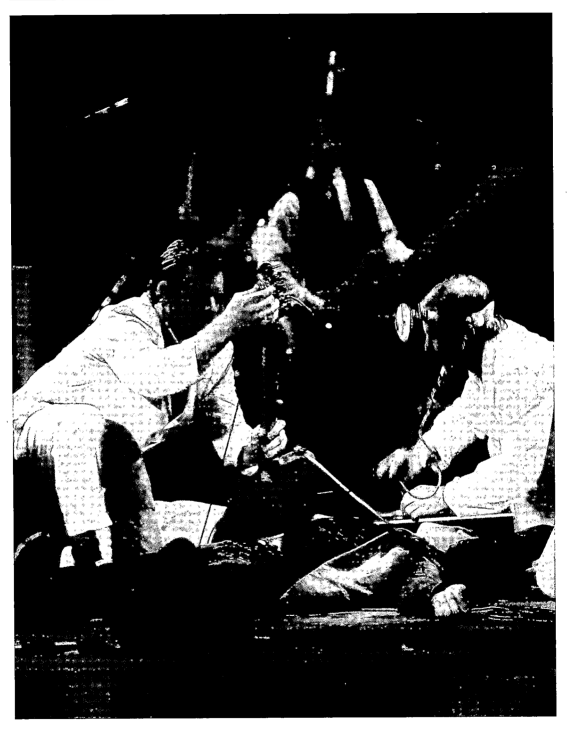

"Paramedics" attempt to revive a spent Springsteen and his guitar in hopes of extending the encore of a *Darkness* tour stop at the Masonic Temple in Detroit in September 1978.

Clarence Clemons, Springsteen, and, well, a bear embellish one of Springsteen's trademark ambling mid-show tales during the *Born in the U.S.A.* tour stop in Detroit in July 1984.

leased songs such as "Seeds" and the instrumental "Paradise by the 'C'"; and covers of "War," Eddie Floyd's "Raise Your Hand," Woody Guthrie's "This Land Is Your Land," and Tom Waits's "Jersey Girl." The set also included an example of the good-humored patter that was regularly part of "Growin' Up," as well as Springsteen's poignant memories of his draft board exam that preceded "The River." Some, however, found the presence of eight tracks from *Born in the U.S.A.*—which, despite its massive popularity, was just two-and-a-half years old at the time—to be excessive.

Live/1975–85 was Springsteen's first album to debut at No. 1 (where it spent seven weeks) and was the first album by anyone to do so since Stevie Wonder's *Songs in the Key of Life* in 1976. It was also the first multi-record set to top the charts since *The River* in 1980. Sales slowed by the spring of 1987, however; *Rolling Stone* magazine reported that an estimated 700,000 copies were sitting unsold at stores around the country, while "Fire" became the first Springsteen single to miss the Top 40 since "Badlands" in 1978. Columbia placed an indefinite moratorium on returns for *Live/1975–85*, though it agreed to give retailers until October 1987 to pay for them.

The album was also accompanied by rumors of some sort of companion video collection, possibly using footage of the Los Angeles Coliseum shows shot by NFL Films. Some of that cropped up in videos for "My Hometown," "War," and "Born to Run," but the collection has never been released in its entirety. —*GG*

Nils Lofgren

E Street Band guitarist, 1984–present

t the beginning of May 1984, Nils Lofgren was three days away from starting rehearsals for his ninth solo album, *Flip*. Then the phone rang and gave him something to really flip over—Bruce

Springsteen was on the other line, inviting him to join the E Street Band to replace the departed Steve Van Zandt. "It was just something I really wanted to do," said Lofgren, who had visited Springsteen not long before that, shortly after the *Born in the U.S.A.* album was completed. "At the time there were lots of rumors that Steve may go on his own. I told (Springsteen) if he ever needed a guitar player, I wanted to audition. I love his music, and I wanted to be in a band."

Winding up on E Street was just another turn in Lofgren's circuitous and eventful career in which he's been a band leader and solo artist. In addition to his work with Springsteen, Lofgren has logged time in the bands of Neil Young and ex-Beatle Ringo Starr and in studios with George Benson, Rod Stewart, Carl Perkins, and E Street bandmates Danny Federici and Patti Scialfa.

Born in Chicago on June 21, 1951, Lofgren's first musical experience came from accordion lessons, which he started when he was five and continued for ten years. But when he was thirteen—his family by then had moved to the Maryland suburbs of Washington, D.C.—Lofgren saw the Beatles on *The Ed Sullivan Show* and took up both rock 'n' roll and the guitar. "I picked (guitar) up as a hobby," he said. "By seventeen I was pretty good at it, and then I saw Jimi Hendrix live and that was it. I knew that's what I wanted to do. I dropped out of school and ran away to Greenwich Village." He had also heard the great local guitarist, Roy Buchanan. With Buchanan, Lofgren said, "I first heard harmonic sounds, like bells." Lofgren eventually returned home and formed Grin, a trio that later added his younger brother Tom on second guitar; the Lofgrens met Springsteen in 1970, when Grin and Springsteen's Steel Mill took part in an audition night at the Fillmore East in New York City. A planned trip to Los Angeles was sidetracked, however, when Neil Young—who had seen Grin perform in a D.C. club—asked Lofgren (then seventeen) to play piano and sing on his *After the Goldrush* album. Eventually, Lofgren became an unofficial member of Young's backing band, Crazy Horse.

Lofgren used his new musical credential to get Grin a contract, and the quartet recorded four underappreciated albums before breaking up in 1974. Before that, however, Lofgren again worked with Young, playing on the *Tonight's the Night* tour in 1973—he appeared on the album of the same name in 1975. After Grin, Lofgren struck out on his own and recorded a series of albums that varied in quality (his musical plea to drug-addled Rolling Stones guitarist Keith Richards was his biggest "hit"). Lofgren's live shows—which included a trademark backflip off of a trampoline during guitar solos—were what truly captured a strong cult following that included fellow musicians like Springsteen—who called Lofgren "the most over-qualified second guitarist in show business" at his Rock and Roll Hall of Fame induction—and the Rolling Stones. Accepting Springsteen's E Street invitation in

Guitarist Nils Lofgren was one of the most respected guitar players in the music business when he was asked to join the E Street Band in May 1984. While he still records solo albums and tours on his own when not busy with the band, he says that "whenever [Bruce] needs me, I'll be there." Here Lofgren plays his 1962 Stratocaster in his Scottsdale, Arizona, studio on January 4, 2004.

1984 was a no-brainer, according to Lofgren. "I've been a fan since the early '70s. I would go and see him play and admire the band and the whole thing Bruce does—being as great a songwriter as there's ever been, as well as a great performer and bandleader. That's a lethal combination in a band like that ... I think he's a great guitarist, a great musician and an excellent keyboard player—which most people don't know. But he knows what sets him apart from everybody is that he's a brilliant writer."

Though he didn't record on *Born in the U.S.A.*, Lofgren fit in well with the E Street Band from the get-go and became a crowd favorite with not only his playing but with antics that included wearing a massive cowboy hat for "Cadillac Ranch" and a patented flip on a trampoline during band introductions. He didn't actually go into the studio with the E Street Band until sessions for 1995's *Greatest Hits* album, though he did play the guitar solo on the title track of Springsteen's 1987 solo album, *Tunnel of Love*. The E Street connection also gave his solo career a boost, shining a spotlight on his 1985 album *Flip*—released during the summer leg of the *Born in the U.S.A.* tour—while Springsteen guested on "Valentine" from Lofgren's 1991 album *Silver Lining*.

Lofgren continues to play and record as a solo artist when time permits. But he's made it clear that when it comes to setting priorities, E Street always has the right of way: "My commitment's to Bruce and the band. Whenever he needs me, I'll be there. When the band's not working, I'll do my own thing. When they're working, I want to be there." —*GG*

Vini Lopez

E Street Band drummer, 1973–74

 longtime Jersey Shore musician, Vini Lopez was the original drummer in Bruce Springsteen's E Street Band and a catalyst for the band's early success. Nicknamed "Mad Dog" for his feisty temper and demeanor, Lopez recalled only partly in jest in 1985, "I was the only drummer I knew with 360-degree hair. And I was a homicidal, schizophrenic, paranoid Roman Catholic. That says it all." Despite his wildman reputation—which, after his departure from the E Street Band in 1974 was more myth than reality—Lopez ranks as one of the Jersey Shore's most popular bandleaders and one of its best drummers.

Mostly self-taught on drums, Lopez began his career with the group Sonny and the Starfires, which featured local hotshot guitarist Sonny Kenn. After his stint with the Starfires, Lopez moved in and out of local bands, the most noted being the Moment of Truth, which included singer-guitarist Billy Chinnock, bass player Garry Tallent, and keyboardist Danny Federici. When the Moment of Truth disbanded in early 1968, Lopez sought out new Jersey Shore musicians with whom to form a new band. "I had heard about Bruce," remembered Lopez, "so me and a friend went to this place called the I.A.M.A., an Italian-American club where Bruce was playing with his band, Earth. I introduced myself, told him I was thinking of putting together an origi-

Off of E Street …
Nils Lofgren

George Benson, *Standing Together* (1998)
Buckshot LeFonque, *Buckshot LeFonque* (1994)
Crazy Horse, *Crazy Horse* (1971)
Tim Curry, *Read My Lips* (1978)
John Eddie, *John Eddie* (1986)
Danny Federici, *Flemington* (1997)
Steve Forbert, *Streets of This Town* (1988)
Grin, *Grin* (1971), *1 + 1* (1972), *All Out* (1972), *Gone Crazy* (1974), *The Best of Grin Featuring Nils Lofgren* (1979), *The Very Best of Grin* (1999)
Carl Perkins, *Go Cat Go* (1996)
Patti Scialfa, *Rumble Doll* (1993), *23rd Street Lullaby* (2004)
Martin Sexton, *Live Wide Open* (2000)
Ringo Starr, *All-Star Band* (1990), *Live From Montreux, Vol. 2.* (1994)
Rod Stewart, *Every Beat of My Heart* (1986), *Rod Stewart* (1986)
Stephen Stills, *Stephen Stills 2* (1971)
Neil Young, *After the Goldrush* (1970), *Tonight's the Night* (Reprise), *Trans* (1983), *Unplugged* (1993)

nal band and invited him down to the [Asbury Park after-hours musicians' club] Upstage. Months later we finally hooked up at the Upstage and played together for the first time."

With the demise of Springsteen's power trio, Earth, he and Lopez formed Child, a Jersey Shore band that included Federici and "Little Vini" Roslyn on bass. In addition to being the band's drummer, Lopez also acted as Child's manager until local surfboard manufacturer Carl "Tinker" West assumed the duties. (Springsteen and Lopez lived together in West's surfboard factory.) Child became Steel Mill a few months later, when Springsteen and Lopez heard that another Jersey band was also calling itself Child.

With a hard-driving, rocking blues sound, Steel Mill became one of New Jersey's top original bands; while Springsteen soared on guitar and vocals, Lopez provided powerful backbeats and often frenzied solos. Steel Mill disbanded in 1971, and Springsteen formed Dr. Zoom and the Sonic Boom followed by the Bruce Springsteen Band, both of which featured Lopez behind the drumkit. It was Lopez who tipped West off to a pair of New York City songwriters—Mike Appel and Jim Cretecos—who were looking for new talent to manage and produce; after Springsteen signed his recording contract with Columbia Records in 1972, he asked Lopez to play drums on his debut album, *Greetings from Asbury Park, N.J.* Lopez toured in Springsteen's backing band in 1973, which eventually became the E Street Band, and also played on Springsteen's second album, *The Wild, the Innocent & the E Street Shuffle*.

Suspicious of Appel, Lopez had frequent run-ins with the manager, which caused friction with Springsteen. Lopez told the *Asbury Park Press* in 1998, "I did all the running to New York for the money. I did all the bickering to get money for this and that. Bruce didn't do any of that. I did. And I guess because I did that, I became more inquisitive about what Mike was doing with the bucks. And I wouldn't sit back, I'd say something. And in those days I was in my twenties and the real Mad Dog." The Lopez-Appel conflict came to a head on Valentine's Day in 1974 when Springsteen fired the drummer after a physical scuffle between Lopez and Appel's brother. Lopez "resented" the firing but said, "There was nothing I could do except ask for a second chance, which I did. But I didn't get it." Springsteen hired another Jersey Shore musician, Ernest "Boom" Carter, to take Lopez's place. Then, with Carter's departure from the E Street Band ten months later, Max Weinberg replaced him and remains the band's drummer.

Stunned by Springsteen's actions, Lopez fell back into the Asbury Park music scene, playing in a number of bands, including Cold Blast & Steel, the Shakes, and the Lord Gunner Group. Although Lopez remained popular in Jersey Shore music circles and his bands were top draws in area clubs such as the Stone Pony in Asbury Park, none of them matched the status enjoyed by the E Street Band. Eventually Lopez turned to another love, golf, and split his time between caddying on Jersey Shore greens and playing drums in bands such as J.P. Gotrock and the Disco Rejects. Lopez still lives on the Jersey Shore, playing drums in area bar bands. His stormy relationship with Springsteen has long since healed, and every so often Lopez jams with his former bandmate at Asbury Park Christmas shows presented by Springsteen and at other special events involving the two musicians. —*RS*

Los Angeles, California

Hotbed for Springsteen history and occasional residence

ruce Springsteen stopped in San Francisco first (where his parents and youngest sister moved in the early '70s) and had a more partisan audience in Phoenix, but Los Angeles was the western U.S. city he ultimately came to embrace. "It's a place where a man can really feel his success," he sang in a 1991 song called "Goin' Cali." Let the record show that in this town Springsteen earned it first. Start with concerts. Since 1972, he has performed roughly fifty times in L.A., including three shows that were broadcast on the radio and another that was filmed for MTV, and before that, a 1973 showcase that was filmed for CBS Records. He played a whopping twenty nights there on *The River* and *Born in the U.S.A.* tours, and some of Springsteen's most notable career performances took place in Los Angeles as well: the 1978 broadcast from the Roxy; *A Night for the Vietnam Veteran* in 1981; and his four-night stand at the Coliseum in 1985 that closed the *Born in the U.S.A.* tour, yielding a large chunk of songs—including his version of Edwin Starr's "War"—that appeared on *Live/1975–85*. That same year, dope-rocker comics Cheech and Chong recorded and released the Springsteen parody single "Born in East L.A."

When Springsteen wasn't busy packing the Sports Arena or Coliseum, he was holed up in his Hollywood Hills bungalow. In 1983, he set up a home studio there and commenced recording by himself, taking initial stabs at songs like "Johnny Bye Bye" and "Shut Out the Light." By 1990, Springsteen had moved to Los Angeles full-time, taking a sabbatical of sorts from New Jersey and for a while, his craft. He and Patti Scialfa started a family, and Springsteen kept a low profile. "In Los Angeles I could still have my cars and motorcycles," he wrote in *Songs*, "be thirty minutes from the mountains, ocean and desert, meet some new people, and relax amidst the anonymity of the big city." It also put him in closer proximity to his parents and particularly his father, with whom he'd patched up old differences and developed a "loving" relationship. Springsteen emerged from seclusion to perform benefit concerts with Bonnie Raitt and Jackson Browne at the Shrine Auditorium in November 1990, his only official appearance between 1988–92. There, Springsteen debuted six new songs, including "57 Channels" and "Real World," but another sixteen months passed until he released the albums *Human Touch* and *Lucky Town.* In 1992, he kicked off his new tour with a radio broadcast from Los Angeles and taped his electric *Plugged* set for MTV as well.

The time residing in Los Angeles had a discernible impact on Springsteen's music. At first, Springsteen poked fun at himself and his "bourgeois house in the Hollywood Hills." By 1995, he had completed the acoustic *The Ghost of Tom Joad*, a record steeped in dusty Western imagery. Songs from that era told tales of Mexican immigrants, border patrol agents, and itinerants who rode the rails in the San Joaquin Valley. The album's liner notes cited articles in the *Los Angeles Times* that influenced two songs in particular, "Sinaloa Cowboys" and "Balboa Park." Topics he had already covered got Western treatment, including the Vietnam veterans in "Brothers Under the Bridge," whose real-life characters lived in the San Gabriel mountains.

The mid-'90s also found Springsteen contributing to movie soundtracks such as Sean Penn's *The Crossing Guard* and most successfully, Jonathan Demme's *Philadelphia*; Springsteen's elegiac "Streets of Philadelphia" opened the film and won an Academy Award for Best Original Song in 1993. These songs and others, like a version of "Gypsy Woman" for the 1994 Curtis Mayfield tribute *All Men Are Brothers*, found him experimenting with drum loops and other percussive elements, a stark contrast to his straight-ahead rock and acoustic projects. —*JP*

Lucky Town

Released: March 31, 1992
Producers: Bruce Springsteen, Jon Landau, Chuck Plotkin, Roy Bittan
Tracks: "Better Days," "Lucky Town," "Local Hero," "If I Should Fall Behind," "Leap of Faith," "The Big Muddy," "Living Proof," "Book of Dreams," "Souls of the Departed," "My Beautiful Reward"
Chart peak: No. 3

Lucky Town is Bruce Springsteen's *other* 1992 album, released in tandem with *Human Touch* but recorded in a much less exacting fashion and achieving a more organic, gritty sound than its companion. While *Human Touch*, a full year in the making, was what Springsteen called "an exercise to get myself back into writing and recording," *Lucky Town* flexed renewed creative muscles and was made in a fraction of the time in the fall of 1991 with a core band that included E Street Band survivor Roy Bittan (who received coproducer credits on three songs) and seasoned drummer Gary Mallaber, with Springsteen's wife Patti Scialfa and Soozie Tyrell—who was to become a fixture in Springsteen's creative world—providing backing vocals. According to Springsteen, *Lucky Town* started with the song "Living Proof," a piece inspired by Bob Dylan's "Series of Dreams" that he intended to put on *Human Touch*; instead it lit a creative fire that, as he writes in *Songs*, resulted in an entirely new album in just three weeks. "It was a release from the long process of making *Human Touch.* I set up home recording equipment and everything came together very quickly, as on *Nebraska* and *Tunnel of Love*. *Lucky Town* had the ease that came with the relaxed writing and recording of its songs."

Springsteen considers the album's ten songs to be about "second chances," mostly in relationships and undoubtably inspired by his still-fresh marriage to Scialfa. He also touches on larger social and political issues in songs such as "The Big Muddy" and "Souls of the Departed." Ultimately he decided to release *Lucky Town* simultaneously with *Human Touch* because, he told *Rolling Stone* magazine, "I realized that the two albums together kind of tell one story." That tale? He relates in *Songs*, "[They're] both about the blessings and the unanswerable questions that come with adult life, mortality, and human love."

And, he pointed out to *Rolling Stone*, Guns N' Roses had released simultaneous albums—*Use Your Illusion I & II*—as well. "I basically said … maybe I'll try it!'"

Though at concerts he bemoaned the sluggish sales of both albums (an *Entertainment Weekly* story asked, "What Ever Happened to Bruce?"), Springsteen did everything he could to promote them. He launched the projects with a special soundstage performance for contest winners in Los Angeles, pressing the flesh and signing autographs afterwards. He played his first live television appearance on May 9, 1992, on "Saturday Night Live." He even conducted interviews in his dressing room during intermission of his concerts and opened his preshow soundchecks to reporters.

> **"W**here *Human Touch* is dense and highly worked, *Lucky Town* has an infectious swagger characterised by the gospel chorusing of the female voices, hammering acoustic guitars and comparatively loose delivery. There are more smiles here, and certainly less desperation … (B)oth albums have their misfires, their occasional lapses into kitsch and sometimes a lack of harmonic colour, but as the age span of the rock audience grows too wide to be meaningfully encompassed by any one artist, they find Springsteen thundering off into middle age, leading with his chin, his recklessness unimpaired."
> —*Q*

> **"D**edicated to (Patti) Scialfa and the couple's two children, the album's 10 songs paint a convincing—and only rarely cloying—portrait of domestic life and its contents."
> —*Rolling Stone*

> **"** … comparatively more intimate, with delicate acoustic tracks, nods to folk rock and twang …"
> —*Entertainment Weekly*

Springsteen took to the road with a new band to promote *Human Touch* and *Lucky Town* in 1992 and 1993.

"Everyone likes to be at the top of the charts," he noted backstage at a show in East Rutherford, New Jersey, one night, "but that has never been my fundamental reason for being on that stage at night ... For me, it's a bit of a sideshow. People just forget that everything recycles itself, even all of the criticisms ... After *Born to Run*, I remember reading all of the 'What happened to?' articles, and it just kind of goes around and around and around ... every time you do something different or go into a big change." —*GG*

LuckyTown Digest. See Luckytown.org.

Luckytown.org

Fan website

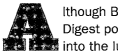lthough Bruce Springsteen has no official fan club, the LuckyTown Digest popped up in 1991 as an e-mail list for fans and expanded into the luckytown.org website in the mid-'90s. (Its original name was *BackStreets Digest*, but it changed names in roughly 1994.) Until owner Kevin Kinder shut it down due to time constraints in 2003, it was a place for opinionated, articulate Springsteen obsessives to rank bootlegs, post concert reviews, and discuss general-admission concert seating in near-fanatical detail. The website's Frequently Asked Questions page lives on at http://www.luckytown.org/faq.html; while dated, it's a pre–*The Rising* fount of information, including contact numbers for Springsteen's publicist and record label, bootleg sources, and answers to questions both stupid and intricate.

When Kinder ceased publishing, other websites mourned. "Kevin may be right that Luckytown will not be missed. But only in the same way that the Continental Congress isn't missed, or the Works Progress Administration, or the League of Nations," eulogized The Hitter (http://users.erols.com/smithsvoboda/). "Reading about a show like the March 23, 1993, Count Basie benefit ... was like receiving a coded message from another planet, in a way that people today might find hard to understand." —*SK*

Southside Johnny Lyon. *See* Southside Johnny & the Asbury Jukes.

Madam Marie

Asbury Park fortune teller

adam Marie, a longtime Asbury Park fortune teller, was made famous in New Jersey rock circles after Bruce Springsteen wrote her into his song, "4th of July, Asbury Park (Sandy)," on his second album, *The Wild, the Innocent & the E Street Shuffle*. But the line, "Did you hear, the cops finally busted Madam Marie for tellin' fortunes better than they do," was entirely fictional; Marie Castello, aka Madam Marie, was never arrested for telling fortunes—good, bad, or otherwise. But she's done countless palm and tarot card readings during a fortune-telling career that began in the late 1930s, and her name is permanently etched into Asbury Park rock 'n' roll history because of her Springsteen connection.

Madam Marie's Temple of Knowledge, a small, one-room concrete structure, is located on the Asbury Park boardwalk, a stone's throw from the city's most famous rock club, the Stone Pony. With the exception of the Springsteen reference, Castello had little else to do with the Asbury Park music scene. Springsteen fans, however, turned the Temple of Knowledge into an Asbury Park rock landmark by making it a point to have their fortunes read by Madam Marie during visits to the seaside resort. In the '70s and '80s Castello did a brisk business with Springsteen tourists, but with the city in continued economic decline, Madam Marie closed the doors of the Temple of Knowledge in 1998. She reopened them on July 4, 2004, for the board-walk summer season amid widespread media coverage. Weekend readings range in price from $5 to $35. "I did close it down for a while, because it was getting pretty slow up there," Castello told the Associated Press. "But I always had people coming around asking for me. I really never left." —*RS*

Terry Magovern

Springsteen's assistant, 1987–present

ruce Springsteen's longtime assistant, Terry Magovern, has been a fixture on the Jersey Shore music scene since the mid-'60s when he first began managing bars and booking bands there. Born in Teaneck, New Jersey, and raised in the resort town of Belmar, Magovern began working in area bars after his discharge from the U.S. Navy in 1962. Among the bars he managed were DJ's in Belmar, the Riptide in Pt. Pleasant Beach, and the Captain's Garter (later the Headliner) in Neptune.

Magovern first met Springsteen in the late '60s at the Asbury Park after-hours musicians' club the Upstage. "Right from the first time I heard him play, I believed in him and his music," recalled Magovern. In late 1971, when Magovern was managing the Captain's Garter, a popular Top 40 club, he hired the Bruce Springsteen Band to open for a Philadelphia cover group, Superheat. Despite the presence of Springsteen's fans at the club the first night he played it, the owner of the Captain's Garter forced Magovern to fire the band, claiming Springsteen's music wasn't any good. "He played one night, but I made sure he got paid for the full two weeks I booked him," said Magovern.

In 1981, E Street Band saxophonist Clarence Clemons opened Big Man's West in Red Bank, and he hired Magovern to run it. Though the club closed two years later, Magovern continued to work for Clemons, going on the road with him and his band, the Red Bank Rockers. When Springsteen took the E Street Band on tour in support of his 1987 album *Tunnel of Love*, Magovern accompanied him and has remained part of the greater Springsteen family ever since; he was credited with "research" on *The Ghost of Tom Joad* and as road manager for the subsequent solo acoustic tour, and as a "project coordinator" on *The Rising* album. But even after working for Springsteen for nearly twenty years and knowing him for almost twice as long, Magovern's job description has remained vague. Once, when Springsteen was asked exactly what role Magovern played in his camp, Springsteen replied, "Terry Magovern is Terry Magovern." —*RS*

Jesse Malin

Former D Generation frontman turned solo artist

hen Jesse Malin left the New York glam rock outfit D Generation and issued his first solo album in 2003, *Entertainment Weekly* christened him "the Springsteen of Avenue D." The comparison wasn't off base; on his own, Malin stepped forward as a rock 'n' roll troubadour with a knack for crafting finely drawn stories and morality plays. At the same time, the songs on Malin's two solo albums—2003's *The Fine Art of Self-Destruction* and 2004's *The Heat*—drew inspiration from other sources as well, most clearly Neil Young, Steve Earle, and the new wave of Americana embodied by *Self-Destruction* producer and former Whiskeytown leader Ryan Adams. Nevertheless, Malin's music made a fan of Springsteen; the two met at the 2003 Light of Day benefit in Asbury Park, New Jersey, where Malin—who had contributed a version of "Hungry Heart" to the *Light of Day: A Tribute to Bruce Springsteen* album—gave Springsteen a copy of *Self-Destruction* "Then he rang a week later and left a message on my machine," Malin related. "When I called him back, he just said, 'Tell me everything!'" Springsteen subsequently invited Malin to be part of his 2003 holiday shows in Asbury Park, joining the E Street Band in backing the younger musician on his own "Queen of the Underworld" and "Wendy."

A native of Queens, New York, Malin co-founded D Generation in the early '90s. The group recorded three albums and provided a spark for successors the Strokes but broke up in 1999. Malin began playing around town and developed a more songwriter-oriented approach that lured Adams's patronage. *Self-Destruction* actually came out in Great Britain nearly four months before its U.S. release, but back home it was nominated for the prestigious Shortlist Music Prize. Adams also recruited Malin to be part of a hard-rocking side project called The Finger. —*GG*

Manfred Mann's Earth Band

British rock group

South Africa native, keyboardist Manfred Lubowitz changed his name and his country, moving to England, where he and drummer Mike Hugg formed the group Manfred Mann, which racked up an impressive number of hits in the mid-'60s. Among their successes were "5-4-3-2-1" (which became the theme song of the TV program "Ready Steady Go!"), "Do Wah Diddy Diddy" (a No. 1 hit in both England and America), "Pretty Flamingo," and a cover of Bob Dylan's "The Mighty Quinn." The band's membership was often in flux, however, and it split up in 1967.

Manfred Mann's Earth Band formed in 1970 and took a completely different direction from the earlier group. Mann's initial intention as a musician was to play jazz, and he at least was able to make instrumental virtuosity a characteristic of the prog-rocking Earth Band. The group did enjoy some radio hits however—most notably "Blinded by the Light," a cover of the *Greetings from Asbury Park, N.J.* track that appeared on the Earth Band's 1976 album *The Roaring Silence.* Led by Mann's wooshing synthesizers, the song was wildly divergent from Springsteen's lean, rambling original. More curious was guitarist/vocalist Chris Thompson's rendering of the lyric, "Cut loose like a deuce," which somehow became "Wrapped up like a douche." Nevertheless, the song became a No. 1 hit in the U.S., the first song penned by Springsteen to achieve that distinction.

"Blinded by the Light" was bookended by two other Earth Band covers of *Greetings from Asbury Park, N.J.* songs. A year earlier, for the album *Nightingales and Bombers*, Mann had covered "Spirit in the Night," a remixed version of that recording made it to No. 40 in 1977. The group returned to Springsteen's catalog again in 1980, covering "For You" on the album *Chance.* All three Springsteen covers appear on 1984's *Budapest Live.*

The Earth Band broke up in the mid-'80s but reunited briefly a decade later. —*DD*

The Mansion on the Hill

1997 book by Fred Goodman

Written by Fred Goodman, a former *Rolling Stone* editor and music business reporter for top magazines and newspapers, *The Mansion on the Hill* is a meticulously documented look at how rock 'n' roll grew from underground innocence into a cutthroat corporate business. Bruce Springsteen, Neil Young, Bob Dylan, and mogul David Geffen are Goodman's case studies, and the inside dirt is insightful and revealing.

The Mansion on the Hill shows how Springsteen began as a raw talent sired by an abrasive manager, former songwriter-for-hire Mike Appel, and upgraded to the more sympathetic rock-critic-turned-producer/manager Jon Landau. The ambitious Landau won Springsteen's trust with his 1974 concert review proclaiming, "I saw rock and roll future and its name is Bruce Springsteen," and latched on as an important creative adviser. Goodman's book chronicles Landau's personal history—he married writer Janet Maslin and, before joining *Rolling Stone*, was a liaison during intense labor negotiations at the *Phoenix* in Boston—and traces the evolution of his partnership with The Boss, beginning during the *Born to Run* album sessions.

Eventually, Landau's influence grew to the extent that he produced Springsteen's albums and guided him to key artistic works such as Flannery O'Connor short stories and John Ford movies. (These would play a creative role in shaping the subsequent *Darkness on the Edge of Town*, not to mention *Nebraska* and *The Ghost of Tom Joad.*) Meanwhile, Appel's influence waned to the extent that Springsteen sued to break his management contracts. The long, emotional court battle ended in a settlement that, Goodman reports, gave $800,000 in royalties to Appel in exchange for relinquishing his control over Springsteen.

Although Goodman gives Landau credit for helping to inspire some of Springsteen's greatest works—Landau, of course, remains with The Boss to this day—he's hardly painted as benevolent. Goodman relays an incident in which Springsteen's old friend, photographer-turned-publishing executive Jeff Albertson, arrived at a 1978 show and tried to socialize with Springsteen. Springsteen was game, but Landau declared, "Look, will you leave Bruce alone right now?" According to the book, Landau's sentiment took over, and Albertson never saw Springsteen again. —*SK*

Marah

Rock 'n' roll kids from Philly

Brothers Serge and Dave Bielanko, who lead the Philadelphia rock group Marah, are dedicated Bruce Springsteen fans who have become his friends and have even worked with him a bit. Springsteen played the guitar solo and sang backing vocals on "Float Away," a song from the group's 2002 album *Float Away with the Friday Night Gods*, and he called the brothers on stage with him to play and sing on "Raise Your Hand" at the August 30, 2003, show at Giants Stadium in East Rutherford, New Jersey. "He's been an amazing guy to us," Dave Bielanko said. "To meet someone of that stature and have him be that cool of a person really is cool. He's way accessible and very, very humble; he'll drink his beer and talk about Sam & Dave the same way we do."

Marah met Springsteen when it played the Stone Pony while supporting its second album, *Kids in Philly*, and while finishing *Float Away*. "We just asked Bruce if he wanted to come out and play on a song, and he did. It was so cool."

The Bielanko brothers were raised in Conshocken, Pennsylvania, about eleven miles outside Philadelphia. Guitarist Dave actually started the group as a trio with two other musicians, subsequently adding Serge to sing and play guitar and harmonica in 1995. The group recorded its first album, 1998's *Let's Cut the Crap and Hook Up Later On Tonight*, for the Black Dog label owned by Blue Mountain's Cary Hudson; after a dynamic performance at that year's South By Southwest Festival, Steve Earle signed them to his E-Squared imprint—and subsequently hooked the band up with tickets for one of the Philadelphia Spectrum shows on the 1999 leg of the E Street Band reunion tour. In 2004, the band released *20,000 Streets Under the Sky.* —*GG*

While playing at longtime Springsteen hangout the Stone Pony in support of their album *Kids in Philly*, the band Marah met and became friends with the rock icon, who subsequently helped out by singing and playing guitar on the band's next album, *Float Away with the Friday Night Gods*. Shown here at the band's rehearsal space in July 2004 are, from left, Kirk Henderson, Serge Bielanko, Jon Wurster, Dave Bielanko, and Mike "Slo-Mo" Brenner.

Dave Marsh

Writer, critic, activist

n outlandishly feisty music journalist and a zealous political and cultural activist, Dave Marsh is Bruce Springsteen's de facto biographer. Marsh's first book was 1979's *Born to Run: The Bruce Springsteen Story*, which became a *New York Times* best-seller. Its 1987 sequel, *Glory Days: Bruce Springsteen in the 1980s*, also hit the best-seller list. In 2003, they were combined as *Bruce Springsteen: Two Hearts (The Definitive Biography, 1972–2003)*. Marsh was also with Jon Landau when they met Springsteen for the first time at an April 1974 gig at Charley's in Cambridge, Massachusetts. And Barbara Carr, Marsh's wife, co-manages Springsteen with Jon Landau.

Born in 1950, Marsh left Detroit's Wayne State University in 1969 to become a founding editor of *Creem*, an early and influential magazine on the still-emerging rock journalism scene. In 1973, he left the Motor City to become *New York Newsday*'s pop music critic. Marsh was also music editor of Boston's *Real Paper* before joining *Rolling Stone* in 1975, where he became one of its star staffers and an associate editor; he profiled Springsteen for *Rolling Stone* as well as for *Musician* magazine. In 1983, Marsh started publishing the anti-censorship *Rock and Roll* (now *Rock and Rap*) *Confidential* newsletter. In 1987, he started a five-year stint as rock critic for the syndicated radio show "Rock Today." He's now a regular contributor to *Playboy* magazine's album review section, and his freelance work appears in many print and online publications. He's also a sought-after lecturer and panelist on a variety of music-related subjects.

Marsh has also written books about the Who, Elvis Presley, Michael Jackson, Woody Guthrie, and "Louie, Louie" (that's right, an entire book about a song even the FBI deemed full of unintelligible lyrics). He's also edited and contributed to many others, including *Mid-Life Confidential: The Rock Bottom Remainders Tour America with Three Chords and an Attitude*, which chronicles the adventures of several authors masquerading as a rock band, including Stephen King, Amy Tan, Dave Barry, Barbara Kingsolver, and, at one time, Dave Marsh. Marsh is the stepfather of Carr's daughters, Kristen and Sasha, whom he helped to raise since Kristen was three and Sasha was a baby. In 1993, when she was twenty-one, Kristen died of liposarcoma, a rare form of cancer. Her family established the Kristen Ann Carr Fund in her honor. The family resides at homes in Connecticut and New York. —*LM*

Max's Kansas City

New York City music club, 1965–81

efore Bruce Springsteen played his pivotal 1975 *Born to Run* showcases at New York's Bottom Line, some his most important Big Apple gigs took place at Max's Kansas City, which he used as a forum to try out new material and work on his stage schtick. Throughout 1972 Springsteen opened for veteran folkie Dave Van Ronk, among others, performing as a solo balladeer. In 1973 he brought the E Street Band and played the kinds of raucous shows that would make him famous. Springsteen's earliest appearance at Max's was on August 30, 1972; he returned from January 31 to February 5, 1973 (opening for Biff Rose), and again from July 18–23 (coheadlining with Bob Marley & the Wailers) and November 6–10. *Rolling Stone* editor (and future Springsteen manager) Jon Landau sent writer Stu Werbin to check out one of the early-'73 shows, and Werbin—

whose April 26, 1973, report was the magazine's first coverage of Spring-steen's music—was so knocked out he made Landau accompany him the next night.

The shows were apparently so exciting that John Hammond, the man who signed Springsteen to Columbia Records, suffered his third heart attack while at one of the early '73 shows. Hammond told *Rolling Stone* that although he thought the cardiac arrest was brought on by a heavy work schedule and weakness from a virus he'd caught in Paris, his doctor disagreed and said it was due to Hammond's enthusiasm at the Spring-steen show.

The club opened in 1965 on Manhattan's lower east side and was named for the man who ran off with owner Mickey Ruskin's first wife and the city where they'd gone. As time went on it became notorious for early punk shows by Iggy and the Stooges, the New York Dolls, and the Velvet Under-ground with Nico (who held court upstairs in the late '60s). Along with its pri-mary competitor, CBGB, Max's spent sixteen years developing its own drug-gy, counter-cultural mythology. Deborah Harry of Blondie was a waitress there, and performance artist Lance Loud, the troubled kid from the docu-mentary *An American Family*, formed a group there called the Mumps. Celebrity hangers-on included John Lennon and Yoko Ono, Warren Beatty, Mick Jagger, Jane Fonda, and transvestite Candy Darling. Wayne County recalled his flamboyant adventures there in a terrific punk anthem called, "Max's Kansas City 1976." "I met Iggy Pop at Max's Kansas City in 1970 or 1971," David Bowie recalled on the club's historical website, maxskansasci-ty.com. "Me, Iggy, and Lou Reed at one table with absolutely nothing to say to each other, just looking at each other's eye makeup."

For his part, a young Springsteen delivered future recorded classics such as "Spirit In the Night," "4th of July, Asbury Park (Sandy)," and "Does This Bus Stop at 82nd Street?" in addition to raucous rarities like "Thunder-crack," "Zero & Blind Terry," and "Something You Got." Max's closed in 1981, and while eulogies touch on Springsteen's early appearances, it remains best known as a ground zero for punk rock. —*SK/LM*

The Meadowlands. *See* **Continental Airlines Arena.**

The Miami Horns

Horn section from 1976 and 1977 tours

Bruce Springsteen and the E Street Band have toured with full horn sections two times—the most famous of which was the Miami Horns that played on the latter part of the *Born to Run* tour in 1976

The Miami Horns (left) join Springsteen, Steve Van Zandt, and the rest of the E Street Band on "Tenth Avenue Freeze-Out" at a November 1976 concert at the Palladium in New York City. The Horns were a staple of 1977's Chicken Scratch Tour.

and on the 1977 Chicken Scratch Tour dates while Springsteen was prevented from recording while fighting manager Mike Appel in court. Named for E Street Band guitarist Miami Steve Van Zandt—who joined the group after arranging the horn parts on *Born to Run*'s "Tenth Avenue Freeze-Out"—the Miami Horns were first organized to play with Southside Johnny & the Asbury Jukes. It's this ensemble—saxophonists Carlo Novi and Ed Manion and trumpeters Tony Palligrosi and Rick Gazda—that joined the E Street Band for shows on August 1976 in Red Bank, New Jersey, and Waterbury, Connecticut.

When the E Street Band hit the road again on September 26 in Phoenix, Arizona, however, that quartet had rejoined the Jukes. A new horn section was in place consisting of Philadelphia players Ed De Palma on saxophone, Joe Benkley and Steve Paraczky on trumpet, and trombonist Dennis Orlock. The four were on the road through the tour's end on March 25, 1977, in Boston, Massachusetts, but Springsteen tended not to introduce the players by name.

Van Zandt and another set of Miami Horns—saxophonists Manion and Stan Harrison, trumpeter Mark Pender and trombonist Richie "La Bamba" Rosenberg—were special guests at Springsteen's August 20, 1984, concert at Brendan Byrne Arena in East Rutherford, New Jersey; their rendition of "Tenth Avenue Freeze-Out" is preserved on the *Live/1975-85* album. Rosenberg, Pender, and Manion returned as part of the Horns of Love section for 1988's Tunnel of Love Express Tour, joined by Mike Spengler on trumpet and Mario Cruz on saxophone. Pender and Rosenberg are now part of the Max Weinberg 7, the house band for NBC's "Late Night with Conan O'Brien." —*GG*

Monmouth Memorial Hospital

Where Springsteen was born

Bruce Springsteen was born in the U.S.A.—but not in Freehold, New Jersey, as is commonly believed (and which he's even put as his birthplace in his tour books). His actual place of birth on September 23, 1949, was at Monmouth Memorial Hospital in Long Branch, which is now known as Monmouth Medical Center. Springsteen was delivered by Dr. Frank Niemtzow. Copies of his birth certificate and other medical records were subsequently obtained by an unidentified collector who auctioned them through the New York City house Leland's.

The Monmouth Medical Center is a 527-bed facility whose history dates back to the early 1900s. The MMC is one of New Jersey's largest community teaching hospitals, with eight residency training programs. Part of the Saint Barnabas Health Care System, MMC handles almost 13,000 surgeries, 3,200 baby deliveries, and more than 150,000-plus patient visits each year, servicing not only Monmouth County but also portions of nearby Middlesex and Ocean counties. —*GG*

Van Morrison

Irish singer, songwriter, iconoclast, Rock and Roll Hall of Fame member

mong the most intriguing, innovative, and occasionally vexing figures in music, Van Morrison stands at the nexus of rock, jazz, blues, soul, and Celtic folk. On the one hand his work is spirited and street-smart, full of knowledge picked up in the neighborhoods of his hometown of Belfast, Northern Ireland, and on the vintage American blues and jazz records collected by his father. On the other hand, Morrison is a profoundly spiritual artist drawing from sources such as visionary English poet William Blake and the texts of various religions and philosophies. In short, he's a soul man, however you want to define the term.

Morrison's influence can be found all over Bruce Springsteen's work—in the punchy horn arrangement of "Tenth Avenue Freeze-Out" and the cool R&B flavor of "Spirit in the Night"; in the ecstatic lyrical babble of the first two albums; and in Springsteen's soulful vocal delivery. And of course, The Boss has been known to throw down a fine cover version of "Gloria," too.

Morrison, however, has not been particularly charitable in acknowledging Springsteen's fondness for his work. He claimed in a 1985 interview that he had not heard Springsteen's music until that year—and wasn't impressed: "He's definitely ripped me off. There's no doubt about that … I mean, he's even ripped off my movements as well. My '70s movements, you know what I mean? … I feel pissed off now that I know about it." Some felt that Springsteen was one of the targets Morrison intended on his 1986 song "A Town Called Paradise," which begins, "Copycats ripped off my words, copycats ripped off my songs…."

Morrison quit school at age fifteen and played saxophone in an R&B band, the Monarchs, which toured Europe. Afterwards, he ran an R&B club in Belfast and formed the group Them to perform as the house band. Them cracked the British charts with a version of Big Joe Williams's "Baby Please Don't Go," after which the group moved to London and scored with "Here Comes the Night" and "Gloria" (a Morrison song made popular in the U.S. by the Shadows of Knight). Morrison left Them in 1966.

As a solo artist, Morrison hit the U.S. charts in 1967 with "Brown Eyed Girl," then signed with Warner Bros. and recorded the enigmatic classic *Astral Weeks*. He followed that with a string of great albums, mostly in an R&B vein: *Moondance*, *His Band and Street Choir*, *Tupelo Honey*, and *Saint Dominic's Preview*. In 1974, backed by the eleven-piece Caledonia Soul Orchestra, Morrison released *It's Too Late to Stop Now*, widely hailed as one of rock's greatest live albums.

Morrison's late-'70s work is less distinguished, but it does include a triumphant appearance at The Band's farewell concert, *The Last Waltz*. His albums of the '80s dealt more with Morrison's passionate yet vague spiritual quest. In 1988, he sought to reconnect with his Celtic roots by recording with traditional Irish band the Chieftains on *Irish Heartbeat*. He also reached back to his pop past, taking "Whenever God Shines His Light on Me," recorded with former U.K. teen idol Cliff Richard, into the British Top 20. Recent efforts have found Morrison bringing his daughter Shana into the act. His output continues to be prodigious as he releases albums that follow his ever-unpredictable muse. He did not attend his induction into the Rock and Roll Hall of Fame in 1993—the same ceremony at which Springsteen inducted Creedence Clearwater Revival. —*DD*

Bob Muller. *See A Night for the Vietnam Veteran.*

Murder Incorporated
Rumored album considered for release in 1983

One year after *Nebraska*, Bruce Springsteen and the E Street Band already had enough material for several albums. Springsteen himself split time between Hollywood, where he was cutting even more elaborate multi-track demos than he had for *Nebraska*, and New York City, where the newly written songs were recorded with the band and added to the pile cut the previous year. By the second half of 1983, a tentative collection of the "best" of these tracks was assembled and cassette copies of that track list, as legend has it, were placed in the hands of the band, management, and perhaps even Columbia. The proposed album featured songs that would later appear on *Born in the U.S.A.*, including its powerful title track and "Glory Days," and many that didn't, such as the suggested title track for this incarnation—"Murder Incorporated," an out-and-out rocker the theme of which is summed up in the lyric, "Everywhere you look life ain't got no soul." There was also "This Hard Land," a sweet piece of farm belt Americana; "Frankie," a romantic epic penned and played live in 1976 and recorded first for *Darkness on the Edge of Town* before resurrection here; and "My Love Will Not Let You Down," an urgent and passionate plea to a lover with a driving beat to match.

The result was an album that had fewer upbeat songs than *Born in the U.S.A.* eventually did, but felt more like the logical extension of the tone of *Nebraska*. Conventional wisdom holds that *Murder Incorporated* was considered for release in 1983, but only briefly, as the prolific Springsteen kept writing and recording into early 1984.

The title track and "This Hard Land" were eventually released officially on 1995's *Greatest Hits*, though the latter was rerecorded. The original "This

Hard Land," "Frankie," and "My Love Will Not Let You Down" came out on *Tracks.* The eight-minute original electric version of "Born in the U.S.A." remains unreleased but pops up on several bootlegs, including the *Lost Masters* series. The original 1983 lineup of the album as reportedly circulated on cassette at that time can be found on the bootleg *This Hard Land*. —*EF*

Elliott Murphy

Long Island–born singer-songwriter, now based in Europe

In 1973, not long after Bruce Springsteen released his first album to intimidating "new Dylan" plaudits, Elliott Murphy's *Aquashow* was tagged by one critic as "the best new Dylan since 1968." If nothing else, it's clear that both musicians share similar influences, outlooks, and life experiences (Murphy is just six months older than Springsteen). They also cut their performance teeth playing the same circuit around New Jersey and New York City's Greenwich Village. And while Springsteen enjoyed the far more celebrated career, he's acknowledged Murphy's influence on his work, and vice versa.

The two have maintained a friendship that includes some memorable collaborations. An October 21, 1994, show at the Playpen in Sayerville, New Jersey, was particularly interesting, with Springsteen joining Murphy, Marshall Crenshaw, John Eddie, and Greg Kihn for a rowdy covers set that included Creedence Clearwater Revival's "Hey Tonight," Elvis Presley's "Suspicious Minds," T. Rex's "Get It On (Bang a Gong)," Bobby Troup's "Route 66," and Them's "Gloria." Springsteen has also made a point of calling Murphy—who resides in Europe—on stage during his most recent tour stops in Paris, France, hosting him twice each on the 1999 E Street Band reunion tour and on the 2002–2003 tour for *The Rising*. "His stage is so nice," Murphy told *Point Blank* magazine founder Salvador Trepat in 2000. "Everyone up there is so great … It's amazing, really. Bruce has got the best fans, I really think … No, *I've* got the best fans, but after me … he's got the best, and he's got a *lot* of 'em. When you look out there, it's an *ocean*. On 'Hungry Heart,' they sing every word. Every word almost to every song, and that's amazing."

Springsteen and Murphy have worked together on record, too; Springsteen dueted on "Everything I Do" from Murphy's 1995 album *Selling the Gold*. A bonus CD5 in France also included Murphy's acoustic versions of Springsteen's "Stolen Car" and "Drive All Night."

Murphy was born and raised on Long Island and used to watch musicians play at the Aqua Show, a club his father owned in Queens, New York. He was fronting bands by the time he was thirteen; one of them, the Rapscallions, won a state battle of the bands contest in New York. He spent time in Europe before returning to New York in the early '70s, forming Elliott Murphy's

Aquashow and signing with Polydor in 1972. Despite critical acclaim—including an Album of the Year prize for his *Party Girls/Broken Poets* at the 1984 New York Music Awards—his albums didn't sell well, and his major label career ended in the late '70s. He emigrated to Paris in 1990, where he continues to write and record. Murphy has also written liner notes for the Velvet Underground and the Violent Femmes, and articles for *Rolling Stone, Spin*, and other periodicals. He's published two collections of short stories and a novel, *Cold and Electric.* —*GG*

Anne Murray
Canadian pop and country singer

Bruce Springsteen was a late addition to the Central Park Music Festival on August 3, 1974; he was added as a replacement for Boz Scaggs, who was scheduled to close the show. But according to Springsteen's then-manager Mike Appel, the manager for Canadian singer Anne Murray "made a real big deal" out of the fact that *his* artist should close the show because she was more commercially successful at that point, with hits such as "Songbird," a cover of the Beatles' "You Won't See Me," and a cover of Kenny Loggins's "Danny's Song." The promoter acquiesced, but it proved to be a mistake for Murray.

Springsteen played a shortened (seventy-five minute) but typically energetic opening set that went over well with the hometownish crowd. Then, as Appel told it, "literally ninety percent of the crowd left. There were maybe 150 people left. Murray came on, and even the crowd that was left started screaming 'Bruce!,' which she thought was boos."

Neither artist suffered greatly for the "controversy." Murray, a regular on "Glen Campbell's Goodtime Hour" TV series, went on to have some of her biggest hits, including 1978's chart-topping "You Needed Me." All told she charted forty-one Adult Contemporary hits and fifty-four country songs. She also had her own show, "Sing Along Jubilee," on Canadian TV. —*GG*

Musicians on Call. *See* Kristen Ann Carr Fund.
Musicians United for Safe Energy Foundation (MUSE). *See* No Nukes.

"My Hometown"
Single release: November 21, 1985
Album: *Born in the U.S.A.* (Columbia, 1984)
Also on: *Live/1975–85* (Columbia, 1986), *Greatest Hits* (Columbia, 1995)
Chart peak: No. 6

Bruce Springsteen didn't have a lot on his mind when he wrote "My Hometown"—just "the harshness of Reaganism, post-industrial America, memories of my childhood and my town," as he wrote in the liner notes for *Greatest Hits*. In *Songs*, he expanded on the subject matter, explaining that it "was based on childhood memories of driving down Main Street on my dad's lap, the closing of a local mill, and a racial incident that occurred near my house in Freehold during my adolescence." In concert, however, Springsteen told audiences that the song meant even more than that: "I thought I was writing this song about the town I grew up in, but it turned out to be about responsibility. Whether it's done here or thousands of miles away, it's done in your name, and you share the shame and the glory." He hammered that theme in at shows by frequently speaking out about local charities to which he was making contributions, encouraging his fans to do the same.

Springsteen recorded "My Hometown" in February 1984 during a short session at the Hit Factory in New York City. The somber, sentimental ballad brought *Born in the U.S.A.* to a thoughtful and pensive close. It also proved to be the album's last commercial note—its seventh and final single (tying Michael Jackson's record from *Thriller*), backed with his rendition of "Santa Claus Is Comin' to Town." A performance video for the song was shot by Arthur Rosato at the tour-concluding shows in Los Angeles, which also produced the video for "War" from the *Live/1975–85* box set. —*GG*

National Organization for Women (NOW)

Lobbying and consciousness-raising entity

In the early '80s it wasn't easy to find someone who didn't like Bruce Springsteen and his music, which was finally taking hold in the pop mainstream thanks to the "Hungry Heart" single. But the New York chapter of the National Organization for Women (NOW) was among the exceptions. Unhappy about Springsteen's references to "little girls" in his songs, the organization began a telephone and letter-writing appeal in the spring of 1982 to demand that he use more respectful terms for women. "He is writing and singing sexist music," Virginia Cornue, NOW's New York chapter executive director, told *Rolling Stone* magazine.

Kathy Tepes, one of NOW's national task force members, was the creator of the Springsteen campaign. In one of her letters to him, Tepes wrote, "When you call us 'little girls,' you perpetuate the myth that we women do things in a 'small' way." She also told Springsteen that she refers to him as "Brucie" and "a Twinkie."

An anonymous spokeswoman in Springsteen's office defended "little girls" as "a rock 'n' roll term." The NOW campaign never really gained momentum and quietly faded away. —*GG*

Nebraska

Released: October 4, 1982
"Producer": Bruce Springsteen
Tracks: "Nebraska," "Atlantic City," "Mansion on the Hill," "Johnny 99," "Highway Patrolman," "State Trooper," "Used Cars," "Open All Night," "My Father's House," "Reason to Believe"
Chart peak: No. 3

The most surprising album of Bruce Springsteen's career was not conceived as an album at all. In early 1982 he asked his guitar tech, Mike Batlan, to bring some recording equipment to the new house Springsteen was renting in Colts Neck, New Jersey. Batlan brought over a Teac Tascam Series 144 four-track recorder and set up a couple of microphones. Springsteen sat in a chair, recording what he thought were fifteen demos for his next album with the E Street Band. Most of the songs were finished in three or four takes, with occasional overdubs—harmony vocals, a second guitar, tambourine—added to the basic voice-and-guitar recordings. He stuck the cassette in his back pocket and went off to teach the material to the E Street Band.

But those sessions, held in April, did not go as well as Springsteen hoped. Some of the earliest songs for *Born in the U.S.A.*, including the title track, surfaced, but the band was not getting what he wanted on selections such as "Atlantic City" and "Mansion on the Hill." Drummer Max Weinberg noted to *Rolling Stone* magazine, "It became obvious fairly soon that what Bruce wanted on the record was what he already had on the demo. The band, though we played the hell out of them, tended to obscure the starkness and the vibe he was going for." Even an attempt by Springsteen to cut the songs again in a professional recording studio was deemed unsatisfactory.

In June, Springsteen and manager Jon Landau discussed the possibility of simply turning the bare bones demo tape into an album. Helmed by Chuck Plotkin, it was an arduous process that was hampered by changing tape speeds and other vagaries caused by the low-tech recording process. But a master recording was finally achieved, while Springsteen chose a strikingly, and appropriately, different kind of album cover than his previous releases—a black-and-white landscape photo shot in the Midwest by David Kennedy.

The album's title was initially *January 3, 1982*, in reference to the date Springsteen started working on it. Some of the other song titles were also considered before he settled on *Nebraska*. The song list was also knocked down to ten tracks, with "Born in the U.S.A." and "Downbound Train" later surfacing in a full-band version on *Born in the U.S.A.*, "Pink Cadillac" popping up as a B-side, and "Child Bride" and "Losin' Kind" winding up in Springsteen's already brimming vault of outtakes.

While some initially saw the stripped-down approach of *Nebraska* as a reaction to the success of *The River* and "Hungry Heart," Springsteen felt he'd sown the creative seeds on his 1980 double album. "There was a natural link between the songs on *The River* and those on *Nebraska*," he writes in *Songs*. "'Stolen Car,' 'Wreck on the Highway,' 'Point Blank' and 'The River' reflected a shift in my songwriting style." And while the *Nebraska* songs may have not sounded like big rock songs, he noted that "their depictions of characters out on the edge contextualized them as rock and roll."

And while many external sources influenced *Nebraska*—including the stories of Flannery O'Connor and films such as *True Confessions* and *Badlands*, Terrence Malick's chronicle of the Charles Stark-weather–Caril Fugate murders that became the album's title track—Springsteen called this his most personal album to date, "connected to my childhood more than any other record I'd made." Many of the songs, he explained, came from his own feeling of isolation after the phenomenon of *The River* subsided, reflecting "the thin line between stability and that moment when ... the things that connect you to your world ... fail you." He also used the works of John Lee Hooker and Robert Johnson as touchstones for the aural impact he wanted *Nebraska* to have. "I wanted to let the listener hear the characters think, to get inside their heads, so you could hear and feel their thoughts, their choices ... I wanted the music to feel like a waking dream and the record to move like poetry."

It seemed like *Nebraska* would be a difficult sell, hardly the expected follow-up to the monumental commercial showing of *The River*. But it did sell, thanks to rave reviews, strong word of mouth, and even some airplay on some 170 rock stations around the country that helped drive sales over the platinum mark. The then-fledgling MTV, hungry for superstars on its playlist, was also happy to air Springsteen's first conceptual video, a black & white travelogue for "Atlantic City" that did not include a single image of the artist.

It was a mark of pride for Springsteen that Johnny Cash covered two of *Nebraska*'s songs, "Johnny 99" and "Highway Patrolman." Steve Earle covered "State Trooper," and in 2000 a group of artists—including Cash—par-

> "**T**his is the bravest of Springsteen's six records; it's also his most startling, direct and chilling...."
> —*Rolling Stone*

> "**N**ebraska, an acoustic bypass through the American heartland, sounds a little like a Library of Congress field recording made out behind some shutdown auto plant."
> —*Time*

> "(Springsteen's) most personal record, and his most disturbing ... It's been a long time since a mainstream rock star made an album that asks such tough questions and refuses to settle for easy answers—let alone an album suggesting that perhaps there *are* no answers."
> —*New York Times*

ticipated in the tribute album *Badlands: A Tribute to Bruce Springsteen's Nebraska*. —*GG*

New York Yankees

Storied Major League Baseball franchise; Springsteen's favorite team?

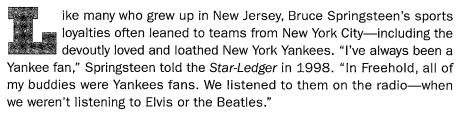

ike many who grew up in New Jersey, Bruce Springsteen's sports loyalties often leaned to teams from New York City—including the devoutly loved and loathed New York Yankees. "I've always been a Yankee fan," Springsteen told the *Star-Ledger* in 1998. "In Freehold, all of my buddies were Yankees fans. We listened to them on the radio—when we weren't listening to Elvis or the Beatles."

Springsteen, who wrote about "a friend who was a big baseball player back in high school" in "Glory Days," played a bit of ball himself on the E Street Kings softball team, which played intermittently during the '70s. Springsteen's most active public embrace of the game was in 1998, however, during what he called his oldest son Evan's "first real baseball summer"—which included playing on a Little League team that Springsteen coached. The two surfaced at a Yankees–Minnesota Twins game that August, visiting both teams' clubhouses. They also hit a late season St. Louis Cardinals–Chicago Cubs game when sluggers Mark McGwire and Sammy Sosa were vying to break Roger Maris's single-season home run record. "Never mind McGwire and Maris," Cardinals manager Tony LaRussa told reporters after the game. "Something really important happened today. Bruce Springsteen was in our clubhouse."

Former Yankees pitcher Al Leiter was skeptical of Springsteen's true loyalty to the Bronx Bombers, however. After singing "Rosalita" with Springsteen at New York's Shea Stadium on October 3, 2003, he told the *White Plains (N.Y.) News*, "When people say Bruce is a big Yankees fan, that's wrong. I think he just went there more often as a kid because it was closer to Jersey. Everybody on the Shore went to more Yankees games." Then again, Leiter was pitching for New York's *other* team, the Mets, at the time, so that might have impacted his perspective. —*GG*

***Newsweek* magazine. *See Time/Newsweek* Covers.**

Nick's Fat City

Pittsburgh club and concert venue

fter nearly three decades of arena and stadium shows, Bruce Springsteen clearly relishes opportunities to get back to the beer-soaked barrooms where the crowds get as sweaty as the band

and there's no need for rings of security or insulating managers. Nick's Fat City, a 550-person capacity joint on Pittsburgh's south side, has been the site of three of those blowouts—all with Joe Grushecky & the Houserockers, Pittsburgh's "rock and real" icons (to quote an album title).

Nick's, located at 1601–1605 E. Carson Street, originally was owned by Bob Pessolano (his ex-wife, Mona, later got it in the divorce), who created the club—named after one of their kids as well as a long-gone rock joint—as his own little memorabilia-filled Hard Rock Cafe wannabe. "Pittsburgh's Rock 'n' Roll Hall of Stars" is one of the city's only remaining live music stages that accommodates both local and national acts. Springsteen is definitely the most renowned artist who ever graced its stage, behind which hangs a giant, neon-edged reproduction of a Les Paul guitar. Walls and glass cases are filled with relics from music icons; Springsteen mementos occupied an honored spot well before he ever showed up in the place.

Springsteen's first two performances were back-to-back shows in 1995 to promote Grushecky's *American Babylon*, which Springsteen produced, cowriting eight songs and performing on two. The third was for Grushecky's 1998 release *Coming Home*, for which Springsteen cowrote four songs. During that show, as the band rocked through the Springsteen-Grushecky tune "Idiot's Delight," Springsteen slid into a bit of "She's About a Mover," after which he teased trivia fans to name that Sir Douglas Quintet tune. —*LM*

Wolfgang Niedecken

German rock musician and Dylan aficionado

n the summer of 1995, to help promote Bruce Springsteen's *Greatest Hits* collection in Europe, a decision was made to release "Hungry Heart" as a single on the continent. But a video was required. So Springsteen flew to Berlin in early July to shoot a performance clip for the song with German musician Wolfgang Niedecken and a band he assembled for the occasion.

Springsteen met Niedecken in April 1995, when he interviewed Springsteen at Sony Studios in New York City. With his band BAP, Niedecken was well-established as a rock star in his own country, and he and Springsteen bonded over a mutual regard for Bob Dylan; Niedecken even operated a side band called Leopardefellband (Leopard Skin Band) which had recently recorded an album of Dylan covers. When the decision was made to shoot the video, Springsteen contacted Niedecken to join him, and the German musician recruited two members from Leopardefellband (bassist Ken Taylor and drummer Bertram Engel) and keyboardist Pasqual Kravetz, who regularly played with German singer Udo Lindenberg.

The video was shot on July 9, 1995. The directing team of DoRo—Austrians Rudi Dolezal and Hannes Rossacher, who had previously worked with Queen and the Rolling Stones—shot footage of Springsteen driving around Berlin's historic Brandenburger Tor and other locations in the city before repairing for the evening performance at the Cafe Eckstein in eastern Berlin. The four-hour shoot in the sweaty club included seven attempts at "Hungry Heart" along with "Down the Road Apiece," John Lee Hooker's "Boom Boom," Dylan's "Knockin' on Heaven's Door" and "Highway 61 Revisited," the Rolling Stones' "Honky Tonk Women" and "Jumping Jack Flash," a Springsteen solo version of "Thunder Road," and the Isley Brothers' "Twist and Shout." The "Hungry Heart" video, with the E Street Band dubbed under Springsteen's live vocal, was broadcast in Europe only but appeared on the 2001 DVD *The Complete Video Anthology 1978–2000.* —GG

A Night for the Vietnam Veteran

August 20, 1981, benefit concert

In 1981, Bruce Springsteen took a battered nonprofit group under his wing, turning one night on *The River* tour—a sold-out show at the Sports Arena in Los Angeles—into a fundraiser and consciousness-starter. The group, the Vietnam Veterans of America Foundation, had been trying for several years to secure benefits for veterans of the war and embark on a campaign of education and healing. According to Vietnam veteran Bobby Muller, the group's founder, its efforts were stymied by a lack of funds and a nation not yet ready to face the legacy of Vietnam. Springsteen met Muller in July during a six-show stand at the Brendan Byrne Arena at the Meadowlands in East Rutherford, New Jersey; he had invited the VVA leader after reading Ron Kovic's book *Born on the Fourth of July* and was looking for a way to help. The two hatched the idea of a benefit concert at the first of six shows in Los Angeles. Before the August 20 show, officially called "A Night for the Vietnam Veteran," he and Muller visited a veterans center. At the venue, Springsteen's crew constructed special ramps alongside the stage to accommodate veterans in wheelchairs. "He gave us $100,000 that night," Muller told *Backstreets* magazine in 2001. "But more important, we got made cool. The press around what Bruce did was a tremendous boost for us. We never looked back." Within months, Pat Benatar and Charlie Daniels performed benefits for VVA, too.

Springsteen wasn't just a conscientious benefactor that night. Although it wasn't his first benefit performance, it did mark the first time he publicly explained why he was doing something like this. Before the music began, Springsteen, appearing nervous, spoke to the hushed crowd; prior to introducing Muller, Springsteen talked about the war's legacy, the struggle its shunned veterans faced, and the need for his audience to beware. "It happened once," he said, "and it can happen again."

The music that followed was explosive: opening with an impassioned version of Creedence Clearwater Revival's "Who'll Stop the Rain," Springsteen delivered a thirty-two-song set that built mightily on its purposeful start. Regularly performed numbers such as "Darkness on the Edge of Town" sounded especially powerful; during "The River," clearly moved by the night's emotion, he stopped singing for one line to regain his composure. The set also included a one-off: a spare arrangement of the Byrds' "Ballad of Easy Rider."

"We celebrated that night," Muller said. "We could not have held on had it not been for Bruce." Revitalized, the group pushed for revamped legislation that addressed the needs of the Vietnam veteran, including health and Agent Orange–related issues, education, and employment provisions. "Had VVA not made it, there would have been a rehabilitation in the public's mind of the Vietnam veteran," Muller said, "but I don't think it would have been as purposeful in its outcome." In 1997, the organization shared in the Nobel Peace Prize for its work to ban land mines. Springsteen quietly donated money in the years after his landmark concert in Los Angeles. Other artists, including Emmylou Harris, Bruce Cockburn, Patty Griffin, and Steve Earle, later supported the group, too, with concerts of their own. —JP

Willie Nile

Buffalo, New York–born singer-songwriter and Springsteen protege

When Willie Nile's debut album came out in 1980, it was termed "Dylan-turned-early-Springsteen folk rock"—comparisons Nile had been hearing since he started playing in Greenwich Village folk clubs in the late '60s. Nile and Springsteen were natural friends and associates, and Nile was one of the myriad guests on the fall 2003 stadium leg of *The Rising* tour, jamming on "Glory Days" on September 20 at the Darien Lake Amusement Park in his home town of Buffalo, New York, then taking part in the October 3 and 4 shows at Shea Stadium—racing to the latter after his own concert in Amagansett, New York, two-and-a-half hours away. He made it in time to guest on encores of "Dancing in the Dark," "Quarter to Three," and "Twist and Shout." "Bruce is a generous guy and a great rocker and it was a real pleasure to be up there with him," Nile e-mailed one fan after the final Shea show. "Can you imagine singing 'Twist and Shout' at Shea Stadium, where the Beatles sang? What a hoot!" Nile also recorded "I'm on Fire" for the Springsteen tribute album *Light of Day*, and the two sang together again in November 2003 at the fourth annual Light of Day benefit concert at the Stone Pony in Asbury Park, New Jersey.

Born Robert Noonan, Nile kicked around New York City before strong word of mouth—particularly a rave review from the *New York Times*'s Robert Palmer—brought record companies sniffing around. Throughout his career he's enjoyed some high-profile associations: Simon & Garfunkel engineer Roy Hallee produced his debut; Nile opened concerts for the Who in 1980 at the personal invitation of Pete Townshend; and players on his albums have included the Byrds' Roger McGuinn, Loudon Wainwright III, Richard Thompson, Paul Shaffer, Terry and Suzzy Roche, and members of Television and the Patti Smith Group. He's remained a cult artist, however, and in 1999 he started his own River House Records; his first release, *Beautiful Wreck of the World*, was a critical favorite that made the Top 10 in the *Village Voice*'s prestigious annual Pazz and Jop Critics Poll. —*GG*

1992–93 Bruce Springsteen Touring Band

Backing musicians on tour supporting *Human Touch* and *Lucky Town*

In 1989 Bruce Springsteen shocked his fans—and, indeed, the entire music industry—by releasing the members of his E Street Band. "I decided it was time to mix it up," he explained to *Rolling Stone* magazine three years later. "I just had to cut it loose a little bit so I could have something new to bring to the table. I wanted to get rid of some of the old expectations." He recorded his next two albums, 1992's twin projects *Human Touch* and *Lucky Town*, with mostly studio-honed musicians, so when it came time to tour in support of them he had to hire yet another band of players—in effect the only fixed group of musicians other than the E Street Band that he's toured with since signing with Columbia Records in 1972. Springsteen assembled the core band—E Street keyboardist Roy Bittan, guitarist Shane Fontayne, bassist Tommy Sims, and drummer Zachary Alford—in April 1992; the quintet debuted on May 6 at a Bottom Line showcase in New York City and then played May 9 on "Saturday Night Live"—which was also Springsteen's first-ever live television appearance. In mid-May, Springsteen expanded the band for the tour with his wife and E Street Band member Patti Scialfa, multi-instrumentalist Crystal Taliefero, and five backing vocalists. "The musicians are basically real, real accomplished," Springsteen explained in his dressing room during intermission of a July 1992 show at the Brendan Byrne Arena in East Rutherford, New Jersey. "I was looking for musicians who could spread out over soul, rock 'n' roll, just a lot of different types of music. I picked people both on the basis of their musicianship and how they *felt*. I want to maintain the kind of emotional communication that I felt we had over the years with the E Street Band." Fontayne told *Backstreets* magazine that the vote of confidence from Springsteen allowed the band to largely ignore any hostile feelings from E Street Band fans: "If he hadn't been so certain of us, then, yeah, it would have been a different matter. But I didn't have to worry about that."

All of the musicians came into the band with established credits, however, making for a diverse but well-seasoned ensemble:

Zachary Alford (drums): A New York native, Alford had logged credits with the B-52's, ex-Bangle Susanna Hoffs, Manic Street Preachers, and Maggie's Dream prior to working with Springsteen. Since then he's worked with Billy Joel, David Bowie, They Might Be Giants, Zucchero, and Patti Scialfa.

Gia Ciambotti (vocals): The Hollywood-born Ciambotti maintained her musical aspirations while her family moved to San Francisco and Champaign, Illinois. She was in a trio called the Graces with former Go-Go's member Charlotte Caffey and future solo star Meredith Brooks, and she also recorded with Belinda Carlisle (another former Go-Go), Patty Smyth, and Lucinda Williams (her father was Williams's bass player for many years). After touring with Springsteen, Ciambotti did sessions with Chicago, Catie Curtis, Mary Lou Lord, Buckcherry, Badly Drawn Boy, and Roger Clyne & the Peacemakers.

Carolyn Dennis (vocals): The Los Angeles–born Dennis came to Springsteen's band with some of the most impressive credentials of any of its members. She had toured and recorded with Bob Dylan, Stevie Wonder, Smokey Robinson, Art Garfunkel, Minnie Ripperton, Olivia Newton-John, Dee Dee Bridgewater, the Carpenters, Kenny Loggins, Jackson Browne, Harry Chapin, and actor-turned-singer David Soul. She'd also originated the role of Sister Carrie in the off-Broadway musical *Mama I Want to Sing*, was on Broadway in *Big River*, provided the singing voice for Lynn Whitfield's Josephine Baker in HBO's 1990 biopic *The Josephine Baker Story*, and was a gospel soloist with the Los Angeles Philharmonic conducted by Zubin Meta. After the Springsteen tour Dennis continued to work with Donna Summer, Candi Staton, Paul Kelly, Andrae Crouch, and Yolanda Adams. She did more than sing with Dylan, too; on January 31, 1986, she gave birth to his youngest child, a daughter named Desiree Gabrielle Dennis-Dylan. The couple married on June 4, 1986, and divorced in the fall of 1992, while Dennis was on the road with Springsteen.

The band that accompanied Springsteen on the road in 1992 and 1993 included guitarist Shane Fontayne (left), formerly of Lone Justice, and multi-instrumentalist Crystal Taliefero, a veteran of tours with many rock musicians.

The Dylan-Dennis relationship was kept largely secret until 2001 publication of Howard Sounes's book *Down the Highway: The Life of Bob Dylan*.

Shane Fontayne (guitar): Born Mick Barakan in London, England, Fontayne moved to the U.S. with his family. He first recorded with a group called Byzantium in 1972 and also played in the Merchants of Venus. He logged session work with Steve Forbert, Mick Ronson, Ian Hunter, Garland Jeffreys, Billy Burnette, and ex-Rolling Stone Mick Taylor before joining Lone Justice in 1987, in time for the group's tour opening for U2. Springsteen was turned on to Fontayne after watching a rerun of Lone Justice's performance on "Saturday Night Live"; he contacted the guitarist through producer Jimmy Iovine, who'd worked with the band. Fontayne continued his relationship with Springsteen after the 1992–93 tour, recording on the never-released "hip-hop" album known to fans as *Waiting on the End of the World* (after the title of a song recorded for the album) and playing on the Springsteen-produced *American Babylon* album by

Although he was accompanied by a new band for the first time in two decades, fans still turned out for Springsteen's tour to promote *Human Touch* and *Lucky Town*, including this August 1992 show in Auburn Hills, Michigan.

Joe Grushecky & the Houserockers. Since working with Springsteen, Fontayne has recorded with John Waite, Chris Botti, Peter Himmelman, and Marc Cohn, among others. He released his first solo album, *What Nature Intended*, in 2003.

Cleopatra Kennedy (vocals): A Birmingham, Alabama, native, Kennedy was a gospel singer and civil rights activist before moving to Los Angeles in the late '70s. She toured with Diana Ross, Graham Nash, the Rev. James Cleveland, and Paul Williams; she also performed at the 1979 No Nukes concerts in New York City, where she met Springsteen.

Bobby King (vocals): The middle of thirteen children born in Lake Charles, Louisiana, King was the most established performer in the 1992–93 band—and the only member to have actually recorded with Springsteen, on *Human Touch*'s "Roll of the Dice" and "Man's Job." King was in the cast of the musical *Don't Bother Me* when he came to Los Angeles in 1973. He recorded with Bob Dylan, George Harrison, John Fogerty, Boz Scaggs, Ry Cooder, Billy Preston, Maria Muldaur, Burton Cummings, and many others; King also released two solo albums—*Bobby King* in 1981 and *Love in the Fire* in 1984—before uniting with fellow singer Terry Evans for 1988's *Live and Let Live!* and 1990's *Rhythm, Blues, Soul & Grooves*. His post-Springsteen credits include Richard Thompson, Moon Martin, and the late John Lee Hooker.

Angel Rogers (vocals): Chosen to hit the high registers on the 1992–93 band's harmonies, Rogers was born in Port Arthur, Texas—also birthplace of singing legend Janis Joplin. She attended Texas Southern University and sang with the band 101 North before moving to Los Angeles, where she racked up credits with Stevie Wonder, Paula Abdul, Dizzy Gillespie, Anita Baker, Peabo Bryson, George Benson, Jermaine Jackson, Vanessa Williams, Stephanie Mills, Jody Watley, Gladys Knight, and Yanni, among others. After touring with Springsteen, she recorded with Freddie Jackson, Frankie Knuckles, Sheila E., and the late TLC member Lisa "Left-Eye" Lopes, and she toured and recorded with Mary J. Blige.

Tommy Sims (bass): Chicago native Sims was something of a late-comer to Springsteen's music; he claimed he had never heard, or heard of, "Born to Run" until the mid-'80s, after which he bought 1987's *Tunnel of Love*. He also hadn't been on the road with a group before 1992. Sims had chalked up some impressive studio credentials, however, for Divinyls, Pat Benatar, Amy Grant, and a number of Christian music acts. Subsequently Sims went back to the studio, where he worked with Michael Bolton, K.T. Oslin, Michael McDonald, Steve Wariner, B.J. Thomas, Kevon Edmonds, the Neville Brothers, and Garth Brooks on his *In the Life of Chris Gaines* project. Sims also released his own album, *Peace and Love*, in 2000.

Crystal Taliefero (vocals, percussion, guitar, saxophone): Hailing from Gary, Indiana, Taliefero studied opera and jazz at Indiana University before making her mark as part of John Mellencamp's band (starting with him when he was still John Cougar). She also toured with Billy Joel, Bob Seger, and Joe Cocker, and recorded with the Bee Gees, Julian Lennon, and Foreigner's Mick Jones. She told *Rolling Stone,* "I was in a blur for the first month" of the Springsteen experience. "Bruce never does the same thing. We learn songs at sound check." Post-Springsteen, Taliefero worked with Brooks & Dunn, Deana Carter, Beth Nielsen Chapman, John Mayall & Friends, on Garth Brooks's *In the Life of Chris Gaines* album, and in Las Vegas showman Danny Gans's band. —*GG*

The 1978 Live Album

"Lost" album

For many fans, the *Darkness on the Edge of Town* tour remains the peak of Springsteen and the E Street Band's live prowess, a legend that owes much to the decision by Columbia and Springsteen's management to broadcast (as mixed by Jimmy Iovine) four of the shows live on regional radio stations, from which they were dutifully bootlegged and traded. One of these shows, August 9, 1978, from the Agora in the Springsteen hotbed of Cleveland, Ohio, was suggested as a possible source for a live album.

So when the tour took a month off in October 1978 before its final leg, legend has it Springsteen and producer Jon Landau spent time in a Los Angeles studio remixing the Cleveland show for possible release. Pre-FM or nonbroadcast copies of the show have circulated, and at least one bootleg claims to use these remixed tapes as its source. From there, the story dies, and we can only assume that at that point in his career, Springsteen felt it was too early for a live album, especially one that would have needed three slabs of vinyl to capture. *Summertime Bruce* on the E Street bootleg label is said to come from the remixed Agora tapes. The show has also been bootlegged many times over from broadcast recordings. —*EF*

No Nukes

Benefit concerts, September 1979, Madison Square Garden in New York City

In 1979 a coalition of performers and activists opposed to the use of nuclear power staged five consecutive concerts at New York's Madison Square Garden. The Musicians United for Safe Energy (MUSE) called the September 19–23 shows the MUSE Concerts for a Non-Nuclear Future, but the album and film created from the project were titled *No Nukes.*

Springsteen perches on Roy Bittan's piano during the Detroit stop of the *Darkness* tour on September 1, 1978. Springsteen contemplated releasing a show from an earlier stop on the tour—August 9 in Cleveland—as a live album, but ultimately decided against the project.

The Ties That Bind

The goal of the concerts and an accompanying rally was to spread aware-ness about the dangers of radioactive-fueled energy and raise funds for an anti-nuclear/pro-solar campaign.

Bruce Springsteen and the E Street Band topped a list of twenty acts invited to play at the event. MUSE's Tom Campbell broached the subject in June 1979, while Springsteen was in Los Angeles to attend the wedding of his lighting director, Marc Brickman. But it was event coproducer Jackson Browne who is credited with convincing Springsteen—who had written the harrowing "Roulette," inspired by the meltdown at Pennsylvania's Three Mile Island nuclear plant, for his next album—to join the bill, which also included the Doobie Brothers, Tom Petty & the Heartbreakers, Bonnie Raitt, James Taylor and Carly Simon, and Crosby, Stills & Nash, among others.

Taking a break from recording for *The River*, Springsteen and company headlined the final two nights of the campaign—the second of which was his thirtieth birthday. They were the group's first concerts in almost a year, a pair of ninety-minute sets (short by E Street standards) during which the band played "The River" for the first time and Springsteen dedicated "The Promised Land" to Browne "and his sense of purpose and conviction." He contributed a pair of songs—"Detroit Medley" and "Stay," with Browne and Rosemary Butler—to the *No Nukes* album, while the film included perfor-mance footage of "The River," "Thunder Road," and Gary U.S. Bonds's "Quar-ter to Three."

Still not entirely comfortable with his political footing, Springsteen approached the shows cautiously. According to *Rolling Stone* magazine, he insisted that no politicians be given microphone time or money from the shows' proceeds, which were estimated at about $600,000. He also was the only artist among the twenty acts who declined to contribute statements for an accompanying program book (though others are missing from the LP booklet and more were cut from the 1997 CD reissue). Manager Jon Landau said that Springsteen believed his presence and music said enough.

The September 22 show was the only sellout of the five nights, and the September 23 show included an incident in which a perturbed Spring-steen pulled photographer Lynne Goldsmith on stage only to announce, "This is my ex-girlfriend." *Rolling Stone* also noted that the Springsteen nights were the most exciting of the five: "The MUSE principals have been searching all week for the vibe, the feeling. Springsteen doesn't have to search for it; he walks onstage and it's there." Sometimes it's to the detriment of the other artists, however; "I learned never to open for Bruce Springsteen," Graham Nash noted afterwards, while Petty was told by Browne that what sounded liked booing was merely the crowd calling for "Brooooooce." His response: "What's the difference?" —*LM/GG*

On September 19–23, 1979, a group of artists who called themselves Musicians United for Safe Energy (MUSE) gathered to play five concerts at New York's Madison Square Garden to help drum up opposition to the use of nuclear power. Springsteen (shown here at the September 22 concert) and the E Street Band were the headliners in a lineup that also featured Tom Petty & the Heartbreakers, Bonnie Raitt, and several other big-name acts. The show was recorded and filmed for release under the title *No Nukes.*

Brendan O'Brien

Record producer and engineer

After Brendan O'Brien helmed Stone Temple Pilots' six-times platinum 1992 album *Core*, he went from a highly regarded recording engineer in Atlanta (working with the Black Crowes, among others) to one of America's foremost producers. In short order he accumulated a resume that included albums by Pearl Jam, Rage Against the Machine, Incubus, the Offspring, and Train, as well as mixes for Aerosmith, Soundgarden, Slayer, Ben Folds Five, Limp Bizkit, Lifehouse, and the Geto Boys. A multi-instrumentalist, O'Brien played guitar on Mick Jagger's 1993 solo album *Wandering Spirit* and guitar, bass, and keyboards on "Dignity," a track on Bob Dylan's *Greatest Hits, Volume III* in 1994; O'Brien coproduced that song with Daniel Lanois and subsequently played on Dylan's 1995 *MTV Unplugged* session.

In *Songs*, Springsteen writes that Sony Music president Don Ienner recommended O'Brien to Springsteen in the '90s. An outside producer didn't seem to be in the cards for him, however; Springsteen had taken charge of his studio affairs with *Born to Run* in 1975 and held control—with cohorts such as manager Jon Landau, E Street Band guitarist Steve Van Zandt, and Chuck Plotkin—ever since. But, he told the *New York Times*, he was ready for a change when it came time for *The Rising* in early 2002: "My own abilities, I felt like I had reached my limits with them. The basic sound of things that you hear on the radio changes at least every five to ten years. Brendan had all my references so I could refer back to something from 1966 or 1980. And then he had the following ten and twenty years." He also liked O'Brien's preference for analog rather than digital recording processes.

Springsteen and O'Brien met first at Springsteen's home studio in New Jersey to listen to demos. Then he and the E Street Band went to Atlanta to work at Southern Tracks Studio, O'Brien's favored facility. There, Springsteen wrote, O'Brien "brought a fresh power and focus to the band's sound and playing"—including a more prominent guitar sound as well as an appreciation for Springsteen's desire for more textures, primarily from Soozie Tyrell's violin and other strings. O'Brien also wasn't afraid to direct Springsteen to write more songs when he felt the material they were working on had run its course.

The association continued after *The Rising*. O'Brien was a guest at Springsteen and company's December 2, 2002, show in Atlanta, playing guitar on "Glory Days" and "Born to Run." O'Brien also produced Springsteen's 2005 release, *Devils & Dust*, playing bass and other instruments on several tracks.

O'Brien's interest in music started as a source of "curiosity" when he was as young as nine; he once said, "I have always wanted to be the guy who helps get records together. I've always appreciated that as a kid, just as much as I liked guitar players." O'Brien's first production credit was the Coolies' 1988 album *Doug (A Rock Opera)*, though it was the Stone Temple Pilots album that gave him star standing in the field. His status also allowed him to start his own label, a Sony subsidiary called 57 Records whose artists included Pete Droge and Michael Penn. —*GG*

Conan O'Brien

David Letterman's successor on late-night TV; Max Weinberg's other boss

If Bruce Springsteen's late-night TV loyalties seem to lie with David Letterman—for whom he's played on five shows—Conan O'Brien certainly has a piece of his heart—and his band. When O'Brien took over NBC's "Late Night" show in 1993 following Letterman's departure for CBS—which happened to be during the E Street Band's hiatus—he hired drummer Max Weinberg to be the musical director. In addition to keeping the show rocking with the Max Weinberg 7, the drummer also became one of O'Brien's comic foils, appearing in live and taped skits.

So when Springsteen decided to take the E Street Band back on the road in 1999, he had to ransom Weinberg away from "Late Night"—which he did with a performance on February 26, playing "Working on the Highway" before ushering Weinberg out of the studio and onto the road. O'Brien didn't require a similar stunt for *The Rising* tour in 2002, but Springsteen obliged later that year, with a legendary December 11 appearance that featured "Merry Christmas Baby" and a surprising rendition of the rarely performed "Kitty's Back."

O'Brien's stock went up considerably in September 2004 when "The Tonight Show"'s Jay Leno announced that he would be bequeathing that most high-profile of late-night spots to O'Brien in 2009. —*GG*

Ocean County College

Home of Springsteen's short-lived attempt at higher education

Though music was his passion, Bruce Springsteen made an attempt—a brief one—at higher education. After graduating from Freehold Regional High School, he enrolled in the fall of 1967 at Ocean County College, a two-year community institution in Toms River, New Jersey. He did not last long there, thanks to a first-term meeting with a guidance counselor who called Springsteen in to talk about his attire—a greaser-style ensemble of leather jacket, white T-shirt, jeans, and sneakers. By Springsteen's own telling the conversation went something like this: "'You've got trouble at home, right?' 'Look, things are great. I feel fine.' 'Then why do you look like that?' 'What are you talking about?' 'There are some students who have … complained about you.' 'Well, that's their problem, you know?' Goodbye, college."

Ocean County College was relatively new when Springsteen attended. It was chartered by Ocean County and the State of New Jersey, with three campuses and some off-site locations where classes were offered throughout the county. Students can earn Associate degrees, with an emphasis on business education and continuing education programs in a variety of fields. About seventy-five percent of the students transfer to four-year institutions. —*GG*

"One Step Up"

Single release: February 1988
Album: *Tunnel of Love* (Columbia, 1987)
Chart peak: No. 13

Bruce Springsteen brought out the third single from *Tunnel of Love*, the gently brooding "One Step Up," just a few weeks before he launched the Tunnel of Love Express Tour in Worcester, Massachusetts. It was one of the tracks, he writes in *Songs*, that "tell[s] the story of men whose inner sense of themselves is in doubt"; in this case it was a protagonist sitting in a bar, pondering a failing relationship—which he terms "our dirty little war." Springsteen-watchers noted the irony that the only other performer on the track was E Street Band singer Patti Scialfa, with whom Springsteen would begin an affair that led to the breakup of his marriage with Julianne Phillips.

The video for "One Step Up" was shot on February 15, 1988, at the Wonder Bar in Asbury Park, New Jersey. The "One Step Up" single featured as its B-side the previously unreleased "Roulette," a fan-favorite outtake from The River that would also become a regular set-list inclusion on the Tunnel of Love Express Tour. British musicians Clive Gregson and Christine Collister covered the A-side as a duet on their 1990 album Love Is a Strange Hotel. —GG

Roy Orbison

Early rock icon, Rock and Roll Hall of Fame inductee

Bruce Springsteen makes no secret of how great an impact Roy Orbison had on his music. No doubt it was Orbison's persona as a brooding outsider and his sense of cool—the dark glasses, the jet-black pompadour, the leather outfits—that appealed to Springsteen. Orbison's operatic sense of drama is evident in many Springsteen songs—especially on Born to Run. Springsteen even name-checks him in "Thunder Road" ("Roy Orbison singin' for the lonely/Hey that's me and I want you only"). When he inducted Orbison into the Rock and Roll Hall of Fame in January 1987, Springsteen revealed, "I rode for fifteen hours in the back of a U-Haul truck to open for Roy Orbison at the Nashville Music Festival … In 1975, when I went in to the studio to make Born to Run, I wanted to make a record with words like Bob Dylan that sounded like Phil Spector. But, most of all, I wanted to sing like Roy Orbison."

Springsteen played with Orbison at the jam that followed the induction ceremony. But he had a more extensive and satisfying experience nine months later, on September 30 at the Coconut Grove in Los Angeles as part of an all-star band backing Orbison for a Cinemax special that came to be known as A Black & White Night—because it was filmed in elegant black & white rather than color. Springsteen joined Elvis Costello, Bonnie Raitt, Tom Waits, Jennifer Warnes, T-Bone Burnett, k.d. lang, J.D. Souther, Jackson Browne, and others in saluting their mutual hero. Springsteen played guitar throughout the show and shared the mic with Orbison on several songs. Afterwards he said, "When I was a kid, his music took me out of my little town. And you don't always get a chance to sing harmony with Roy Orbison and play guitar with James Burton. That's a dream."

An unlikely pop star due to his ungainly looks and thick eyeglasses, Roy Orbison triumphed in the age of Elvis Presley thanks to his tremulous

Roy Orbison performs at Farm Aid in 1985. The sense of epic drama Orbison brought to his music proved a great influence on Springsteen's early work, particularly _Born to Run_.

neo-operatic voice and sexy growl. Orbison was born in Vernon, Texas, in 1936. By age eight, he was performing on local radio shows. Initially a country performer who formed the Wink Westerners at the age of thirteen in 1949 in his hometown of Wink, Texas, Orbison switched to rock 'n' roll at the urging of his college friend, Pat Boone. Sam Phillips signed Orbison to Sun Records after hearing his song "Ooby Dooby," but Orbison's greatest successes came at the Monument label, where he unleashed a string of Top 40 hits—"Only the Lonely," "Running Scared," "Crying," "In Dreams," "Blue Bayou," "It's Over," "Oh, Pretty Woman"—that were elaborately produced, full of tension and drama, and often featured Orbison's voice rising to a breathtaking soprano. A smash in Europe, he toured with the Beatles in 1963.

Orbison's career came to a halt in 1966, when his wife, Claudette, was killed in a motorcycle accident. Two years later, two of his sons died in a fire. Orbison continued to work and had occasional success. In 1982, a cover version of "Oh, Pretty Woman" became a hit for Van Halen; later, it served as the title song for the Richard Gere/Julia Roberts film *Pretty Woman.*

In the late '80s, Orbison's career surged when his song "In Dreams" was featured prominently in the David Lynch film *Blue Velvet.* Orbison joined Bob Dylan, Jeff Lynne, George Harrison, and Tom Petty in the pseudonymed supergroup the Traveling Wilburys and also released new material and remakes of earlier works. His duet remake of "Crying" with k.d. lang was a hit on the country charts.

In 1989, Orbison recorded the album *Mystery Girl* with contributions from Jeff Lynne, Tom Petty, U2 members Bono and The Edge, T-Bone Burnett, and others. But on December 6, 1988, before the album was released, Orbison died of a heart attack; eventually, *Mystery Girl* became the highest charting release of his career and sold over a million copies, with the single "You Got It," penned by Lynne, Petty, and Orbison, reaching the Top 20. —*DD/GG*

The Oscars. See The Academy Awards.

The Palace

Asbury Park boardwalk attraction

alace Amusements, aka the Palace, was the focal point of Asbury Park's once-thriving enclave of boardwalk attractions and a popular hangout for generations of Jersey Shore teens. It also looms large as a direct or implied image in three of Bruce Springsteen's most popular songs—"4th of July, Asbury Park (Sandy)," "Born to Run," and "Tunnel of Love." The structure was built in 1888 and demolished in mid-2004 after a valiant struggle by historians and Springsteen fans who united in a campaign to "Save Tillie"—the cartoon-like caricature painted on the building's side that symbolized Asbury Park to tourists and residents alike. The Palace housed one of the world's oldest Ferris wheels; built in 1895, just a few years after its invention, it spun right through the building's roof. At the top of its rotation, it provided a spectacular view of the Atlantic Ocean. Legend has it that a weapons collector used the Ferris wheel to arrange arms shipments to the Middle East during the war for Israel's statehood in 1948 because its gondolas provided protection against eavesdroppers.

Tillie's supporters got the building listed on the National Register of Historic Places, and Springsteen backed preservation efforts with fundraising Christmas concerts. But the city eventually granted permission to shoreline developer Asbury Partners to raze the structure. A zoning permit for the planned residential-retail-entertainment complex included a condition that any new construction must incorporate Tillie's image if it were salvageable. In June

2004, the Save Tillie group removed the ten-ton mural in one piece and placed it in storage until it can regain its status as a boardwalk beacon. —*LM*

Paramount Theatre
Asbury Park music, theater, and film venue

ocated on the Asbury Park boardwalk adjacent to Convention Hall, the 1,600-seat Paramount Theatre has been an important film, theater, and music venue in the seaside resort town since the 1920s. Boasting the best acoustics of any Asbury Park concert venue and an opulent design that recalls the golden age of vaudeville and film, the Paramount was never truly a part of the Asbury Park music scene until Bruce Springsteen and the E Street Band used it to rehearse for concert tours in the '80s and '90s and local promoters began presenting occasional rock concerts there. Much more the rock concert venue was the Paramount's neighbor, the Convention Hall, which seats more than 3,600 and since the '60s hosted hundreds of acts, including Bob Dylan, the Rolling Stones, Janis Joplin, the Who, the Beach Boys, the Clash, Southside Johnny & the Asbury Jukes, and, of course, Springsteen and the E Street Band for special performances, including his annual Christmas show.

Springsteen stopped at the Paramount for a three-night stand November 24–26, 1996, for three shows during his solo acoustic tour to support *The Ghost of Tom Joad*. They were special nights during which Springsteen pulled out quite a bit of rarely played material, including the tour debut of "Independence Day," "Wild Billy's Circus Story," "Rosalita," and "4th of July, Asbury Park (Sandy)." In April 2005 Springsteen played two "warm up" shows at the Paramount prior to launching the tour to support *Devils & Dust*.

Due to its small size, the Paramount is an intimate venue for pop and rock concerts, and usually acts must play multiple dates at the Paramount in order for promoters to recoup expenses and make a profit. Rock acts looking for a Jersey Shore theater with a larger capacity are more apt to play the Count Basie Theater in nearby Red Bank, which has nearly 1,550 seats. —*RS/GG*

The Paris Concert for Amnesty International. *See* **Amnesty International Human Rights Now! Tour.**
Pearl Jam. *See* **Vote for Change Tour.**

Sean Penn
Academy Award-winning actor and director

e may have made his name as surfer dude–stoner Jeff Spicoli in 1982's *Fast Times at Ridgemont High*, but Sean Penn is a lifelong Bruce Springsteen fan (and he also briefly dated Springsteen's younger sister, Pamela). *Nebraska's* "Highway Patrolman," in fact, provided the inspiration for *The Indian Runner*, the 1991 film Penn wrote and produced. It was also the first movie he ever directed; nine years later he used scenes from the movie to create a moody visual interpretation of the song that was included on the 2001 DVD version of *The Complete Video Anthology 1978–2000*. Penn also tapped Springsteen to write a song, the Oscar-nominated "Missing," for his next directorial outing, *The Crossing Guard,* in 1995. Springsteen, meanwhile, declared that "my friend Sean Penn is very cool" when he presented him with the 2004 Steinbeck Award, bestowed annually by the Center for Steinbeck Studies at San Jose State University to artists whose creativity addresses social and human issues (Springsteen himself received the inaugural prize in 1996). Accepting the honor, Penn reiterated that Springsteen was "one of the most important creative inspirations in my life."

Born in 1960, Penn boasts a Hollywood pedigree. His parents are director Leo Penn and actor Eileen Ryan; older brother Michael is a musician and younger brother Chris an actor. The middle Penn joined the Los Angeles Repertory Theater after graduating from high school. He made his professional debut in 1979 on TV's "Barnaby Jones" and came to the big screen in 1981's *Taps* before *Fast Times* trumpeted his arrival as a leading man. For a time considered one of Hollywood's hot-tempered bad boys—he spent time in jail for reckless driving and for assaulting a photographer—he was married to Madonna from 1985–89; they appeared together in one film, the 1987 bomb *Shanghai Surprise*. But Penn has rebounded nicely both personally and professionally, with a marriage to actress Robin Wright Penn and a diverse body of work that includes roles in *I Am Sam, Bukowski: Born into This, Dead Man Walking, The Thin Red Line, Sweet and Lowdown, Being John Malkovich*, and his Academy Award–winning turn in 2003's *Mystic River*.   —GG

Tom Petty

Singer, songwriter, Rock and Roll Hall of Fame member

om Petty hails from Florida, and Bruce Springsteen from New Jersey, yet their music, which speaks of and to blue-collar folks yearning for a better life as they try and survive the one they've been handed, has been tagged "heartland rock." Geography aside, they're joined by the likes of Bob Seger and John Mellencamp—actual Midwesterners whose work and sensibilities have a similarly populist bent. Photographer Lynn Goldsmith saw a definite Springsteen influence on Petty—particularly in his live performance style. She reminisced to *Backstreets*, "This guy used to come to the *Darkness* shows and sit in the front a lot; he came to quite a few. Then I went to see *his* show. Tom picked so much stuff off of Bruce. Big time … And he'd do these moves—like, did you go to the Springsteen school of dance?" Springsteen has shared the stage with Petty, including a guest appearance on March 1, 1990, during the Los Angeles stop of the Heartbreakers' tour with Bob Dylan; Springsteen's cameo included Creedence Clearwater Revival's "Travelin' Band" and a bit of the Animals' "I'm Cryin'." Nearly eight months later, on October 29, Springsteen joined the jamming at Petty's fortieth birthday party in Encino, California, playing with Roger McGuinn, Jeff Lynne, and members of the Heartbreakers.

But Petty and Springsteen crossed paths most famously at the 1979 No Nukes concerts staged by Musicians United for Safe Energy (MUSE) at New York's Madison Square Garden. The Heartbreakers preceded Springsteen on the bill; according to Petty's account, while Jackson Browne was walking the group to the stage, he told Petty that what sounded like booing was actually the crowd calling for "Bruuuuuuuce!" Petty's response: "What's the difference?"

That chin-out attitude has been a staple in Petty's life. Born in 1950, he dropped out of high school at seventeen to join Mudcrutch with guitarist Mike Campbell and keyboardist Benmont Tench. He moved to Los Angeles and signed with Shelter Records. The group followed but disbanded before recording; Campbell and Tench went on to work with bassist Ron Blair and drummer Stan Lynch, and after Petty heard a demo they were preparing, they came together as the Heartbreakers. Their self-titled debut was released in 1976. Despite a quintessentially American sound that drew heavily on the Byrds and Bob Dylan, the group remained in obscurity until a tour of England made them a sensation overseas. Only then did their debut single, "Breakdown," make it to the U.S. charts. The group also received a morale boost when former Byrd Roger McGuinn recorded their song "American Girl." The big commercial breakthrough came with the group's third album, 1979's *Damn the Torpedoes*, which sold more than two million copies and launched hit singles such as "Don't Do Me Like That" and "Refugee."

Ironically, *Torpedoes*'s success came after one of Petty's skirmishes with the record industry; when the Heartbreakers' original label, Shelter, went bust, he protested the automatic shift to Shelter's parent company, MCA, by declaring bankruptcy and holding on to the album until a satisfactory deal could be negotiated. He held out again for 1981's *Hard Promises* when the label wanted to release it at a then-high $9.98 list price; he even threatened to title the record *$8.98.* He won. Petty has also remained one of the few superstar rockers—Springsteen is another—who has made a genuine effort to keep his ticket prices relatively inexpensive. In addition to albums with the Heartbreakers and on his own, Petty has populated his career with interesting collaborations. He wrote and performed on Fleetwood Mac singer Stevie Nicks's first solo hit, "Stop Draggin' My Heart Around." He coproduced an album for personal hero Del Shannon, "Drop Down and Get

Me." After playing with Bob Dylan at the 1985 Farm Aid concert, Petty and the Heartbreakers went on the road with Dylan the following year. And in 1988, Petty joined Dylan, George Harrison, Jeff Lynne, and Roy Orbison (who Springsteen inducted into the Rock and Roll Hall of Fame) to form the Traveling Wilburys (Petty was Charlie T. Wilbury, Jr., a.k.a. Muddy). Guitarist Mike Campbell produced and played on Patti Scialfa's first album, *Rumble Doll*, in 1992. Campbell and Tench are also much in demand session players. Bass player Howie Epstein died from drug-related causes in 2003, and was replaced by original bassist Ron Blair.

Petty has earned a reputation for inventive videos for his songs—particularly the twisted *Alice in Wonderland* fantasy "Don't Come Around Here No More," and he's tried his hand at acting as well, including a turn in the Kevin Costner vehicle *The Postman*. Petty and the Heartbreakers were inducted into the Rock and Roll Hall of Fame in 2003. An authorized semi-biography, *Conversations with Tom Petty* by Paul Zollo, is scheduled for publication in late 2005. —*DD*

Tom Petty's music shares themes and sensibilities similar to Springsteen's, as does his touring ethic.

Philadelphia. See **Johnathan Demme; "Streets of Philadelphia."**

Julianne Phillips

Springsteen's first wife, 1985–89

ruce Springsteen was playing one of the highlight stands of the early *Born in the U.S.A.* tour—a seven-night run in the fall of 1984 at the Los Angeles Sports Arena—when his booking agent, Barry Bell, took him to dinner to meet model/actress Julianne Phillips. The two began dating—as much as they could, given each of their work schedules—and within seven months they would be married.

It was a relationship that ran afoul of what many Springsteen fans seemed to expect from their hero. Phillips, ten years Springsteen's junior, was not a Jersey girl, after all; born in Evanston, Illinois, she was the youngest of six children, and her father was a wealthy stockbroker. The family subsequently moved to the affluent Portland suburb of Lake Oswego, Oregon, and after high school Phillips studied at Brooks College in Long Beach, California, before returning home to act in community theater and begin her modeling career. The latter took off first, and the Elite Modeling Agency hired her to come to New York City, where she became one of its top clients. By 1984 her acting prospects were also improving; that year she appeared in four made-for-television movies—*He's Not Your Son*, *Jealousy*, *His Mistress*, and *Summer Fantasy*—and appeared with Ted Danson in the Blake Edwards comedy *A Fine Mess*, which came out in 1985. She also appeared in Springsteen's "Glory Days" video.

The Springsteen-Phillips courtship was quick; they began to talk marriage during a Hawaiian vacation after the first leg of the *Born in the U.S.A.* tour and told friends and family they were engaged in early May 1985. They also wanted to get married quickly; they pulled it off after midnight on May 13 in a traditional Catholic ceremony at the Our Lady of the Lakes church in Lake Oswego, faking out press and paparazzi that had learned that the couple's wedding was imminent. Jon Landau, Clarence Clemons, and Steve Van Zandt attended Springsteen, while his younger sister Pam was a bridesmaid. A full reception was held on May 15 in Tualitin, Oregon, with the media out in full force—some employing helicopters that were issued warnings by the Federal Aviation Administration for flying too close to the party. Phillips continued to spend time on the road with the E Street Band, and when the *Born in the U.S.A.* tour wrapped up on October 2 at the Los Angeles Coliseum, Springsteen pulled his wife out of the wings to join him for "Dancing in the Dark" ("Had to save the last dance for her!" he told the crowd, and the moment was captured in the subsequent "Born to Run" video.)

Still, Phillips was conscious of keeping an identity separate from being just Mrs. Springsteen: "It's real important, but I don't want *that* to be why people are interested in me," she told *Rolling Stone* magazine. "I want to be thought of as an actor." Fans and observers began wondering about the strength of the marriage, however, when the dark *Tunnel of Love* album emerged in the fall of 1987. Springsteen denied that it signaled trouble in the relationship, claiming he was "happier than I've ever been." He told *Rolling Stone* in March 1988 that the *Tunnel* songs dealt with the concept of being married and the emotions he had to overcome in order to commit himself to that kind of relationship: "I wanted to make a record ... about really letting another person in your life and trying to be part of someone else's life. That's a frightening thing ... You have to find the strength to sustain it and build on it and work for it and constantly pour energy into it." He noted, "[T]here's days when you're real close and days when you're real far away," but added, "I've been married for three years, just about. And I feel like we just met."

Things came apart two months later, however. During the Tunnel of Love Express Tour he began growing closer to E Street Band singer Patti Scialfa; reviewers noted the heat the two generated together on stage, especially when they faced off to harmonize on "Tougher Than the Rest." Springsteen told Phillips about the affair in May, and the couple agreed to separate. It didn't become public until mid-June, when tabloids printed paparazzi shots of Springsteen and Scialfa nuzzling on a hotel balcony in Rome. Springsteen issued a hasty statement that acknowledged his separation and apologized to Phillips—and also denied that differing desires for children (rumor was she didn't want them) had anything to do with the rift. Phillips filed for divorce on August 30; it was made final on March 1, 1989. In 1992, Springsteen told *Rolling Stone,* "I didn't really know how to be a husband. She was a terrific person, but I just didn't know how to do it ... I really needed something, and I was giving it a shot. Anybody who's been through a divorce can tell you what that's about. It's difficult, hard, and painful for everybody involved."

Phillips continued her acting career following the divorce. She starred opposite Chevy Chase in 1989's *Fletch Lives* and from 1991–96 played Francesca "Frankie" Reed Margolis on the NBC drama "Sisters." Other credits include an appearance on HBO's "The Larry Sanders Show" and roles in *Big Bully* (1996), *Allie & Me,* (1997) and *Colin Fritz* (1997), and in the made-for-TV movies *Getting Up and Going Home* (1992) and *Tidal Wave: No Escape* (1997). —*GG/SD*

"Pink Cadillac." See Natalie Cole.

Pittsburgh Ballet Theatre

Steel City dance company

 wan Lake met Greasy Lake in April 2004, when the Pittsburgh Ballet Theatre premiered *Springsteen & Seeger*, a production that featured two newly choreographed pieces set to Bruce Springsteen music. The show ran for four days at the PBT's regular home at the Benedum Center in downtown Pittsburgh and was reprised for a summer stop that August at the suburban Hartwood Acres. Springsteen's friend Joe Grushecky and his Iron City Houserockers performed at intermission of the Benedum Center dates.

Derek Deane, a principal dancer with Great Britain's Royal Ballet, set "Hungry Heart ... We All Have One" in a late '50s/early '60s diner, interpreting a variety of characters' stories through dance pieces set to "Darkness on the Edge of Town," "The River," "Secret Garden," "I Wanna Be With You," "A Good Man Is Hard to Find (Pittsburgh)," "Blood Brothers," "Dancing in the Dark," and "Hungry Heart." Dean described his work as "earthy, grounded, about real people, not superficial ... all about feeling." Meanwhile, Canadian choreographer Matjash Mrozewski conceived "Straight Life" as a more athletic and abstract interpretation of Springsteen's music, tapping songs such as "State Trooper," "Atlantic City," "Straight Time," and "New York City Serenade."

Announcing the Springsteen ballet pieces, PBT Artistic Director Terrence S. Orr said, "Springsteen's music has an earnestness and soulfulness that transports the listener, which will work to our advantage. The magic to his music is in the lyrics. His music has tremendous energy, whether it be a full-out rock song or one of his slower ballads, the emotions are palatable."

The Seeger portion of *Springsteen & Seeger* was Lynne Taylor-Corbett's "Ballad of You and Me," which was set to staples of Pete Seeger's repertoire such as "This Land Is Your Land," "Talkin' Union," "Die Gedanken Sind Frei (My Spirit Is Free)," "Ballad of You and Me," "We Shall Overcome," and "If I Had a Hammer." —*GG*

Chuck Plotkin

Producer, engineer

Chuck Plotkin first received a coproducing credit on Bruce Springsteen's 1984 album *Born in the U.S.A.* but his involvement dates back to 1978's *Darkness on the Edge of Town*, which he was brought in to mix. "Chuck Plotkin ... came in near the end of the album and helped us get a tighter, more modern mix," Springsteen wrote in *Songs*. "He helped us focus the songs in a way we'd been unable to and allowed us to bring the record to completion." Plotkin also mixed 1980's *The River* and subsequently became a more active part of the production team

Born in Los Angeles to a musician father, Plotkin learned to play guitar, bass, keyboards, drums, and banjo. In college he played in a jug band. After earning an undergraduate degree in philosophy and literature, Plotkin attended law school at the University of Southern California. But he never took the bar exam, deciding to give music a shot first. While he was studying law, he realized he'd be more useful behind the scenes than as an actual musician, and when he discovered singer-songwriter Wendy Waldman working as a singing waitress, he made his first official foray into the biz.

Plotkin helped create the band Bryndle with Waldman and fellow troubadours Andrew Gold, Karla Bonoff, and Kenny Edwards (a cofounder of the Stone Poneys, which featured Linda Ronstadt). Plotkin brokered a deal for Bryndle with A&M but was not allowed to produce what was to be its 1970 debut album—until another producer created an unsatisfactory version. He took a quick shot at it, and though the label loved Plotkin's version, it let veteran mogul Lou Adler give it a try. The album went unreleased for twenty-five years, until after each of the members built their own solo careers. After that experience, Plotkin decided to begin recording on his own and built Clover Studios (aka Clover Recorders), where he produced Waldman's first solo album. His next production project was a Steve Ferguson album for David Geffen's Asylum Records. Eventually, he became an A&R man for Asylum, where he charted with two acts he also produced, Andrew Gold and Orleans.

Plotkin met Jon Landau in 1976 when Landau, fresh from coproducing Springsteen's *Born to Run*, was in Los Angeles producing Jackson Browne's *The Pretender*. In 1978, Plotkin quit Asylum to help Springsteen and Landau finish *Darkness*, and he's said he's never regretted that decision. That same year, Plotkin produced the Cowsills' reunion effort, *The Cocaine Drain Album*, which was never released.

In the early '80s, Springsteen helped Plotkin secure a production deal at Columbia Records, where he coproduced Bob Dylan's 1981 release *Shot of Love*. When Plotkin married in 1990, Springsteen played at his wedding; the set list reportedly included: "I Think It's Gonna Work Out Fine," "Glory Days," and, with Tom Waits, "The Fever," and "Jersey Girl." Plotkin's production credits also include projects with Bette Midler, Harry Chapin, Tommy Tutone, Dwight Twilley, and Dan Bern. Plotkin also is listed as assistant producer (with Tom Petty & the Heartbreakers' Mike Campbell) of *Rumble Doll*, Patti Scialfa's 1994 solo debut. —*LM/GG*

Point Blank Magazine

Spanish fan magazine and companion website

Thunder Road was the first and *Backstreets* is the longest running, but Springsteen fanzines have cropped up all over the world for years. One of the most respected is Spain's *Point Blank*, which has been published continuously under that name since 1991 by Salvador Trepat. Trepat has kept the Springsteen flag flying in Spain for over twenty years with his magazine and its fanzine predecessor; the associated website (www.pointblankmag.com); concert, convention, and record fair activities; and his mail-order record store specializing in Springsteen-related items, now called Buffalomail.com (formerly Buffalo Records). Buffalomail.com also sells handpicked music from the rock, folk, alt-country, and roots genres.

The *Point Blank* website provides up-to-date Springsteen news, while the magazine is known for its interviews and its in-depth coverage of Springsteen's activities in Spain, such as his October 16, 2002, concert at the Palau Sant Jordi in Barcelona, preserved for all to see on the official double DVD *Live in Barcelona*. Spanish fans are among Springsteen's most fervent in Europe, so it's no surprise that he released a DVD from a show in Spain and chose to start the 1999 reunion tour there, again at the Palau Sant Jordi, April 9 and 11.

Trepat is a particularly strong supporter of artists associated with Springsteen, including Joe Grushecky and Elliott Murphy; he helped to promote Grushecky's 2004 Spanish tour and ran Murphy's official web store. He is also a major Springsteen collector and dedicated fan who rarely misses a tour opener, closer, or special show no matter the continent on which it takes place. —*EF*

The Pointer Sisters

R&B vocal group

ith their sisterly harmonies, retro fashions, and songs that mixed Andrews Sisters–style jazz and pop with more contemporary R&B sounds, the Pointer Sisters—Ruth, Anita, Bonnie, and June—hailed from Oakland, California. As children they sang in church (both of their parents were ministers). Later, Bonnie and June sang in Bay Area nightclubs; Anita was the third sister to get in on the act, and the trio sang backup for Elvin Bishop, Taj Mahal, Boz Scaggs, and others. They recorded a couple of unsuccessful singles before Ruth completed the quartet. Eventually, they hit with Allen Toussaint's "Yes We Can Can" in 1983.

The mid-'70s brought struggles with their record label and within the group (June suffered a nervous breakdown; Bonnie went solo). The group sought to update their image and sound on the 1978 album *Energy*, which contained a cover of Bruce Springsteen's "Fire." The Pointers' version was a No. 2 pop hit and reached No. 7 on the R&B chart. It also brought Springsteen, through association, some much-needed exposure on the airwaves.

The Pointers went on to more success with songs like "He's So Shy," "Slow Hand," and "I'm So Excited." The sisters would have one more encounter with Springsteen, though; they sang together on the USA for Africa charity single, "We Are the World," in 1985. —*DD*

Polar Music Prize

Awarded May 5, 1997

stablished in 1989 by ABBA manager Stig Anderson and administered by the Royal Swedish Academy of Music, the Polar Music Prize is one of the most prestigious creative honors in the world—it's even been called the Nobel Prize of music. Named for Anderson's record label and recognizing "exceptional achievements in the creation and advancement

Called the "Nobel Prize of music," the Polar Music Prize, awarded by the Royal Swedish Academy of Music (after being created by ABBA manager Stig Anderson), is one of the most prestigious honors in the music business. Springsteen won the 1 million kronor (U.S. $133,000) prize in 1997. Here Swedish monarch King Karl Gustav XVI awards Springsteen with the prize; later in the ceremony, Springsteen played "Thunder Road" and "The Ghost of Tom Joad" for the appreciative crowd.

of music," it is given each year to two recipients from any discipline of music, feting them at a televised ceremony each spring and a $125,000 prize.

Bruce Springsteen received the Polar Music Prize from Swedish King Karl Gustav XVI on May 5, 1997, along with Swedish conductor Eric Ericson. In its citation, the Polar committee saluted Springsteen "for an outstanding career as singer and stage performer. His authority in rock music is unshakeable. For two decades now he has been one of the most colorful personalities at the very center of the genre, and he is an uncompromising steward of the essential qualities of rock: its heavy beat and 'groovy' sound—a harsh sometimes crude but at the same time spiritual sound ideal rooted in black rhythm and blues. In his lyrics he focuses on the little man's winding path through life with a certain melancholy and profound compassion. In a world of music where styles are fluctuating all the time, Bruce Springsteen stands with both feet firmly planted on the ground of rock 'n' roll. Although his records have sold in vast quantities, the live concert remains his natural medium. Bruce Springsteen, with his social pathos, is also a singer of the people, a modern 'bard.' He stands up straight and hits hard, but he does so with discretion and not without tenderness."

Springsteen—who performed "The Ghost of Tom Joad" and "Thunder Road" at the ceremony—accepted the honor with typical grace and brevity, thanking the assembled Swedish royalty and the Polar committee "for honoring my music tonight" and saying it was "an additional source of joy" to be recognized alongside Ericson, who was the first Swedish musician to receive the award. Other Polar Music Prize winners from the popular music world include Sir Paul McCartney, Dizzy Gillespie, Quincy Jones, Sir Elton John, Joni Mitchell, Ray Charles, Stevie Wonder, Bob Dylan, and Burt Bacharach. —*GG*

The Power Station

Famed New York City recording studio

 ow known as Avatar Studios, the Power Station is the famed New York City recording studio where Bruce Springsteen and the E Street Band recorded their double-album epic *The River* as well as significant portions of *Born in the U.S.A.* In a 2003 *Mix* magazine story, writer Maureen Droney said the band's nightly recording set-ups for *The River* had to be struck and redone daily because the studio was used for other sessions during the day (back then, artists did not commandeer studios as their own for the duration of a project). Engineer Neil Dorfsman told her he and his assistants eventually got so good at it that he could walk into the console room and be ready to go in twenty minutes.

The River sessions went from April 1979 through August 1980; during that time the group was visited by New Jersey Senator Bill Bradley. *Born in the U.S.A.* was recorded on and off from early 1982 to April 1984; some sessions were also recorded at the Hit Factory in New York City. Arthur Baker remixed the latter album's first single, "Dancing in the Dark," at the Power Station as well. Dozens of bootlegs, many included in contraband series *The Lost Masters*, are available from the sessions for both albums. In May 2004, the auction house Leland's sold four reel-to-reel master tapes from *The River* sessions for $2,937.50.

Besides Springsteen, many of the most legendary artists in the history of pop music have recorded in the former Consolidated Edison electric factory, including Eric Clapton, the Rolling Stones, Bob Dylan, the Ramones, and Madonna. Located on 53rd Street in New York's infamous Hell's Kitchen district, the building's first entertainment-industry use was as a home for "Let's Make a Deal," the TV game show hosted by Monty Hall. The facility was turned into the Power Station in 1977 by Tony Bongiovi—whose cousin, Jon Bon Jovi, used to sweep floors there in exchange for studio time. It became Avatar in 1996. The 33,000-square-foot space contains four studios, but Studio A is the one where most of the magic has been created. With room for a sixty-piece orchestra, it easily contained the entire E Street Band during *The River* sessions, which were recorded mostly live. —*LM*

Elvis Presley

The King, 1935–1977. 'Nuf said.

 lvis Presley is the man who started it all—arguably for rock 'n' roll, definitely for Bruce Springsteen. It was when an almost seven-year-old Springsteen saw Elvis Presley perform on *The Ed Sullivan Show* in 1956 that he decided what he wanted to do with his life. "On came Elvis," Springsteen recalled at the 1981 Night for the Vietnam Veteran benefit in Los Angeles, "(and) I said 'I wanna be just … like … that." Springsteen was so inspired that he begged his mother to get him a guitar, which she did when he was nine years old; on the 2002 NBC TV special "Elvis Lives," he recalled, "The first thing I did was take it out of its case, hold it in front of me, standing front of the mirror and try to move like [Presley]."

When it came to Presley, Springsteen was lured in by the same aspects as everyone else—the energy, the sexuality, the rebellion, and the sense of forbidden experience. But over time he became a student of the deeper implications of Presley's stardom. "He was not primitive, like people think," Springsteen told *Rolling Stone* in 1977, after Presley's death. "He was an artist, and he was into being an artist. Of course, he was also into rockin' his ass, but that was part of it." Two decades later, he told *DoubleTake* magazine that Presley was "one of the most socially conscious artists in the second half of (the twentieth) century," not so much as a political activist but as a cultural force who blended together aspects of black and white America in a seamless fashion that, to Springsteen, made him "one of the people … who led to the sixties and the civil rights movement … this poor white kid from Mississippi who connected with black folks through their music, which he made his own and then gave to others." On "Elvis Lives," he also noted that Presley "really was a harbinger of wearing your sexuality, of not being ashamed, frightened of it, of *enjoying* it … It was a real outward signifying of a very sensual, feminine side of men."

The East Tupelo, Mississippi–born Presley was indeed the king of rock 'n' roll, even if his acquired claim to recording the first rock song—"That's All Right" on July 5, 1954, at Sam Phillips's Memphis Recording Service—is the subject of great debate. He was unquestionably the first of a new era of singers to be embraced by a fevered mass fan base, creating a new "teen audience" of such baby-boomer proportions that media and corporate America could not help but court it. That machine drove Presley as much as—if not more than—Presley drove himself. And in the late '50s, Springsteen was as caught up by it as fervently as any other young person looking for a cultural identity separate from that of his parents.

That Springsteen played Presley's music was certainly to be expected; over the years, even after he became a recording artist and superstar in his own right, the New Jersey admirer would pull out Presley tunes such as "Heartbreak Hotel," "Can't Help Falling in Love," "Mystery Train," "Hound Dog," "Love Me Tender," and "Good Rockin' Tonight" in his shows. In the early '80s he wrote his own version of "Follow That Dream," the title song of Presley's 1961 movie, although the song was never officially released. And shortly after breaking up the E Street Band in 1989, Springsteen recorded "Viva Las Vegas" (which he'd reportedly done with the group in 1977) with another set of musicians—including former Faces keyboardist Ian McLagan and the late Toto drummer Jeff Porcaro—for the 1990 benefit tribute album *The Last Temptation of Elvis.*

The specter of Presley is apparent in much of Springsteen's songwriting and stagecraft and haunts some of his own music in more direct fashion. His "Johnny Bye Bye," a B-side for the 1985 single "I'm on Fire," was written in the early '80s about Presley's death. Another B-side, 1984's "Pink Cadillac," has its roots in one of Presley's favorite rides. "57 Channels (and Nothin' On)" from *Human Touch* in 1992 finds Springsteen firing a bullet into his television "in the blessed name of Elvis"—a reference to legends about Presley shooting up his own TVs when he wasn't happy with what was on. He's occasionally performed an unreleased song called "I'm Turning into Elvis," a good-humored, seven-verse rumination that even makes mention of Presley's taste for peanut butter and banana sandwiches. On the cover of *Born to Run* he sports a fan club button from a New York outfit known as The King's Court, while the cover of *Live in New York City* employed star graphics that were used for a 1956 Presley concert poster. Then there's "Fire," the popular Springsteen non-album track—recorded by the Pointer Sisters and Robert Gordon—that, legend has it, was written in the mid-'70s with Presley in mind. After Presley's death, Springsteen told concert audiences, "I always wanted Elvis Presley to record it." But there's no hard evidence to confirm the numerous reports that he had sent a demo of "Fire" to Graceland for Presley's consideration.

Springsteen and Presley never met, though the former tried once. It was in the wee hours of April 30, 1976, after a concert in Memphis; Springsteen, E Street Band guitarist Steve Van Zandt, and publicist Glen Brunman, initially hunting for something to eat, had their cab detour to Presley's Graceland estate—where Springsteen, seeing a single light on upstairs, hopped the stone wall and began walking down the driveway towards the house. He was stopped by security guards who were polite but unimpressed by this guy who was, as Springsteen put it, "pulling out all the cheap shots" and (truthfully) professed to being a recording artist himself, with his picture on the covers of *Time* and *Newsweek*. They escorted him off the property through the front gates, and the story is now part of *The Official Visitor's Guide to Graceland*.

Interestingly, Springsteen declined an invitation from concert promoters to meet Presley before his May 28, 1977, performance in Philadelphia. "I never liked ... going backstage and stuff. I just feel uncomfortable when that happens—I don't know why," Springsteen told the late Philadelphia DJ Ed Sciaky, who attended the concert with him. That was actually the second time Springsteen saw Presley in concert; the first was in June 1972 at New York's Madison Square Garden, just after Springsteen signed his contract with Columbia Records. He attended that show with his then-manager and producer Mike Appel; the latter told *Backstreets*, "After the concert, Bruce turned to me and said 'The King.' That was it. That was all that needed to be said. 'The King.'" Springsteen was less impressed with the Philadelphia concert—which, coincidentally, happened on the same day he settled the bitter lawsuit with Appel that had kept his recording career in limbo; he told an East Rutherford, New Jersey, audience in 1981, "I felt disappointed because he didn't play the old songs like I remembered them."

Springsteen and the E Street Band were off the road when Presley died on August 16, 1977. When he heard the news, Springsteen told *Rolling Stone*, "[I]t was like somebody took a piece out of me." Over the years he's commemorated both the anniversary of Presley's death and his birthday (January 8) by playing his music and ruminating on his demise. "I used to think back," he said in 1981 in East Rutherford, "and try and understand what happened to him, why he ended up like he did and how easy it is to get everything and to lose that thing inside you that keeps you alive. This is for Elvis, 'cause he deserved better than he got." —*GG*

John Prine

Singer-songwriter

 mart, literate, and laugh-out-loud funny, John Prine is a one-of-a-kind singer/songwriter. In the late '60s, the Kentucky native and army veteran supported himself working as a Chicago mailman while trying his luck on the folk-music scene. Prine's self-titled debut album in 1971 included an impossibly sad song about old people ("Hello in There"), an outraged environmental anthem ("Paradise"), and a trenchant tale of a Vietnam vet/drug addict ("Sam Stone"). Subsequent albums found him working all styles of humor, from dark cynicism to whimsy, into songs like "Dear Abby," "That's the Way That the

Like Springsteen, folk icon John Prine was given the "new Dylan" label early in his career; also like Springsteen, he survived the hype to forge a respected career as a writer and performer.

World Goes 'Round," and "Come Back to Us Barbara Lewis Hare Krishna Beauregard." Other artists took notice of Prine and covered his songs, including the Everly Brothers ("Paradise"), Bette Midler and Joan Baez ("Hello in There"), Bonnie Raitt ("Angel from Montgomery"), and Prine's Chicago buddy Steve Goodman ("You Never Even Call Me by My Name," which the two cowrote). Due to Prine's lyrical acuity, he was given the "new Dylan" tag that simultaneously boosted and destroyed many a singer/songwriter's career—including Bruce Springsteen's. In fact, the two were among those singled out by fellow troubadour Loudon Wainwright III in his 1992 song "Talking New Bob Dylan": "I got a deal and so did John Prine/Steve Forbert and Springsteen all in a line/They were looking for you, signing up others/We were the new Bob Dylans, your dumbass kid brothers."

Springsteen and Prine got together in 1991 as Prine was recording *The Missing Years*, his first effort after a five-year hiatus. Springsteen sang backup vocals on the track "Take a Look at My Heart," joining an all-star group of contributors that included Raitt, Tom Petty, and Phil Everly. The album won a Grammy Award for Best Folk Album.

Surviving a cancer scare in the late '90s, Prine has continued to write, record, and perform. He started his own record company, Oh Boy Records, and added acting to his bag of tricks in 1992, appearing in the John Mellencamp film *Falling from Grace* and Billy Bob Thornton's *Daddy and Them*. —*DD*

Prodigal Son

Unauthorized compilation of early demos and studio recordings

hen Bruce Springsteen told *Rolling Stone* magazine in 1984 that he had lots of "good" unreleased material "that should come out," he did not have in mind *Prodigal Son* and its myriad other incarnations—*The Early Years*, *Unearthed,* and *Before the Fame,* among others. These were proposed releases of early demo and studio recordings that were unauthorized and that, in all but one case, Springsteen was able to block from coming out in the late '90s, around the same time he was preparing his career-spanning *Tracks* box set. "The music that you come up with when you are sitting in your room alone with your guitar late at night is one of the most personal things in your life," Springsteen said during the court proceedings, explaining why he worked so aggressively to stop the other packages. "I have told a long story throughout my career, and a big part of that story has been fashioned by the way the records have been released, as well as what is on them."

It's never been established where the *Prodigal Son* material—demos he recorded with original producers Mike Appel and Jim Cretecos as well as recordings from sessions for his first two albums at 914 Sound Studios in Blauvelt, New York—came from. Among the tracks were alternate versions of "4th of July, Asbury Park (Sandy)," "Growin' Up," "For You," "New York City Serenade," and "Kitty's Back," as well as unreleased songs such as "Hey Santa Ana," "Jesse," "War Nurse," and "Prodigal Son." Britain's Dare International fingered Cretecos as the source, claiming he sold the tapes to the company in the mid-'90s;

A nattily dressed Springsteen testified in October 1998 before London's Royal Court of Justice in his lawsuit against Masquerade Music Ltd., which claimed that the singer/songwriter had signed away the rights to his early material. The British court sided with Springsteen and awarded significant monetary damages while also ordering Masquerade to cease its attempts to release the early tracks.

Cretecos denied this. Once word of the impending releases leaked out, however, Springsteen and his attorneys swung into action against Dare, Masquerade Music Ltd., and Flute International Ltd. in Britain and against Pony Express Records Inc. and JEC Music USA Inc. in the states. The companies claimed that Springsteen had signed away his rights to the recordings—which he indeed had early in his career. However, through subsequent legal actions in the '70s against Appel—who had bought out Cretecos's interests—Springsteen began to retain ownership of them. He regained all of his copyrights completely in 1983.

In January 1994 Springsteen was able to obtain an injunction to keep Dare from releasing its *Prodigal Son* package; they reached an out-of-court settlement the following December. In the case against Masquerade Music,

Springsteen testified in October 1998 at the Royal Courts of Justice in London; wearing a suit and tie, he spoke at length about his career and particularly his early days with Appel, Cretecos, and their Laurel Canyon Productions firm. When one of the record companies' attorneys tried to get him to acknowledge private recording sessions with Cretecos, Springsteen stood firm, telling the barrister, "I know what you're getting at. Nice try, sir—but *no.*" In a humorous moment during the trial, a defense attorney asked Springsteen if he wanted a drink to clear his throat; Springsteen's response—"No thank you sir, I don't think it will help. I sound like this most of the time anyway"—drew laughs in the courtroom.

The Royal Court ruled in Springsteen's favor in December 1998, ordering the companies to pay his court costs as well as £2 million in damages. A three-judge panel subsequently upheld the ruling on appeal. "I really didn't come here for the money," Springsteen said after the initial verdict. "I came here for the music. It took a long time, but I will not hesitate to do it again."

The American companies instigated their fight with Springsteen, claiming he "used his stature and position as a famous recording artist" to discourage distributors from handling their albums. Springsteen countersued and was eventually victorious. He later told the *New York Times*, "[T]here's a reason I don't put out the stuff I don't put out—I don't think it's good enough or focused enough. You try to have some control over your releases … They were attempting to put it out as an actual legal release and they simply didn't have the right to do that. I don't have any strong feelings about the material one way or the other. There were some good things and some stinkers on the tape, and some day I'd like to get some of it out. But your editing is part of your aesthetic process."

Though the material wound up appearing on a variety of bootlegs over the years, there was one legitimate release—*The Early Years,* on the Dutch label Early. However, it was withdrawn after Springsteen's legal victories. —*GG*

"Protection." *See* **Donna Summer.**

"Prove It All Night"

Single release: June 9, 1978
Album: *Darkness on the Edge of Town* (Columbia, 1978)
Also on: *Live in New York City* (Columbia, 2001)
Chart peak: No. 33

he first single from *Darkness on the Edge of Town* did not climb as high on the charts as "Born to Run," but "Prove It All Night" still gave Bruce Springsteen some radio exposure—and his second Top 40 hit. It was not one of the *Darkness* tracks that was previewed before

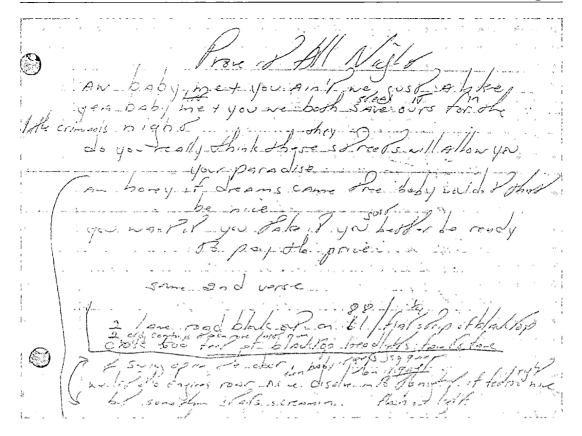

This copy of a draft of the handwritten lyrics to "Prove It All Night," from Springsteen's fourth album, *Darkness on the Edge of Town*, were displayed as part of an exhibit titled *Springsteen—Troubadour of the Highway* at the Newark Museum in New Jersey. The exhibit ran in Newark from June 17 to August 29, 2004, after stops in three other cities.

the album's release, but in concert it became a tour de force, opening with long piano and guitar solos that built to the song's explosive start. Columbia planned to release a live version of the song as a promotional single to radio stations but later canceled those plans. It was surprisingly not included on *Live/1975–85*, but the rendition from the 2000–2001 tour did wind up on *Live in New York City*.

One aspect of the song Springsteen liked was Clarence Clemons's saxophone solo. He told *Rolling Stone* magazine, "The saxophone's a very urban instrument ... On some of the songs, it collided with the texture or just the particular character of what was happening in a funny way. You can make it work—it worked on 'Born to Run' and it works on 'Prove It All Night'—but it's tricky."

The "Prove It All Night" single was backed with the *Darkness* track "Factory." —*GG*

Bonnie Raitt

Singer, songwriter, performer, activist, red-headed woman

Since 1974, Bonnie Raitt has been in a kind of sidecar position for some notable moments in Bruce Springsteen's career. He opened for her on May 9, 1974, at the Harvard Square Theater in Cambridge, Massachusetts—the show from which Jon Landau wrote his "rock and roll future" column. She was also on the bill at the September 1979 No Nukes concerts at New York's Madison Square Garden; she's caught in the film sitting backstage, listening to the crowd chant for "Bruuuuuuuuce!" Her reaction: "It's a good thing his name isn't Melvin." Raitt joined Springsteen and Jackson Browne at the Christic Institute benefit concerts on November 16–17, 1990, at the Shrine Auditorium in Los Angeles, where each artist performed a solo acoustic set, then joined forces at the end of Springsteen's for "Highway 61" and "Across the Borderline." And on September 3, 1999, Raitt and Browne and their entire touring company at the time—including Bruce Hornsby, Shawn Colvin, and Mary Chapin Carpenter—got up on stage with Springsteen and the E Street Band in Washington, D.C., for renditions of "Hungry Heart" and, appropriately enough, "Red Headed Woman."

The daughter of Broadway star John Raitt (*Oklahoma, Carousel*), Raitt was raised a Quaker and adopted a liberal and pacifistic worldview. Inspired by folk and blues artists, she began performing while studying at Radcliffe College in the late '60s and signed a recording contract with Warner Bros. in 1971. In addition to making her own music, Raitt used her platform to champion her heroes, including Sippie Wallace, Charles Brown, Ruth Brown, and John Lee Hooker, with whom she

.

.

.

won a Grammy in 1990. Though she had modest success during the '70s and '80s—and was admittedly addled at times by substance addictions—she began a string of hits with 1989's multiple-Grammy-winning *Nick of Time* and has maintained her career at a high level ever since. She's a guiding force of the Rhythm and Blues Foundation. Raitt was inducted into the Rock and Roll Hall of Fame in 2000, and she joined Springsteen and several other musicians as part of the Vote for Change tour in 2004. —*GG*

Ronald Reagan

Fortieth president of the United States

lectoral candidates co-opting popular culture for their own benefit is nothing new in American politics. So with Bruce Springsteen at the peak of his commercial fame in the fall of 1984, it was only a matter of time before that the year's presidential candidates would attempt to attach themselves to him in some way. Ironically, it was the incumbent, Ronald Reagan—whose conservative, elitist rule had inspired much of Springsteen's dark *Nebraska* album and some of *Born in the U.S.A.*—who moved first. At a September 19 campaign rally in Hammonton, New Jersey—which Cellar Door Productions, a concert promotion firm, asked Springsteen to attend—Reagan told a crowd, "America's future rests in the message of hope in the songs of a man that so many young Americans admire, New Jersey's own Bruce Springsteen. Helping you make these dreams come true is what this job of mine is all about."

This, of course, did not go down well with Springsteen. After all, on the night Reagan was elected to his first term—November 4, 1980—Springsteen told a crowd in Tempe, Arizona, "I don't know what you guys think about what happened last night, but I think it's pretty frightening. You guys are young. There's gonna be a lot of people depending on you comin' up, so this is for you," before launching into a ferocious, pointed version of "Badlands." He chose the stage to address Reagan's campaign remark, too; playing in Pittsburgh on September 21, 1984, he told the audience, "The president was mentioning my name the other day, and I kinda got to wondering what his

Bonnie Raitt has shared the stage with Springsteen on several occasions, in support of causes ranging from safe energy to progressive politics and as a special guest during the encore of an E Street Band performance.

favorite album must've been. I don't think it was the *Nebraska* album." The following night Springsteen made a more subtle retaliation by dedicating his performance of "The River" to the staunchly anti-Reagan United Steelworkers of America Local 1397 and making a donation to the organization.

In a subsequent interview with *Rolling Stone* magazine, Springsteen explained his response to Reagan's comments: "You see the Reagan reelection ads on TV—you know, 'It's morning in America.' And you say, well, it's not morning in Pittsburgh. It's not morning on 125th Street in New York. It's midnight, and, like, there's a bad moon risin'. And that's why when Reagan mentioned my name in New Jersey, I felt it was another manipulation, and I had to disassociate myself from the president's kind words." But given the opportunity to criticize Reagan, Springsteen was relatively restrained, calling him the embodiment of "a nostalgia for a mythical America" and saying, "I don't know if he's a bad man. But I think there's a large group of people in this country whose dreams don't mean much to him, that just get indiscriminately swept aside."

Walter Mondale, Reagan's Democratic opponent in the 1984 election, seized on Reagan's misstep as an opportunity to woo the Springsteen audience himself; he told an October 1, 1984, crowd in New Jersey, "Bruce may have been born to run, but he wasn't born yesterday." Maybe so, but it didn't earn him Springsteen's public backing; on October 2 Springsteen's management issued a statement saying, "Bruce has not, and has no intention of endorsing any political candidate."

Reagan—a former actor and broadcaster who had switched party affiliations and was governor of California before running for the White House—won the 1984 election handily and served out his term. Alzheimer's Disease limited his activities after he left office, however, and he passed away on June 5, 2004. —*GG*

Red Bank Rockers. *See* **Clarence Clemons.**
R.E.M. *See* **Vote for Change Tour.**

The Rising

Released: July 30, 2002
Producer: Brendan O'Brien
Tracks: "Lonesome Day," "Into the Fire," "Waitin' on a Sunny Day," "Nothing Man," "Countin' on a Miracle," "Empty Sky," "Worlds Apart," "Let's Be Friends (Skin to Skin)," "Further On (Up the Road)," "The Fuse," "Mary's Place," "You're Missing," "The Rising," "Paradise," "My City of Ruins"
Key outtakes: "I'll Stand By You Always"
Chart peak: No. 1

 ollowing the reinvigorating 1999–2000 reunion tour with the E Street Band, Bruce Springsteen was ready to hit the studio again. He had some strong material he'd rolled out during the tour, includ-

"**W**ith its bold thematic concentration and penetrating emotional focus, (*The Rising*) is a singular triumph. I can't think of another album in which such an abundance of great songs might be said to seem the least of its achievements."

—*Rolling Stone*

"**O**bsessed with mortality and suffused with grief, *The Rising* is the most eloquent artistic response yet to the World Trade Center tragedy."

—*Spin*

"**R**eunited with the E Street Band for their first full album together in nearly two decades, he drips inspiration ... *The Rising* is a ghost story, but it's more, too—past and present, celebration and wake—and few others could have pulled it off."

—*Entertainment Weekly*

"**T**he Rising is about September 11, and it is the first significant piece of pop art to respond to the events of that day ... The songs are sad, but the sadness is almost always matched with optimism, promises of redemption, and calls to spiritual arms. There is more rising on *The Rising* than in a month of church."

—*Time*

"**T**he Rising is the most poignant musical commentary yet to be made in the wake of September 11 ... The tragedy seeps into nearly every note as Springsteen soaks himself in dark, unfathomable loss and in the effort to endure, recover, and live again."

—*Oakland (Michigan) Press*

"... a song cycle about duty, love, death, mourning and resurrection. *The Rising* provides comfort without flinching from sadness and bitter fury. In a way the album brings together the topics that have occupied Mr. Springsteen for two decades: work and love."

—*New York Times*

ing "Land of Hope and Dreams," the controversial "American Skin (41 Shots)," "Code of Silence," and "Further On (Up the Road)." The group went into the studio in the fall of 2000, but despite productive sessions, Springsteen wrote in *Songs* that he felt "something was missing." He later confessed to the *New York Times* he was "having a hard time locating my rock voice." It took tragedy to help him find it.

Like hundreds of millions around the globe, Springsteen watched the September 11, 2001, terrorist attacks on New York City and Washington, D.C., with shock, horror, and disbelief. For him they hit home literally, because Monmouth County, New Jersey, where he resides with his family, suffered one of the highest death tolls of any population center. Springsteen read some of the obituaries in which the deceased were identified as his fans; he wound up calling some of the families to express his condolences and even sent a tape of himself performing a solo version of "Thunder Road" to the family of one victim. A few days following the attack, when Springsteen was leaving a beachfront parking lot in Sea Bright, New Jersey, a man drove by and shouted, "We need you!" out of his car window. After that, the elusive voice began to come into focus.

"Our band was built well over many years, for difficult times," Springsteen wrote. "When people wanted a dialog, a conversation of events, internal and external, we developed a language that suited those moments, a language I hoped would entertain, inspire, comfort, and reveal ... I always believed that it was this conversation, this language, that was at the heart of our resilience with our audience."

The Rising drew deeply on September 11 and its aftermath, though certain

Springsteen's tour to support *The Rising* mixed songs from that emotionally charged album with others throughout his career to explore themes of loss and despair, redemption and hope.

songs—such as "My City of Ruins," "Nothing Man," and "Waitin' on a Sunny Day"—had been in motion well before the attacks. The "genesis" song proved to be "Into the Fire," a song Springsteen wrote with an eye towards performing on the September 21 benefit telethon but didn't finish in time, so he instead performed "My City of Ruins," a song he had written earlier about the decline of Asbury Park. But "Into the Fire," with its "grittiness and sacrifice of the blues giving the gospel elements … their meaning," ultimately "unlocked the rest of the album" for Springsteen. "You're Missing" came shortly thereafter. Some of the songs dealt with the pain of loss; others reveled in the stoic joy—and necessity—of living.

"The songs I wrote sort of occur in that context" of September 11, Springsteen said to the Associated Press. "It's more of an emotional feeling that I felt—and that I felt was in the air at that time. (Some songs) deal more directly with it than others, but the stories all happen in a post–September 11 context. If you were writing at that point, it's in everything in some fashion." He told the *New York Times*, "You have to come to grips with the real horrors that are out there. And then all people have is hope. That's what brings the next day and whatever that day may bring. You can't be uncritical, but just a hope grounded in the real world of living, friendship, work, family, Saturday night. And that's where it resides. That's where I always found faith and spirit … I've really tried to write about that basic idea my whole life." There were some surprises within that framework. "Worlds Apart" utilized Pakistani Kawaii singers and exotic Eastern rhythms; one of the characters in the hushed "Paradise" is a suicide bomber preparing for attack. "I wanted other voices, other situations than just the American ones," Springsteen explained. "The eleventh was ultimately an international tragedy … I wanted to find a place where worlds collide and meet."

The Rising had great musical significance for Springsteen besides its central subject matter. It was his first new studio album and his first recordings with the E Street Band in seven years, and his first full-length effort with the group since *Born in the U.S.A.* in 1984. It also marked the first change in his production approach since 1975's *Born to Run*, as he handed the reins over to Atlanta-based Brendan O'Brien, who had made his name with modern rock bands such as Pearl Jam and Rage Against the Machine but had also worked with Bob Dylan. All of that, Springsteen told *Entertainment Weekly*, made *The Rising* "an important record to me. It's the first record in such a long time with the band, and I wanted to make it really good, a record that could stand shoulder to shoulder with all our others. The whole idea with the band was to get back together but move very consciously forward … The band's playing as good—as committed and intense—as at any time in its history, and making a record that carried on those values and ideals was very important."

Not trusting that radio would automatically spread the word, Springsteen launched an unprecedented promotional blitz to support *The Rising*, utilizing special prerelease listening parties, America Online, and

Filled with the emotions that resulted from the horrific events of September 11, 2001, *The Rising* album was hailed by critics and fans alike as one of Springsteen's best and most important albums. Here, Springsteen, Patti Scialfa, and Steve Van Zandt perform the album's title track at Giants Stadium on July 21, 2003.

particularly TV, staging a special release-day edition of NBC's "Today" live from the beach at Asbury Park and performing on "Late Night with David Letterman" (two nights in a row) and on "Saturday Night Live." It paid off with a No. 1 debut on the *Billboard* 200 chart and double-platinum sales. *The Rising* also won three Grammy Awards—Best Rock Album and, for the title track, Best Rock Song and Best Male Rock Vocal Performance—but surprisingly lost out to Norah Jones's debut album in the Album of the Year category.

A special, limited edition version of *The Rising* was also produced, looking like a small, cloth-bound book and containing a forty-page booklet with photos and handwritten lyrics. The first pressing sold out quickly, prompting Springsteen and Columbia Records to order a second printing in the fall of 2002. —*GG*

"The Rising"

Single release: July 16, 2002
Album: *The Rising* (Columbia, 2002)
Chart peak: No. 52

The title track of Bruce Springsteen's eighteenth album was, by his account written late in the project, as a kind of "bookend" to one of the album's first tracks, "Into the Fire." The songs dealt with similar themes stemming from the September 11, 2001, terrorist attacks on New York City; as Springsteen wrote in *Songs*: "Of the many tragic images of that day, the picture I couldn't let go of was of the emergency workers going up the stairs as others rushed down to safety. The sense of duty, the courage. Ascending into ... what?" The song is full of such images, as well as fire department jargon such as "sixty pound stone," referring to an oxygen tank and "half a mile of line," referring to the hose. He also worked in themes of "the religious image of ascension. The crossing of the line between this world, the world of blood, work, family, your children, earth, the breath in your lungs, the ground beneath your feet."

The anthemic track preceded the release of *The Rising* album and was met with heavy initial airplay, though it only wound its way to No. 52 on the *Billboard* Hot 100—and was, in fact, the only one of the album's singles to chart. It did win two Grammy Awards—Best Rock Song and Best Male Rock Vocal Performance. The single's B-side was the version of "Land of Hope and Dreams" that appeared on the *Live in New York City* album in 2001. —*GG*

The River

Released: October 17, 1980
Producers: Bruce Springsteen, Jon Landau, Steve Van Zandt
Tracks: Disc One—"The Ties That Bind," "Sherry Darling," "Jackson Cage," "Two Hearts," "Independence Day," "Hungry Heart," "Out in the Street," "Crush on You," "You Can Look (But You Better Not Touch)," "I Wanna Marry You," "The River"; Disc Two—"Point Blank," "Cadillac Ranch," "I'm a Rocker," "Fade Away," "Stolen Car," "Ramrod," "The Price You Pay," "Drive All Night," "Wreck on the Highway"
Key outtakes: "Roulette," "Loose Ends," "Take 'Em as They Come," "Cindy," "Restless Nights," "Where the Bands Are," "Mary Lou"; alternate versions of "The Ties That Bind," "You Can Look (But You Better Not Touch)," "Stolen Car"
Chart peak: No. 1

When Bruce Springsteen and the E Street Band entered New York's Power Station in early April 1979 to begin recording what would become *The River*, talk was of a quick project that would come out later that year. After taking nearly three years between *Born to Run*

and *Darkness on the Edge of Town*, Springsteen and company wanted to make up for lost time and start putting out music on a regular and frequent basis. Despite those intentions, however, *The River* became an epic undertaking, a year and a half in the making with some ninety songs considered and recording costs reported at $500,000. It was worth the effort, however, as the double-album became Springsteen's first No. 1 and yielded his first Top 10 hit in "Hungry Heart."

Springsteen has termed *The River* "both a reaction to and an extension of the ideas explored in *Darkness on the Edge of Town*." After the serious tone of that album, he mostly wanted his fifth release to tap into the exuberance of his live shows, capturing the more lighthearted spirit of fun while retaining the brooding introspection that marked his growth as a writer on *Darkness*. He wrote in *Songs*, "I wanted to give myself a lot more flexibility with the emotional range of the songs I chose. Our shows had always been filled with fun, and I didn't want to see that left out this time around."

Springsteen tour to support *The River*, his first album to top the charts, included New Year's Eve 1980 stop at Nassau Coliseum, where the set list topped out at an incredible thirty-eight songs.

Springsteen walked into the studio with some strong material already prepared. He had previewed "Point Blank," "The Ties That Bind," "Independence Day," "Sherry Darling," and "Ramrod" at shows on the *Darkness* tour. "Roulette," which wouldn't make the album, was written just after the March 1979 nuclear emergency at the Three Mile Island plant in Pennsylvania. With old friend, kindred spirit, and guitarist Steve Van Zandt a full-fledged member of the production team and the E Street Band in fit form after the *Darkness* tour—and from nonstudio nights jamming at the Fast Lane club in Asbury Park—the optimism for a quick album wasn't misplaced. "*The River* was the first record where I felt we were comfortable enough to start capturing what the band was all about," recalled Van Zandt, adding that the producers deployed "extensive room mics ... to capture the sound of the band live." Springsteen concurred; as he wrote in *Songs*, "If anything, I wanted to create songs that would sound good played by a bar band. To me, that was basically what we remained ... On *The River* I was determined to let the band play live and let the music happen."

"**S**cope, context, sequencing, and mood are everything here. Bruce Springsteen didn't title his summational record *The River* for nothing ... When the surface looks smooth, watch out for dangerous undercurrents. You may believe you're splashing about in a shallow stream and suddenly find yourself in over your head."

—*Rolling Stone*

" ... the condensed songcraft makes this double album a model of condensation—upbeat enough for the radio here, delicate enough for a revery there, he elaborates a myth about the fate of the guys he grew up with that hits a lot of people where they live."

—*Village Voice*

"**T**he River is ... Bruce Springsteen's best album ... It sums up seven years of work, and it does not shy away from the errors of his career thus far, nor does it disown them. He remains a romantic and bit of a juvenile after all this, for who but a romantic juvenile could conceive of a purposeless car thief as a genuine figure of tragedy? But he is also capable now of tying together his hopes and fears—the most joyous songs are awash with brutal undercurrents."

—*Musician*

"**U**nable or unwilling to cast off the cliches of his past records, *The River*'s attempt to Make a Statement is buried in an avalanche of repetition and evident lack of inspiration."

—*Trouser Press*

" ... there are a few tracks, most notably 'Hungry Heart,' which at least reveal that Bruce can sing in a voice that suits his tunes."

—*Audio*

He would come up with songs during the day and introduce them in the studio that night, in sessions that often dragged into the wee hours. "I saw the sun come up almost every day," drummer Max Weinberg told *Billboard*. But he added, "It was the first record where we really started to play as a band, all live in the studio, all of us playing simultaneously."

Work on the album continued at a steady clip despite some delays—including a three-week break in mid-April to allow Springsteen to recuperate from a leg injury sustained when he crashed a three-wheeler into a tree. The band also took a West Coast sojourn to attend and play at the wedding reception for lighting designer Marc Brickman, and it played two nights of the Musicians United for Safe Energy (MUSE) No Nukes shows in September at Madison Square Garden. In October, Springsteen delivered a single-disc album to Columbia called *The Ties That Bind*, with a track lineup that included "The Ties That Bind," "Cindy," "Hungry Heart," "Stolen Car," "To Be True," "The River," "You Can Look (But You Better Not Touch)," "The Price You Pay," "I Wanna Marry You," and "Loose Ends." Cover mockups were reportedly created, with images by *Darkness* photographer Frank Stefanko. Columbia planned a pre-Christmas release—and then Springsteen pulled the plug. "I felt that it just wasn't good enough," he wrote in *Songs.* "The songs lacked the kind of unity and conceptual intensity I liked my music to have." He told the *Los Angeles Times* that *The Ties That Bind* simply "wasn't personal enough."

Recording continued into 1980; the Clash even had to relocate to Electric Ladyland studios because Springsteen continued to occupy the Power Station. "Many songs were cut, and many were judged not up to par," Springsteen recalled, acknowledging that his "less meticulous, more instinctive" songwriting approach was yielding a lot of material, but not necessarily a lot of material he wanted to put out. But he did have twenty-five songs to mix when he, Van Zandt, and Jon Landau flew to Los Angeles in early May to work with Chuck Plotkin; it was then that they hatched the idea of making *The River* a double album, allowing Springsteen the opportunity for an even greater emotional range and a poignant contrast of moods and feels, from the buoyancy of "Cadillac Ranch," "Ramrod," "I'm a Rocker," and "Out in the Street" to the dark hues of "Independence Day," "Fade Away," "The Price You Pay," and "Wreck on the Highway." "The River" itself, Springsteen acknowledged, drew heavily on the life of his sister Ginny and the economic hardships her family experienced after her husband lost his job in the late '70s. "I finally got to a the place where I realized life had paradoxes, a lot of them, and you've got to learn to live with them," Springsteen told the *Los Angeles Times*. He expanded in *Mojo*, explaining, "By the time we got to *The River* adulthood was imminent, if it hadn't arrived already, so I knew I was gonna be following my characters over a long period of time. I thought it would be interesting and fun for my audience to have a certain sort of ... loose continuity from record to record."

Ultimately, Springsteen wouldn't finish *The River* until September, doing some more recording in the summer and tinkering with the song list right up to zero hour; "Held Up Without a Gun," later to appear as the B-side to "Hungry Heart," was withdrawn so late that elements of the package had to be reprinted. Meanwhile, Landau and Columbia were busy issuing cease-and-desist orders to radio stations who were airing the live version of *The River*'s title track taken from the *No Nukes* film. And while the album did become his first chart-topper, Springsteen maintained that was not the measure of its success. "Doing it is the goal," he told *Musician* magazine. "It's not to play some big place, or for a record to be Number One. Doing it is the end, not the means; ... bigness—that is no end." —*GG*

Tim Robbins. *See Dead Man Walking.*

"Rock and Roll Future"

Proclamation by Jon Landau, 1974

 saw rock and roll future and its name is Bruce Springsteen." When, in 1974, marketers at Columbia Records got a load of that line, written by a prominent rock critic, the proverbial dollar signs flashed in their eyes. "I guess somebody at the ad department said, 'This is it!'" Springsteen once explained, "and it went out. I guess that's their job."

Before it was removed from its original context and plastered on promotional material, before it became the bane of Springsteen's existence as a tag no one could live up to, it was part of a lengthy, introspective column by Jon Landau in the *Real Paper* titled, "Growing Young with Rock and Roll." Landau would go on to become Springsteen's manager, coproducer, and close friend; at the time of the column, published on May 22, 1974, he was still a year away from entering a studio with Springsteen and had only met him a month before. In the spring of 1974, Springsteen was more "past" than "future" in the view of his label. With two records that had sold below expectations despite regional fanaticism, he was, by several accounts, in danger of being dropped. Landau was reviews editor at *Rolling Stone* and had a column called "Loose Ends" in the *Real Paper*, a Boston alternative weekly. The two met for the first time on April 10 outside Charley's in Cambridge, Massachusetts, where Springsteen was to play that night. He happened to be reading Landau's review of *The Wild, the Innocent & the E Street Shuffle*, which was posted in the club's window; the author approached Springsteen and said, by way of introduction, "I wrote that." Though Landau saw the show that night, it was Springsteen's return to Cambridge a month later—the May 9 show at the Harvard Square Theatre, opening for Bonnie Raitt—that actually inspired the soon-to-be famous line. Landau later talked to MTV about seeing the live show: "I just knew Bruce from the [first two] records—you wouldn't call them rock records in tone. I didn't quite know what to expect. The show—and there were maybe twenty people there—was so phenomenal, and it was so vibrant, it was so energetic, and it was such a rock show, is what it was. And so this was such a revelation, because it hadn't really come across from those initial records."

Inspired by that revelation, the May 22, 1974, "Growing Young with Rock and Roll" piece was a lengthy confessional, detailing both Landau's "all-encompassing obsession" with rock 'n' roll music, and the inevitable and disheartening "detachment" that came with writing about it professionally. "There are months when I hate it," Landau wrote, "going through the routine just as a shoe salesman goes through his." After describing at length the flow and inevitable ebb of his musical passions, he came to what inspired this four-in-the-morning rumination: "But tonight there is someone I can write of the way I used to write, without reservations of any kind. Last Thursday, at the Harvard Square Theatre, I saw my rock and roll past flash before my eyes. And I saw something else: I saw rock and roll future and its name is Bruce Springsteen. And on a night when I needed to feel young, he made me feel like I was hearing music for the very first time."

That this dark-hour-of-the-soul epiphany would be quickly transformed into what Springsteen soon called "one of the stupidest campaigns of all time" and "a kiss of death" didn't prevent him from seeing the writer's intent. Springsteen told WNEW in 1976, "It was an article that meant a lot to me, because if you read the article, what was made of it was not what it was."

Landau's column has since become as legendary as a brief piece of music journalism can get; Kurt Loder described it as possibly "the single most famous review in rock history." Thirty years later, Nick Hornby would write a piece for the *New York Times* largely inspired by "Growing Young with Rock and Roll," describing the original as "influential, exciting, career-changing, and subsequently much derided and parodied." Springsteen himself was often the one making jokes, trying to deflate the hype if nothing else; he laughed about the quote in interviews even as he admitted it "dogged" him for years.

In 1999, freshly inducted into the Rock and Roll Hall of Fame, Springsteen thanked his longtime manager with a flip of the infamous phrase: "I've seen the future of rock and roll management, and its name is Jon Landau." He laughed and continued, "That quote was managing. It was a mite burdensome for me, but as he often said, 'That's your job.'" —*CP*

Rock and Roll Hall of Fame Induction Ceremony

Site of Springsteen appearances as inductee, inductor, jam-session participant

Bruce Springsteen was inducted into the Rock and Roll Hall of Fame on March 15, 1999, in his first year of eligibility, during ceremonies at the Waldorf-Astoria Hotel in New York City. Because his first album, *Greetings from Asbury Park, N.J.*, was billed to Springsteen alone, the E Street Band was not inducted with him, which angered many fans. The other performers inducted in the class of '99 were Billy Joel, Curtis Mayfield, Paul McCartney, Del Shannon, Dusty Springfield, and the Staples Singers. Charles Brown and Bob Wills & His Texas Playboys were honored as early influences. Beatles producer Sir George Martin was inducted as a nonperformer. U2 lead singer Bono inducted Springsteen, declaring, "More than The Boss, he's the owner. He owns America's heart." After a warm speech during which he dedicated the trophy to his mother, Adele, and called the E Street Band onto the dais, Springsteen and company teamed up for a celebratory set that included "Tenth Avenue Freeze-Out," "Darkness on the Edge of Town," and "The Promised Land." Later that night, Springsteen also joined 1991 inductee Wilson Pickett for a raucous version of "In the Midnight Hour" before adjourning to an upstairs suite to party with McCartney, Joel, and others.

A smiling Springsteen expresses his honor and gratitude after being inducted into the Rock and Roll Hall of Fame and Museum in 1999.

Springsteen has been a presenter four times at Hall of Fame induction ceremonies, ushering in Roy Orbison in 1987, Bob Dylan in 1988, Creedence Clearwater Revival in 1993, and Jackson Browne in 2004. "In 1970, I rode for fifteen hours in the back of a U-Haul truck to open for Roy Orbison at the Nashville Music Festival," Springsteen recalled in his January 21, 1987, speech for Orbison. "It was a summer night and I was twenty years old and he came out in dark glasses, a dark suit, and he played some dark music. When I went into the studio to make *Born to Run*, most of all I wanted to sing like Roy Orbison." Springsteen capped that evening as part of an all-star jam session, singing lead on Orbison's "Oh Pretty Woman" and Ben E. King's "Stand By Me."

His Dylan speech on January 20, 1988, was even more memorable. Like many successful singer-songwriters of the 1970s, Springsteen had been declared a "new Dylan" early in his career. He didn't seem to mind on this night, however. With fellow inductees like the Beatles and the Beach Boys in the audience, Springsteen said, "Without Bob, the Beatles wouldn't have made *Sgt. Pepper*, the Beach Boys wouldn't have made *Pet Sounds*. The Sex Pistols wouldn't have made "God Save the Queen," U2 wouldn't have made "Pride (In the Name of Love)," Marvin Gaye wouldn't have done "What's Goin' On," the Count Five would not have done "Psychotic Reaction," and Grandmaster Flash might not have done "The Message." And there would never have been a group named the Electric Prunes. To this day, whenever great rock music is being made, there is the shadow of Bob Dylan." Springsteen—along with E Street Band members Roy Bittan, Danny Federici, Garry Tallent, Max Weinberg, and Patti Scialfa—finished the night on stage with George Harrison, Ringo Starr, Mick Jagger, Elton John, the Beach Boys, and others on a jam-session medley that included "Twist and Shout," "I Saw Her Standing There," "(I Can't Get No) Satisfaction," and Creedence Clearwater Revival's "Born on the Bayou."

The latter was a good warm-up for Springsteen's next inducting gig, for CCR on January 12, 1993, in Los Angeles. Springsteen—who joined forces with CCR frontman John Fogerty to perform "Long Tall Sally" at the 1990 induction ceremony in New York—saluted the band in his speech, noting, "They played no-frills American music for the people. In the late '60s and early '70s, they weren't the hippest band in the world—just the best." But Springsteen subsequently angered bassist Stu Cook, drummer Doug Clifford, and the family of late guitarist Tom Fogerty by playing as part of an ad hoc group organized by John Fogerty—with whom they were at odds both legally and personally. Cook said that Springsteen later apologized for the slight.

In 2004, five years after his own induction in 1999, Springsteen stepped to the podium to usher Jackson Browne into the Hall. He joked, "Jackson drew an enormous amount of good-looking women. Great lookin' women who stood there starting at the stage, entranced. I also noticed that while the E Street Band and I were sweatin' our asses off for four hours to put some fannies in the seats, that obviously due to what must have been some strong homoerotic undercurrent in our music, we were drawing rooms filled with men—not that great lookin' men either! Meanwhile, Jackson is drawing more women than an Indigo Girls show!" Springsteen elected not to perform that night, however.

Springsteen became the first Hall of Fame member to induct an act that had inducted him, taking the stage at the 2005 ceremony with a speech for U2 that was as moving as it was humorous. "In their music, you hear the spirituality as home and as quest," Springsteen noted. "How do you find God unless he's in your heart, in your desire, in your feet? I believe this is a big part of what's kept their band together all of these years. See, bands get formed by accident, but they don't survive by accident. It takes will, intent, a sense of shared purpose and a tolerance for your friends' fallibilities and they of yours. And that only evens the odds. U2 has not only evened the odds but they've beaten them by continuing to do their finest work and remaining at the top of their game and the charts for twenty-five years. I feel a great affinity for these guys as people as well as musicians." He later joined the band on stage to trade vocals with Bono on "I Still Haven't Found What I'm Looking For."

Springsteen has also attended the Hall of Fame ceremony when he wasn't inducting anybody and has often wound up on stage those nights, too, performing tributes to the late Roy Orbison in 1989 and the injured Curtis Mayfield in 1991. An unscheduled performance of John Lennon's "Come Together" with Guns N' Roses frontman Axl Rose at the 1995 ceremony in New York celebrated the ex-Beatle's induction as a solo artist. The song was supposed to have been sung by Rod Stewart and Elton John, but Stewart didn't make the induction because of an earthquake in Los Angeles shortly before the ceremony. Hall of Fame officials scrambled to find a replacement, finally convincing Rose who, in turn, invited Springsteen. The two rehearsed the song at their table in hotel's Grand Ballroom before performing it on stage. —*MN/GG*

Everyone wants to be a rock star, including Stephen King (left) and Scott Turow, performing at a 2000 charity fund-raising event. The best-selling authors are part of a loose collective of writers who form the Rock Bottom Remainders. During the band's show at the 1994 American Booksellers Association convention, Springsteen made a surprise guest appearance when he strapped on a guitar and joined in on a rousing rendition of the rock standard "Gloria."

The Rock Bottom Remainders

Authors' pick-up band

The Rock Bottom Remainders, the most literary band of pseudo-musicians on the planet, are a bunch of famous authors and journalists who get on stage and take pride in wrecking classic rock songs. Formed in 1992, the collective actually released an album and still tours for one week each year. One of those tours became the subject of a book by Bruce Springsteen biographer and Remainder member Dave Marsh. Most of the group's appearances, however, take place at the annual American Booksellers Association convention.

The band's performances normally include the likes of Stephen King, Amy Tan, Roy Blount, Jr., Scott Turow, and *The Simpsons* creator Matt Groening. But during their 1994 convention gig, Springsteen—who had never writ-ten a book—strapped on a guitar to join the group, which wasn't checking his credentials. As Remainder Dave Barry described in a subsequent column: "Just as we were about to start, Stephen King tapped me on the shoulder and said, 'We have a special guest.' I turned around, and there was Bruce Springsteen. I still don't know how he came to be at this convention; I don't believe he's a bookseller. All I know is, he was picking up the other guitar. 'Bruce,' I said to him, 'Do you know the guitar part to "Gloria"?' 'I think so,' he said." The Remainders' website now contains the following Springsteen quote: "Your band's not too bad. It's not too good either. Don't let it get any better otherwise you'll just be another lousy band."

The Remainders, sans Springsteen, were also the featured act at 1995's opening-weekend, $1,000-a-ticket gala for the Rock and Roll Hall of Fame and Museum in Cleveland. They were joined for part of the performance by Springsteen sideman Nils Lofgren, who performed with Springsteen the fol-lowing night at the Rock and Roll Hall of Fame's opening concert.

In October 2004, the group, with special guest Roger McGuinn, hit the road on a four-city "WannaPalooza" tour, with proceeds benefiting America Scores, an organization that develops programs that use soccer to energize and inspire public school students nationwide in their lessons. "We are going to rock the nation's Heartland so hard that there could be bruising as far away as the nation's Spleenland, and possibly even the nation's Kidney-land," said Dave Barry, lead guitar. —*LM*

Angel Rogers. *See* 1992–93 Bruce Springsteen Touring Band.

The Rogues

Springsteen's first band

Though most Bruce Springsteen biographers point to the Castiles as his first band, he actually spent nearly a year in the Rogues as a young teen growing up in the mid-'60s in Freehold, New Jersey. Little is known about the Rogues other than Springsteen joined the group in his freshman year at Freehold Regional High School. At the time he was merely a novice guitarist with little or no indication of the rock 'n' roll acumen he'd demonstrate a few years later in bands such as Child and Steel Mill.

The Rogues performed a few times, mostly at local teen dances. But with many bands sprouting up all across the Jersey Shore, inspired in large measure by the arrival of the Beatles in 1964 and the resulting British Inva-sion, the Rogues attracted little attention beyond Freehold. After Spring-steen's departure in 1965 to join the Castiles, the Rogues continued as a band, though it never matched the popularity enjoyed by their guitarist's new band. In 1966, the two groups performed in a local battle of the bands, though neither won. Within the next two years, the Rogues faded from the Jersey music scene. —*RS*

"Rosalita (Come Out Tonight)"

Released: November 5, 1973
Album: *The Wild, the Innocent & the E Street Shuffle* (Columbia, 1973)
Also on: *Live/1975–85* (Columbia, 1986), *The Essential Bruce Spring-steen* (Columbia, 2003)
Chart peak: Album track only; never released as a single

"Rosalita" is arguably Bruce Springsteen's most important song that wasn't a single—at least in terms of mass aware-ness. Rowdy and robust, it was one of his first songs to receive significant airplay prior to "Born to Run." And a 1978 video filmed at a concert in Phoenix, Arizona, gave the world a taste of the energy and onstage interplay that made his concerts so special. In *Songs*, Springsteen described "Rosalita"—which surfaced in writing sessions for *The Wild, the Innocent & the E Steet Shuffle*—as "my musical biography ... I wrote it as a kiss-off to everybody who counted you out, put you down or decided you weren't good enough." The song soon took a vaunted place in the E Street Band set, spending the better part of 1973–84 as the main-set closer, lengthened by instrumental vamps and band introductions. "Rosalita" stopped being a playlist automatic during the second half of the *Born in the U.S.A.* tour, though it resurfaced for 1988's Tunnel of Love Express Tour and in the latter stages of *The Rising* tour in 2003. —*GG*

Rumson Country Day School Benefits

Private fundraising concerts

Some private school parents give money—lots of it. Bruce Springsteen chose to give music—and lots of it—in order to raise money. At a black-tie fundraiser for the Rumson Country Day School (RCDS) in February 2002, Springsteen announced a special contribution for the organiza-tion; a pair of $1,000-per-couple concerts at the Stone Pony in Asbury Park. The April 13 show would benefit the RCDS lower school, while the next night's performance would benefit the upper school; the shows were open only to RCDS parents and staff, and teachers were admitted without charge. Many non-RCDS-affiliated Springsteen fans gathered outside the club to listen.

The RCDS benefits became an annual tradition, with shows taking place each April in 2003, 2004, and 2005 at the Stone Pony. Asbury Jukes guitarist Bobby Bandiera provided the house band to back Springsteen and Scialfa; Southside Johnny Lyon appeared all three years, while E Street Band drummer Max Weinberg performed on the second night of the 2002 shows and Jon Bon Jovi showed up in 2003. The same admission restrictions have applied every year.

The performances themselves were special because they were dominated by rock and soul covers—Moon Mulligan's "Seven Nights to Rock," Bob Seger's "Ramblin' Gamblin' Man" and "Get Out of Denver," Aretha Franklin's "Respect," Van Morrison's "Domino," Sam & Dave's "Soul Man," the Exciters' "Tell Him," Smokey Robinson & the Miracles' "You Really Got a Hold on Me," the Beatles' "Tell Me Why," the Isley Brothers' "Twist and Shout," "The Detroit Medley," "Son of a Preacher Man," and many more. Springsteen played a few of his own songs at each benefit, too; "Darlington County" made the setlist all four years, while he and Scialfa performed an acoustic version of "Thunder Road" in 2002.

The benefits were not the first time Springsteen used his music to help raise money for the school. In 1999 he donated a guitar to RCDS's annual auction, along with a thirty-minute lesson. The package fetched a winning bid of $27,000. *—GG*

Rumson, New Jersey

Springsteen's place of residence

One of the Jersey Shore's most affluent communities, Rumson is the home of Bruce Springsteen and Jon Bon Jovi. The town boasts multimillion dollar homes, large and immaculately kept estates, and white-fenced horse farms. The nearby Navesink and Shrewsbury Rivers give Rumson added charm. While most of Monmouth County has succumbed to large-scale development and tourism, Rumson has retained its patrician character despite the fact that Asbury Park and Long Branch, the north Jersey Shore's most depressed communities, are only minutes away. Rumson was originally part of Shrewsbury Township; it became a Monmouth County borough in 1907. During the early twentieth century, wealthy families from northern New Jersey and New York built large summer homes in Rumson. While neighboring communities created swim clubs and touted their ocean beaches, Rumson's summer residents were more apt to sail in the local rivers and to ride horses through the town's rolling fields and polo grounds. Today, little has changed.

Springsteen made Rumson his permanent residence in the mid-'90s after he returned to New Jersey from his short-lived move to California. (Springsteen still keeps a house in Beverly Hills.) In Rumson, Springsteen could enjoy the financial fruits of his music yet be close enough to his Asbury Park roots and to late night jams at the Stone Pony whenever the urge touched him. Springsteen also owns a large farm in Colts Neck Township in western Monmouth County, offering him and his family a more rural retreat than his relatively modest (at least by his neighbors' standards) Rumson home—and a place for daughter Jessica to practice her equestrian skills. —*RS*

Mitch Ryder

Rock singer, 1965–present; inspiration for the "Detroit Medley"

 itch Ryder's pioneering rock career of the mid-'60s had been consigned to the oldies circuit by the late '70s, when Bruce Springsteen turned several of Ryder's hits into the popular "Detroit Medley" encore. But Springsteen's nod to the rock pioneer and one of his stylistic mentors raised Ryder's profile to a new high point, especially when the "Detroit Medley" was committed to record in 1980.

Ryder's music was no stranger to Springsteen's performances before "Detroit Medley"; Springsteen had frequently covered the 1966 hit "Little Latin Lupe Lu" in his concerts. But the "Detroit Medley" was the true Ryder spotlight, splicing together the Ryder hit combination of "Devil With a Blue Dress On" and Little Richard's "Good Golly Miss Molly" with another Ryder pairing of Richard's "Jenny Jenny" and Chuck Willis's "C.C. Rider" (aka "Jenny Take a Ride!"). The medley first surfaced on September 16, 1978, at the Palladium in New York City during the *Darkness on the Edge of Town* tour and was a staple for some time after, occasionally adding other songs or vamps onto the end. The most famous performance of the "Detroit Medley" was at the 1979 No Nukes concerts in New York; the number was included on the subsequent album souvenir of the event (listed as "Devil With a Blue Dress Medley") and received heavy airplay from radio stations happy to finally have some authorized Springsteen live material to put on the air.

It was certainly a boon to Ryder—who joined Springsteen for a performance of the medley on August 12, 1981, at Joe Louis Arena in Detroit. Born William Levise, Jr., in the metro Detroit area, Ryder emerged in 1965 with the Detroit Wheels and began cranking out a string of hits in 1966, supporting them with ferocious performances that often ended in staged fistfights. Ryder's career arc dipped in 1967, however, when manager Bob Crewe broke up the Wheels and tried to establish Ryder as a solo act, with little success. In 1973 Ryder even left music and moved to Denver, though he came back in the late '70s, just as "Detroit Medley" was rekindling his reputation. Another

Veteran rocker and Motown native Mitch Ryder, right, joins Springsteen and the band for the "Detroit Medley" encore during a performance at Detroit's Joe Louis Arena on August 12, 1981.

fan, John Cougar Mellencamp, produced a new major label album for Ryder, 1983's "Never Kick a Sleeping Dog," and he's maintained a career ever since, with a particularly strong following in Germany. —*GG*

St. Rose of Lima

Parish and parochial school in Freehold, New Jersey

Bruce Springsteen offered a lighthearted observation about his time at St. Rose of Lima parochial school in Freehold, New Jersey, when he played a benefit concert for the Hispanic community there on November 8, 1996. Debuting "In Freehold," a song he wrote espe-cially for the occasion, Springsteen sang: "Well I got a good Catholic educa-tion here in Freehold/Led to an awful lot of masturbation here in Freehold/Now Father it was just something I did for a smile ...." His actual memories were not quite that warm or comical, however.

Springsteen spent his first eight school years at St. Rose of Lima, on the corner of South and Lincoln streets, not far from the Springsteen family home at South and Institute streets. Shy and rebellious, he was not exactly a model stu-dent for the strict nuns—and was treated accordingly. He's told stories about one of the nuns stuffing him in a trash can under her desk in third grade "because, she said, that's where I belonged." A couple of years later he was sent to a first grade class for misbehaving, where he received a literal slap in the face from one of the younger students, on orders from another nun. He also told biographer Dave Marsh that, while serving as a neophyte altar boy, he was knocked down by one of the priests at mass because he didn't know the proper rituals. Not surpris-ingly, he was happy to leave in 1963 for the public Freehold Regional High School.

The time at St. Rose certainly made an impact on Springsteen's music, however. Religious references and images run throughout his song catalog; in his 1988 essay, "The Catholic Imagination of Bruce Springsteen," Father Andrew M. Greeley calls him "a Catholic minstrel" and writes that "his work is profoundly Catholic ... because his creative imagination is permeated by Catholic symbolism he absorbed, almost necessarily, from the Sacraments." That was evident even at Springsteen's 1972 audition with Columbia Records' John Hammond, when he played the still unreleased "If I Was the Priest," ripe with angry, anti-religion fervor. His body of work is peppered with nods to God, Jesus, prayer, ritual, holy grace, and redemption and figures such as the pope ("Local Hero"), Moses ("Leap of Faith"), and the Virgin Mary ("The Rising"). In his highly complimentary essay, Greeley lamented that "the failure of the church to understand Springsteen's importance and to embrace him ... shows how profound is the alienation of the church from the fine and lively arts ...."

Springsteen, however, re-embraced the church and apparently forgave his childhood torment twenty-three years later, when he played a special show at the St. Rose gymnasium as part of his tour supporting *The Ghost of Tom Joad*. The acoustic concert—featuring his wife, Patti Scialfa, and future E Street Band associate Soozie Tyrell as guests—was announced just five days in advance, and tickets were sold only to residents of Freehold Borough; $150 tickets were also sold for a pre-show fundraising cocktail party at which Springsteen appeared. Several songs—including "The River," "Two Hearts," "Open All Night," "Growin' Up," "When You're Alone," "Racing in the Street," and, of course, "In Freehold"—were performed for the first time on the tour. Springsteen peppered the show with remembrances, noting, "When I told my friend Steve I was playing my old Catholic school ... Steve said 'Revenge, huh?' I said 'No ... well, maybe just a little.'" He called it "a night of sin and redemption; I'll handle the sin, and Father McCarron's gonna handle the redemption." He later apologized to McCarron for swearing in his introduction to "Straight Time," but the religious specter did not prevent him from singing the oral-sex reference in "Red Headed Woman." Springsteen also paid tribute to his first manager, the late Tex Vinyard, and he dedicated "The Ghost of Tom Joad" to one of his former teachers, Sister Charles Marie, who he described as "very lovely, very compassionate."

Springsteen told the *Asbury Park Press* that he had wanted to do a Freehold show for awhile and felt the time was appropriate because issues dealing with the town's Hispanic community were echoed in some of the *Tom Joad* songs. Springsteen said, "We just had an election where people used issues like immigration divisively. But inclusiveness, that's where this country got its power and its beauty, with its mix of cultures. You could come here, you could find acceptance, promise, possibility. That's what my music is about." —*GG*

David Sancious (left) has enjoyed a prolific post–E Street career, releasing solo albums and serving as an accomplished sideman to artists including Sting (right).

David Sancious

Musician, songwriter, early E Street Band member

An early architect of the E Street Band sound, David Sancious was a New Jersey organist who escaped before the big money rolled in. He never complained about it, though, releasing solo albums of funk, jazz, and classical piano and hooking up as a sideman with Sting, Peter Gabriel, Eric Clapton, and many others. Born in 1953 in Long Branch, New Jersey, Sancious studied classical piano as a kid and started playing in Asbury Park bands around 1965. In the early '70s, he was at an Asbury Park bar with a guitarist friend when Springsteen invited the friend on stage to jam; the friend introduced Sancious to Springsteen, and the pianist soon became an anchor of Springsteen's Dr. Zoom and the Sonic Boom. That wild, unfocused outfit slowly morphed into the E Street Band as we know it, and after a few stabs at a solo career, Sancious stayed on.

Off of E Street ...
David Sancious

Jon Anderson, "Animation" (1983)
Patti Austin, "Patti Austin" (1984)
Jack Bruce, "I've Always Wanted to Do This"
(1980)
Eric Clapton, "One More Car: One More Rider"
(2002)
Stanley Clarke, "Journey to Love" (1975),
"School Days" (1975), "Live (1976–1977),"
"Hideaway" (1986)
Clarence Clemons & the Red Bank Rockers,
"Hero" (1985)
Marshall Crenshaw, "#447" (1999)
Bryan Ferry, "Taxi" (1993)
Aretha Franklin, "Aretha" (1980)
Peter Gabriel, "Passion" (1989), "Us" (1992),
"Up" (2002)
Hall & Oates, "Do it For Love" (2003)
Angelique Kidjo, "Oremi" (1998)
Patti LaBelle, "Be Yourself" (1989)
Living Colour, "Collideoscope" (2003)
Youssou N'Dour, "Lion" (1989)
Santana, "Beyond Appearances" (1985)
Seal, "Human Being" (1998)
Billy Squier, "Tale of the Tape" (1980)
Sting, "Soul Cages" (1991), "Ten Summoner's
Tales" (1993)

Sancious performed on *Greetings from Asbury Park, N.J.* and *The Wild, the Innocent & the E Street Shuffle*, and his elaborate piano frills remain some of the albums' most distinctive bits. (Check out the opening to "Growin' Up" and the jazz-classical run that links "Incident on 57th Street" to "Rosalita.") But Sancious had solo ambitions and, with the help of Springsteen's Columbia Records connections, he released albums such as *Forest of Feelings*, *Transformation and Tone*, and *Dance of the Age of Enlightenment*. During the *Born to Run* sessions, he left Springsteen on amicable terms and Roy Bittan replaced him; one of Sancious's final sessions, in fact, was the August 1974 recording of that album's title track.

Sancious's albums never sold particularly well, however, so he supplemented his solo work by recording and touring with other artists. While in Peter Gabriel's band on the 1988 Amnesty International Human Rights Now! tour, Sancious occasionally joined Springsteen and the E Streeters on stage. He also collaborated with Springsteen in 1992, adding organ to the song "Soul Driver" from the *Human Touch.* album. —*SK*

"Santa Claus Is Comin' to Town"

Released: 1975 (radio); 1981 (commercial)
Appears on: *In Harmony 2* (1981), "My Hometown" B-side (1985), *Christmas of Hope* (1995), *Now That's What I Call Christmas* (2001)

jovial version of the holiday classic built from Phil Spector's 1963 arrangement, "Santa Claus Is Comin' to Town" was a regular holiday feature in Springsteen's shows before this version was recorded during a college show on the *Born to Run* tour. The recording was quickly released to radio stations as a promotional-only track and became a staple during the holiday season. It also became a popular bootleg item as Springsteen fans clamored for its release. A live version recorded at C.W. Post College in New York in December 1975 finally saw a commercial release in

1981, when it was included on the children's album *In Harmony 2*. It was also included on a twelve-inch promotional disc in 1984 for "Born in the U.S.A.," and the following year it popped up as a B-side on the "My Hometown" 45. Springsteen continues to perform the song, when seasonally appropriate, at his concerts. —*GG*

Robert Santelli

Historian, musicologist, author

Robert Santelli had the good fortune to grow up in the right place at the right time. A native of Point Pleasant Beach, New Jersey, about five miles south of Asbury Park, he witnessed the evolution of Bruce Springsteen and other area musicians who became part of the E Street Band, and he still counts some of them—particularly Max Weinberg, Steve Van Zandt, and Garry Tallent—as close friends. But Santelli occupies a significant niche in the music community for other reasons; a respected author and educator, he is the director of public programs at the Experience Music Project in Seattle, where he also served as director and chief executive officer. Prior to that he was vice president of educational programs at Cleveland's Rock and Roll Hall of Fame and Museum.

When Springsteen was preparing to write *Songs*, his 1998 coffee table book of lyrics and insights into his creative process, he chose Santelli as his collaborator, sculpting the book via lengthy discussions at Springsteen's house nearly every weekend for a year. Santelli also coauthored Max Weinberg's 1984 book *The Big Beat: Conversations with Rock's Greatest Drummers*.

Santelli heard Springsteen for the first time in 1968, playing solo at a coffee house in Red Bank, New Jersey. Springsteen also performed at Santelli's 1969 freshman orientation at Monmouth College (now University). Santelli is among a handful of people who have seen every Springsteen performing incarnation, with two early exceptions—the Rogues, which he describes as "like an eighth-grade/freshman band," and the Castiles. The first time the two spoke, "on a quasi-professional basis," was when Santelli was a budding journalist working on a story about the Bruce Springsteen Band for the college newspaper. Santelli, also an aspiring rock guitarist, was a fan, calling that particular group "the second greatest band to come out of New Jersey, with the E Street Band being first."

In 1973, just after *The Wild, the Innocent & the E Street Shuffle* was released, Santelli started freelancing as a rock critic for the *Asbury Park Press*, the local daily, and the alternative *Aquarian Weekly*. (He went on to write for *Rolling Stone*, *Playboy*, the *New York Times*, *Downbeat*, *Billboard*, and many other publications, and has published travel guides to the Jersey

Shore.) Santelli surfed with Springsteen and original E Street Band drummer Vini Lopez, and he played touch football on the same Jersey Shore team as Steve Van Zandt. While singing backup in the Asbury Jukes, Patti Scialfa babysat one of Santelli's children. He also played for a year on the E Street Kings softball team. Nevertheless, Santelli said Springsteen was very aware he was a journalist and therefore kept a certain distance.

His passion for Springsteen did help to shape Santelli's career as an educator. After giving a lecture at Monmouth about Springsteen, Santelli—who earned a master's degree in American studies from the University of Southern California and is working on a doctorate from New York University (where his dissertation is on Springsteen)—was asked to teach a course about rock 'n' roll history. He wound up creating the popular music studies program at Monmouth and went on to teach courses in music and New Jersey history at Rutgers University, where E Street Band members periodically delivered guest lectures.

According to Santelli, Springsteen did two "critical" favors for him over the years. In 1987, Springsteen agreed to play at the second Jersey Shore Jazz and Blues Festival and Foundation show organized by Santelli and some local musicians and club owners; he delivered what Santelli calls one of the most amazing blues sets he's ever heard Springsteen play, and possibly the only complete set of blues Springsteen has ever done. His appearance helped to raise enough money to keep the foundation going to this day. The second favor was also a performance, at a 1996 Rock and Roll Hall of Fame and Museum–sponsored conference and celebration of Woody Guthrie's career. Springsteen performed at the tribute concert and appears on 'Til We Outnumber 'Em, an album culled from the show. Springsteen also contributed footage for American Roots Music, a public television documentary Santelli worked on.

Santelli, who has authored several books about blues music, was instrumental in persuading the U.S. Congress to declare 2003 as the Year of the Blues and helped conceive and execute a massive multimedia project to chronicle the genre. The married father of three also was instrumental in organizing the nonprofit Music Museum Alliance, a coalition of musicologists at sixty-four institutions. —LM

"Saturday Night Live"

Long-lived late-night comedy and music show on NBC

Though Bruce Springsteen performance footage had aired periodically on television in the '70s and '80s, it took him twenty years into his recording career to make a live televised performance. On May

9, 1992, Springsteen was the musical guest on NBC's "Saturday Night Live," promoting *Human Touch* and *Lucky Town*, his first releases since dismissing the E Street Band in 1989. The "SNL" team certainly realized the significance of the occasion, allowing Springsteen to play three songs—"Lucky Town," "57 Channels (And Nothin' On)," and "Living Proof"—rather than the two normally given to most performers on the show. Springsteen, who snuck in a surprise performance at the Bottom Line in New York City to warm up for the "SNL" broadcast, told *Rolling Stone* magazine that the live TV experience "was intense. You rehearse ... but when we actually did it, it was like 'Okay, you've got three songs. You got to give it up.' It was different, but I really enjoyed it. I mean, I must not have been on TV for all this time for some reason, but now that I've done it, it's like 'Gee, why didn't I do this before?' "

Springsteen had been a presence on "SNL" prior to his own appearance, from Bill Murray's lounge lizard version of "Badlands" to various other cast members' imitations in skits. The man himself returned to the show again on October 5, 2002—this time with the E Street Band—to promote *The Rising* with performances of "Lonesome Day" and "You're Missing." —*GG*

Save Tillie

Campaign to preserve Asbury Park landmark
Palace Amusements

illie is the name of a cartoonish face painted on the side of Palace Amusements, a beloved Asbury Park boardwalk attraction that members of the Save Tillie organization valiantly tried to save from the wrecking ball. The Palace is referenced in several of Bruce Springsteen's songs, including "4th of July, Asbury Park (Sandy)," "Born to Run," and "Tunnel of Love." Tillie and the Palace also appear in Springsteen's "Lonesome Day" video and on T-shirts and other tour images. The band is standing under Tillie's neon-illuminated visage in a photo on page six of the *Tracks* box set booklet.

The Save Tillie campaign was already in the works when the Asbury Partners development firm bought the dilapidated, long-vacant Palace and announced plans to raze it. A coalition of Springsteen fans banded together and began efforts to save the image and building. Eventually, the organization numbered more than 1,000 members, with the Springsteen devotees joined by historic preservationists and amusement park–lovers worldwide. They got the building listed on the National Register of Historic Places and managed to keep it standing until mid-2004. Springsteen supported Save Tillie's efforts with publicity and cash, including some of the proceeds from the Springsteen/Max Weinberg 7 Asbury Park Convention Hall Christmas concerts.

The face of Tillie on the side of the Palace Amusements building in Asbury Park is a familiar one to Springsteen fans. When Palace Amusements was torn down in June 2004, workers carefully prepared the portion of the façade that contained the mural for removal and preservation, a result of efforts by the Save Tillie campaign. As of late 2004, the wall was in storage.

In 2003, the group listed the building on eBay for $2.5 million in an effort to put potential buyers into contact with its owners. No buyers willing to meet the owners' demands surfaced, but state officials compelled Asbury Partners to reuse Tillie as part of its future development plans. In June 2004, Save Tillie members managed to remove the 16-foot-by-14-foot, 10-ton concrete-block Tillie face and haul it to a storage area to await the development's construction. —*LM*

John Sayles

Film and video director, screenwriter

hat Bruce Springsteen is to American rock 'n' roll, John Sayles is to American independent film. Like Springsteen, for whom he directed three music videos in 1984 and 1985, Sayles's wide-ranging body of work focuses on populist themes, often tackling social issues, though rarely at the expense of character. The director's artistic integrity is generally viewed as second-to-none, with "independent" being the key word. Sayles has gone to great efforts to position himself outside of the Hollywood studio system, for the same reason Springsteen battled in the courts in the '70s—to have complete control over their art. The lesson of Springsteen's lawsuit was not lost on Sayles, as he told interviewer Cynthia Rose: "One of the interesting things I learned when I made that first video with Bruce Springsteen was that here's this guy who got really burned early on. But who also has some instincts and who became very careful. So ever since, he's pretty much been able to control what goes out there with his name on it. That doesn't mean it's gonna always be the greatest thing in the world. But at least it will be close to what you really want to do. And it's not going to be the way it is because some marketing guy or some computer was whispering in your ear."

Best known as a director, Sayles has worked as a novelist, screenwriter, actor, editor, producer, and script doctor. "To get what you want," he said, "you have to master a lot of other things." In 1998, Sayles was the second recipient of the annual Steinbeck Award; Springsteen was the first.

Born and raised in Schenectady, a factory town in upstate New York, Sayles later made his home in Hoboken, and New Jersey has featured prominently in his work. His first film as a director, *Return of the Secaucus 7*, was released in 1980. He received the MacArthur Foundation "Genius Grant" in 1983, and his connection with Springsteen began that year with his third film, *Baby It's You*. Set on the Jersey Shore in the '60s, *Baby It's You* was the first film authorized to use Springsteen's music, making effective (if anachronistic) use of "It's Hard to Be a Saint in the City," "She's the One," "Adam Raised a Cain," and "The E Street Shuffle." Sayles told *Backstreets* that year, "We sent him the script and he really liked it. He sent his manager to see it and then Bruce said we could have [the songs]. We didn't even have to pay a whole bunch of money for them. I was really honored."

The two met face-to-face the following year, for dinner at Sayles's house the night after the *Born in the U.S.A.* album was mastered, and the director was soon behind the camera for a trilogy of videos to promote the album. His first was for the title track, *Born in the U.S.A.*'s third single. ("Dancing in the Dark" was directed by Brian De Palma; there was no video for "Cover Me.") Sayles filmed Springsteen's Los Angeles Sports Arena performances in the fall of 1984, blending the live "Born in the U.S.A." footage with scenes he shot around their shared home state.

Hired again for "I'm on Fire," Sayles filmed Springsteen's Syracuse, New York, shows in January 1985, with the initial intent of a live performance video. Instead, Sayles and Springsteen collaborated on a storyline, and "I'm on Fire" became Springsteen's first narrative video (with his first speaking lines in character), shot in February 1985. Sayles donated his $10,000 fee to a fund aiding Sandinistas in Nicaragua. After playing an auto mechanic in "I'm on Fire," Springsteen played a construction worker in "Glory Days," filmed in May 1985. Again, the two developed the storyline together, with Springsteen playing both a blue-collar, baseball-obsessed family man as well as "himself" as a bar band rocker. In Sayles's Hoboken hometown, Springsteen and the E Street Band (along with then-alumnus Little Steven Van Zandt) were shot lip-syncing onstage at Maxwell's; Sayles used two additional Jersey locations for "Glory Days," West New York and Secaucus.

"Glory Days" was the director's final music video; a decade and a half later, Springsteen would return the favor by contributing a new song, "Lift Me Up," to Sayles's feature *Limbo* (1999).

In the years in between, Sayles built an impressive filmography. His subject matter has ranged widely, from sci-fi allegory (1984's *Brother from Another Planet*) to fairy tale (*The Secret of Roan Inish* a decade later), but his films are consistently populated by realistically drawn, recognizably human characters. As such, these films have often mined similar territory to Springsteen's, particularly *Matewan* (1987), *City of Hope* (1991), *Lone Star* (1996), *Limbo* (1999), and *Sunshine State* (2002). All reflected communities of individuals with intertwined fates, inextricable from a sense of place and the weight of history. Distinct echoes of Springsteen's work appear in his films: *City of Hope*, like "Born in the U.S.A.," has a protagonist whose brother was killed in Vietnam; *Lone Star*'s clash of cultures in a border town shares themes with *The Ghost of Tom Joad.* —*CP*

Ed Sciaky

Philadelphia radio DJ

 long with WMMS-FM's Kid Leo in Cleveland, Philadelphia disc jockey Ed Sciaky (pronounced SHOCK-ee) is credited with having the biggest role in helping to break Bruce Springsteen to a mass audience. Both played his music when other stations wouldn't touch the then-unknown New Jersey rocker. Born in New York and raised in Philadelphia—where he received a mathematics degree from Temple University—Sciaky worked at the influential WMMR-FM and later at WIOQ-FM. He freely and proudly admitted his status as a fan and often introduced Springsteen and the E Street Band when they played the Philadelphia area, which they did frequently as they built their following. The onetime host of the syndicated "King Biscuit Flower Hour" concert series also conducted several on-air interviews and, according to fellow Philadelphia-area disc jockey Rob Charry, even let Springsteen bunk on his couch after some of those early shows. On the day he settled his lawsuit with former manager Mike Appel, on May 28, 1977, Springsteen attended an Elvis Presley concert with Sciaky at the Philadelphia Spectrum.

At the time of his death on January 29, 2004, from diabetes complications, Sciaky, who was fifty-five, hosted the weekly "Sunday with Springsteen" show on classic-rock station WMGK-FM. Springsteen issued the following statement: "Ed Sciaky was the kind of DJ whose passion was the lifeblood for artists like myself. His support for my work brought me to an audience in Philadelphia that has remained one of my strongest to this day. Ed was the DJ as true rock 'n' roll fan—the very spirit of the music he loved. He will be greatly missed."

E Street Band drummer Max Weinberg spoke at Sciaky's funeral, and Steve Van Zandt, whose syndicated "Underground Garage" radio show followed Sciaky's on WMGK, told reporters, "As long as the music of the bands he played lives, he lives ... Ed Sciaky will never die." —*LM*

Patti Scialfa

**Singer, songwriter,
Springsteen's wife, E Street
Band member, 1984–present**

P atti Scialfa plays three roles in the life of Bruce Springsteen. She is his wife, the mother of his three children, and a member of his E Street Band. She is also a recording artist in her own right. An original Jersey girl, Scialfa grew up at the Shore and, as a teen, sang in her brother's rock band. After graduating from Asbury Park High School, Scialfa attended the University of Miami to study jazz vocals, where she met future producer and recording artist Michael Narada Walden. Impatient to get her singing career on track, Scialfa transferred to New York University in 1972, the year Springsteen was playing the city's downtown clubs as a solo artist prior to his signing with Columbia Records. Scialfa graduated in 1975, just a few months before Springsteen and the E Street Band's famous *Born to Run* shows at the Bottom Line, a club located in the middle of the NYU city campus.

After spending the *Born in the U.S.A.* tour positioned on a rear-stage riser, Patti Scialfa earned a spot at the front of the stage with Springsteen during the Tunnel of Love Express Tour; the pair harmonize at a March 1988 concert at Detroit's Joe Louis Arena.

Scialfa remained in New York during Asbury Park's mid-'70s golden years, making demos and hoping for a recording deal. She sang backup for Walden, after he too left Miami for New York, and with David Johansen, former member of the glam-punk band the New York Dolls. Scialfa also spent time singing with the jazz-fusion band Tone, which included former E Street Band members David Sancious and Ernest "Boom" Carter and Jersey Shore bass player Gerald Carboy.

In 1979 she got a call from high school classmate Billy Rush, who played guitar for Southside Johnny & the Asbury Jukes; Rush told her the Jukes needed female vocals on their soon-to-be-released album, *Love Is a Sacrifice* and offered the job to Scialfa and two of her friends, Soozie Tyrell and Lisa Lowell, with whom she'd formed a band called Trickster. Together, the three singers joined the Jukes in the studio and on the road in 1980 to promote the album. Scialfa, Tyrell, and Lowell stayed with the Jukes for two years, also adding their voices to the live album *Reach Up and Touch the Sky.*

Alternating her work as a member of the E Street Band with her own solo career, Patti Scialfa performs on NBC's "Today" show on June 15, 2004, in support of her album *23rd Street Lullaby*.

After her stint with the Jukes, Scialfa split her time between New York and the Jersey Shore and continued to do session work. In 1984 she occasionally sang with Cats on a Smooth Surface, the Stone Pony house band with whom Springsteen frequently jammed on Sunday nights. "I met Bruce there," Scialfa told *Backstreets* magazine. "I was doing a lot of Motown stuff and all. I just sort of bumped into him. He asked me to sing on his record." Scialfa added background vocals to an unused version of "Dancing in the Dark," one of the singles from *Born in the U.S.A.* In June 1984, two days before Springsteen and the E Street Band were to embark on a world tour to support the album, he asked Scialfa to join the band; she sang backup vocals on the tour, giving the E Street Band a new sound and a new look. In 1987, Scialfa—who did some session work with the Rolling Stones and Johansen's alter-ego, Buster Poindexter—was offered what she had always wanted: a recording contract of her own with Columbia Records. She had always written songs and was anxious to begin work on her album, but when Springsteen called the E Street Band together the following year to tour in support of his recently released solo album, *Tunnel of Love*, Scialfa put her album on hold and went back on the road.

This time, in addition to singing backup, Scialfa was moved to the front of the stage and also began playing some acoustic guitar in the show. She was given a bit more attention from Springsteen, too, on stage—and off. Springsteen, who was married to but separated from actress-model Julianne Phillips at the time, became romantically involved with Scialfa; their budding relationship quickly found its way into the tabloids and created plenty of juice for the gossip columnists. Springsteen and Phillips divorced in 1989; two years later Springsteen and Scialfa married.

Despite becoming the wife of Bruce Springsteen, Scialfa was determined to resume work on her long overdue debut album, called *Rumble Doll*. Although the couple began having children almost at once, Scialfa worked in the recording studio through her pregnancies with son Evan James and daughter Jessica Rae. (Their third child, Sam Ryan, was born after the 1993 release of *Rumble Doll*.) The album revealed a sweeter and more personal side of Scialfa that she only hinted at while with onstage with the E Street Band. The album was critically lauded, and Scialfa was praised for not exploiting her relationship with Springsteen. (Springsteen appears on the album only sparingly.)

Scialfa and Springsteen spent much of the '90s raising their family. When Springsteen released *The Ghost of Tom Joad* in 1995 and did a solo tour in support of it, Scialfa stayed home with the kids. However, when Springsteen called together the E Street Band for a reunion tour, Scialfa resumed her role in the band—with the children in tow for much of the tour. She also performed on both *The Rising* album, released in 2002, and the resulting world tour.

In 2004, Scialfa, after appearing on albums by Tyrell and Emmylou Harris, released *Rumble Doll*'s follow-up album, *23rd Street Lullaby*—again with a

Off of E Street ... Patti Scialfa

Don Cherry, *Hear and Now* (1976)
Emmylou Harris, *Red Dirt Girl* (2000)
David Johansen/Buster Poindexter, *Sweet Revenge* (1984), *Buster Poindexter* (1987)
Keith Richards, *Talk Is Cheap* (1988)
The Rolling Stones, *Dirty Work* (1986)
Soozie Tyrell, *White Lines* (2003)
Southside Johnny & the Asbury Jukes, *Love Is a Sacrifice* (1980), *Reach Up and Touch the Sky* (1981)
Narada Michael Walden, *Garden of Love Light* (1977), *Awakening* (1979)

modicum of contributions from her husband—which one reviewer called "an appealing, tightly knit collection that functions as both a memoir of her pre–E Street life and a valentine to pre–September 11 Manhattan." Scialfa also provided backing vocals on several tracks for Springsteen's 2005 release, *Devils & Dust.—RS*

Toby Scott

Springsteen recording engineer since 1978

ecording engineer Toby Scott has worked with Bruce Springsteen since 1978, providing him with the studio know-how necessary to produce best-selling and critically acclaimed albums such as *The River, Nebraska, Born in the U.S.A.,* and *The Rising.* Born October 30, 1948, in Pasadena, California, Scott began his career in music first as a guitarist, then as a manager. After he purchased a tape recorder in the late '60s in order to record local Santa Barbara rock bands, Scott became interested in recording studio engineering and enrolled at the Los Angeles–based Recording Institute of America. While there Scott met Chuck Plotkin, a former record company executive who opened Clover Recording Studio in Hollywood in the early '70s; Plotkin hired Scott to be Clover's main engineer in 1975.

Scott became connected to Springsteen when Plotkin began his long-time recording relationship with the New Jersey rocker in the late '70s. In 1978, while Springsteen was finishing *Darkness on the Edge of Town*, Scott assisted with the studio mix of the eventual single "Prove It All Night." Two years later Springsteen contacted Scott to work on his album *The River*; not satisfied with the existing mix, Springsteen asked Scott to remix every track except for "Hungry Heart." "That really was the start of my relationship with Springsteen," Scott recalled. "I was fortunate enough to come up with the kind of sound Springsteen was after for the songs he was recording. I was able to understand his musical vision and give the album what Bruce felt it needed."

In addition to working with Springsteen, Scott went into the studio with Steve Van Zandt and Gary U.S. Bonds, mixing the former's *Men Without Women* album and the latter's *On the Line* in the early '80s. But it would be Scott's contributions to a pair of seminal Springsteen albums, *Nebraska* and *Born in the U.S.A.*, that would not only solidify his recording studio role with Springsteen but also make him one of the most respected studio engineers in popular music. Upon Springsteen's urging, Scott left Los Angeles and moved to New York in 1984, where in addition to working on albums he also helped Springsteen create song demos and supervised the recording of live shows. He also worked on the *Live/1975–85* box set.

In late 1987, Springsteen and Scott sequestered themselves in Springsteen's Rumson, New Jersey, home recording studio, during which time Scott engineered the recording of the songs that would comprise *Tunnel of Love*. Scott next returned to Los Angeles to work on Springsteen's non–E Street Band albums *Human Touch* and *Lucky Town*. By this time it was rare for Springsteen to do anything in the studio without Scott; few music people outside of the E Street Band and Jon Landau, Springsteen's manager and coproducer, have enjoyed such an intimate working relationship with the artist.

In the '90s Scott was behind the studio board for Springsteen's Grammy and Academy Award–winning song "Streets of Philadelphia," as well as Springsteen's *Greatest Hits, The Ghost of Tom Joad,* and *Live in New York City*. Scott also worked on Patti Scialfa's first solo album, 1993's *Rumble Doll*, and went on the road to record Springsteen's 1999–2000 reunion tour with the E Street Band. In 2002, Scott did some engineering for *The Rising*, though he did not work on the full album, on which Springsteen went outside his usual camp and worked with producer Brendan O'Brien. Still, Scott, who resides in Montana, remains Springsteen's primary recording engineer. —*RS*

The Searchers

British pop band

When you think about bands from Liverpool, the Searchers is not the first one that comes to mind. But after the Beatles, it shouldn't take too long for the name to come up. The clean-cut, close-harmonied quartet—guitarist/vocalist John McNally, guitarist/vocalist Mike Pender (né Michael Pendergast), bassist/vocalist Tony Jackson, and drummer/vocalist Chris Curtis—formed in 1961 and followed in the Fab Four's footsteps, plying their trade at the Star Club in Hamburg, Germany, and returning to England ready to record. Their breakthrough record was "Needles and Pins," which reached No. 1 in England and No. 13 in the U.S. Subsequent hits included "Don't Throw Your Love Away," "Love Potion Number Nine," and "When You Walk in the Room," the latter tune written and originally performed by Jackie DeShannon. With its ringing guitars, sweet harmonies, and lyrics of romantic longing, the song caught the ear of a young Bruce Springsteen, who in later years would cover the tune with the E Street Band.

One further connection between the Searchers and Springsteen: the band was named after the 1956 John Ford film starring John Wayne, which was also a favorite of Springsteen's. —*DD*

"Secret Garden"

Single release: Spring 1995
Album: *Greatest Hits* (Columbia, 1995)
Chart peak: No. 19

how me the money!" was the most famous tag line to come out of Cameron Crowe's 1996 film *Jerry Maguire.* But it's a phrase Bruce Springsteen could have uttered as well, thanks to what the movie did for his song "Secret Garden."

One of four new tracks included on 1995's *Greatest Hits* set, "Secret Garden" languished when it was first released as a single, making it only to No. 63 on the *Billboard* Hot 100 chart in April that year. But when Crowe included it as the love theme for *Jerry Maguire*, which starred Tom Cruise as a sports agent in the midst of a crisis of conscience, there was renewed interest in the song; a remix that incorporated dialogue from the film vaulted it into the Top 20 in the spring of 1997.

In *Songs*, Springsteen wrote that "Secret Garden" was written and recorded for an album he was working on in 1994 that was never released; he brought it to the E Street Band at the reunion sessions in January 1995, letting the group provide accents to what remains a hushed and spare arrangement—though in the liner notes of *Greatest Hits* he praises Clarence Clemons's contribution as "the Big Man sweeter than ever." "It was darkly erotic," Springsteen wrote of the song, "and centered on the mysteries that remain between partners, even the closest of relationships."

The initial single release of "Secret Garden" featured "Thunder Road" as a B-side. A subsequent EP included two versions of the song (the second with a string arrangement), a live version of "Murder Incorporated" with the E Street Band, the live take of "Thunder Road" from the *In Concert MTV Plugged* performance, and "Pink Cadillac," the non-album B-side from 1984's "Dancing in the Dark." *—GG*

Pete Seeger

American folk music icon

ete Seeger, one of the deans of American folk music, has been a primary influence on Bruce Springsteen ever since Springsteen first encountered the music of the legendary folksinger in the 1970s. Like Woody Guthrie, a folksinger of even greater stature whose impact on Springsteen can be heard in albums such as *Nebraska* and *The Ghost of Tom Joad*, Seeger's influence has been long-lasting. It's most evident in Springsteen's narratives about the plight of the common man and the use of the acoustic rather than the electric guitar to present such themes. Springsteen has also admired Seeger's deep knowledge of the American folk music tradition, his personal humility, and his never-ending battle via music for essential American principles of justice, opportunity, equality, and freedom.

Over the years, Springsteen and Seeger have corresponded and socialized, and on occasion, have performed on the same bill. In 1995 at the Rock and Roll Hall of Fame and Museum in Cleveland, the two shared the same stage when the museum honored Woody Guthrie in the first of the shrine's annual American Music Masters series. And although Seeger, a music traditionalist, is less enamored with rock 'n' roll than with the many other American roots music forms, he has publicly expressed admiration for Springsteen's work. Springsteen, meanwhile, contributed a version of "We Shall Overcome" to the 1999 tribute album *Where Have All the Flowers Gone: The Songs of Pete Seeger.*

Folk legend Pete Seeger, whose works inspired Springsteen's socially conscious style of music, is pictured on his porch overlooking the Hudson River in Beacon, New York, on July 27, 2004.

Born in 1919, Seeger began his lifelong passion for American folk music began at home with his father, a musicologist, and his mother, a violin teacher. Seeger worked with the legendary folk archivist Alan Lomax, attended Harvard University, and absorbed traditional folk music styles by attending folk festivals, particularly in the South. His interest in musical activism was further spurred after meeting Woody Guthrie in 1940; the two traveled and performed together and were members of the Almanac Singers, a politically active group that sang at union rallies and supported political candidates that ascribed to a socialist agenda. Seeger later formed the group the Weavers, which did much to bring folk music into the American pop music mainstream. In the early '50s, the Weavers achieved pop success with their renditions of the folk standard "On Top of Old Smokey" and the Leadbelly classic "Goodnight Irene."

But with McCarthyism in full swing in America in the 1950s, Seeger was brought in front of the House Un-American Activities Committee for his socialist sympathies and was eventually blacklisted. In the early '60s he emerged again, this time as a hero to young folksinging political activists such as Bob Dylan, Odetta, and Phil Ochs. In 1965 the folk-rock group the Byrds made Seeger's song "Turn! Turn! Turn!" into a chart-topping pop hit. Throughout the '60s, Seeger was active in the anti-war movement, and with the ending of the Vietnam War turned much of his attention to environmental and human rights causes.

For more than twenty-five years, Seeger has toured and performed with Woody Guthrie's son, Arlo. Despite his age—he turned eighty-five in 2004—Seeger plays his banjo and sings with the same spirit and commitment to social and political change that he had more than a half century ago. —*RS*

Bob Seger

Rock singer-songwriter from Detroit

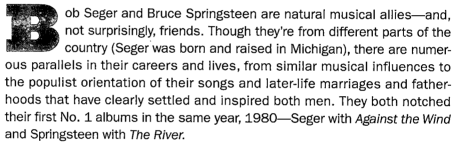ob Seger and Bruce Springsteen are natural musical allies—and, not surprisingly, friends. Though they're from different parts of the country (Seger was born and raised in Michigan), there are numerous parallels in their careers and lives, from similar musical influences to the populist orientation of their songs and later-life marriages and fatherhoods that have clearly settled and inspired both men. They both notched their first No. 1 albums in the same year, 1980—Seger with *Against the Wind* and Springsteen with *The River.*

Though he once saluted Springsteen as "our fearless leader when it comes to courage," Seger—who's four-and-a-half years Springsteen's senior—already had his career well in motion when *Greetings from Asbury Park, N.J.* was released in 1973. After some regional hits in the Midwest, including the anti-war "2 + 2 = ?," Seger signed with Capitol Records in 1968 and hit the Top 20 with "Ramblin' Gamblin' Man"—a feat he wouldn't accomplish again until 1976's "Night Moves" ushered him into the superstar realm. Yet he continued to record and developed a reputation as a dynamic, hard-working live act, another ethic he shared with Springsteen.

The two men met on September 2, 1978, at the Pine Knob Music Theatre in the Detroit suburb of Independence Township. Springsteen had played Detroit's Masonic Auditorium on September 1 and had an off night; he asked Ken Calvert, Columbia Records' regional album promotion manager out of Chicago, to take him to the Seger show. Calvert and photographer Thomas Weschler, Seger's former road manager, introduced the two men backstage, and they struck up a friendship after a warm conversation. Their most famous encounter, however, was on the first night of *The River* tour,

Springsteen used a rare night off during the *Darkness* tour to take in a Bob Seger concert, meeting the legendary Detroit rocker, left, backstage at the Pine Knob Music Theater in Independence Township, Michigan, on September 2, 1978.

October 3, 1980, in Ann Arbor, Michigan. Seger joined Springsteen and the E Street Band on stage to close the show with "Thunder Road," which had also been performed in the first set.

There was some ruffled feathers between the Seger and Springsteen camps over the 1985 Peter Bogdanovich film *Mask*, which starred Cher and Eric Stoltz. Bogdanovich wanted to use some of Springsteen's music in the film, but when an agreement couldn't be reached, the studio approached Seger—without revealing the prior negotiations with Springsteen, resulting in inaccurate but still damaging speculation that Seger had gotten his songs in the film by undercutting Springsteen's price. Seger ultimately pulled his songs from the soundtrack album, while a special edition of the *Mask* DVD in 2004 reinstated the Springsteen songs that Bogdanovich originally intended to use.

The incident caused no lasting damage, however. Rolling through Detroit in August 1992, Springsteen paid tribute to Seger with an encore version of "Ramblin' Gamblin' Man"—which he dedicated to Seger's manager Ed "Punch" Andrews, pointing to him in the stands. Seger and his family were Springsteen's special guests at the latter's September 2003 concert at Detroit's baseball stadium, Comerica Park, watching from side stage as Springsteen sang "Local Hero" as a nod to his friend. (Interestingly, Springsteen played Seger's "Get Out of Denver" at the next show in—where else?— the Mile High City.) Springsteen, introducing Jackson Browne, was also present on March 15, 2004, when Seger was inducted into the Rock and Roll Hall of Fame. Springsteen has also covered Seger at various other appearances, including the annual Rumson Country Day School Benefits. —*GG*

Shore Fire Media

Brooklyn Heights, New York, publicity firm

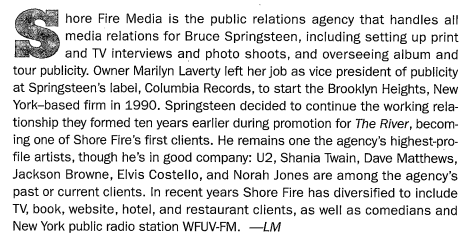 hore Fire Media is the public relations agency that handles all media relations for Bruce Springsteen, including setting up print and TV interviews and photo shoots, and overseeing album and tour publicity. Owner Marilyn Laverty left her job as vice president of publicity at Springsteen's label, Columbia Records, to start the Brooklyn Heights, New York–based firm in 1990. Springsteen decided to continue the working relationship they formed ten years earlier during promotion for *The River*, becoming one of Shore Fire's first clients. He remains one the agency's highest-profile artists, though he's in good company: U2, Shania Twain, Dave Matthews, Jackson Browne, Elvis Costello, and Norah Jones are among the agency's past or current clients. In recent years Shore Fire has diversified to include TV, book, website, hotel, and restaurant clients, as well as comedians and New York public radio station WFUV-FM. —*LM*

Tommy Sims. See 1992–93 Bruce Springsteen Touring Band.

Frank Sinatra

The Chairman of the Board, the other New Jersey icon

orn in Hoboken, New Jersey, Frank Sinatra has often been more associated with New York, New York, than with his home state. But every good Jersey boy and Jersey girl surely knows the truth. Sinatra and Bruce Springsteen—with all due respect to Count Basie, Bon Jovi, Yo La Tengo, Southside Johnny, and Whitney Houston—are the brightest stars in the Garden State's musical sky. While few would ever confuse the two, in voice or in craft—Sinatra interpreted Dietz & Schwartz's "Dancing in the Dark," Springsteen wrote his own—there's a great affinity between The Boss and the Chairman of the Board: New Jerseyans, Italian-Americans, Columbia recording artists, international superstars, each with a "My Way" style that served their careers well. But the nearly two generations that separated them made for an almost unbridgeable gap; their paths nearly never crossed. Perhaps the difference Sinatra perceived between the pop and rock milieus was a factor; in 1957 he raged to *Western World* magazine, "Rock 'n' roll smells phony and false. It is sung, played, and written for the most part by cretinous goons and is the most brutal, ugly, desperate, vicious form of expression it has been my misfortune to hear." In any case, for all their similarities and proximities, and the reverence Springsteen and his generation had for Sinatra, the two never met until shortly before the end of Sinatra's life.

Though it came late, they finally seemed to share a kinship. In 1995, Springsteen was given the honor of opening Sinatra's birthday celebration, "80 Years My Way" (an event broadcast on ABC); where the younger icon put their relative claims to New Jersey in perspective: "I'm here tonight not just to salute Frank's artistry—because, well, he is the patron saint of New Jersey. Since his rise from the streets of Hoboken, Frank has basically owned the place. He has been gracious enough to loan me a small piece of it by the beach. We first met at a party about six months ago, and we talked about the Jersey Shore, and I was glad to find that his conversation was still peppered with the kind of words that made our state great." Springsteen went on to recall the first time he heard Sinatra's voice ("coming out of a jukebox, it was in a dark bar on a Sunday afternoon, when my mother and I went in searching for my father"), to imagine Sinatra's postscript to every song ("And if you don't like it, here's a punch in the kisser") and to reveal his favorite Sinatra album (*Frank Sinatra Sings for Only the Lonely*). "It was the deep blueness of Frank's voice that affected me the most," Springsteen said. "On behalf of all of New Jersey, Frank, I want to say, 'Hail, brother. You sang out our soul.'" And, leading into a song from *Only the Lonely*: "From one Italian singer to another, for Ol' Blue Eyes, this is 'Angel Eyes.'"

It was also for Sinatra's eightieth birthday that Springsteen and wife Patti Scialfa were invited to dinner at his house. Springsteen later told ABC's

The legendary Frank Sinatra is certainly as much a part of the New Jersey musical legacy as Springsteen, with whom he shared a record label (Columbia). Here Sinatra (with wife Barbara, left) is the guest of honor at a taping of the television special "80 Years My Way" at the Shrine Auditorium in Los Angeles in November 1995, at which Springsteen performed "Angel Eyes."

"Nightline" host Ted Koppel: "We started to play the piano after dinner, and Patti sang. It was a big kick. I sort of stood by the side because I don't know those songs, I can't sing like that, and man, she sang those standards, and it was fun watching Frank Sinatra listening to my wife sing. It was like, whoa!" Sinatra died just two-and-a-half years later (on May 14, 1998); Springsteen attended the May 20 funeral at Good Shepherd Catholic Church in Beverly Hills, California, to pay his respects.

Since then, Springsteen's speech from "80 Years My Way" was printed as liner notes for *Classic Sinatra*. The two artists have also shared space on a handful of compilation albums, including *God Bless America* and one of the companion albums for HBO's series-"The Sopranos." On the summer 2003 leg of *The Rising* tour, Springsteen and the E Street Band often took the outdoor stage—most often in New Jersey—to the strains of Sinatra's "Summer Wind." —*CP*

The Ties That Bind

Patti Smith

Singer, songwriter, performer, artist, poet, playwright, critic, "punk priestess"

hough she was the purported "priestess of punk" and he was the savior of rock 'n' roll, Patti Smith and Bruce Springsteen had much in common. Both were born in New Jersey, three years apart (Smith is older). They both drew inspiration from some of the same sources, including Bob Dylan and the Rolling Stones. Smith sang "Rosalita" with Springsteen onstage on October 30, 1976, at the Palladium in New York City. And come 2004 they were both recording for the same label (Columbia).

In 1977 they also shared producer/engineer Jimmy Iovine, who was responsible for the two singer-songwriters' most direct connection— "Because the Night." It was a song Springsteen introduced in the early stages of his *Darkness on the Edge of Town* album, when he was recording at Atlantic Studios in New York City. Iovine was engineering those sessions and also producing Smith's third album, *Easter*. Iovine told a reporter that Springsteen knew *Easter* "was my first real break as a producer ... One night while lounging around the Hotel Navarro in New York, I told Bruce I desperately wanted a hit with Patti, that she deserved one. He agreed. As he had no immediate plans to put 'Because the Night' on an album, I said 'Why not give it to Patti?' Bruce replied, 'If she can do it, she can have it.'"

Springsteen told a Philadelphia disc jockey that he actually offered Smith another song but Iovine played her "Because the Night," "and she said she liked it. I said, 'I don't have all the words done or anything,' and she said, 'Oh,' and she wrote the words. And that's pretty much how it went down." For public consumption, however, Iovine recalled that Smith embellished the tale: "Patti being Patti, she said that Bruce pestered her to record it, but that's not how it was." Springsteen didn't mind, however; he performed the song with Smith on December 30, 1977, at CBGB's, and several times thereafter, and he has also included it in his shows over the years, most frequently during the *Darkness* tour dates. (During the 2004 Vote for Change Tour, R.E.M. frontman Michael Stipe joined Springsteen in a particularly impassioned version of the song, as well as a show-closing rendition of Smith's "People Have the Power.")

And it did become the hit Iovine was looking for, reaching No. 13 on the *Billboard* Hot 100 in the spring of 1978—higher than any Springsteen single had charted up to that time. "I'm actually grateful to that song," Smith said in 2000. "It was my most popular song, of course, and in hard times, because so many people have recorded it (including 10,000 Maniacs) and it's been used in so many ways, it's helped me make a living. The song's been good for me."

Patti Smith's version of Springsteen's "Because the Night" reached No. 13 on the *Billboard* Hot 100 in 1978, making it the highest-charting Springsteen song at that time. Despite her many albums and cult following, it remains her most popular song.

Smith partly returned the favor by introducing Springsteen to Frank Stefanko, the photographer who shot the cover for *Darkness*.

Smith was already a press and underground darling when she recorded "Because the Night." In fact, she was a well-regarded poet, playwright, and music critic when she started making music in the mid-'70s, bringing an aggressive, poetic sensibility to the burgeoning punk rock scene. Her first two albums, 1975's *Horses* and 1976's *Radio Ethiopia*, won a strong cult and critical following—R.E.M.'s Michael Stipe and the members of U2 are among the legion of later rockers who cite her as an influence—before "Because the Night" and *Easter* hit commercial pay dirt.

Smith dropped out of the scene in 1980, however, moving to the Detroit suburbs with her husband, former MC5 guitarist Fred "Sonic" Smith, and raising two children. She recorded just one album over the next sixteen years, 1988's *Dream of Life*, but she revived her active career after Smith's death in 1994 and has released a steady stream of highly touted albums such as *Gone Again, Peace & Noise, Gung Ho,* and *Trampin'* in addition to nonmusical writings and visual art projects. —*GG/LM*

Songs

Springsteen lyric book, published 1998, updated 2003

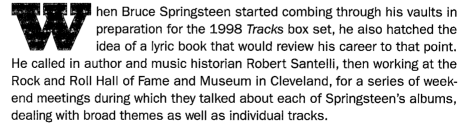

hen Bruce Springsteen started combing through his vaults in preparation for the 1998 *Tracks* box set, he also hatched the idea of a lyric book that would review his career to that point. He called in author and music historian Robert Santelli, then working at the Rock and Roll Hall of Fame and Museum in Cleveland, for a series of weekend meetings during which they talked about each of Springsteen's albums, dealing with broad themes as well as individual tracks.

Emerging in the fall of 1998, *Songs* was an insightful 306-page tome that, in addition to the lyrics from each of his albums (save *Tracks* and the live albums), contained some of Springsteen's most detailed and incisive comments about his songwriting and recording process. The book also featured scores of photographs from shooters who have chronicled his career, including Annie Leibovitz, Lynn Goldsmith, Neal Preston, Frank Stefanko, and his sister Pam Springsteen, along with some candid snapshots by his mother, Adele Springsteen, the late *Billboard* editor Timothy White, and Springsteen himself. *Songs* was dedicated to Springsteen's father, Douglas, who had passed away earlier in the year.

A paperback edition of *Songs* was published in October 2003; *Tracks* was once again absent from its pages, but Springsteen and Santelli did craft new chapters for the two new songs on the *Live in New York City* album and for *The Rising*. Springsteen also held a special book signing on June 23, 2004, at Antic Hay Books in Asbury Park, with proceeds going to the Merchants Guild of Asbury Park. —*GG*

Southside Johnny & the Asbury Jukes

Jersey Shore band, 1974–present

outhside Johnny Lyon will always be tied to Bruce Springsteen. They were friends and contemporaries on the New Jersey bar circuit. They played together in Dr. Zoom and the Sonic Boom, in the Sundance Blues Band, and in countless jams in and around Asbury Park. And when Southside launched his own band, the Asbury Jukes, in 1974, the already well-established Springsteen was an indispensable patron, contributing some of the group's best-known songs.

Raised next door to Asbury Park in Ocean Grove, New Jersey, Southside (whose nickname came from his devotion to blues from Chicago's south side) won an early reputation for his powerful voice—an instrument steeped in R&B influences such as Otis Redding and James Brown—and his personality. Springsteen wrote about the latter in the liner notes to the Jukes' debut, *I Don't Want to Go Home:* "Southside Johnny—One of the weirdest guys I ever saw. He used to dress just like my old man. He was definitely comin' in from the outside. First time I saw him he was playin' bass behind one of the early legends in Asbury, a guy named Sonny Kenn. Johnny was terrible. This was a person that could not play the bass. But he could sing and play harp and he knew a lot about the blues. Once I talked to him, I realized he wasn't as weird as he looked—he was weirder, and his general conversation consisted of insulting everyone within fifty feet. But he was the only white kid on the Jersey Shore that you could stand to hear sing straight R&B five sets a night."

After working with several other groups, Southside put the Jukes together with guitarist Steve Van Zandt, another Jersey Shore music fixture

Southside Johnny Lyon (shown here performing in Indianapolis on July 5, 2002) and his band the Asbury Jukes are a key part of Jersey Shore lore. Lyon and Springsteen played together in several bands in the 1970s, and they remain close friends and musical collaborators.

who also served as the group's manager and producer—and who wound up joining Springsteen's E Street Band before the 1976 release of *I Don't Want to Go Home*. The rest of the original Jukes lineup included guitarist Billy Rush, keyboardist Kevin Kavanaugh, bassist Alan Berger, drummer Kenny Pentifallo, saxophonist Carlo Novi, and the Miami Horns: Bob Malach, Louie "The Lover" Parente, Rick Gazda, and Deacon Earl Gardner. The Miami Horns also played with Springsteen on tour in 1976–77.

With Van Zandt producing, the Springsteen stamp was all over the Jukes' first albums for Epic Records. *I Don't Want to Go Home* featured two Springsteen songs, "The Fever" and "You Mean So Much to Me," while Van Zandt contributed three tunes; Ronnie Spector and Lee Dorsey were also special guests. The Jukes' next album, 1977's *This Time It's for Real*, featured three collaborations between Springsteen and Van Zandt and five songs written solely by Van Zandt. The seminal *Hearts of Stone*, released in

1978, sported six by Van Zandt, two by Springsteen (including the title track), and the Springsteen/Van Zandt/Lyon collaboration "Trapped Again."

After being dropped by Epic and suffering a temporary falling-out with Van Zandt, the Jukes moved to Mercury and became a more self-contained unit, with Rush becoming the dominant songwriter. (Springsteen's future wife, Patti Scialfa, became one of the band's backup singers.) *The Jukes* in 1979 was their highest charting record, but after that sales began to slide and the group began label-hopping. Chic's Nile Rogers produced 1983's *Trash It Up* in an attempt to modernize the Jukes' sound, which rang false. Southside went solo on 1988's *Slow Dance* but has continued to keep the Jukes rolling on the road and on record (guitarist Bobby Bandiera, who joined in 1985, is his chief creative foil these days). The old friends, meanwhile, came out in force for 1991's *Better Days*, with Van Zandt producing and playing guitar, Springsteen and fellow Jerseyan Jon Bon Jovi—who toured with the Jukes the previous year—providing duets, and the E Street Band rhythm section of Garry Tallent and Max Weinberg playing on the entire album.

Southside continues to hit the stage with Springsteen at various Jersey benefits and club jams, and occasionally during E Street Band tours. And he's at peace with being the "little brother" of the Asbury Park scene. "There was a period ... when I felt, 'Hey, what about me?'" he told *Backstreets* magazine in 1984. "It can be bothersome, but it could be a lot worse. If it has to be anybody, I can't think of anyone better than Bruce. He's one of the most honest, straightforward guys with the most integrity and he's given me some great songs and some good advice. He's been decent to me all these years." —*GG/DD*

Phil Spector

Producer, songwriter, musician, Wall of Sound architect

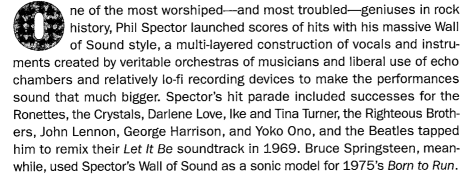

ne of the most worshiped—and most troubled—geniuses in rock history, Phil Spector launched scores of hits with his massive Wall of Sound style, a multi-layered construction of vocals and instruments created by veritable orchestras of musicians and liberal use of echo chambers and relatively lo-fi recording devices to make the performances sound that much bigger. Spector's hit parade included successes for the Ronettes, the Crystals, Darlene Love, Ike and Tina Turner, the Righteous Brothers, John Lennon, George Harrison, and Yoko Ono, and the Beatles tapped him to remix their *Let It Be* soundtrack in 1969. Bruce Springsteen, meanwhile, used Spector's Wall of Sound as a sonic model for 1975's *Born to Run*.

A native of New York's Bronx borough, Spector achieved his first musical success at age seventeen as the writer of the Teddy Bears' "To Know Him Is to Love Him" before undertaking a tutelage with the writing and production team of Jerry Leiber and Mike Stoller. With them Spector cowrote Ben E. King's 1960 hit "Spanish Harlem" and played guitar for the Drifters' "On Broadway." Spector moved on to the Dunes and Atlantic Records before cofounding Philles Records in late 1961, where he had his most consistent string of success.

Springsteen never sought to work with Spector himself—which, according to those who have, may not be a bad thing. Spector's story is filled with tales of wild, erratic, and dangerous behavior, allegedly firing a gun into a studio ceiling during a recording session with Lennon and pointing a pistol at a sideman during a Leonard Cohen session. The Ramones also reported Spector threatened them with a gun, and Dee Dee Ramone claimed Spector held him captive for days. Spector's ex-wife, the Ronettes' Ronnie Spector, claimed that he was so intent on keeping her imprisoned and controlling her life that he hid all of her shoes; when she finally decided to leave him, she ran out of their Hollywood mansion barefoot.

In 2003, Spector was accused of murdering actress Lana Clarkson at his hilltop mansion in Los Angeles. By then, he had become a notorious recluse himself, but he got out occasionally (producing some tracks for the British band Starsailor's 2004 release *Silence Is Easy*) and was frequently spotted at Los Angeles Lakers basketball games. The *Guardian of London* reported that Spector had been linked with Nancy Sinatra shortly before Clarkson's death and that the pair had been spotted at a Springsteen concert.

Springsteen and Spector did have one memorable meeting, in 1975 at Gold Star Recording Studios in Hollywood—where Spector recorded many of his biggest hits—not long after *Born to Run* was released. According to reported accounts, Spector, who had invited Springsteen to watch him work in a new Dion DiMucci single, stared at the New Jersey rocker before shaking hands and saying, "You're a very talented man." Springsteen had brought along E Street Band guitarist Steve Van Zandt, another fan, and they endured some gentle taunting from Spector, who told the musicians playing the sessions, "Bruce Springstreet is here. He's on the cover of *Time* and he's born to run, so let's show him how to make a record." Spector also told Springsteen that what he was working on "will make 'Born to Run' suck" and opined, "If I were with you, your records would be clearer and better, and you'd sell five times as many!" *Rolling Stone* magazine reported that when a friend compared the meeting to famed pitcher Sandy Koufax to up-and-comer Don Sutton, Spector raised the bar, saying, "No, it's more like Babe Ruth and Hank Aaron."

Springsteen again gave a direct nod to Spector's influence by covering "Santa Claus Is Comin' to Town" at his concerts—and later on record—with the arrangement Spector did for the Ronettes on *A Christmas Gift for You* in 1963. —*LM*

Ronnie Spector

Singer, primary Ronette

onnie Spector's influence looms large in rock 'n' roll history. The Ronette whose doo wop–influenced "wha-ho-oh-oh" choruses in "Be My Baby" became one of the most beloved—and imitated—song refrains has been revered not only by countless female vocalists but also by the Beatles, the Rolling Stones, the Ramones, Eddie Money, Billy Joel, Brian Wilson, and Bruce Springsteen and the E Street Band. Most of these artists recognized that the former Veronica Bennett's talent existed independent of her ex-husband, producer Phil Spector, the man who crafted the Ronettes' string of hits and who is similarly worshipped as one of rock's greatest sonic architects for his Wall of Sound approach to recording.

Springsteen's association with Ronnie Spector came through Steve Van Zandt and Southside Johnny & the Asbury Jukes. Van Zandt was producing the Jukes' first album, *I Don't Want to Go Home*, with engineer Jimmy Iovine at New York's famed Record Plant. Spector knew Iovine through her friend John Lennon (the Beatles and the Ronettes had toured together). Iovine invited her to the Jukes session; Spector liked what she heard and wound up recording a duet with Southside Johnny on the Springsteen-composed "You Mean So Much to Me." Van Zandt had Springsteen rewrite the lyrics to accommodate a male-female duet, and Springsteen, a huge Phil Spector fan himself, came to the studio to meet Ronnie and grilled her for production information about some of her ex's famous projects.

At the same time, Steve Popovich, who ran Epic Records' A&R department, headed back to his native Cleveland to start Cleveland International Records. He signed Ronnie Spector, then gave her a demo of "Say Goodbye to Hollywood," a song Billy Joel had written for the Ronettes. With backing by Springsteen and the E Street Band and production by Van Zandt in the Wall of Sound style, the 1977 song became the company's first release. At the time, Springsteen was enjoined from recording because he was embroiled in his lawsuit with ex-manager Mike Appel; he is uncredited on the song (though his picture appears on the single's sleeve), but the E Street Band received its first official recording credit on it. To date, it remains the band's only non-Springsteen credit.

Springsteen subsequently invited Spector to join him on stage at several of his concerts. The November 4, 1976, show at New York's Palladium Theater, recorded by Boston radio station WCOZ-FM, featured Spector singing her hits "Baby I Love You," "Walking in the Rain," and "Be My Baby." On February 17, 1977, in Cleveland, both Spector and Flo & Eddie of the Turtles sang those tunes as well as "Say Goodbye to Hollywood." On May 12 and 13, 1977, at the Monmouth Arts Center in Red Bank, New Jersey, Springsteen, Spector, and Van Zandt were backed by the Asbury All-Star Revue. Springsteen and Spector sang "You Mean So Much to Me." Spector also performed Springsteen's "Brilliant Disguise" on the 2001 tribute album, *Made in the U.S.A.*.

In 1990, Spector published a memoir, *Be My Baby: How I Survived Mascara, Miniskirts and Madness*, in which she wrote candidly about her life working and living with Phil Spector. A revised paperback edition was released in June 2004. Her most notable recording work since the E Street Band sessions was her guest appearance on Eddie Money's 1986 hit "Take Me Home Tonight," the chorus of which referenced "Be My Baby."

In the '90s, Spector made a Joey Ramone–produced EP on the Kill Rock Stars label titled *She Talks to Rainbows*; the disc included a cover of New York Doll Johnny Thunders's "You Can't Put Your Arms Around a Memory" and the Beach Boys' "Don't Worry Baby," which Brian Wilson wrote as an answer to "Be My Baby." In 1998, Phil Spector was ordered to pay Ronnie and the other Ronettes $3 million in back royalties and licensing fees, but an appeals court overturned the verdict, giving Spector the right to continue using the group's songs without paying them. Ronnie Spector is not allowed to rerecord or perform her songs in films or on video, but she still makes live appearances, including Christmas shows in New York City. In the early '80s, she married Jonathan Greenfield; they live in Connecticut with their two sons. —*LM*

Rick Springfield

Songwriter, musician, actor

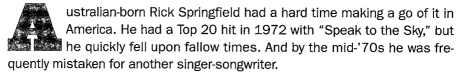 ustralian-born Rick Springfield had a hard time making a go of it in America. He had a Top 20 hit in 1972 with "Speak to the Sky," but he quickly fell upon fallow times. And by the mid-'70s he was frequently mistaken for another singer-songwriter.

"Twice in one week I went out for interviews for an acting part," Springfield recalls. "There was some girl looking at me, and as I was walking out the door she called me Bruce. And then right after that, after another acting interview, I was sitting on a curb and waiting for a cab and some kid came up and started talking to me about some record he liked—*Born to Run*. I was having a tough time."

Springfield vented his frustration in the darkly comic song "Bruce," which recounted these cases of mistaken identity: "You see I've got this name and he's got this name too/And they're kind of close, only a blind crazy fool/Would think I was him, it's like saying green is blue ...." He recorded it in

1978 without necessarily meaning for it to come out; however, after Springfield hit it big a former manager released it on an unauthorized 1984 compilation called *Beautiful Feelings*. The song hit No. 27 on the *Billboard* Hot 100, while the album reached No. 78 on the *Billboard* 200 chart.

"It was funny back when I wrote it, but by (1984) it was a little embarrassing," Springfield says. "I took it with a sense of humor. Some girl came up to me once and said, 'As one of two women who's ever lived with Bruce Springsteen, I find that song very offensive.' I said 'Tough shit.'"

Acting—particularly as Dr. Noah Drake on "General Hospital"—gave Springfield (born Rick Sprinthrope on August 23, 1949, in Sydney) the profile he needed to finally make a go of it in music. His 1981 album *Working Class Dog* launched the hit "Jessie's Girl" (which, ironically, beat out Springsteen's *The River* for a Grammy Award for Best Male Rock Vocal Performance) and started a three-year platinum streak. Things subsequently cooled for Springfield, though he continues to record, tour, and act. —*GG*

Adele Springsteen

Mother, optimistic influence

When Bruce Springsteen was inducted into the Rock and Roll Hall of Fame in 1999, he dedicated his statue to a smiling woman in the audience—his mother, Adele (Zirilli) Springsteen. She was the one who bought him the "brand new Japanese guitar" immortalized in his song "The Wish." At one point Springsteen described "The Wish"—a *Tunnel of Love* outtake—as the song drawn most directly from his life; in it he sings of standing outside a run-down music store window, eyeing that guitar, then finding it underneath the family Christmas tree. His mother is the loving, upbeat heroine in the song, looking proud and happy as she walks home from work: "If Pa's eyes were windows into a world so deadly and true/You couldn't stop me from lookin', but you kept me from crawlin' through." He sings about his mom in "pink curlers and matador pants," pulling him up to do the twist for his uncles and aunts.

Springsteen has described Adele, a legal secretary for Lawyer's Title, a land title company in Freehold, as an encouraging parent—"real smart, real strong, real creative." She was able to smile through tough times. In his Rock and Roll Hall of Fame induction speech, he noted, "She protected me and provided for me … she gave me a sense of work as something that was joyous and that filled you with pride and self-regard and that committed you to your world." He told biographer Dave Marsh, "My mother is the great energy—she's the energy of the show. The consistency, the steadiness, day after day—that's her. And the refusal to be disheartened, even though she was really up against it a lot of the time." In a joint 1995 interview with the TV show "60 Minutes," mother and son talked about the junky family car that wouldn't even go in reverse. They had to push it backwards out of parking places. "We weren't used to luck," Bruce said, adding that his mom and dad "worked like crazy their whole lives." Nevertheless, Springsteen was drawn to his mother's optimism, a counterpoint to his dad's often negative view of life. As he told *Time* magazine in 2002: "When I was growing up, we didn't have very much, but I saw by my mom's example that a step into the next day was very important. Hey, some good things might happen."

She could be tough, too; when she rented her son a first guitar when he was nine years old, she also insisted he take lessons—which he disliked so much that he gave up, resuming when he was fourteen years old with another instrument he bought for eighteen dollars at the Western Auto Store in Freehold. The guitar purchase from "The Wish," meanwhile, came when Springsteen was sixteen. Adele took out a sixty-dollar loan to buy her son a "barely tunable" Kent six-string and a small amplifier for Christmas. "It was a very defining moment," he later recalled, "standing in front of the music store with someone who's going to do everything she can to give you what you needed that day, and having the faith that you were going to make sense of it." He was reminded of his mother's sacrifice each week, when she went to the finance company to pay on the loan.

As Bruce found success, his mother often attended his concerts, jumping around to the music and greeting fans. She long kept a scrapbook of his accomplishments and even wrote thank-you notes to some reviewers for their kind words about her son. She's gotten into the act a couple of times, too. On August 23, 1978, at the final show of a three-night Madison Square Garden run, she "dragged" Bruce back to the microphone for one more encore, with him protesting "Aw, Mom!' I can't do anymore! I just played four hours! I can't do no more!" And at the June 11, 1999, stop of the E Street Band reunion tour in Genoa, Italy, she joined him for an onstage dance during "Tenth Avenue Freeze-Out."

"The Wish" ends with Springsteen contemplating "all those things that guitar brought us." He calls his mother "baby" and tells her he'll take requests "here in the kitchen." But he also warns her: If she's looking for a sad song, "well, I ain't gonna play it." —*JZ/GG*

Douglas Springsteen

Father, inspiration for poignant, very personal songs

hen Douglas "Dutch" Springsteen died in 1998, one obituary writer dubbed him "the most famous father in the history of rock 'n' roll." His relationship with Bruce, his only son and the oldest of his three children, was contentious, complicated, and loving in its own painful way. He railed against Bruce's long hair, his headstrong ways, his "goddamned guitar." And yet Bruce saw himself in his father; in "Independence Day" he sang of a home that could no longer hold a father and son: "I guess we were just too much of the same kind."

Born of mostly Irish ancestry, though the family surname is Dutch, Douglas "Dutch" Springsteen married Adele Zirilli shortly after returning home to Freehold, New Jersey, from World War II; recalling an early photo of his father—who was known as a "sure-money man" at pool—Bruce told *Rolling Stone*, "He looked just like John Garfield. He wore this great suit; he looked like he was gonna eat the photographer's head off. And I couldn't even remember him looking that proud, or that defiant, when I was growing up." Money was tight and life was hard in the Springsteen home. "I lived in a house where there was a struggle to find work," Bruce told *New Musical Express*. Douglas worked a variety of jobs—in a rug factory, at a mental hospital, in the local Nestle plant, as a prison guard and a gardener, at a race track. As Bruce sang in "Adam Raised a Cain," "My daddy worked his whole life for nothing but the pain/Now he walks these empty rooms looking for something to blame." He also drove cabs and buses and passed on his passion for driving to his family. "My daddy was a driver," Bruce recalled. "He liked to get in the car and just drive. He got everybody else in the car, too, and he made us drive." Bruce once told New Jersey concert promoter John Scher that his embittered father always complained about his bosses: "He'd be saying, 'My boss this' and 'My boss that.' And I'd say to myself, 'When I grow up, I'm gonna be the fuckin' boss!'"

Douglas was the inspiration for songs such as "Used Cars," "Mansion on the Hill," "My Father's House," "Factory," "My Hometown," and the appreciative "Walk Like a Man," as well as a thousand Springsteen monologues told slowly and thoughtfully in darkened arenas. He recalled to one New York audience, "We'd start talking about nothin' much, how I was doing. Pretty soon he'd ask me what I thought I was doin' with myself, and we'd always end up screaming at each other." One of Bruce's most poignant reminiscences was captured in the long preamble to "The River" from *Live/1975–85*; in it, Springsteen talked about the rancor between them but recalled that when he was rejected by the draft board, his father simply said, "That's good." Bruce reportedly wrote a verse to "Glory Days" about the glories his dad never experienced, but the verse didn't make it into the final song.

Over time, father and son began to reconcile. When Bruce made the covers of *Time* and *Newsweek* in the same week in 1975, his father told him, "Well, better you than another picture of the president." After the *Born in the U.S.A.* tour in 1985 they took a week-long fishing trip in Mexico. After his dad died at age seventy-three, Bruce issued a statement. He described his parents' fifty-year marriage as "warm and caring," and said he and his father had "a very loving relationship ... I feel lucky to have been so close to my dad as I became a man and a father myself."

As Bruce ages, he has said, he has come to resemble his dad. Sometimes, he's noted, he feels as if his father's face is looking back at him in the mirror. —*JZ/GG*

Evan, Jessica, and Sam Springsteen

Children of Bruce Springsteen and Patti Scialfa

Bruce Springsteen and Patti Scialfa have two sons and a daughter, all born in Los Angeles: Evan James, born July 25, 1990; Jessica Rae, born December 30, 1991; and Sam Ryan, born January 5, 1994. In 1992, Springsteen described the transition to parenthood to *Rolling Stone* magazine: "Engagement. Engagement. Engagement. You're afraid to love something so much, you're afraid to be that in love ... It's funny, because the night my little boy (Evan) was born, it was amazing. I've played onstage for hundreds of thousands of people, and I've felt my own spirit really rise some nights. But when he came out, I had this feeling of a kind of love that I hadn't experienced before." He also noted that parenthood brought him closer to his own parents, particularly his father.

Like many offspring of celebrities, the Springsteen children's privacy is carefully guarded—although the family is active at the Rumson Country Day School, for which Springsteen has donated auctioned items and performed fundraising concerts. Jessica has also garnered some attention as a junior equestrian who's taken part in competitions around the country, usually accompanied by her parents.

In 2001, Springsteen said that part of the inspiration for reuniting the E Street Band two years prior was to give his children a chance to see the band in action. "Basically they think we're big showoffs!" he said with a laugh. "But it was nice, because my kids were young, so they'd really only had a memory of me playing acoustically. Before we toured I played them a few of the videos, and they were just getting to an age where it really started to register with them a little bit. So they came to rehearsal, and they saw the band, and that was one of the great things about it—my kids got to know Clarence, they got to know Steve, they got to know Nils, Danny, Roy. It was 'These guys are daddy's best friends. These are the people I spent such an enormous part of my life with, and we made something together that was very special.' And so they got to see that, and to see Patti and me alongside each other. It was nice." —*GG*

Pamela Springsteen

Youngest sister

ruce Springsteen's youngest sister, Pamela, was born on September 7, 1962—thirteen years after her brother—in Freehold, New Jersey. She spent most of her growing-up years in San Mateo, California, where her parents moved in early 1969 (Bruce and another sister, Virginia, stayed in New Jersey). She was thirteen when he hit the covers of *Time* and *Newsweek*; she was quoted in the latter, telling a reporter, "Only one girl at school has his record." In 1978, he dedicated a performance of "Sweet Little Sixteen" to her from the stage of New York's Madison Square Garden, then brought her onstage. That same year he told Britain's *New Musical Express*, "My sister, my youngest sister, she's sixteen and she's very pretty and very popular. There's no way that she's gonna sit in her room for every waking hour. I didn't have that problem."

She may not have spent hours writing songs and playing a guitar, but she eventually did earn a tiny measure of fame as an actor before turning her attention toward photography. Among her acting credits are roles in the film *Fast Times at Ridgemont High* and on the TV show "Family Ties." She also starred as the killer in the teen slasher flicks *Sleepaway Camp 2: Unhappy Campers* and *Sleepaway Camp 3: Teenage Wasteland*, a couple of practically straight-to-video films that have cult status today. One online critic wrote of her performance in *Camp 2*: "Pamela Springsteen's perfect comic timing and manic clean-cut chirpiness (like a revivalist Christian on Prozac) holds the whole thing together nicely."

Her photographs adorn the booklets of her brother's *Lucky Town* and *The Ghost of Tom Joad* albums and appear in his book *Songs*. She has shot album covers and/or inner sleeve photos and publicity stills for a diverse array of artists from Alan Jackson to Ice Cube, and has served as on-set photographer for several films. Perhaps her greatest photographic achievement to date is her *Tom Joad* series, a collection of black & white prints that were edited together for a thirty-second commercial, then an entire music video. They were shot along lonely highways in the Mojave Desert—including Route 66, the road used by the fictional Joads for their western migration in John Steinbeck's book *The Grapes of Wrath*. Those prints were interspersed with images she shot in Los Angeles following the Rodney King verdict in 1992, when rioting gripped the city. Forty-one of her photographs were included in a photo exhibit titled *Springsteen—Troubadour of the Highway*, which opened in the fall of 2002 at the University of Minnesota's Weisman Art Museum in Minneapolis and traveled to other museums beginning the following year.

Coincidentally, Bruce Springsteen dated a photographer (Lynn Goldsmith) and married an actress (Julianne Phillips). Pam Springsteen married a musician, David Ricketts of David + David fame; they are no longer together but remain friends according to David Baerwald, the other half of the musical duo. Previously, she had been engaged to an actor she met while filming *Fast Times*—Sean Penn, in his pre-Madonna days. She resides in Los Angeles. —*LM*

Virginia Springsteen

Younger sister

Born December 8, 1950, Virginia Springsteen was the second child in the family, almost fourteen months younger than Bruce and just under twelve years older than youngest child Pam. Much less of a public figure than either of her siblings, Ginny was nevertheless partly responsible for helping to forward her brother's career; while growing up in Freehold, New Jersey, she was wooed by George Theiss, who played in a local band called the Castiles. Through his romantic overtures towards Ginny, Theiss met Bruce, which led to his joining the Castiles in 1965.

Ginny was immortalized as "Mary" in her brother's song "The River," in which he sings of her pregnancy and subsequent marriage at age seventeen. Her husband, meanwhile, is also echoed in the verses, as Bruce wrote in *Songs:* "I based ('The River') on the crash of the construction industry in late '70s New Jersey and the hard times that fell on my sister and her family. I watched my brother-in-law lose his good-paying job and work hard to survive without complaint. When my sister first heard it, she came backstage, gave me a hug and said 'That's my life.'"

Bruce also pays tribute to Ginny in a lighter vein in the unreleased song "In Freehold": "Well, my sister got pregnant at seventeen in Freehold/Back then people they could be pretty mean/Now honey you had a rough road to go/Now you ain't made of nothin' but soul/I love you more than you'll ever know/We both survived Freehold." —*GG*

The Bruce Springsteen Band

Short-lived big band, 1971–72

The Bruce Springsteen Band emerged after the breakup of the short-lived Dr. Zoom and the Sonic Boom, a carnivalesque big band based in Asbury Park that included not just musicians, but also baton twirlers, an emcee, and an ongoing Monopoly game center stage. The Bruce Springsteen Band formed in 1971 and didn't experience much commercial success, but it was a hot, eleven-piece, multi-racial rock and soul outfit with backup singers (Barbara Dinkins, Francine Daniels, and Delores Holmes) and a small horn section (Harvey Cherlin on trumpet and Bobby Feigenbaum on sax). The rest of the band—keyboardists Danny Federici and David Sancious, drummer Vini Lopez, bassist Garry Tallent, and guitarist Steve Van Zandt—had been with Springsteen in one musical form or another for the previous couple of years.

Like Dr. Zoom and the Sonic Boom, the Bruce Springsteen Band was short-lived. With the exception of a concert it gave in Richmond, Virginia, where some members of the Jersey Shore music scene were planning to relocate, the Bruce Springsteen Band played mostly at the Asbury Park club the Student Prince and at nearby Monmouth College in West Long Branch. The band blended R&B and blues classics such as "C.C. Rider," "Route 66," "Bright Lights, Big City," and "Walking the Dog" with Springsteen originals such as "Goin' Back to Georgia"—originally performed by the Springsteen-led hard-rock band Steel Mill—and "You Mean So Much to Me," a song Southside Johnny & the Asbury Jukes would later record for their 1976 debut album, *I Don't Want to Go Home.* Springsteen had performed "You Mean So Much to Me" live with the E Street Band in 1973–74; a studio version of the song was considered for but eventually cut from *Tracks.*

Although Springsteen could not keep the group together—having ten musicians in the band limited everyone's earning potential—the Bruce Springsteen Band paved the way for the E Street Band and the Jukes, the two most successful groups to hail from the Jersey Shore in the '70s. —RS

Springsteen—Troubadour of the Highway

Photo exhibit, September 2002–present

 pringsteen—*Troubadour of the Highway* is a photo exhibit that opened in September 2002 at the University of Minnesota's Weisman Art Museum in Minneapolis. It is the brainchild of Colleen Sheedy, one of the museum's curators and a casual Springsteen fan since she first heard the *Born to Run* album. A concentration in American studies and an interest in Springsteen's frequent use of highway and travel themes, both in his music and in his imaging, stoked Sheedy's interest in exploring the connection. "I've been very interested in the American landscape and the mythology of the highway, so going back and listening to his music, so many things came together," Sheedy said in 2003. "I knew that there were a number of key visual images related to the road that had been used for album covers and some other materials, and I just started exploring to what extent this visual material existed and found there was plenty to do an exhibition."

In September 2002, curator Colleen Sheedy created the exhibit *Springsteen—Troubadour of the Highway* at the Weisman Art Museum in Minneapolis, Minnesota. The multimedia display, which included photographs, videos, and music, expanded on the common Springsteen themes of travel and the open highway. The exhibit itself did some traveling, stopping in Detroit and Seattle before landing at the Newark Museum, where this airbrush-tinted 1978 photo of Springsteen by photographer Frank Stefanko was on display in June 2004.

Sheedy found a treasure trove, in fact. With the help of Sandra Choron, Springsteen's personal art director, the curator constructed an exhibit of seventy works by photographers such as Annie Leibovitz, Frank Stefanko, David Rose, Joel Bernstein, and former Springsteen girlfriend Lynn Goldsmith, who's published two photo books dedicated to Springsteen. The exhibit also features the work of Springsteen's sister Pamela, whose photos have appeared on some of his albums. Among *Troubadour of the Highway*'s highlights is a series of previously undisplayed images the younger Springsteen took for 1995's Grammy-winning *The Ghost of Tom Joad* album.

Besides the photos, Sheedy also incorporated music and videos for the songs "I'm on Fire" (directed by John Sayles) and "Atlantic City" (Arnold Levine) into the exhibit. "I didn't set out to do an overview of Springsteen's

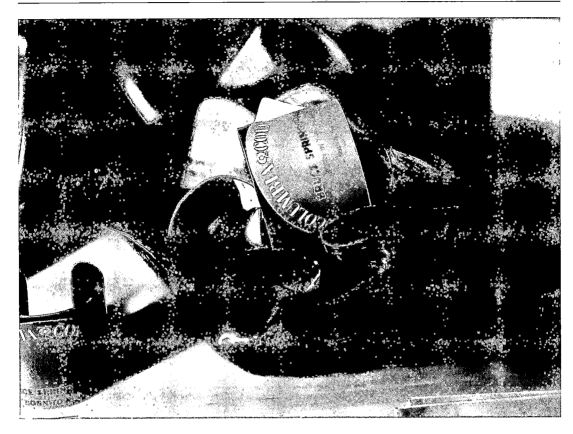

At the traveling museum exhibit called *Springsteen: Troubadour of the Highway*, fans could enjoy the displays and then also take home their very own bracelets and bowls made out of old vinyl Springsteen records.

career," Sheedy said. "I really wanted to approach him as an artist and look at how he created these images, and then how those were also expressed in the visual materials that he was very much a collaborator on."

Springsteen and a small entourage checked out the exhibit in its opening weeks in Minneapolis, when his tour in support of *The Rising* hit town. Sheedy escorted Springsteen around the gallery and said he was generally "quiet" throughout the tour. "He sent a note to our opening saying he was a little 'spooked' to be hanging in a museum," Sheedy recalled, "and I think there was an element that he felt it was maybe a little unbelievable he was in an art museum. But I know he really enjoyed seeing the section of his sister's photographs, and he had a lot of reactions to seeing these images of himself at different points in his career."

After its run in Minneapolis, *Troubadour of the Highway* made its way to Detroit and Seattle before landing closer to Springsteen's home turf with a stint at the Newark Museum in New Jersey in the summer of 2004. —*GG*

Charles Starkweather

Heartland serial killer

T he subject of the title track from Springsteen's *Nebraska* album, Charles Starkweather is infamous not merely for the number of people he killed—eleven—but for the shocking brutality and seeming nonchalance with which he carried out the executions.

On December 1, 1957, Starkweather robbed and murdered gas station attendant Robert Colvert in Lincoln, Nebraska. Two months later, he shot and killed the mother and stepfather of his girlfriend, Caril Ann Fugate, while waiting for her to come home. After Fugate arrived, he strangled to death her two-year-old sister. He hid the bodies outside and the couple remained in the house for two days before fleeing. His other victims included a high-school couple (he had also attempted to rape the girl), a friend from whom he demanded guns and ammunition, and a wealthy couple and their housekeeper (he stabbed the women and shot the man).

Starkweather and Fugate fled to Wyoming, where the crime spree continued. Starkweather shot a man napping in his car, firing nine bullets into his skull. He was finally captured by a sheriff's deputy and betrayed by Fugate, who yelled, "It's Starkweather, he's going to kill me." Starkweather was executed by electrocution on June 25, 1959, at age nineteen. Fugate drew a life sentence but was paroled in 1977.

In "Nebraska," Springsteen lowers the death toll to ten but perfectly captures Starkweather's swagger, asking the sheriff that when he's put in the electric chair his girlfriend be placed on his lap. It is perhaps Springsteen's most bone-chilling song. —*DD*

Steel Mill

Springsteen's hard-rock band from late '60s and early '70s that featured Danny Federici, Vini Lopez, and Steve Van Zandt

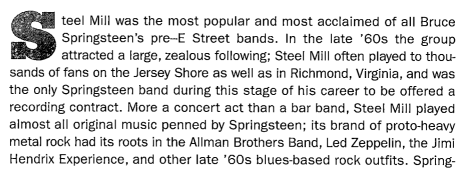

S teel Mill was the most popular and most acclaimed of all Bruce Springsteen's pre–E Street bands. In the late '60s the group attracted a large, zealous following; Steel Mill often played to thousands of fans on the Jersey Shore as well as in Richmond, Virginia, and was the only Springsteen band during this stage of his career to be offered a recording contract. More a concert act than a bar band, Steel Mill played almost all original music penned by Springsteen; its brand of proto-heavy metal rock had its roots in the Allman Brothers Band, Led Zeppelin, the Jimi Hendrix Experience, and other late '60s blues-based rock outfits. Springsteen himself described it as "a Humble Pie-type band" to *Crawdaddy* magazine in 1973.

Steel Mill was actually a transformation of Child, another early Springsteen band that was already playing heavy rock. Child was formed from the late-night jams that occurred at the Upstage, an Asbury Park after-hours musicians' club where the Jersey Shore's best rock players congregated each weekend in the late '60s. Child was born at the Upstage in 1969 when drummer Vini Lopez and keyboards player Danny Federici, both members of the Jersey Shore rock group the Moment of Truth, teamed up with Vini Roslyn, the bass player from the Motifs, and Springsteen, who had recently ended his hard-rock power trio Earth. Child performed a number of times at the Upstage as well as on the beach and at nearby Monmouth College in West Long Branch. When Springsteen and Lopez discovered that another Jersey Shore band also went by the name Child, the two musicians decided to change the name of their band to Steel Mill, a name suggested by mutual friend Chuck Dillion.

As important a member of Steel Mill as any musician in it was the group's manager, Carl "Tinker" West, a local surfboard manufacturer. Not only did West provide a place to live for Springsteen and the other members of Steel Mill in his surfboard factory, but, being a businessman, he instilled a degree of professionalism in the band, handling contracts, organizing concerts, and pushing the group to broaden its reach beyond New Jersey. As a result, Steel Mill made the mid-Atlantic region its stomping grounds, finding a second home in Richmond, where Steel Mill became so popular it could attract nearly 5,000 fans to a concert there.

Steel Mill even performed in California, hoping to attract the kind of attention in San Francisco that it already had in New Jersey and Virginia. After driving across country, Steel Mill planned to stay on the West Coast if it met with success. The group played the popular San Francisco club the Matrix, owned by Marty Balin of the Jefferson Airplane; its performance there was reviewed favorably by Phil Elwood of the *San Francisco Examiner*, who wrote that the members of Steel Mill "deserve and demand attention." Shortly thereafter, Steel Mill was invited to perform at Bill Graham's Fillmore West and was offered a recording contract from Graham. West and Springsteen considered the terms meager and turned the deal down. Homesick, Steel Mill returned to New Jersey, where it replaced bass player Vini Roslyn with another Upstage regular, Steve Van Zandt, and quickly picked up where it had left off a couple of months earlier. Before one of its Virginia performances, Steel Mill added Richmond's Robbin Thompson to its lineup; Thompson, a guitarist and singer, complemented Springsteen in both areas and was a budding songwriter. His presence in Steel Mill made the band's connection to Virginia even stronger.

Despite its continued success, Steel Mill ended in 1971 after Springsteen grew weary of the band's sound. With the peak of late '60s blues-rock passed, Springsteen sought a new musical direction, one that included elements of R&B and soul music and featured horns and backup singers. He would pursue that path first with the theatrical Dr. Zoom and the Sonic Boom and then the Bruce Springsteen Band. —*RS*

John Steinbeck. *See The Grapes of Wrath*.

Sting

Police man, solo artist, humanitarian, actor, tantric sexualist

ruce Springsteen and Sting had met "casually" prior to 1988's worldwide Human Rights Now! tour for Amnesty International. But on that tour they became much closer; in 2004 Sting noted, "Now our families are very close. Our children and our wives are very close. We see each other. It's lovely." The tour, according to Sting, "made us feel much less isolated than you normally feel as a sort of rock icon. For the first time in any of our careers we were kind of forced to share the bubble—sharing hotels, sharing the plane, sharing dressing rooms, sharing the stage. Those friendships have stayed firm and grown from that." Springsteen even told his pal that the first album by Fiction Plane, Sting's son Joe Sumner's band, was "the best debut record he'd heard in many a year."

Sting and Springsteen started sharing the stage about a week before the tour started, on August 25, 1988, when Sting was performing at New York's Madison Square Garden. Telling the crowd, "I'm pretty angry at all of this business about a rivalry between Bruce and myself—maybe this will put an end to it." Springsteen then came on stage for acoustic versions of "The River" and the Police's "Message in a Bottle," with Sting commenting to *Rolling Stone* magazine, "He sings so loud, I couldn't believe it!" Afterwards, the two musicians and their girlfriends (now wives), Trudie Styler and Patti Scialfa, attended a dinner party at the Canal Bar with Madonna and Jodie Foster.

After that auspicious start, it didn't take the two men much time to start collaborating on the Human Rights Now! tour (which also featured Peter Gabriel, Tracy Chapman, and Youssou N'Dour). Sting started performing "The River" with Springsteen and the E Street Band at the tour's second show, September 4 in Paris. Starting September 17 in Montreal, Springsteen began singing the Police hit "Every Breath You Take" with Sting and his band. On the final night of the tour, Sting and Gabriel donned *Born in the U.S.A.*–style tour attire to sing "Twist and Shout" with Springsteen and company.

Born Gordon Matthew Sumner on October 2, 1951, in Newcastle, England, Sting started as a jazz musician; it was some jazz colleagues, in fact, who gave him his nickname after a favorite black-and-yellow jersey. He worked as a school teacher, civil servant, and ditch digger before forming the Police in 1977, in the midst of the British punk movement; the Police, however, was a sophisticated and musically accomplished outfit, blending jazz and reggae into its energetic rock. The group split up in 1985, at the peak of its success, and has reunited publicly for only three shows on the 1986 Amnesty International Conspiracy of Hope tour and for the trio's 2003 induction into the Rock and Roll Hall of Fame.

Sting released his first solo album in 1985, backed by a group of jazz musicians. He's continued to experiment with different musical styles and flavors over the course of his career. He's also acted in films (*Dune*, *Stormy Monday*, *Lock, Stock and Two Smoking Barrels*) and on the Broadway stage (*Threepenny Opera*). An off-the-cuff remark about practicing hours-long sessions of tantric sex grew quite a bit of attention, too. On a more serious

Icons of the pop-music world in the 1980s who remain relevant as songwriters and performers, Sting and Springsteen forged their friendship in 1988 during the Amnesty International Human Rights Now! tour.

front, he and Styler established the Rainforest Foundation, which raises funds through an annual all-star concert in New York City and for which he was honored as Musicares' Person of the Year in 2004. "You Will Be My Ain True Love," which Sting wrote for the *Cold Mountain* film soundtrack, was nominated for an Academy Award, and in 2003 Sting was named a Commander of the British Empire (CBE) by Queen Elizabeth II. But, he noted, "I haven't found anybody I can command yet. They all ignore me." —*GG*

The Stone Pony

Legendary Asbury Park club

he Stone Pony, affectionately known to longtime Springsteen fans as the House That Bruce Built, is Asbury Park's legendary rock club. Located at 913 Ocean Avenue, across the street from the

Asbury Park boardwalk, the Stone Pony is the unofficial headquarters for all things rock 'n' roll in the city. Since its opening in 1974, the club has featured countless local, national, and international rock acts. But by far its most noted performer has been Springsteen, whose connection to the club permanently placed it on the American music map; so known and respected is the Stone Pony that many music historians rank it with the greatest rock clubs of all time, adding it to a list that includes such landmarks as CBGB's and the Bottom Line in New York City, the Whiskey and Roxy in Los Angeles, and the Cavern Club in Liverpool, England.

The opening of the Stone Pony was the start of the golden age of Asbury Park's music scene. A previous scene in the late '60s that evolved from another Asbury Park club, the Upstage, ended abruptly in 1970 when race riots plagued the city. Unable to recover economically, Asbury Park lost its reputation as a thriving seaside resort and plunged into a prolonged period of closed businesses, depreciating property values, increased crime, and general urban blight that continues today despite numerous attempts to turn the seaside resort around. The one bright spot in the city's recent history has been its music scene, and the center of that scene has been, and still is, the Stone Pony.

The Pony, as locals have always called the club, was never a pretentious establishment. Original owners Butch Pielka and Jack Roig prided themselves on running a blue-collar club that featured R&B and soul-influenced rock on its stage, and shots and beer at its bar. Its first house band, Southside Johnny & the Asbury Jukes, played the club a few nights weekly and quickly began to attract a loyal local following. The Jukes' set list included R&B, soul, rock, and reggae standards along with original songs penned by its leader, Miami Steve Van Zandt, aka Little Steven.

Van Zandt, along with singer-harmonica player Southside Johnny Lyon, were part of the Upstage crowd and therefore already popular local musicians, which helped attract patrons to the Pony. From the start, the Jukes reflected Van Zandt's and Southside's love of black music. The band became synonymous with the Stone Pony, and when Springsteen and members of his E Street Band began hanging out and occasionally jamming with the Jukes at the club between concert tours in 1974–75, the club's reputation grew substantially.

In late 1975, when *Time* and *Newsweek* simultaneously featured cover stories on Springsteen that included detailed descriptions of the Asbury Park music scene and the Stone Pony, the club's popularity shot well beyond the Jersey Shore. Suddenly music journalists looking for a Springsteen scoop and record company executives looking for the next big thing out of Asbury Park were rubbing shoulders with Shore fishermen, local factory workers, Monmouth College students, and other area rock fans at the Stone Pony bar.

After the Asbury Jukes signed a recording contract with Columbia Records, Van Zandt decided to celebrate the release of the band's debut record *I Don't Want to Go Home* with a live broadcast from the Stone Pony over Memorial Day weekend in 1976. The event featured Southside Johnny & the Asbury Jukes with plenty of guests, including Springsteen and E Street Band members. Once the Jukes gave up their house-band status to go on tour to promote their album, other Jersey Shore bands vied for Stone Pony dates. Hot local acts such as the Lord Gunner Group, the Shakes, Paul Whistler & the Wheels, Cold Blast & Steel, and Billy Chinnock competed with more obvious Jukes-influenced bands such as Cahoots, the Shots, and one called the Atlantic City Expressway that featured an underage singer named John Bongiovi, later to become famous as Jon Bon Jovi.

In the late '70s, the mere possibility of a Springsteen jam caused huge crowds to descend on the Pony. Club merchandise, especially T-shirts and jackets, were prized by rock fans who began making the pilgrimage to the Pony as if it were a rock 'n' roll shrine. The success of the Pony prompted new rock clubs to open in Asbury Park; one of them, the Fast Lane, rivaled the Pony in the early '80s by attracting a younger crowd with a more stylistically diverse array of acts—including New Wave bands from England. Still, the Stone Pony remained the most prestigious rock club in all New Jersey.

In 1984, with the release of Springsteen's monumental *Born in the U.S.A.* album, interest in Asbury Park and the Stone Pony in particular peaked all over again. A new generation of Asbury Park bands attracted followings at both the Pony and the Fast Lane, including the George Theiss Band, Hot Romance, John Eddie & the Front Street Runners, the Rest, and two acts from outside Jersey who made Asbury Park their home away from home, Pittsburgh's Norman Nardini & the Tigers and Rhode Island's Beaver Brown. But it was the Pony's latest house band, Cats on a Smooth Surface, that got the lion's share of attention from the national rock press; the band played Sunday nights at the Pony, and Springsteen liked to sneak out for some late-night jamming. For awhile it was the best kept rock 'n' roll secret on the Jersey Shore, but once *Rolling Stone* magazine reported in its Random Notes section that Springsteen often jammed with Cats at the Pony, the large crowds the club experienced a decade or so earlier were back—at least on Sunday nights.

As the '80s wore on, the Stone Pony's fortunes hinged on Springsteen. When he moved to California, temporarily abandoning his Jersey roots, interest in the club diminished. When he moved back to the Jersey Shore in the '90s and reestablished his Asbury Park legacy, the Pony's popularity rose dramatically. The possibility of catching Springsteen perform in a small club setting was a special treat for fans willing to ride out the rumors of a late-night appearance.

The Stone Pony, which first opened in 1974, is practically considered holy ground by Springsteen fans, who call the Asbury Park landmark "the House that Bruce Built." Early in his career, Springsteen frequently performed at the small, unpretentious rock club, and even after he became a huge star he would often pop in for unannounced concerts. The club, shown here in 1999, fell on hard times in the late 1990s but was still open and hosting rock acts in 2004.

Despite the Stone Pony's Springsteen-related success, the continued economic malaise of Asbury Park endangered its survival. By the late '80s, Asbury Park had suffered through at least two failed attempts at urban renewal. Surrounding the Stone Pony were empty lots and half renovated buildings whose owners had run out of money or simply given up on Asbury Park as a comeback city. In 1988, unable to pay the bills, Pielka and Roig filed for Chapter 11 bankruptcy, preventing the club from being taken over by creditors and hoping for a turnaround which never came. In late 1991, the Pony closed its doors, but not permanently; a year later, Steven Nasar purchased the club and reopened it, helped in large measure by the decision of Southside Johnny to film a video in the club for the title track of the Jukes' newest album, the aptly titled *Better Days*. The special event featured guest performances by Springsteen, Bon Jovi, and Van Zandt and reignited media attention in the Stone Pony. Though Nasar worked hard to restore the Pony's rich tradition of blue-collar rock 'n' roll, the club's original magic was gone, and the Pony again found itself in jeopardy of closing. Nasar's tenure as owner of the Stone Pony was short-lived; by the mid-'90s the club was being run by Dominic Santana, who also swore to bring back the Pony's glory days.

For most of the '90s, the Stone Pony suffered from an identity crisis. While longtime Springsteen fans considered the club holy ground, many of them were now too busy with family obligations or too old to frequent the club regularly and pour money into its coffers. To survive, the Pony had to attract a young clientele, featuring punk rock, dance, techno, and heavy metal on its stage. Only when the Jukes came back to perform at the club or Springsteen launched a surprise performance did the Pony shows signs of its original vitality. Nevertheless, the Stone Pony continues to feature music on a regular basis; it celebrated its thirtieth anniversary in 2004, though under new ownership—this time developers intent on making over the Asbury Park oceanfront. —*RS*

"Streets of Philadelphia"

Released: December 1994
Album: *Music from the Motion Picture Philadelphia* (Columbia, 1994)
Also on: *Greatest Hits* (Columbia, 1995), *The Essential Bruce Springsteen* (Columbia, 2003)
Chart peak: No. 9

arly in 1993, Bruce Springsteen was approached by director Jonathan Demme to write a song for his upcoming film *Philadelphia*, which starred Tom Hanks as an AIDS-stricken lawyer teaming with a colleague (Denzel Washington) to sue his firm for unlawful dismissal. Springsteen, who was in the midst of a world tour at the time and had never written a song specifically for a movie, did not initially commit but agreed to consider it. And Demme was persistent. "Jonathan told him not simply about the story, but about the atmosphere and the main character in such sufficient depth that it began to work on Bruce," coproducer Chuck Plotkin told *Billboard*. Springsteen, who was a fan of Demme's films, already had "some lyrics I had partially written dealing with the death of a close friend," so he started working on the song in the home studio at his Rumson, New Jersey, estate.

"I spent a day or so trying to accommodate, but the lyrics I had seemed to resist being put to rock music," he wrote in *Songs*. "So I began to fiddle with the synthesizer, playing over a hip-hop influenced beat I programmed on the drum machine. As soon as I slowed the rhythm down over some basic minor chords, the lyrics fell into place and the voice I was looking

Springsteen won four Grammy Awards for "Streets of Philadelphia" at the 1997 ceremony, including Song of the Year, Best Rock Song, Best Male Rock Vocal Performance, and Best Song Written for a Motion Picture or Television.

for came forward." Springsteen did try to flesh the arrangement out with other musicians, but ultimately he stuck with the spare demo version of the song, keeping only tour bassist Tommy Sims's subtle backing vocals.

"Streets of Philadelphia" benefited from high interest surrounding Demme's film, which was the first major, mainstream motion picture to deal directly with AIDS; it was his first Top 10 hit since "Tunnel of Love" six-and-a-half years earlier, and logged fifteen weeks in the Top 40, Springsteen's longest stay since "Dancing in the Dark" in 1984. Demme shot the video for the song on December 6–7, 1993, in the City of Brotherly Love, and Springsteen performed it on January 27, 1994, at the annual benefit for AIDS Project Los Angeles.

It also became his most decorated song, winning a Golden Globe and becoming the first song by a rock 'n' roll artist to win the Academy Award for Best Original Song. At the former he told the audience, "I hope that this film, and in some smaller way this song, might take away a little chip out of the fear and intolerance and lack of compassion that we show for one another." Accepting his Oscar on March 21, 1994, he noted that he had to "share" it with Neil Young, who wrote *Philadelphia*'s title song, and noted, "This is the first song I ever wrote for a motion picture, so I guess it's all downhill from here. You do your best work and you hope that pulls out the best in your audience and some piece of it spills over into the real world and into people's everyday lives and it takes the edge off the fear and allows us to recognize each other through our veil of differences. I always thought that was one of the best things popular art was supposed to be about, along with the merchandising and other stuff."

"Streets of Philadelphia" had one more moment in the spotlight—on March 1, 1995, the day after Springsteen's *Greatest Hits* album arrived in stores, when it won four Grammy Awards, including Song of the Year, Best Rock Song, Best Male Rock Vocal Performance, and Best Song Written for a Motion Picture or Television. The song has also been covered by an eclectic group of artists, ranging from MOR orchestrator Ray Conniff to singer-songwriter Richie Havens and pianist Richard Clayderman. —*GG*

Donna Summer

Multi-platinum R&B/disco singer

In 1981, Donna Summer and producer Quincy Jones were looking for songs for her second album for Geffen Records. "Quincy said 'We should do something with The Boss,'" Summer recalled, and through label chief David Geffen, who was friendly with Springsteen's manager Jon Landau, the request was made. Springsteen custom-wrote "Cover Me" with

Springsteen and disco icon Donna Summer forged an unlikely link when she recorded his song "Protection" for her album *Donna Summer* in 1981. Summer is shown here performing at the Universal Amphitheater in Los Angeles in 1979.

Summer in mind—demoing it with the E Street Band while they were recording Gary U.S. Bonds's *On the Line*—but when Landau heard the song he nixed the idea, insisting that Springsteen keep it for his next album (it wound up being the second single from 1984's *Born in the U.S.A.*). In its stead Springsteen gave Summer another song he was working on, "Protection," and even played guitar on it.

"It was kind of cool, I must say, sitting down and having The Boss teach me the song," Summer said. "I kept thinking, 'I think I'm gonna plotz. Oh, no, this isn't happening. Yes it is ...' Let's face it; sometimes celebrities are bigger fans than fans themselves. We recognize greatness in other people. I'd been to several of Bruce Springsteen's concerts and was a total fan. To work with him was more than a delight and a pleasure. It was an honor." Springsteen biographer Dave Marsh quoted Jones as calling Springsteen "one of the nicest people I have ever worked with" and complimented him for doing "every take like it was the last show at Madison Square Garden." The Springsteen connection gave the *Donna Summer* album some crossover newsworthiness, but the album stalled at No. 20 on the *Billboard* charts and hastened Summer's departure from Geffen.

Born Adrian Donna Gaines in Boston, Summer made her mark in the '70s as disco's leading diva, racking up a string of hits with producer Giorgio Moroder—"I Feel Love," "Love to Love You Baby," "Last Dance"—before broadening her sound with the rock-oriented "Hot Stuff," an epic treatment of "MacArthur Park," and a chart-topping duet with Barbra Streisand, "No More Tears (Enough Is Enough)." Summer became a born-again Christian in the late '70s, renouncing disco's decadent tendencies. The move from Geffen in 1982 paid off; in 1983 she and her new label, Mercury, scored a big hit with "She Works Hard for the Money." In the mid-'90s she moved to Nashville with her husband, musician Bruce Sudano; she continues to record and perform, including a rendition of "God Bless America" at Fenway Park during the 2004 World Series. —*GG*

"Sun City"

All-star anti-apartheid awareness-raising single organized by Little Steven Van Zandt

In the summer and fall of 1985, former E Street Band guitarist Little Steven Van Zandt wrote, produced, and organized "Sun City," an all-star project created to raise awareness of the continuing racist and segregationist policies of the South African government. As the vehicle for his message, Van Zandt chose Sun City, the opulent resort located in the otherwise impoverished Bophuthatswana, an "independent homeland"—or glorified ghetto—within South African territory. Acts such as Queen and Rod Stewart had used that status as an excuse to take hefty paydays to play at Sun City, arguing that it wasn't really part of South Africa. Van Zandt, who'd traveled to South Africa, didn't buy that, arguing that Sun City was a gross monument to apartheid: "To forcibly relocate people is bad enough, but to erect a $90-million showplace to celebrate their imprisonment is beyond all conscience." The message of his song was simple—fifty-four singers, musicians, and rappers, the Artists United Against Apartheid, promising the world, "I ain't gonna play Sun City!"

As Van Zandt was one of his closest friends since the mid-'60s, Springsteen of course signed on to be part of "Sun City." In a statement for the book that accompanied the project (written by Springsteen biographer Dave Marsh), he said, "I don't think I could just sit back and watch what was going on without feeling like I had to say something about it. The funny thing about it is that (apartheid) is so out in the open down there, but I was hoping that by helping bring attention to what's going on in South Africa, it'd also make us look in our own backyards, at the terrible problems we have with racism right here in this country. So when Steve said, 'Come on!' I said 'Sure!'"

"Sun City" was a herculean effort for Van Zandt and coproducer Arthur Baker. Van Zandt sent six weeks recruiting musicians and organizing logistics. Recording began on July 31 and was done over several weeks in New York, Los Angeles, and London; Springsteen recorded his part on August 29, 1985, after a scheduled concert at Giants Stadium in nearby East Rutherford, New Jersey, was canceled because of inclement weather. All told, the "Sun City" performances filled up thirteen master tapes and 300 tracks. Springsteen praised the final result as "a great rock record … For me, music was always informative, educational, and fun, and I think that's what this record is."

He was in good company. The rock world was represented on "Sun City" by Bob Dylan, Rolling Stones guitarists Keith Richards and Ron Wood, Beatles drummer Ringo Starr and his son Zak Starkey, Who guitarist Pete Townshend, U2 frontman Bono, Jackson Browne, Joey Ramone, former J. Geils Band singer Peter Wolf, Daryl Hall and John Oates, Peter Gabriel, Lou

Reed, Bonnie Raitt, Bob Geldof, Van Zandt's former E Street Band mate Clarence Clemons, Pat Benatar, Midnight Oil's Peter Garrett, former Dead Boy Stiv Bator, and Hanoi Rocks' Michael Monroe. A corps of rappers included Run-DMC, Afrika Bambaataa, the Fat Boys, Grandmaster Melle Mel, Scorpio, Gil Scott-Heron, Big Youth, Kurtis Blow, Duke Bootee, and Fats Comet. Former Temptations Eddie Kendricks, and David Ruffin led the R&B delegation that included Bobby Womack, George Clinton, Will Downing, Nona Hendrix, Kashif, and Tina B. Miles Davis, Herbie Hancock, Stanley Jordan, and Ron Carter brought jazz to the mix. Latin singer Ruben Blades and reggae legend Jimmy Cliff were in the house, as was the South African band Malopoets.

Many of the Artists United Against Apartheid (including a leather-jacketed Springsteen) turned out for the video shoot on October 10 and 11, to coincide with a major anti-apartheid rally in New York City. Van Zandt spoke on an apartheid panel at the New Music Seminar in Manhattan shortly before that, and the song's mid-October release was greeted with considerable attention, although its hot-button political topic limited its potential for airplay. Besides the "Sun City" book, there was also a companion album with additional tracks contributed by artists who took part in the single. Van Zandt and Artists United Against Apartheid subsequently received commendations from the United Nations and Nobel Prize–winning South African Bishop Desmond Tutu, while Van Zandt also won an audience before the U.S. Senate to talk about apartheid.

In 1987, Van Zandt told *Backstreets*, "I'm happy with the way it reached people. We accomplished everything we set out to accomplish. Our main goal was to reach our own people—those in the entertainment world … We wanted also to increase awareness about the issue and we wanted to give the whole issue a little push … to send a message to the South African people that we care." —*GG*

Doug Sutphin. See Mike Batlan and Doug Sutphin.

Edwin Sutphin

Rumson, New Jersey, resident who helped to inspire
The Rising

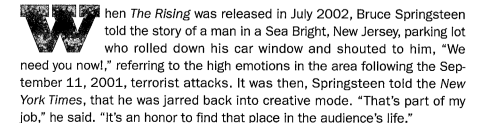 hen *The Rising* was released in July 2002, Bruce Springsteen told the story of a man in a Sea Bright, New Jersey, parking lot who rolled down his car window and shouted to him, "We need you now!," referring to the high emotions in the area following the September 11, 2001, terrorist attacks. It was then, Springsteen told the *New York Times*, that he was jarred back into creative mode. "That's part of my job," he said. "It's an honor to find that place in the audience's life."

Sutphin's appeal made him part of the Springsteen story, if only for a brief moment. He was interviewed during the NBC "Today" show broadcast on July 30, 2002, from Asbury Park, New Jersey, telling the program that when he saw Springsteen, "I rolled down the window, and I yelled as loud and as hard as I could, 'We need you now!'" Springsteen, according to Sutphin, didn't respond verbally, but he nodded—and then, apparently, went to work. "Bruce has given us so much," Sutphin told "Today." "If anyone can bring us together, he can." —*GG*

Crystal Taliefero. *See 1992–93 Bruce Springsteen Touring Band.*

Garry Tallent

E Street Band bass player, 1973–present

arry Tallent told one of his fan websites, "I think it's needless to have a rest from music itself, at least for me." He's proven that throughout his career, from his early days of gigging on the Jersey Shore to his time both with and without the E Street Band.

He was born Garry Wayne Tallent on October 27, 1949, in Detroit, Michigan, as one of seven children. The family moved around the U.S. before winding up for most of his high-school years in Neptune, New Jersey, where he was nicknamed the Tennessee Terror because of a family stop in Chattanooga. His classmates included not-yet-Southside Johnny Lyon and future E Street Band drummer Vini "Mad Dog" Lopez. Tallent played tuba in the school band but, smitten by rock and soul, he noticed that bass players seemed scarce, so he switched instruments, schooling himself on recordings by the Beatles' Paul McCartney, Motown's James Jamerson, the Rolling Stones' Bill Wyman, and Stax/Volt's Donald "Duck" Dunn. He told *Bass Player* magazine, "I stole from everyone"; in the late '70s he even took lessons from Atlantic Records house bassist Jerry Jemmot. Tallent was also a rockabilly fiend who amassed a large collection of early rock 'n' roll singles.

Once he picked up bass Tallent had no problem finding work—especially with other future E Street Band members. He and saxophonist

E Street bassist Garry Tallent, center, is flanked by Springsteen and violin player Soozie Tyrell at the band's performance at Boston's Fenway Park on September 6, 2003, in the final stretch of *The Rising* tour.

Clarence Clemons were in Little Melvin & the Invaders in the mid-'60s. Tallent worked with Lopez and keyboardist Danny Federici in the Downtown Tangiers Band and in the Moment of Truth. He played with guitarist Steve Van Zandt in the Jaywalkers and original E Street Band keyboardist David Sancious in Glory Road. The latter led him to Dr. Zoom and the Sonic Boom, Springsteen's performance art concept group, in 1971, and then to the Bruce Springsteen Band. When the latter disbanded Tallent joined the Sundance Blues Band with Van Zandt, Lopez, Sancious, Southside Johnny, and occasionally Springsteen before the E Street Band became a going concern in 1972.

Former Springsteen manager and coproducer Mike Appel described Tallent as "the right kind of bass player for this raggedy set of musicians. And he was a very obedient, low-key kind of guy who never had a problem." Tallent's own assessment about his contribution to the band is,

"Nobody notices I'm there until I'm not," but he was unquestionably around—not only to work with Springsteen but also doing sessions for Ronnie Spector, Ian Hunter, and Little Steven & the Disciples of Soul; Tallent also produced "We Got Love," an all-star benefit single by Jersey Artists for Mankind (J.A.M.) that included Springsteen, Clemons, Max Weinberg, and Nils Lofgren.

There was no questioning the warmth Springsteen felt toward Tallent; in his 1999 speech at the Rock and Roll Hall of Fame induction ceremony, Springsteen called the bassist "My lovely friend. Great bass player. Rock and roll aficionado whose quiet and dignity graced my band and my life." Behind that quiet veneer, however, was plenty of musical energy. When Springsteen disbanded the E Streeters in 1989, Tallent became one of the group's busiest alumni, moving to Nashville, where he set himself up as a producer and a session player. He established MoonDog Studios, named in tribute to early rock 'n' roll DJ Alan Freed and to John Lennon's first band with Paul McCartney. He racked up a resume that included work with Steve Earle, Emmylou Harris, Rodney Crowell, Steve Forbert, Robert Gordon, Clifford Curry, Jim Lauderdale, Sonny Burgess, Buddy and Julie Miller, the Delevantes (who he toured with in 1997), Kelly Willis, and others. Tallent also set up a record label, D'Ville Record Group, with engineer Tim Coats and singer-songwriter Ron LaSalle, which subsequently closed down. Tallent also joined Springsteen on stage on December 17, 1992, at Rupp Arena in Lexington, Kentucky, during the *Human Touch/Lucky Town* tour and also played on 1995's *The Ghost of Tom Joad*. —GG

Off of E Street ... Garry Tallent

The Believers, *I'm Your Prisoner* (1992)
Billy Pilgrim, *Bloom* (1995)
Gary U.S. Bonds, *Dedication* (1981), *On the Line* (1982)
Sonny Burgess, *Sonny Burgess* (1996)
Paul Burlison, *Train Kept A-Rollin'* (1997)
The Burns Sisters, *In This World* (1997)
Marshall Crenshaw, *La Bamba* soundtrack (1987)
Rodney Crowell, *Thing Called Love* soundtrack (1993)
Clifford Curry, *Clifford's Blues* (1996)
The Delevantes, *Postcards from Along the Way* (1997)
Francis Dunnery, *Tall Blond Helicopter* (1995)
Steve Earle, *I Feel Alright* (1996), *SideTracks* (2002)
Danny Federici, *Flemington* (1997)
Steve Forbert, *Streets of This Town* (1988), *Mission of the Crossroad Palms* (1995), *Live at the Bottom Line* (2001), *Any Old Time: Songs of Jimmie Rodgers* (2001)
Foster & Lloyd, *Version of the Truth* (1990)
Robert Gordon, *Live Fast, Die Young* (1989), *All for the Love of Rock 'n' Roll* (1994), *All for the Love of Money* (1999)
Henry Gross, *Nothing but Dreams.* (1992), *Hearing Things* (2001)
Emmylou Harris, *Brand New Dance* (1990)
Ian Hunter, *You're Never Alone with a Schizophrenic* (1979)
Evan Johns & His H-Bombs, *Evan Johns & His H-Bombs* (1986), *Bombs Away* (1989), *Love Is Murder* (1997)
Robert Earl Keen, Jr., *A Bigger Piece of the Sky* (1993), *Gringo Honeymoon* (1994)
Jim Lauderdale, *Persimmons* (1996), *Whisper* (1998), *Onward Through It All* (1999), *The Other Sessions* (2001), *The Hummingbirds* (2002)

Continued on next page...

The Temple of Soul

The Big Man's dressing room

he Temple of Soul is the name that E Street Band saxophonist Clarence Clemons has given his on-tour dressing room. He explained to *Backstreets* magazine: "It's a place that's created. It's an atmosphere that's created, where we can go and have fun and come out with something rewarding ... the Temple of Soul is a spiritual place—it's not like most dressing rooms. Mostly I meditate. And get treatments, stretching and stuff, before I go on stage. It's a pretty sane place, and we just try to take that energy on stage."

It's a well-stocked place, too, according to the rider from *The Rising* tour. According to the contract, "This room is for the sole use of Clarence Clemons" from a half-hour before the E Street Band hits the stage until after the equipment has been loaded out. The Temple of Soul is to be "suitably decorated, have a private restroom and shower and should be properly heated or air conditioned." It must also be equipped with: a couch and two matching chairs, one straight back chair, one coffee table, two side tables, a clothing rack, a full-length mirror, two table lamps, a standing lamp, two large floor plants, and two table plants. The Temple of Soul food order includes six twenty-ounce bottles of Green Gatorade, six cans of Coca-Cola, six cans of Diet Coke, eight one-liter bottles of Poland Spring water, Fiji water "big bottles," six red wine glasses, one wine opener, ice, one box of Carr's water biscuits, and one small tin of Beluga caviar. A whole fresh roasted chicken was to be boxed and placed in the room at 9:45 p.m. each show night.

Clemons also used the Temple of Soul as the name for his most recent band, which recorded two *Live from Asbury Park* CDs released in 2002 and 2004, with Springsteen jamming on Eddie Floyd's "Raise Your Hand" on the second volume. —*GG*

Clarence Clemons as Springsteen's maraca-wielding foil in a performance of "She's the One" at the Palladium in New York City in November 1976.

"Tenth Avenue Freeze-Out"

Single released: December 12, 1975
Album: *Born to Run* (Columbia, 1975)
Also on: *Live/1975–85* (Columbia, 1986), *Live in New York City* (Columbia, 2001)
Chart peak: No. 83

ruce Springsteen's "band bio and block party" has been a fan favorite since its release on 1975's breakthrough *Born to Run* album. The song itself was very much a product of its time; when Springsteen sang, "I'm running on the bad side/And I got my back to the wall," he was indeed feeling the pressure to make a great—and successful—album amidst rumors that his label, Columbia Records, was ready to drop him. But he managed to circumvent the tension with an R&B-fueled, good-time vibe that bolstered E Street Band saxophonist Clarence Clemons with the Brecker brothers—horn players Michael and Randy—and saxophonist David Sanborn.

"Tenth Avenue Freeze-Out" was also the song that brought Steve Van Zandt—a longtime friend who'd played with Springsteen in other New Jersey bands—into the E Street fold. When he decided to use a full horn section for the song, he called in Van Zandt, who happened to be managing, producing, and playing in another horn band, Southside Johnny & the Asbury Jukes, at the time. Van Zandt shocked everyone in the studio by telling the horn players to put away the charts that had been written for the song; instead he sang each player the part he wanted them to play. After that, Springsteen announced, "It's time to put the boy on the payroll."

Though it made only minor impact as a single, peaking at No. 83, "Tenth Avenue Freeze-Out" became a highlight of his live shows. Early on it was one of the moments when he'd venture into the audience; during his 1999–2000 reunion tour with the E Street Band it became an epic showpiece into which he incorporated the band introductions. —*GG*

3M

Manufacturer of electronics, recording tapes, and other products

n his Top 10 hit "My Hometown," Bruce Springsteen sang about the shutting down of a rug mill in Freehold, New Jersey, and its devastating economic impact on the town. But in October 1985, about seven weeks before that single was released, Springsteen became aware of another plant closing about to take place in Freehold—the town's Minnesota Mining and Manufacturing (3M) facility, which made professional audio and video tape. The company had notified the Oil, Chemical and Atomic Workers (OCAW)

Union Local 8-760 of its plans to shut down rather than modernize; the local's president, Stanley Fischer, wrote Springsteen a letter invoking the sentiments of "My Hometown" to ask him to join a campaign to keep the plant open.

Springsteen agreed, affixing his name to a series of open-letter ads that were published in the *New York Times, Asbury Park Press, St. Paul Pioneer Press*, and the entertainment trade publication *Variety*. Springsteen was joined in the first ad by Willie Nelson; the cast of TV's "Hill Street Blues" signed a second ad, while a third featured signatures from Springsteen, Nelson, the "Hill Street" cast, John Mellencamp, Joan Jett, Ed Asner, Robert Foxworth, the Blasters, and others.

On January 19, 1986, Springsteen and most of the E Street Band (sans Roy Bittan and Nils Lofgren, who were out of town) performed at a benefit for the 3M plant workers organized by Jersey Artists for Mankind at the Stone Pony in Asbury Park. Before starting his set, Springsteen told the crowd, "The marriage between a community and a company is a special thing that involves a special trust ... I'm here to say that I think that after twenty-five years of service from a community, there is a debt owed to the 3M workers and to my hometown." His set began, appropriately, with "My Hometown" and also included "The Promised Land," "Badlands," "Darkness on the Edge of Town" (which he dedicated to Fischer and the Local 8-760 members), "Stand on It," "Ramrod," and "Twist and Shout." The efforts, unfortunately, were not successful. 3M closed the Freehold plant in phases over the next couple of years, and the OCAW was thwarted in its attempts to sue 3M and to convince New Jersey politicians to pass legislation on plant closings. —*GG*

Thrill Hill

Springsteen's home studio

Thrill Hill is wherever Bruce Springsteen decides it is at any given time. It's the name he gave his home studio, whose locations have shifted with each of his moves. The low-fi *Nebraska*, for instance, was recorded at Thrill Hill—which was essentially a four-track recorder and a chair. Thrill Hill relocated to Los Angeles for the 1992 releases *Human Touch* and *Lucky Town*, and for 1995's *The Ghost of Tom Joad*. Thrill Hill, back in New Jersey, was also listed as a mixing site for some of the 1998 box set *Tracks* and as one of the studios at which 2002's *The Rising* was recorded. Currently it can be found in the nineteenth-century farmhouse in which Springsteen and his family reside in New Jersey's Monmouth County.

The Thrill Hill name is used on other aspects of Springsteen's operations. Thrill Hill Productions handles tour business management and also received a production credit on Springsteen's DVDs. The Thrill Hill Foundation distributes money to various charities Springsteen supports. And on the unsanctioned front, one active bootleg label operates under the moniker Thrill Hill Records. —*GG*

Thunder Road

Original Springsteen fanzine

he father of all Springsteen fanzines was *Thunder Road*, founded by the bicoastal duo of Lou Cohan (California) and Ken Viola (New Jersey) in 1977. While it didn't include the tour reports and set lists like we've come to expect from fanzines, *Thunder Road* did offer interviews and features focused around Springsteen, the E Street Band, and associated musicians. Interviewees across the issues included former E Streeter David Sancious; Columbia A&R legend and the man who signed Springsteen to Columbia, John Hammond; Springsteen's first manager, Tex Vinyard; and Springsteen musical influences such as Chuck Berry and Bo Diddley. *Thunder Road* truly excelled with its photography, and each issue brimmed with previously unpublished photos. Alas, *Thunder Road* published just five issues before going out in style with a farewell double issue in late 1982 that covered *The River* tour and the recently released *Nebraska*. —*EF*

"Thunder Road"

Released: September 1, 1975
Album: *Born to Run* (Columbia, 1975)
Also on: *Live/1975–85* (Columbia, 1986); *Greatest Hits* (Columbia, 1995); *In Concert MTV Plugged* (Columbia, 1997); *The Essential Bruce Springsteen* (2003)
Chart peak: Album track; never released as a single

hough it was never released as a single, Bruce Springsteen felt it was important to include "Thunder Road" on his 1995 *Greatest Hits* collection. "It seemed central," he explained to the *New York Times*, and it's unquestionably a song that conveys themes that he's explored throughout his career—those being, as he wrote in *Songs*, "Do you want to take a chance? On us? On life?" The vocal approach, meanwhile, was intended as an homage to Roy Orbison, who's name-checked in the song's first verse ("Roy Orbison singin' for the lonely ..."). When Springsteen first envisioned *Born to Run* as a "day in the life" concept album, "Thunder Road"—the title of which came from a 1958 bootlegging drama that starred Robert Mitchum—was slated to appear twice, opening the album in an acoustic arrangement and closing it as a full-band anthem.

The version of "Thunder Road" that appeared on *Born to Run* took a bit of work before Springsteen was satisfied; in fact, it was one of the first songs to benefit from his new association with music journalist Jon Landau as coproducer. Landau suggested shortening the song from more than seven minutes to a more concise 4:49 and moving Clarence Clemons's saxophone solo from the middle of the song to the end to better facilitate its compositional flow. Springsteen was so pleased with the final result that he hired Landau as coproducer of the album the next day.

The acoustic arrangement of the song lived on, however. At his famous Bottom Line concerts in 1975 in New York City, Springsteen opened the show with "Thunder Road" accompanied by just Roy Bittan on piano; a similar arrangement from October of that year at the Roxy in Los Angeles appears on *Live/1975–85*, and the song has been played in that fashion on other tours. Several cover versions of the song have been recorded—by Mary Lou Lord, the Smithereens, and country singer John Berry—and Springsteen joined Melissa Etheridge on her performance of the song for her 1995 episode of MTV's "Unplugged." —*GG*

Ticket Drop

Regular practice by which last-minute concert tickets become available

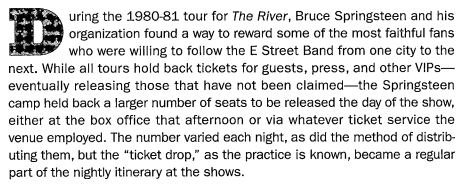

uring the 1980-81 tour for *The River*, Bruce Springsteen and his organization found a way to reward some of the most faithful fans who were willing to follow the E Street Band from one city to the next. While all tours hold back tickets for guests, press, and other VIPs—eventually releasing those that have not been claimed—the Springsteen camp held back a larger number of seats to be released the day of the show, either at the box office that afternoon or via whatever ticket service the venue employed. The number varied each night, as did the method of distributing them, but the "ticket drop," as the practice is known, became a regular part of the nightly itinerary at the shows.

Fans can find rewards once inside the venues as well. Springsteen crew members often roam the upper deck and "cheap seat" areas prior to the show's start, randomly passing out tickets for considerably better seats, usual in the first few rows. Fans nicknamed these individual rock 'n' roll Santa Clauses "Men in Black" (or M.I.B.), and *Backstreets* magazine once noted, "The M.I.B. was known to favor attractive women, as there are few reports of unaccompanied men receiving ticket upgrades." —*GG*

The Ties That Bind

Single-disc album from 1979. Never released.

fter spending the late spring and early summer of 1979 cutting dozens of songs with the E Street Band at the Power Station in New York City, and on the eve of the band's appearance at the No Nukes benefit concert, Bruce Springsteen wrote up a track list for a single-LP follow-up to *Darkness on the Edge of Town*. This time the effort went so far as to have a Power Station engineer assemble a master tape of the ten-song lineup of what was to be called *The Ties That Bind*. Photo sessions for the album's cover were convened with Frank Stefanko, who shot the *Darkness* cover, and even Columbia hinted publicly that a new Springsteen album would be out before the end of 1979. While the lineup was tinkered with, the version that was submitted to Columbia was as follows: Side one—"The Ties That Bind," "Cindy," "Hungry Heart," "Stolen Car," "To Be True"; Side two—"The River," "You Can Look (But You Better Not Touch)," "The Price You Pay," "I Wanna Marry You," "Loose Ends." Like all of Springsteen's lost albums, plans for *The Ties That Bind* were eventually abandoned as Springsteen kept writing and the band kept recording new songs. "I felt that it just wasn't good enough," he wrote of *The Ties That Bind* in *Songs*. "The songs lacked the kind of unity and conceptual intensity I liked my music to have." Eventually, the core of *Ties* was expanded into a double album, *The River*, in 1980. But not all the songs made the cut and a few underwent significant changes. "Stolen Car" bore a completely different arrangement some refer to as the "Son You May Kiss the Bride" version; this arrangement eventually saw the light of day on *Tracks*, as did the album-closing "Loose Ends." But the album's rockabilly arrangement of "You Can Look" remains unreleased to this day, as does "Cindy," a lilting tale of a hopeless and hapless romantic. "The Price You Pay" also features a different verse to the released take.

Amazingly, reel-to-reel copies of *The Ties That Bind* from the Power Station itself found their way into the hands of bootleggers, who released a version of the album under that title in remarkable quality and featuring reproductions of the tape boxes on the front and back cover. —*EF*

Time/Newsweek Covers

October 1975

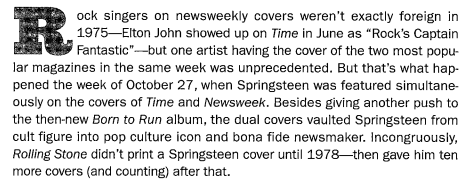

ock singers on newsweekly covers weren't exactly foreign in 1975—Elton John showed up on *Time* in June as "Rock's Captain Fantastic"—but one artist having the cover of the two most popular magazines in the same week was unprecedented. But that's what happened the week of October 27, when Springsteen was featured simultaneously on the covers of *Time* and *Newsweek*. Besides giving another push to the then-new *Born to Run* album, the dual covers vaulted Springsteen from cult figure into pop culture icon and bona fide newsmaker. Incongruously, *Rolling Stone* didn't print a Springsteen cover until 1978—then gave him ten more covers (and counting) after that.

The two articles took markedly different courses. *Time*'s interview piece called Springsteen "Rock's New Sensation," while *Newsweek* weighed in with "Making of a Rock Star," focusing on the hype surrounding Springsteen and the *Born to Run* album. Were the simultaneous covers a coincidence? Not according to Dave Marsh's biography *Born to Run: The Bruce Springsteen Story*, which accuses *Newsweek* writer and "glamour sniper" Maureen Orth of deliberately discrediting Springsteen with her story. *Time*'s Jay Cocks, a Springsteen fan, learned about Orth's plans and convinced his editors to commission a more upbeat one. *Newsweek* ran an editorial piece the following week denying that the two publications colluded at all in putting Springsteen on the cover, while *Time* editor-in-chief Henry Gruenwald, according to Marsh, was overheard calling the Springsteen cover the greatest embarrassment of his career.

Springsteen, who characteristically avoids boasting about media attention, famously tried to co-opt the magazine covers for his own purposes in 1976. Seeking an audience with Elvis Presley, he hopped the fence at Graceland, ran to the door, knocked ... and was intercepted by security. Attempting to convince the guards of his status as a recording star, he mentioned the *Time* and *Newsweek* covers—but ultimately failed in his quest. As he recounted the story on stage: "Later on, I used to wonder what I would have said if I had knocked on the door and if Elvis had come to the door. Because it really wasn't Elvis I was goin' to see, but it was like he came along and whispered some dream in everybody's ear and somehow we all dreamed it."

Springsteen also made light of the notoriety in his concert performances, occasionally altering the "Rosalita" lyric to "Tell your papa I ain't no freak/'cause I got my picture on the cover of *Time* and *Newsweek*!"

Springsteen's second *Newsweek* cover came ten years later, during the *Born in the U.S.A.* hype cycle, on August 5, 1985. *Time* waited twenty-seven years, giving Springsteen the cover for *The Rising* on August 5, 2002. Commented the *Media Industry Newsletter* in 2002: "As far as we know, that is the longest cover 'gap' in Time's seventy-eight-year history for people still active in their craft." —*SK*

Tougher Than the Rest

Promotional album

In June 1992, with Bruce Springsteen's first post–E Street Band tour about to come to the U.K., Sony Music's British branch released this sixteen-track promotional album to help hype the dates. The career-spanning collection reached from "For You" from *Greetings from Asbury Park, N.J.* all the way to his then-current releases *Human Touch* and *Lucky Town*.

The sampler was pressed in very limited quantities and is hotly pursued by collectors. —*GG*

Pete Townshend

Guitarist, chief songwriter and leader of the Who

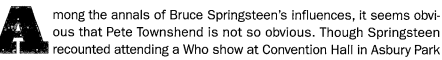

Among the annals of Bruce Springsteen's influences, it seems obvious that Pete Townshend is not so obvious. Though Springsteen recounted attending a Who show at Convention Hall in Asbury Park in the mid-'60s, his public comments about the Who and its dynamic leader have been few. More easily compared to Bob Dylan and Elvis Presley, the comparisons between Springsteen and Townshend take a little effort to trace. Few would argue that Springsteen's guitar playing, for example, shares much with the aggressive rhythmic slashing style Townshend pioneered. Yet Springsteen's occasional swings of his right arm windmill style seem more like a tribute to Townshend than anything else. Both musicians demonstrated respect for blues music, and for the ability to perform it credibly: early Who records and performances were blues-based, and Springsteen fronted a short-lived blues band in 1971. And of course, both have played "My Generation": Springsteen's first band, the Castiles, occasionally performed the groundbreaking song in the mid-'60s.

Where the two musicians intersect, perhaps, is in their songwriting. Springsteen and Townshend have both created bodies of work steeped in introspection. Even as the Who put the brakes on in 1982, Townshend was adamant in his belief that rock 'n' roll still had to "face the issues," something Springsteen had been doing in his own work since *Darkness on the Edge of Town*.

The two performed together once; Townshend attended several Springsteen concerts in the U.K. in 1981 and sat in with the E Street Band for "Born to Run" and the "Detroit Medley" on June 7 in Birmingham, England. Steve Van Zandt's Little Steven & the Disciples of Soul, meanwhile, opened shows in Cleveland on the first Who "farewell" tour in 1982, which Springsteen attended (but alas, did not play).

Townshend, meanwhile, has been a vociferous admirer *and* critic of Springsteen. In 1975, following the release of *Born to Run*, he noted, "When Bruce Springsteen sings on his new album, that's not 'fun'; that's fucking triumph, man." In 1996, he told *Wall of Sound,* "I had such an extraordinary engagement with Springsteen, mainly through his concerts. I like the early, anthemic stuff, but when I saw him in 1981 what I really liked was the poetry, the demand he made of his audience to 'listen to this.' He put you in another place ...." Townshend wasn't quite as enamored with Springsteen's "stadium rock" turn with 1984's *Born in the U.S.A.* ("... it became like an adrenaline-addicted experience. Next thing you know, he was pumping iron and I just thought, the guy's a casualty") but he was intrigued by *The Ghost of Tom Joad* and the subsequent solo tour: "What he has done now is pretty much what I think I did, which is he's destroyed everything and gone back to square one. This first step is not a very comfortable one ... I think you have to dig really deep to find the worms. I'm waiting, in a way, for him to get through the other side of this." —JP

Tracks

Released: November 10, 1998
Producers: Bruce Springsteen, Chuck Plotkin
Tracks: Disc 1—"Mary Queen of Arkansas," "It's Hard to Be a Saint in the City," "Growin' Up," "Does This Bus Stop at 82nd Street?," "Bishop Danced," "Santa Ana," "Seaside Bar Song," "Zero & Blind Terry," "Linda Let Me Be the One," "Thundercrack," "Rendezvous," "Give the Girl a Kiss," "Iceman," "Bring on the Night," "So Young and in Love," "Hearts of Stone," "Don't Look Back"; Disc 2—"Restless Nights," "A Good Man Is Hard to Find (Pittsburgh)," "Roulette," "Dollhouse," "Where the Bands Are," "Loose Ends," "Living on the Edge of the World," "Wages of Sin," "Take 'Em as They Come," "Be True," "Ricky Wants a Man of Her Own," "I Wanna Be With You," "Mary Lou," "Stolen Car," "Born in the U.S.A.," "Johnny Bye Bye," "Shut Out the Light"; Disc 3—"Cynthia," "My Love Will Not Let You Down," "This Hard Land," "Frankie," "TV Movie," "Stand on It," "Lion's Den," "Car Wash," "Rockaway the Days," "Brothers Under the Bridges ('83)," "Man at the Top," "Pink Cadillac," "Two for the Road," "Janey Don't You Lose Heart," "When You Need Me," "The Wish," "The Honeymooners," "Lucky Man"; Disc 4—"Leavin' Train," "Seven Angels," "Gave It a Name," "Sad Eyes," "My Lover Man," "Over the Rise," "When the Lights Go Out," "Loose Change," "Trouble in Paradise," "Happy," "Part Man, Part Monkey," "Goin' Cali," "Back in Your Arms," "Brothers Under the Bridge"
Chart peak: No. 27

n 1984, Bruce Springsteen told Kurt Loder, "We record a lot of material, but we just don't release it all ... I always tell myself that some day I'm gonna put an album out with all this stuff on it that didn't fit in. I think there's good material there that should come out. Maybe at some point I'll do that." That point came in 1998, when Springsteen released *Tracks*, a lavishly packaged four-CD set that liberated sixty-six songs from his brimming vaults, fifty-six of which were previously unreleased.

The impetus for the project was inertia; Springsteen was working on a follow-up to *The Ghost of Tom Joad* and, he told *Mojo* magazine, he "got stuck." Conscious that a great deal of time could pass before he had a new album ready to release, he asked engineer Toby Scott to crack open the vaults and start sending tapes. "I said 'Gee, if it's going to be a year or

Springsteen included a rare performance of "Frankie" at an April 4, 1976, show in East Lansing, Michigan. He finally released a studio version of the song as part of the *Tracks* collection in 1998.

longer in between records, I have all this unreleased music that I know is very good and I should release some of it,'" Springsteen explained. He and longtime coproducer Chuck Plotkin listened and came up with about 100 possible tracks for the album; Bob Benjamin, a friend who manages Pittsburgh rocker Joe Grushecky, also contributed some ideas and recordings from his personal collection. Springsteen then presented the box-set idea to manager Jon Landau—who was supportive but insisted that the material be freshly mixed. It was a daunting request, to say the least; "I said 'Mixed, oh my God ... has *anybody* ever done eighty mixes?" Springsteen told *Mojo*.

He noted, "*Tracks* didn't take a lot of thinking," but it did take a great deal of work. Springsteen and Plotkin kept three studios going throughout the process, communicating by phone with mixing engineer Bob Clearmountain in California. Another engineer, Ed Thacker, was also instru-

The Ties That Bind

mental in keeping things flowing. "For the fans who'd heard these things, it's just a very different presentation of the music, much more fully realized and powerful," Springsteen said.

As for the song selection, he explained to *Mojo*, "I based my choices on what was pretty much finished and what I felt were the best things we had done that hadn't come out." Hence a heavily desired outtake like "The Promise" didn't make the cut because Springsteen didn't have a version he felt was good enough to release (though he wound up recording a new one for the subsequent *18 Tracks* single-disc set), while he left off "The Fever" because "it was never one of my favorite songs" (though it, too, surfaced on *18 Tracks*). But *Tracks* is still brimming with treasures, starting with his 1972 audition for Columbia Records' John Hammond and going in chronological order through outtakes, rarities, and some alternate versions of songs. *Tracks* also includes several selections that popped up as Springsteen B-sides, including "Be True," "Pink Cadillac," and "Shut Out the Light."

Columbia began teasing *Tracks* in a July 13, 1998, *Billboard* magazine ad about new releases that ended with one word: "Bruuuuuuuuuuuuce!" Springsteen attended the Sony Music convention on July 16 in Miami, Florida, to officially announce the *Tracks* and play a tape of three of the songs—"Where the Bands Are," "Loose Ends," and "I Wanna Be with You." He also hinted that an E Street Band tour would be in the offing for 1999. In mid-September, the mastered *Tracks* tapes were delivered to the label, right around the time Rock and Roll Hall of Fame ballots—with Springsteen's name among the finalists—were mailed to voters. *Tracks*'s November 10 release coincided with the announcement that he'd been elected to the Hall of Fame for induction in March 1999. —*GG*

"**W**hat's apparent is that Springsteen left more good songs off his studio albums than most composers write in their entire recording careers ... He's had to make hard choices in deleting some absolute gems, which are finally collected in this project."
—*Boston Globe*

"**B**ruce Springsteen sounds like one of his lesser imitators on *Tracks* ... most of the songs are clunkers, low on melody and full of labored metaphors and painfully earnest cliches. With barely one CD's worth of new songs worth saving, *Tracks* belatedly reveals what a superb self-editor Mr. Springsteen has been until now."
—*New York Times*

"**T**racks certainly goes beyond the tip of the iceberg, but it also misses its share of gems in favor of lesser pieces, which makes it a fascinating and in places frustrating exercise that is nonetheless a worthy addendum to Springsteen's body of work."
—*Wall of Sound*

"**T**racks adds to Mr. Springsteen's legacy as the best of America's post-Dylan singer-songwriters. Much more than a collection of miscellaneous and unconnected recordings, it shows an artist who's looked inward to find a superior means of expression."
—*Wall Street Journal*

Reggae legend Jimmy Cliff performs in Berne, Switzerland, in July 2003. Springsteen first performed his version of Cliff's song "Trapped" during *The River* tour in 1981.

"Trapped"

Cover version of Jimmy Cliff song, released April 1985 on *USA for Africa: We Are the World*

In 1985, Bruce Springsteen sang on USA for Africa's "We Are the World," an all-star charity single for Ethiopian famine relief. Various artists, including Springsteen, contributed tracks for the *USA for Africa* album as well. Springsteen's selection was a live recording of "Trapped," a reworking of a Jimmy Cliff reggae song he recorded in August 1984 in New Jersey.

Cliff, born James Chambers in St. Catherine, Jamaica, is one of reggae's seminal artists. He had hit records as a teenager and moved to France and then England in an attempt to reach an international audience. The plan worked to an extent, but Cliff gained greater fame as an actor, staring in the film *The Harder They Come*, the soundtrack of which became an enduring reggae classic. His many hits include "You Can Get It If You Really Want It," "Many Rivers to Cross," and "The Harder They Come." Cliff also took part in Steve Van Zandt's all-star "Sun City" protest song in 1985.

Springsteen first heard "Trapped" on a cassette tape around 1980 and began incorporating it into his shows the following year, while touring in support of *The River*. Cliff's song is about a doomed relationship, but Springsteen's impassioned delivery of new lines he wrote for the song, such as— "I'll teach my eyes to see/Beyond these walls in front of me/Someday I'll walk out of here again"—gave it a greater sense of hope and made it an apt choice for the *USA for Africa* album. (Not to mention that fans were clamoring for a version of it, too.) A documentary of the making of the album was also released featuring a clip of "Trapped." Until the song surfaced again on the 2003 anthology *The Essential Bruce Springsteen*, the *USA for Africa* album and video were the only place his version was available. —*DD*

George Travis

Springsteen tour director

eorge Travis, one of the most respected tour directors in pop music, began his relationship with Bruce Springsteen in 1978, when he was hired as a rigger for the *Darkness on the Edge of Town* tour. (A rigger hangs the cables, motors, trusses, and most everything else suspended above the artist's and audience's heads during a concert.) After that, Travis ascended to the ranks of stage manager, production manager, and tour manager before assuming the title of tour director in 1984. In more than a quarter century of Springsteen shows and tours, Travis has missed only one Springsteen performance—the one that occurred the day after he got married.

Raised in upstate New York, Travis grew up a gadget guy whose interest in rock 'n' roll music was mild by comparison to other roadies and crew members. After he and some friends found themselves stranded in San Francisco in the early '70s, Travis got a job driving a truck and working as a rigger for a circus and made his way back across the country. His first rigger's gig in rock was with the Rolling Stones in 1975; it was followed by road stints with Emerson, Lake & Palmer, Kiss, Crosby, Stills & Nash, and Elvis Presley on his last tour in 1977. He landed with Springsteen in 1978.

Travis and other members of Springsteen's road crew—who Billy Joel called "the best" in the business in 1999—have joined other tours when Springsteen was off the road. Among the artists Travis has worked with are Madonna, Shania Twain, Ringo Starr, and the Rolling Stones. He has also worked for the two US Festivals, Farm Aid, the Amnesty International Tour Human Rights Now! tour in 1988, and Van Halen's Monsters of Rock tour. —*RS*

Salvador Trepat. *See Point Blank Magazine.*

Tunnel of Love

Released: October 6, 1987
Producers: Bruce Springsteen, Jon Landau, Chuck Plotkin
Tracks: "Ain't Got You," "Tougher Than the Rest," "All That Heaven Will Allow," "Spare Parts," "Cautious Man," "Walk Like a Man," "Tunnel of Love," "Two Faces," "Brilliant Disguise," "One Step Up," "When You're Alone," "Valentine's Day"
Chart peak: No. 1

or twenty years I'd written about the man on the road," Bruce Springsteen noted in *Songs*. "On *Tunnel of Love* that changed, and my music turned to the hopes and fears of the man in the house." This shift in gears resulted in one of the most fascinating rides of Springsteen's career, as well as the beginning of a twelve-year stretch as a solo recording artist.

Tunnel of Love parallels the creative decision Springsteen made in 1982, when he was following up the multi-platinum success of *The River*. In the wake of the phenomenon of *Born in the U.S.A.* and the massive *Live/1975–85* project, Springsteen was determinedly looking for a way to dial things down and perhaps serve notice that he understood the fragile and potentially perilous position his career was in at the time. "Trying to keep the kind of success we had with *Born in the U.S.A.* going would have been a losing game," he explained. "In 1987 … I decided to reintroduce myself to my fans as a songwriter." He also opted to pursue the project as his second solo album rather than a full-blown E Street Band outing, though the group members would show up throughout *Tunnel of Love*.

The newlywed Springsteen—he'd married actress/model Julianne Phillips on May 13, 1985—first started recording in January 1987 at A&M Studios in Los Angeles, with members of former Byrd and Flying Burrito Brother Chris Hillman's New Rose Band; "One Step Up," which in its final form featured just Springsteen and Patti Scialfa, was all that would make it from those sessions. After a brief attempt at recording at Kren Studios in New York City, Springsteen then returned to the studio he'd built atop the carriage house at his home in Rumson, New Jersey, to work on the rest of the material that would fill the album. "I wanted to get back to the intimacy of home recording," he wrote, adding that most of the album was done in a three-week period. "The songs … came out of a single place in a short period of time. The songs and the record happened very fast." The E Street Band members were brought in to add colors, textures, and the occasional solo (á la Nils Lofgren's guitar break in the title track); Max Weinberg replaced the electronic drums Springsteen had used to write to on eight of the twelve tracks. The album's intimate, hushed sound was disarming, especially after the full-scale band attack of *Born in the U.S.A.* and *Live/1975–85*.

But that was only part of the story. *Tunnel of Love*'s lyrics gripped listeners just as much, as they received what was perceived as a deep look into the state of Springsteen's life and especially his still-young marriage—which did not seem to be a smooth ride at all but rather one filled with doubt, darkness, and fear. As he sang in the title track, "The house is haunted and the ride gets rough/And you've got to learn with what you can't rise above." Springsteen contended in *Songs*, "The writing was not painful, and though some thought so, not literally autobiographical." Rather, he wrote, *Tunnel of Love* delved into "an inner life and unresolved feelings" he had not yet embraced significantly in his music. So rather than an album of maudlin love songs to his new bride, Springsteen was writing what he told *Rolling Stone* magazine was "a different type of romantic song, one that I felt took in the different types of emotional experience of any real relationship ... Letting another person into your life, that's a frightening thing. That's something that's filled with shadows and doubts, and also wonderful things and beautiful things, things you cannot experience alone." There's certainly a universality to the emotions Springsteen examines in *Tunnel of Love*, but anyone listening to it recognized it was not the work of a happily married man. And this proved to be the case; in mid-June 1988, during the Roman stop of the European leg of the *Tunnel of Love* tour, paparazzi snapped photos of Springsteen and Scialfa canoodling on a hotel balcony. Phillips filed for divorce on August 30.

Fans still felt the love, though. *Tunnel* hit No. 1 on the *Billboard* Top 200 chart in its third week of release, bumping Michael Jackson's *Bad* out of the top spot. It gave Springsteen his fourth consecutive chart-topper and made him the only artist to log four No. 1 albums in the '80s. —*GG*

"**I**t is a record Springsteen has staked a lot on. It follows no formulas and does not provide what many fans may first expect. But right now, anyhow, it sounds like the best record he has ever made."
—*Time*

"**I**t's not that Springsteen is the first writer to address the confusions of the heart ... but putting out such an introspective and intimate collection on the heels of the hard-charging *Born in the U.S.A.* and the heroically structured *Live* set is an intriguing move. It contains some of Springsteen's most personal work and could very well provide the demythologizing he must crave."
—*Washington Post*

"**F**ar from being a series of hymns to cozy domesticity, *Tunnel of Love* is an unsettled and unsettling collection of hard looks at the perils of commitment. A decade or so ago, Springsteen acquired a reputation for romanticizing his subject matter. Now he doesn't even romanticize romance."
—*Rolling Stone*

"Tunnel of Love"

Released: October 1987
Album: *Tunnel of Love* (Columbia, 1987)
Also on: *The Essential Bruce Springsteen* (Columbia, 2003)
Chart peak: No. 9

Though it's positioned in the middle, the title track of Bruce Springsteen's eleventh album crystallizes its theme, using a carnival thrill ride as the metaphor for a relationship—an experience fraught with twists, turns, and, in the worst case scenario, a premature end. As he sings in the song's midsection, "It's easy for two people to lose each other/In this tunnel of love."

Like most of the other songs on *Tunnel of Love*, this one began as a demo-style home recording onto which Springsteen added other musicians—in this case the fullest and most "band"-style arrangement of anything on the album. Max Weinberg played percussion, Roy Bittan provided synthesiz-

Springsteen abandoned the muscle shirts and jeans of the *Born in the U.S.A.* tour for a suited-up style for the Tunnel of Love Express Tour.

ers, and Patti Scialfa brought echoing backing vocals. In addition to acoustic guitar, Springsteen is credited with "sound effects," and the rollercoaster sounds came courtesy of the Schiffer Family amusement company in Pt. Pleasant Beach, New Jersey. Springsteen also called in E Street Band guitarist Nils Lofgren, who joined the group after the completion of *Born in the U.S.A.* in 1984, for his first studio recording with The Boss. "My wife and I were visiting Bruce in Jersey for a couple of days," Lofgren recalled. "He was working on that record in another house, and he said, 'Hey, tomorrow afternoon, if you've got a little time, I've got this song and I'd like you to take a shot at the solo.'" Springsteen rejected Lofgren's initial attempt as "too standard," and the two musicians worked up a markedly different tone for his performance. "He plugged me into all these foot pedals, all these flangers and distortions, and started turning all the dials," Lofgren said. "He came up with this funky, flangy sound ... I have no idea how he got the sounds, though; Bruce turned about eighteen knobs until it was weird."

"Tunnel of Love" was Springsteen's tenth Top 10 single. The song's video, directed by Meiert Avis, was shot in November 1987 on the boardwalk in Asbury Park, New Jersey. —*GG*

Tunnel of Love Express Tour **CD**

Released: February 1988
Producers: Bruce Springsteen, Jon Landau, Chuck Plotkin, Steve Van Zandt
Tracks: "All That Heaven Will Allow," "One Step Up," "Roulette," "Be True," "Pink Cadillac"

ne of Bruce Springsteen's most treasured promotional items is this five-song CD issued to promote the first leg of the 1988 Tunnel of Love Express Tour. The CD includes a pair of songs from the *Tunnel of Love* album—"All That Heaven Will Allow" and "One Step Up"—but

The Ties That Bind

is most notable for its three rare tracks: the B-sides "Be True" and "Pink Cadillac," and the unreleased "Roulette."

The CD included the dates of the first twenty-one shows on the tour on both the back cover and the CD itself. The cover showed a black-suited Springsteen sporting a bolo tie and holding a bouquet of roses. —*GG*

2 Live Crew

Controversial Florida rap troupe

ore than a decade before Bruce Springsteen threw his support behind the Dixie Chicks, he took a stand for freedom of speech by aiding a more disparate act, 2 Live Crew. A Miami, Florida, rap group formed in 1987 and known for its unrepentantly lewd, crude, and lascivious lyrics, 2 Live Crew was an underground sensation in the late '80s; as is often the case, it took attempted censorship to bring them more widespread recognition. As with Eminem a decade later, what was funny to some was outrageous and even pornographic to others. In June 1990, a Broward county judge declared 1989's *As Nasty as They Wanna Be* (featuring songs like "Me So Horny" and "Dirty Nursery Rhymes") legally obscene—meaning that record-store sales in Miami could lead to arrest and prosecution.

Led by Luther Campbell (aka Luke Skyywalker, aka Luke), 2 Live Crew recorded "Banned in the U.S.A." the following month, with a chorus sung to the melody of "Born in the U.S.A." and a recurring riff lifted from the Springsteen song. "Banned in the U.S.A." was a simple yet effective anti-censorship retort: "The First Amendment gave us freedom of speech/So what are you sayin'? It didn't include me? ... Wisen up, 'cause on Election Day/ We'll see who's banned in the U.S.A.!"

After reviewing the song, Springsteen gave his permission "enthusiastically," according to the group's lawyer. Springsteen's manager Jon Landau said his client found "Banned in the U.S.A." to be a "quality" song and told *Rolling Stone* magazine, "Bruce is not unmindful of the fact that Luke is on the spot. He's happy to lend a hand." Florida attorney general Jack Thompson, who led the campaign against 2 Live Crew, was unhappy, retorting, "Bruce and Luther Campbell can go to hell together. Bruce Springsteen is facilitating the sexual abuse of women and the mental molestation of children by giving 2 Live Crew the use of his music."

"Banned in the U.S.A." was released as a single and became the title track of an album (the group's first to be distributed by a major label) later in the year. The obscenity ruling was later overturned on appeal, but not before an outcry from free speech advocates around the country and a nationwide

Off of E Street ...
Soozie Tyrell

Shawn Colvin, *Steady On* **(1989)**

Sheryl Crow, *C'mon C'mon* **(2002)**

John Hammond, Jr., *Found True Love* **(1996),**
Ready for Love (2003)

Buster Poindexter, *Buster Poindexter* **(1987),**
***Buster's Happy Hour* (1994),** *Buster's Spanish*
***Rocketship* (1997)**

Patti Scialfa, *Rumble Doll* **(1993),** *23rd Street*
***Lullaby* (2004)**

Train, *My Private Nation* **(2003)**

Uptown Horns, *Uptown Horns Revue* **(1994)**

debate on obscenity in song lyrics. *As Nasty as They Wanna Be*, meanwhile, went triple-platinum.

An unlikely First Amendment champion, Campbell later won a 1993 Supreme Court case against Acuff-Rose Music, with 2 Live Crew's "Pretty Woman" parody being judged a case of "fair use." —*CP*

Soozie Tyrell

Singer, songwriter, multi-instrumentalist

ntil 2002, Soozie Tyrell listed Bruce Springsteen as one of her many session clients, having played on *Lucky Town* and *The Ghost of Tom Joad*. But when he set to work on *The Rising*, Springsteen told Tyrell, "Sooz, I'm just hearing violins on everything now," and brought the multi-instrumentalist deeper into the fold than ever before, making her a key player on that album and incorporating her into the E Street Band for the 2002–2003 world tour supporting *The Rising*.

Tyrell was cautious about her status, however. "It's a funny thing," she said. "I don't think that officially I am, but when I'm up there playing with them I feel a part of the band. I know it sounds trite, but it's a real honor and a privilege—and a complete joy. And Bruce's fans have been so accepting of me, really taken me in as an added new sound to the E Street Band. But I don't think officially I'm allowed to say I'm a member; I haven't earned that right yet. Probably by the second or third tour, if I'm ever asked again, I may be. But, as you know, he goes through a lot of changes."

Tyrell was born in Italy and moved around the world with her father's U.S. Army career. She moved to New York City in 1977 and formed a group, Trickster, with Springsteen's future wife, Patti Scialfa, and fellow singer Lisa Lowell. Tyrell also filled her resume working with Carole King, Shawn Colvin, Judy Collins, Buster Poindexter, Sheryl Crow, Train, and others, along with commercial sessions for ad agencies.

In 2003, while out on the road with the E Street Band, Tyrell released her first solo album, *White Lines*. Scialfa, of course, helped out with backing vocals, and Springsteen played guitar on the rocking title track and joined his wife to sing on the gently melodic "St. Genevieve." Tyrell also provided strings and vocals to Springsteen's 2005 release, *Devils & Dust*.—*GG*

The Upstage

Asbury Park club and musicians' proving ground, 1968–71

An after-hours, amateur musician's club in Asbury Park, New Jersey, the Upstage launched a number of late '60s Jersey Shore rock bands, including Bruce Springsteen's hard-rock outfit Steel Mill. The Upstage was also a musician's proving ground; only the best area players were invited onto the club's stage to jam. Competition for a place on stage was keen. The music—mostly long, extended blues jams that lasted until four or five o' clock in the morning—was like none heard anywhere else on the Jersey Shore at that time. While most of the Shore's bars and nightclubs featured Top 40 cover bands, the Upstage encouraged musicians to leave convention at the door, bringing into the club only their ability to play and their determination to shine.

In many ways, the Upstage, which was only open for about three years, was more like a great jazz club, where jamming and improvisation rules, than any rock club of its time. With the Stone Pony, it created an internationally famous rock scene in Asbury Park. Springsteen, along with future E Street Band members including bassist Garry Tallent, guitarist Steve Van Zandt, keyboardist/guitarist David Sancious, and organist Danny Federici, were Upstage regulars. Other prominent Jersey Shore musicians often found jamming at the Upstage included guitarists Billy Chinnock, Ricky DeSarno, and Billy Ryan; harmonica player and singer Southside Johnny Lyon; bassists Vini Roslyn, Gerald Carboy, and Johnny Luraschi; and keyboards player Kevin Kavanaugh. Together, these musicians went on to form the nucleus of the

Jersey Shore music scene in the early and mid-'70s, the area's golden age of rock.

The Upstage opened in 1968 above a Thom McAn shoe store on Cookman Avenue in Asbury Park. Run by Tom and Margaret Potter, it was open on Friday, Saturday, and Sunday nights; while Tom took care of the club's business side, Margaret's band, Margaret and the Distractions, kept the Upstage full of music before the early morning jams began. The first "session" at the Upstage started around 9 p.m. and lasted until just after midnight; if the Distractions didn't perform, other local bands did, for an audience of mostly minors under the age of eighteen. The club's second "session" began around 1 a.m. and featured just jams, and only those musicians and music fans over eighteen were permitted to stay. The Upstage closed at daybreak, after which some musicians then went to the beach to sleep until the lifeguards and bathers arrived.

"You could go there and work all night for five bucks," Van Zandt recalled. "If you were exceptional and ran the jams, you'd get fifteen bucks for eight hours' work. If you were working somewhere else by some miracle, you could come there after your normal bar gig. Most of the other clubs closed by one or two."

The Upstage remained open until early 1971. Race riots the previous year destroyed Asbury Park's downtown section, causing millions of dollars in damage and fracturing the relationship between the city's black and white residents. Although the Upstage was not physically damaged by the riots, the general uneasiness from the wake of the violence ended the carefree spirit of the club. Some six months after the riots, the Upstage closed. —*RS*

USA for Africa. *See* **"We Are the World."**

U2

Rock band from Dublin, Ireland

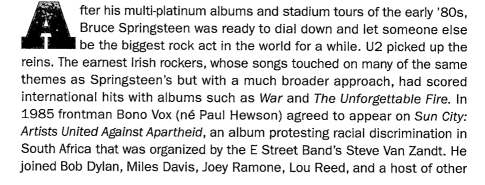 fter his multi-platinum albums and stadium tours of the early '80s, Bruce Springsteen was ready to dial down and let someone else be the biggest rock act in the world for a while. U2 picked up the reins. The earnest Irish rockers, whose songs touched on many of the same themes as Springsteen's but with a much broader approach, had scored international hits with albums such as *War* and *The Unforgettable Fire*. In 1985 frontman Bono Vox (né Paul Hewson) agreed to appear on *Sun City: Artists United Against Apartheid*, an album protesting racial discrimination in South Africa that was organized by the E Street Band's Steve Van Zandt. He joined Bob Dylan, Miles Davis, Joey Ramone, Lou Reed, and a host of other

rockers and rappers on the single and video of the title song, and contributed another track, "Silver & Gold," with help from Rolling Stones Keith Richards and Ron Wood.

Launched in the late '70s in Dublin, U2 rose to superstar status with 1987's *The Joshua Tree*—which got the quartet its own *Time* magazine cover (but no *Newsweek*)—and remained at the top of the rock heap through efforts such as *Achtung Baby* and *All That You Can't Leave Behind.* They crossed paths occasionally with Springsteen, often at charity and tribute concerts such as 2001's September 11 benefit telethon "America: A Tribute to Heroes" and a 1999 show paying homage to Johnny Cash. Springsteen also joined U2 on stage on September 25, 1987, for an encore performance of Ben E. King's "Stand by Me" at Philadelphia's John F. Kennedy Stadium.

When Springsteen was inducted into the Rock and Roll Hall of Fame in 1999, Bono did the honors: "Bruce made you believe that dreams were still out there, but after loss and defeat, they had to be braver, not just bigger," Bono said. He added that Springsteen "saved music from the phonies, saved lyrics from the folkies, and saved black leather jackets from the Fonz."

Springsteen returned the favor in 2005, inducting U2 into the Hall with a speech that was both reverential and amusing. "A great rock band searches for the same kind of combustible force that fueled the expansion of the universe after the big bang," Springsteen surmised. "You want the earth to shake and spit fire, you want the sky to split apart and for God to pour out ... This is music meant to take on not only the powers that be but on a good day, the universe and God himself, if he was listening. It's man's accountability, and U2 belongs on this list." After poking fun at Bono's choice of hairstyles and the band's tie-in with the iPod ("Smart, wily Irish guys. Anybody—anybody—can do an ad and take the money. But to do the ad and not take the money, that's smart"), Springsteen joined U2 for a verse of "I Still Haven't Found What I'm Looking For." U2 worked another Bruce element into the night's performance of "Pride (In the Name of Love)," with Bono borrowing lyrics from "The Promised Land" to close the song, singing, "No I ain't a boy/No I'm a man/And I believe in the promised land."

U2 continues to make music today, while Bono has become a statesman in the continuing effort to achieve Third World debt forgiveness. The band remains one of the few groups whose work is as literate, impassioned, important, and durable as Springsteen's. —*DD*

Steve Van Zandt

**Guitarist, songwriter, producer, E Street Band member
1975–1984 and 1999–present, *Sopranos* hitman,
garage rock guru**

O n his 1999 album *Born Again Savage*, Steve Van Zandt sings, "I ain't afraid of hellfire/I'm only afraid of wasting my time." That hasn't been much of an issue over the course of his career, with a range of accomplishments—and even identities—that have made him the E Street Band's most prolific and adventurous member. He has, over the years, been Miami Steve, Sugar Miami Steve, and Little Steven. He's been the fedora-wearing guitarist in the E Street Band, the early creative force behind the Asbury Jukes, and the bandanaed leader of the Disciples of Soul. Viewers of the acclaimed HBO mob series "The Sopranos" know him as henchman Silvio Dante; radio listeners tune in weekly to hear what Little Steven has under the hood in his "Underground Garage." "I tend to live in artistic chaos," Van Zandt said. "I never looked at my stuff like a career. I never looked at it like a money-earner. Maybe that was a little bit stupid or naive, but I didn't relate to it that way."

Born December 22, 1950, in Boston and raised in Middletown, New Jersey, Van Zandt grew up on a diet of '60s rock and soul, particularly favoring British Invasion rockers such as the Yardbirds, the Animals, John Mayall's Bluesbreakers, the Rolling Stones, the Kinks, and the Who, as well as American counterparts like the Young Rascals (who Van Zandt inducted into the Rock and Roll Hall of Fame in 1997). He toted his guitar down to the Jersey

Shore, where he worked on a road crew by day and played guitar by night. Early on he met fellow aspiring musician Bruce Springsteen and discovered a truly kindred spirit: "In those days, if you were in a band you were already friends. If you had long hair, you were friends. There were so few freaks, as we were known, that there was a common philosophy before you spoke to each other."

Springsteen and Van Zandt were the two main guitar slingers and band leaders on the circuit—Van Zandt's outfits included the Shadows, the Source, and the Jaywalkers—as well as regular participants in the after-hours jam sessions at the Upstage in Asbury Park. In 1970, Springsteen approached Van Zandt (known as Miami after returning from a Florida vacation wearing a tropical-print shirt) about joining his current band Steel Mill to replace bassist Vini Roslyn, and Van Zandt decided to cast his lot with the man who was essentially his main musical competition in the area. "Basically, it was a big decision for me to dedicate my life to him," he said. "But I always felt he was something special, more than just a local whatever."

Van Zandt played with Springsteen in Steel Mill and its successors, the oddball collective Dr. Zoom and the Sonic Boom, and the Bruce Springsteen Band. When Springsteen went solo and signed his deal with Columbia Records, Van Zandt went back to the Jersey Shore to tour with the Dovells and play in the Blackberry Booze Band with Southside Johnny Lyon; he did, however, "appear" on *Greetings from Asbury Park, N.J.*, punching an amplifier head to create feedback at the beginning of "Lost in the Flood." Van Zandt and Lyon went on to form the soulful, brass-fueled Asbury Jukes in 1974, but the guitarist's status in the band changed from member to producer/mentor thanks to another call from Springsteen—this time to visit the studio during the *Born to Run* sessions, where he helped arrange the horn parts for "Tenth Avenue Freeze-Out." "That was a fluke thing," Van Zandt recalled. "I was hanging around the studio, and what he was doing just wasn't working. I knew how to make it work, and I was too naive to know my place and stay there and shut up. So I said, 'This sucks, why don't you fix it?' And Bruce was like, 'Why don't you give it a shot? Nothing else is working.'" Van Zandt surprised everybody—including horn players David Sanborn and brothers Michael and Randy Brecker—by telling them to put away their charts and then singing each of their individual parts to them. An impressed Springsteen made him a full-time member of the E Street Band, and Van Zandt was on the road when the *Born to Run* tour kicked off on July 20, 1975.

For the next five years Van Zandt, along with saxophonist Clarence Clemons, played Springsteen's visual foil and settled into a supporting musical role. "Mostly I'd play rhythm, and when he wasn't playing, I'd do a solo," Van Zandt explained. "I had decided that I was gonna work *for* him. He was something special, and I just wanted to help him become a success. I felt he deserved it; I had an emotional stake in it because he was my friend." Van

Springsteen and guitarist Steve Van Zandt perform a rain-soaked rendition of "The Rising" at the Museum of Natural History's Hayden Planetarium in New York City to open the 2002 MTV Video Music Awards.

In addition to his work with the E Street Band, Steve Van Zandt has earned substantial credit as a songwriter, producer, political activist, and actor.

Zandt had more at stake than the E Street Band, however, and he often got Springsteen involved as a writing and performing contributor to his other projects, including work with Southside Johnny & the Asbury Jukes, Gary U.S. Bonds, and Ronnie Spector. By the early '80s, however, Van Zandt was starting to feel a bit restless. He experienced a profound political awakening during the E Street Band's tour of Europe in 1981, which included a solemn visit to Checkpoint Charlie on the border between East and West Germany. When then–EMI Records president David Gersh broached the idea of a solo album, Van Zandt started recording *Men Without Women* with E Street Bandmates Danny Federici, Garry Tallent, and Max Weinberg. About halfway into it, however, he decided to form a full-scale band and the Disciples of Soul were born, with an initial lineup that included former Young Rascals drummer Dino Danelli, former Plasmatics bassist Jean Beauvoir, percussionist Monti Louis Ellison from the Alvin Ailey dance troupe, keyboardist Rusty Cloud, and the Jukes' horn section, led by trombonist Richie "La Bamba" Rosenberg. At this point Van Zandt also knew his days with the E Street Band were coming to an end. Though he didn't formally leave until 1984, after the recording of *Born in the U.S.A.*, he told *Backstreets* in December 1982 that the group is "not my central focus. Miami has retired, really ... My central focus and my first priority is my own work now."

The Disciples of Soul would take many forms over Van Zandt's five albums, which after *Men Without Women* included *Voice of America* (1984), *Freedom No Compromise* (1987) (featuring Springsteen on the track "Native American"), *Revolution* (1989), and *Born Again Savage* (1999)—the latter recorded with a rhythm section of U2's Adam Clayton and Jason Bonham, the son of the late Led Zeppelin drummer John Bonham. Each of the albums presented passionate treatises on political, social, religious, and environmental issues; when he started his LittleSteven.com website, Van Zandt even prepared lengthy essays about how these topics were covered on the individual albums. Van Zandt's politicization came to full fruition in the summer of 1985, when he formed Artists United Against Apartheid to protest the human rights violations of South Africa's bantustan regime and to tacitly criticize musicians who performed—often for massive paydays—at the country's lavish Sun City resort. The all-star "Sun City" single featured Springsteen along with Bob Dylan, Jackson Browne, U2's Bono, Bonnie Raitt, Joey Ramone, Pat Benatar, Lou Reed, former Temptations David Ruffin and Eddie Kendricks, and rappers such as Run-DMC, Kurtis Blow, and Afrika Bambaataa. Van Zandt and producer Arthur Baker recorded the song throughout the summer, and most of the artists gathered on October 10 and 11 to shoot a video. The project also yielded an album and a book (by Springsteen biographer Dave Marsh). For his efforts, Van Zandt received commendations from the United Nations and Nobel Prize–winning South African Bishop Desmond Tutu, as well as an audience before the U.S. Senate.

Liberalism in the Ronald Reagan/George Bush '80s was a hard sell, of course—and political rock was not exactly a big seller, either. Little Steven wound up without a major label deal but instead established the Renegade Nation imprint, for which he produced the debut album by punk rockers Demolition 23 and on which he released *Born Again Savage*. He also produced albums for Lone Justice, the Arc Angels, former Hanoi Rocks frontman Michael Monroe, Nigerian artist Majek Fashek, and Southside Johnny's *Better Days* "come-

Off of E Street ... Steve Van Zandt

Gary U.S. Bonds, *Dedication* (1981), *On the Line* (1982)

Chesterfield Kings, *Mindbending Sounds of the Chesterfield Kings* (2003)

David Darling, *Eight String Religion* (1993)

Face to Face, *Confrontation* (1985)

Iron City Houserockers, *Have a Good Time but Get Out Alive* (1980)

Lone Justice, *Lone Justice* (1985)

Meat Loaf, *Welcome to the Neighborhood* (1995)

Michael Monroe, *Not Fakin' It* (1989), *Peace of Mind* (2000)

Southside Johnny & the Asbury Jukes, *I Don't Want to Go Home* (1976), *This Time It's for Real* (1977), *Hearts of Stone* (1978), *Better Days* (1991)

back effort." The "Sopranos" offer came after creator and producer David Chase saw Van Zandt's *Joisey*-centric Hall of Fame induction for the Rascals; giving the musician a pompadour and a pistol, he had his hit man—and subsequently cast Van Zandt's real-life wife, Maureen, as Silvio's squeeze. Van Zandt described the TV production schedule, with its early and long hours, as "a shock to my system," but he loved it nonetheless. Of course, at the time he wasn't anticipating a full-fledged return of the E Street Band, but Van Zandt was able to make his commitments to both work with a minimum of conflict—and occasional flights to "The Sopranos" set during off-days on tour.

Van Zandt's other great passion in recent years has been championing great rock 'n' roll—including the music of his past as well as newcomers. In the late '90s he helped to produce the Cavestomp! concert series in New York City, which provided a stage for forgotten garage rock veterans as well as up-and-comers. He then launched "Little Steven's Underground Garage," a weekly syndicated radio show that plays everything from vintage Animals and Seeds—among the more well-known bands—to new music by the Strokes, the White Stripes, the Von Bondies, and many others. "The normal, major label record business was not interested in this kind of rock 'n' roll," Van Zandt says. "It's fun and it's interesting. I think it's important to encourage this new scene and also to let people see these classic groups—some of whom are quite good at it, still." The show has been a ratings winner most everywhere it's aired, which Van Zandt said should send a message to the radio industry as well as the music business: "I really am a big, big radio fan, and I miss what radio used to be when DJs had personality and could put together their own sets of music."

Since his return to the E Street fold, however, Van Zandt's membership in the band has once again become a dominant force in his life—whether he wants it to be or not. At his 1999 Rock and Roll Hall of Fame induction, Springsteen told the audience, "We haven't played together in fifteen years, and if it's up to me that's never going to happen again." —*GG*

Vietnam Veterans of America. *See* **A Night for the Vietnam Veteran.**

Tex and Marion Vinyard

Managers of the Castiles, an early Springsteen band

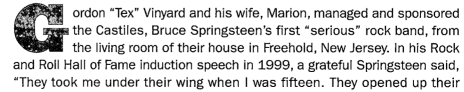

ordon "Tex" Vinyard and his wife, Marion, managed and sponsored the Castiles, Bruce Springsteen's first "serious" rock band, from the living room of their house in Freehold, New Jersey. In his Rock and Roll Hall of Fame induction speech in 1999, a grateful Springsteen said, "They took me under their wing when I was fifteen. They opened up their home to a bunch of rock and roll misfits and let us make a lot of noise and practice all night long." In fact, the Vinyards had already opened their house to the Castiles before Springsteen knocked on the door in 1965, "one night (when) it was raining like cows pissin' on a flat rock," according to Tex's memory—a description that Springsteen has noted is "better than reality." Vinyard recalled that he initially refused Springsteen's request to be in the band since he didn't know any songs; he told the fledgling musician to learn five, and Springsteen "returned the next night, ready to go."

The Vinyards' house was located at 35 Center Street; they didn't have children, so the couple was happy to clear the furniture out of their living room and provide not only a place for the Castiles to practice but also make sure they were fed. Founding member George Theiss told *Backstreets* magazine, "Marion and Tex were like second parents to us. They didn't have any children of their own and I think they kind of felt that we had become almost like their own children. They were very protective of us and supervised us." Tex would find and transport the Castiles to their gigs; despite making just $21 a week strike pay at the time, he put down $5 to buy the group a $300 amplifier with four inputs, which was for a time the Castiles' entire sound system. After some success playing local bars, Tex managed to book the band at the Cafe Wha? in New York City's Greenwich Village.

By late 1967, however, the psychedelic sound had taken hold, rendering the Castiles obsolete by music business standards. It also became clear that Springsteen was more intent on a career in music then the other members, who seemed headed for college or marriage. After the group disbanded, Tex became involved with several other groups—though none as special as the Castiles. Springsteen and Tex continued to enjoy a close relationship, and Tex even cosigned on a loan several years later for Bruce to upgrade his musical gear. By the time Tex Vinyard died in 1988, he and Marion had not only helped a slew of local bands but also aided several youngsters with college tuition. On May 18, 2002, a park was dedicated in Tex's honor near the spot where the Vinyards' home once stood. At the opening ceremony, Springsteen thanked the couple whose generosity provided mentorship to kids with big dreams but little cash: "Tex was someone who opened his house completely and let us come in and turn it up as loud as we wanted when everybody else was trying to get us to turn it down." —*ML*

Vote for Change Tour

2004 political action tour

 rior to 2004, Bruce Springsteen had never endorsed a U.S. presidential candidate, though some—notably incumbent Ronald Reagan in 1984—had attempted to co-opt his music and/or reputation for their own ends. Even when John Kerry entered the 2004 Democratic National Convention in Boston to the strains of "No Surrender" to formally accept the party's nomination against President George W. Bush, Springsteen had not publicly spoken out in support of the challenger. But that changed quickly.

In early August, Springsteen announced he was joining forces with eighteen other acts—including the Dave Matthews Band, Pearl Jam, the Dixie Chicks, James Taylor, Jackson Browne, Bonnie Raitt, and John Mellencamp—for the Vote for Change tour, which comprised thirty-eight shows on ten separate days in eleven battleground states in that year's election. Springsteen and the E Street Band played six dates on the tour, including a televised October 11 show in Washington, D.C., that featured most of the artists on the tour. Former Creedence Clearwater Revival leader John Fogerty was a special guest who played with Springsteen and company during their sets; R.E.M. opened five of the shows, Bright Eyes appeared on four, and Tracy Chapman and Jackson Browne each appeared on one. Proceeds from the tour went to America Coming Together (ACT), an organization devoted to getting out the vote for "progressive" candidates. MoveON PAC, a 2.5 million member populist political group, presented the shows.

"We're trying to put forward a group of progressive ideals and change the administration in the White House," Springsteen told the Associated Press when the tour was announced. "That's the success or failure, very clear cut and very simple ... We're chipping in our two cents. That's all we're trying to do."

Jon Landau, Springsteen's manager, was one of the architects of the tour. He was among a group of fifty managers called to Washington, D.C., by Pearl Jam overseer Kelly Curtis to coordinate the activities of like-minded artists who he thought would be interested in speaking out in the election year. Together the managers decided on the mobile tour idea rather than one big show or a series of large-scale concerts. "The artists we represent all wanted to find the right forum to promote their ideas and be heard," Landau told *Billboard*. "We'll do our best to make our contribution to the discussion. These artists are very educated and sophisticated people. They will have some impact, somewhere."

From the start Springsteen was a leading spokesman for Vote for Change. He appeared on "Nightline," wrote an op-ed piece in the *New York Times* and filmed a video explaining his position that was shown at tour stops. "He is a very committed individual; once he commits to something, he's there 100 percent," noted R.E.M.'s Mike Mills. At the shows themselves Springsteen joined R.E.M. singer Michael Stipe in welcoming the audiences and explaining the purpose of the tour and the need to "fight for a govern-

United for a cause, R.E.M. frontman Michael Stipe welcomed Springsteen into his band's set during each of the stops on the Vote for Change tour to trade vocals on "Man on the Moon." Stipe later joined the E Street Band's set to voice an epic rendition of "Because the Night."

ment that is open, forward-looking, rational and humane." He also dubbed each arena "a no 'Brooooooce' zone" in deference to the other bands on the bill. During his own set Springsteen made several pointed remarks, including

Bruce Springsteen A to E to Z   **405**

The final show of the Vote for Change tour in Washington, D.C., featured a lineup including almost all of the acts that had fanned out to perform at multiple venues during the tour's previous stops. Springsteen joined fellow rockers (from left) Dave Matthews, John Fogerty, and Eddie Vedder on stage to perform a powerful version of Patti Smith's "People Have the Power" for the show's finale.

some localized observations about the economic and political circumstances of the state they were playing in and a nightly "public service announcement" during "Mary's Place," employing a schtick in which he pulled up a conservative-looking undecided voter (a plant) from the audience and executed a preacher-style conversion to the Kerry camp.

Musically it was one of the most unique, interesting, and collaborative tours Springsteen has ever done. It featured some of the shortest E Street Band sets—about two hours each night—since the 1988 Amnesty International Human Rights Now! tour. The repertoire was carefully stocked with topical selections; Springsteen began his performances on acoustic guitar with a quasi-flamenco treatment of "The Star Spangled Banner," then led the band into "Born in the U.S.A.," "Badlands," and "No Surrender." "The Rising" and "Mary's Place" were also constants, while an array of other appropriate songs shifted in and out of the shows, including "Lonesome Day," "Darkness on the Edge of Town," "The River," "The Ties That Bind," "Lost in the Flood," "Prove It All Night," and a particularly rollicking arrangement of *Nebraska's* "Johnny 99." The Fogerty portion of the shows included "Centerfield," the politically pointed title track and first single of his then-new album *Deja Vu All Over Again,* and CCR's "Fortunate Son." Fogerty also dueted with Springsteen on "The Promised Land" and, during the encores, played CCR songs such as "Bad Moon Rising," "Travelin' Band," and "Proud Mary."

Springsteen, meanwhile, joined R.E.M. each night for "Man on the Moon" as well as "Bad Day" and "Permanent Vacation." R.E.M.'s Stipe joined Springsteen for "Because the Night," while Mills and guitarist Peter Buck jammed on "Born to Run," with Mills playing fuzz bass. The shows ended with the assemblage joining forces for Nick Lowe's "(What's So Funny 'Bout) Peace, Love and Understanding" and Patti Smith's "People Have the Power." Other notable guest appearances during the short tour included: the Dixie Chicks, after performing nearby, on "People Have the Power" in Detroit; Neil Young ("Any Canadians for Kerry in the house?") in St. Paul, Minnesota, on "Souls of the Departed," Bob Dylan's "All Along the Watchtower" and his own "Rockin' in the Free World," as well as the regular encores; and Tracy Chapman on "My Hometown" in Orlando, Florida.

The final show at the Continental Airlines Arena in East Rutherford, New Jersey—a late addition to the itinerary—was even more intertwined. Springsteen sang two songs during his wife Patti Scialfa's set and "Running on Empty" with Jackson Browne. Pearl Jam's Eddie Vedder showed up in the E Street Band set for "No Surrender" and "Darkness on the Edge of Town" as well as his band's "Betterman." Browne sang on "Racing in the Street."

Springsteen's participation in the Vote for Change tour polarized some of his audience, and those who didn't agree with his politics or social viewpoint found themselves torn about attending the shows. Many also vented their feelings on Internet chat sites. But, as Springsteen noted to *Backstreets*, "I think if you followed us over the past thirty years, our positions on most social issues have been consistent and straightforward." And, he added, he fully accepted the dissent: "It's pretty simple. I don't need people cheering everything I'm doing—I don't go out expecting that, and we've done enough that I've seen both sides of the coin. And that's all right. The show is a forum of ideas. That's one of the things that we try to provide over the course of the evening. And as such, that's part of what you're getting when you walk through the doors." —*GG*

Tom Waits

Idiosyncratic California singer-songwriter who penned "Jersey Girl"

F ew other songwriters have composed a song so perfect for Bruce Springsteen to cover than Tom Waits did with "Jersey Girl." "That's the same guy that's on the boardwalk in 'Sandy,'" Springsteen told biographer Dave Marsh, "the same guy in 'Rosalita'—you know, he got that Jersey girl ... When I listened to that song, I'd always see myself riding through Asbury (Park). There'd be people I know a little bit on the corner, and we'd just drive by. I guess that you feel in some way you've changed forever. But you also have all those connections, so you feel really at home."

Waits wrote "Jersey Girl" in the late '70s for his then-new wife and future collaborator Kathleen Brennan, who he said "saved" him after a two-year relationship with Rickie Lee Jones. The song appeared on Waits's *Heartattack and Vine* album in 1989, and Springsteen started playing it live—albeit with some modified lyrics—on July 2, 1981, the first show of a six-night stand at the Brendan Byrne Arena in East Rutherford, New Jersey. On August 24, 1981, Waits sang it with Springsteen at the Los Angeles Sports Arena. Springsteen included a live take of "Jersey Girl" as the B-side of "Cover Me" in 1984, then included it as the closing track on 1986's *Live/1975–85* boxed set.

Born in Ponoma, California, Waits established himself with a bourbon-and-sandpaper voice and songs that flaunted compositional influences from Stephen Foster, George Gershwin, and Bertoldt Brecht and lyrics culled from a stew of Jack Kerouac, Charles Bukowski, and Bob Dylan. After setting up in the Los Angeles club scene in the late '60s, Waits began recording in 1973 and ever since has mixed album releases with acting gigs, including films such as *Paradise Alley*, *Short Cuts*, *Ironweed*, *Bram Stoker's Dracula*, *Mystery Train*, and *Rumblefish*. His 1992 album *Bone Machine* won a Grammy award for Best Alternative Music Album, while 1999's *Mule Variations* was named Best Contemporary Folk Album. He's collaborated with playwright Robert Wilson on *The Black Rider* and a 1993 update of *Alice in Wonderland*. Waits's songs have been covered by Rod Stewart, Johnny Cash, Bette Midler, the Eagles, the Ramones, Dion, and others. —*GG*

The Wallflowers

Rock group featuring Bob Dylan's son, Jakob

Bruce Springsteen and Jakob Dylan should have a natural affinity for each other. Early in his career, Springsteen was dubbed "the new Bob Dylan"; Jakob, both when he was born in 1970 and when he debuted with his band, the Wallflowers, in 1990, quite literally *was* the new Dylan.

The Wallflowers—the lineup of which, besides guitarist/vocalist Dylan keyboardist Rami Jaffee and bassist Greg Richling, has been fairly fluid over the years—is a roots-rock styled outfit inspired by the sounds of The Band (who famously backed the elder Dylan in the '60s and '70s), Tom Petty & the Heartbreakers, and Springsteen, to whom Jakob Dylan bears something of a vocal resemblance. The Wallflowers' self-titled debut flopped in 1992, but the group came back strong in 1996 with *Bringing Down the Horse* thanks to the hits "6th Avenue Heartache" and "One Headlight"; the latter song won two Grammys, for Best Rock Song and Best Rock Performance by a Duo or Group with Vocal. After a long period of touring, the group returned in 2000 with *Breach* and in 2002 with *Red Letter Days*.

In 1997 Springsteen joined the Wallflowers onstage twice. The first was on March 8, at the Tradewinds in Sea Bright, New Jersey, where he traded vocals with Dylan on "My Girl" and "God Don't Make Lonely Girls." Jon Bon Jovi sat in as well. In September, Springsteen appeared with the band on the MTV Video Music Awards, performing "One Headlight."

Springsteen has remained an inspiration for Dylan. In 2002, he told VH1.com, "I like Bruce Springsteen's record [*The Rising*]. He's the only one who could do that. He's such an incredibly genuine artist. He means it. I'm glad that a lot of other artists haven't felt required to make that record.

Springsteen shares the stage with Wallflowers singer Jakob Dylan to perform that band's
hit "One Headlight" at the 1997 MTV Video Music Awards.

Artists tend to feel a responsibility to react to important things. The problem
is that most of them are not educated or sincere about it. But you can't
argue with Bruce Springsteen's sincerity." —DD

"War"

Single released: November 1986
Album: *Live/1975–85* (Columbia, 1986)
Chart peak: No. 8

Bruce Springsteen's rendition of this Motown anti-war protest song—a No. 1 hit for Edwin Starr in the summer of 1970—was the first single from the *Live/1975–85* box set. It reached No. 8 on the *Billboard* Hot 100. It was one of four songs on a cassette that manager Jon Landau presented to his client to encourage him to release a live album, which the oft-bootlegged Springsteen had long resisted.

Springsteen, who was staunchly critical of then–President Ronald Reagan's foreign policy, added "War" to some of his shows during the final North American leg of his marathon 1984–85 *Born in the U.S.A.* tour. The version of the song on *Live/1975–85* came from the September 30, 1985, show during a tour-closing run at the Los Angeles Coliseum.

Springsteen told biographer Dave Marsh, "[I]t was a song Jon suggested maybe a year before. And we just couldn't get it down—it seemed too hard to play or we didn't have the patience at the time. Or at the moment, it didn't make enough sense. And then we just tried 'War' one afternoon and we got it fine. So I taped the words to my arm and we did it."

Drummer Max Weinberg told *Billboard* that on the day Springsteen introduced the song to the set, "Bruce called us into his dressing room and said he wanted to do 'War.' We all knew the tune, so we went out and rehearsed it very briefly because we had never played it before in concert." He did not, however, tell the band that he planned to speak before they played the song. "He came back to me and said 'Just watch my hand,'" Weinberg recalled. "He went through this long, incredibly beautiful and touching monologue and he started to raise his hand. When he brought his hand down, everybody in the E Street Band hit that downbeat perfectly. It was awesome."

"War" was first considered for the B-side of "My Hometown," the final single from *Born in the U.S.A.*, but was held back when Landau began hatching the idea for the live album. —*GG*

"We Are the World"/USA for Africa

1985 benefit single and charity project

On January 28, 1985, Bruce Springsteen was one of the stars who took part in the recording of "We Are the World," a benefit single by an ad hoc group of superstar singers dubbed USA for Africa to raise money for famine relief in Africa. But according to Ken Kragen, the artist manager who coordinated the project, Springsteen's contribution was far greater than just singing. "The turning point was Bruce Springsteen's commitment," Kragen told *Rolling Stone* magazine. "That legitimized the project in the eyes of the rock community." When producer Quincy Jones asked Springsteen to join the effort, however, his response was, "You sure you really want me to do this?"

"We Are the World" was the American response to "Do They Know It's Christmas?," the 1984 British all-star single organized by the Boomtown Rats' Bob Geldof that raised more than $20 million for famine relief and became the top-selling single in British history. Singer Harry Belafonte was impressed—and embarrassed that a group of mostly white British performers had served an issue he felt the African-American community should have led the world in addressing. Belafonte contacted Kragen, who had managed the late Harry Chapin and helped coordinate the singer-songwriter's World Hunger Year drive. Michael Jackson and Lionel Richie wrote the song, and Jones agreed to produce it. Recording was scheduled for the night of the American Music Awards—which, Kragen and Jones figured, would make it easier for stars to participate—and was held at A&M Records' studio on the old Charlie Chaplin sound stage on Sunset Strip in Los Angeles. Springsteen—who flew to Los Angeles after finishing a leg of the *Born in the U.S.A.* tour the night before in Syracuse, New York—didn't attend the awards show, where "Dancing in the Dark" was named Best Pop/Rock Single. Instead he arrived at Los Angeles International Airport, rented a Corvette, and drove to the studio, parking in a lot across the street. In a humorous anecdote from his autobiography, *Is That It?*, Geldof recalled that Kragen at one point walked in and said, "'Bruce Springsteen has just parked his car on the other side of the road and walked across—by himself—to the studio. Can you believe it?' I could believe it. 'No, I mean he drove himself, no chauffeur, no limo. Then The Boss walked across himself, no bodyguards, no security.'"

Springsteen—who during the tour had donated more than $225,000 to food banks and other groups serving the hungry—was in good company for "We Are the World"; the session featured a who's who of American musical nobility that included Jackson, Richie, Bob Dylan, Stevie Wonder, Diana Ross, Daryl Hall and John Oates, Smokey Robinson, Ray Charles, Billy Joel, Bette Midler, Willie Nelson, Tina Turner, and many others. Springsteen chatted with friends such as Dylan, Simon, and Joel; the Pointer Sisters, who had a hit with "Fire," sat on his lap at one point.

Springsteen was part of the song's soaring chorus and was also tapped to be one of the soloists, reentering the studio just after 6 a.m. to sing the line "We are the world, we are the children." Asking the producer for some guidance, Jones advised him, "[I]t's like being the cheerleader of the chorus." After the first run-through, Springsteen asked Jones, "Something like that?," to which the producer said "*Exactly* like that." Springsteen's performance appeared twice in the song, the second time blended with Wonder's. When he finished, Richie declared that Springsteen "is now officially on vacation"; Springsteen replied, "That sounds goooooood. I want to get a soda." He then left the studio and turned down an A&M security guard's offer of escort to the parking lot across the street.

Speaking of the event and of the issue, Springsteen said, "Any time somebody asks you to take one night of your time to help people who are starving to death, it's pretty hard to say no ... There's all this senseless suffering in the world. Either you're tearing something down or building something up. I want to be part of the building process, holding back the flood a little bit." "We Are the World" hit No. 1 on the *Billboard* Hot 100 and sold more than five million copies. In addition to his participation in the song, Springsteen also donated a live recording of Jimmy Cliff's "Trapped" taken from the *Born in the U.S.A.* tour to a subsequent *USA for Africa* album. The USA for Africa effort raised an estimated $200 million for famine relief.

Springsteen was, however, a surprising no-show for the Live Aid concerts that took place in July 1985 in London and Philadelphia. Geldof confesses to pursuing him aggressively and even changing the date in order to accommodate Springsteen's schedule. In the end, it seems that burnout from the lengthy *Born in the U.S.A.* tour and a desire to spend time with his then-new wife, Julianne Phillips, overrode any desire to perform at one of the shows. Springsteen and his organization did donate the staging from their recent shows at Wembley Stadium to be used at the London show, however. —*GG*

Max Weinberg

Drummer, E Street Band member 1974–present, music director for "Late Night with Conan O'Brien"

 ax Weinberg, aka the Mighty Max, has been drumming with the E Street Band since taking over for Ernest "Boom" Carter in 1974. In 1993, he also became band leader and music director for NBC's "Late Night with Conan O'Brien," heading a gang of old New Jersey and New York friends assembled for his audition and labeled the Max Weinberg 7.

Born April 13, 1951, in Newark, New Jersey, Weinberg started drumming at age five, after hearing drummer D.J. Fontana performing with Elvis Presley on "The Milton Berle Show." By the time he was seven, Weinberg was playing in a bar mitzvah band—and getting paid for it. He was close to graduating from college—and playing in various lounge and theater pit bands—when he got around to answering a month-old "drummer wanted" ad he saw

Drummer Max Weinberg joined the E Street Band in 1974. Weinberg also doubles as the bandleader on the "Late Night with Conan O'Brien" show, taking extended leaves from the show in order to tour with Springsteen.

in the *Village Voice* that read, "No junior Ginger Bakers, must encompass R&B and jazz."

Weinberg had never seen Springsteen perform, though they were in bands that once appeared on the same bill (Weinberg fell ill and left the gig early), and his band played a couple of Springsteen covers—including "Blinded by the Light" and "4th of July, Asbury Park (Sandy)," which he played at his New York audition for the E Street Band. After two auditions, Weinberg got the job, beginning with the recording of *Born to Run*.

In between *The River* and *Born in the U.S.A.*, Weinberg teamed with writer Robert Santelli on a book titled *The Big Beat: Conversations with Rock's Great Drummers*, which was published in 1984; in it, Weinberg chats with luminaries such as Ringo Starr, Charlie Watts of the Rolling Stones, Dave Clark of the Dave Clark Five, and D.J. Fontana and dissects their styles. The book led to a three-CD series for Rhino Records entitled *Max Weinberg Pre-*

Off of E Street ... Max Weinberg

Gary U.S. Bonds, *Dedication* (1981), *On the Line* (1982)

Ian Hunter, *You're Never Alone with a Schizo-phrenic* (1979)

Johnnie Johnson, *Johnnie Be Back* (1995)

Carole King, *City Streets* (1980)

Little Steven & the Disciples of Soul, *Men Without Women* (1982)

Meat Loaf, *Bat Out of Hell* (1977), *Dead Ringer* (1981), *Midnight at the Lost and Found* (1983)

Southside Johnny & the Asbury Jukes, *Hearts of Stone* (1978), *Better Days* (1991)

Jim Steinman, *Bad for Good* (1981)

Barbra Streisand, *Emotion* (1984)

Bonnie Tyler, *Faster than the Speed of Night* (1983), *Secret Dreams & Forbidden Fire* (1986)

sents: *Let There Be Drums*. He also became an in-demand session performer, with credits that include Carole King, Southside Johnny, Gary U.S. Bonds, Meat Loaf, and Ian Hunter. He suffered a scare in the early '80s, however, developing severe tendonitis that threatened to end his career. Seven operations and numerous therapies led to recovery.

In 1985, a *Playboy* magazine poll gave Weinberg its Best Drummer honors, which was echoed by *Rolling Stone* magazine critics in 1986. When Springsteen temporarily disbanded the E Streeters in 1989, Weinberg decided to enter law school, following in his dad's career footsteps. "All I had was an advanced degree in Bruce Springsteen music, and the market for used drummers was slim," he said at the time; still, he made it into law school but didn't stay long.

Weinberg started his own record label, Hard Ticket Entertainment, in 1990, and in 1991 released *Killer Joe's Scene of the Crime*, which featured guest performances by fellow Jerseyans Steve Van Zandt, Jon Bon Jovi, and Southside Johnny, among others. He also toured with 10,000 Maniacs and performed at President Bill Clinton's 1992 and 1996 inauguration galas (accompanied at one point by the sax-playing chief executive) and at the 1995 Grammy Awards. That was the same year the E Street Band reunited to record new tracks for Springsteen's *Greatest Hits* album and play a few shows, including the Rock and Roll Hall of Fame and Museum's opening weekend concert in Cleveland, Ohio.

By then, Weinberg was leading the Max Weinberg 7, the house band for Conan O'Brien's show. He got the gig in 1993, when O'Brien was preparing to take over the show from David Letterman. Weinberg spotted O'Brien while leaving a restaurant, and his wife, Becky, encouraged him to ask the new host for an audition. O'Brien had to be convinced, but as soon as the audition began, he reportedly told his producers, "Buy me this band." The other six members include: former Asbury Jukes trombonist Richie "La Bamba" Rosenberg, guitarist Jimmy Vivino; trumpeter Mark "Love Man" Pender; sax player Jerry Vivino; keyboardist Scott Healy; and bassist Mike Merritt.

Tom Shales of the *Washington Post* dubbed the group the "best band in late night TV." In 2000 the group released a self-titled CD containing favorite "Late Night" songs, including some in Weinberg's favored jump-blues style and the original "Caught 'em in the Act." Besides leading the band, Weinberg also became one of "Late Night"'s comic personalities, appearing in many parodies and bits—which partially helped lead to a guest appearance on "Hollywood Squares." O'Brien and his produces have been kind enough to allow Weinberg leaves of absence to record and tour with Springsteen, and Springsteen has returned the favor with some memorable "Late Night" performances. "I will always desire to play with Bruce Spring-steen," Weinberg once told *Backstreets*. "He's the most inspirational, most dedicated, most committed, and most focused artist I've ever seen. I like to be around people like that, and there aren't many people like that."

Weinberg's other credits include acting as music director for the Comic Relief 8 fundraiser as well as delivering the Rock and Roll Hall of Fame's first educational lecture (he has since talked about his career at more than 150 colleges and universities).

Max and Becky Weinberg reside in Middletown, New Jersey, with their two children, Ali (a pianist who's made occasional guest appearances with the E Street Band) and Jay. *—LM*

Carl "Tinker" West

Early Springsteen manager

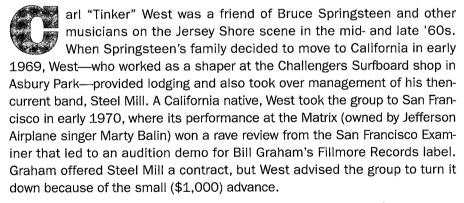

arl "Tinker" West was a friend of Bruce Springsteen and other musicians on the Jersey Shore scene in the mid- and late '60s. When Springsteen's family decided to move to California in early 1969, West—who worked as a shaper at the Challengers Surfboard shop in Asbury Park—provided lodging and also took over management of his then-current band, Steel Mill. A California native, West took the group to San Francisco in early 1970, where its performance at the Matrix (owned by Jefferson Airplane singer Marty Balin) won a rave review from the San Francisco Examiner that led to an audition demo for Bill Graham's Fillmore Records label. Graham offered Steel Mill a contract, but West advised the group to turn it down because of the small ($1,000) advance.

West also managed Dr. Zoom and the Sonic Boom and the Bruce Springsteen Band—advising him to drop the horn section of the latter at one point in order to pare expenses. But West's greatest contribution was sending Springsteen to his future manager, Mike Appel. West was referred to Appel by Steel Mill/Bruce Springsteen Band drummer Vini Lopez, who had heard about them from friends; West ended up meeting Appel through another band he managed, Montana Flintlock (aka Tumbleweed). West put in a call to Appel to ask him to listen to Springsteen, and the meeting took place in November

1971 in New York City. In his 1999 Rock and Roll Hall of Fame acceptance speech, Springsteen thanked West for being "another one of my early managers whose support I couldn't have done without" and for connecting him to Appel, who secured Springsteen's deal with Columbia Records, managed him into 1976, and coproduced his first three albums. —*GG*

The Wild, the Innocent & the E Street Shuffle

Released: November 5, 1973
Producers: Mike Appel, Jim Cretecos
Tracks: "The E Street Shuffle," "4th of July, Asbury Park (Sandy)," "Kitty's Back," "Wild Billy's Circus Story," "Incident on 57th Street," "Rosalita (Come Out Tonight)," "New York City Serenade"
Chart peak: No. 59

iving the lengthy and exacting recording processes that would become Bruce Springsteen's basic creative modus, the idea of *two* albums coming out in the same year seems mind-boggling now. But Springsteen's sophomore album followed his debut by exactly ten months and revealed a more confident performer and more ambitious songwriter, he and his bandmates fortified by hard touring both before and during the sessions to record *The Wild, the Innocent & the E Street Shuffle*." In *Songs*, Springsteen notes that at this juncture, "I was intent on taking control of the recording process ... I was determined to take the reins and go in the creative direction I wanted ... I was determined to call on my songwriting ability and my bar band experience."

Recording in the summer of 1973, again at 914 Sound Studios in Blauvelt, New York, Springsteen came to *The Wild, the Innocent & the E Street Shuffle* with more songs than he would need and many that had the benefit of being road-tested. Among those that *didn't* make the cut were fan favorites such as "The Fever" (recorded as a publishing demo and later given to Southside Johnny & the Asbury Jukes), "Thundercrack," "Zero & Blind Terry," and "Bishop Danced." Springsteen's work at the time was also displaying a tendency towards the epic, both in theme and arrangement; the long pieces came from his performing sensibility and "were arranged to leave the band and the audience gasping for breath." They invoked the spirit of old soul revues and jazz workouts that careened cheerfully from one segment to the next, finding some new direction to go in just as they seemed to be coming to an end.

The Wild, the Innocent was also an even more Jersey-centric album than its predecessor, *Greetings from Asbury Park, N.J.* The inspirations came directly from Springsteen's past, including the cast of characters in "The E

Although *The Wild, the Innocent & the E Street Shuffle* was not a commercial hit, Springsteen continued their hard-touring ways after the album's release, including a free outdoor show at Kean College in Union Township, New Jersey, in September 1974.

Street Shuffle," the childhood memories that informed "Wild Billy's Circus Story," and, in "New York City Serenade" and "Incident on 57th Street," the sense of his hometown's limitations that sent him across the river looking for broader vistas. And "4th of July, Asbury Park (Sandy)" was written in a garage apartment in Bradley Beach, New Jersey, as "a goodbye to my adopted hometown" after Springsteen was evicted from his apartment in Asbury Park. The album's enduring highlight, however, is "Rosalita," the "musical autobiography" that became a staple, and often the finale, of Springsteen's live shows for many years.

Like *Greetings*, *The Wild, the Innocent* made few commercial ripples and didn't chart until 1975, amidst the building *Born to Run* fervor. Yet there's a sense of boldness and abandon that informs *The Wild, the Innocent*, which Springsteen noted came from a feeling he had nothing to lose: "I had no success, so I had no real concerns about where I was going."

"**F**olkie trappings behind him, Springsteen has created a funky, vivacious rock and roll that's too eager and zany ever to be labeled tight, suggesting jazz heard through an open window with one R&B saxophone, or Latin music out in the street with zero conga drums ... This guy may not be God yet, but he has his sleeveless undershirt in the ring."
—*Village Voice*

"**T**he *Wild, the Innocent & the E Street Shuffle* takes itself more seriously [than *Greetings from Asbury Park, N.J.*]. The songs are longer, more ambitious and more romantic; and yet, wonderfully, they lost little of *Greetings*'s rollicking rush. Having released two fine albums in less than a year, Springsteen is obviously a considerable new talent."
—*Rolling Stone*

"**"** ... The most under-rated album so far this year, an impassioned and inspired street fantasy that's as much fun as it is deep ... The subways he sings so much about keep rolling all night long; and the way this boy rocks, it's just a matter of time before he starts picking up passengers."
—*Real Paper*

But he did recognize that the album marked welcome progress. "I started slowly to find out who I am and where I wanted to be," he said in a 1981 interview. "It was like coming out of the shadow of various influences and trying to be yourself." —*GG*

George Will

Commentator, columnist, broadcaster, baseball enthusiast

Bruce Springsteen was hit with a double whammy from the conservative side of American politics in September 1984. First, President Ronald Reagan, running for a second term, invoked Springsteen and his music during a campaign speech in New Jersey. Then conservative commentator George Will published a syndicated newspaper column extolling his virtues, concluding that "if all Americans ... made their product with as much energy and confidence as Springsteen and his merry band make music, there would be no need for Congress to be thinking about protectionism."

Will came to see Springsteen live via E Street Band drummer Max Weinberg, a friend who invited him to a *Born in the U.S.A.* tour show in August 1984 in Landover, Maryland. An admitted fish out of water ("I may be the only forty-three-year-old American so out of swim that I do not even know what marijuana smells like," he wrote), he was nevertheless impressed by what he saw, from the duration of the show to the connection with the audience to the post-show odor of Ben-Gay backstage. "Springsteen is an athlete draining himself for every audience," Will observed. And although Will wrote, "I have not a clue about Springsteen's politics," he was also taken with the parade of American values he felt were expressed in Springsteen's songs—up to and including cars and girls.

A native of Champaign, Illinois, Will taught philosophy at Michigan State University and the University of Toronto and served on the staff of the U.S. Senate before concentrating on journalism. In addition to the Pulitzer Prize–winning newspaper column, he's been a regular essayist in *Newsweek* and a contributing analyst to ABC News (including weekly appearances on Sunday morning's "This Week"). Will has published several collections of his writings and in 1989 penned *Men at Work: The Craft of Baseball.* —GG

Hank Williams

Early country music icon

ne of country music's most influential artists, Hank Williams was an essential figure in helping the genre to achieve nationwide popularity in the late '40s and early '50s. Williams was a riveting live performer, a dependable hitmaker—three dozen of his songs topped the country charts—and a songwriter of astounding emotion and intensity. While many of his songs were upbeat honky-tonk classics such as "Hey Good Lookin'" and "Jambalaya (On the Bayou)," others displayed remarkable world-weariness, sorrow, and fatalism. "I'll Never Get Out of This World Alive" and "I'm So Lonesome I Could Cry," for example, stand as some of the most personal (and saddest) songs to ever grace the charts.

Legendary singer-songwriter Hank Williams influence can clearly be heard on numerous Springsteen albums, including *The River, Nebraska,* and *The Ghost of Tom Joad.*

Williams, whose birth name was Hiram, was born in southeastern Alabama. As a preteen, he developed an interest in gospel music (by singing in his church choir), country (by attending local dances), and blues (by learning from a black street performer named Rufe "Tee-Tot" Payne). Williams won an amateur contest in Montgomery and appeared on a radio show there. He later formed a band, the Drifting Cowboys, and played all over the region. In 1948, Williams traveled to Nashville to begin his recording career. Eventually, his song "Lovesick Blues" went to No. 1, kicking off a string of major hits. He joined the popular radio show "Louisiana Hayride," later switching to "The Grand Ole Opry," where he was a huge success.

But with fame came problems, including alcoholism, a dependence on painkillers, and divorce from his wife, Audrey, whom he had married in 1944. Williams was fired from the Opry for repeatedly missing his scheduled performances. His life came to an abrupt end when he died of a heart attack in the backseat of a Cadillac on the way to a show. He was only twenty-nine years old.

Williams's influence on Bruce Springsteen's work became noticeable in the late '70s and early '80s, when he began overtly embracing the works of folk and country icons such as Williams, Jimmie Rodgers, and Woody Guthrie. Springsteen has acknowledged that some of the lyrics to "The River" were inspired by a particularly dark Williams song, "Long Gone Lonesome Blues." The stark arrangements and general feel of the albums *Nebraska* and *The Ghost of Tom Joad* owe a debt to Williams as well. In terms of artistic fearlessness, personal charisma, and occasionally, sartorial splendor (his string-tie and suit coat period), Springsteen is most certainly one of Williams's most prominent heirs. —*DD*

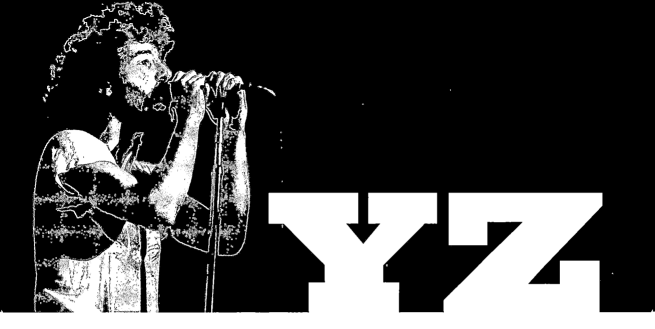

Walter Yetnikoff

Former CBS Records chief

From the beginning of his career-long association with Columbia Records, Bruce Springsteen enjoyed the support of its top executives, from famed talent scout John Hammond in 1972 to today's chief, Don Ienner. Perhaps the most colorful, as well as of the most service to Springsteen, is Walter Yetnikoff, the Brooklyn-raised lawyer who headed CBS Records from 1975 to 1990. Yetnikoff and Springsteen shared a cordial relationship that lasted nearly as long as the former's tenure at the top. In addition to good relations, however, the two enjoyed Springsteen's commercial peak in the mid-'80s, culminating with *Born in the U.S.A.* and *Live/1975-85*.

Before the runaway success of those records, however, Yetnikoff—who came up through the label's legal department—oversaw the campaigns behind *The River* and *Nebraska*. Yetnikoff told *Backstreets* magazine in 2004 how he visited the musician he often refers to as "the ultimate artist" in a Los Angeles studio in mid-1980 and learned of Springsteen's intention to make a double record: "I said, 'Ah, shit! Why?' On a number of occasions, he came up with very good answers, which went something like, 'I can't put everything I have to say creatively on one record, okay? So you're going to have to figure out the rest, like how you sell two records, how you price it and promote it.' The example I've used a million times about why at that period of time I regarded him as the ultimate artist was that I said to him, 'You know how much money you're spending on this? You're spending a fortune! You know something? It's your money. We lay it out, but it's an advance against royalties.' And his response was, 'How should I spend my money better than on my art?' You can't argue with that, nor should you."

The follow-up record was one on which Springsteen spent far less money, but invested no less in sweat equity: *Nebraska*. Yetnikoff visited Springsteen in mid-1982 at Jon Landau's office in New York; the record chief listened by himself. "Bruce was outside walking back and forth. He didn't know how I was going to react," Yetnikoff said. He liked it and reassured Springsteen that he would support it: "As I recall, I said, 'This record doesn't have a band, it's not a rock and roll record, and we're not going to sell a zillion copies for that reason. But we are going to sell a respectable amount.'" Yetnikoff put his own capital behind the record: some colleagues at CBS expected an E Street Band record and were dubious about the record's commercial viability. "This was one time I did impose my will, because there was some resistance to it. People weren't going to argue with me because I was too crazy," Yetnikoff recalled. "To a certain extent it fostered Bruce's career. But I wanted to do a good job." Yetnikoff, a man of considerable charm and humor, gave the collection of serious songs a pet name that he uses to this day: *Omaha*.

The most fruitful period of Springsteen's career coincided with Yetnikoff's rise as one of the music industry's most successful leaders: in the course of a few short years, his Epic label released Michael Jackson's *Thriller*; he helped Marvin Gaye to the top of the charts for the last time; and he signed the Rolling Stones. By the time *Born in the U.S.A.* and *Live/1975-85* hit, Yetnikoff says that Springsteen's career was largely beyond the need of his day-to-day attention. As the '80s came to an end, Yetnikoff was physically burned out: he spent time in rehab in 1989 and was fired in 1990, only two years after Sony bought CBS Records. By then his relationship with Springsteen had soured, or as Jon Landau said in a statement to *Billboard* at the time, "had ended."

Yetnikoff said he felt alienated by Springsteen's decision to undertake a tour on behalf of Amnesty International in 1988; a staunch supporter of Israel, Yetnikoff believed the human rights organization was no friend to the Jewish state. "Bruce maybe didn't even know what I was pissed at," he said. "But I did pull back in terms of taking their calls. Part of that had to do with my own arrogance, my own ego. He was doing things I don't like, but hey, his politics are his politics. He has the right to do that. At the time, if I had called Bruce and said, 'Hey, let's sit down and work this out,' I'm sure he would have said yes. I owe him an apology."

After being ousted by Sony, Yetnikoff founded the short-lived Velvel Records, a boutique label, then helped run another small imprint, Commotion Records. He continued to work on a number of music and other arts pro-jects and joined the New York board of the Caron Foundation addiction treat-ment facility. In 2004 he collaborated with writer David Ritz on a colorful memoir, *Howling at the Moon.* —*JP*

Pete Yorn

Singer, songwriter, record company director

Although Pete Yorn grew up in New Jersey, he did not cultivate his affinity for Bruce Springsteen until later, when he was attending Syracuse University. "An elder advised, via telephone, that I smoke a marijuana cigarette, put on *The Wild, the Innocent & the E Street Shuffle*, specifically a song called 'New York City Serenade,' and lie on the floor in the dark while listening to it," Yorn noted. "That is the day I became a Bruce fan …There's a line in that song about walking tall; 'Walk tall, or baby don't walk at all.' That line inspires me."

Yorn's inspiration has turned into tribute on the 2003 *Light of Day* album, to which he contributed a cover of "New York City Serenade." The song had already appeared, along with "Dancing in the Dark," on a special limited edition of his 2001 debut album *musicforthemorningafter*. He also covered "Atlantic City" on his 2004 double CD *Live from New Jersey*. Critics have often cited Springsteen's influence on Yorn's music, and on his live shows. "I don't think we sound alike," Yorn told VH1, "but he was always singing about love and heartache in a way that was kind of tough. When I do those kind of songs, I try to keep it that way. When songs get really sappy, it turns me off."

Born in 1975 into a musical family—his mother was a concert pianist and two older brothers played in bands—Yorn picked up guitar and piano early and started writing songs as a teenager. He moved to California in 2000 and, with the help of his brother Rick, a Hollywood talent agent, landed gigs writing and performing music for television and film, including *Me, Myself, and Irene* and "Dawson's Creek" before snagging a record contract with Columbia Records. *Musicforthemorningafter* was certified gold and was followed by the less commercially successful *Day I Forgot* in 2003. Yorn also became co-owner of Trampoline Records, which started by putting out sam-plers and holding showcase concerts in Los Angeles.

Yorn's brother also provided the fledgling musician's first two in-per-son introductions to Springsteen. "After I met Springsteen for the first time, I remember thinking he was as cool as I thought he would be," Yorn said. "The first time I clammed up. It was before *musicforthemorningafter* had come out. We'd been signed in a similar way, off playing acoustic for people at the

Warren Zevon recorded Springsteen's "Jeannie Needs a Shooter" for his 1980 album *Bad Luck Streak in Dancing School.* Their collaboration on "Disorder in the House", from Zevon's final album *The Wind*, earned a Grammy in 2004.

label and he said, 'I didn't know they still did that.' I met him again at a Columbia Grammy party in New York and we talked for a long time and he invited me down to his farm and I was like, 'Sweet! Let's go!'"
—MC/GG

Warren Zevon

Singer-songwriter

 singer-songwriter whose work was noir-ish, literary, politically incorrect, and poetically violent, Warren Zevon was Bruce Springsteen's friend and artistic collaborator, writing two songs with him—"Jeannie Needs a Shooter" and the Grammy-winning "Disorder in the House." Zevon was born in Chicago but reared in Los Angeles and Arizona as the son of a professional gambler. He studied classical music at an early age but switched to pop and recorded in the late '60s as part of the folk-rock duo Lyme and Cybelle. He landed a track on the soundtrack of the Oscar-winning film *Midnight Cowboy*, but his first solo album, *Wanted Dead or Alive*, bombed. Zevon also did session work and played piano on the road with the Everly Brothers before moving to Spain for several years. He returned to the states to record *Warren Zevon*, produced by his friend, Jackson Browne, who had gotten him a record deal. From that album (released in 1976), Linda Ronstadt covered "Poor Poor Pitiful Me" and "Carmelita" on her 1977 best-selling album, *Simple Dreams.* His second album, *Excitable Boy,* was also produced by Browne and contained Zevon's best known songs, "Werewolves of London" and "Roland the Headless Thompson Gunner." *Bad Luck Streak in Dancing School*, released in 1980, featured the Springsteen collaboration "Jeannie Needs a Shooter." "I'd heard this Springsteen song title from his manager, Jon Landau. I asked Bruce about it so many times, he finally said, 'You like it so much, why don't you write it?'" Zevon wrote in the liner notes to his best-of anthology, *I'll Sleep When I'm Dead.* "I did write a few lines, T-Bone Burnett added something, I cut a track and actually put strings on it, then showed up at Bruce's house in Asbury Park in the middle of the night. He was asleep on the sofa in front of a videotaped baseball game. I roused him and played what I had for him. 'It's nice,' he said, 'but where are all the other verses?' I just smiled."

Zevon struggled with alcoholism, and albums such as *Sentimental Hygiene* and *Mr. Bad Example* address his own failings with honesty and gallows humor. He continued to record and tour, mostly on his own, and made frequent appearances on "The Late Show with David Letterman," sitting in for musical director Paul Shaffer.

In 2002 Zevon was diagnosed with mesothelioma, a fatal form of cancer. Given three months to live by his doctors, Zevon immediately began work on *The Wind*, which would be his final album. Among the guests who came to support him was Springsteen, who cowrote and played guitar on "Disorder in the House." "I love Bruce very much," Zevon says in the VH1 documentary *Keep Me in Your Heart* (released on DVD as *Inside Out*). "The thing about Springsteen is that he's the person that everybody hopes he would be. He's stuck by me through some weird stuff. Some real bad times." Later, after Springsteen rips through a wicked guitar solo, Zevon looks at him and marvels, "You *are* him!" The track won a Grammy Award in 2004 for Best Rock Performance By a Duo or Group with Vocal.

Zevon outlived his doctors' prediction but died on September 7, 2003, having witnessed both the release of his album and the birth of his twin grandchildren. Springsteen and the E Street Band contributed a live version of Zevon's "My Ride's Here" on *Enjoy Every Sandwich: The Songs of Warren Zevon*, a tribute album released in October 2004 produced by Zevon's son, Jordan, and long-time collaborator Jorge Calderon. —*DD*

Further On (Up the Road):
Springsteen Live, 1971-2005

1971

March
18 Deal Park, Deal, NJ
27 Sunshine Inn, Asbury Park, NJ

April
16–17, 23–24 The Upstage, Asbury Park, NJ

May
14 Sunshine Inn, Asbury Park, NJ
15 Newark State College, Union, NJ
21 Sunshine Inn, Asbury Park, NJ
22 The Upstage, Asbury Park, NJ

July
10 Brookdale Community College, Lincroft, NJ
11 Sunshine Inn, Asbury Park, NJ (opening for Humble Pie)
22 D'Scene, South Amboy, NJ
23 Damrosch Park, Lincoln Center, New York, NY
29 D'scene, South Amboy, NJ

August
7 Sunshine Inn, Asbury Park, NJ
27–29 Student Prince, Asbury Park, NJ

September
1 City Park, Long Branch, NJ
3–5, 10–12, 17–19, 24–26 Student Prince, Asbury Park, NJ

October
1–3 Student Prince, Asbury Park, NJ
8 Rutgers University, New Brunswick, NJ
15–17 Student Prince, Asbury Park, NJ
23 Keller Hall, University of Richmond, Richmond, VA
25 Richmond Arena, Richmond, VA
29 St. Jerome School, West Long Branch, NJ
29 The Upstage, Asbury Park, NJ
30 Virginia Commonwealth University, Richmond, VA
31 National Guard Armory, Long Branch, NJ

November
11, 13–14, 19–21, 23 Student Prince, Asbury Park, NJ
23 New Plaza Theater, Linden, NJ
24, 26–28 Student Prince, Asbury Park, NJ

December
3, 5 Student Prince, Asbury Park, NJ
9 Freehold Township High School, Freehold, NJ
10–12 Student Prince, Asbury Park, NJ
17 Rutgers University, New Brunswick, NJ
18–19 Student Prince, Asbury Park, NJ

1972

January
28–30 The Captain's Garter, Neptune, NJ

February
4–6 The Back Door, Richmond, VA

12, 14 Sunshine Inn, Asbury Park, NJ
16 Monmouth College, Long Branch, NJ
18–20, 25, 26–27 The Back Door, Richmond, VA

March
3 St. Joseph High School, Metuchen, NJ
17 Richmond Arena, Richmond, VA
18 Hampden–Sydney College, Hampden–Sydney, VA

April
15 The Ledge, Rutgers University, New Brunswick, NJ

May
2 The Gaslight Club, New York, NY

June
17 The Shipbottom Lounge, Point Pleasant, NJ (with Norman Seldin & the Joyful Noyze)

July
1 The Shipbottom Lounge, Point Pleasant, NJ (with Norman Seldin & the Joyful Noyze)
5 Cinema III, Red Bank, NJ (George McGovern campaign benefit)

August
9–14 Max's Kansas City, New York, NY

September
2 Huddy Park, Highlands, NJ (with Odin)
4 Max's Kansas City, New York, NY
4 The Bitter End, New York, NY (with Jackson Browne and David Blue)

October
25 The Shipbottom Lounge, Point Pleasant, NJ
28 West Chester College, West Chester, PA
29 National Guard Armory, Long Branch, NJ

November
11 York College of Pennsylvania, York, PA
12 unknown venue, York, PA
31 unknown venue, York, PA

December
5–6 Kenny's Castaways, New York, NY
7 Ossining Correctional Facility, Ossining, NY
8–10 Kenny's Castaways, New York, NY
22 Rutgers University, New Brunswick, NJ
29 Dayton Hara Arena, Dayton, OH
30 Ohio Theatre, Columbus, OH

1973

January
3–6 The Main Point, Bryn Mawr, PA
8–14 Paul's Mall, Boston, MA
16 Villanova University, Villanova, PA
18–21 My Father's Place, Roslyn, NY
24–28 The Quiet Knight, Chicago, IL
31 Max's Kansas City, New York, NY

February
1–5 Max's Kansas City, New York, NY
10 Student Prince, Asbury Park, NJ
11 Seton Hall University, South Orange, NJ
14 Virginia Commonwealth University, Richmond, VA
16 Monmouth College, West Long Branch, NJ (Save a Tree Concert)
26 The Troubadour, Los Angeles, CA
28 Memorial Civic Auditorium, Stockton, CA (opening for Paul Butterfield)

March
2 Community Theatre, Berkeley, CA (opening for Blood, Sweat & Tears)
3 Santa Monica Civic Auditorium, Santa Monica, CA (opening for Blood, Sweat & Tears)
4 Paramount Northwest Theater, Portland, OR
5 Paramount Theater, Seattle, WA
12–17 Oliver's, Boston, MA
18 University of Rhode Island, Kingston, RI
23 Palace Theatre, Providence, RI
24 Niagara University, Lewiston, NY
29 Kutztown University, Kutztown, PA

April
1 The Ledge, Rutgers University, New Brunswick, NJ
7 Scope Arena, Norfolk, VA
11 Omni Coliseum, Atlanta, GA
14 unknown venue, Richmond, VA
18 Christian Brothers Academy, Lincroft, NJ
23 Bushnell Memorial Hall, Hartford, CT
24–25 The Main Point, Bryn Mawr, PA
27 Convocation Center, Ohio University, Athens, OH
28 University of Maryland Field House, College Park, MD (opening for Chuck Berry and Jerry Lee Lewis)

May
1 Ahmanson Theatre, Los Angeles, CA
5 Providence College, Providence, RI

6 Alumni Stadium, University of Massachusetts, Amherst, MA (opening for It's a Beautiful Day)
11 Ohio State University, Columbus, OH
12 Niagara University, Lewiston, NY
16 Minnesota State University, Mankato, MN
24–26 Childe Harold, Washington, DC
30 Cumberland County Civic Centre, Fayetteville, NC (opening for Chicago)
31 Coliseum, Richmond, VA (opening for Chicago)

June
1 Hampton Roads Coliseum, Hampton, VA (opening for Chicago)
2 Civic Center, Baltimore, MD (opening for Chicago)
3 Veterans Memorial Coliseum, New Haven, CT (opening for Chicago)
6 The Spectrum, Philadelphia, PA (opening for Chicago)
8–9 Boston Garden, Boston, MA (opening for Chicago)
10 Civic Centre, Springfield, MA (opening for Chicago)
13 Broom County Memorial Arena, Binghamton, NY (opening for Chicago)
14–15 Madison Square Garden, New York, NY (opening for Chicago)
22–24 Fat City, Seaside Heights, NJ

July
5–9 The Main Point, Bryn Mawr, PA
18–23 Max's Kansas City, New York, NY (co-headline with Bob Marley & the Wailers)
27 CBS Annual Sales Convention, San Francisco, CA
31 My Father's Place, New York, NY

August
1–2 My Father's Place, New York, NY
4 Convention Hall, Asbury Park, NJ
14 Erlton Lounge, Cherry Hill, NJ
16 Mr. D's, East Paterson, NJ
20–26 Oliver's, Boston, MA
31 Fat City, Seaside Heights, NJ

September
1–2 Fat City, Seaside Heights, NJ
6 Dean College, Franklin, MA
7 Penn State University, University Park, PA
8 University of Pittsburgh, Pittsburgh, PA
22 Jai Alai Fronton, Miami, FL
28 Hampden Sydney College, Hampden Sydney, VA

29 Waynesburg College, Waynesburg, PA
30 State University of New York, Stony Brook, NY

October
6 Villanova University, Villanova, PA
7 Avery Fisher Hall, Lincoln Center, New York, NY
13 Kennedy Center, Washington, DC
15–19 Oliver's, Boston, MA
20 Franklin Pierce College, Rindge, NH
26 Hobart College, Geneva, NY
30–31 The Main Point, Bryn Mawr, PA

November
3 Ricker College, Houlton, ME
6–10 Max's Kansas City, New York, NY
11 Trenton State College, Trenton, NJ
14–16 My Father's Place, Roslyn, NY
17 The Roxy, Manayunk, PA
25 University of Massachusetts, Amherst, MA (opening for John Mayall)
30 Virginia Commonwealth University, Richmond, VA

December
1 Quinnipiac College, Hamden, CT
6–8 Childe Harold, Washington, DC
14 Pine Crest Country Club, Shelton, CT
15 Nassau Community College, Garden City, NY
17–18 Student Prince, Asbury Park, NJ
20 Roger Williams University, Providence, RI
21 Sandy's, Beverly, MA
22 Erlton Lounge, Cherry Hill, NJ
23 Rova Farms, Jackson, NJ
27–30 The Main Point, Bryn Mawr, PA

1974

January
4–6 Joe's Place, Boston, MA
12 The Joint in the Woods, Parsippany, NJ
19 Kent State University, Kent, OH
25 Mosque, Richmond, VA
26 Chrysler Theatre, Norfolk, VA
29–30 Muther's Music Emporium, Nashville, TN

February
1 Allen Theatre, Cleveland, OH
2 Springfield College, Springfield, MA
7–9 Richard's, Atlanta, GA
12 University of Kentucky, Lexington, KY
23 Satellite Lounge, Cookstown, NJ
24–25 The Main Point, Bryn Mawr, PA

March

3–4 Gaston Hall, Georgetown University, Washington, DC
7–10 Liberty Hall, Houston, TX
15–16 Armadillo World HQ, Austin, TX
18–21 Gertie's, Dallas, TX
24 Celebrity Theatre, Phoenix, AZ

April

5 Widener College, Chester, PA
6 Burlington County College, Pemberton, NJ
7 Seton Hall University, South Orange, NJ
9–12 Charley's Bar, Cambridge, MA
13 The Joint in the Woods, Parsippany, NJ
19 State Theatre, New Brunswick, NJ
20 Ursinus College, Collegeville, PA
26 Brown University, Providence, RI
27 University of Connecticut, Storrs, CT
28 Swarthmore College, Swarthmore, PA
29 Roxy Theatre, Northampton, PA

May

4 Montclair State University, Montclair, NJ
5 Kent State University, Kent, OH
6 Bucks County Community College, Newtown, PA
9 Harvard Square Theatre, Cambridge, MA (opening for Bonnie Raitt)
10 Palace Theatre, Providence, RI
11 Fairleigh Dickenson University, Rutherford, NJ
24 War Memorial Theatre, Trenton, NJ
25 Archbishop John Carrol High School, Radnor, PA
28–29 The Main Point, Bryn Mawr, PA
31 The Agora, Columbus, OH

June

1 Kent State University, Kent, OH
2 The Agora, Toledo, OH
3 The Agora, Cleveland, OH
13 Civic Center Music Hall, Oklahoma City, OK
14 Texas Hall, Arlington, TX
15 Armadillo World Head Quarters, Austin, TX
21–22 Le Garage, Spray Beach, NJ

July

12–14 The Bottom Line, New York, New York, NY
25 Santa Monica Civic Auditorium, Santa Monica, CA (opening for Dr. John)
26 Civic Theatre, San Diego, CA
27 Celebrity Theatre, Phoenix, AZ
28 Tucson Community Center Theatre, Tucson, AZ

30 The Troubadour, Los Angeles, CA

August

3 Schaefer Music Festival, Central Park, New York, NY (opening for Anne Murray)
13 The Stone Ballroom, Newark, DE
14 Carlton Theatre, Red Bank, NJ

September

9 The Stone Pony, Asbury Park, NJ
19 The Main Point, Bryn Mawr, PA
20 The Tower Theatre, Upper Darby, PA
21 State University of New York, Oneonta, NY
22 Kean University, Union, NJ

October

4 Avery Fisher Hall, Lincoln Center, New York, NY
5 Albright College, Reading, PA
6 Clark University, Worcester, MA
11 Shady Grove Music Fair, Gaithersburg, MD
12 Alexander Hall, Princeton University, NJ
18 Capitol Theatre, Passaic, NJ
19 Union College, Schenectady, NY
20 Dickinson College, Carlisle, PA
25 Dartmouth College, Hanover, NH
26 Springfield College, Springfield, MA
27 Millersville University, Millersville, PA
29 Music Hall, Boston, MA

November

1–2 Tower Theatre, Philadelphia, PA
6–7 Armadillo World Headquarters, Austin, TX
8 Ritz Music Hall, Corpus Christi, TX
9 Music Hall, Houston, TX
15 Lafayette College, Easton, PA
16 Gaston Hall, Georgetown University, Washington, DC
17 University of Virginia, Charlottesville, VA
21 Camden Community College, Camden, NJ
22 West Chester College, West Chester, PA
23 Salem State College, Salem, MA
29–30 War Memorial Theatre, Trenton, NJ

December

6 State Theatre, New Brunswick, NJ
7 Hobart & William Smith College, Geneva, NY
8 University of Vermont, Burlington, VT
14 Rutgers University, New Brunswick, NJ
29 The Stone Pony, Asbury Park, NJ

1975

January
5, 12, 19 The Stone Pony, Asbury Park, NJ

February
5 The Main Point, Bryn Mawr, PA
6–7 Widener College, West Chester, PA
18 John Carroll University, Cleveland, OH
19 Penn State University, University Park, PA
20 Syria Mosque, Pittsburgh, PA
23 Westbury Music Fair, Westbury, NY

March
7 Painters Mill Music Fair, Owings Mills, MD
8–9 Constitution Hall, Washington, DC
25 Township Auditorium, Columbia, SC

July
20 Palace Theatre, Providence, RI
22 Geneva Theatre, Geneva, NY
23 Music Inn, Lenox, MA
25–26 Keystone Hall, Kutztown State College, Kutztown, PA
28–30 Carter Barron Amphitheatre, Washington, DC

August
1 Mosque Theatre, Richmond, VA
2 Chrysler Theatre, Norfolk, VA
8 Civic Theatre, Akron, OH
9 Syria Mosque, Pittsburgh, PA
10 Allen Theatre, Cleveland, OH
13–17 Bottom Line, New York, NY (two shows per night)
21–23 Electric Ballroom, Atlanta, GA

September
6 Performing Arts Center, New Orleans, LA
7 Ya Ya Lounge, New Orleans, LA
12 Municipal Auditorium, Austin, TX
13–14 Music Hall, Houston, TX
16 Convention Center Theatre, Dallas, TX
17 Oklahoma City Music Hall, Oklahoma City, OK
20 Grinnell College, Grinnell, IA
21 Guthrie Theatre, Minneapolis, MN
23 Hill Auditorium, University of Michigan, Ann Arbor, MI
25 Chicago Auditorium Theatre, Chicago, IL
26 Hancher Auditorium, University of Iowa, Iowa City, IA
27 Ambassador Theatre, St. Louis, MO
28 Memorial Hall, Kansas City, MO
30 Music Hall, University of Nebraska, Omaha, NE

October
2 Uptown Theatre, Milwaukee, WI
4 Michigan Palace, Detroit, MI
11 Monmouth Arts Center, Red Bank, NJ
16–19 The Roxy, Los Angeles, CA
26 Paramount Theatre, Seattle, OR
27 Paramount Theatre, Portland, OR
29 Memorial Auditorium, Sacramento, CA
31 Paramount Theatre, Oakland, CA

November
1 Robertson Gym, University of California, Santa Barbara, CA
3–4, 6 Arizona State University, Phoenix, AZ
9 Jai Alai Fronton, Tampa, FL
11 Jai Alai Fronton, Miami, FL
18 Hammersmith Odeon, London, England
21 Konserthus, Stockholm, Sweden
23 RAI, Amsterdam, The Netherlands
24 Hammersmith Odeon, London, England

December
2–3 Boston Music Hall, Boston, MA
5–7 Georgetown University, Washington, DC
10 Bucknell University, Lewisburg, PA
11 Seton Hall University, South Orange, NJ
12 C.W. Post College, Greenvale, NY
16 State University of New York, Oswego, NY
17 Kleinhans Music Hall, Buffalo, NY
19 Place De Arts, Montreal, Canada
20 National Arts Centre, Ottawa, Canada
21 Seneca College, Toronto, Canada
27–28, 30–31 Tower Theatre, Upper Darby, PA

1976

January
1 The Stone Pony, Asbury Park, NJ (with Southside Johnny & the Asbury Jukes)

March
7 Beacon Theatre, New York, NY (with Carole King)
21 The Stone Pony, Asbury Park, NJ
25 Township Auditorium, Columbia, SC
26 Fox Theatre, Atlanta, GA
28 Duke University, Durham, NC
29 Oven's Auditorium, Charlotte, NC

April
1 University of Ohio, Athens, OH
2 Macauley Theatre, Louisville, KY
4 Michigan State University, East Lansing, MI
5 Ohio Theatre, Columbus, OH

7–9 Allen Theatre, Cleveland, OH
9 Colgate University, Hamilton, NY
10 Choate School, Wallingford, CT
12 Memorial Auditorium, Johnstown, PA
13 Penn State University, University Park, PA
15 Syria Mosque, Pittsburgh, PA
16 Allegheny College, Meadville, PA
17 University of Rochester, Rochester, NY
20 Freedom Hall, Johnson City, TN
21 Knoxville Civic Auditorium, Knoxville, TN
22 Burruss Hall, Virginia Poly–Tech Institute, Blacksberg, VA
24 Appalachian State University, Boone, NC
26 Soldiers & Sailors Memorial Auditorium, Chattanooga, TN
28 Grand Ol' Opry, Nashville, TN
29 Ellis Auditorium, Memphis, TN
30 Municipal Auditorium, Birmingham, AL

May
4 Mississippi Coliseum, Jackson, MS
6 Hirsch Municipal Auditorium, Shreveport, LA
8 Louisiana State University, Baton Rouge, LA .
9–10 Municipal Auditorium, Mobile, AL
11 Auburn University, Auburn, AL
13 Municipal Auditorium, New Orleans, LA
27 Eisenhower Hall, West Point, NY
28 Naval Academy, Annapolis, MD
30 The Stone Pony, Asbury Park, NJ (with Southside Johnny & the Asbury Jukes)

July
20 CBS Annual Sales Convention, Los Angeles, CA (with Southside Johnny)

August
1–3, 5–7 Monmouth Arts Centre, Red Bank, NJ
21 Palace Theatre, Waterbury, CT
22 Springfield Civic Center, Springfield, MA

September
4 The Stone Pony, Asbury Park, NJ (with Southside Johnny & the Asbury Jukes)
26 Memorial Coliseum, Phoenix, AZ
29–30 Civic Center, Santa Monica, CA
30 The Roxy, Los Angeles, CA (with Dion)

October
2 Paramount Theatre, Oakland, CA
3 Santa Clara University, Santa Clara, CA
5 County Bowl, Santa Barbara, CA
9 Notre Dame University, South Bend, IN
10 Miami of University, Oxford, OH

12 Rutgers University, New Brunswick, NJ
13 Kean College, Union, NJ
16 William And Mary University, Williamsburg, VA
17–18 Georgetown University, Washington, DC
25, 27 The Spectrum, Philadelphia, PA
28–30 The Palladium, New York, NY

November
2–4 The Palladium, New York, NY
26 The Bottom Line, New York, NY (with Patti Smith, two shows)

1977

February
7 Palace Theatre, Albany, NY
8 Auditorium Theatre, Rochester, NY
9 Kleinhans Auditorium, Buffalo, NY
10 Memorial Auditorium, Utica, NY
12 Civic Centre, Ottawa, Canada
13 Maple Leaf Gardens, Toronto, Canada
15 Masonic Temple Auditorium, Detroit, MI
16 Veterans Auditorium, Columbus, OH
17 Richfield Coliseum, Cleveland, OH
19 Civic Center, St. Paul, MN
20 Dane County Coliseum, Madison, WI
22 Arena Auditorium, Milwaukee, WI
23 Auditorium Theatre, Chicago, IL
25 Purdue University, Lafayette, IN
26 Convention Center, Indianapolis, IN
27 Riverfront Coliseum, Cincinnati, OH
28 Fox Theatre, St. Louis, MO

March
2 Civic Center, Atlanta, GA
4 Auditorium, Jacksonville, FL
5 Jai Alai Fronton, Orlando, FL
6 Jai Alai Fronton, Miami, FL
10 Sports Arena, Toledo, OH
11 St. Vincent College, La Trobe, PA
13 Towson State University, Baltimore, MD
14 Mid-Hudson Civic Center, Poughkeepsie, NY
15 Community Arena, Binghamton, NY
18 Memorial Coliseum, New Haven, CT
19 Central Maine Youth Center, Lewiston, ME
20 Alumni Hall, Providence College, Providence, RI
22–25 Music Hall, Boston, MA

April
17 The Stone Pony, Asbury Park, NJ (with Southside Johnny & the Asbury Jukes)

May
12–13 Monmouth Arts Center, Red Bank, NJ (Asbury All–Star Review, two shows on May 13)

September
4 The Stone Pony, Asbury Park, NJ (with the Shots)
13 The Stone Pony, Asbury Park, NJ (with Southside Johnny & Asbury Jukes and the E Street Band)

October
13 The Stone Pony, Asbury Park, NJ (with Southside Johnny & the Asbury Jukes)

December
2 NYU Loeb Student Center, New York, NY (with Robert Gordon and Link Wray)
30 CBGB's, New York, NY (with Patti Smith)
31 Capitol Theatre, Passaic, NJ (with Southside Johnny and the E Street Band)

1978

May
19 Paramount Theatre, Asbury Park, NJ
23 Shea Theater, Buffalo, NY
24 Palace Theater, Albany, NY
26–27 The Spectrum, Philadelphia, PA
29–31 Music Hall, Boston, MA

June
1 U.S. Naval Academy, Annapolis, MD
3 Nassau Coliseum, Uniondale, NY
5 Centennial Arena, Toledo, OH
6 Convention Center, Indianapolis, IN
8 Dane County Coliseum, Madison, WI
9 Milwaukee Arena, Milwaukee, WI
10 Met Center, Bloomington, MN
12 unknown venue, La Crosse, WI
13 University of Iowa, Iowa City, IA
14 Music Hall, Omaha, NE
16 Municipal Auditorium, Kansas City, MO
17 Kiel Opera House, St. Louis, MO
20 Red Rocks Amphitheater, Morrison, CO
22 unknown venue, Salt Lake City, UT
24 Paramount Theater, Portland, OR
25 Paramount Arena, Seattle, WA
26 Queen Elizabeth Theatre, Vancouver, Canada
29 Performing Arts Centre, San Jose, CA
30 Community Theater, Berkeley, CA

July
1 Community Theater, Berkeley, CA
3 unknown venue, Santa Barbara, CA

5 The Forum, Los Angeles, CA
6 Sundance Club, Los Angeles, CA (with unknown cover band)
7 The Roxy, Los Angeles, CA
8 Veterans Memorial Coliseum, Phoenix, AZ
9 Sports Arena, San Diego, CA
12 Convention Center, Dallas, TX
14 Municipal Auditorium, San Antonio, TX
15 Sam Houston Coliseum, Houston, TX
16 The Warehouse, New Orleans, LA
18 Civic Center, Jackson, MI
19 Ellis Auditorium, Memphis, TN
21 Municipal Auditorium, Nashville, TN
28 Jai Alai Fronton, Miami, FL
29 Bayfront Civic Center Auditorium, St. Petersburg, FL
31 Township Auditorium, Columbus, SC

August
1 Gaillard Municipal Auditorium, Charleston, SC
2 Charlotte Coliseum, Charlotte, NC
4 Civic Center, Charleston, WV
5 Louisville Gardens, Louisville, KY
7 Wings Auditorium, Kalamazoo, MI
9 The Agora, Cleveland, OH
10 War Memorial, Rochester, NY
12 Civic Center, Augusta, ME
14 Hampton Roads Coliseum, Hampton, VA
15 Capital Centre, Landover, MD
18–19 The Spectrum, Philadelphia, PA
21–23 Madison Square Garden, New York, NY
25 Veteran's Memorial Coliseum, New Haven, CT
25 Toad's Place, New Haven, CT (with Beaver Brown)
26 Civic Center, Providence, RI
28–29 Stanley Theater, Pittsburgh, PA
30 Richfield Coliseum, Cleveland, OH
31 The Agora, Cleveland, OH (with Southside Johnny & the Asbury Jukes)

September
1 Masonic Temple Auditorium, Detroit, MI
3 Civic Center, Saginaw, MI
5 Veterans Memorial Auditorium, Columbus, OH
6 Uptown Theater, Chicago, IL
9 University of Notre Dame, South Bend, IN
10 Riverfront Coliseum, Cincinnati, OH
12 War Memorial Auditorium, Syracuse, NY
13 Civic Center, Springfield, MA
15–17 The Palladium, New York, NY
19–21 Capitol Theater, Passaic, NJ

25 Boston Gardens, Boston, MA
29 Boutwell Auditorium, Birmingham, AL
30 Fox Theater, Atlanta, GA

October
1 Fox Theater, Atlanta, GA
17 The Troubadour, Los Angeles, CA (with the Knack)

November
1 Princeton University, Jadwin Gym, Princeton, NJ
2 Capitol Centre, Landover, MD
4 University of Vermont, Burlington, VT
5 University of New Hampshire, Durham, NH
7 Cornell University, Ithaca, NY
8 The Forum, Montreal, Canada
10 St. Bonaventure University, Olean, NY
12 Rensselaer Polytechnic University, Troy, NY
14 Utica Memorial Auditorium, Utica, NY
16 Maple Leaf Gardens, Toronto, Canada
17 Michigan State University, East Lansing, MI
18 Miami University, Millet Hall, Oxford, OH
20 University of Illinois, Champaign, IL
21 Northwestern University, Evanston, IL
25 Kiel Opera House, St. Louis, MO
27 Milwaukee Arena, Milwaukee, WI
28 Dane County Coliseum, Madison, WI
29 Civic Center, St. Paul, MN

December
1 Lloyd Noble Center, University of Oklahoma, Norman, OK
3 Southern Illinois University, Carbondale, IL
5 Louisiana State University, Baton Rogue, LA
7 University of Texas, Austin, TX
8 The Summit, Houston, TX
9 Convention Center, Dallas, TX
11 University of Colorado, Boulder, CO
13 Community Center, Tucson, AZ
15–16 Winterland, San Francisco, CA
19 Paramount Theater, Portland, OR
20 Seattle Center Arena, Seattle, WA
27–28 Stanley Theater, Pittsburgh, PA
30 Cobo Hall, Detroit, MI
31 Richfield Coliseum, Cleveland, OH

1979

January
1 Richfield Coliseum, Cleveland, OH

March
14 The Fast Lane, Asbury Park, NJ (with Robert Gordon)

April
13, 15 The Fast Lane, Asbury Park, NJ (with Beaver Brown)

May
27 Paramount Theater, Asbury Park, NJ (with Robert Gordon)

June
6 The Whisky, Los Angeles, CA (wedding of lighting director Marc Brinkman)

September
22–23 Madison Square Garden, New York, NY (MUSE "No Nukes" benefit concerts)

October
5–6 The Fast Lane, Asbury Park, NJ (with Beaver Brown)

December
12 NYU Loeb Auditorium, New York, NY (with Robert Gordon)

1980

January
9 The Fast Lane, Asbury Park, NJ (with Jon Bon Jovi's Atlantic City Expressway)

May
1 The Fast Lane, Asbury Park, NJ (with David Johansen)

August
16 The Forum, Los Angeles, CA (with Jackson Browne)

October
3 Crisler Arena, Ann Arbor, MI
4, 6, 7 Riverfront Coliseum, Cincinnati, OH
9 Cobo Hall, Detroit, MI
10–11 Uptown Theater, Chicago, IL
13 Civic Center, St. Paul, MN
14 Milwaukee Arena, Milwaukee, WI
17–18 Kiel Opera House, St. Louis, MO
20 McNicholls Arena, Denver, CO
23 Old Timer's Cafe, Seattle, WA (with the Lost Highway Band)
24 Seattle Center Coliseum, Seattle, WA
25 Coliseum, Portland, OR
27–28 Coliseum, Oakland, CA
30–31 Sports Arena, Los Angeles, CA

November
1, 3 Sports Arena, Los Angeles, CA
5 Arizona State University, Tempe, AZ

8 Reunion Arena, Dallas, TX
9 Frank Erwin Center, Austin, TX
11 LSU Assembly Center, Baton Rogue, LA
14–15 The Summit, Houston, TX
20 Rosemont Horizon, Chicago, IL
23–24 Capital Centre, Landover, MD
27–28 Madison Square Garden, New York, NY
30 Civic Arena, Pittsburgh, PA

December
1 Civic Arena, Pittsburgh, PA
2, 4 War Memorial, Rochester, NY
6, 8–9 The Spectrum, Philadelphia, PA
11 Civic Center, Providence, RI
12 Civic Center, Hartford, CT
15–16 Boston Gardens, Boston, MA
18–19 Madison Square Garden, New York, NY
28–29, 31 Nassau Coliseum, Uniondale, NY

1981

January
20–21 Maple Leaf Gardens, Toronto, Canada
23 The Forum, Montreal, Canada
24 Civic Centre, Ottawa, Canada
26 University of Notre Dame, South Bend, IN
28 Checkerdome, St. Louis, MO
29 Hilton Coliseum, Ames, IA

February
1 St. Paul Civic Arena, St. Paul, MN
2 Dane County Coliseum, Madison, WI
4 Southern Illinois University, Carbondale, IL
5 Kemper Arena, Kansas City, MO
7 University of Illinois, Champaign, IL
12 Municipal Auditorium, Mobile, AL
13 Mississippi State University, Starkville, MS
15–16 Civic Center, Lakeland, FL
18 Coliseum, Jacksonville, FL
20 Sportatorium, Hollywood, FL
22 Carolina Coliseum, Columbia, SC
23 The Omni, Atlanta, GA
25 Mid–South Coliseum, Memphis, TN
26 Municipal Auditorium, Nashville, TN
28 Greensboro Coliseum, Greensboro, NC

March
2 Hampton Roads Coliseum, Hampton, VA
4 Rupp Arena, Lexington, KY
5 Market Square Arena, Indianapolis, IN

April
7 Congress Centrum, Hamburg, West Germany
8 ICC Halle, West Berlin, West Germany
11 Hallenstadion, Zurich, Switzerland
14 Festhalle, Frankfurt, West Germany
16 Olympiahalle, Munich, West Germany
18–19 Palais Des Sports, Paris, France
21 Palacio de Deportes, Barcelona, Spain
24 Palais Des Sport, Lyon, France
26 Vorst National, Brussels, Belgium
28–29 Sportspaleis Ahoy, Rotterdam, The Netherlands

May
1 Forum, Copenhagen, Denmark
2 Brondbyhallen, Copenhagen, Denmark
3 Scandinavium, Gothenberg, Sweden
5 Drammenshallen, Oslo, Norway
7–8 Johannsehovg Isstadion, Stockholm, Sweden
11 Newcastle City Hall, Newcastle, England
13–14 Apollo Theatre, Manchester, England
16–17 Playhouse Theatre, Edinburgh, Scotland
20 New Bingley Hall, Stafford, England
26–27 Brighton Centre, Brighton, England
29–30 Wembley Arena, London, England

June
1–2, 4–5 Wembley Arena, London, England
7–8 NEC Arena, Birmingham, England
14 Hollywood Bowl, Los Angeles, CA (Survival Sunday with Jackson Browne and Gary U.S. Bonds)
15 Old Waldorf, San Francisco, CA (with Gary U.S. Bonds)

July
2–3, 5–6, 8–9 Brendan Byrne Arena, East Rutherford, NJ
11 Big Man's West, Red Bank, NJ (with Clarence Clemons & the Red Bank Rockers)
13, 15–16, 18–19 The Spectrum, Philadelphia, PA
29–30 Richfield Coliseum, Cleveland, OH

August
4–5 Capital Centre, Landover, MD
6 Bayou Club, Washington, DC (with Robbin Thompson)
7 Capital Centre, Landover, MD
11–12 Joe Louis Arena, Detroit, MI
16–17 Red Rocks Amphitheater, Denver, CO

20 Sports Arena, Los Angeles, CA (A Night for the Vietnam Veteran benefit)

21, 23–24, 27–28 Sports Arena, Los Angeles, CA

September
2 Sports Arena, San Diego, CA
5 Perkin's Palace, Pasadena, CA (with the Pretenders)
8, 10–11 Rosemont Horizon, Chicago, IL
13–14 Riverfront Coliseum, Cincinnati, OH

1982

January
5 The Stone Pony, Asbury Park, NJ (with the Lord Gunner Group)
12 Royal Manor North, New Brunswick, NJ (with Nils Lofgren)

February
20 Big Man's West, Red Bank, NJ (with Beaver Brown)

April
9–10 Big Man's West, Red Bank, NJ (with Beaver Brown)
11 Big Man's West, Red Bank, NJ (with John Eddie & the Frontstreet Rockers)
16 Big Man's West, Red Bank, NJ (with Clarence Clemons & the Red Bank Rockers)
25 The Stone Pony, Asbury Park, NJ (with Cats on a Smooth Surface)

May
2 The Stone Pony, Asbury Park, NJ (with Cats on a Smooth Surface)
8 The Fast Lane, Asbury Park, NJ (with Beaver Brown)
16 Big Man's West, Red Bank, NJ (with Clarence Clemons & the Red Bank Rockers)
23 The Fast Lane, Asbury Park, NJ (with Cats on a Smooth Surface)
29 Big Man's West, Red Bank, NJ (with Beaver Brown and Southside Johnny)

June
6 The Stone Pony, Asbury Park, NJ (with Cats on a Smooth Surface)
12 Central Park, New York, NY (rally for disarmament with Jackson Browne)
12 Big Man's West, Red Bank, NJ (with Sonny Kenn)
13 The Stone Pony, Asbury Park, NJ (with Cats on a Smooth Surface)
20 The Stone Pony, Asbury Park, NJ (with Cats on a Smooth Surface)

26 Big Man's West, Red Bank, NJ (with Billy Chinnock)
27 Big Man's West, Red Bank, NJ (with Clarence Clemons & the Red Bank Rockers)
27 The Stone Pony, Asbury Park, NJ (with Cats on a Smooth Surface)

July
17 Big Man's West, Red Bank, NJ (with the Iron City Houserockers)
23 Monmouth County Fair, Freehold, NJ (with Sonny Kenn & the Wild Ideas)
23 The Fast Lane, Asbury Park, NJ (with the Stray Cats)
25 The Stone Pony, Asbury Park, NJ (with Cats on a Smooth Surface)
31 Big Man's West, Red Bank, NJ (Sonny Kenn & the Wild Ideas)

August
1 The Stone Pony, Asbury Park, NJ (with Cats on a Smooth Surface)
6–7 Big Man's West, Red Bank, NJ (with Beaver Brown)
8, 15 The Stone Pony, Asbury Park, NJ (with Cats on a Smooth Surface)
23 Brighton Bar, NJ (with Mama Tried)
31 Jon Jon's, Wall, NJ (with Cats on a Smooth Surface)

September
4 Big Man's West, Red Bank, NJ (with Beaver Brown)
18 Big Man's West, Red Bank, NJ (with Dave Edmunds)
19 The Stone Pony, Asbury Park, NJ (with Cats on a Smooth Surface)
21 Peppermint Lounge, New York, NY (with Dave Edmunds)
25 The Stone Pony, Asbury Park, NJ (with Cats on a Smooth Surface)
29 On Broadway, Westwood, NJ (with Billy Rancher and the Unreal Gods)

October
3 The Stone Pony, Asbury Park, NJ (with Cats on a Smooth Surface)

November
27 Club Lingerie, Los Angeles, CA (with Jimmy and the Mustangs)

December
3 The Keystone, Palo Alto, CA (with Clarence Clemons & the Red Bank Rockers)

31 Harkness House, New York, NY (Steven Van Zandt's wedding party)

1983

January
8 Big Man's West, Red Bank, NJ (closing night of Big Man's West)

April
24 The Stone Pony, Asbury Park, NJ (with Cats on a Smooth Surface)
27 The Stone Pony, Asbury Park, NJ (with the Diamonds)

June
18 The Stone Pony, Asbury Park, NJ (with the Diamonds)

July
10 The Stone Pony, Asbury Park, NJ (with Cats on a Smooth Surface)
16 The Headliner, Neptune, NJ (with Midnight Thunder)

August
2 Madison Square Garden, New York, NY (with Jackson Browne)
14 The Stone Pony, Asbury Park, NJ (with Cats on a Smooth Surface)
19 Brighton Bar, Long Branch, NJ (with John Eddie)

November
6 The Stone Pony, Asbury Park, NJ (with Cats on a Smooth Surface)

December
28 Monmouth Arts Center, Red Bank, NJ (La Bamba's Holiday Hurrah)

1984

January
8 The Stone Pony, Asbury Park, NJ (with Cats on a Smooth Surface)
14 Patrix, New Brunswick, NJ (with John Eddie)

March
25 The Stone Pony, Asbury Park, NJ (with Cats on a Smooth Surface)

April
8 The Stone Pony, Asbury, NJ (with Cats on a Smooth Surface)
13 Ripley Music Hall, Philadelphia, PA (with Clarence Clemons & the Red Bank Rockers)
21 Expo, Mount Ivy, NY (with Clarence Clemons & the Red Bank Rockers)

22 The Stone Pony, Asbury Park, NJ (with Cats on a Smooth Surface)

May
19 The Stone Pony, Asbury Park, NJ (with Clarence Clemons & the Red Bank Rockers)
26 Xanadu, Asbury Park, NJ (with Bystanders)

June
1 The Stone Pony, Asbury Park, NJ (with John Eddie)
8 The Stone Pony, Asbury Park, NJ
10 The Stone Pony, Asbury Park, NJ (with Nils Lofgren, Cats on a Smooth Surface)
21 The Village, Lancaster, PA
29 St. Paul Civic Arena, St. Paul, MN

July
1–2 St. Paul Civic Arena, St. Paul, MN
5–6 Riverfront Coliseum, Cincinnati, OH
8–9 Richfield Coliseum, Cleveland, OH
12–13 Alpine Valley Music Theater, East Troy, WI
15, 17–18 Rosemont Horizon, Chicago, IL
21 The Forum, Montreal, Canada
23–24, 26 CNE Grandstand, Toronto, Canada
27 Performing Arts Center, Saratoga Springs, NY
30–31 Joe Louis Arena, Detroit, MI

August
5–6, 8–9, 11–12, 16–17, 19–20 Brendan Byrne Arena, East Rutherford, NJ
22 The Stone Pony, Asbury Park, NJ (with La Bamba & the Hubcaps)
23 Brighton Bar, Long Branch, NJ (with Mama Tried)
25–26, 28–29 Capital Centre, Landover, MD

September
3 The Stone Pony, Asbury Park, NJ (with John Eddie)
4–5 The Centrum, Worcester, MA
7–8 Civic Center, Hartford, CT
11–12, 14–15, 17–18 The Spectrum, Philadelphia, PA
20 The Decade, Pittsburgh, PA
21–22 Civic Arena, Pittsburgh, PA
24–25 War Memorial Auditorium, Buffalo, NY
26 Morris Community Theatre, Morristown, NJ (with Southside Johnny & the Asbury Jukes)

October

7 The Stone Pony, Asbury Park, NJ (with Cats on a Smooth Surface)
15 PNE Coliseum, Vancouver, Canada
17, 19 Tacoma Dome, Tacoma, WA
21–22 Coliseum, Oakland, CA
25–26, 28–29, 31 Sports Arena, Los Angeles, CA

November

2, 4 Sports Arena, Los Angeles, CA
8 Arizona State University Activities Center, Tempe, AZ
11–12 McNicholls Arena, Denver, CO
15 The Arena, St. Louis, MO
16 Hilton Coliseum, Ames, IA
18 Bob Devaney Sports Center, Lincoln, NE
19 Kemper Arena, Kansas City, MO
23 Frank Erwin Center, Austin, TX
25–26 Reunion Arena, Dallas, TX
29–30 The Summit, Houston, TX

December

2 LSU Assembly Center, Baton Rouge, LA
6 Jefferson Civic Center, Birmingham, AL
7 Civic Center, Tallahassee, FL
9 James T. Murphy Center, Murfreesboro, TN
11 Rupp Arena, Lexington, KY
13–14 Mid–South Coliseum, Memphis, TN
16–17 The Omni, Atlanta, GA

1985

January

4–5 Hampton Roads Coliseum, Hampton, VA
7–8 Market Square Arena, Indianapolis, IN
10 Freedom Hall Arena, Louisville, KY
13 Carolina Coliseum, Columbia, SC
15–16 Charlotte Coliseum, Charlotte, NC
17 Rhinoceros Club, Greensboro, NC (with the Del Fuegos)
18–19 Greensboro Coliseum, Greensboro, NC
23–24 Civic Center, Providence, RI
26–27 Carrier Dome, Syracuse, NY

March

21 Entertainment Centre, Sydney, Australia
22 Entertainment Centre, Sydney, Australia (with Neil Young)
23–24, 27–28 Entertainment Centre, Sydney, Australia
31 QE2 Stadium, Brisbane, Australia

April

3–4 Royal Melbourne Showgrounds, Melbourne, Australia
10–11, 13, 15–16 Yoyogi Olympic Pool, Tokyo, Japan
19 Furitsu Taiikukan, Kyoto, Japan
21–22 Castle Hall, Osaka, Japan

June

1 Slane Castle, Dublin, Ireland
4–5 St. James Park, Newcastle, England
8–9 Ullevi Stadium, Gothenberg, Sweden
12–13 Stadion Feynoord, Rotterdam, The Netherlands
15 Waldstadion, Frankfurt, West Germany
18 Olympic Stadium, Munich, West Germany
21 San Siro Stadium, Milan, Italy
23 Stade Richter, Montpellier, France
25 Stade Geoffrey Guichard, St. Etienne, France
29–30 La Courneuve, Paris, France

July

3–4, 6 Wembley Stadium, London, England
7 Roundhay Park, Leeds, England
30 Big Man's West, Red Bank, NJ

August

1 Big Man's West, Red Bank, NJ
5 RFK Stadium, Washington, DC
7 Municipal Stadium, Cleveland, OH
9 Soldier Field, Chicago, IL
11 Three Rivers Stadium, Pittsburgh, PA
14–15 Veterans Stadium, Philadelphia, PA
18–19, 21–22 Giants Stadium, East Rutherford, NJ
26–27 CNE Stadium, Toronto, Canada
31 Giants Stadium, East Rutherford, NJ

September

1 Giants Stadium, East Rutherford, NJ
4 Silverdome, Pontiac, MI
6 Hoosier Dome, Indianapolis, IN
9–10 Orange Bowl, Miami, FL
13–14 Cotton Bowl, Dallas, TX
18–19 Oakland Stadium, Oakland, CA
23–24 Mile High Stadium, Denver, CO
27, 29, 30 Memorial Coliseum, Los Angeles, CA

October

2 Memorial Coliseum, Los Angeles, CA

1986

January
19 The Stone Pony, Asbury Park, NJ (benefit for workers at Freehold, NJ, 3M plant)

March
2 The Stone Pony, Asbury Park, NJ ("E Street Band sneak attack," minus Roy Bittan)

October
13 Shoreline Amphitheater, Mountain View, CA (Bridge School Benefit concert)

November
5 Le Zenith, Paris, France (with Bob Geldof and Huey Lewis)

1987

January
20 Waldorf–Astoria Hotel, New York, NY (Rock and Roll Hall of Fame induction ceremony)

April
12 The Stone Pony, Asbury Park, NJ ("E Street Band sneak attack," with Jon Bon Jovi)

July
29 Key Largo, Belmar, NJ (with Jah Love)
30 Green Parrot, Neptune, NJ (with Jah Love)
31 The Stone Pony, Asbury Park, NJ (with Marshall Crenshaw)

August
2 The Stone Pony, Asbury Park, NJ ("E Street Band sneak attack," without Nils Lofgren)
9 The Stone Pony, Asbury Park, NJ ("E Street Band sneak attack")
14 The Stone Pony, Asbury Park, NJ (with Ernest "Boom" Carter and the Fairlanes)
21 The Stone Pony, Asbury Park, NJ (with Little Steven)
22 The Stone Pony, Asbury Park, NJ (with Levon Helm's All-Stars)
26 Key Largo, Belmar, NJ (with Jah Love)
26 The Columns, Avon, NJ (with the Cherubs)
27 The Tradewinds, Sea Bright, NJ (with Cats on a Smooth Surface)

September
25 JFK Stadium, Philadelphia, PA (with U2)

30 Coconut Grove, Los Angeles, CA (with Roy Orbison)

October
8 The Ritz, New York, NY (with Little Steven)
31 McLoone's Rumrunner, Sea Bright, NJ ("E Street Band sneak attack," minus Nils Lofgren and Clarence Clemons)

November
6 Rumson Country Day School, Rumson, NJ (benefit concert, with the Fabulous Grease Band)
20 The Stone Pony, Asbury Park, NJ (with Bobby Bandiera)

December
5 The Stone Pony, Asbury Park, NJ (with Cats on a Smooth Surface)
7 Carnegie Hall, New York, NY (Tribute to Harry Chapin)
13 Madison Square Garden, New York, NY (benefit for the homeless, with Paul Simon, Billy Joel, Dion, Paul Schafer, and others)

1988

January
20 Waldorf Astoria Hotel, New York, New York, NY (Rock and Roll Hall of Fame induction ceremony)
28 Eatontown, NJ

February
25, 28–29 The Centrum, Worcester, MA

March
3–4 Dean Smith Center, Chapel Hill, NC
8–9 The Spectrum, Philadelphia, PA
13–14 Richfield Coliseum, Cleveland, OH
16–17 Rosemont Horizon, Chicago, IL
20 Civic Arena, Pittsburgh, PA
22–23 The Omni, Atlanta, GA
26 Rupp Arena, Lexington, KY
28–29 Joe Louis Arena, Detroit, MI

April
1–2 Nassau Coliseum, Uniondale, NY
4–5 Capital Centre, Landover, MD
12–13 The Summit, Houston, TX
15 Frank Erwin Center, Austin, TX
17 St. Louis Arena, St. Louis, MO
20 McNicholls Arena, Denver, CO
22–23, 25, 27–28 Sports Arena, Los Angeles, CA

May
2–3 Shoreline Amphitheater, Mountain View, CA

5–6 Tacoma Dome, Tacoma, WA

9–10 Met Center, Bloomington, MN

11 Maple Leaf Club, New Orleans, LA (with the New Orleans Blues Department)

13 Market Square Arena, Indianapolis, IN

16, 18–19, 22–23 Madison Square Garden, New York, NY

26 Irvine Meadows, Irvine, CA (with John Mellencamp)

June

11 Stadio Comunale, Turin, Italy

13 Piazza Di Spangna, Rome, Italy (with street musicians)

15–16 Stadio Flamminio, Rome, Italy

18 Chateau de Vincennes, Paris, France (SOS Racism benefit)

19 Hippodromes De Vincennes, Paris, France

21–22 Aston Villa Football Ground, Birmingham, England

25 Wembley Stadium, London, England

28–29 Stadion Feynoord, Rotterdam, The Netherlands

July

2–3 Olympic Stadium, Stockholm, Sweden

7 RDS Jumping Enclosure, Dublin, Ireland

9–10 Bramall Lane Stadium, Sheffield, England

12 Waldstadion, Frankfurt, West Germany

14 St. Jakob Stadion, Basel, Switzerland

17 Olympic Riding Stadium, Munich, West Germany

19 Weissensee Cycling Track, East Berlin, East Germany

22 Walbuehne Ampitheater, West Berlin, West Germany

23 Strøget, Copenhagen, Denmark (with street musician John Magnusson)

25 Idrætsparken, Copenhagen, Denmark

27 Valle Hovin Stadion, Oslo, Norway

30 Weser Stadion, Bremen, West Germany

August

2 Viecente Calderon Stadium, Madrid, Spain

3 Camp Nou Stadium, Barcelona, Spain

21 The Stone Pony, Asbury Park, NJ (with Cats on a Smooth Surface)

25 Madison Square Garden, New York, NY (with Sting)

September

2 Wembley Stadium, London, England (Human Rights Now!)

4–5 Palais Omnisports Bercy, Paris, France (Human Rights Now!)

6 Nepstadion, Budapest, Hungary (Human Rights Now!)

8 Stadio Comunale, Turin, Italy (Human Rights Now!)

10 Camp Nou Stadium, Barcelona, Spain (Human Rights Now!)

13 Estadio Nacional, San Jose, Costa Rica (Human Rights Now!)

15 Maple Leaf Gardens, Toronto, Canada (Human Rights Now!)

17 Olympic Stadium, Montreal, Canada (Human Rights Now!)

19 J.F.K. Stadium, Philadelphia, PA (Human Rights Now!)

21 Coliseum, Los Angeles, CA (Human Rights Now!)

23 Oakland Stadium, Oakland, CA (Human Rights Now!)

27 Tokyo Dome, Tokyo, Japan (Human Rights Now!)

30 Jawaharlal Nehru Stadium, New Delhi, India (Human Rights Now!)

October

3 New Olympic Stadium, Athens, Greece (Human Rights Now!)

7 National Sports Stadium, Harare, Zimbabwe (Human Rights Now!)

9 Houphouet–Boigny Stadium, Abidjan, Cote D'Ivoire (Human Rights Now!)

12 Palmeiras Stadium, Sao Paulo, Brazil (Human Rights Now!)

14 Estadio Mundialista Mendoza, Mendoza, Argentina (Human Rights Now!)

15 River Plate Stadium, Buenos Aires, Argentina (Human Rights Now!)

November

12 Music Hall, Tarrytown, NY (with John Prine)

26 The Stone, San Francisco, CA (with Southside Johnny & the Asbury Jukes)

December

18 The Stone Pony, Asbury Park, NJ (Jersey Artists for Mankind benefit)

1989

June

2 The Stone Pony, Asbury Park, NJ (with Killer Joe, Roy Bittan, Patti Scialfa, and the Horns of Love)

3 Hotel Carlyle, New York, NY (a friend's wedding)

9 The Stone Pony, Asbury Park, NJ (with Nils Lofgren)

14 Jones Beach State Park, Long Island, NY (with Neil Young)

20 Martells, Pt. Pleasant Beach, NJ (with Bobby Bandiera)

24 The Stone Pony, Asbury Park, NJ (with Bobby Bandiera)

29 The Headliner, Neptune, NJ (with the Fabulous Grease Band)

30 Bally's Grandstand Under the Stars, Atlantic City, NJ (with Jackson Browne)

July

1 The Stone Pony, Asbury Park, NJ (with La Bamba & his Big Band)

3 Cafe Bar, Long Branch, NJ (with Gary U.S. Bonds)

9 The Stone Pony, Asbury Park, NJ (with Cats on a Smooth Surface)

12 Pennsauken, NJ (with Gary U.S. Bonds)

15 T–Birds Cafe, Asbury Park, NJ (with the X–Men)

22 McLoone's Rumrunner, Sea Bright, NJ (with Peter Hartung & the Remakes)

23 The Stone Pony, Asbury Park, NJ (with Cats on a Smooth Surface)

27 The Headliner, Neptune, NJ (with the Fabulous Grease Band)

August

2 Cheers, Long Branch, NJ (with Bobby Bandiera)

11 Garden State Arts Center, Holmdel, NJ (with Ringo Starr & His All-Starr Band)

16 Cheers, Long Branch, NJ (with Bobby Bandiera)

September

22 The Stone Pony, Asbury Park, NJ (with Jimmy Cliff)

23 McLoone's Rumrunner, Sea Bright, NJ (Springsteen's fortieth birthday party, with the E Street Band and Little Steven)

29 Matt's Saloon, Prescott, AZ

December

17 Ventura Theatre, Ventura, CA

1990

January

17 Waldorf-Astoria Hotel, New York, NY (Rock and Roll Hall of Fame induction ceremony)

February

12 The China Club, Hollywood, CA (An Evening in Brazil benefit)

March

1 The Forum, Los Angeles, CA (with Bob Dylan and Tom Petty & the Heartbreakers)

October

29 Tom Petty's house, Encino, CA (Petty's 40th birthday party, with Roger McGuinn, Jeff Lynne, and others)

November

16–17 Shrine Auditorium, Los Angeles, CA (Christic Institute benefit with Jackson Browne and Bonnie Raitt)

1991

January

16 Waldorf-Astoria Hotel, New York, NY (Rock and Roll Hall of Fame induction ceremony)

20 McLoone's Rumrunner, Sea Bright, NJ (benefit for singer Jim Faulkner)

February

17 Malibu, CA (private party with Stephen Stills, John McEnroe, and Bruce Willis)

July

12 McLoone's Rumrunner, Sea Bright, NJ (with Bobby Bandiera)

August

4 Cheers, Long Branch, NJ (with the Outcry)

September

26 The Stone Pony, Asbury Park, NJ (video shoot for Southside Johnny & the Asbury Jukes' "It's Been a Long Time," with Little Steven and Jon Bon Jovi)

1992

February

2 The Maple Leaf, New Orleans, LA (with the Iguanas)

May

6 The Bottom Line, New York, NY (for Columbia Records staff)

June

5 Hollywood Sound Stage, Los Angeles, CA

15, 17 Globen, Stockholm, Sweden

20–21 Milano Forum, Milan, Italy

25–26 Festhalle, Frankfurt, Germany

29–30 Palais Omnisports, Paris, France

July

3–4 Plaza De Toros, Barcelona, Spain
6, 9–10, 12–13 Wembley Arena, London, England
23, 25–26, 28, 30–31 Brendan Byrne Arena, East Rutherford, NJ

August

2, 4, 6, 7, 10 Brendan Byrne Arena, East Rutherford, NJ
13–14 The Centrum, Worcester, MA
17–18 The Palace, Auburn Hills, MI
21–22 Richfield Coliseum, Richfield, OH
25–26 Capital Centre, Landover, MD
28–29 The Spectrum, Philadelphia, PA

September

2–3 World Music Theater, Tinley Park, IL
22 MTV Studios, Los Angeles, CA ("Plugged" concert)
24–25, 28 Sports Arena, Los Angeles, CA
29 San Diego Sports Arena, San Diego, CA

October

2–3 America West Arena, Phoenix, AZ
6 ARCO Arena, Sacramento, CA
12–23 Tacoma Dome, Tacoma, WA
15 Pacific National Exhibition Stadium, Vancouver, Canada
17 Olympic Saddledome, Calgary, Canada
18 Northlands Coliseum, Edmonton, Canada
21–22 Shorline Ampitheater, Mountain View, CA
26 McNichols Arena, Denver, CO
30 Hilton Arena, Ames, IA
31 Target Center, Minneapolis, MN

November

3 Bradley Center, Milwaukee, WI
5–6 Skydome, Toronto, Canada
9–10 Nassau Coliseum, Uniondale, NY
13 Carrier Dome, Syracuse, NY
15 Civic Center, Hartford, CT
17 Dean Smith Center, Chapel Hill, NC
18 Charlotte Coliseum, Charlotte, NC
23 Orlando Arena, Orlando, FL
24 Miami Arena, Miami, FL
30 The Omni, Atlanta, GA

December

2 Reunion Arena, Dallas, TX
3 Checkerdome, St. Louis, MO
5 Market Square Arena, Indianapolis, IN
7–8 The Spectrum, Philadelphia, PA
13–14 Boston Gardens, Boston, MA
16 Civic Arena, Pittsburgh, PA
17 Rupp Arena, Lexington, KY

27 The Stone Pony, Asbury Park, NJ (with Southside Johnny & the Asbury Jukes)

1993

January

6 St. Bartholomew's Church, New York, NY (funeral for Kristen Ann Carr)
12 Century Plaza Hotel, Los Angeles, CA (Rock and Roll Hall of Fame induction ceremony)

March

23 Count Basie Theater, Red Bank, NJ
31 SECC, Glasgow, Scotland

April

3–4 Westfalenhalle, Dortmund, Germany
7–8 Hallenstadion, Zurich, Switzerland
11 Bentegodi Stadium, Verona, Italy
13 Halle Tony Garnier, Lyon, France
15–16 The Arena, Sheffield, England
19–20 Ahoi Sportspaleis, Rotterdam, The Netherlands
23–24 Flanders Expo Center, Gent, Belgium

May

1 Stadium of Lights, Lisbon, Portugal
5 Estadio Vincente Calderon, Madrid, Spain
7 Estadio El Molinon, Gijon, Spain
9 Estadio Compostela, Santiago, Spain
11 Olympic Stadium, Barcelona, Spain
14 Waldbuehne Ampitheater, Berlin, Germany
15 Bayerischer Hof, Munich, Germany (with the Hetti Schneider Band)
16 Airfield Rien, Munich, Germany
17 Maimarkthalle, Mannheim, Germany
19 The Stadium, Dublin, Ireland (with Joe Ely)
20 RDS Jumping Enclosure, Dublin, Ireland
22 National Bowl, Milton Keynes, England
24 Stanhope Arms, London, England (karaoke)
25 Flaminio Stadium, Rome, Italy
28 Olympic Stadium, Stockholm, Sweden
30 Gentofte Stadium, Copenhagen, Denmark

June

1 Valle Hovin, Oslo, Norway
24 Brendan Byrne Arena, East Rutherford, NJ (A Concert to Fight Hunger benefit with Joe Ely, Little Steven, Clarence Clemons, the Miami Horns, and Southside Johnny)

26 Madison Square Garden, New York, NY (Kristen Ann Carr Fund benefit with Joe Ely and Terence Trent D'Arby)

28 Tradewinds, Sea Bright, NJ (with Clarence Clemons & the Red Bank Rockers)

1994

January
20 Waldorf–Astoria Hotel, New York, NY (Rock and Roll Hall of Fame induction ceremony)

27 Universal Amphitheatre, Los Angeles, CA (The Concert for Life)

March
1 Radio City Music Hall, New York, NY (Grammy Awards ceremony, Curtis Mayfield tribute)

21 Dorothy Chandler Pavilion, Los Angeles, CA (66th Academy Awards)

April
29 House of Blues, Los Angeles, CA (with John Fogerty)

30 House of Blues, Los Angeles, CA (with various artists)

May
29 Hollywood Palladium, Los Angeles, CA (with the Rock Bottom Remainders)

June
18 McCabe's Guitar Shop, Santa Monica, CA (with John Wesley Harding)

27 House of Blues, Los Angeles, CA (with the House of Blues Band)

July
16 The Stone Pony, Asbury Park, NJ (with Southside Johnny & the Asbury Jukes, Patti Scialfa, Max Weinberg, and Jon Bon Jovi)

August
20 Marz American Style, Long Branch, NJ (with Joe Grushecky)

26 Classics Cafe, Westfield, NJ (with Stand and Deliver, and Max Weinberg)

September
8 Radio City Music Hall, New York, NY (MTV Video Music Awards)

20 House of Blues, Los Angeles, CA (with John Fogerty)

October
20 Roseland Ballroom, New York, NY (with Bob Dylan and Neil Young)

21 The Playpen, Sayerville, NJ (with John Eddie, Greg Kihn, Marshall Crenshaw, and Elliott Murphy)

November
12 Lake Castaic, Los Angeles, CA (The Love Ride XI with Jackson Browne)

December
20 Tradewinds, Sea Bright, NJ (with the Holiday Express Band featuring Tim McLoone)

1995

February
15 Brooklyn Academy of Music (Melissa Etheridge "MTV Unplugged" performance)

21 Tramps Nightclub, New York, NY (E Street Band "Murder Incorporated" video shoot)

March
1 Shrine Auditorium, Los Angeles, CA (Grammy Awards)

6 Tramps Nightclub, New York, NY (with Soul Asylum)

24 House of Blues, Los Angeles, CA (with The Blasters)

April
5 Sony Studios, New York, NY (E Street Band reunion concert)

12 Carnegie Hall, New York, NY (Rainforest Benefit with Elton John, Sting, Billy Joel, and Jessye Norman)

July
9 Cafe Eckstein, Berlin, Germany (video shoot for "Hungry Heart" with Wolfgang Niedecken and his Leopardfellband)

22 Tradewinds, Sea Bright, NJ (with Joe Grushecky & the Houserockers, Little Steven, and Max Weinberg)

August
6 Cheers, Long Branch, NJ (private party for Patti Scialfa, with Bobby Bandiera and others)

10 Cheers, Long Branch, NJ (with Solar Circus)

14 Jack's Sugar Shack, Los Angeles, CA (with unknown band)

September
2 Cleveland Stadium, Cleveland, OH (Concert for the Rock and Roll Hall of Fame)

14 The Viper Room, Los Angeles, CA (with Joe Ely)

October

17 The Stone Pony, Asbury Park, NJ (with Joe Grushecky & the Houserockers)
18 Tramps, New York, NY (Joe Grushecky & the Houserockers)
19 The Electric Factory, Philadelphia, PA (Joe Grushecky & the Houserockers)
20–21 Nick's Fat City, Pittsburgh, PA (Joe Grushecky & the Houserockers)
24 Park West, Chicago, IL (Joe Grushecky & the Houserockers)
28 Shoreline Amphitheater, Mountain View, CA (Bridge School Benefit concert)

November

19 Shrine Auditorium, Los Angeles, CA (Frank Sinatra's 80th birthday tribute concert)
21 State Theater, New Brunswick, NJ
22 Count Basie Theater, Red Bank, NJ
22 The Stone Pony, Asbury Park, NJ (with John Eddie)
26–27 Wiltern Theater, Los Angeles, CA
29–30 Berkley Community Theater, San Francisco, CA

December

3 The Rosemont, Chicago, IL
5–6 Constitutional Hall, Washington, DC
8–9 Tower Theater, Philadelphia, PA
12–13 The Beacon Theater, New York, NY
15–16 The Orpheum, Boston, MA
17 The Beacon Theater, New York, NY

1996

January

7 Place des Artes, Montreal, Canada
8 Massey Hall, Toronto, Canada
10–11 Fox Theater, Detroit, MI
12 Stambaugh Theater, Youngstown, OH
16–17 Music Hall, Cleveland, OH
18 Fox Theater, St. Louis, MO
22 The Sangor Theater, New Orleans, LA
23 Jones Hall, Houston, TX
25 Music Hall, Austin, TX
26 Bronco Bowl, Dallas, TX
28 Fox Theater, Atlanta, GA

February

12 Alte Opera, Frankfurt, Germany
14 Kulturpalast, Dresden, Germany
15 Rudi–Sedimayer Halle, Munchen, Germany

May

17 CCH Halle 1, Hamburg, Germany
18 Phillipshalle, Dusseldorf, Germany

21–22 Le Zenith, Paris, France
25 De Doelen, Rotterdam, The Netherlands
26 The Carre Theatre, Amsterdam, The Netherlands
28 Apollo Theatre, Manchester, England
29 Symphony Hall, Birmingham, England

March

2 City Hall, Newcastle, England
3 Playhouse, Edinburgh, Scotland
13 The Cirkus, Stockholm, Sweden
14 The Spektrum, Oslo, Norway
16 Falkoner–Teatret, Copenhagen, Denmark
17 The Mean Fiddler, Dublin, Ireland (with Joe Ely)
19 Kings Hall, Belfast, Northern Ireland
20 The Point Theatre, Dublin, Ireland
25 Dorothy Chandler Pavilion, Los Angeles, CA (68th Academy Awards)

April

10 Auditorium di S. Cecilia, Rome, Italy
11 Teatro Smeraldo, Milan, Italy
13 Teatro Carlo Felice, Genova, Italy
16–17 Royal Albert Hall, London, England
19 ICC Halle, Berlin, Germany
20 Queen Elizabeth Hall, Antwerp, Belgium
22 Royal Albert Hall, London, England
24–25 Brixton Academy, London, England
27 Royal Albert Hall, London, England
30 Palais De La Musique et Des Congres, Strasbourg, France

May

1 Palais Van Schone Kunsten, Brussels, Belgium
2 Kongresshaus, Zurich, Switzerland
6–7 Teatre Tivoli, Barcelona, Spain
8 Palacio de Congresos y Exposiciones, Madrid, Spain

August

9 Great Northern Bar and Grill, Whitefish, MT (with the Fanatics)
10 Grand Mountain Lodge, Whitefish, MT (Toby Scott's wedding, with the Fanatics)

September

16 Benedum Center, Pittsburgh, PA
18 Oakdale Theater, Wallingford, CT
19 Performing Arts Center, Providence, RI
24 Miller Auditorium, Kalamazoo, MI
25 EJ Thomas Hall, Akron, OH
26 Hill Auditorium, Ann Arbor, MI
29 Severance Hall, Cleveland, OH (Woody Guthrie tribute show)

October

1 Braden Auditorium, Normal, IL
2 Riverside Auditorium, Milwaukee, WI
2 Bradley Center, Milwaukee, WI (with Melissa Etheridge)
3 Northrup Auditorium, Minneapolis, MN
15 Abravnel Hall, Salt Lake City, UT
16–17 Paramount Theater, Denver, CO
19 Kiva Auditorium, Albuquerque, NM
21 Gammage Auditorium, Tempe, AZ
22 Civic Theater, San Diego, CA
23 Saroyan Theater, Fresno, CA
25 Arlington Theater, Santa Barbara, CA
26 San Jose Event Center, San Jose, CA
27 Westwood Federal Building, Los Angeles, CA (rally against proposed Proposition 209 to abolish affirmative action in California)
28 Schnitzer Auditorium, Portland, OR
29 Paramount Theater, Seattle, WA

November

1 St. Rose of Lima, Freehold, NJ (benefit)
12 Shea's Performing Arts Center, Buffalo, NY
13 Landmark Theater, Syracuse, NY
14 Lowell Memorial Auditorium, Lowell, MA
19 Dixon–Myers Hall, Memphis, TN
20 Palace Theater, Louisville, KY
21 Murat Theater, Indianapolis, IN
24–26 Paramount Theatre, Asbury Park, NJ

December

2–3 Sunrise Theater, Miami, FL
5 Township Auditorium, Columbia, SC
6 Concert Hall, Birmingham, AL
10 Music Hall, Cincinnati, OH
11 Veteran's Auditorium, Columbus, OH
12 Ryman Auditorium, Nashville, TN
14 Oven's Auditorium, Charlotte, NC

1997

January

27, 29–31 Kokusai Forum Hall, International Forum, Tokyo, Japan

February

4–5 Concert Hall, Brisbane, Australia
7–8, 10–12 Capitol Theatre, Sydney, Australia
15–17 Palais Theatre, Melbourne, Australia
8 Tradewinds, Sea Bright, NJ (with the Wallflowers)

May

5 Grand Hotel, Stockholm, Sweden (Polar Music Prize ceremony)

6–7 Austria Center, Vienna, Austria
9–10 Sala Kongresowa, Warsaw, Poland
12 Congress Centre, Prague, Czech Republic
15 Auditorium Maurice Ravel, Lyon, France
16 Le Corum, Montpellier, France
18 Acropolis, Nice, France
19 Zenith–Omega, Toulon, France
21 Teatro Verdi, Florence, Italy
22 Teatro Augusteo, Naples, Italy
22 Balcony of Teatro Augusteo, Naples, Italy (post-show performance for crowd gathered underneath the theater balcony)
25–26 Palais Des Congres, Paris, France

August

28 The Derby, Los Angeles, CA (with Jimmy & the Gigolos)

September

4 Radio City Music Hall, New York, NY (MTV Video Music Awards, with the Wallflowers)
26 Cheers, Long Branch, NJ (with Bobby Bandiera)

December

7 Kennedy Center, Washington, DC (Kennedy Center Honors gala for Bob Dylan)
13 Cheers, Long Branch, NJ (with Joe Grushecky)
16 Rumrunners, Sea Bright, NJ (private Christmas party with Bobby Bandiera's band)

1998

January

31 Count Basie Theater, Red Bank, NJ (Come Together benefit with E Street Band members, Jon on Jovi, Southside Johnny, and others)

February

6 Tradewinds, Sea Bright, NJ (with Steve Earle)

March

2 Nick's Fat City, Pittsburgh, PA (Joe Grushecky & the Houserockers)

April

4 Bay Street Theatre, Sag Harbour, NY (Elaine Steinbeck Tribute)

October

11 Springsteen's farm, Colts Neck, NJ (Springsteen birthday party with Little

Steven, Max Weinberg, Jon Bon Jovi, and Sheryl Crow)

27 The Saint, Asbury Park, NJ (BBC documentary taping)

November

6 Club 251, West Palm Beach, FL (with Clarence Clemons)

December

10 Bercy, Paris, France (concert marking the fiftieth anniversary of Amnesty International's Declaration of Human Rights)

1999

March

11 Convention Hall, Asbury Park, NJ

15 Waldorf-Astoria Hotel, New York, NY (Rock and Roll Hall of Fame induction ceremony)

18–19 Convention Hall, Asbury Park, NJ

April

9, 11 Palau Sant Jordi, Barcelona, Spain

13 Olympiahalle, Munich, Germany

15 Kolnarena, Cologne, Germany

17 Palasport, Bologna, Italy

19–20 Forum, Milan, Italy

23 Donauarena, Regensburg, Germany

24 Stadthalle, Vienna, Austria

26 Hallenstadion, Zurich, Switzerland

28 Halle Tony Garnier, Lyon, France

May

1–2 Manchester Evening News Arena, Manchester, England

16 NEC, Birmingham, England

18–19, 21, 23 Earls Court, London, England

25 RDS, Dublin, Ireland

27 Flanders Expo, Gent, Belgium

29–30 Wuhlheide, Berlin, Germany

June

2–3 Bercy, Paris, France

5 Estadio la Romareda, Zaragosa, Spain

7 Estadio de la Comunidad, Madrid, Spain

11 Marassi Stadium, Genova, Italy

13 Bruno–Platche Stadion, Leipzig, Germany

15 OFC Stadion Bieberer Berg, Offenbach, Germany

17 Weserstadion, Bremen, Germany

19–20 Gelredome, Arnhem, The Netherlands

23–24 Olympic Stadium, Stockholm, Sweden

24 Olympic Stadium, Stockholm, Sweden

26 Parken, Copenhagen, Denmark

27 Valle Hovin Stadion, Oslo, Norway

July

9 Hooligans, Long Branch, NJ (with Joe Grushecky)

10 Cheers, Long Branch, NJ (with Joe Grushecky)

15, 18, 20, 24, 26–27, 29 Continental Airlines Arena, East Rutherford, NJ

August

1–2, 4, 6–7, 9, 11–12 Continental Airlines Arena, East Rutherford, NJ

21–22, 24, 26–27 Fleet Center, Boston, MA

31 MCI Center, Washington, DC

September

1, 3 MCI Center, Washington, DC

8–9 The Palace, Auburn Hills, MI

13, 15, 20–21, 24–25 First Union Center, Philadelphia, PA

27–28, 30 United Center, Chicago, IL

October

15 America West Arena, Phoenix, AZ

17–18, 21, 23 Staples Center Arena, Los Angeles, CA

25–26, 28 Oakland Arena, Oakland, CA

November

6 Fargo Dome, Fargo, ND

9 Bradley Center, Milwaukee, WI

10 Conseco Fieldhouse, Indianapolis, IN

14–15 Gund Arena, Cleveland, OH

17 Jerome Schottenstein Center, Columbus, OH.

19 Marine Midland Arena, Buffalo, NY

21 Pepsi Arena, Albany, NY

28–29 Target Center, Minneapolis, MN

December

4 Colts Neck, NJ (private benefit show organized by Jon Bon Jovi)

20 McLoone's Rumrunner, Sea Bright, NJ (with Bobby Bandiera, Springsteen's personal Christmas party)

2000

February

28 Bryce Jordan Center, State College, PA

March

4 Orlando Arena, Orlando, FL

6 Ice Palace, Tampa, FL

9–10 NCR Center, Ft. Lauderdale, FL

13 Reunion Arena, Dallas, TX

14 Altel Arena, Little Rock, AR

18 Pyramid Arena, Memphis, TN
19 New Orleans Arena, New Orleans, LA
30–31 Pepsi Arena, Denver, CO

April
3 Rose Garden Arena, Portland, OR
4 Tacoma Dome, Tacoma, WA
8 Kiel Center, St. Louis, MO
9 Kemper Arena, Kansas City, MO
12 Nashville Arena, Nashville, TN
15 Freedom Hall, Louisville, KY
17 Frank Erwin Center, Austin, TX
18 Compaq Arena, Houston, TX
21 Charlotte Coliseum, Charlotte, NC
22 Raleigh Entertainment Center, Raleigh, NC
25–26 Mellon Arena, Pittsburgh, PA
30 Firstar Center, Cincinnati, OH

May
3–4 Air Canada Arena, Toronto, Canada
7–8 Civic Center, Hartford, CT
21–22 Arrowhead Pond, Anaheim, CA
27 MGM Grand Garden, Las Vegas, NV
29 Delta Center, Salt Lake City, UT

June
3–4 Philips Arena, Atlanta, GA
12, 15, 17, 20, 22–23, 26–27, 29 Madison Square Garden, New York, NY

July
1 Madison Square Garden, New York, NY

October
14 Springsteen's farm, Colt's Neck, NJ (Springsteen's birthday party, with the Gotham Playboys)
21 Hedgerow Stables, Middletown, NJ (with Bobby Bandiera)

November
3 The Stone Pony, Asbury Park, NJ (with Joe Grushecky)

December
17–18 Convention Hall, Asbury Park, NJ (holiday shows)

2001

May
27 The Stone Pony Landing, Asbury Park, NJ (with Southside Johnny & the Asbury Jukes)

July
31 Count Basie Theater, Red Bank, NJ (with Bruce Hornsby)

August
18 Asbury Park, NJ (Clearwater Music Festival)
18 The Stone Pony Landing, Asbury Park, NJ (with Nils Lofgren)
18 The Stone Pony, Asbury Park, NJ (with John Eddie)

September
1 The Stone Pony, Asbury Park, NJ (with Clarence Clemons Temple of Soul)
3 Donovan's Reef, Sea Bright, NJ (with Brian Kirk & the Jirks)

October
18–19 Count Basie Theatre, Red Bank, NJ (Alliance of Neighbors benefit for Monmouth County victims of September 11)

November
3 Tradewinds, Sea Bright, NJ (with Joe Grushecky & the Houserockers)

December
3–4, 6–8 Convention Hall, Asbury Park, NJ (holiday shows)
15 Continental Airlines Arena, East Rutherford, NJ (Tim McLoone's Holiday Express)

2002

January
12 Foxwoods Resort and Casino, Mashantucket, CT (Clarence Clemons's sixtieth birthday party, with B.B. King)

April
13–14 The Stone Pony, Asbury Park (Rumson Country Day School benefit concerts)

July
24 Sonny's Southern Cuisine, Asbury Park, NJ (with the Alliance Singers, for NBC's "Today" show)
25 Convention Hall, Asbury Park, NJ (private rehearsal show)
26 Convention Hall, Asbury Park, NJ (rehearsal show for radio contest winners)
26 Sonny's Southern Cuisine, Asbury Park, NJ (surprise appearance for rehearsal show radio contest winners)
30 Convention Hall, Asbury Park, NJ (for NBC's "Today" show)

August
2 Convention Hall, Asbury Park, NJ

5, 7 Continental Airlines Arena, East Rutherford, NJ
10 MCI Arena, Washington, DC
12 Madison Square Garden, New York, NY
14 Gund Arena, Cleveland, OH
15 The Palace, Auburn Hills, MI
18 Thomas and Mack Center, Las Vegas, NV
20 The Rose Garden, Portland, OR
21 Tacoma Dome, Tacoma, WA
24 The Forum, Los Angeles, CA
25 America West, Phoenix, AZ
27 Compaq Center, San Jose, CA
29 Hayden Planetarium, New York, NY (MTV Video Music Awards)
30 Savvis Center, St. Louis, MO

September
22 Pepsi Center, Denver, CO
24 Kemper Arena, Kansas City, MO
25 United Center, Chicago, IL
27 Bradley Center, Milwaukee, WI
29 Fargo Dome, Fargo, ND
30 Xcel Energy Center, St. Paul, MN

October
4 Zakim Bunker Hill Bridge, Boston, MA (Zakim Bunker Hill Bridge dedication)
4 Fleet Center, Boston, MA
6 First Union Center, Philadelphia, PA
7 HSBC Arena, Buffalo, NY
14 Bercy, Paris, France
16 Palau Sant Jordi, Barcelona, Spain
18 Palamalaguti, Bologna, Italy
20 Velodrom, Berlin, Germany
22 Ahoy, Rotterdam, The Netherlands
24 Globen, Stockholm, Sweden
27 Wembley Arena, London, England

November
2 Tradewinds, Sea Bright, NJ (Light of Day benefit)
3 American Airlines Arena, Dallas, TX
4 Compaq Center, Houston, TX
12 US Bank Arena, Cincinnati, OH
14 Rupp Arena, Lexington, KY
16 Greensboro Coliseum, Greensboro, NC
19 BJCC, Birmingham, AL
21 TD Waterhouse, Orlando, FL
23 American Airlines Arena, Miami, FL
24 Ice Palace, Tampa, FL

December
2 Philips Arena, Atlanta, GA
4 Mellon Arena, Pittsburgh, PA
5 Air Canada Center, Toronto, Canada
8 Charlotte Coliseum, Charlotte, NC

9 Carolina Center, Columbia, SC
13 Pepsi Arena, Albany, NY
16 Schotenstein Arena, Columbus, OH
17 Conseco Fieldhouse, Indianapolis, IN

2003

February
19–20 Somerville Theatre, Somerville, MA (*DoubleTake* magazine benefits)
23 Madison Square Garden, New York, NY (Grammy Awards)
28 The Arena at Gwinnett Center, Duluth, GA

March
2 Frank Erwin Center, Austin, TX
4 Jacksonville Coliseum, Jacksonville, FL
6 Richmond Coliseum, Richmond, VA
7 Boardwalk Hall, Atlantic City, NJ
10 Dunkin Donuts Center, Providence, RI
11 Blue Cross Arena, Rochester, NY
20 Telstra Dome, Melbourne, Australia
22 Cricket Ground, Sydney, Australia
25–26 Brisbane Entertainment Centre, Brisbane, Australia
28 Western Springs Stadium, Auckland, New Zealand

April
9 Arco Arena, Sacramento, CA
11 Pacific Coliseum, Vancouver, Canada
13 Pengrowth Saddledome, Calgary, Canada
14 Skyreach Centre, Edmonton, Canada
18 The Corel Centre, Ottawa, Canada
19 Bell Centre, Montreal, Canada
29 Count Basie Theater, Red Bank, NJ (Hope Concert benefit for Robert Bandiera Jr.)
30 The Stone Pony, Asbury Park, NJ (Rumson Country Day School benefit)

May
2 The Stone Pony, Asbury Park, NJ (with Soozie Tyrell)
6, 8 Feyenoord Stadion, Rotterdam, The Netherlands
10 Südweststadion, Ludwigshafen, Germany
12 Koning Boudewijnstadion, Brussels, Belgium
15 Estadio de el Molinon, Gijon, Spain
17 Estadi Olimpic Lluis Companys, Barcelona, Spain
19 Estadio De La Comunidad, Madrid, Spain

22 Arena AufSchalke, Gelsenkirchen, Germany

24 Stade de France, Paris, France

26–27 Crystal Palace National Sports Arena, London, England

29 Old Trafford Cricket Ground, Manchester, England

31 RDS, Dublin, Ireland

June

8 Stadio Artemio Franchi, Florence, Italy

10 Olympiastadion, Munich, Germany

12 Hamburger AOL Arena, Hamburg, Germany

14 Parken, Copenhagen, Denmark

16–17 Olympic Stadium, Helsinki, Finland

19 Valle Hovin, Oslo, Norway

21–22 Ullevi Stadium, Gothenburg, Sweden

25 Ernst–Happel Stadium, Vienna, Austria

28 San Siro Stadium, Milan, Italy

July

15, 17–18, 21, 24, 26–27 Giants Stadium, East Rutherford, NJ

August

1–2 Gillette Stadium, Boston, MA

6 PNC Park, Pittsburgh, PA

8–9, 11 Lincoln Financial Field, Philadelphia, PA

13 Comiskey Park, Chicago, IL

16 Pacific Bell Park, San Francisco, CA

17 Dodger Stadium, Los Angeles, CA

28, 30–31 Giants Stadium, East Rutherford, NJ

September

6–7 Fenway Park, Boston, MA

10 Skydome, Toronto, Canada

13 FedEx Field, Washington, DC

14 Kenan Stadium, Chapel Hill, NC

16, 18 Rentschler Field, Hartford, CT

20 Darien Lake Performing Arts Center, Buffalo, NY

21 Comerica Park, Detroit, MI

25 Invesco Field, Denver, CO

27 Miller Park, Milwaukee, WI

October

1, 3–4 Shea Stadium, New York, NY

November

1 The Stone Pony, Asbury Park, NJ (Light of Day benefit)

8 Aberdeen, NJ (Muscular Dystrophy Association gala)

December

5, 7–8 Convention Hall, Asbury Park, NJ (holiday shows)

2004

March

16 Beacon Theater, New York, NY (with Jackson Browne)

April

18 The Hit Factory, New York, NY (with Patti Scialfa)

26 The Stone Pony, Asbury Park, NJ, (Rumson Country Day School benefit)

July

17 The Stone Pony, Asbury Park, NJ (with Joe Grushecky & the Houserockers and Patti Scialfa)

September

15 Paramount Theater, Asbury Park, NJ (with Patti Scialfa)

21 Bowery Ballroom, New York, NY (with Patti Scialfa)

25 The Roxy, Los Angeles, CA (with Patti Scialfa)

October

1 Wachovia Center, Philadelphia, PA (Vote for Change)

2 Gund Arena, Cleveland, OH (Vote for Change)

3 Cobo Arena, Detroit, MI (Vote for Change)

5 Xcel Energy Center, St. Paul, MN (Vote for Change)

8 TD Waterhouse Centre, Orlando, FL (Vote for Change)

11 MCI Center, Washington, DC (Vote for Change)

13 Continental Airlines Arena, East Rutherford, NJ (Vote for Change)

28 West Washington Avenue, Madison, WI (John Kerry campaign rally)

28 Ohio State University, Columbus, OH, (John Kerry campaign rally)

30 Bayfront Park Amphitheater, Miami, FL, (John Kerry campaign rally)

November

1 Cleveland, Ohio (John Kerry campaign rally)

6 The Stone Pony, Asbury Park, NJ (Light of Day benefit)

December

2 Heinz Hall, Pittsburgh, PA (Flood Aid '04 with Joe Grushecky & the Houserockers, others)

19 Harry's Roadhouse, Asbury Park, NJ (two holiday benefit shows)

2005

March

14 Waldorf-Astoria Hotel, New York, NY (Rock and Roll Hall of Fame induction ceremony)

April

4 Two Rivers Theater, Red Bank, NJ (VH1 "Storytellers" taping)

10 The Stone Pony, Asbury Park, NJ (Rumson County Day School benefit)

21 Paramount Theater, Asbury Park, NJ (*Devils & Dust* tour rehearsal)

22 Paramount Theater, Asbury Park, NJ (*Devils & Dust* tour rehearsal)

There's Magic in the Night:
Springsteen Guest Performances (Live)

Asbury All-Star Revue: May 12–13, 1977, Monmouth Arts Center, Red Bank, NJ ("The Fever," "I Don't Wanna Go Home," "Havin' a Party," "Thunder Road," "Rendezvous," "Backstreets," "Born to Run," "Higher and Higher," "Amen," "You Mean So Much to Me")

Atlantic City Expressway (featuring Jon Bon Jovi): January 9, 1980, The Fast Lane, Asbury Park, NJ ("Prove It All Night," "The Promised Land")

Joan Baez: September 23, 1988, Oakland Stadium, Oakland, CA ("Blowin' in the Wind")

Bobby Bandiera: November 20, 1987, The Stone Pony, Asbury Park, NJ ("Little Latin Lupe Lu," "Stand By Me," "Carol"); June 20, 1989, Martells, Pleasant Beach, NJ ("Kansas City"); June 24, 1989, The Stone Pony ("Hound Dog," "Under the Boardwalk," "Glory Days"); August 2, 1989, Cheers, Long Branch, NJ ("Willie and the Hand Jive"); August 16, 1989, Cheers ("New Orleans," "From Small Things [Big Things One Day Come]," "I Hear You Knockin'," "Light of Day," "Land of 1000 Dances"); July 12, 1991, McLoone's Rumrunner, Sea Bright, NJ ("Travelin' Band," "Under the Boardwalk," "Jersey Girl," "Glory Days," "From Small Things [Big Things One Day Come]"); September 26, 1997, Cheers ("Mustang Sally," "Lucille"); December 16, 1997, Rumrunners, Sea Bright, NJ (private Christmas party, "Run, Rudolph, Run," "Merry Christmas Baby," "Land of 1,000 Dances," "Gloria"); October 21, 2000, Hedgerow Stables, Middletown, NJ, (also Patti Scialfa, Max Weinberg and Jon Bon Jovi, "Havin' a Party," "Rockin' All Over the World," "Proud Mary," "You Really Got a Hold on Me," "Hungry Heart," "Mustang Sally," "Twist and Shout")

Beaver Brown: August 26, 1978, Providence Civic Center, Providence, RI; April 13 and 15, 1979, The Fast Lane, Asbury Park, NJ; October 5–6, 1979, The Fast Lane ("Rosalita," "Twist and Shout"); February 20, 1982, Big Man's West, Red Bank, NJ ("Ain't That a Shame," "Money," "You Can't Sit Down"); February 20, 1982, Big Man's West, ("Ain't That a Shame," "Money," "You Can't Sit Down"); April 9–10, 1982, Big Man's West ("Lucille," "Jersey Girl," "Jole Blon," "Twist and Shout"); May 8, 1982, The Fast Lane ("Jole Blon," "Jersey Girl," "Lucille," "Around and

Around"); May 29, 1982, Big Man's West (with Southside Johnny Lyon, "Little Latin Lupe Lu," "Summertime Blues," "Around and Around," "High School Confidential"); August 6–7, 1982, Big Man's West ("Ready Teddy," "Lucille," "Jersey Girl," "Twist and Shout," "From Small Things [Big Things One Day Come]," "Do You Wanna Dance"); September 4, 1982, Big Man's West ("From Small Things [Big Things One Day Come]," "Come On Let's Go," "Lucille")

The Blasters: March 24, 1995, House of Blues, Los Angeles, CA ("American Music," "High School Confidential")

David Blue: September 4, 1972, The Bitter End, New York, NY

Gary U.S. Bonds: June 14, 1981, Survival Sunday benefit, Hollywood Bowl, Los Angeles, CA ("This Land Is Your Land," "Promised Land," "Jole Blon," "Hungry Heart," "Brother John Is Gone"); June 15, 1981, Old Waldorf, San Francisco, CA ("Jole Blon," "This Little Girl," "Quarter to Three," "School's Out," "New Orleans"); July 3, 1989, Cafe Bar, Long Branch, NJ ("This Little Girl," "Angelyne," "Bony Moronie," "Your Love," "Dedication," "New Orleans," "Quarter to Three"); July 12, 1989, Pennsauken, NJ; November 2, 2002, Tradewinds, Sea Bright, NJ (Light of Day benefit, "Jole Blon," "Quarter to Three")

Jackson Browne: September 4, 1972, The Bitter End, New York, NY; August 16, 1980, The Forum, Los Angeles, CA ("Sweet Little Sixteen," "Stay"); June 14, 1981, Survival Sunday benefit, Hollywood Bowl, Los Angeles, CA ("This Land Is Your Land," "Promised Land," "Jole Blon," "Hungry Heart," "Brother John Is Gone"); June 12, 1982, Rally for Disarmament, Central Park, New York, NY ("Promised Land," "Running on Empty"); August 2, 1983, Madison Square Garden, New York, NY ("Stay," "Running on Empty," "Sweet Little Sixteen"); June 30, 1989, Bally's Grandstand Under the Stars, Atlantic City, NJ ("Stay," "Sweet Little Sixteen," "Running on Empty"); December 17, 1989, Ventura Theatre, Ventura, CA (with Clarence Clemons, "Glory Days," "Cadillac Ranch," "Sweet Little Sixteen"); November 12, 1994, Lake Castaic, Los Angeles, CA (The Love Ride XI, "Running on Empty," "Born to Run," "Route 66," "Gloria," "Born to Be Wild"); March 16, 2004, Beacon Theater, New York, NY ("Take It Easy"); October 13, 2004, Continental Airlines Arena, East Rutherford, NJ (Vote for Change concert, "Running on Empty")

Bystander: May 26, 1984, Xanadu, Asbury Park, NJ ("Dancing in the Dark")

Cats on a Smooth Surface: April 25, 1982, The Stone Pony, Asbury Park, NJ; May 2, 1982, The Stone Pony ("Long Tall Sally," "Twist and Shout"); May 23, 1982, The Fast Lane, Asbury Park, NJ ("Carol," "Long Tall Sally," "Twist and Shout"); June 6, 1982, The Stone Pony; June 13, 1982, The Stone Pony ("Heartbreak Hotel," "Around and Around," "Lucille," "Kansas City," "Twist and Shout"); June 20, 1982, The Stone Pony ("Come On, Let's Go," "Little Latin Lupe Lu," "Sweet Little Sixteen," "Around and Around," "Lucille," "Twist and Shout"); July 25, 1982, The Stone Pony ("From Small Things [Big Things One Day Come]," "Come On, Let's Go," "Ramrod," "Lucille," "Around and Around," "The Wanderer," "Long Tall Sally," "Twist and Shout"); August 1, 1982, The Stone Pony ("Rip it Up," "Come on Over to My Place," "Come On Let's Go," "Lucille," "Around and Around," "Twist and Shout"); August 8, 1982, The Stone Pony ("Ready Teddy," "From Small Things [Big Things One Day Come]," "Come On Let's Go," "Come on Over to My Place," "Around and Around," "Lucille"/"On the Prowl," "Twist and Shout"); August 15, 1982, The Stone Pony ("Detroit Medley," "Ready Teddy," "From Small Things [Big Things One Day Come]," "Around and Around," "Jersey Girl," "You Can Look [But You Better Not Touch]," "Havin' a Party," "Detroit Medley"/"Shake"/"Sweet Soul

Music"); August 31, 1983, Jon Jon's, Wall, NJ; September 19, 1982, The Stone Pony ("Ready Teddy," "From Small Things [Big Things One Day Come]," "Come On Let's Go," "Lucille," "Come On Over to My Place," "Around and Around," "Havin' a Party," "Jersey Girl," "Wooly Bully," "Louie, Louie," "High Heeled Sneakers," "Twist and Shout"); September 25, 1982, The Stone Pony ("Ready Teddy," "From Small Things [Big Things One Day Come]," "Come on Over to My Place," "Around and Around," "Lucille," "Twist and Shout"); October 3, 1982, The Stone Pony ("From Small Things [Big Things One Day Come]," "Come On Let's Go," "Around and Around," "Open All Night," "Jersey Girl," "On the Prowl," "Do You Wanna Dance," "Lucille," "Wooly Bully," "Louie, Louie," "Rock Baby Rock," "Come On Over to My Place," "Havin' a Party," "Twist and Shout"); April 24, 1983, The Stone Pony ("From Small Things [Big Things One Day Come]," "Around and Around," "Lucille," "Twist and Shout"); July 10, 1983, The Stone Pony; August 14, 1983, The Stone Pony ("Ready Teddy," "Around and Around," "Jersey Girl," "Lucille," "Twist and Shout," "Ain't That Lovin' You Baby"); November 6, 1983, The Stone Pony ("It's All Over Now"); January 8, 1984, The Stone Pony ("Lucille," "Carol"); March 25, 1984, The Stone Pony ("I'm Bad, I'm Nationwide," "Lucille"); April 8, 1984, The Stone Pony ("Proud Mary," "Dirty Water," "I'm Bad, I'm Nationwide," "Lucille"); April 22, 1984, The Stone Pony ("I'm Bad, I'm Nationwide," "Little Latin Lupe Lu," "Jersey Girl"); June 10, 1984, The Stone Pony (with Nils Lofgren, "Gloria," "Boom Boom," "We Gotta Get Out of This Place," "The Last Time," "Rockin' All Over the World"); October 7, 1984, The Stone Pony; August 27, 1987, Tradewinds, Sea Bright, NJ ("Light of Day," "Proud Mary," "Fortunate Son," "I'll Be There," "Around and Around," "Lucille"); December 5, 1987, The Stone Pony ("Carol," "Stand By Me," "Wooly Bully," "Around and Around," "Little Latin Lupe Lu," "Twist and Shout"); August 21, 1988, The Stone Pony ("Stand By Me," "Around and Around"); July 9, 1989, The Stone Pony ("Travelin' Band"); July 23, 1989, The Stone Pony ("Old Time Rock 'n' Roll," "Hound Dog," "From Small Things [Big Things One Day Come]," "Under the Boardwalk," "Sweet Little Sixteen," "Glory Days," "Carol")

The Cherubs: August 26, 1987, The Columns, Avon, NJ ("Lucille," "Stand By Me")

Billy Chinnock: June 26, 1982, Big Man's West, Red Bank, NJ ("Lucille")

Clarence Clemons/Red Bank Rockers/Temple of Soul: April 16, 1982, Big Man's West, Red Bank, NJ ("Tenth Avenue Freeze-Out"); May 16, 1982, Big Man's West ("Tenth Avenue Freeze-Out"); June 27, 1982, Big Man's West ("Tenth Avenue Freeze-Out"); December 3, 1982, the Keystone, Palo Alto, CA ("Lucille," "From Small Things [Big Things One Day Come]"); January 8, 1983, Big Man's West ("Rockin' All Over the World," "Lucille"); April 13, 1984, Ripley Music Hall, Philadelphia, PA ("Fire," "Rockin' All Over the World"); April 21, 1984, Mount Ivy (NY) Expo; May 19, 1984, The Stone Pony, Asbury Park, NJ ("Fire," "In the Midnight Hour," "Lucille," "Twist and Shout"); December 17, 1989, Ventura Theatre, Ventura, CA (with Jackson Browne, "Glory Days," "Cadillac Ranch," "Sweet Little Sixteen"); June 28, 1993. Tradewinds, Sea Bright, NJ ("Rockin' Pneumonia and the Boogie Woogie Flu," "From Small Things [Big Things One Day Come]," "Jersey Girl," "Glory Days," "Twist and Shout"); November 6, 1998, Club 251, West Palm Beach, FL ("Shake, Rattle and Roll," "Got My Mojo Working," "Pink Cadillac," "Down the Road Apiece"); September 1, 2001, The Stone Pony ("Pink Cadillac," "Raise Your Hand," "Mustang Sally," "Glory Days"); January 12, 2002, Foxwoods Resort and Casino, Mashantucket, CT (Clemons' sixtieth birthday party, "Raise Your Hand," "Pink Cadillac," "Mustang Sally," "Glory Days" [with B.B. King])

Jimmy Cliff: September 22, 1989, The Stone Pony, Asbury Park, NJ ("Trapped")

Marshall Crenshaw: August 1, 1987, The Stone Pony, Asbury Park, NJ ("You Can't Sit Down," "La Bamba," "Twist and Shout"); October 21, 1994, The Playpen, Sayerville, NJ (with John Eddie, Greg Kihn and Elliott Murphy, "Hey Tonight," "Suspicious Minds," "Get It On," "Route 66," "Gloria")

Crosby, Stills, Nash & Young: October 13, 1986, Bridge School Benefit, Shoreline Amphitheater, Mountain View, CA ("Teach Your Children")

Del Fuegos: January 17, 1985, Rhinoceros Club, Greensboro, NC ("Hang on Sloopy," "Stand by Me")

The Diamonds: April 27, 1983, The Stone Pony, Asbury Park, NJ ("Lucille," "Long Tall Sally"); June 18, 1983, The Stone Pony ("Around and Around," "Lucille," "Twist and Shout")

Dion DiMucci: September 30, 1976, The Roxy, Los Angeles, CA ("Teenager in Love")

Bob Dylan: March 1, 1990, The Forum, Los Angeles, CA (with Tom Petty & the Heartbreakers, "Rainy Day Women," "Travelin' Band," "I'm Cryin'"); October 20, 1994, Roseland Ballroom, New York, NY (also Neil Young, "Rainy Day Women #12 & 35," "Highway 61 Revisited")

Steve Earle: February 6, 1998, Tradewinds, Sea Bright, NJ ("Everybody's Trying to Be My Baby," "Sweet Virginia," "Guitar Town," "I Ain't Ever Satisfied," "Dead Flowers," "Johnny Come Lately")

John Eddie: April 11, 1982, Big Man's West, Red Bank, NJ ("Long Tall Sally," "Rockin' All Over the World," "Proud Mary," "Carol"); August 19, 1983, Brighton Bar, Long Branch, NJ ("Blue Suede Shoes," "Rockin' All Over the World," "Ain't That Lovin' You Baby," "Jersey Girl," "Carol"); January 14, 1984, Patrix, East Brunswick, NJ ("Rockin' All Over the World," "Ain't Too Proud to Beg," "Boom Boom," "Proud Mary," "Twist and Shout"); June 1, 1984, The Stone Pony, Asbury Park, NJ ("I'm Bad, I'm Nationwide," "Proud Mary," "Bright Lights, Big City," "Carol"); September 3, 1984, The Stone Pony ("Travelin' Band," "Proud Mary," "I'm Bad, I'm Nationwide," "Twist and Shout"); October 21, 1994, The Playpen, Sayerville, NJ (with Greg Kihn, Marshall Crenshaw and Elliott Murphy, "Hey Tonight," "Suspicious Minds," "Get It On," "Route 66," "Gloria"); November 22, 1995, The Stone Pony ("Wild Thing"); August 18, 2001, The Stone Pony ("Suspicious Minds")

Dave Edmunds: September 18, 1982, Big Man's West, Red Bank, NJ ("From Small Things [Big Things One Day Come]," "Johnny B. Goode," "Lucille," "Let's Talk About Us," "Carol," "Bama Lama Bama Loo"); September 21, 1982, Peppermint Lounge, New York, NY ("From Small Things [Big Things One Day Come]")

Joe Ely: May 19, 1993, The Stadium, Dublin, Ireland ("Dusty Old Roads," "I Keep My Fingernails Long," "Settle for Love"); September 14, 1995, The Viper Room, Los Angeles, CA ("All Just to Get to You"); March 17, 1996, The Mean Fiddler, Dublin, Ireland ("All Just to Get to You," "Oh Boy," "Long Tall Sally," "I Keep My Fingernails Long," "Settle for Love," "Dusty Old Roads")

Melissa Etheridge: February 15, 1995, Brooklyn Academy of Music, NY (MTV *Unplugged*, "Thunder Road"); October 2, 1996, Bradley Center, Milwaukee, WI ("Pink Cadillac")

Fabulous Grease Band: November 6, 1987, Rumson Country Day School, Rumson, NJ ("Carol," "Lucille," "Twist and Shout," "Stand By Me"); June 29, 1989, Headliner, Neptune, NJ ("Twist and Shout"); July 27, 1989, Headliner ("Long Tall Sally," "Under the Boardwalk," "Sweet Little Sixteen," "Glory Days")

The Fairlanes (with Ernest "Boom" Carter): August 14, 1987, The Stone Pony, Asbury Park, NJ ("Savin' Up")

The Fanatics: August 9, 1996, Great Northern Bar and Grill, Whitefish, MT ("Shake, Rattle and Roll," "Mustang Sally"); August 10, 1996, Grand Mountain Lodge, Whitefish, MT (Toby Scott's wedding, "Around and Around," "You Sent Me," "Hold On, I'm Coming," "Mustang Sally," "Long Tall Sally," "Shake, Rattle and Roll")

John Fogerty: April 29, 1994, House of Blues, Los Angeles, CA; September 20, 1994, House of Blues, Los Angeles ("In the Midnight Hour")

Robert Gordon: December 2, 1977, Loeb Student Center, New York University ("Heartbreak Hotel"); March 14, 1979, The Fast Lane, Asbury Park, NJ ("Heartbreak Hotel," "Fire"); May 27, 1979, Paramount Theater, Asbury Park, NJ ("Fire," "Heartbreak Hotel")

Joe Grushecky/Iron City Houserockers: July 17, 1982, Big Man's West, Red Bank, NJ ("Mony Mony," "Shout," "Johnny Bye Bye," "Whole Lotta Shakin' Goin' On"); August 20, 1994, Marz American Style, Long Branch, NJ ("Lucky Town," "Darkness on the Edge of Town," "Chain Smoking," "Never Be Enough Time," "Brown Eyed Girl," "Mustang Sally," "Atlantic City," "Diddy Wah Diddy," "Living Proof," "Glory Days," "Around and Around," "Bama Lama Bama Loo," "The Wanderer," "Kansas City"); July 22, 1995, Tradewinds, Sea Bright, NJ (also Little Steven and Max Weinberg, "Lucky Town," "Atlantic City," "Never Be Enough Time," "Labour of Love," "Dark and Bloody Ground," "Diddy Wah Diddy," "Mustang Sally," "Murder Incorporated," "Darkness on the Edge of Town," "What Did You Do in the War Daddy," "American Baby-lon," "Cadillac Ranch," "Pumping Iron," "Gloria," "Ramrod"); October 17, 1995, The Stone Pony, Asbury Park, NJ (as full-set member traveling with the band); October 18, 1995, Tramps, New York, NY (as full member traveling with the band); October 19, 1995, The Electric Factory, Philadelphia, PA (as full member traveling with the band); October 20–21, 1995, Nick's Fat City, Pittsburgh, PA (as full member traveling with the band); October 24, 1995, Park West, Chicago, IL (as full member traveling with the band); December 13, 1997, Cheers, Long Branch, NJ ("Homestead," "Never Be Enough Time"); March 2, 1998, Nick's Fat City ("Never Be Enough Time," "Talking to the King," "What Did You Do in the War Daddy," "Homestead," "Chain Smoking," "Labour of Love," "Murder Incorporated," "Idiot's Delight," "Pumping Iron," "Ramrod," "Light of Day"); July 9, 1999, Hooligans, Long Branch, NJ; July 10, 1999, Cheers, Long Branch, NJ ("Never Be Enough Time," "Brown Eyed Girl," "Pumping Iron," "Talking to the King"); November 3, 2000, The Stone Pony ("Labour of Love," "Brand New Cadillac," "Never Be Enough Time," "Homestead," "Pumpin' Iron Sweatin' Steel," "Murder Inc.," "Talking to the King," "Down the Road Apiece," "Diddy Wah Diddy," "Everything's Gonna Work Out Right," "I Hear You Knockin'," "Light of Day"/"Land of 1000 Dances," "Twist and Shout," "I Don't Wanna Go Home"); November 3, 2001, Tradewinds ("Talking to the King," "Fire," "Ramrod," "Light of Day," "Twist and Shout," "Lucille"); July 17, 2004, The Stone Pony ("Never Be Enough Time," "Homestead," "Code of Silence," "Johnny 99," "Pumpin' Iron," "Mustang Sally"/"Walking the Dog," "Talking to the King," "Down the Road Apiece," "Have a Good Time (But Get Out Alive)," "Murder Incorporated")

John Wesley Harding: June 18, 1994, McCabe's Guitar Shop, Santa Monica, CA ("Wreck on the Highway")

Paul Hartung & the Remakes: July 22, 1989, McLoone's Rumrunner, Sea Bright, NJ ("Twist and Shout," "Glory Days")

Levon Helm's All Stars: August 22, 1987, The Stone Pony, Asbury Park, NJ ("Lucille," "Up On Cripple Creek")

Bruce Hornsby: July 31, 2001, Count Basie Theater, Red Bank, NJ ("Cadillac Ranch")

House of Blues Band: June 27, 1994, House of Blues, Los Angeles, CA ("Ride Your Pony," "Just to Be With You," "Tobacco Road," "Bama Lama Bama Loo," "Happen to Love You")

The Iguanas: February 2, 1992, The Maple Leaf, New Orleans, LA ("Ain't That a Shame," "Save the Last Dance for Me," "Betty Jean")

Jah Love: July 29, 1987, Key Largo, Belmar, NJ ("Born in the U.S.A.," "My Hometown"); July 30, 1987, Green Parrot, Neptune, NJ ("One Love, One Heart," "Born in the U.S.A.," "My Hometown"); August 26, 1987, Key Largo ("Jersey Girl," "My Hometown," "Born in the U.S.A.)

Jimmy & the Gigolos: August 28, 1997, The Derby, Los Angeles, CA

Jimmy & the Mustangs: November 27, 1982, Club Lingerie, Los Angeles, CA.

David Johansen: May 1, 1980, The Stone Pony, Asbury Park, NJ ("Personality Crisis," "Lucille")

Sonny Kenn: June 12, 1982, Big Man's West, Red Bank, NJ ("Walking the Dog," "Route 66," "Carol"); July 23, 1982, Monmouth County Fair, Freehold, NJ ("Sweet Little Sixteen," "Long Tall Sally," "Carol," "Shake," "Land of 1,000 Dances"); July 31, 1982, Big Man's West ("Sweet Little Sixteen," "Ready Teddy," "Rip It Up," "Around and Around," "Sweet Little Rock 'n' Roller")

Greg Kihn: October 21, 1994, The Playpen, Sayerville, NJ (with John Eddie, Marshall Crenshaw and Elliott Murphy: "Hey Tonight," "Suspicious Minds," "Get It On," "Route 66," "Gloria")

Killer Joe: June 2, 1989, The Stone Pony, Asbury Park, NJ ("You Never Can Tell," "Lucille," "Boom Boom," "Travelin' Band")

Carole King: March 7, 1976, Beacon Theatre, New York, NY ("The Loco-Motion")

Brian Kirk & the Jirks: September 3, 2001, Donovan's Reef, Sea Bright, NJ (also Patti Scialfa, "Rosalita," "Tenth Avenue Freeze-Out," "Mustang Sally," "Jersey Girl")

Huey Lewis & the News: November 5, 1986, Le Zenith, Paris, France (with Bob Geldof, "Barefootin'")

Little Steven & the Disciples of Soul: December 31, 1982, Little Steven's wedding party, Harkness House, New York, NY ("Jole Blon," "I'm a Rocker," "Hungry Heart," "Save the Last Dance for Me," "Rockin' All Over the World," "Shout"); August 21, 1987, The Stone Pony, Asbury Park, NJ ("Native American," "Sun City"); October 8, 1987, The Ritz, New York, NY ("Native American," "Sun City")

Nils Lofgren: January 12, 1982, Royal Manor North, New Brunswick, NJ ("Lucille," "Carol"); June 9, 1989, The Stone Pony, Asbury Park, NJ ("Not Fade Away," "In the Midnight Hour," "Lean on Me," "Glory Days"); August 18, 2001, Stone Pony Landing, Asbury Park, NJ ("If I Should Fall Behind," "It's All Over Now," "Boom Boom," "Shine Silently")

Lord Gunner Group: January 5, 1982, The Stone Pony, Asbury Park, NJ ("In the Midnight Hour," "Jole Blon")

The Lost Highway Band: October 23, 1980, Old Timer's Cafe, Seattle, WA ("Route 66," "Gloria," "In the Midnight Hour")

Malurt: May 1, 1981, Forum, Copenhagen, Denmark ("Hungry Heart")

Mama Tried: August 23, 1984, Brighton Bar, Long Branch, NJ ("Twist and Shout")

Tim McLoone: December 20, 1994, Tradewinds, Sea Bright, NJ (Tim McLoone's Holiday Express, "Santa Claus Is Comin' to Town," "Run, Rudolph, Run," "Merry Christmas Baby"); December 15, 2001, Continental Airlines Arena, East Rutherford, NJ (Tim McLoone's Holiday Express, "Merry Christmas Baby," "Santa Claus Is Comin' to Town")

John Mellencamp: May 26, 1988, Irvine Meadows, Irvine, CA ("Like a Rolling Stone")

Midnight Thunder: July 16, 1983, The Headliner, Neptune, NJ ("Lucille," "I Hear You Knockin'," "Wooly Bully," "Sweet Little Sixteen," "Twist and Shout," "Louie Louie")

Mighty Hornets: March 10, 1989, Rubber, Los Angeles, Calif. ("C.C. Rider")

Mile High Band: September 19, 1989, Matt's Saloon, Prescott, AZ ("I'm on Fire," "Don't Be Cruel," "Route 66, "Sweet Little Sixteen")

Elliott Murphy: October 21, 1994, The Playpen, Sayerville, NJ (also John Eddie, Greg Kihn and Marshall Crenshaw: "Hey Tonight," "Suspicious Minds," "Get It On," "Route 66," "Gloria")

New Orleans Blues Department: May 11, 1988, Maple Leaf Club, New Orleans, LA ("Boom Boom")

Wolfgang Niedecken and his Leopardfellband: July 9, 1995, Cafe Eckstein, Berlin, Germany ("Hungry Heart" (six times for video shoot), "Down the Road Apiece," "Boom Boom," "Honky Tonk Women," "Thunder Road," "Glory Days," "Jumpin' Jack Flash," "Twist and Shout")

Odin: September 2, Huddy Park, Highlands, NJ ("Maybelline," "New Orleans")

Roy Orbison: September 30, 1987, A Black and White Night, Coconut Grove, Los Angeles, CA ("Only the Lonely," "Dream Baby," "The Comedian," "Ooby Dooby," "Lean," "Running Scared," "Uptown," "In Dreams," "Crying," "Candy Man," "Down the Line," "Mean Woman Blues," "It's Over," "Oh Pretty Woman," "(All I Can Do Is) Dream You")

The Outcry: August 4, 1991, Cheers, Long Branch, NJ ("Ain't That a Shame," "People Get Ready," "Not Fade Away," "Stand By Me," "Travelin' Band")

Tom Petty & the Heartbreakers: March 1, 1990, The Forum, Inglewood, CA (with Bob Dylan, "Travelin' Band," "I'm Cryin'")

The Pretenders: September 5, 1981, Perkin's Cow Palace, Pasadena, CA ("Higher and Higher")

John Prine: November 12, 1988, Tarrytown Music Hall, Tarrytown, NJ ("Paradise")

Billy Rancher & the Unreal Gods: September 29, 1982, Westwood, NJ

R.E.M.: October 1, 2004, Wachovia Center, Philadelphia, PA (Vote For Change concert, "Man on the Moon"); October 2, 2004, Gund Arena, Cleveland, OH (Vote For Change concert, "Bad Day," "Man on the Moon"); October 3, 2004, Cobo Arena, Detroit MI (Vote For Change concert, "Bad Day," "Man on the Moon"); October 5, Xcel Energy Center, St. Paul, MN ("Bad Day," "Man on the Moon"); October 8, 2004, TD Waterhouse Arena, Orlando, FL ("Permanent Vacation," "Man on the Moon"); October 11, 2004, MCI Center, Washington, DC ("Man on the Moon")

Rock Bottom Remainders: May 29, 1994, Hollywood Palladium, Los Angeles, CA ("Gloria")

Richie "La Bamba" Rosenberg/La Bamba & the Hubcaps/La Bamba & His Big Band: December 28, 1983, Holiday Hurray, Monmouth Arts Center, Red Bank, NJ ("From Small Things [Big Things One Day Come]," "Santa Claus Is Comin' to Town," "Twist and Shout"); August 22, 1984, The Stone Pony, Asbury Park, NJ ("Travelin' Band," "I'm Bad, I'm Nationwide"); July 1, 1989, The Stone Pony ("Long Tall Sally")

Hetti Schneider Band: May 15, 1993, Bayerischer Hof, Munich, Germany ("Lucille," "Twist and Shout")

Patti Scialfa: April 18, 2004, The Hit Factory, New York, NY ("Love (Stand Up)," "As Long As I (Can Be With You)"); September 15, 2004, Paramount Theater, Asbury Park, NJ ("Love (Stand Up)," "As Long As I (Can Be With You)"); September 21, 2004, Bowery Ballroom, New York, NY ("Love (Stand Up)," "As Long As I (Can Be With You)"); September 25, 2004, The Roxy, Los Angeles, CA ("Love (Stand Up)," "As Long As I (Can Be With You)"); October 13, 2004, Continental Airlines Arena, East Rutherford, NJ (Vote For Change concert, "As Long As I (Can Be With You)," "Love (Stand Up)")

Norman Selden & the Joyful Noyze: June 17 and July 1, 1972, The Shipbottom Lounge, Point Pleasant, NJ

The Shots: September 4, 1977, The Stone Pony, Asbury Park, NJ ("Funky Broadway," "Further On Up the Road")

Patti Smith: December 26, 1975, The Bottom Line, New York, NY ("Gloria"); November 26, 1976, The Bottom Line ("Gloria," "My Generation"); December 30, 1977, CBGB's, New York, NY ("Because the Night")

Solar Circus: August 10, 1995, Cheers, Long Branch, NJ ("Better Things," "Mustang Sally," "Stems and Seeds," "All Along the Watchtower," "Not Fade Away")

Soul Asylum: March 6, 1995, Tramps Nightclub, New York, NY ("Tracks of My Tears")

Southside Johnny & the Asbury Jukes: September 8, 1974, The Stone Pony, Asbury Park, NJ; January 1, 1976, The Stone Pony; May 30, 1976, The Stone Pony ("Havin' a Party"); July 20, 1976, CBS Annual Sales Convention, Los Angeles, CA ("I Don't Want to Go Home"); September 4, 1976, The Stone Pony ("Havin' a Party"); April 17, 1977, The Stone Pony; September 13, 1977, The Stone Pony; October 13, 1977, The Stone Pony ("Ain't Too Proud to Beg," "Soothe Me," "Let the Good Times Roll," "Carol"); December 31, 1977, Capitol Theater, Passaic, NJ ("Havin' a Party," "Higher and Higher," "Little Latin Lupe Lu," "You Can't Sit Down"); August 31, 1978, The Agora, Cleveland, OH ("The Fever," "I Don't Wanna Go Home," "Havin' a Party"); September 26, 1984, Morris Community Theatre, Morristown, NJ ("In the Midnight Hour," "Mustang Sally," "Twist and Shout"); November 26, 1988, the Stone, San Francisco, CA ("In the Midnight Hour," "Hearts of Stone," "Keep a Knockin'," "Little Queenie"); September 26, 1991, The Stone Pony (video shoot for "It's Been a Long Time" with Little Steven and Jon Bon Jovi, plus "Havin' a Party," "Talk to Me"); December 27, 1992, The Stone Pony ("The Fever," "Oh Caroline," "All the Way Home," "I Don't Wanna Go Home," "This Time It's For Real," "It's Been a Long Time," "Havin' a Party"); July 16, 1994, The Stone Pony, (with Patti Scialfa, Max Weinberg and Jon Bon Jovi, "I Played the Fool," "Funky Broadway," "Land of 1,000 Dances," "It's Been a Long Time," "Jersey Girl," "I've Been Working Too Hard," "Havin' a Party"); May 27, 2001, Stone Pony Landing, Asbury Park, NJ ("The Fever," "I Don't Want to Go Home," "I've Been Working Too Hard," "Sex Machine," "Trapped Again," "Chain of Fools"/"Born on the Bayou," "Havin' a Party")

Stand and Deliver: August 26, 1994, Classics Cafe, Westfield, NJ (with Max Weinberg, "In the Midnight Hour," "Mustang Sally," "Slowdown," "Hippy Hippy Shake," "Twist and Shout," "Boom Boom")

Ringo Starr & His All-Starr Band: August 11, 1989, Garden State Arts Center, Holmdel, NJ ("Get Back," "Long Tall Sally," "Photograph," "With a Little Help From My Friends")

Sting: August 25, 1988, Madison Square Garden, New York, NY ("The River," "Message in a Bottle")

The Stray Cats: July 23, 1982, The Fast Lane, Asbury Park, NJ ("Twenty Flight Rock," "Be Bop a Lula," "Long Tall Sally")

Robbie Thompson: August 6, 1981, Bayou Club, Washington, DC ("Carol")

Soozie Tyrell: May 2, 2003, The Stone Pony, Asbury Park, NJ ("Ste. Genevieve," "It's All Over Now")

U2: September 25, 1987, JFK Stadium, Philadelphia, Pa. ("Stand By Me")

Tom Waits: August 24, 1981, Los Angeles (CA) Sports Arena ("Jersey Girl")

The Wallflowers: March 8, 1997, Tradewinds, Sea Bright, NJ ("God Don't Make Lonely Girls," "My Girl," "Brand New Cadillac," "Bring It on Home to Me," "Not Fade Away"); September 4, 1997, Radio City Music Hall, New York, NY (MTV Video Music Awards, "One Headlight")

X-Men: July 15, 1989, T-Birds Cafe, Asbury Park, NJ ("Little Sister," "Gloria")

Neil Young: March 22, 1985, Entertainment Centre, Sydney, Australia ("Down by the River"); October 13, 1986, Bridge School Benefit, Shoreline Amphitheater, Mountain View, CA ("Helpless"); June 14, 1989, Jones Beach, Wantagh, NY ("Down by the River"); October 28, 1995, Shoreline Amphitheater (Bridge School Benefit, "Down by the River," "Rockin' in the Free World"); October 5, 2004, Xcel Energy Center, St. Paul, MN (Vote For Change concert, "Souls of the Departed," "All Along the Watchtower," "Rockin' in the Free World")

The Price You Pay:
Springsteen as an Opening Act

July 11, 1971: for Humble Pie, Sunshine Inn, Asbury Park, NJ

February 28, 1973: for Paul Butterfield, Memorial Civic Auditorium, Stockton, CA

April 28, 1973: for Chuck Berry and Jerry Lee Lewis, University of Maryland Field House, College Park, MD

March 2, 1973: for Blood, Sweat & Tears, Community Theater, Berkeley, CA

March 3, 1973: for Blood, Sweat & Tears, Santa Monica Civic Center, Santa Monica, CA

November 11, 1973: for David Bromberg, Kendall Hall, Trenton State College, Trenton, NJ (Bromberg, aware of Springsteen's dynamic performances, reportedly backed out of the show when he heard Springsteen was opening)

May 6, 1973: for It's a Beautiful Day, Alumni Stadium, University of Massachusetts, Amherst, MA

May 30, 1973: for Chicago, Cumberland County Civic Center, Fayetteville, NC

May 31, 1973: for Chicago, Richmond Coliseum, Richmond, VA

June 1, 1973: for Chicago, Hampton Coliseum, Hampton, VA

June 2, 1973: for Chicago, Baltimore Civic Center, Baltimore, MD

June 3, 1973: for Chicago, Veterans Memorial Coliseum, New Haven, CT

June 6, 1973: for Chicago, The Spectrum, Philadelphia, PA

June 8–9, 1973: for Chicago, Boston Garden, Boston, MA

June 10, 1973: for Chicago, Civic Center, Springfield, MA

June 12, 1973: for Chicago, Broome County Memorial Arena, Binghamton, NY

June 14–15, 1973: for Chicago, Madison Square Garden, New York, NY

November 25, 1973: for John Mayall, University of Massachusetts, Amherst, MA

May 9, 1974: for Bonnie Raitt, Harvard Square Theater, Cambridge, MA

July 25, 1974: for Dr. John, Santa Monica Civic Center, Santa Monica, CA

August 3, 1974: for Anne Murray, Central Park Music Festival, New York, NY

Rendezvous: Springsteen Guest Performances (Recorded)

Artists United Against Apartheid: *Sun City* (Manhattan, 1985), vocals ("Sun City")

Gary U.S. Bonds: *Dedication* (EMI, 1981), co-producer, vocals and guitar ("Jole Blon," "This Little Girl," "Your Love," "Dedication"); *On the Line* (EMI 1982), co-producer, backing vocals ("Love's on the Line"), guitar ("Out of Work," "Angelyne"); *Back in 20* (MC, 2004), backing vocals and guitar ("Can't Teach an Old Dog New Tricks")

Clarence Clemons & the Red Bank Rockers: *Rescue* (Columbia, 1983), guitar ("Savin' Up")

Clarence Clemons Temple of Soul: *Live in Asbury Park Vol. II* (Valley, 2004), vocals and guitar ("Raise Your Hand")

The Dictators: *Bloodbrothers* (Asylum, 1978), count-in ("Faster and Louder")

Joe Ely: *Letter to Laredo* (MCA, 1995), backing vocals ("All Just to Get to You," "I'm a Thousand Miles from Home")

The Epidemics (Shankar & Caroline): *Eye Catcher* (Tokuma, 1989), harmonica ("Up to You," live from Human Rights Now! tour stop in New Delhi, India)

Robert Gordon: With Link Wray, *Fresh Fish Special* (Private Sock, 1978), piano ("Fire")

Joe Grushecky & the Houserockers: *American Babylon* (Razor & Tie, 1995), producer, co-writer ("Dark and Bloody Ground," "Homestead"), vocals ("Chain Smokin'"), guitar ("Chain Smokin'," "Labor of Love," "Homestead"), mandolin ("Labor of Love," "Homestead," "Billy's Waltz"), harmonica ("Homestead"); "Labor of Love" (UK single), guitar and backing vocals (including bonus tracks "Talking to the King," "Labor of Love," "Never Be Enough Time," "Gimme Shelter," "Pumping Iron," live from October 1995); *Down the Road Apiece: Live* (Schoolhouse CD, 1999), guitar and vocals ("Talking to the King," "Pumping Iron," "Down the Road Apiece," live from October 1995)

John Wesley Harding: *Awake* (Appleseed reissue, 2000), vocals and acoustic guitar ("Wreck on the Highway," live at McCabe's Guitar Shop, Santa Monica, CA, June 18, 1994)

Emmylou Harris: *Red Dirt Girl* (Nonesuch, 2000): harmony vocals ("Tragedy," with Patti Scialfa)

Jersey Artists for Mankind (J.A.M. 86): "We've Got the Love"/"Save Love, Save Life" (Arista), guitar solo ("We've Got the Love")

Little Steven & the Disciples of Soul: *Men Without Women* (Manhattan, 1982), backing vocals ("Angel Eyes," "Men Without Women," "Until the Good Is Gone")

Little Steven: *Freedom No Compromise* (Manhattan, 1987), duet vocal ("Native American")

Nils Lofgren: *Silver Lining* (Rykodisc, 1992), backing vocals ("Valentine")

Jesse Malin: *Messed Up Here Tonight* (One Little Indian, 2004), guitar and backing vocals ("Wendy," live from Convention Hall, Asbury Park, NJ, December 7, 2003)

Marah: *Float Away with the Friday Night Gods* (Artemis, 2002), guitar and backing vocals ("Float Away")

Elliott Murphy: *Selling the Gold* (Dejadisc, 1995), duet vocal ("Everything I Do")

Mike Ness: *Cheating at Solitaire* (Time Bomb, 1999), duet vocal ("Misery Loves Company")

Roy Orbison & Friends: *A Black and White Night: Live* (Virgin, 1989), guitar and backing vocals throughout

Graham Parker: *The Up Escalator* (Arista, 1980), backing vocals ("Endless Night")

John Prine: *The Missing Years* (Oh Boy, 1991), backing vocals ("Take a Look at My Heart")

Lou Reed: *Street Hassle* (Arista, 1978), vocals ("Street Hassle")

Patti Scialfa: *Rumble Doll* (Columbia, 1993), guitar, keyboards, production ("Big Black Heaven," "Talk to Me Like the Rain"); *23rd Street Lullaby* (Columbia, 2004), guitar and keyboards ("You Can't Go Back", "Rose," "Love (Stand Up)," "As Long as I (Can Be with You)" [live bonus track from the Hit Factory, New York City, April 18, 2004])

Southside Johnny & the Asbury Jukes: *Hearts of Stone* (Epic, 1978), backing vocals and guitar solo ("Hearts of Stone"); *Better Days* (Impact, 1991), duet vocal ("It's Been a Long Time"), backing vocals, guitar, and synthesizers ("All the Way Home")

Ronnie Spector & the E Street Band: "Say Goodbye to Hollywood"/"Baby Please Don't Go" (Epic, 1977), acoustic guitar on both songs

Donna Summer: *Donna Summer* (Geffen, 1982), guitar and vocals ("Protection")

Soozie Tyrell: *White Lines* (Treasure/Valley, 2003), guitar ("White Lines"), backing vocals ("St. Genevieve," with Patti Scialfa)

USA for Africa: *We Are the World* (Columbia, 1985), vocals ("We Are the World")

Various Artists: The Concert for the Rock and Roll Hall of Fame: (Columbia, 1996): "Great Balls of Fire" and "Whole Lotta Shakin' Goin' On" with Jerry Lee Lewis (live at Cleveland Stadium, Cleveland, OH, September 2, 1995)

Warren Zevon: *The Wind* (Artemis, 2003), guitar and backing vocals ("Prison Grove," "Disorder in the House"); *Enjoy Every Sandwich: The Songs of Warren Zevon* (Artemis, 2004), rendition of "My Ride's Here" for tribute album

Cover Him:
Acts Who Have Recorded Springsteen Songs

A Boat: "Born in the U.S.A."
Stephen Ackless: "From Small Things (Big Things One Day Come)"
Acoustic Sound Orchestra: "Streets of Philadelphia"
After Dark: "Streets of Philadelphia"
Afterhours: "State Trooper"
Air Supply: "4th of July, Asbury Park (Sandy)"
Alabama 3 (aka A3): "Nebraska" (labeled as "Badlands")
The All Stars: "Bruce Springsteen Mix" (medley)
Dave Alvin: "Seeds"
Tori Amos: "I'm on Fire"
Janne Anderson: "For You" (as "Till Dig," Swedish)
John Anderson: "Atlantic City"
Jaime Anglada: "Thunder Road"
Any Trouble: "Growin' Up"
The Apple Pirates: "Two for the Road"
Aram: "Something in the Night"
Arizona Smoke Revue: "Factory"
Atabala: "Brilliant Disguise"
Australian Blonde: "I'm on Fire"
Avila: "Streets of Philadelphia"
Babyface: "Fire" (with Des'ree)
Backseat Boys: "From Small Things (Big Things One Day Come)"
The Badlees: "Atlantic City"
Badly Drawn Boy: "Thunder Road"
The Band: "Atlantic City"
BAP: "Hungry Heart"

Luca Barbarossa: "Tougher Than the Rest" (with Alexi Lalas)
John Bayless: "Born in the U.S.A.," "Born to Run," "Candy's Room," "4th of July, Asbury Park (Sandy)," "Hungry Heart," "Jungleland," "My Hometown," "Rosalita (Come Out Tonight)"
The Beat Farmers: "Reason to Believe"
Howie Beck: "I Wish I Were Blind"
Pierre Belmonde: "Streets of Philadelphia"
Dan Bern: "Nebraska," "Thunder Road"
John Berry: "The Fever," "Thunder Road"
Bestaff: "Cover Me"
Dave Bielanko (of Marah): "Streets of Philadelphia"
Big Country: "I'm on Fire"
Big Daddy: "Born to Run," "Dancing in the Dark"
Billboard Hits 13: "Dancing in the Dark"
Bimbo Du Jour: "No Surrender"
Carol Black Band: "Fire"
Frank Black & the Catholics: "I'm Goin' Down"
Blackeyed Susans: "State Trooper"
Blue Emotions: "The River"
The Bluebeat: "Fire"
Blueberry Hill: "When You Need Me"
The Blue Bonnets: "The Angel"
Bob 'n' Bob: "I'm on Fire"
Boiled in Lead: "State Trooper"
Alex Bollard Assembly: "Dancing in the Dark"
Beki Bondage: "Because the Night"

Gary U.S. Bonds: "All I Need," "Angelyne," "Club Soul City," "Dedication," "Hold On (To What You Got)," "Love's on the Line," "Out of Work," "Rendezvous," "This Little Girl," "Your Love"

The Boss: "Dancing in the U.S.A." (medley)

Boss & the Bandits: "Born in the U.S.A." (as "Born in North Van"), "Dancing in the Dark" (as "Stranded in the Dark")

David Bowie: "Growin' Up," "It's Hard to Be a Saint in the City"

Boyz Nite Out: "Fire"

Billy Bragg: "Mansion on the Hill"

Johnny Brian: "No Surrender"

Paul Brooks: "Streets of Philadelphia"

Patrick Bruel and Jean Louis Aubert: "Streets of Philadelphia"

The Buccaneers: "Factory"

Cindy Bullens: "If I Should Fall Behind"

Bumping Uglies: "My Beautiful Reward"

Eric Burdon: "Factory"

Sonny Burgess: "Tiger Rose"

Luther Campbell & 2 Live Crew: "Born in the U.S.A." (as "Banned in the U.S.A.")

Canyon: "Used Cars"

Carillion: "Factory"

Rob Carlson: "Born to Run" (as "(These Eggs Were) Born to Run")

Carlton Sisters: "Fire"

Mary Chapin Carpenter: "Dancing in the Dark"

Michael Carpenter: "I Wish I Were Blind"

Deana Carter: "State Trooper"

Rossana Casale: "I'm on Fire"

Johnny Cash: "Highway Patrolman," "I'm on Fire," "Johnny 99"

Paul Cebar: "One Step Up"

CFD: "Pink Cadillac"

Cheech and Chong: "Born in the U.S.A." (as "Born in East L.A.")

Cher: "Tougher Than the Rest"

Ava Cherry & the Astronettes: "Spirit in the Night"

Kenny Chesney: "I'm on Fire," "One Step Up"

Chicken Mambo: "Nebraska"

The Chipettes: "Pink Cadillac" (with the Chipmunks)

The Chipmunks: "Pink Cadillac" (with the Chipettes)

Choice: "For You"

Dawn Chorus & the Blue Tits: "I'm Goin' Down"

Doug Church: "Pink Cadillac"

Circo Fantasma: "Factory" (as "La Babrica," Italian)

Claire: "Dancing in the Dark"

Louis Clark & the London Philharmonic Orchestra: "Dancing in the Dark"

Allan Clarke: "Blinded by the Light," "Born to Run," "If I Were the Priest"

Paula Clarke: "Fire"

Stanley Clarke: "Born in the U.S.A."

Richard Clayderman: "Streets of Philadelphia"

Clarence Clemons: "Paradise by the C" (with Temple of Soul), "Pink Cadillac" (with Temple of Soul), "Savin' Up" (with the Red Bank Rockers), "Summer on Signal Hill" (with the Red Bank Rockers)

The Clumsy Lovers: "I'm on Fire"

Joe Cocker: "Human Touch"

Colby 9: "Streets of Philadelphia"

Natalie Cole: "Pink Cadillac"

Sean Collins: "One Step Up"

Christine Collister: "One Step Up" (with Clive Gregson)

Tammy Comstock: "Reason to Believe"

Marco Conidi & the Rockin' Chairs: "One Step Up" (as "Un passo via da te," Italian)

Ray Coniff: "Streets of Philadelphia"

Brian Conley: "Pink Cadillac"

The Gary Cooper Combo: "Highway Patrolman"

Lanny Cordola: "My Beautiful Reward"

CO.RO featuring Tarlisa: "Because the Night"

Elvis Costello: "Brilliant Disguise"

Neal Coty: "Sad Eyes"

The Countdown Singers: "My Hometown," "Sad Eyes," "Streets of Philadelphia"

Cowboy Junkies: "My Father's House," "State Trooper," "Thunder Road"

Cracker: "Sinaloa Cowboys"

Siobahn Crawley: "Because the Night"

Crazysloth: "Candy's Room"

Marshall Crenshaw: "All or Nothing at All"

Crooked Fingers: "Mansion on the Hill," "The River"

Cultercide: "Dancing in the Dark"

Joey Curtin: "Meeting Across the River"

Mary Cutrufello: "Stolen Car"

Cutt Glass: "Fire"

Sonny Day & the All Stars: "Savin' Up"

Carrie Davis: "Tougher Than the Rest"

Kris De Bruyne: "Tougher Than the Rest" ("Taaier dan de rest," Belgian)

Richard De Groot: "Because the Night," "Born in the U.S.A.," "Born to Run," "Dancing in the Dark," "Fire," "For You," "Thunder Road"

De Pascale/Terzani: "The Fever"

The Debonaires: "I'm on Fire"

The Del Lords: "Johnny 99"

Frank DeLima: "I'm on Fire" (as "Bruce Springroll," a parody)

Des'ree: "Fire" (with Babyface)

Dick Tool Company: "Streets of Fire"

Ani DiFranco: "Used Cars"

Dimit: "My Hometown"

Dioni: "Book of Dreams," "If I Should Fall Behind"

Joe Dolan: "Brilliant Disguise"

Tomaz Domicelj: "Tougher Than the Rest" ("Tebi bom pa zvest," Slovenian)

Minnie Driver: "Hungry Heart"

Duessenberg: "For You"

Joe D'Urso & Stone Caravan: "Badlands," "Johnny Bye Bye" ("Bye Johnny Bye [Dead Rock Stars])," "The River"

The Dynatones: "Savin' Up"

Steve Earle: "Nebraska," "State Trooper"

Earthling: "Because the Night"

Eddie & the Hotrods: "The Ties That Bind"

Dave Edmunds: "From Small Things (Big Things One Day Come)"

Electralane: "I'm on Fire"

O'Brian Eselu: "Fire"

Melissa Etheridge: "Born to Run"

Everything But the Girl: "Tougher Than the Rest"

Barbara Fasano: "Thunder Road"

Mirella Felli: "Because the Night"

The Fevers: "Sherry Darling"

Matthew Fisher & the Downliners Sect: "Cadillac Ranch"

Raffaele Fiume: "Jeannie Needs a Shooter" (as "Jeannie Sparami," Italian)

The Floating Men: "Darkness on the Edge of Town"

Flor: "Wreck on the Highway"

Rosie Flores: "Lucky Town"

The Flying Mules: "If I Should Fall Behind"

The Flying Pickets: "Factory"

Fokke: "Tougher Than the Rest" ("Ik lit dy nea wer gean," Frisian)

Dean Ford: "The Fever"

4 Hr. Ramona: "I'm on Fire"

Kim Fox: "Atlantic City"

Mikael Fox: "Streets of Philadelphia"

Francine: "I'm on Fire"

Frankie Goes to Hollywood: "Born to Run"

Scott Free: "Streets of Philadelphia"

Frischhol: "Streets of Philadelphia" ("I Dene Schtrasse," Swiss)

Manel Fuentes: "Nothing Man"

Full Tilt Boogie Band: "Pink Cadillac"

Funkstar De Luxe: "Blinded by the Light"

Richie Furay: "If I Should Fall Behind"

Paul Fuster: "Used Cars"

Michael Garson Ensemble: "Streets of Philadelphia" (ensemble)

Gay Men's Chorus of Los Angeles: "Streets of Philadelphia"

Thea Gilmore: "Cover Me"

Arthur Godfrey: "The Ghost of Tom Joad"

Sandra Goldner: "The Fever"

Carmen Gomez: "I'm on Fire"

Tim Goodman: "Growin' Up"

Robert Gordon: "Fire"

Grand Drive: "Hearts of Stone"

Clive Gregson: "One Step Up" (with Christine Collister)

Sid Griffin: "Highway Patrolman"

Patti Griffin: "Stolen Car"

Timm Grimm: "Johnny 99"

The Groovers: "Factory," "Stolen Car"

Joe Grushecky & the Houserockers: "Cheap Motel," "Dark and Bloody Ground," "Homestead," "Idiot's Delight," "I'm Not Sleeping," "Light of Day," "1945"

Guana Batz: "I'm on Fire"

Gundermann: "Atlantic City" (as "Atlantik City"), "Badlands" (as "Steinland," instrumental), "Downbound Train" (as "War dein Freund," German instrumental)

Guns 'N Charoses: "Born to Run" (as "Born to Shop"), "Hungry Heart" (as "Everybody's Got a Jewish Mom")

1/2 Japanese: "Tenth Avenue Freeze-Out"

Klaus Hallen: "Streets of Philadelphia"

The Hamburg Rock Band: "Cover Me"

Andy Hamilton: "Hungry Heart" (instrumental)

George Hamilton IV: "My Hometown"

Albert Hammond: "Rendezvous"

Paul Hann: "Racing in the Street"

Ed Harcourt: "Atlantic City"

Mike Harding: "Factory"

John Wesley Harding: "Jackson Cage," "Wreck on the Highway"

Ben Harper: "My Father's House"

Emmylou Harris: "Across the Border" (with Linda Ronstadt), "Mansion on the Hill," "My Father's House," "The Price You

Pay," "Racing in the Street," "Tougher Than the Rest"

Duscan Huscava: "The River"

Richie Havens: "Streets of Philadelphia"

Greg Hawks & Tremblers: "Tougher Than the Rest"

Head Like a Hole: "I'm on Fire"

Heinäsirkka: "Because the Night" (as "Tama Yo," Finnish)

Hem: "Valentine's Day"

Hero's: "Growin' Up"

The Hesh: "Blinded by the Light"

John Hiatt: "Johnny 99"

Faith Hill: "If I Should Fall Behind"

Hip Cats: "Fire"

Lou Hobbs: "Fire"

The Hollies: "4th of July, Asbury Park (Sandy)"

Hollywood Star Orchestra & Singers: "Streets of Philadelphia"

Hon'nu'a: "Fire"

Jeff Hughes & Chaparral: "My Beautiful Reward"

Ashley Hutchings: "No Surrender"

Chrissie Hynde: "Nebraska" (with Adam Seymour)

Enrique Iglesias: "Sad Eyes" (English and Spanish, as "Mas Es Amar")

Georges Imbert: "The Promised Land"

Io vorrei la pelle nera: "Your Love" (Italian)

The Irrationals: "Because the Night"

William Jansen: "Sad Eyes" (as "Mas Es Amar," Spanish)

Jawadde: "Fire" (as "Vrijen," Belgian)

J.B.O.: "Born in the U.S.A." (as "Born in Der Nase," German parody)

Garland Jeffreys: "Streets of Philadelphia"

Waylon Jennings: "I'm on Fire"

Jet Lag: "Hungry Heart"

Joan Jett: "Light of Day"

Jive Bunny and the Mastermixers: "Blinded by the Light," "Dancing in the Dark"

The Joint Chiefs: "Atlantic City"

Jenny Jones: "If I Should Fall Behind"

Jubilant Bridge: "Independence Day"

Damien Jurado: "Wages of Sin" (with Rose Thomas)

Tom Juravich: "Used Cars"

Cindy Kallet: "My Hometown"

Harold Kama, Jr.: "Fire"

Keel: "Because the Night"

Kirk Kelly: "Downbound Train"

Andras Kern: "Born in the U.S.A." (as "Born in Budapest," Hungarian)

Bob Khaleel: "Streets of Philadelphia"

Greg Kihn: "For You," "Rendezvous," "Thunder Road"

Killer Joe: "Club Soul City," "Summer on Signal Hill"

Ben E. King: "4th of July, Asbury Park (Sandy)"

The Knack: "Don't Look Back"

Solly Kramer: "Fire"

Serge Kuhm: "Better Days," "Factory," "Nebraska," "No Surrender"

Henning Kvitnes' Next Step: "Mansion on the Hill"

Johnny La Rosa: "Savin' Up"

Jimmy LaFave: "Valentine's Day"

Alexi Lalas: "If I Should Fall Behind," "Tougher Than the Rest" (with Luca Barbarossa)

James Last: "Blinded by the Light"

Jerry Lawson: "Born to Run"

Russ Le Roq & the Romantics: "Fire"

Marti Lebow: "Hearts of Stone"

Chris LeDoux: "Tougher Than the Rest"

Keiko Lee: "Pink Cadillac"

Lena-Maria: "Fire"

Lili and Susie: "Fire" (as "Feber," Swedish)

Little Milton: "I'm on Fire"

Little Rock Country Band: "Tougher Than the Rest"

Chuck Loeb: "Fire"

Nils Lofgren: "Man at the Top," "Wreck on the Highway"

London Symphony Orchestra: "Born in the U.S.A."/"Dancing in the Dark," "Born to Run"

Mary Lou Lord: "Thunder Road"

Lord Horror with the Savoy Hitler Youth Band: "Cadillac Ranch" (lyrics only to "Blue Monday" melody)

Los Lobos: "Johnny 99"

Lost Weekend: "Highway Patrolman"

Mike Love: "Hungry Heart"

Gary Lucas' Gods and Monsters: "Ain't Got You"

Lucky 7: "Valentine's Day"

Ulf Lundell: "4th of July, Asbury Park (Sandy)" ("Sanna nyarsafton," Swedish)

Wolf Maahn & Die Deserteure: "Racing in the Street" (as "Blinder Passadier," German)

Jesse Malin: "Hungry Heart"

Raul Malo: "Downbound Train"

Aimee Mann: "Reason to Believe" (with Michael Penn)

Billy Mann: "Two Hearts"

Manfred Mann's Earth Band: "Blinded by the Light," "For You," "Spirit in the Night"

Marah: "Streets of Philadelphia"

The Gino Marinello Synthesizer: "Fire"

Greg Martin & Friends: "Paradise by the C"

Iain Matthews: "Sad Eyes" (with Elliott Murphy)

The Mavericks: "All that Heaven Will Allow"

Sally Mayes: "Meeting Across the River"

Robin McAuley: "My Hometown"

Boris McCutcheon: "If I Should Fall Behind"

John McCutcheon: "Reasons to Believe" (medley of separate "Reason to Believe" songs by Bruce Springsteen and Tim Hardin)

Mel McDaniel: "Stand on It"

Mark McKay: "Atlantic City"

Grant McLennan: "If I Should Fall Behind"

El McMeen: "I Wish I Were Blind," "Sad Eyes"

Megajam5: "Loose Ends"

Ulla Meinecke: "One Step Up" (as "Ein Schritt Vor," German)

The Mendoza Line: "Tougher Than the Rest"

Meredith: "Fire"

Merv & Maria: "All that Heaven Will Allow"

Bette Midler: "The E Street Shuffle"

The Mighty Echoes: "Factory"

Mighty Pope: "Because the Night"

Sylvia Millecamp: "Fire" (as "Brand!!," Dutch parody)

Frank Mills: "Streets of Philadelphia"

Mirage: "Pink Cadillac"

Mr. Fun/Tina & the B-Side Movement: "Janey Don't You Lose Heart"

Kevin Montgomery: "I Wish I Were Blind," "No Surrender"

More Trouble Band: "Reason to Believe"

Betty Mthombeni: "Fire"

Elliott Murphy: "Better Days," "Sad Eyes" (with Iain Matthews), "Stolen Car"

Pate Mustajärvi: "Born to Run" (as "Synnyimme lähtemään," Finnish)

The Mystic Knights of the Sea: "Johnny 99"

Tove Naess: "Hearts of Stone"

Natcha: "Human Touch" (as "Monschehand," Swiss)

Casey Neill Trio: "I'm on Fire"

Kurt Neumann: "Atlantic City"

Nicotine: "Born in the U.S.A."

The Nightshift Trio: "Cadillac Ranch"

Willie Nile: "I'm on Fire"

"97434" Johansen: "Factory" (as "Arbeidsdag," Norwegian)

Nitty Gritty Dirt Band: "Angelyne," "Cadillac Ranch," "From Small Things (Big Things One Day Come)"

Mojo Nixon: "The Big Payback"

Michael Nold Band: "Across the Border"

Heather Nova: "I'm on Fire"

Oblivion Dust: "Born in the U.S.A."

***Only the Lonely: The Roy Orbison Story* Original Cast:** "Born to Run"

Ostbahn-Kurti & die Chefpartie: "Factory" (as "Arbeit," Austrian); "Fire," "Hearts of Stone" (as "Stadt Aus Stan," Austrian), "Independence Day" (as "Feiertog," Austrian), "One Step Up" (as "An Schriat fiere," Austrian), "Point Blank" (as "Blattschuss," Austrian); "Rendezvous"

Anna Oxa: "Because the Night"

Papa Bueno: "Tenth Avenue Freeze-Out"

Fausto Papeti: "I'm on Fire"

Paradise Brothers: "Souls of the Departed"

Graham Parker: "Pink Cadillac"

Paul Parker: "Streets of Philadelphia"

The Party Boys (with Marc Hunter): "Cover Me"

The Party Boys (with Richard Clapton): "I'm a Rocker"

Petra Pasl: "One Step Up" (as "Ein Schritt vor und zwei Zurück," German)

Patti O'Doors: "Factory"

Kevin Pearce: "Pink Cadillac"

Pearl Jam: "Growin' Up"

PeCH: "Blinded by the Light"

Pele: "Highway Patrolman"

Michael Penn: "Reason to Believe" (with Aimee Mann)

Carl Perkins: "Pink Cadillac"

The Persuasions: "This Little Girl"

Ingrid Peters: "Fire" (as "Feigling," German)

Philadelphia Project: "Streets of Philadelphia"

Pickin' On Springsteen (session musicians): "Atlantic City," "Badlands," "Blinded by the Light," "Born in the U.S.A.," "Born to Run," "Brilliant Disguise," "Cover Me," "Dancing in the Dark," "Glory Days," "Growin' Up," "Hungry Heart," "I'm on Fire," "Independence Day," "My Beautiful Reward," "One Step Up," "Pink Cadillac," "Prove It All Night,"

"The Rising," "Streets of Philadelphia," "Tenth Avenue Freeze-Out," "Tunnel of Love"

Joe Piscopo: "Born to Run"

Pointer Sisters: "The Fever" (as "(She's Got) The Fever"); "Fire"

Bill Power: "Streets of Philadelphia"

Precious Metal: "Two Hearts"

The Pride: "Johnny 99"

P.J. Proby: "I'm on Fire"

Purple Ivy Shadows: "Does this Bus Stop at 82nd Street?"

Quantize: "Because the Night"

Suzi Quatro: "Born to Run"

Rage Against the Machine: "The Ghost of Tom Joad"

The Rankins: "All That Heaven Will Allow"

The Razorbacks: "I'm Goin' Down" (as "Goin' Down"), "Stand on It"

Refrigerator: "State Trooper"

Reilly & Maloney: "Cadillac Ranch," "Dancing in the Dark"

The Reivers (aka Zeitgeist): "Atlantic City"

Rhonda: "She's the One" (as "He's the One")

Allan Rich: "The Fever" (as "Fever for the Girl")

Mikael Rickfors: "Club Soul City"

Eric Rigler: "Born in the U.S.A."

Mike Rimbaud: "Atlantic City"

Jason Ringenberg: "My Hometown"

The River Detectives: "Factory"

Bob Rivers: "Glory Days" (as "Diaper Days," a parody), "I'm on Fire" (as "I Perspire," a parody)

Rock Afire Explosion: "Born to Run"

Rock Hotel: "Fire" (as "Teesklus," Estonian)

Rocking Chairs: "Restless Nights"

Rollin' in the Hay: "Atlantic City"

Graziano Romani: "All I Need," "Cadillac Ranch," "Don't Back Down," "Drive All Night," "Frankie," "Jesse," "Leap of Faith," "My Beautiful Reward," "Night," "None but the Brave," "Point Blank," "The Promise," "Soul Driver," "Streets of Fire," "Walk Like a Man," "The Way"

Linda Ronstadt: "Across the Border" (with Emmylou Harris); "If I Should Fall Behind"

Jan Rot: "If I Should Fall Behind" (as "Wacht op Mij," Dutch), "I'm on Fire" (as "Ik Word Gek," Dutch)

Kevin Rowland: "Thunder Road"

JW Roy: "Better Days"

Royal Philharmonic Orchestra with Joey Tempest: "Born to Run"

Gerd Rube: "Because the Night," "I'm on Fire"

Tom Russell Band: "I'm on Fire," "Shut Out the Light"

Matthew Ryan: "Something in the Night"

Salamander Crossing: "Two Faces Have I"

Sanne Salomonsen: "The Fever"

Santa's Dead: "Hungry Heart," "No Surrender"

Dean Sapp & The Hartford Express: "Sinaloa Cowboys," "Youngstown"

SAS Band: "For You"

Jane Saunders: "If I Should Fall Behind"

Helen Schneider: "Hearts of Stone"

Joe Schwach: "Tougher Than the Rest"

Seasons: "Cover Me"

The Section: "Atlantic City," "4th of July, Asbury Park (Sandy)," "Independence Day," "Into the Fire," "Mansion on the Hill," "My Hometown," "Nebraska," "Streets of Philadelphia," "The River," "Something in the Night," "Thunder Road"

Seldom Scene: "One Step Up"

Patrizio Sepe & the Chain Gang: "No Surrender"

Sesame Street's Bruce Stringbean & the S Street Band: "Born in the U.S.A." (as "Barn in the U.S.A."); "Born to Run" (as "Born to Add")

17th Avenue Allstars: "I'm on Fire"

Adam Seymour: "Nebraska" (with Chrissie Hynde)

The Shadows: "Dancing in the Dark"

Richard Shindell: "4th of July, Asbury Park (Sandy)"

Shot in the Dark: "Because the Night"

Frank Sidebottom: "Born in the U.S.A." (as "Born in Timperley")

Nikolas Sirkis: "Two Faces Have I"

SKAndalous All-Stars: "Because the Night"

Skilt: "Born in the U.S.A." (as "Born in the Norway")

Joe Slomp: "All the Way Home," "Living Proof," "Tenth Avenue Freeze-Out"

Smackee: "Born to Run"

Small Time Dave & the Windy City Groove: "Tenth Avenue Freeze-Out"

Patti Smith Group: "Because the Night"

The Smithereens: "Downbound Train"

Smokie: "Hungry Heart"

Solfa: "Fire"

Son Volt: "Open All Night"

Southern Pacific: "Pink Cadillac"

Southside Johnny: "Fade Away"

Southside Johnny & the Asbury Jukes: "All the Way Home," "The Fever," "Hearts of Stone," "Little Girl So Fine," "Love on the Wrong Side of Town," "Talk to Me," "Trapped Again," "Walking Through Midnight," "When You Dance," "You Mean So Much to Me"

Spanner Banner featuring Tanya Stephens: "Fire"

Ronnie Spector: "Brilliant Disguise"

Alvin Stardust: "Growin' Up"

Angie Stardust: "Streets of Philadelphia"

The Eddy Starr Orchestra: "Fire"

The Starshine Orchestra and Singers: "Streets of Philadelphia"

Stars on 45: "Fire"

Starsound: "Fire"

Startrax: "Because the Night"

Status Quo: "Cadillac Ranch"

Sandra Stephens: "Adam Raised a Cain"

Jeff Stevens & the Bullets: "Angelyne," "Darlington County," "From Small Things (Big Things One Day Come)"

The Studio Sound Orchestra: "Streets of Philadelphia"

Shakin' Stevens: "Fire"

Suzi Stevens: "Pink Cadillac"

Stolen Shack: "I'm on Fire"

Little Bob Story: "Seaside Bar Song"

Strange Fruit: "Kitty's Back"

Stranzinger: "All or Nothing at All" (as "Ois Oda Nix," Austrian)

Syd Straw: "Meeting Across the River"

Henning Staerk Band: "Fire," "One Step Up"

Donna Summer: "Protection"

Sunrize: "Fire"

Pablo Surja & Cambio de Planes: "Lucky Town"

John Swank: "The Fever"

Jubilant Sykes: "If I Should Fall Behind"

Tahures Zurdos: "Because the Night" (as "La Noches es…," Spanish)

Werner Tauber: "Streets of Philadelphia"

Roger Taylor: "Racing in the Street"

10,000 Maniacs: "Because the Night"

The Tesca Allstars: "Streets of Philadelphia"

Todd Thibaud: "Lucky Town"

Rose Thomas: "Wages of Sin" (with Damien Jurado)

Chris Thompson: "Blinded by the Light," "For You"

Robbin Thompson: "Guilty," "Train Song"

Jun Togawa: "Because the Night"

Rick Trevino: "Cadillac Ranch"

Travis Tritt: "Tougher Than the Rest"

The Turtles: "Growin' Up"

Bonnie Tyler: "Human Touch" (with the City of Prague Philharmonic Orchestra)

Two Tons of Steel: "Red Headed Woman"

UA: "Because the Night"

John Valby: "Hungry Heart," "I'm on Fire"

Alexandra van Marken: "No Surrender"

Townes Van Zandt: "Racing in the Street"

Tom Varner: "With Every Wish"

Lars Vegas Trio: "Fire"

Bamses Venner: "Janey Don't You Lose Heart" (as "Ikke være bange," Danish); "Sherry Darling"

Victoria Y Sus Chikos: "Fire" (as "Fuego," Tejano)

Voce: "Fire"

Voicebox: "Pink Cadillac" (medley with "Greased Lightnin'")

Walk the Walk: "Because the Night"

Jason Walker: "I Wish I Were Blind"

The Waterboys: "Because the Night," "Independence Day"

Helen Watson: "Ain't Got You"

Jan Wayne: "Because the Night"

Casell Webb: "Reason to Believe"

Zueri West: "Point Blank" (as "Flachgleit," Swiss)

When the Cats Away: "Fire"

Nick White: "Born in the U.S.A.," "Cover Me," "Dancing in the Dark," "Glory Days," "Human Touch," "Hungry Heart," "I'm on Fire," "My Hometown," "The River," "Streets of Philadelphia," "Thunder Road"

Goran Wiklund: "Savin' Up"

Kim Wilde with the Royal Philharmonic Orchestra: "Because the Night"

Pepe Willberg: "Blinded by the Light" (Finnish, as "Mennaan Rooperiin")

Dar Williams: "Highway Patrolman"

Hank Williams III: "Atlantic City"

Robin Williams: "Fire"

Robin and Linda Williams: "If I Should Fall Behind"

Aretha Wilson: "Pink Cadillac"

Ray Wilson: "Born to Run"

Wolfsbane: "Born to Run"

The Woolridge Brothers: "Fade Away"

Link Wray: "Fire"

Dusty Wright: "Mary, Queen of Arkansas"

Mark Wright: "Two Hearts"

Steve Wynn: "State Trooper"
XXX Century: "Because the Night"
Trisha Yearwood: "Sad Eyes"
The Yell Leaders: "I Wish I Were Blind"
Pete Yorn: "Atlantic City," "Dancing in the Dark," "New York City Serenade"

Martin Zellar: "Darkness on the Edge of Town"
Warren Zevon: "Cadillac Ranch," "Jeannie Needs a Shooter"
Teddy Zig Zag: "57 Channels (and Nothin' On)"

Cover Me:
Springsteen Songs Recorded by Other Acts

"Across the Border": Emmylou Harris and Linda Ronstadt; Michael Nold Band

"Adam Raised a Cain": Sandra Stephens

"Ain't Got You": Gary Lucas' Gods and Monsters; Helen Watson

"All I Need": Gary U.S. Bonds; Graziano Romani

"All or Nothing at All": Marshall Crenshaw; Stranzinger (as "Ois Oda Nix," Austrian)

"All That Heaven Will Allow": The Mavericks; Merv & Maria; The Rankins

"All the Way Home": Joe Slomp; Southside Johnny & the Asbury Jukes

"The Angel": The Blue Bonnets

"Angelyne": Gary U.S. Bonds; Nitty Gritty Dirt Band; Jeff Stevens & the Bullets

"Atlantic City": John Anderson; The Badlees; The Band; Kim Fox; Gundermann ("Atlantik City"); Ed Harcourt; The Joint Chiefs; Mark McKay; Kurt Neumann; Pickin' On Springsteen (session musicians); The Reivers (aka Zeitgeist); Mike Rimbaud; Rollin' in the Hay; The Section; Hank Williams III; Pete Yorn

"Badlands": Joe D'Urso and Stone Caravan, Gundermann (as "Steinland," instrumental); Pickin' On Springsteen (session musicians)

"Because the Night": Beki Bondage; CO.RO featuring Tarlisa; Siobahn Crawley; Richard De Groot; Earthling; Mirella Felli, Heinäsirkka (Finnish, as "Tämä Yö"); The Irrationals; Keel; Mighty Pope; Anna Oxa; Quantize; The Royal Philharmonic Orchestra with Kim Wilde; Gerd Rube; Shot in the Dark; SKAndalous All-Stars; Patti Smith Group; Startrax; Tahures Zurdos (as "La Noche es...," Spanish); 10,000 Maniacs; Jun Togawa; UA; Walk the Walk; The Waterboys; Jan Wayne; XXX Century

"Better Days": Serge Kuhm; Elliott Murphy; J.W. Roy

"The Big Payback": Mojo Nixon

"Blinded by the Light": Allan Clarke; Funkstar De Luxe; The Hesh; James Last; Jive Bunny and the Mastermixers; Manfred Mann's Earth Band; PeCH; Pickin' On

Springsteen (session musicians); Chris Thompson; Pepe Willberg (as "Menaan Rooperiin," Finnish)

"Book of Dreams": Dion

"Born in the U.S.A.": A Boat; John Bayless; Stanley Clarke, Richard De Groot; London Symphony Orchestra; Nicotine; Oblivion Dust; Pickin' On Springsteen (session musicians); Eric Rigler; Nick White

"Born in the U.S.A."–inspired: The Boss ("Dancing in the U.S.A." medley); Boss & the Bandits ("Born in North Van"); Luther Campbell & the 2 Live Crew ("Banned in the U.S.A."); Cheech and Chong ("Born in East L.A."); J.B.O. ("Born in Der Nase," German); Andras Kern ("Born in Budapest" ["Pesten Szulettem"], Hungarian); Frank Sidebottom ("Born in Timperley"); Skilt ("Born in the Norway"); *Sesame Street's* Bruce Stringbean & the S Street Band ("Barn in the U.S.A.")

"Born to Run": John Bayless; Big Daddy; Allan Clarke; Richard De Groot; Melissa Etheridge; Frankie Goes to Hollywood; Jerry Lawson; London Symphony Orchestra; Pate Mustajärvi ("Synnyimme lähtemään," Finnish); Original Cast of *Only the Lonely: The Roy Orbison Story*; Pickin' On Springsteen (session musicians); Joe Piscopo; Suzi Quatro; Rock Afire Explosion; Royal Philharmonic Orchestra with Joey Tempest; Smackee; Ray Wilson; Wolfsbane

"Born to Run"–inspired: Rob Carlson ("[These Eggs Were] Born to Run"); Guns 'N Charoses ("Born to Shop"); *Sesame Street's* Bruce Stringbean & the S Street Band ("Born to Add")

"Brilliant Disguise": Atabala; Elvis Costello; Joe Dolan; Pickin' On Springsteen (session musicians); Ronnie Spector

"Cadillac Ranch": Matthew Fisher & the Downliners Sect; Lord Horror with the Savoy Hitler Youth Band (lyrics only, to "Blue Monday" melody); The Nightshift Trio; Nitty Gritty Dirt Band; Reilly & Maloney; Graziano Romani; Status Quo; Rick Trevino; Warren Zevon

"Candy's Room": John Bayless; Crazysloth

"Cheap Motel": Joe Grushecky & the Houserockers

"Club Soul City": Gary U.S. Bonds; Killer Joe; Mikael Rickfors

"Cover Me": Bestaff; Thea Gilmore; The Hamburg Rock Band; The Party Boys (with Marc Hunter); Pickin' On Springsteen (session musicians); Seasons; Nick White

"Dancing in the Dark": Big Daddy; Billboard Hits 13; Alex Bollard Assembly; The Boss; Mary Chapin Carpenter; Claire; Louis Clark & the London Philharmonic Orchestra; Cultercide; Jive Bunny & the Mastermixers; Pickin' On Springsteen (session musicians); Richard De Groot; Reilly & Maloney; The Shadows; Nick White; Pete Yorn

"Dark and Bloody Ground": Joe Grushecky & the Houserockers

"Darkness on the Edge of Town": The Floating Men; Martin Zellar

"Darlington County": Jeff Stevens & the Bullets

"Dedication": Gary U.S. Bonds

"Does This Bus Stop at 82nd Street?": Purple Ivy Shadows

"Don't Back Down": Graziano Romani

"Don't Look Back": The Knack

"Downbound Train": Gundermann (as "War dein Freund," German instrumental); Kirk Kelly; Raul Malo; The Smithereens

"Drive All Night": Graziano Romani

"Factory": Arizona Smoke Revue; The Buccaneers; Eric Burdon; Carillion; Circo Fantasma (as "La Babrica," Italian); The Flying Pickets; The Groovers; Mike Harding; Serge Kuhm; Ostbahn-Kurti und die Chefpartie (as "Arbeit," Austrian); The Mighty Echoes; "97434" Johansen (as "Arbeidsdag," Norwegian); Patti O'Doors; The River Detectives

"Fade Away": Southside Johnny; The Woolridge Brothers

"The Fever": John Berry; De Pascale/Terzani; Dean Ford; Sandra Goldner; Pointer Sisters (as "[She's Got] The Fever"); Allan Rich (as "Fever for the Girl"); Sanne Salomonsen; Southside Johnny & the Asbury Jukes; John Swank

"57 Channels (and Nothin' On)": Teddy Zig Zag

"Fire": John Berry; Carol Black Band; The Bluebeat; Boyz Nite Out; Carlton Sisters; Paula Clarke; Cutt Glass; Richard De Groot; Des'ree and Babyface; O'Brian Eselu; Robert Gordon; Hip Cats; Lou Hobbs; Hon'nu'a; Harold Kama, Jr.; Russ Le Roq & the Romantics; Lena-Maria; Lili and Susie (as "Feber," Swedish); Chuck Loeb; Jawadde (as "Vrijen," Belgian); Solly Kramer; The Gino Marinello Synthesizer; Meredith; Sylvia Millecamp (as "Brand!!," Dutch parody); Betty Mthombeni; Ingrid Peters (as "Feigling," German); Ostbahn-Kurti und die Chefpartie (as "Feuer," Austrian); Pointer Sisters; Rock Hotel (as "Teesklus," Estonian); Solfa; Spanner Banner featuring Tanya Stephens; The Eddy Starr Orchestra; Stars on 45; Starsound; Shakin' Stevens; Henning Stærk Band; Sunrize; Lars Vegas Trio; Victoria Y Sus Chikos (as "Fuego," Tejano); Voce; When the Cats Away; Robin Williams; Link Wray

"For You": Janne Andersson (as "Till Dig," Swedish); Choice; Richard De Groot; Duessenberg; Greg Kihn Band; Manfred Mann's Earth Band; SAS Band; Chris Thompson

"4th of July, Asbury Park (Sandy)": Air Supply; John Bayless; The Hollies; Ben E. King; Ulf Lundell (as "Sanna nyarsafton," Swedish); The Section; Richard Shindell

"Frankie": Graziano Romani

"From Small Things (Big Things One Day Come)": Stephen Ackless; Backseat Boys; Dave Edmunds; Nitty Gritty Dirt Band; Jeff Stevens & the Bullets

"The Ghost of Tom Joad": Arthur Godfrey; Rage Against the Machine

"Glory Days": Pickin' On Springsteen (session musicians); Bob Rivers (as "Diaper Days," a parody); Nick White

"Growin' Up": Any Trouble; David Bowie; Tim Goodman; Hero's; Pearl Jam; Pickin' On Springsteen (session musicians); Alvin Stardust; The Turtles

"Guilty": Robbin Thompson

"Hearts of Stone": Grand Drive; Marti Lebow; Tove Naess; Ostbahn-Kurti und die Chefpartie (as "Stadt Aus Stan," Austrian); Helen Schneider; Southside Johnny & the Asbury Jukes

"Highway Patrolman": Johnny Cash; The Gary Cooper Combo; Sid Griffin; Lost Weekend; Pele; Dar Williams

"Hold On (to What You Got)": Gary U.S. Bonds

"Homestead": Joe Grushecky & the Houserockers

"Human Touch": Joe Cocker; Natcha (as "Monschehand," Swiss); Bonnie Tyler (with the City of Prague Philharmonic Orchestra); Nick White

"Hungry Heart": BAP; John Bayless; Minnie Driver; Guns 'N Charoses (as "Everybody's Got a Jewish Mom," parody); Andy Hamilton (instrumental); Jet Lag; Mike Love; Jesse Malin; Pickin' On Springsteen (session musicians); Santa's Dead; Smokie; John Valby; Nick White

"I Wish I Were Blind": Howie Beck; Michael Carpenter; El McMeen; Kevin Montgomery; Jason Walker; The Yell Leaders

"Idiot's Delight": Joe Grushecky & the Houserockers

"If I Should Fall Behind": Cindy Bullens; Dion; The Flying Mules; Richie Furay; Faith Hill; Jenny Jones; Alexi Lalas; Grant McLennan; Boris McCutcheon; Linda Ronstadt; Jan Rot (as "Wacht op Mij," Dutch); Jane Saunders; Jubilant Sykes; Robin and Linda Williams

"If I Were the Priest": Allan Clarke

"I'm a Rocker": The Party Boys (with Richard Clapton)

"I'm Goin' Down": Frank Black & the Catholics; Dawn Chorus & the Blue Tits; the Razorbacks (as "Goin' Down")

"I'm Not Sleeping": Joe Grushecky & the Houserockers

"I'm on Fire": Tori Amos; Australian Blonde; Big Country; Bob 'n' Bob; The Clumsy Lovers; Rossana Casale; Johnny Cash; Kenny Chesney; The Debonaires; Frank DeLima (as "Bruce Springroll," a parody); Electralane; 4 Hr. Ramona; Francine; Carmen Gomez; Guana Batz; Head Like a Hole; Waylon Jennings; Little Milton; Casey Neill Trio; Willie Nile; Heather Nova; Fausto Papeti; Pickin' On Springsteen (session musicians); P.J. Proby; Bob Rivers (as "I Perspire," a parody); Gerd Rube; Tom Russell Band; Jan Rot (as "Ik Word Gek," Dutch); 17th Avenue Allstars; Stolen Shack; John Valby; Nick White

"Independence Day": Jubilant Bridge; Ostbahn-Kurti und die Chefpartie (as "Feiertog," Austrian); Pickin' On Springsteen (session musicians); The Section; The Waterboys

"Into the Fire": The Section

"It's Hard to Be a Saint in the City": David Bowie

"Jackson Cage": John Wesley Harding

"Janey Don't You Lose Heart": Bamses Venner (as "Ikke være bange," Danish); Mrs. Fun/Tina & the B-Side Movement

"Jeannie Needs a Shooter": Raffaele Fiume (as "Jeannie Sparami," Italian); Warren Zevon

"Jesse": Graziano Romani

"Johnny 99": Johnny Cash; Timm Grimm; The Del Lords; John Hiatt; Los Lobos; The Mystic Knights of the Sea; The Pride

"Johnny Bye Bye ("Bye Johnny Bye [Dead Rock Stars])": Joe D'Urso and Stone Caravan

"Jungleland": John Bayless

"Kitty's Back": Strange Fruit

"Leap of Faith": Graziano Romani

"Light of Day": Joe Grushecky & the Houserockers; Joan Jett

"Little Girl So Fine": Southside Johnny & the Asbury Jukes

"Living Proof": Joe Slomp

"Loose Ends": Megajam5

"Love on the Wrong Side of Town": Southside Johnny & the Asbury Jukes

"Love's on the Line": Gary U.S. Bonds

"Lucky Town": Rosie Flores; Pablo Surja & Cambio de Planes; Todd Thibaud

"Man at the Top": Nils Lofgren

"Mansion on the Hill": Billy Bragg; Crooked Fingers; Emmylou Harris; Henning Kvitnes' Next Step; The Section

"Mary, Queen of Arkansas": Dusty Wright

"Meeting Across the River": Joey Curtin; Sally Mayes; Syd Straw

"My Beautiful Reward": Bumping Uglies; Lanny Cordola; Jeff Hughes & Chaparral; Pickin' On Springsteen (session musicians); Graziano Romani

"My Father's House": Cowboy Junkies; Ben Harper; Emmylou Harris

"My Hometown": John Bayless; The Countdown Singers; Dimit; George Hamilton IV; Cindy Kallet; Robin McAuley; Jason Ringenberg; The Section; Nick White

"Nebraska": Alabama 3 (labeled as "Badlands"); Dan Bern; Chicken Mambo; Steve Earle; Chrissie Hynde and Adam Seymour; Serge Kuhm; The Section

"New York City Serenade": Pete Yorn

"Night": Graziano Romani

"1945": Joe Grushecky & the Houserockers

"No Surrender": Bimbo Du Jour; Johnny Brian; Ashley Hutchings; Serge Kuhm; Kevin Montgomery; Santa's Dead; Patrizio Sepe & the Chain Gang; Alexandra van Marken

"None but the Brave": Graziano Romani

"Nothing Man": Manel Fuentes

"One Step Up": Paul Cebar; Kenny Chesney; Sean Collins; Marco Conidi & the Rockin' Chairs (as "Un passo via da te," Italian); Clive Gregson and Christine Collister; Ostbahn-Kurti und die Chefpartie (as "An Schriat fiere," Austrian); Ulla Meinecke (as "Ein Schritt Vor," German); Petra Pasl (as "Ein Schritt vor und zwei Zurück," German); Pickin' On Springsteen (session musicians); Seldom Scene; Henning Stærk Band

"Open All Night": Son Volt

"Out of Work": Gary U.S. Bonds

"Paradise by the C": Clarence Clemons (with Temple of Soul); Greg Martin & Friends

"Pink Cadillac": CFD; The Chipmunks and the Chipettes; Doug Church; Clarence Clemons (with Temple of Soul); Natalie Cole; Brian Conley; Full Tilt Boogie Band; Keiko Lee; Mirage; Graham Parker; Kevin Pearce; Carl Perkins; Pickin' On Springsteen (session musicians); Southern Pacific; Suzi Stevens; VoiceBox (medley with "Greased Lightnin'"); Aretha Wilson

"Point Blank": Ostbahn-Kurti & die Chefpartie (as "Blattschuss," Austrian); Graziano Romani; Zueri West (as "Flachgleit," Swiss)

"The Price You Pay": Emmylou Harris

"The Promise": Graziano Romani

"The Promised Land": Georges Imbert

"Protection": Donna Summer

"Prove It All Night": Pickin' On Springsteen (session musicians)

"Racing in the Street": Paul Hann; Emmylou Harris; Wolf Maahn & Die Deserteure (as "Blinder Passadier," German); Roger Taylor; Townes Van Zandt

"Reason to Believe": The Beat Farmers; Tammy Comstock; Aimee Mann & Michael Penn; John McCutcheon ("Reasons to Believe" medley of Bruce Springsteen and Tim Hardin songs with same time); More Trouble Band; Casell Webb

"Red Headed Woman": Two Tons of Steel

"Rendezvous": Gary U.S. Bonds; Albert Hammond; Greg Kihn Band; Ostbahn-Kurti

"Restless Nights": Rocking Chairs

"The Rising": Pickin' On Springsteen (session musicians)

"The River": Blue Emotions; Crooked Fingers; Joe D'Urso & Stone Caravan; Duscan Huscava; The Section; Nick White

"Rosalita (Come Out Tonight)": John Bayless

"Sad Eyes": Neal Coty; The Countdown Singers; Enrique Iglesias (English and Spanish, as "Mas Es Amar"); William Jansen (as "Mas Es Amar," Spanish); El McMeen; Elliott Murphy and Iain Matthews; Trisha Yearwood

"Savin' Up": Clarence Clemons & The Red Bank Rockers; Sonny Day & the All Stars; The Dynatones; Johnny La Rosa; Goran Wiklund

"Seaside Bar Song": Little Bob Story

"Seeds": Dave Alvin

"Sherry Darling": The Fevers; Bamses Venner

"She's the One": Rhonda (as "He's the One")

"Shut Out the Light": Tom Russell Band

"Sinaloa Cowboys": Cracker; Dean Sapp & The Hartford Express

"Something in the Night": Aram; Matthew Ryan; The Section

"Soul Driver": Graziano Romani

"Souls of the Departed": Paradise Brothers

"Spirit in the Night": Ava Cherry & The Astronettes; Manfred Mann's Earth Band

"Stand on It": Mel McDaniel; The Razorbacks

"State Trooper": Afterhours; Blackeyed Susans; Boiled in Lead; Deana Carter; Cowboy Junkies; Steve Earle; Refrigerator; Steve Wynn

"Stolen Car": Mary Cutrufello; Patti Griffin; The Groovers; Elliott Murphy

"Streets of Fire": Dick Tool Company; Graziano Romani

"Stranded in the Park" (based on "Dancing in the Dark"): Boss & the Bandits

"Streets of Philadelphia": Acoustic Sound Orchestra; After Dark; Sergio Avila; Pierre Belmonde; Dave Bielanko (of Marah); Paul Brooks; Patrick Bruel and Jean Louis Aubert; Richard Clayderman; Colby 8; Ray Coniff; The Countdown Singers; Frischhohl ("I Dene Schtrasse," Swiss); Mikael Fox; Scott Free; Michael Garson

Ensemble (instrumental); Gay Men's Chorus of Los Angeles; Klaus Hallen; Richie Havens; Hollywood Star Orchestra & Singers; Garland Jeffreys; Bob Khaleel; Marah; Frank Mills; Paul Parker; Philadelphia Project; Pickin' On Springsteen (session musicians); Bill Power; The Section; Angie Stardust; The Starlight Orchestra; The Starshine Orchestra and Singers; The Studio Sound Orchestra; Werner Tauber; The Tesca Allstars; Nick White

"Summer on Signal Hill": Clarence Clemons & the Red Bank Rockers; Killer Joe

"Talk to Me": Southside Johnny & the Asbury Jukes

"Tenth Avenue Freeze-Out": 1/2 Japanese; Papa Bueno; Pickin' On Springsteen (session musicians); Joe Slomp; Small Time Dave & the Windy City Groove

"This Little Girl": Gary U.S. Bonds; The Persuasions

"Thunder Road": Jaime Anglada; Badly Drawn Boy; Dan Bern; John Berry; Cowboy Junkies; Richard De Groot; Barbara Fasano; Greg Kihn; Mary Lou Lord; Kevin Rowland; The Section; Nick White

"The Ties That Bind": Eddie & the Hotrods

"Tiger Rose": Sonny Burgess

"Tougher Than the Rest": Luca Barbarossa and Alexi Lalas; Cher; Carrie Davis; Kris De Bruyne ("Taaier dan de rest," Belgian); Tomaz Domicelj ("Tebi bom pa zvest," Slovenian); Everything but the Girl; Fokke ("Ik lit dy nea wer gean," Frisian); Emmylou Harris; Greg Hawks & Tremblers; Chris LeDoux; Little Rock Country Band; The Mendoza Line; Joe Schwach; Travis Tritt

"Train Song": Robbin Thompson

"Trapped Again": Southside Johnny & the Asbury Jukes

"Tunnel of Love": Pickin' On Springsteen (session musicians)

"Two Faces Have I": Salamander Crossing; Nikolas Sirkis

"Two for the Road": The Apple Pirates

"Two Hearts": Billy Mann; Precious Metal; Mark Wright

"Used Cars": Canyon; Ani DiFranco; Paul Fuster; Tom Juravich

"Valentine's Day": Hem; Jimmy LaFave; Lucky 7

"Wages of Sin": Damien Jurado and Rose Thomas

"Walk Like a Man": Graziano Romani

"Walking Through Midnight": Southside Johnny & the Asbury Jukes

"The Way": Graziano Romani

"When You Dance": Southside Johnny & the Asbury Jukes

"When You Need Me": Blueberry Hill

"With Every Wish": Tom Varner

"Wreck on the Highway": Flor; John Wesley Harding; Nils Lofgren

"You Mean So Much To Me": Southside Johnny & the Asbury Jukes

"Youngstown": Dean Sapp & The Hartford Express

"Your Love": Gary U.S. Bonds; Io vorrei la pelle nera (Italian)

His Beautiful Rewards: Industry Honors

Grammy Awards

1984: Best Male Rock Vocal Performance, "Dancing in the Dark"

1987: Best Male Rock Vocal Performance, *Tunnel of Love*

1994: Song of the Year, "Streets of Philadelphia;" Best Male Rock Vocal Performance, "Streets of Philadelphia;" Best Rock Song, "Streets of Philadelphia"; Best Song Written Specifically For a Motion Picture or Television, "Streets of Philadelphia"

1996: Best Contemporary Folk Album, *The Ghost of Tom Joad*

2002: Best Male Rock Vocal Performance, "The Rising"; Best Rock Album, *The Rising*; Best Rock Song, "The Rising"

2003: Best Rock Performance by a Duo or Group with Vocal, "Disorder in the House" with Warren Zevon

2004: Best Solo Rock Vocal Performance, "Code of Silence"

American Music Awards

1985: Favorite Pop/Rock Single, "Born in the U.S.A."

1986: Favorite Pop/Rock Male Artist; Favorite Pop/Rock Album, *Born in the U.S.A.*; Favorite Pop/Rock Male Video Artist

For You: Springsteeen Tribute Albums

Cover Me: Songs by Bruce Springsteen (Rhino, 1984)

The first Springsteen tribute album collected versions of Springsteen songs written for and/or recorded by others, including hits such as Patti Smith's "Because the Night" and the Pointer Sisters' "Fire."

Tracks: "From Small Things (Big Things One Day Come)," Dave Edmunds; "Talk to Me," Southside Johnny & the Asbury Jukes; "Club Soul City," Gary U.S. Bonds with Chuck Jackson; "Reason to Believe," the Beat Farmers; "The Fever," Southside Johnny & the Asbury Jukes; "Because the Night," Patti Smith Group; "For You," Greg Kihn; "Fire," Pointer Sisters; "Love on the Wrong Side of Town," Southside Johnny & the Asbury Jukes; "4th of July, Asbury Park (Sandy)," the Hollies; "This Little Girl," Gary U.S. Bonds; "Johnny 99," Johnny Cash; "Rendezvous," Greg Kihn Band; "Atlantic City," the Reivers; "Hearts of Stone," Southside Johnny & the Asbury Jukes.

The Bruce Springsteen Songbook (Connoisseur, 1996)

Like 1984's *Cover Me*, a collection of previously recorded Springsteen covers.

Tracks: "Blinded by the Light," Manfred Mann's Earth Band; "For You," Greg Kihn; "Fire," Pointer Sisters; "Jeannie Needs a Shooter," Warren Zevon; "Light of Day," Little River Band; "Angelyne," Gary U.S. Bonds; "From Small Things (Big Things One Day Come)," Dave Edmunds; "Born to Run," Frankie Goes to Hollywood; "Reason to Believe," Beat Farmers; "State Trooper," Cowboy Junkies; "Factory," Arizona Smoke Revue; "Tougher Than the Rest," Everything but the Girl; "Mansion on the Hill," Emmylou Harris & the Nash Ramblers; "Homestead," Joe Grushecky.

One Step Up/Two Steps Back: The Songs of Bruce Springsteen (The Right Stuff, 1997)

An ambitious collection, with one disc of Springsteen favorites and another of rare and unrecorded songs, plus an EP that was released prior to the album. A dollar from the sale of each copy was donated to Harry Chapin's World Hunger Year.

Tracks: CD 1—"Something in the Night," Aram; "Downbound Train," the Smithereens; "Atlantic City," Kurt Neumann; "Jackson Cage," John Wesley Harding; "Wreck on the Highway," Nils Lofgren; "Johnny 99," John Hiatt; "Seeds," Dave Alvin; "Light of Day," Joe Grushecky & the Houserockers; "Darkness on the Edge of Town," Martin Zellar; "Janey Don't You Lose Heart," Mrs. Fun and Tina & The B-Side Movement; "All or Nothin' at All," Marshall Crenshaw; "Meeting Across the River," Syd Straw; "4th of July, Asbury Park (Sandy)," Ben E. King; "One Step Up," Paul Cebar.

CD 2—"Don't Look Back," the Knack; "Protection," Donna Summer; "Human Touch," Joe Cocker; "Stolen Car," Elliott Murphy; "It's Hard to Be a Saint in the City," David Bowie; "Restless Nights," Rocking Chairs; "Guilty," Robbin Thompson; "Tiger Rose," Sonny Burgess; "Love's on the Line," Gary U.S. Bonds; "Savin' Up," Clarence Clemons & the Red Bank Rockers.

EP—"Atlantic City," Kurt Neumann; "I Wish I Were Blind," the Yell Leaders; "My Beautiful Reward," the Bumpin' Uglies; "Mary, Queen of Arkansas," Dusty Wright; "Bye Bye Johnny" (alternate Cajun version), Joe D'Urso & Stone Caravan.

Pickin' On Springsteen (CMH, 1999)

This group of Nashville players—led by producer and multi-instrumentalist David West—has picked on seemingly everybody, up to and including Metallica. Springsteen got picked on not once but twice, with a second volume in 2003.

Tracks—"Prove It All Night," "I'm on Fire," "Cover Me," "Born to Run," "Hungry Heart," "Tunnel of Love," "Glory Days," "Blinded by the Light," "Born in the U.S.A.," "Brilliant Disguise," "Dancing in the Dark," "Streets of Philadelphia."

The Songs of Bruce Springsteen (Capitol, 2000)

A separate release of the first disc from 1997's two-CD tribute *One Step Up/Two Steps Back: The Songs of Bruce Springsteen.*

Tracks: "Something in the Night," Aram; "Downbound Train," the Smithereens; "Atlantic City," Kurt Neumann; "Jackson Cage," John Wesley Harding; "Wreck on the Highway," Nils Lofgren; "Johnny 99," John Hiatt; "Seeds," Dave Alvin; "Light of Day," Joe Grushecky & the Houserockers; "Darkness on the Edge of Town," Martin Zellar; "Janey Don't You Lose Heart," Mrs. Fun and Tina & The B-Side Movement; "All or Nothin' at All," Marshall Crenshaw; "Meeting Across the River," Syd Straw; "4th of July, Asbury Park (Sandy)," Ben E. King; "One Step Up," Paul Cebar.

Badlands: A Tribute to Bruce Springsteen's Nebraska (Sub Pop, 2000)

Producer Jim Sampas took a unique approach to his Springsteen tribute by paying homage to just one album, 1982's surprising solo release, *Nebraska*. It is widely regarded as one of the most successful Springsteen tributes.

Tracks: "Nebraska," Chrissie Hynde and Adam Seymour; "Atlantic City," Hank Williams III; "Mansion on the Hill," Crooked Fingers; "Johnny 99," Los Lobos; "Highway Patrolman," Dar Williams; "State Trooper," Deana Carter; "Used Cars," Ani DiFranco; "Open All Night," Son Volt; "My Father's House," Ben Harper; "Reason to Believe," Aimee Mann and Michael Penn; "I'm on Fire," Johnny Cash; "Downbound Train," Raul Malo; "Wages of Sin," Damien Jurado and Rosie Thomas.

Bruce Springsteen Tribute: Made in the U.S.A. (Purple Pyramid, 2001)

An eclectic set of interpretations—Uillean pipes on "Born in the U.S.A.," a Beach Boy singing "Hungry Heart," a former Guns N' Roses touring band member's rootsy take on "57 Channels (And Nothin' On)." Many of the songs surfaced two years later on the truncated *A Tribute to Bruce Springsteen*.

Tracks: "Born in the U.S.A.," Eric Rigler; "Born to Run," Jerry Lawson and Jimmy Hayes; "Hungry Heart," Mike Love; "I'm on Fire," Little Milton; "Brilliant Disguise," Ronnie Spector; "Interlude #1," Lanny Cordola; "If I Should Fall Behind," Richard Furay; "Adam Raised a Cain," Sandra Stephens; "Streets of Philadelphia," Khaleel and Bob Bronx Style; "Interlude #2"/"57 Channels (and Nothin' On)," Teddy Zig Zag; "My Hometown," Robin McAuley; "My Beautiful Reward," Lanny Cordola; "Born in the U.S.A." (reprise), Eric Rigler.

Reason to Believe: A Country Music Tribute to Bruce Springsteen (Rhino, 2002)

Exactly what the title says it is, with previously recorded covers of Springsteen songs by some of Nashville's finest, plus former Hollies singer Allan Clarke's version of "Blinded by the Light."

Tracks: "Thunder Road," John Berry; "Tougher Than the Rest," Travis Tritt; "Cadillac Ranch," Nitty Gritty Dirt Band; "The Price You Pay," Emmylou Harris; "Atlantic City," Hank Williams III; "Pink Cadillac," Southern Pacific; "Reason to Believe," the Beat Farmers; "State Trooper," Steve Earle; "Angelyne," Nitty Gritty Dirt Band; "Blinded by the Light," Allan Clarke.

Hometown: The String Quartet Tribute to Bruce Springsteen (Vitamin, 2002)

The String Quartet hasn't found too many artists it isn't willing to pay homage to, and Springsteen certainly falls within the chamber ensemble's aesthetic parameters. "Mansion on the Hill" is performed solo by violinist Eric Gorfain.

Tracks: "4th of July, Asbury Park (Sandy)," "Thunder Road," "Something in the Night," "Nebraska," "Atlantic City," "Mansion on the Hill," "Independence Day," "The River," "My Hometown," "Streets of Philadelphia," "Into the Fire."

A Tribute to Bruce Springsteen (Big Eye, 2003)

Selections from 2001's *Bruce Springsteen Tribute: Made in the U.S.A.* with other songs performed by an undistinguished house band.

Tracks: "Born in the U.S.A.," Eric Rigler; "Into the Fire"; "Cover Me"; "Streets of Philadelphia," Bob Khaleel; "Born to Run," Jerry Lawson and Jimmy Hayes; "Hungry Heart," Mike Love; "Paradise"; "Glory Days"; "57 Channels (and Nothin' On)," Teddy Zig Zag; "Pink Cadillac"; "I'm on Fire," Little Milton; "You're Missing"; "Dancing in the Dark."

Light of Day (Schoolhouse, 2003)

An outgrowth of the annual Light of Day benefit shows organized by Bob Benjamin, a friend of Springsteen and former manager of Joe Grushecky, to benefit the Parkinson's Disease Foundation. Proceeds from the album also went to the Kristen Ann Carr Fund. Singer-songwriter Elliott Murphy served as the artistic director for the two-CD collection of new and previously released covers.

Tracks: CD 1—"Better Days," Elliott Murphy; "Book of Dreams," Dion; "Valentine's Day," Lucky 7; "Thunder Road," Dan Bern; "Candy's Room," Crazysloth; "Johnny 99," Mystic Knights of the Sea; "Man at the Top," Nils Lofgren; "If I Should Fall Behind," Cindy Bullens; "Something in the Night," Matthew Ryan; "Atlantic City," Mike Rimbaud; "Highway Patrolman," Sid Griffin; "Mansion on the Hill," Billy Bragg & the Blokes; "Badlands," Joe D'Urso & Stone Caravan; "State Trooper," Steve Wynn; "I Ain't Got You," Gary Lucas' Gods and Monsters; "Bobby Jean," Jennifer

Glass; "The River," the Clarks; "Back in Your Arms," Marc Broussard; "The E Street Shuffle," John Cafferty & the Beaver Brown Band.

CD2—"Brilliant Disguise," Elvis Costello; "New York City Serenade," Pete Yorn; "Pink Cadillac," Graham Parker; "Streets of Philadelphia," Garland Jeffreys; "My Hometown," Jason Ringenberg; "Light of Day," Joe Grushecky & the Houserockers; "Lucky Town," Rosie Flores; "I'm on Fire," Willie Nile; "Downbound Train," Kirk Kelly; "Stolen Car," Patty Griffin; "Souls of the Departed," Paradise Brothers; "Two Hearts," Mark Wright; "The Promise," Graziano Romani; "For You," the Format; "Hungry Heart," Jesse Malin; "Secret Garden," Tom Cochrane and Damhnait Doyle; "Born to Run," Cowboy Mouth; "Working on the Highway," Joe Ely.

Pickin' On Springsteen, Vol. 2 (CMH, 2003)

David West and his company of Nashville musicians goes back to the Springsteen well a second time, even tossing in an original—"Jersey Beat"—inspired by The Boss.

Tracks: "Pink Cadillac," "One Step Up," "Atlantic City," "The Rising," "Tenth Avenue Freeze-Out," "Independence Day," "Growing Up," "Badlands," "My Beautiful Rewards," "Jersey Beat."

The B Street Band

The B Street Band was formed in May of 1980 in Asbury Park, New Jersey, as Backstreets. Its first gig drew 2,000 fans to an Asbury Park club called Park Place and
established the tribute act as a viable commodity. The group carved out a market
that encompasses 400 venues and 150 colleges in fifteen states, plus the
Bahamas. Several E Street Band members have sat in with the B Streeters, who
have also played on television's "Late Night with Conan O'Brien" and on Howard
Stern's radio show. (www.bmaent.com/b_street_band.htm)

Born to Run

A five-piece band from the U.K. led by Mark Priestley, Born to Run works with a repertoire of more than three dozen songs, including rarities such as "Stand on It,"
"Back in Your Arms," and "Seven Angels." (www.born-to-run.co.uk)

Brooce: The Show

Brooce: The Show's frontman Jerry Castello worked in New York's World Trade Center
until the September 11 terrorist attacks in 2001, after which he was inspired to
create this tribute to his musical hero. Recruiting some ace players, including former George Benson bassist Stanley Banks and Sony recording artist Dominico on
backing vocals, Brooce: The Show built its ninety-minute "Rock and Roll Opera"
with songs from throughout Springsteen's career, right up to *The Rising*.
(www.brooce.net)

Lucky Town Band

Fronted by singer-guitarist Tim Sigler, the group from Minnesota's Twin Cities area
works with a wide array of Springsteen material, including songs from *The Rising*.
(www.luckytownband.com)

Steel Mill Retro featuring Vini Lopez

If anyone has the right to do a Springsteen tribute band, it's one of the musicians who
played with him. Original E Street Band drummer Vini "Mad Dog" Lopez's venture

is a different animal, however; with Springsteen's blessings, Lopez is recreating Steel Mill, the hard rock band that featured the two men—along with future E Streeters Danny Federici and Steve Van Zandt—in 1969–70. Lopez's quartet recreates Steel Mill's repertoire along with "some songs that we just like to play." (www.steelmillretro.com)

Stone Pony

This is the band, not the club—in fact, a nine-piece Cleveland ensemble that pays tribute to the Jersey Shore scene with a repertoire that mixes Springsteen tunes with selections from the Southside Johnny & the Asbury Jukes catalog, along with the Ides of March's *Vehicle*. (www.stoneponyband.com)

Tramps Like Us

This New York sextet has one of the most ambitious repertoires of any Springsteen tribute band, with more than sixty songs in its catalog. Original E Street Band drummer Vini "Mad Dog" Lopez has sat in with the group, along with members of the Asbury Jukes and the Beaver Brown Band. Tramps' Web site even boasts a fawning testimonial from original Springsteen manager Mike Appel. (http://members.aol.com/trampslike/)

The Hungry and the Hunted:
Lyric Index

The Ladies

Angel ("Don't Look Back," *Tracks*)

Angel from Innerlake, an ("Thundercrack," *Tracks*)

Aunt, my ("Cadillac Ranch," *The River*)

Backstreet girls, the ("Jungleland," *Born to Run*)

Barefoot girl ("Jungleland," *Born to Run*)

Blonde girls pledged sweet sixteen ("The E Street Shuffle," *The Wild, the Innocent & the E Street Shuffle*)

Bloodshot forget-me-not, some ("Blinded by the Light," *Greetings from Asbury Park, N.J.*)

Bride, my ("Walk Like a Man," *Tunnel of Love*)

Broadway Mary ("Does This Bus Stop at 82nd Street?," *Greetings from Asbury Park, N.J.*)

Candy ("Candy's Room," *Darkness on the Edge of Town*)

Carol ("County Fair," *The Essential Bruce Springsteen*)

Catherine LeFevre ("Car Wash," *Tracks*)

Cherry ("Meeting Across the River," *Born to Run*)

Counter girl, a ("Living on the Edge of the World," *Tracks*)

Crazy Janey ("Spirit in the Night," *Greetings from Asbury Park, N.J.*)

Cynthia ("Cynthia," *Tracks*)

Diamond Jackie ("New York City Serenade," *The Wild, the Innocent & the E Street Shuffle*)

Dinah ("Bishop Danced," *Tracks*)

Dirty Annie ("You Can Look [But You Better Not Touch]," *The River*)

Doreen ("With Every Wish," *Human Touch*)

Factory girls, the ("4th of July, Asbury Park [Sandy]," *The Wild, the Innocent & the E Street Shuffle*)

Fire alley virgins ("So Young and in Love," *Tracks*)

Fish lady ("New York City Serenade," *The Wild, the Innocent & the E Street Shuffle*)

Fleshpot mascot, some ("Blinded by the Light," *Greetings from Asbury Park, N.J.*)

Fontaine, Joan ("Does This Bus Stop at 82nd Street?," *Greetings from Asbury Park, N.J.*)

Frankie ("Frankie," *Tracks*)

Girl in Calgary, a ("Lucky Man," *Tracks*)

Girl standing by the band, a ("None but the Brave," *The Essential Bruce Springsteen*)

Girl that lives down the block, a ("Glory Days," *Born in the U.S.A.*)

Gloria ("Gloria's Eyes," *Human Touch*)

Gypsy, the ("Lucky Man," *Tracks*)

Hard girl over on Easy Street, the ("Incident on 57th Street," *The Wild, the Innocent & the E Street Shuffle*)

Tainted women in Vistavision ("Does This Bus Stop at 82nd Street?," *Greetings from Asbury Park, N.J.*)

Thumbscrew woman, a ("Bishop Danced," *Tracks*)

Terry ("Backstreets," *Born to Run*)

Waitress I was seeing, that ("4th of July, Asbury Park [Sandy]," *The Wild, the Innocent & the E Street Shuffle*)

Wanda ("Open All Night," *Nebraska*)

Wendy ("Born to Run," *Born to Run*)

Wife, my ("Darkness on the Edge of Town," *Darkness on the Edge of Town*)

The Dudes

All-hot half-shot, some ("Blinded by the Light," *Greetings from Asbury Park, N.J.*)

Bad Scooter ("Tenth Avenue Freeze-Out," *Born to Run*)

Barker, the ("Wild Billy's Circus Story," *The Wild, the Innocent & the E Street Shuffle*)

Big baseball player, a ("Glory Days," *Born in the U.S.A.*)

Big Bones Billy ("Rosalita [Come Out Tonight]," *The Wild, the Innocent & the E Street Shuffle*)

Bill Horton ("Cautious Man," *Tunnel of Love*)

Billy ("Spirit in the Night," *Greetings from Asbury Park, N.J.*; "New York City Serenade," *The Wild, the Innocent & the E Street Shuffle*; "Bishop Danced," *Tracks*; "Seaside Bar Song," *Tracks*; "Rockaway the Days," *Tracks*; "Gave It a Name," *Tracks*; "The Big Muddy," *Lucky Town*)

Billy Devon ("Brothers Under the Bridge," *Tracks*)

Billy Sutter ("Galveston Bay," *The Ghost of Tom Joad*)

Black boys, them ("Incident on 57th Street," *The Wild, the Innocent & the E Street Shuffle*)

Blind Terry ("Zero & Blind Terry," *Tracks*)

Bobby ("Shut Out the Light," *Tracks*; "Glory Days," *Born in the U.S.A.*; "Spare Parts," *Tunnel of Love*; "Stand on It," *Tracks*; "With Every Wish," *Human Touch*; "Murder Incorporated," *Greatest Hits*; "The Big Payback," *The Essential Bruce Springsteen*)

Bobby Jean ("Bobby Jean," *Born in the U.S.A.*)

Bobby Ramirez ("The Line," *The Ghost of Tom Joad*)

Border boys, the ("Balboa Park," *The Ghost of Tom Joad*)

Boss man, the ("Night," *Born to Run*)

Boy prophets, the ("The E Street Shuffle," *The Wild, the Innocent & the E Street Shuffle*)

Boys from the casino dance, the ("4th of July, Asbury Park [Sandy]," *The Wild, the Innocent & the E Street Shuffle*)

Brimstone baritone anticyclone rolling stone preacher from the East, some ("Blinded by the Light," *Greetings from Asbury Park, N.J.*)

Bronx's best apostle ("Lost in the Flood," *Greetings from Asbury Park, N.J.*)

Bus driver ("Does This Bus Stop at 82nd Street?," *Greetings from Asbury Park, N.J.*)

Cannoneer, the ("Bishop Danced," *Tracks*)

Charles ("American Skin [41 Shots]," *Live in New York City*)

Charlie ("Straight Time," *The Ghost of Tom Joad*)

Circus boss, the ("Wild Billy's Circus Story," *The Wild, the Innocent & the E Street Shuffle*)

Circus boy ("Wild Billy's Circus Story," *The Wild, the Innocent & the E Street Shuffle*)

City dude, a ("Kitty's Back," *The Wild, the Innocent & the E Street Shuffle*)

Cochise ("Balboa Park," *The Ghost of Tom Joad*)

D.A., the ("Atlantic City," *Nebraska*)

Daddy, my ("Mansion on the Hill," *Nebraska*; "Youngstown," *The Ghost of Tom Joad*)

Daddy, your ("Book of Dreams," *Lucky Town*)

Damn fool with a guitar, some ("Held Up Without a Gun," *The Essential Bruce Springsteen*)

Dan, a handsome ("Tougher Than the Rest," *Tunnel of Love*)

Darlin' yearling sharp boy, the ("New York City Serenade," *The Wild, the Innocent & the E Street Shuffle*)

Downtown Boys, them ("It's Hard to Be a Saint in the City," *Greetings from Asbury Park, N.J.*)

Dude from L.A., this ("Racing in the Street," *Darkness on the Edge of Town*)

Dude in white ("Kitty's Back," *The Wild, the Innocent & the E Street Shuffle*)

Dude with a calling card, some ("Blinded by the Light," *Greetings from Asbury Park, N.J.*)

E Street brats ("The E Street Shuffle," *The Wild, the Innocent & the E Street Shuffle*)

Eddie ("Meeting Across the River," *Born to Run*; "Linda Let Me Be the One," *Tracks*)

Eighth Avenue sailors ("Lost in the Flood," *Greetings from Asbury Park, N.J.*)

Fat man sitting on a little stool ("Tunnel of Love," *Tunnel of Love*)

Fire eater, the ("Wild Billy's Circus Story," *The Wild, the Innocent & the E Street Shuffle*)

Foreman, my ("From Small Things [Big Things One Day Come]," *The Essential Bruce Springsteen*)

Foreman, the ("Out in the Street," *The River*; "My Hometown," *Born in the U.S.A.*)

Frank ("This Hard Land," *Greatest Hits* and *Tracks*; "The New Timer," *The Ghost of Tom Joad*)

Frankie ("Independence Day," *The River*; "Highway Patrolman," *Nebraska*)

Fresh-sown moonstone, some ("Blinded by the Light," *Greetings from Asbury Park, N.J.*)

Friend, a ("The Big Muddy," *Lucky Town*)

Friend of mine, a ("Valentine's Day," *Tunnel of Love*)

Gamblin' commissioner, the ("Atlantic City," *Nebraska*)

Gasoline boys, them ("It's Hard to Be a Saint in the City," *Greetings from Asbury Park, N.J.*)

Gavachos, the ("Balboa Park," *The Ghost of Tom Joad*)

Golden-heeled fairies, them ("Incident on 57th Street," *The Wild, the Innocent & the E Street Shuffle*)

Greasers, the ("4th of July, Asbury Park [Sandy]," *The Wild, the Innocent & the E Street Shuffle*)

Groom ("Reason to Believe," *Nebraska*)

Gypsy, the ("Brilliant Disguise," *Tunnel of Love*)

Gypsy man, the ("Over the Rise," *Tracks*)

Hazard from Harvard, some ("Blinded by the Light," *Greetings from Asbury Park, N.J.*)

Hazy Davy ("Spirit in the Night," *Greetings from Asbury Park, N.J.*)

Hired hand, the ("Wild Billy's Circus Story," *The Wild, the Innocent & the E Street Shuffle*)

Hiring man ("Born in the U.S.A.," *Born in the U.S.A.*)

Hueros, the ("Sinaloa Cowboys," *The Ghost of Tom Joad*)

Human cannonball, the ("Wild Billy's Circus Story," *The Wild, the Innocent & the E Street Shuffle*)

Iceman, the ("Iceman," *Tracks*)

Jack Knife ("Kitty's Back," *The Wild, the Innocent & the E Street Shuffle*)

Jack the Rabbit ("Rosalita [Come Out Tonight]," *The Wild, the Innocent & the E Street Shuffle*)

Jazz man (aka vibes man) ("New York City Serenade," *The Wild, the Innocent & the E Street Shuffle*)

Jimmy Lee ("Stand on It," *Tracks*)

Jimmy the Saint (aka the pure American brother) ("Lost in the Flood," *Greetings from Asbury Park, N.J.*)

Joe ("Downbound Train," *Born in the U.S.A.*)

Joe, a good-lookin' ("Tougher Than the Rest," *Tunnel of Love*, "Nothing Man," *The Rising*)

Joe Roberts ("Highway Patrolman," *Nebraska*)

Joey ("Brothers Under the Bridges," *Tracks*)

Johnny ("Johnny Bye Bye," *Tracks*; "Reason to Believe," *Nebraska*; "When You're Alone," *Tunnel of Love*)

Johnny 99 (aka Ralph) ("Johnny 99," *Nebraska*)

Johnson (Johnny) Leneir ("Shut Out the Light," *Tracks*)

Judge, the ("Working on the Highway," *Born in the U.S.A.*; "57 Channels [and Nothin' On]," *Human Touch*)

Junk man, your ("New York City Serenade," *The Wild, the Innocent & the E Street Shuffle*)

Kidnapped handicap, some ("Blinded by the Light," *Greetings from Asbury Park, N.J.*)

Killer Joe ("Spirit in the Night," *Greetings from Asbury Park, N.J.*)

King on a white horse ("Gloria's Eyes," *Human Touch*)

Real and Literary Figures

Houston, Sam ("Santa Ana," *Tracks*)
James Bond ("I'm a Rocker," *The River*)
Jesus ("It's Hard to Be a Saint in the City," *Greetings from Asbury Park, N.J.*; "Wild Billy's Circus Story," *The Wild, the Innocent & the E Street Shuffle*; "The New Timer," *The Ghost of Tom Joad*)
Jesus's son ("Leap of Faith," *Lucky Town*)
Junior Johnson ("Cadillac Ranch," *The River*)
Kid Colt ("Santa Ana," *Tracks*)
King Farouk ("Ain't Got You," *Tunnel of Love*)
Kojak ("I'm a Rocker," *The River*)
Lee, Bruce ("Local Hero," *Lucky Town*)
Moses ("Leap of Faith," *Lucky Town*)
Orbison, Roy ("Thunder Road," *Born to Run*)
Presley, Elvis ("Johnny Bye-Bye," *Tracks*; "57 Channels [and Nothin' On]," *Human Touch*)
Pope, the ("Local Hero," *Lucky Town*)
Prince Charming ("Gloria's Eyes," *Human Touch*)
Queen Isabella ("Stand on It," *Tracks*)
Rambo ("Real Man," *Human Touch*)
Rembrandt ("Ain't Got You," *Tunnel of Love*)
Reynolds, Burt ("Cadillac Ranch," *The River*)
Rockefeller ("Crush on You," *The River*)
Romeo, a sweet-talkin' ("Tougher Than the Rest," *Tunnel of Love*)
Romeo and Juliet ("Point Blank," *The River*; "Fire," *Live/1975–85*)
Samson and Delilah ("Fire," *Live/1975–85*)
Santa Ana ("Santa Ana," *Tracks*)
Satan ("Santa Ana," *Tracks*; "Wages of Sin," *Tracks*)
Sleeping Beauty ("Countin' on a Miracle," *The Rising*)
Tom Joad ("The Ghost of Tom Joad," *The Ghost of Tom Joad*)
Venus de Milo ("Crush on You," *The River*)
Virgin Mary ("The Rising," *The Rising*)

Roads

A and Twelfth ("The Big Muddy," *Lucky Town*)
Alvarado Street ("Dry Lightning," *The Ghost of Tom Joad*)
Avenue, the ("Point Blank," *The River*; "Streets of Philadelphia," *Greatest Hits*)
Baker Street ("Don't Look Back," *Tracks*)
Bleecker Street ("Kitty's Back," *The Wild, the Innocent & the E Street Shuffle*)
Bluebird Street ("Ramrod," *The River*)
Bond Street ("The Wish," *Tracks*)
Broadway ("New York City Serenade," *The Wild, the Innocent & the E Street Shuffle*)
Cason Street ("Linda Let Me Be the One," *Tracks*)
Chelsea Road ("Frankie," *Tracks*)
Dixie highway, that ("Darlington County," *Born in the U.S.A.*)
Dusty beach road, this ("Thunder Road," *Born to Run*)
Dusty road from Monroe to Angeline ("Prove It All Night," *Darkness on the Edge of Town*)
E Street ("The E Street Shuffle," *The Wild, the Innocent & the E Street Shuffle*)
Easy Street ("Incident on 57th Street," *The Wild, the Innocent & the E Street Shuffle*)
Eighth Avenue ("Lost in the Flood," *Greetings from Asbury Park, N.J.*)
82nd Street ("Does This Bus Stop at 82nd Street?," *Greetings from Asbury Park, N.J.*)
Eldridge Avenue ("Stolen Car," *The River*)
Flamingo Lane ("Jungleland," *Born to Run*)
Fifty-third Street ("Sherry Darling," *The River*)
57th Street ("Incident on 57th Street," *The Wild, the Innocent & the E Street Shuffle*)
Highway, the ("Night," *Born to Run*; "Born to Run," *Born to Run*; "Sherry Darling," *The River*; "Independence Day," *The River*; "Cadillac Ranch," *The River*; "The Price You Pay," *The River*; "Reason to Believe," *Nebraska*; "Valentine's Day," *Tunnel of Love*; "The Ghost of Tom Joad," *The Ghost of Tom Joad*; "The Fuse," *The Rising*; "Seaside Bar Song," *Tracks*; "Take 'em as They Come," *Tracks*; "Brothers Under the Bridges," *Tracks*; "County Fair," *The Essential Bruce Springsteen*)
Highway One ("Held Up Without a Gun," *The Essential Bruce Springsteen*)
Highway 9 ("Born to Run," *Born to Run*)
Highway 29 ("Highway 29," *The Ghost of Tom Joad*)
Highway 31 ("Reason to Believe," *Nebraska*)
Interstate, the ("The Angel," *Greetings from Asbury Park, N.J.*; "Racing in the Street," *Darkness on the Edge of Town*)

You Can Look...:
Promotional Music Videos

"Rosalita (Come Out Tonight)"
Director: Arnold Levine
Filmed: July 8, 1978, Veterans Memorial Coliseum, Phoenix, AZ
B-roll: Used mostly for TV, this did not become an "official" clip until its May 16, 1984, appearance on MTV.

"Atlantic City"
Director: Arnold Levine
Filmed: Fall 1982, Atlantic City, NJ
B-roll: Springsteen's first "official" video to promote an album.

"Dancing in the Dark"
Director: Brian DePalma
Filmed: June 28–29, 1984, Civic Centre, St. Paul, MN
B-roll: A live performance video during which Springsteen pulls future "Friends" star Courteney Cox on stage to dance with him at the end of the song.

"Born in the U.S.A."
Director: John Sayles
Filmed: October–November, 1984, Sports Arena, Los Angeles, CA, and various New Jersey locations.
B-roll: Sayles filmed performances during a seven-night stand in Los Angeles. The E Street Band members had to wear the same clothes for continuity and Springsteen's beard stubble had to be trimmed to the same length each day.

"I'm on Fire"
Director: John Sayles
Filmed: February 1985, Los Angeles, CA
B-roll: Springsteen's "acting" debut earned Best Male Video honors at the 1985 MTV Music Video Awards.

"Glory Days"
Director: John Sayles
Filmed: May 1985, West New York, Hoboken, and Secaucus, NJ
B-roll: Steve Van Zandt returns to the E Street Band to play his mandolin solo in the bar scene.

"My Hometown"
Director: Arthur Rosato
Filmed: September 27–October 2, 1984, Los Angeles Coliseum, Los Angeles, CA
B-roll: The first of the *Born in the U.S.A.* videos to be ready and out before the single was actually released.

"War"
Director: Arthur Rosato
Filmed: September 27–October 2, 1984, Los Angeles Coliseum, Los Angeles, CA
B-roll: Nominated for Best Stage Performance at the 1987 MTV Video Music Awards. Lost to fellow New Jerseyan Bon Jovi's "Livin' on a Prayer."

"Fire"
Editor: Arthur Rosato

Filmed: October 13, 1986, Shoreline Amphitheatre, Mountain View, CA

B-roll: Footage comes from Springsteen's acoustic performance at Neil Young's Bridge Benefit Concert. E Street Band members Nils Lofgren and Danny Federici also appear.

"Born to Run"
Director: Arthur Rosato

Filmed: Various locations on the *Born in the U.S.A.* tour

B-roll: Voted Best Officially Released Video Clip by *Backstreets* magazine readers in 1990.

"Brilliant Disguise"
Director: Meiert Avis

Filmed: October 1987, Sandy Hook, NJ

B-roll: Rather than lip-sync, Springsteen sang live for all twenty takes.

"Tunnel of Love"
Director: Meiert Avis

Filmed: November 1987, Asbury Park and Seaside Heights, NJ

B-roll: Partly filmed at Palace Amusements in Asbury Park.

"One Step Up"
Director: Meiert Avis

Filmed: February 1988, the Wonder Bar, Asbury Park, NJ

B-roll: The Wonder Bar is where Springsteen first saw Clarence Clemons play, when the saxophonist was with Norman Seldin's Joyful Noise.

"Tougher Than the Rest"
Director: Meiert Avis

Filmed: April 27–28, 1988, Los Angeles Sports Arena, Los Angeles, CA

B-roll: Filmed for European television before its release on *Video Anthology/1978–88*.

"Spare Parts"
Director: Carol Dodds

Filmed: July 9, 1988, Bramall Lane Stadium, Sheffield, England

B-roll: Another clip done first for European TV.

"Human Touch"
Director: Meiert Avis

Filmed: Late January and early February 1992, New Orleans, LA

B-roll: Springsteen shirtless!

"Better Days"
Director: Meiert Avis

Filmed: Spring 1992, Hollywood Center Studios, Hollywood, CA

B-roll: "American Idol" judge Randy Jackson, who played on the *Human Touch* and *Lucky Town* albums, appears in the video though he was not part of Springsteen's 1992–93 touring band.

"57 Channels (And Nothin' On)"
Director: Adam Bernstein

Filmed: Spring 1992, Los Angeles, CA

B-roll: Bernstein directed the "Saturday Night Live" spin-off movie *It's Pat*.

"Leap of Faith"
Director: Meiert Avis

Filmed: August 6, 1992, Brendan Byrne Arena, East Rutherford, NJ

B-roll: Springsteen and his band performed the song twice at the concert in order to accommodate the video shoot.

"Streets of Philadelphia"
Directors: Jonathan and Ted Demme

Filmed: December 6–7, 1993, Philadelphia, PA and Camden, NJ

B-roll: After filming, Springsteen made a $45,000 donation to the Solomon Sacks Playground, one of the sites used for the video.

"Murder Incorporated"
Director: Jonathan Demme

Filmed: February 21, 1995, Tramps, New York, NY

B-roll: First live performance by the E Street Band in more than six years.

"Secret Garden"
Director: Peter Care

Filmed: Spring 1995, Los Angeles, CA.

B-roll: Nominated for Best Video From a Film at the 1997 MTV Video Music Awards after *Jerry Maguire* made the song a belated hit.

"Hungry Heart (Berlin '95)"
Directors: Rudi Dolezal and Hannes Rossacher

Filmed: July 9, 1995, Cafe Eckstein and other locations, Berlin, Germany

B-roll: Filmed performance with German musicians for European TV.

"Dead Man Walking"
Director: Tim Robbins

Filmed: January 22, 1996, Saeingor Center, New Orleans, LA

B-roll: Sister Helen Prejean, the subject of Robbins' film, was in the audience at the *Tom Joad* tour show where the video was filmed.

"The Rising"

Director: Danny Clinch

Filmed: Spring 2002, New Jersey

B-roll: Surprisingly, never released as an "official" promotional clip.

"Lonesome Day"

Director: Mark Pellington

Filmed: September 2002, Belmar, Sandy Hook, and other New Jersey locations

B-roll: Occasionally aired on Country Music Television (CMT).

"Countin' on a Miracle"

Director: Danny Clinch

Filmed: 2002, Southern Tracks Studio, Atlanta, GA

B-roll: Solo acoustic performance shown at end of shows on *The Rising* tour.

"Waitin' on a Sunny Day"

Director: Chris Hilson

Filmed: October 16, 2002, Palau Sant Jordi, Barcelona, Spain

B-roll: Footage from show filmed for *Live in Barcelona* DVD.

Home Entertainment Was My Baby's Wish: Springsteen on Television

July 7, 1978

KABC-TV Los Angeles

Interview and live footage of "Prove It All Night" and "Rosalita (Come Out Tonight)"

July 19, 1988

DDR2 (East Germany)

Taped concert from earlier in the evening at Weissensee Cycling Track, East Berlin, minus six songs

May 9, 1992

"Saturday Night Live" (NBC)

"Lucky Town," "57 Channels (And Nothin' On)," "Living Proof" (Springsteen's first-ever live TV performance)

June 25, 1993

"Late Night with David Letterman" (NBC)

"Glory Days" (Letterman's last show for NBC)

March 1, 1994

"The 1994 Grammy Awards" (CBS)

Tribute to Curtis Mayfield

March 21, 1994

"The 66th Annual Academy Awards" (ABC)

"Streets of Philadelphia"

September 9, 1994

"MTV Music Video Awards" (MTV)

"Streets of Philadelphia"

February 15, 1995

"MTV Unplugged" (MTV)

"Thunder Road" with Melissa Etheridge

February 23, 1995

"Nulle Part Ailleurs" (France)

Interview and performance of "The Ghost of Tom Joad"

March 1, 1995

"The 1995 Grammy Awards" (CBS)

"Streets of Philadelphia"

April 5, 1995

"The Late Show with David Letterman" (CBS)

"Murder Incorporated," "Tenth Avenue Freeze-Out" (off camera), "Secret Garden"

November 27, 1995

"The Tonight Show" (NBC)

"The Ghost of Tom Joad"

December 14, 1995

"The Late Show with David Letterman" (CBS)

"Youngstown"

December 14, 1995

"Sinatra: 80 Years My Way" (ABC)

"Angel Eyes" (taped November 19, 1995)

March 25, 1996

"The 68th Annual Academy Awards" (ABC)

"Dead Man Walking"

January 21, 1996

"60 Minutes" (CBS)

Interview with Ed Bradley

February 20, 1996

"San Remo Song Festival" (Italy)

"The Ghost of Tom Joad"

September 4, 1997

"MTV Video Music Awards" (MTV)

"One Headlight" with the Wallflowers

May 21, 1998

"Rolling Stone State of the Union" (ABC)

"The Ghost of Tom Joad," "Across the Border"

December 6, 1998

"Dateline NBC" (NBC)

Interview with Bob Costas

December 7–8, 1998

"Today" (NBC)

Segments from Bob Costas interview

December 8, 1998

"Sen Kvall med Luuk (Late Night with Luuk)" (TV Sweden)

"Born in the U.S.A."

December 9, 1998

"Nulle Part Ailleurs" (French TV)

"Born in the U.S.A."

December 11, 1998

"Taratata-TV" (Italian TV)

"Born in the U.S.A.," "This Hard Land"

December 14, 1998

"Musica Si" (Spain)

"Born in the U.S.A.," "This Hard Land"

December 28, 1998

"The Charlie Rose Show" (PBS)

Interview and performance of "Born in the U.S.A."

February 26, 1999

"Late Night with Conan O'Brien" (NBC)

"Working on the Highway" (Springsteen ushers "Late Night" bandleader Max Weinberg off the show for the 1999–2000 E Street Band reunion tour)

March 17, 1999

"Rock and Roll Hall of Fame Induction Ceremony" (VH1)

"Darkness on the Edge of Town," "Promised Land," "Tenth Avenue Freeze-Out"

July 15, 1999

"Opening Night Live" from Continental Airlines Arena in East Rutherford, NJ (VH1)

"My Love Will Not Let You Down," "Promised Land"

March 21, 2001

"On the Record" (HBO)

Interview with Bob Costas

September 21, 2001

"America: A Tribute to Heroes" (all broadcast networks)

"My City of Ruins" (from Sony Studios in New York, NY)

December 16, 2001

"Homecoming: Bruce Springsteen and the E Street Band" (VH1)

Interview, "Thunder Road," "Ramrod," "Light of Day," "If I Should Fall Behind" (from "Live in New York City" DVD)

July 30, 2002

"Today" (NBC)

"For You" (acoustic), "The Rising," "Lonesome Day," "Glory Days," "Into the Fire" (live from Asbury Park, NJ)

July 30, 2002

"Nightline" (ABC)

Interview with Ted Koppel; includes performance of "Empty Sky"

July 30, 2002

"Up Close" (ABC)

Continuation of interview with Ted Koppel

August 1, 2002

"The Late Show with David Letterman" (CBS)

"The Rising"

August 2, 2002

"The Late Show with David Letterman" (CBS)

"Lonesome Day," interview (taped August 1)

August 29, 2002

"MTV Video Music Awards" (MTV)

"The Rising" (from Hayden Planetarium at the Museum of Natural History, New York, NY; opens the show)

October 5, 2002

"Saturday Night Live" (NBC)

"Lonesome Day," "You're Missing"

November 28, 2002

"Elvis Lives" (NBC)

Commentary as part of tribute program

February 23, 2003

"The 2003 Grammy Awards" (CBS)

"The Rising," "London Calling" (tribute to Joe Strummer, with Steve Van Zandt, Elvis Costello, and Dave Grohl)

December 11, 2002

"Late Night with Conan O'Brien" (NBC)

"Merry Christmas Baby," "Kitty's Back"

February 28, 2003

"Bruce Springsteen & the E Street Band" (CBS)

One-hour version of October 2002 concert in Barcelona, Spain originally broadcast by MTV Europe

March 21, 2004

"Rock and Roll Hall of Fame Induction Ceremony" (VH1)

Induction speech for Jackson Browne

August 4, 2004

"Nightline" (ABC)

Interview with Ted Koppel after announcement of Vote for Change tour

October 11, 2004

"Vote for Change" (Sundance Channel)

Tour finale concert from Washington, DC

April 23, 2005

"VH1 Storytellers" (VH1)

"Blinded by the Light," "Brilliant Disguise," "The Rising," "Devils & Dust," "Jesus Was an Only Son"

April 25 & 26, 2005

"Today" (NBC)

Interview, "Devils & Dust," "All I'm Thinkin' About"

Sittin' 'Round Here Trying to Write These Books: Springsteen in Print

SPRINGSTEEN BIOGRAPHIES

Born to Run: The Bruce Springsteen Story, Dave Marsh (Doubleday Dolphin, 1979, 1981)

The Boss: Bruce Springsteen, Sharon Starbrooks (New American Library, 1984)

Bruce, Tajfun Zvani (Edicija Posebna Izdanja, 1989)

Bruce Frederick Springsteen, Hugues Barriere and Mikael Ollivier (Librio Musique, 2001; Le Castor Astral, 2003)

Bruce Springsteen, Peter Basham (Pocket Essentials, 2005)

Bruce Springsteen, Teresa Noel Celsi (Armand Eisen, 1994)

Bruce Springsteen, Sergio D'Alesio (Lato Side Editori, 1981)

Bruce Springsteen, Laura Fissinger (Creative Education, 1983)

Bruce Springsteen, Ron Frankl (Chelsea House Publishers, 1994)

Bruce Springsteen, Keith Elliott Greenberg (Lerner Publications, 1986)

Bruce Springsteen, Jordi Sierra i Fabra (Editorial Empuries, 1992)

Bruce Springsteen, Ignacio Julia (Editorial La Mascara, 1995)

Bruce Springsteen, Teresa Koenig (Crestwood House, 1986)

Bruce Springsteen, Joao Lisboa (Assirio e Alvim, 1986)

Bruce Springsteen, Marianne Meyer (Ballantine Books, 1984)

Bruce Springsteen, Toni Murphy (William Collins Sons and Co. Ltd., 1986)

Bruce Springsteen, Javier Perez de Albeniz (Ediciones Jucar, 1985)

Bruce Springsteen, Steve J. Powell (Ediciones Catedra, 1994)

Bruce Springsteen, James R. Rothaus (Creative Education Inc., 1986)

Bruce Springsteen, Michael Stewart (Crescent Books, 1984)

Bruce Springsteen, Petra Zeitz (Moewig KG, 1991)

Bruce Springsteen: An American Classic, Mike Slaughter (Chester Lane Books, 1984)

Bruce Springsteen: An Independent Story in Words and Pictures, Roger St. Pierre (Anabas Publishing, 1985)

Bruce Springsteen: An Illustrated Record, Brian Barron (Proteus, 1985)

Bruce Springsteen: Blinded by the Light, Patrick Humphries and Chris Hunt (Henry Holt and Co., 1985)

Bruce Springsteen: Career of a Rock Legend, Jeff Horn (Zinn, 1999)

Bruce Springsteen de A à Z, Jean-Michel Oullion (Guides Musicbook, 2002)

Bruce Springsteen: Here and Now, Craig MacInnis and Philip Kamin (Barron's Educational Service, 1988)

The Bruce Springsteen Scrapbook, Hank Bordowitz (Citadel Press Books, 2004)

Bruce Springsteen: The Boss, Elianne Halbersberg (Sharon Publications, 1984)

Bruce Springsteen: The Boss, Nancy Robison (Modern Publishing, 1985)

Bruce Springsteen: The Boss, Julia Edenhofer (Bastei Lubbe, 1988)

Bruce Springsteen: The Ultimate Story, Steven Rosen (Castle Communications, 1995)

Bruce Springsteen: Tutti i Testi, Con Traduzione a Fronte, Guido Harari (Arcana Editrice, 1985)

Bruce Springsteen: Tutti i Testi, Con Traduzione a Fronte, Massimo Cotto (Gruppo Editoriale Muzzio, 1988, 1992)

Down Thunder Road: The Making of Bruce Springsteen, Marc Eliot (Simon & Schuster, 1992)

Glory Days: Bruce Springsteen in the 1980s, Dave Marsh (Pantheon Books, 1987, 1991)

Rock & Roll Hall of Famers: Bruce Springsteen, Susie Derkins (Rosen Publishing Group, 2002)

Rock 'n Pop Stars Series: Bruce Springsteen, Zadra (Creative Co., 1986)

Springsteen, Dennis Eichorn (Truman Publishing Co. 1987)

Springsteen, Robert Hilburn (Rolling Stone Press, 1985)

Springsteen, Frank Moriarty (Metro Books, 1998)

Springsteen: Back in the U.S.A., Marty Monroe (Robus Books, 1984)

Springsteen: No Surrender, Kate Lynch (Proteus Books, 1984)

Springsteen: Point Blank, Christopher Sandford (DaCapo Press, 1999)

Tajfun Zvani Bruce ("Typhoon" Bruce), Dragan Todorovic (Beograd, Yugoslavia, 1989)

Two Hearts: The Definitive Biography, 1972–2003, Dave Marsh (Routledge, 2003)

RELATED BIOGRAPHIES

Clive: Inside the Record Business, Clive Davis with James Willwerth (Ballantine Books, 1976)

Cousin Brucie: My Life in Rock 'n' Roll Radio, Cousin Bruce Morrow and Laura Baudo (Beech Tree Books, 1987)

John Hammond on Record: An Autobiography, John Hammond with Irving Townsend (Penguin Books, 1977)

Howling at the Moon: The Odyssey of a Monstrous Music Mogul in an Age of Excess, Walter Yetnikoff (Broadway, 2004)

JERSEY GIRLS—AND BOYS

Beyond the Palace, Gary Wien, Debra Rothenberg (Trafford Publishing, 2003)

Greetings from Asbury Park, N.J.: The Bruce Springsteen Photo Discovery, Chuck Yopp and Donna Fenton (Greetings Publications, 1983)

Guide to the Jersey Shore from Sandy Hook to Cape May, Robert Santelli (Sixth Edition, Globe Pequot Press, 2003)

The Lost Legends of New Jersey, Frederick Reiken (Harvest, 2001)

The Meadowlands, Robert Sullivan (Doubleday Anchor Books, 1998)

A Place to Stand: A Guide to Bruce Springsteen's Sense of Place, Bob Crane (Palace Books, 2002)

Rock & Roll Tour of the Jersey Shore, Stan Goldstein and Jean Mikle (2002)

The Wishbones, Tom Perrotta (Berkley Signature Edition, 1997)

QUOTE BOOKS

Bruce Springsteen: In His Own Words, John W. Duffy (Omnibus Press, 1993)

Bruce Springsteen Talking, John W. Duffy (Omnibus, 2004)

Local Hero: Bruce Springsteen in the Words of His Band, Ermanno Labianca (Great Dane Books, 1993)

PHOTO BOOKS

Bruce Springsteen, A Photo-Bio, Peter Gambaccini (Quick Fox, 1979; Perigee Books, 1985)

Days of Hope and Dreams: An Intimate Portrait of Bruce Springsteen, Frank Stefanko (Billboard Books/Watson-Guptill Publications, 2003)

Photodiary, Lynn Goldsmith (Rizzoli Publishing, 1995)

Photographs, Annie Leibovitz (Pantheon/Rolling Stone Press, 1983)

The Picture Life of Bruce Springsteen, Geri Bain and Michael Leather (Franklin Watts, 1985)

Springsteen—Access All Areas, Lynn Goldsmith (Universe Publishing, 2000)

Springsteen Live, Peter Goddard, Philip Kamin (Stoddart Publishing, 1984)

Springsteen Photographed, Lynn Goldsmith (St. Martin's Press, 1984)

SPRINGSTEEN COMPENDIUMS

Backstreets: Springsteen: The Man and His Music, Charles R. Cross and the editors of *Backstreets* (Harmony Books, 1989, 1992)

Bruce Springsteen Anthology: Tutti i Dischi, Tutte le Cansoni (La Musa Rock Anthology), Stefano Barco (Arcana, 1999)

Bruce Springsteen: The Rolling Stone Files, The Editors of *Rolling Stone* (Hyperion/Rolling Stone Press, 1996)

Racing in the Street: The Bruce Springsteen Reader, June Skinner Sawyers ed. (Penguin Books, 2004)

SPRINGSTEEN MUSIC GUIDES

American Skin, Vita e Musica di Bruce Springsteen, Ermanno Labianca (Giunti Gruppo Editoriale, 2002)

Bruce Springsteen—An Underground Discography, Jolly Roger (1984)

Bruce Springsteen: The Complete Guide to the Music, Patrick Humphries (Omnibus Press, 1996)

The E Street Shuffle: Springsteen & the E Street Band in Performance 1972–1988, Clinton Heylin and Simon Gee (Labour of Love Productions, 1989)

Hungry Heart: The Music of Bruce Springsteen, Jeff Horn (1st Books, 2000)

Roll Your Tapes, Fulvio Fiore and Fulvio Felisi (Born to Run Books, 1994)

Songs, Bruce Springsteen (Avon Books, 1998, 2003)

Wild and Innocent: The Recordings of Bruce Springsteen, 1972–1985, Brad Elliot (Popular Culture Ink, 1996)

You Better Not Touch, Vol. 1, Lynn Elder (Backstreets Publishing)

You Better Not Touch 1991–1994, Vol. 2, Lynn Elder (Backstreets Publishing)

You Better Not Touch 1994–1997, Vol. 3, Lynn Elder (Backstreets Publishing)

FUN AND GAMES

Behind the Scenes with Bruce Springsteen: The Parody Collection, Rich Kortz (Push/Pull Press, 2000)

Bruce! The Ultimate Springsteen Quiz Book, Heather Higgins and Beth Laiderman (M. Evans and Co., 1985)

Dear Bruce Springsteen, Kevin Major (Dell Publishing, 1987)

50 Guaranteed Tips to Great Springsteen Tickets, The Editors of Backstreets (Backstreets)

Prove It All Night: The Bruce Springsteen Trivia Book, Deborah Mayer (Mustang Publishing, 1987)

Rock 'n' Roll Comics: Bruce Springsteen, Jay Allen Sanford (Revolutionary Comics, 1992)

GENERAL MUSIC COMPENDIUMS

American Rock 'n' Roll Tour, Dave Walker (Thunder's Mouth Press, 1992)

Bat Chain Puller: Rock & Roll in the Age of Celebrity, Kurt Loder (St. Martin's Press, 1990)

The Big Beat, Max Weinberg with Robert Santelli (Contemporary Books, 1984, 1991)

The Billboard Book of Number One Albums, Craig Rosen (Billboard Books, 1996)

The Billboard Book of Number One Hits, Fred Bronson (Billboard Books, 5th edition, 2003)

Classic Rock Stories, Tim Morse (St. Martin's Griffin, 1998)

Dick Clark's the First 25 Years of Rock & Roll, Michael Uslan and Bruce Solomon (Dell Publishing, 1981)

Dispatches from the Front Line of Popular Culture, Tony Parsons (Virgin Books, 1994)

Fortunate Son: The Best of Dave Marsh, Dave Marsh (Random House, 1985)

The Gold Record, Lucy Emerson (Fountain Publishing, 1978)

Human Rights Now! The Official Book of the Amnesty International World Concert Tour, James Henke and Annie Leibovitz (Salem House Publishers, 1988)

Idole: Von Hibbing nach Asbury Park, Siegfried Schmidt-Joos (Populare Kultur, 1984)

L'Enfer des Concerts, Humour Libre (ZEP, 1999)

MTV Unplugged, Sarah Malarkey ed. (MTV Books/Pocket Books/Melcher Media, 1995)

Music to My Ears: The Billboard Essays, Timothy White (Henry Holt and Co., 1996)

MusicHound Rock: The Essential Album Guide, Gary Graff and Daniel Durchholz eds. (Schirmer Trade Books, 1999)

100 Pop Rock Stars, David Dachs (Scholastic Book Services, 1980)

The Q/Omnibus Press Rock 'n' Roll Reader, Danny Kelly ed. (Omnibus Press, 1994)

Rock and Roll Is Here to Stay: An Anthology, William McKeen ed. (Norton, 2000)

Rock Lives: Profiles and Interviews, Timothy White (Henry Holt, 1990)

Rock Movers & Shakers, Barry Lazell ed. (Billboard Publications Inc., 1989)

The Rock Musician: The Best of Musican Magazine, Tony Scherman ed. (St. Martin's Press, 1995)

Rock of Ages: The Rolling Stone History of Rock & Roll, Ed Ward, Geoffrey Stokes and Ken Tucker (Summit Books, 1986)

Rock Revolution, The Editors of CREEM Magazine (Popular Library, 1976)

Rock Topicon, Dave Marsh, Sandra Choron and Debbie Geller (Contemporary Books Inc., 1984)

Rock Video Superstars, Daniel and Susan Cohen (Pocket Books, 1985)

The Rock Yearbook 1981, Michael Gross and Maxim Jakubowski eds. (Virgin Books Ltd. 1980)

The Rock Yearbook 1982, Al Clark ed. (St. Martin's Press, 1981)

The Rock Yearbook 1984, Al Clark ed. (St. Martin's Press, 1983)

The Rock Yearbook 1986, Ian Cranna ed. (St. Martin's Press, 1986)

The Rock Yearbook 1987, Tom Hibbert ed. (St. Martin's Press, 1986)

The Rock Yearbook 1988, Ian Cranna ed. (St. Martin's Press, 1987)

Rockin' Reels: An Illustrated History of Rock & Roll Movies, Jan Stacy and Ryder Syvertsen (Contemporary Books Inc., 1984)

Rocking My Life Away: Writing about Music and Other Matters, Anthony DeCurtis (Duke University Press, 2003)

The Rolling Stone Encyclopedia of Rock & Roll, Holly George-Warren, Patricia Romanowski and Jon Pareles eds. (1983, 1995, 2001)

The Rolling Stone Illustrated History of Rock & Roll, Jim Miller ed. (Random House, 1980)

The Rolling Stone Interviews: The 1980s, The Editors of Rolling Stone (St. Martin's Press, 1989)

Satisfaction: Monografie Rock, Ermanno Labianca (New Digital Music, 1995)

Singer-Songwriters: Pop Music's Performer-Composers from A to Zevon, Dave DiMartino (Billboard Books, 1994)

Songbook, Nick Hornby (McSweeney's Books, 2002)

The Sound and the Fury: 40 Years of Classic Rock Journalism, Barney Hoskins ed. (Bloomsbury, 2003)

Stranded: Rock and Roll for a Desert Island, Greil Marcus ed. (Da Capo Press Edition, 1996)

The Sun Book of Rock, Bob Hart (Sun Books, 1977)

Sun City: The Struggle for Freedom in South Africa, Dave Marsh (Penguin Books, 1985)

They Fought the Law: Rock Music Goes to Court, Stan Soocher (Schirmer, 1999)

VH1 Music First Rock Stars Encyclopedia, Dafydd Rees and Luke Crampton eds. (DK, 1996, 1999)

Video Rock Today, Stuart Matranga (Parachute Press, 1987)

We Are the World: The Photos, Music and Inside Story of One of the Most Historic Events in American Popular Music, David Breskin (Perigee Books, 1985)

Working Musicians, Bruce Pollock (Harper Entertainment, 2002)

Written in My Soul: Conversations with Rock's Great Songwriters, Bill Flanagan (Contemporary Books Inc., 1987)

The Year in Music 1979, Judith Glassman (Columbia House, 1979)

Zagat Survey Music Guide: 1,000 Top Albums of All Time, Pat Blashill, coordinator (Zagat Survey, 2003)

COMMENTARY AND ANALYSIS

Bob Dylan, Bruce Springsteen and American Song, Larry David Smith (Praeger Publishers, 2002)

Born in the U.S.A.: Bruce Springsteen and the American Tradition, Jim Cullen (HarperCollins, 1997)

Born in the U.S.A.: The Myth of America in Popular Music from Colonial Times to the Present, Timothy E. Scheurer (University Press of Mississippi, 1991)

Bruce Springsteen: Learn from the Greats and Write Better Songs, Rikky Rooksby (Backbeat, 2005)

Bruce Springsteen's America: The People Listening, A Poet Singing, Robert Coles (Random House, 2003)

A Change Is Gonna Come: Music, Race and the Soul of America, Craig Werner (Penguin Group, 1999)

Highway 61 Revisited: The Tangled Roots of American Jazz, Blues, Rock & Country Music, Gene Santoro (Oxford University Press, 2004)

Hit Men: Power Brokers and Fast Money Inside the Music Business, Fredric Danner (Times Books, 1990)

In the Fascist Bathroom, Punk in Rock Music 1977–1992, Greil Marcus (Harvard University Press, 1993)

It Ain't No Sin to Be Glad You're Alive: The Promise of Bruce Springsteen, Eric Alterman (Little, Brown and Co., 1999)

The Mansion on the Hill: Dylan, Young, Geffen, Springsteen and the Head-on Collision of Rock and Commerce, Fred Goodman (Times Books, 1997)

The Moral Passion of Bruce Springsteen, Patrick Primeaux (International Scholars Publications, 1996)

Music for Pleasure: Essays in the Sociology of Pop, Simon Frith (1988)

Night Beat: A Shadow History of Rock & Roll, Mikal Gilmore (Bantam, Doubleday, Dell, 1998)

Present Tense: Rock & Roll and Culture, Anthony DeCurtis ed. (Duke University Press, 1992)

A Race of Singers: Whitman's Working-Class Hero from Guthrie to Springsteen, Bryan K. Carman (University of North Carolina Press, 2000)

The Rock Styles of Bruce Springsteen, arranged by John Cerullo (Warner Bros. Publications, 1983)

Rockin' in Time: A Social History of Rock-and-Roll, David P. Szatmary (Prentice Hall, 1991)

Rockonomics: The Money Behind the Music, revised and updated edition, Mark Eliot (Citadel Press Book, 1993)

Rhythm and Resistance: The Political Uses of American Popular Music, Ray Pratt (The Smithsonian Institute, 1990)

Springsteen: Visions of America, Adam Sweeting (Horborn Group, 1985)

Tramps Like Us: Music and Meaning among Springsteen Fans, Daniel Cavicchi (Oxford University Press, 1998)

Writing Work: Writers on Working-Class Writing, various contributors (Bottom Dog Press, 1999)

SONGBOOKS (ALL FROM WARNER BROS. PUBLICATIONS)

The Best of Bruce Springsteen

Born in the U.S.A.

Born to Run

Bruce Springsteen Complete

Bruce Springsteen (Guitar Anthology Series)

Darkness on the Edge of Town

18 Tracks

The Ghost of Tom Joad

Greatest Hits

Guitar Anthology Series

Human Touch

Lucky Town

Nebraska

The New Best of Bruce Springsteen for Guitar

The Rising

The River

Springsteen/Complete Guitar

Tunnel of Love

TOUR PROGRAMS

MUSE Concerts (1979)

The River Tour (1980–81)

Born in the U.S.A. Tour (1984)

Born in the U.S.A. World Tour (1984–85)

Tunnel of Love Express Tour (1988)

1992–93 World Tour

World Acoustic Tour (1995–96)

The Ghost of Tom Joad Tour (1995–96; Netherlands edition)

E Street Band Reunion Tour (1999–2000)

The Rising Tour (2002–03)

Open All Night:
Springsteen Online

Official Sites

http://www.brucespringsteen.net
http://www.sonymusic.com/artists/
BruceSpringsteen/
http://www.sonymusic.de/brucespringsteen/
(Germany)

E Street Band Sites

Roy Bittan
http://www.mp3.com/Roy-Bittan

Clarence Clemons
http://www.clarenceclemons.com

Danny Federici
http://www.mp3.com/Danny-Federici

Nils Lofgren
http://www.nilslofgren.com

David Sancious
http://www.davidsancious.com

Patti Scialfa
http://www.pattiscialfa.net

Garry Tallent biography
http://www.mp3.com/Gary-Tallent

Soozie Tyrell
http://www.sooozietyrell.com

Steven Van Zandt
http://www.littlesteven.com
http://www.littlestevensundergroundgarage.com

Max Weinberg
http://www.nbc.com/Late_Night_with_Conan_O'
Brien/bios/Max_Weinberg
http://www.maxweinberg7.com

Recommended Fan Sites

***Backstreets* Magazine**
http://www.Backstreets.com

**Badlands: The Italian Bruce
   Springsteen Webzine**
http://www.badlands.it/

The Boots
http://home.TheBoots.net

Bosstime
http://www.springsteennews.net

Brucebase
http://www.brucebase.shetland.co.uk/

Candy's Room
http://www.candysroom.freeservers.com

Greasy Lake
http://www.greasylake.org/index.php

Lost in the Flood
http://www.lostintheflood.priv.at

Luckytown
http://www.luckytown.org

Point Blank Magazine
http://www.pointblankmag.com

The Stone Pony
http://www.stoneponylondon.net/

**Your Hometown Springsteen Site (*Asbury
   Park Press*)**
http://thnt.com/springsteen

Additional Fan Sites

Across the Border
http://home.hetnet.nl/~bruce.springsteen/index.htm

AMBS
http://www.rmasfaq.net/

Badlands (Portugal)
http://badlands.com.sapo.pt/index2.htm

Badlands (U.K.)
http://www.badlands.co.uk

Blood Brothers (Norway)
http://www.springsteen.net

Blood Brothers (Poland)
http://www.blood-brothers.org

Born to Run (Sweden)
http://hem.passagen.se/springsteen/start.htm

The Boss
http://home2.inet.tele.dk/theboss/

Covers of Bruce Springsteen Songs: Matt and Lori's List
http://bruce.orel.ws/covers

Drive All Night (Switzerland)
http://www.driveallnight.com

E Street Band
www.home.att.net/~droboogie1/estreet.htm

Fanatic Records: Rob's Springsteen Artwork Covers
http://fanaticrecords.freeservers.com

Glory Days
http://www.springsteen.de/

The Hitter
http://users.erols.com/smithsvoboda/index

Hultschi's Springsteen Page
http://musik.freepage.de/hultsch/

Jeroen's Bruce Springsteen Page
http://www.xs4all.nl/~maroen/engels/bruce.html

The Jersey Devil (Finland)
http://www.helsinki.fi/~tsmalmbe/bruce_spring-steen/bruce.htm

John's Bruce Springsteen Artwork Page
http://angelfire.com/art2/jsjoyceartwork/artlinks.html

John's Bruce Springsteen Artwork Page
http://www.angelfire.com/art2/jsjoyceartwork/artlinks.html

Killing Floor (Italy)
http://www.brucespringsteen.it/

Land of Hope and Dreams Homepage
http://www.dubbelhuis.nl/

Lebanese Tribute to Bruce Springsteen
http://www.springsteenlyrics.com/

Loose Ends (Italian language site)
http://www.loose-ends.it/

Nebraska
http://nebraska_99.tripod.com/

No. 1 Springsteen News Resource
http://www.springsteen-resource.de/archive.php

Page d'accueil de Spirit in the Night (France)
http://perso.wanadoo.fr/city.lights/spiritinthenight/spirit2.html

Paginas dedicadas a Bruce Springsteen (Spain)
http://personales.mundivia.es/ricard_c/

Bruce Springsteen (Belgium)
http://www.angelfire.com/rock/brummi/bruce/bs1.html

Bruce Springsteen (Canada)
http://www.brucespringsteen.ca/
http://www.canehdian.com/non/brucespringsteen/biography.html

Bruce Springsteen (Spain)
http://www.geocities.com/edug.geo/

Bruce Springsteen (Hungary)
http://www.brucespringsteen.hu/

Bruce Springsteen (Japan)
http://www.shio.org/springsteen/

Bruce Springsteen (The Netherlands)
http://www.brucespringsteen.nl/

Bruce Springsteen Interactive Web Site
http://www.mcs.surrey.ac.uk/cgi-bin/stats/bosspoll/

Bruce Springsteen Setlist Page
http://bruce.archesis.it/

Bruce Springsteen: The Storyteller
http://www.vroegop.org

Springsteen Memorabilia Collectors Page

The Bruce Springsteen Web Ring
http://hem.passagen.se/nm/webring/
http://users.aol.com/sfezuk/index

Springstomania
http://www.springstomania.com

The Stone Pony Bruce Springsteen Magazine, Revista y Club de Fans (Spain)
http://www.ofitecnica.net/stonepony/

Tenth-Avenue (France)
http://www.tenth-avenue.com

This Hard Land (Italian-language site)
http://www.clarence.com/home/bruce/

Unauthorized Bruce Springsteen Web Site
http://www.brucespringsteen.com

Wild and Innocent: Sam's Springsteen page
http://home.att.net/~droboogie1/springsteen.html

Product-Dedicated Sites

Books
http://www.bossbooks.net

Bootlegs
http://mv.com/ipusers/richbreton/main.htm
http://http://www.euronet.nl/~everhaar/thepromise/index.html

http://wksu.org/news/features/springsteen/

DVD/Video

http://www.brucedvds.com

http://www.brucevideos.com

Related New Jersey Sites

Asbury Park

http://www.asburypark.net

Asbury Park Convention Hall/Paramount Theater

http://www.asburyparkconventionhall.com

Asbury Park Press

http://www.app.com

Asbury Park Public Library/Bruce Springsteen Special Collection

http://www.asburypark.lib.nj.us/springsteen_collection_holdings.htm

Asbury Park Then and Now

http://members.tripod.com/gowen2/

Beyond the Palace

http://www.beyondthepalace.com/newjersey/

Brucemaps.com

http://www.brucemaps.com

Freehold Township

http://twp.freehold.nj.us/index.asp

I Love Tillie Asbury Park Palace Amusements

http://mywebpages.comcast.net/ilovetillie/

Meadowlands Fan Page

http://home.att.net/~droboogie1/Meadowlands.htm

My Hometown: Springsteen's Jersey Shore

http://members.aol.com/daboss72/bruce/jbruce.htm

New Jersey Music

http://www.njgang.com/historic_nj/music.htm

Rumson Borough, NJ site

http://www.rumsonboro.com

St. Rose of Lima Church and School/Haddon Heights

http://www.eticomm.net/~strose/

St. Rose of Lima Parish, Freehold

http://www.strosenj.com

Save Tillie

http://www.homestead.com/savetillie/

The Stone Pony

http://www.stoneponyonline.com

General Sites of Springsteen Fan Interest

Cadillac Ranch

http://www.roadsideamerica.com/attract/TXAMAcadillac.html

Experience Music Project

http://www.emplive.com

Max's Kansas City Web

http://www.maxskansascity.com

Nick's Fat City

http://www.nicksfatcity.com

Rock and Roll Hall of Fame and Museum

http://www.rockhall.com

Songwriters Hall of Fame

http://www.songwritershalloffame.org

Selected Media Sites

All Music Guide

http://www.allmusic.com

Ask Men

http://www.askmen.com/men/entertainment_100/109_bruce_springsteen

BBC

http://www.bbc.co.uk/music/profiles/springsteenbruce.shtml

DoubleTake Magazine

http://www.doubletakemagazine.org

Entertainment Weekly

http://www.ew.com

International Movie Database

http://us.imdb.com

IQ451 Music Guide

http://www.iq451.com/music/bruce-springsteen.htm

Launch

http://www.launch.yahoo.com

LiveDaily

http://www.livedaily.com

Metacritic

http://www.metacritic.com/music/

MTV

http://www.mtv.com

New Musical Express

http://www.nme.com

NJ.com

http://www.nj.com/springsteen/

123 Music Stars

http://www.123musicstars.com/music-stars/bruce-springsteen.htm

People

http://people.aol.com/people/

Reason to Rock

http://www.reasontorock.com/artists/bruce_springsteen

Rock and Rap Confidential

http://www.rockrap.com

The Rock Site

http://www.rocksite.info/r-springsteen-bruce.htm

Rolling Stone

http://www.rollingstone.com

Shore Fire Media
http://www.shorefire.com

Undercover
http://www.undercover.com.au

VH1
http://www.vh1.com

Lyric Sites

http://www.amiright.com/misheard/artist/
springsteenbruce.shtml
http://www.azlyrics.com/s/springsteen
http://www.allthelyrics.com/lyrics/bruce_
springsteen/
http://www.brucespringsteen.net/songs/
index.html
http://www.lyricsdepot.com/bruce-springsteen/
http://www.lyricsfreak.com/b/bruce-
springsteen/
http://www.thuismarkt.nl/users/springsteen/
http://www.xs4all.nl/~maroen/engels/
bruce.html

Song Tablature

http://www.guitarists.net/tab/bands.php/spring
steen_bruce
http://www.delafont.com/music_acts/
Bruce-Springsteen.htm
http://www.proguitar.com/bands/bruce
springsteen/brucespringsteen.html
http://www.e-tabs.org/tab/bruce_springsteen

http://springsteen-chords.com

Search Sites

Bruce Springsteen Links Directory
http://www.cbel.com/bruce_springsteen/

Bruce Springsteen Web Ring Hub
http://q.webring.com/hub?ring=theboss

Musicsearcher
http://www.musicsearcher.com/s/
    Springsteen,Bruce.php

Rock on the Net
http://www.rockonthenet.com/artists-s/
brucespringsteen_main.htm

Springsteen Start4All
http://www.springsteen.start4all.com

Springsteen Web Site Directory
http://www.zurl.com/who/bruce-springsteen

Springsteen Web Site Index
http://www.classicrock.about.com/library/artist
s/blspring.htm

Starpulse Entertainment
http://www.starpulse.com/Music/
Springsteen,_Bruce/

Topix
http://www.topix.net/who/bruce-springsteen

Familiar Faces Around Me: Guest Performers at Springsteen Concerts

Bobby Bandiera: July 29, 1999. Continental Airlines Arena, East Rutherford, NJ ("Hungry Heart"); August 23, 2003, Giants Stadium, East Rutherford, NJ ("From Small Things [Big Things One Day Come]")

Jean Beauvoir: June 3, 1999, Bercy, Paris, France ("Hungry Heart")

Richard Blackwell: November 26, 1996, Paramount Theatre, Asbury Park, NJ ("All That Heaven Will Allow," "I Don't Want to Go Home," "Spirit in the Night," "Rosali-ta," "4th of July, Asbury Park [Sandy]")

Gary U.S. Bonds: October 29, 1976, The Palladium, New York City ("Quarter to Three"); June 3, 1981, Brendan Byrne Arena, East Rutherford, NJ ("This Little Girl"); January 18, 1985, Greensboro Coliseum, Greensboro, NC ("Twist and Shout"); October 3, 2003, Shea Stadium, Flushing, NY ("Twist and Shout"); October 4, 2003, Shea Stadium, Flushing, NY ("Quarter to Three," "Twist and Shout")

Laurie Bonds (Gary U.S. Bonds's wife): October 4, 2003, Shea Stadium, Flushing, NY ("Quarter to Three")

Laurie Bonds (Gary U.S. Bonds's daughter): October 3, 2003, Shea Stadium, Flushing, NY ("Twist and Shout"); October 4, 2003, Shea Stadium, Flushing, NY ("Quarter to Three")

Jon Bon Jovi: April 12, 1987, The Stone Pony, Asbury Park, NJ ("Kansas City"); August 12, 1999, Continental Airlines Arena, East Rutherford, NJ ("Hungry Heart"); April 28, 1999, Halle Tony Garnier, Lyon, France ("Hungry Heart")

Bono: November 23, 2002, American Airlines Arena, Miami, FL ("Because the Night")

J.T. Bowen: August 9, 1984, Brendan Byrne Arena, East Rutherford, NJ ("Woman's Got the Power")

Jackson Browne: September 22–23, 1979, MUSE benefit, Madison Square Garden, New York, NY ("Stay"); November 1, 1980, Los Angeles Sports Arena, Los Angeles, CA ("Sweet Little Sixteen"); September 3, 1999, MCI Center, Washington, DC ("Hungry Heart," "Red Headed Woman"); October 13, 2004, Vote for Change show, Continental Airlines Arena, East Rutherford, NJ ("Racing in the Street," "[What's So Funny 'Bout] Peace, Love and Understanding," "People Have the Power")

Peter Buck (R.E.M): October 1, 2004, Vote for Change show, Wachovia Center, Philadelphia, PA ("Born to Run," "[What's So Funny 'Bout] Peace, Love and Understanding," "People Have the Power"); October 2, 2004, Vote for Change show, Gund Arena, Cleveland, OH ("Born to Run," "[What's So Funny 'Bout] Peace, Love and Understanding," "People Have the Power"); October 3, 2004, Vote for Change show, Cobo Arena, Detroit, MI ("Born to Run," "[What's So Funny 'Bout] Peace, Love and Understanding," "People Have the Power"); October 5, 2004, Vote for Change show, Xcel Energy Center, St. Paul, MN ("Born to Run," "Rockin' in the Free World," "[What's So Funny 'Bout] Peace, Love and Understanding," "People Have the Power"); October 8, 2004, Vote for Change show, TD Waterhouse Arena, Orlando, FL ("Born to Run," "[What's So Funny 'Bout] Peace, Love and Understanding," "People Have the Power"); October 11, 2004, Vote for Change show, MCI Center, Washington, DC ("Born to Run," "[What's So Funny 'Bout] Peace, Love and Understanding," "People Have the Power")

Gary Busey: August 18–19, 1978, The Spectrum, Philadelphia, PA ("Rave On," "Quarter to Three")

Mary Chapin Carpenter: September 3, 1999, MCI Center, Washington, DC ("Hungry Heart," "Red Headed Woman")

Barbara Carr: May 23, 1988, Madison Square Garden, New York, NY ("You Can Look [But You Better Not Touch]")

Tracy Chapman: October 8, 2004, Vote for Change show, TD Waterhouse Arena, Orlando, FL ("My Hometown")

Clarence Clemons: June 24, 1993, Brendan Byrne Arena, East Rutherford, NJ ("Tenth Avenue Freeze-Out," "Born to Run")

Shawn Colvin: September 3, 1999, MCI Center, Washington, DC ("Hungry Heart," "Red Headed Woman")

Cousin Frankie: September 3, 1999, MCI Center, Washington, DC ("Ramrod"); April 22, 2000, Raleigh Entertainment Center, Raleigh, NC ("Hungry Heart")

Crosby, Stills, Nash & Young: October 13, 1986, Bridge School Benefit, Shoreline Amphitheater, Mountain View, CA ("Hungry Heart")

Terence Trent D'Arby: June 26, 1993, Madison Square Garden, New York, NY ("Many Rivers to Cross," "I Have Faith in These Desolate Times," "Jole Blond," "Jumping Jack Flash")

Dion: December 2, 1996, Sunrise Theater, Miami, FL ("If I Should Fall Behind"); November 23, 2002, American Airlines Arena, Miami, FL ("If I Should Fall Behind")

Dixie Chicks: October 3, 2004, Vote for Change show, Cobo Arena, Detroit, MI ("People Have the Power")

Bob Dylan: October 4, 2003, Shea Stadium, Flushing, NY ("Highway 61 Revisited")

Steve Eitelberg: August 9, 1999, Continental Airlines Arena, East Rutherford, NJ ("Spirit in the Night")

Joe Ely: May 20, 1993, RDS Jumping Enclosure, Dublin, Ireland ("Settle for Love," "Blowin' Down the Road [I Ain't Going to Be Treated This Way]"); June 26, 1993, Madison Square Garden, New York, NY ("Lonesome in the Valley," "Settle for

Love"); June 24, 1993, Brendan Byrne Arena, East Rutherford, NJ ("I Ain't Got No Home"); April 17, 2000, Frank Erwin Center, Austin, TX ("All Just to Get to You"); March 2, 2003, Frank Erwin Center, Austin, TX ("All Just to Get to You," "Working on the Highway")

John Entwistle: August 11, 1984, Brendan Byrne Arena, East Rutherford, NJ ("Twist and Shout")

Melissa Etheridge: August 12, 1999, Continental Airlines Arena, East Rutherford, NJ ("Hungry Heart")

Danny Federici: November 24, 1996, Paramount Theatre, Asbury Park, NJ ("Wild Billy's Circus Story," "Shut Out the Light," "This Hard Land," "Rosalita," "4th of July, Asbury Park [Sandy]"); November 25, 1996, Paramount Theatre, Asbury Park, NJ ("For You," "Wild Billy's Circus Story," "Shut Out the Light," "Spirit in the Night," "Rosalita," "This Hard Land," "4th of July, Asbury Park [Sandy]"); November 26, 1996, Paramount Theatre, Asbury Park, NJ ("For You," "Wild Billy's Circus Story," "Shut Out the Light," "I Don't Want to Go Home," "Spirit in the Night," "Rosalita," "This Hard Land," "4th of July, Asbury Park [Sandy]")

Flo and Eddie: February 17, 1977, Richfield Coliseum, Richfield, OH ("Baby, I Love You," "Walking in the Rain," "Say Goodbye to Hollywood," "Be My Baby"); December 28, 1980, Nassau Coliseum, Uniondale, NY ("Hungry Heart")

Eddie Floyd: April 29, 1976, Ellis Auditorium, Memphis, TN ("Knock on Wood," "Yum Yum I Want Some," "Raise Your Hand")

John Fogerty: October 1, 2004, Vote for Change show, Wachovia Center, Philadelphia, PA ("Centerfield," "Deja Vu All Over Again," "Fortunate Son," "The Promised Land," "Proud Mary," "[What's So Funny 'Bout] Peace, Love and Understanding," "People Have the Power"); October 2, 2004, Vote for Change show, Gund Arena, Cleveland, OH ("Centerfield," "Deja Vu All Over Again," "Fortunate Son," "The Promised Land," "Bad Moon Rising," "[What's So Funny 'Bout] Peace, Love and Understanding," "People Have the Power"); October 3, 2004, Vote for Change, Cobo Arena, Detroit, MI ("Centerfield," "Deja Vu All Over Again," "Fortunate Son," "The Promised Land," "Travelin' Band," "[What's So Funny 'Bout] Peace, Love and Understanding," "People Have the Power"); October 5, 2004, Vote for Change show, Xcel Energy Center, St. Paul, MN ("Centerfield," "Deja Vu All Over Again," "Fortunate Son," "The Promised Land," "Proud Mary," "Rockin' in the Free World," "[What's So Funny 'Bout] Peace, Love and Understanding," "People Have the Power"); October 8, 2004, Vote for Change show, TD Waterhouse Arena, Orlando, FL ("Centerfield," "Deja Vu All Over Again," "Fortunate Son," "The Promised Land," "Bad Moon Rising," "[What's So Funny 'Bout] Peace, Love and Understanding," "People Have the Power"); October 11, 2004, Vote for Change show, MCI Center, Washington, DC ("Deja Vu All Over Again," "Fortunate Son," "[What's So Funny 'Bout] Peace, Love and Understanding," "People Have the Power"); October 13, 2004, Vote for Change show, Continental Airlines Arena, East Rutherford, NJ ("Centerfield," "Deja Vu All Over Again," "Fortunate Son," "The Promised Land," "Proud Mary," "Bad Moon Rising," "Travelin' Band," "[What's So Funny 'Bout] Peace, Love and Understanding," "People Have the Power")

Al Franken: October 3, 2003, Shea Stadium, Flushing, NY ("Mary's Place")

Big Dan Gallagher: November 26, 1996, Paramount Theatre, Asbury Park, NJ ("Spirit in the Night," "Rosalita," "4th of July, Asbury Park [Sandy]")

Joe Grushecky: March 20, 1988, Civic Arena, Pittsburgh, PA ("Raise Your Hand"); December 16, 1992, Civic Arena, Pittsburgh, PA ("Glory Days," "Santa Claus Is Comin' to Town); September 16, 1995, Benedum Center, Pittsburgh, PA ("Homestead"); April 25, 2000, Mellon Arena, Pittsburgh, PA ("Idiot's Delight"); April 26, 2000, Mellon Arena, Pittsburgh, PA ("Hungry Heart"); December 4, 2002, Mellon Arena, Pittsburgh, PA ("Code of Silence," "Glory Days"); August 6, 2003, PNC Park, Pittsburgh, PA ("Glory Days")

Johnny Grushecky (Joe Grushecky's son): December 4, 2002, Mellon Arena, Pittsburgh, PA ("Glory Days"); August 6, 2003, PNC Park, Pittsburgh, PA ("Glory Days")

Emmylou Harris: November 19, 2002, BJCC, Birmingham, AL. ("My Hometown"); August 30, 2003, Giants Stadium, East Rutherford, NJ ("Across the Border")

Don Henley: November 3, 2002, American Airlines Arena, Dallas, TX ("I Fought the Law")

Bruce Hornsby: September 3, 1999, MCI Center, Washington, DC ("Hungry Heart," "Red Headed Woman"); March 6, 2003, Richmond Coliseum, Richmond, VA ("Let's Go, Let's Go, Let's Go")

Don Ienner: October 4, 2003, Shea Stadium in Flushing, NY ("Twist and Shout")

Garland Jeffreys: July 18, 2003, Giants Stadium, East Rutherford, NJ ("96 Tears"); October 4, 2003, Shea Stadium, Flushing, NY ("Quarter to Three," "Twist and Shout")

Jon Landau: October 2, 1985, Los Angeles Coliseum, Los Angeles, CA ("Glory Days"); May 23, 1988, Madison Square Garden, New York, NY (encores); June 28, 1988, Stadion Feynoord, Rotterdam, The Netherlands ("Glory Days"); September 24, 2002, Kemper Arena, Kansas City, MO ("Kansas City"); May 19, 2003, Estadio De La Comunidad, Madrid, Spain ("Dancing in the Dark"); May 24, 2003, Stade de France, Paris, France ("Dancing in the Dark"); May 27, 2003, Crystal Palace National Sports Arena, London, England ("Dancing in the Dark"); June 28, 2003, San Siro Stadium, Milan, Italy ("Dancing in the Dark"); August 9, 2003, Lincoln Financial Field, Philadelphia, PA ("Dancing in the Dark"); August 31, 2003, Giants Stadium, East Rutherford, NJ ("Dancing in the Dark"); September 6–7, 2003, Fenway Park, Boston ("Dancing in the Dark"); October 3, 2003, Shea Stadium, Flushing, NY ("Dancing in the Dark," "Twist and Shout"); October 4, 2003, Shea Stadium, Flushing, NY ("Dancing in the Dark," "Quarter to Three," "Twist and Shout")

Al Leiter (New York Mets pitcher): October 3, 2003, Shea Stadium, Flushing, NY ("Rosalita")

Jerry Lee Lewis: May 20, 1993, RDS Jumping Enclosure, Dublin, Ireland ("Great Balls of Fire," "Whole Lotta Shakin' Goin' On")

Vini "Mad Dog" Lopez: November 25, 1996, Paramount Theatre, Asbury Park, NJ ("Spirit in the Night," "Rosalita"); November 26, 1996, Paramount Theatre, Asbury Park, NJ ("Spirit in the Night," "Rosalita," "4th of July, Asbury Park [Sandy]"); July 21, 2003, Giants Stadium, East Rutherford, NJ ("Spirit in the Night")

Southside Johnny Lyon: July 29–30, 1981, Richfield Coliseum, Richfield, OH ("I Don't Wanna Go Home"); August 12, 1984, Brendan Byrne Arena, East Rutherford, NJ ("Twist and Shout"); June 24, 1993, Brendan Byrne Arena, East Rutherford, NJ ("It's Been a Long Time," "Havin' a Party," "It's All Right"); August 7, 1992, Brendan Byrne Arena, East Rutherford, NJ ("All the Way Home"); October 28, 1999, Oakland Coliseum, Oakland, CA ("Hungry Heart")

John Magnusson (Danish street musician): July 23, 1988, Stroget, Copenhagen, Denmark ("I'm on Fire," "The River," "Dancing in the Dark")

Marah (Serge and Dave Bielanko): August 30, 2003, Giants Stadium, East Rutherford, NJ ("Raise Your Hand")

Malurt: The Forum, Copenhagen, Denmark ("Hungry Heart")

Miami Horns: August 20, 1984, Brendan Byrne Arena, East Rutherford, NJ ("Tenth Avenue Freeze-Out"); June 24, 1993, Brendan Byrne Arena, East Rutherford, NJ ("It's Been a Long Time," "Tenth Avenue Freeze-Out," "Havin' a Party," "It's All Right")

Mike Mills (R.E.M.): October 1, 2004, Vote for Change show, Wachovia Center, Philadelphia, PA ("Born to Run," "[What's So Funny 'Bout] Peace, Love and.Understanding," "People Have the Power"); October 2, 2004, Vote for Change show, Gund Arena, Cleveland, OH ("Born to Run," "[What's So Funny 'Bout] Peace, Love and Understanding," "People Have the Power"); October 3, 2004, Vote for Change show, Cobo Arena, Detroit, MI ("Born to Run," "[What's So Funny 'Bout] Peace, Love and Understanding," "People Have the Power"); October 5, 2004, Vote for Change show, Xcel Energy Center, St. Paul, MN ("Born to Run," "Rockin' in the Free World," "[What's So Funny 'Bout] Peace, Love and Understanding," "People Have the Power"); October 8, 2004, Vote for Change show, TD Waterhouse Arena, Orlando, FL ("Born to Run," "[What's So Funny 'Bout] Peace, Love and Understanding," "People Have the Power"); October 11, 2004, Vote for Change show, MCI Center, Washington, DC ("Born to Run," "[What's So Funny 'Bout] Peace, Love and Understanding," "People Have the Power")

Sam Moore: October 15, 1999, First Union Center, Phoenix, AZ ("Soul Man")

Elliot Murphy: June 30, 1992, Bercy, Paris, France ("Rock Ballad"); May 26, 1997, Palais des Congres, Paris, France ("Diamonds by the Yard," "Blowin' Down That Old Dusty Road"); May 27, 1999, Flanders Expo, Ghent, Belgium ("Hungry Heart," "Born to Run"); June 2, 1999, Bercy, Paris, France ("Hungry Heart"); October 14, 2002, Bercy, Paris, France ("Born to Run"); October 18, 2002, Palamalaguti, Bologna, Italy ("Born to Run"); May 19, 2003, Estadio De La Comunidad, Madrid, Spain ("Better Days," "Born to Run")

Wolfgang Niedecken: April 15, 1999, Kolnarena, Cologne, Germany; June 12, 2003, Hamburger AOl Arena, Hamburg, Germany

Willie Nile: September 20, 2003, Darien Lake Amusement Park, Buffalo, NY ("Glory Days"); October 3, 2003, Shea Stadium, Flushing, NY ("Dancing in the Dark," "Twist and Shout"); October 4, 2003, Shea Stadium, Flushing, NY ("Dancing in the Dark," "Quarter to Three," "Twist and Shout")

Brendan O'Brien: December 2, 2002, Philips Arena, Atlanta, GA ("Glory Days," "Born to Run"); September 25, 2003, Invesco Field, Denver, CO ("Rosalita," "Dancing in the Dark"); October 4, 2003, Shea Stadium, Flushing, NY ("Twist and Shout")

Bonnie Raitt: September 3, 1999, MCI Center, Washington, DC ("Hungry Heart," "Red Headed Woman")

Martha Reeves (with Kim Farinacci): September 21, 2003, Comerica Park, Detroit, MI ("Heatwave")

Mitch Ryder: August 12, 1981, Joe Louis Arena, Detroit, MI ("Detroit Medley")

Richie Sambora: August 12, 1999, Continental Airlines Arena, East Rutherford, NJ ("Hungry Heart")

Boz Scaggs: September 6, 1975, Theater for the Performing Arts, New Orleans, LA ("Twist and Shout")

Bob Seger: October 3, 1980, Crisler Arena, Ann Arbor, MI ("Thunder Road")

Patti Scialfa: June 24, 1993, Brendan Byrne Arena, East Rutherford, NJ ("Brilliant Disguise," "Human Touch"); June 26, 1993, Madison Square Garden, New York, NY ("Brilliant Disguise," "Human Touch"); November 8, 1996, St. Rose of Lima, Freehold, NJ ("Mansion on the Hill," "Two Hearts," "When You're Alone"); November 24, 1996, Paramount Theatre, Asbury Park, NJ ("Mansion on the Hill," "Two Hearts," "When You're Alone," "Shut Out the Light"); November 25, 1996, Paramount Theatre, Asbury Park, NJ ("Tougher Than the Rest," "Two Hearts," "When You're Alone," "Shut Out the Light," "Spirit in the Night"); November 26, 1996, Paramount Theatre, Asbury Park, NJ ("Tougher Than the Rest," "Two Hearts," "When You're Alone," "Shut Out the Light," "I Don't Want to Go Home," "Spirit in the Night," "Rosalita," "4th of July, Asbury Park [Sandy]"); December 12, 1996, Ryman Auditorium, Nashville, TN; May 7, 1997, Austria Center, Austria, Vienna ("Two Hearts")

Patti Smith: October 30, 1976, The Palladium, New York City ("Rosalita")

Ronnie Spector: November 4, 1976,The Palladium, New York City ("Baby, I Love You," "Walking in the Rain," "Be My Baby"); February 17, 1977, Richfield Coliseum, Richfield, OH ("Baby, I Love You," "Walking in the Rain," "Say Goodbye to Hollywood," "Be My Baby")

Adele Springsteen: August 23, 1978, Madison Square Garden, New York, NY; May 3, 1988, Shoreline Amphitheatre, Mountain View, CA

Edwin Starr: June 22, 1988, Aston Villa Football Ground, Birmingham, England ("War"); June 25, 1988, Wembley Arena, London, England ("War"); May 16, 1999, NEC, Birmingham, England ("War")

Dave Stewart: November 23, 2002, American Airlines Arena, Miami, FL ("Because the Night")

Michael Stipe (R.E.M.): October 1, 2004, Vote for Change show, Wachovia Center, Philadelphia, PA ("Because the Night," "[What's So Funny 'Bout] Peace, Love and Understanding," "People Have the Power"); October 2, 2004, Vote for Change show, Gund Arena, Cleveland, OH ("Because the Night," "[What's So Funny 'Bout] Peace, Love and Understanding," "People Have the Power"); October 3, 2004, Vote for Change show, Cobo Arena, Detroit, MI ("Because the Night," "[What's So Funny 'Bout] Peace, Love and Understanding," "People Have the Power"); October 5, 2004, Vote for Change show, Xcel Energy Center, St. Paul, MN ("Because the Night," "Rockin' in the Free World," "[What's So Funny 'Bout] Peace, Love and Understanding," "People Have the Power"); October 8, 2004, Vote for Change show, TD Waterhouse Arena, Orlando, FL ("Because the Night," "[What's So Funny 'Bout] Peace, Love and Understanding," "People Have the Power"); October 11, 2004, Vote for Change show, MCI Center, Washington, DC ("Because the Night," "[What's So Funny 'Bout] Peace, Love and Understanding," "People Have the Power")

Al Tellone (roadie): October 29–31, 1973, The Main Point, Bryn Mawr, PA

Richard Thompson: March 6, 2003, Richmond Coliseum, Richmond, VA ("Let's Go, Let's Go, Let's Go")

Robbin Thompson: January 18, 1985, Greensboro Coliseum, Greensboro, NC ("Twist and Shout"); March 6, 2003, Richmond Coliseum, Richmond, VA ("Let's Go, Let's Go, Let's Go")

Pete Townshend: June 7, 1981, International Arena, Birmingham, England ("Born to Run," "Detroit Medley")

Soozie Tyrell: June 24, 1993, Brendan Byrne Arena, East Rutherford, NJ ("Blowin' Down the Road [I Ain't Going to Be Treated This Way]"); June 26, 1993, Madison Square Garden, New York, NY ("Lonesome in the Valley," "If I Should Fall Behind"); November 8, 1996, St. Rose of Lima, Freehold, NJ ("The River," "Mansion on the Hill," "Two Hearts," "My Hometown," "Racing in the Street"); November 24, 1996, Paramount Theatre, Asbury Park, NJ ("Mansion on the Hill," "Wild Billy's Circus Story," "When You're Alone," "Two Hearts," "Shut Out the Light," "Racing in the Street," "Rosalita"); November 25, 1996, Paramount Theatre, Asbury Park, NJ ("Tougher Than the Rest," "Wild Billy's Circus Story," "Two Hearts," "When You're Alone," "Shut Out the Light," "Racing in the Street," "Spirit in the Night," "Rosalita"); November 26, 1996, Paramount Theatre, Asbury Park, NJ ("Tougher Than the Rest," "All That Heaven Will Allow," "Wild Billy's Circus Story," "Two Hearts," "When You're Alone," "Shut Out the Light," "Racing in the Street," "I Don't Want to Go Home," "Spirit in the Night," "Rosalita," "4th of July, Asbury Park [Sandy]"); December 12, 1996, Ryman Auditorium, Nashville, TN; August 12, 1999, Continental Airlines Arena, East Rutherford, NJ ("Factory"); June 20, 2000, Madison Square Garden, New York, NY ("The Ghost of Tom Joad"); June 22, 2000, Madison Square Garden, New York, NY ("Youngstown," "The Ghost of Tom Joad")

Little Steven Van Zandt: August 20, 1984, Brendan Byrne Arena, East Rutherford, NJ ("Two Hearts," "Drift Away," "Born to Run," "Detroit Medley"/"Travelin' Band," "Twist and Shout," "Do You Love Me"); January 14, 1984, Mid-South Coliseum, Memphis, TN ("Drift Away," "Two Hearts"); December 16–17, 1984, the Omni, Atlanta, GA ("Two Hearts," "Ramrod"); August 22, 1985, Giants Stadium, East Rutherford, NJ ("Two Hearts," "Ramrod," "Twist and Shout," "Do You Love Me"); August 31, 1985, Giants Stadium, East Rutherford, NJ (encores); June 24, 1993, Brendan Byrne Arena, East Rutherford, NJ ("Glory Days," "It's Been a Long Time," "Tenth Avenue Freeze-Out," "Born to Run," "Blowin' Down the Road [I Ain't Going to Be Treated This Way]," "Havin' a Party," "Jersey Girl," "It's All Right"); November 26, 1996, Paramount Theatre, Asbury Park, NJ ("I Don't Want to Go Home," "Spirit in the Night," "Rosalita," "4th of July, Asbury Park [Sandy]")

Eddie Vedder: September 25, 2003, Comiskey Park, Chicago, IL ("My Hometown"); October 13, 2004, Vote for Change show, Continental Airlines Arena, East Rutherford, NJ ("No Surrender," "Darkness on the Edge of Town," "Betterman," "[What's So Funny 'Bout] Peace, Love and Understanding," "People Have the Power")

Ali Weinberg (Max Weinberg's daughter): July 29, 1999, Continental Airlines Arena, East Rutherford, NJ ("Hungry Heart"); August 12, 1999, Continental Airlines Arena, East Rutherford, NJ ("Hungry Heart"); April 19, 2003, Bell Centre, Montreal, Canada ("Ramrod"); May 19, 2003, Estadio De La Comunidad, Madrid, Spain ("Ramrod"); July 24, 2003, Giants Stadium, East Rutherford, NJ ("Ramrod"); June 22, 2000, Madison Square Garden, New York, NY ("Ramrod")

Max Weinberg: June 24, 1993, Brendan Byrne Arena, East Rutherford, NJ ("Jersey Girl")

Peter Wolf: December 14, 1992, Boston Garden, Boston MA ("In the Midnight Hour"); August 27, 1999, Fleet Center, Boston, MA ("Raise Your Hand"); October 4, 2002, Fleet Center, Boston, MA ("Dirty Water"); September 6–7, Fenway Park, Boston, MA ("Dirty Water")

Neil Young: October 5, 2004, Vote for Change show, Xcel Energy Center, St. Paul, MN ("Souls of the Departed," "All Along the Watchtower," "Rockin' in the Free World," "[What's So Funny 'Bout] Peace, Love and Understanding," "People Have the Power")

Pegi Young: October 5, 2004, Vote for Change show, Xcel Energy Center, St. Paul, MN ("Rockin' in the Free World," "[What's So Funny 'Bout] Peace, Love and Understanding," "People Have the Power")

Rock and Roll Hall of Fame Induction and Acceptance Speeches

Bono Inducts Bruce Springsteen, March 18, 1999

"Oh man, Bruce is a very unusual rock star, isn't he? Really, I mean, he hasn't done the things most rock stars do. He got rich and famous, but never embarrassed himself with all that success, did he? No drug busts, no blood changes in Switzerland. Even more remarkable, no golfing! No bad hair period, even in the '80s. No wearing of dresses in videos. But there was those fingerless gloves in the '80s. No embarrassing movie roles, no pet snakes, no monkeys. No exhibitions of his own paintings. No public brawling or setting himself on fire.

"Rock stars are supposed to make soap operas of their lives, aren't they? If they don't kill themselves first. Well, you can't be a big legend and not be dysfunctional. It's not allowed. You should at least have lost your looks. Everyone else has. Have you seen them? *[Gestures backstage]* It's like Madame Tussaud's back there.

"Then there's Bruce Springsteen. Handsome mother with those brooding brown eyes, eyes that could see through America. And a catastrophe of great songs, if you were another songwriter. Bruce has played every bar in the U.S.A., and every stadium. Credibility—you couldn't have more, unless you were dead. But Bruce Springsteen, you always knew, was not gonna die stupid. He didn't buy the mythology that screwed so many people. Instead he created an alternative mythology, one where ordinary lives became extraordinary and heroic. Bruce Springsteen feels familiar to us. But it's not an easy familiarity, is it? Even his band seems to stand taller when he walks in the room. It's complex. He's America's writer, and critic. It's like in *Badlands*, he's Martin Sheen and Terrence Malick. To be so accessible and so private, there's a rubric. But then again, he is an Irish-Italian, with a Jewish-sounding name. What more do you want? Add one big African sax player, and no one in this room is gonna fuck with you!

"In 1974, I was fourteen. Even I knew the '60s were over. It was the era of soft-rock and fusion. The Beatles were gone, Elvis was in Vegas. What was goin' on? Nothin' was goin' on. Bruce Springsteen was comin' on, saving music from the phonies, saving lyrics from the folkies, saving black leather jackets from the Fonz. *[Sings:]* 'Oh, the greasers, they tramp the streets and get busted for sleeping on the beaches all night, and them boys in their high heels, ah Sandy, their skins are so white. Oh Sandy, love me tonight, and I promise I'll love you forever.' In Dublin, Ireland, I knew what he was talking about. Here was a dude who carried himself like Brando, and Dylan, and Elvis. If John Steinbeck could sing, if Van Morrison could ride a Harley-Davidson. But he was something new, too. He was the first whiff of Scorsese, the first hint of Patti Smith, Elvis Costello, and the Clash. He was the end of long hair, brown rice and bell bottoms. He was the end of the twenty-minute drum solo. It was good night, Haight-Ashbury; hello, Asbury Park.

"America was staggering when Springsteen appeared. The president just resigned in disgrace, the U.S. had lost its first war. There was going to be no more oil in the ground. The days of cruising and big cars were supposed to be over. But Bruce Springsteen's vision was bigger than a Honda, it was bigger than a Subaru. Bruce made you believe that dreams were still out there, but after loss and defeat, they had to be braver, not just bigger. He was singing, 'Now you're scared and you're thinking that maybe we ain't that young anymore,' because it took guts to be romantic now. Knowing you could lose didn't mean you still didn't take the ride. In fact, it made taking the ride all the more important.

"Here was a new vision, and a new community. More than a community, because every great rock group is kind of like starting a religion. And Bruce surrounded himself with fellow believers. The E Street wasn't just a great rock group, or a street gang. It was a brotherhood. Zealots like Steve Van Zandt, the bishop Clarence Clemons, the holy Roy Bittan, crusaders Danny Federici, Max Weinberg, Garry Tallent, and later Nils Lofgren. And Jon Landau, Jon Landau, Jon Landau, Jon Landau, Jon Landau. What do you call a man who makes his best friend his manager, his producer, his confessor? You call him the Boss. And Springsteen didn't just marry a gorgeous red-headed woman from the Jersey Shore. She could sing, she could write, and she could tell the Boss off. And that's Patti, right there *[points]*.

"For me and the rest of the U2-ers, it wasn't just the way he described the world. It was the way he negotiated it. It was a map, a book of instructions on how to be in the business but not of it. Generous is a word you could use to describe the way he treated us. Decency is another. But these words can box you in. I remember when Bruce was headlining Amnesty International's tour for prisoners of conscience, I remember thinking, 'Wow, if ever there was a prisoner of conscience, it's Bruce Springsteen.' Integrity can be a yoke, a pain in the ass, when your songs are taking you to a part of town where people don't expect to see you.

"At some point I remember riding in an elevator with gentleman Bruce, where he just stared straight ahead of himself, and completely ignored me. I was crushed. Only when he walked into the doors as they were opening, did I realize the impossible was happening. My god, Bruce Springsteen, the Buddha of my youth, is plastered! Drunk as a skunk! Pissed as a fart! I had to go back to the book of instructions, scratch the bit out about how you held yourself in public. By the way, that was, on a personal note, a great relief.

"Something was going on, though. As a fan, I could see that my hero was beginning to rebel against his own public image. Things got even more interesting on *Tunnel of Love* when he started to deface it. A remarkable bunch of tunes, where our leader starts having a go at himself, and the hypocrisy of his own heart, before anyone else could. But the tabloids could never break news on Bruce Springsteen. Because his fans ... he had already told us everything in the songs. We knew he was spinning. We could feel him free-falling. But it wasn't in chaos or entropy. It was in love.

"We call him 'The Boss.' Well that's a bunch of crap. He's not the boss. He works *for* us. More than a boss—he's the *owner*. Because more than anyone else, Bruce Springsteen owns America's heart."

Bruce Springsteen's Induction Acceptance Speech, March 18, 1999

"You should remember: you always want an Irishman to give your induction speech. I knew I always liked you, Bono. You were scaring me a little bit there, though. I wasn't that good—but I liked the part about my good looks.

"I guess, let me warn you, the records took two years, the show's three hours, so the speech may take a little while.

"I stood on this stage and I inducted Roy Orbison and Creedence Clearwater Revival and Bob Dylan, an artist whose music was a critical part of my own life. And tonight I hope that my music served my audience half as well. If I succeed in doing that, it's been with the help of many, many kindred spirits along the way.

"I'd like to thank my mother, Adele, for that slushy Christmas Eve, for that Christmas Eve night—like the one outside—we stood outside the music store, and I pointed at the sunburst guitar. And she had that sixty bucks, and I said, 'I need that one.' She got me what I needed. And she protected me and provided for me, a thousand other days and nights. As importantly, she gave me a sense of work as something that was joyous and that filled you with pride and self-regard and that committed you to your world. Thanks, Mom, this is yours tonight *[holds up the statue]*. Take it home as a small return on the investment you made in your son. Mama! The Italian side of the family: Mama!

"Now my dad, he passed away this year, but I've got to thank him, because what would I have conceivably written about without him? I mean, you've got to imagine, if everything had gone great between us, it would have been a disaster. I would have written just happy songs—and I tried that in the early '90s and it didn't work. The public didn't like it!

"He never said much about my music, except that his favorite songs were the ones about him. And that was enough, you know? I put on his work clothes, and I went to work. It was the way that I honored him. My parents' experience forged my own. They shaped my politics, and they alerted me to what is at stake when you're born in the U.S.A. I miss you, Dad.

"A lot of other people: Marion and Tex Vinyard, they took me under their wing when I was fifteen. They opened up their home to a bunch of rock 'n' roll misfits and let us make a lot of noise and practice all night long. Thanks, Marion. Carl 'Tinker' West, another one of my early managers whose support I couldn't have done without. He introduced me to Mike Appel, and Mike kicked the doors down when they needed kicking, and I consider him my friend. I want to say, Mike, thanks for everything—mostly everything [laughs]. And thanks for being my guest here tonight. I'm glad you're here with me.

"Mike introduced me to the world of Columbia Records, which has been my home for the past twenty-five years, from the early days with John Hammond and Clive Davis to the high rolling times with Walter Yetnikoff and Al Teller, to the present with my friend Tommy Mottola and Donny Ienner. They created a conduit for a lifetime of thoughts and ideas, a place where I felt safe and supported and encouraged to do my best and my truest work. I've heard enough record company horror stories right from this stage to appreciate the fact that I don't have one. For that I've got to thank all the men and women at Columbia Records around the world for my success. Thanks very much for your efforts.

"I've got to thank my co-producer Chuck Plotkin and engineer, Toby Scott, for a sustained contribution to my recorded work. They remained in the saddle as often years went by wondering if we'd ever get the music out or if they'd ever get a royalty check. They kept their cool and their creativity—of course, they're basket cases now, but we remain friends and great working partners. And no mention of my records would be complete without Bob Clearmountain, the great mixer, who helped me bring my music to a larger audience.

"I want to thank my tour director, George Travis, and the great crews he's assembled on the road over the years. Thank you, George. I want to thank my agents Barry Bell and Frank Barsalona, for a great job.

"All right, thank you, and now, the lawyers. You gotta thank them, you know [laughs]. Peter Parcher and Steve Hayes, they've protected me and my music for twenty-two years; I appreciate it. This next one's a little tough: Alan Grubman and Artie Indursky, names familiar to many in this room. They're the 'money men.' How can I put this? These are great and complicated and misunderstood Americans. They're men that are entrusted with a very, very important task. For the folks that don't know, the money man goes to the record company, and he's in charge in bringing back the pink Cadillac. When Alan and Artie go, they bring back the pink Cadillac, and the blue Cadillac, and the red Cadillac, and the yellow Cadillac. The pink Cadillac with the whitewalls. But then they take the blue Cadillac. And they take the hubcaps off the yellow Cadillac. But, that still leaves you with a few Cadillacs. And they make sure that neither you nor themselves, of course, are gonna be broke when you're riding in the black Cadillac. They do that well.

"I've gotta thank Barbara Carr for her love, loyalty, and dedication. I couldn't get along without you, Barb. My friend, Dave Marsh, thank you so much. And oh, the next guy, this is Jon Landau—or as I sometimes call him, Jon 'Thank God I'm a Country Boy' Landau. *I've seen the future of rock and roll management and its name is Jon Landau.* Return the favor, there *[laughs]*. That quote was managing. It was a might burdensome for me, but as he often said, 'That's your job.' But Jon's given me something beyond friendship and beyond guidance: his intelligence, his sense of the truth, his recognition of my intelligence. We were worlds that collided. His creative ability as producer, and editor—speechwriter earlier this evening—his ability to see through to the heart of matters, both professional and personal, and the love he's given me has altered my life forever. What I hope to give to my fans with my music—a greater sense of themselves and greater freedoms—he with his talents and his abilities has done that for me. There's no 'thank you' tonight that's gonna do the job. It's a debt that I can't repay, one that I treasure owing. Thank you, Jon, I love you. I also want to thank Barbara Landau, and Kate and Charlie, for sharing Jon with me over the years. I know it hasn't been easy.

"Now, last but not least, the men and women—the mighty men and women of the E Street Band. Oh, Lord. Oh, Lord. Who I have reeducated and rededicated, re-animated, resuscitated and reinvigorated with the power, the magic, the mystery, the ministry of rock 'n' roll.

"Vini Lopez, 'Boom' Carter, early drummers of the band. Davey Sancious.

"Nils Lofgren, the most over-qualified second guitarist in show business. He plays ten times better than me, and he still wanders over to hear my solos when I play. I guess he's checking to see if I'm getting any better.

"Danny Federici, the most instinctive and natural musician I ever met, and the only member of the band that can reduce me to a shouting mess. I love you, Danny, your organ and accordion playing brought the boardwalks of Central and South Jersey alive in my music. Thank you.

"Garry Tallent, Southern Man, my lovely friend, great bass player, rock 'n' roll aficionado, whose quiet and dignity grace my band and my life. Thank you, Garry.

"Roy Bittan. Roy's playing formed the signature sound of some of my greatest records. He can play anything. He's always there for me. His emotional generosity and his deep personal support mean a great, great deal to me. Thank you, Roy.

"Max Weinberg, Mighty Max! Star of the Conan O'Brien show. Conan ain't too bad, either. Max found a place where Bernard Perdie, Buddy Rich, and Keith Moon intersected, and he made it his own. I ask, and he delivers for me every night. Thank you, Max.

"Stevie Van Zandt. For those of you who have seen 'The Sopranos' and worry that that's what Steve is like: that's what he's like! A lifetime of rock 'n' roll friendship. We did it all. Great songwriter, producer, great guitarist. We haven't played together in fifteen years, and if it's up to me, that will never happen again. I love you, Steve.

"Patti Scialfa. She busted the boys club *[laughs]*. Big time! Oh ... It went like this: 'Okay, fellas, there's gonna be a woman in the band. We need someone to sing all the high parts. How complicated can it get?' A nice paparazzi photo of me in my Jockey shorts on a balcony in Rome tendered the best years of my life. Evan, Jesse, Sam—three children genealogically linked to the E Street Band—tells the rest of the story. Everybody wants to know how I feel about the band. Hell, I *married* one of 'em. Thank you, baby, you hit all the high notes. You're tougher than the rest.

"Now, last but not least: Clarence Clemons. You wanna be like him, but you can't. The night I met Clarence, and he got on stage, a sound came out of his horn that—it seemed to rattle the glasses behind the bar and threaten to blow out the back wall. The door literally blew off the club in a storm that night, and I knew I'd found my sax player. But there was something else. Something happened when we stood side-by-side. Some energy. Some unspoken story. For fifteen years, Clarence has been a source of myth and light and enormous strength for me on stage. He has filled my heart so many nights, so many nights. I love it when he wraps me in those arms at the end of the night. That night we first stood together, I looked over at 'C' and it looked like his head reached into the clouds, and I felt like a mere mortal scurrying upon the earth. But he always lifted me up. Way, way, way up. Together, we told a story of the possibilities of friendship. A story older than the ones that I would write. And a story I could have never told without him at my side. Thank you, Big Man. I love you so much.

"So, as Stevie Van Zandt says, 'Rock 'n' roll. It's a band thing.' And that includes you, the audience. Thank you for giving me access and entrance into your lives and I hope that I've been a good companion. But right now, my wife, my great friends, my great collaborators, my great band: Your presence tonight honors me, and I wouldn't be standing up here tonight without you, and I can't stand up here now without you. Please join me."

Index

Boldface refers to main entries and the page numbers on which those entries appear.